THE NEW PUBLIC FINANCE

RESPONDING TO GLOBAL CHALLENGES

THE NEW
PUBLIC
FINANCE

RESPONDING TO
GLOBAL CHALLENGES

EDITED BY
INGE KAUL
PEDRO CONCEIÇÃO

Published for
The United Nations Development Programme

New York   Oxford
Oxford University Press
2006

Oxford University Press

Oxford University Press, Inc., publishes works that further Oxford University's
objective of excellence in research, scholarship, and education.

Oxford   New York
Auckland   Cape Town   Dar es Salaam   Hong Kong   Karachi
Kuala Lumpur   Madrid   Melbourne   Mexico City   Nairobi
New Delhi   Shanghai   Taipei   Toronto

With offices in
Argentina   Austria   Brazil   Chile   Czech Republic   France   Greece
Guatemala   Hungary   Italy   Japan   Poland   Portugal   Singapore
South Korea   Switzerland   Thailand   Turkey   Ukraine   Vietnam

Library of Congress Cataloging-in-Publication Data

The new public finance : responding to global challenges / edited by Inge
Kaul and Pedro Conceição.
    p. cm.
"Published for The United Nations Development Programme."
Includes bibliographical references and index.
ISBN 0-19-517997-8 (pbk. : alk. paper) -- ISBN 0-19-517996-X (cloth
: alk. paper)
1. Finance, Public--International cooperation. 2. Public-private sector
cooperation. I. Kaul, Inge. II. Conceição, Pedro.
HJ141.N477 2005
336--dc22
                                2005026365

1 3 5 7 9 8 6 4 2

Printed in the United States of America
on acid-free paper

"This is a bold and penetrating compilation of papers on the most profound challenges of modern public finance—how to construct better partnerships between governments and private sector players and how to strengthen cooperation between nations in pursuit of common interests."

TREVOR A. MANUEL
MP; Minister of Finance, Republic of South Africa

"*The New Public Finance* shows how we can equip people and countries for the future—for a new global economy that combines greater prosperity and fairness both within and across nations. *The New Public Finance* is important reading for today's policymakers."

RT HON GORDON BROWN
MP; Chancellor of the Exchequer, United Kingdom

"As the global economy widens its reach, the principles and instruments of public finance face new problems and tasks. This volume takes an imaginative and down-to-earth look at the problems and the policy instruments needed to resolve them. It is a volume not to be missed."

RICHARD A. MUSGRAVE
Harvard University

"*The New Public Finance* is a real eye-opener. It is a must for everyone with an interest in international developments in economics, law, business, and intergovernmental relations."

SIJBREN CNOSSEN
University of Maastricht

"The problems facing policymakers in a globalized world require international cooperation. But efficient policy design also demands a reconsideration of the respective tasks of the public and private sectors. This is especially so for the need to create incentives for private agents to promote social goals. For those who are looking for a survey of current thinking in this field, *The New Public Finance* is an excellent reference."

AGNAR SANDMO
Norwegian School of Economics and Business Administration

"This book presents the reader with a fascinating option. It shows that through the development of financial markets and financial product innovation, achieving what the world wants to accomplish in terms of human betterment nationally and internationally is *not* beyond our means."

FRANK J. FABOZZI
Yale School of Management

"This book is a welcome and important addition to the review of what we know and do not know about public finance in this new era of globalization. Looking at it through the eyes of a former finance minister, I see it as required reading for both scholars and policymakers."

EDUARDO ANINAT
Ambassador of Chile to Mexico, former Minister of Finance of Chile
(1994–99)

"An essential contribution to shaping public-private partnering and the kind of international cooperation needed to achieve truly prosperous, equitable, and sustainable development. This book is bound to make a significant difference in the way we build our future."

MAURICIO ESCANERO
Facilitator of the UN International Conference for Financing for Development (1999–2002); Consul General of Mexico in Shanghai

"The challenges and opportunities of globalization call for creative new approaches—and for new financing models to fund them. While there's no textbook on how to do this yet, *The New Public Finance* brings together some of today's most insightful thinkers to engage the issue and add considerably to our understanding."

TIMOTHY E. WIRTH
President, United Nations Foundation

"This volume presents recent thinking on policy actions, instruments, and financing technologies that are developing in response to the challenges posed by the intended and unintended openness of borders. It is a timely, well conceived, and very necessary book."

RAJENDRA K. PACHAURI
Director-General, The Energy and Resources Institute (TERI)

"In a world of increasing globalization, the creation, financing, and delivery of global public goods are critical priorities. Existing mechanisms directed at nation states and companies have not been sufficient; innovative models of public-private partnerships are required. Global leaders should examine the analysis and insights contained in *The New Public Finance* and reflect on how to put them into action."

SETH F. BERKLEY
President and Chief Executive Officer, International AIDS Vaccine Initiative (IAVI)

"This book offers practical and highly relevant suggestions for adapting public finance to the conditions of globalization. Policymakers, researchers, and business actors alike stand to gain extraordinary insight from its analyses."

MICHAEL J. INACKER
Vice-President, External Affairs and Public Policy, DaimlerChrysler AG

CONTENTS

Foreword   xi
Mark Malloch Brown

Prologue   xii
Joseph E. Stiglitz

Acknowledgments   xvi

Contributors   xvii

OVERVIEW   1

WHY REVISIT PUBLIC FINANCE TODAY?   3
WHAT THIS BOOK IS ABOUT
Inge Kaul and Pedro Conceição

THE CHANGES UNDER WAY   28
FINANCING GLOBAL CHALLENGES THROUGH INTERNATIONAL COOPERATION
BEHIND AND BEYOND BORDERS
Inge Kaul and Pedro Conceição

1. THE NEW NATIONAL PUBLIC FINANCE   71
TAKING THE OUTSIDE WORLD INTO ACCOUNT

BLENDING EXTERNAL AND DOMESTIC POLICY DEMANDS   73
THE RISE OF THE INTERMEDIARY STATE
Inge Kaul

MAKING POLICY UNDER EFFICIENCY PRESSURES   109
GLOBALIZATION, PUBLIC SPENDING, AND SOCIAL WELFARE
Vito Tanzi

INTERNALIZING CROSS-BORDER SPILLOVERS   131
POLICY OPTIONS FOR ADDRESSING LONG-TERM FISCAL CHALLENGES
Peter S. Heller

MANAGING RISKS TO NATIONAL ECONOMIES   152
THE ROLE OF MACRO MARKETS
Robert J. Shiller

COMBINING FISCAL SOVEREIGNTY AND COORDINATION   167
NATIONAL TAXATION IN A GLOBALIZING WORLD
Peggy B. Musgrave

RECOGNIZING THE LIMITS TO COOPERATION BEHIND
NATIONAL BORDERS   194
FINANCING THE CONTROL OF TRANSNATIONAL TERRORISM
Todd Sandler

2. THE NEW INTERNATIONAL PUBLIC FINANCE   217
RELYING ON PUBLIC-PRIVATE COOPERATION AND COMPETITION

EXPLORING THE POLICY SPACE BETWEEN MARKETS AND STATES   219
GLOBAL PUBLIC-PRIVATE PARTNERSHIPS
Inge Kaul

ACCOMMODATING NEW ACTORS AND NEW PURPOSES
IN INTERNATIONAL COOPERATION   269
THE GROWING DIVERSIFICATION OF FINANCING MECHANISMS
Pedro Conceição

MAKING THE RIGHT MONEY AVAILABLE AT THE RIGHT TIME
FOR INTERNATIONAL COOPERATION   281
NEW FINANCING TECHNOLOGIES
Pedro Conceição, Hari Rajan, and Rajiv Shah

TAKING SELF-INTEREST INTO ACCOUNT   304
A PUBLIC CHOICE ANALYSIS OF INTERNATIONAL COOPERATION
Philip Jones

3. THE NEW INTERNATIONAL PUBLIC FINANCE   325
INVESTING IN GLOBAL PUBLIC GOODS PROVISION ABROAD

IDENTIFYING HIGH-RETURN INVESTMENTS   327
*A METHODOLOGY FOR ASSESSING WHEN INTERNATIONAL COOPERATION PAYS—
AND FOR WHOM*
Pedro Conceição and Ronald U. Mendoza

MAKING INTERNATIONAL COOPERATION PAY   357
FINANCING AS A STRATEGIC INCENTIVE
Scott Barrett

COMPENSATING COUNTRIES FOR THE PROVISION
OF GLOBAL PUBLIC SERVICES   371
THE TOOL OF INCREMENTAL COSTS
Kenneth King

CREATING NEW MARKETS   389
THE CHICAGO CLIMATE EXCHANGE
Richard L. Sandor

USING MARKETS MORE EFFECTIVELY   417
DEVELOPING COUNTRY ACCESS TO COMMODITY FUTURES MARKETS
C. Wyn Morgan

ASSESSING CONTRACTUAL AND STATUTORY APPROACHES   433
POLICY PROPOSALS FOR RESTRUCTURING UNSUSTAINABLE SOVEREIGN DEBT
Barry Eichengreen

PLACING THE EMPHASIS ON REGULATION   453
LESSONS FROM PUBLIC FINANCE IN THE EUROPEAN UNION
Brigid Laffan

4. THE NEW INTERNATIONAL PUBLIC FINANCE   469
ENHANCING AID EFFICIENCY

USING AID INSTRUMENTS MORE COHERENTLY   471
GRANTS AND LOANS
Paul Collier

RECTIFYING CAPITAL MARKET IMPERFECTIONS   486
THE CONTINUING RATIONALES FOR MULTILATERAL LENDING
Yilmaz Akyüz

PULLING NOT PUSHING REFORMS   510
DELIVERING AID THROUGH CHALLENGE GRANTS
Steve Radelet

OVERCOMING COORDINATION AND ATTRIBUTION PROBLEMS   529
MEETING THE CHALLENGE OF UNDERFUNDED REGIONALISM
Nancy Birdsall

REDUCING THE COSTS OF HOLDING RESERVES   549
A NEW PERSPECTIVE ON SPECIAL DRAWING RIGHTS
Jacques J. Polak and Peter B. Clark

CREATING INCENTIVES FOR PRIVATE SECTOR INVOLVEMENT
IN POVERTY REDUCTION   564
PURCHASE COMMITMENTS FOR AGRICULTURAL INNOVATION
Michael Kremer and Alix Peterson Zwane

MITIGATING THE RISKS OF INVESTING IN DEVELOPING COUNTRIES   585
CURRENCY-RELATED GUARANTEE INSTRUMENTS FOR INFRASTRUCTURE PROJECTS
Stephany Griffith-Jones and Ana Teresa Fuzzo de Lima

ANNEXES

FURTHER READING   607

GLOSSARY   613

ABOUT THE CONTRIBUTORS   617

INDEX   624

FOREWORD

Public finance is in transition. For the most part, the world still practices what might be termed conventional public finance—paying to achieve public policy purposes mainly from public revenue, now and in full. And we know that this way of meeting public policy goals often leaves many goals underfunded—something seen most acutely today in the Millennium Development Goals. Recent increased aid commitments notwithstanding, international aid and domestic public finance commitments still fall well short of what is needed to meet the 2015 deadline for the Goals.

Yet, as the provocative and varied analyses in this volume demonstrate, public finance—an area often perceived as rule-ridden and stagnant—is undergoing a vibrant process of innovation. New policy approaches and financing technologies are emerging that could allow us to pursue public policy goals more efficiently— at lower cost and with higher welfare gains. Often involving public-private partnering that builds on the comparative strengths of all partners, these new approaches and tools permit better risk management (avoiding costly crises), more sustainable resource management (avoiding further loss of resources), a better understanding of incentives (motivating actors to abide by agreements and follow rules), and better ways of harnessing private finance and initiative (meeting challenges that would otherwise remain unmet or underfunded).

At the national level many of these new types of public-private partnerships are already visible and familiar. Less common, as the book shows, is international cooperation behind national borders: taking the outside world—both the risks and the opportunities—into account when making national policy. National public policy still has much to accomplish in adjusting to the increasing openness of national borders and to the interdependence of countries that comes with this openness. And cooperation at the international level still has a long way to go in responding to the growing capacity of markets to help deliver many important public policy objectives.

What this book has to say about current trends and future possibilities in the practice of public finance deserves careful consideration by all actors, public and private, national and international. Many of the ideas it presents have enormous potential. Especially in these times of great and growing public finance needs the world over, they merit serious attention by policymakers and practitioners alike.

Mark Malloch Brown
Administrator, United Nations Development Programme
New York, 1 August 2005

PROLOGUE

Joseph E. Stiglitz

Globalization has meant the closer integration of countries, and that in turn has meant a greater need for collective action. This book provides one of the first systematic treatments of public finance for the new era of globalization—with the totally appropriate title *The New Public Finance.*

Over the years the focus of public finance has changed dramatically. At one time it was strictly about what the term proclaimed—how governments should raise money to finance public activity.[1] By the time I began teaching the subject, in the 1970s, it had been redefined to *The Economics of the Public Sector* (the title of the text I first published in the early 1980s; Stiglitz 1986), giving equal weight both to expenditures and taxation. Macroeconomics was left out—not because it wasn't an important area (and earlier texts by Richard and Peggy Musgrave had included the subject) but because the subject had to be circumscribed somehow.

A half century ago Tiebout (1956) opened up the formal study of competition among communities, which I expanded in a paper delivered in 1974 into the general theory of local public goods (Stiglitz 1977), goods whose benefits accrued only to people living in a particular community. Public finance differed fundamentally when factors (labor and capital) could choose where to reside from when factors were not mobile. In the extreme, there was no scope for redistribution (Stiglitz 1986a,b)—a subject that had been at the center of traditional public finance discourse.

The new public finance at the time had to deal with the interplay between national and local public finance, including what activities should be conducted at the national level and what at the local level. It was clear that national public goods, for instance, ought to be provided at the national level, and that responsibility for redistributive taxation also must lie there.

As we move further into a globalized world, analogous issues are again being raised. With increased mobility of factors, redistribution may become more difficult. Having formalized the concept of local public goods, it was natural to extend that to the concept of *global public goods,* goods whose benefits accrue to anyone living anywhere in the world.[2] It would make sense for responsibility for the provision of such goods to rest with a global authority. And yet there is no global body able to meet the needs for global collective action and to organize the provision of global public goods.

This makes the challenge of the new public finance all the greater. There is no pristine theory and no set of well functioning institutions reflecting a common understanding of the role of collective action. There are myriad challenges:

national authorities now must take into account the outside world as they formulate their tax and expenditure policies. With footloose firms, they must worry about how tax and expenditure policies affect the competitiveness of investments in their country.

Financing global collective action is particularly problematic. In the past, for instance, the United Nations has been financed mainly by "dues." The only enforcement mechanism is expulsion from the "club." More recently, however, a number of governments have put on the table a set of innovative proposals, from taxes levied on certain cross-border transactions, to revenues raised from managing global public resources, to income derived from creating a new global currency to replace the current reserve system.

The *New Public Finance*, of course, does not deal with public finance alone, narrowly defined, but with a host of concerns requiring global collective action. In response to the need for collective action, we have developed a system of global governance without global government, a patchwork of institutions and agreements, varying in the effectiveness and efficiency with which they deal with the needs for collective action within their purview. Understanding these *public* failures is no less important than understanding market failures. Just as political economy has become an important part of standard public finance at the national level, so too should it be at the international level. Regrettably, this remains a very underdeveloped area of research.

As a result, international organizations often miss correcting serious market failures—and sometimes even compound them through their actions. Capital market liberalization has been actively promoted and arguably has exposed developing countries to increased risk. Well developed financial markets would presumably shift the burden of that risk from those less able to bear it (the poor) to those better able to do so. But there is massive market failure, with enormous consequences. This is a market failure that the International Monetary Fund and other international organizations should have long ago addressed, but which, as this book shows, is only now emerging as a policy focus.

Still another problem that should have been addressed but that has been allowed to linger is the global reserve system, a system that imposes enormous costs on developing countries, exerts a deflationary bias on the global economy, and contributes to global instability. The dollar reserve system not only has not worked, but it is quickly fraying, as central banks around the world increasingly move out of dollars. The multiple reserve currency system that is evolving, however, does not promise to be much more stable, or any more equitable, than the current system. There are alternatives, including regular emissions of Special Drawing Rights, that need to be considered.

One of the most important areas of market failure is the environment. Without government intervention, firms and households have no incentive to limit their pollution. The new public finance is concerned with *global* externalities—in this case, global environmental problems, the most important being global climate change. Just as a standard topic within traditional public finance is the evaluation of alternative ways of "correcting" these market failures, so too here. The international community, through the Kyoto Protocol, has settled on a particular remedy—tradable permits. But this has involved difficult problems of assigning pollution rights. And while it is remarkable that so many countries have signed on to the protocol, with the largest polluter, the United States, refusing to sign, and with no commitments from developing countries— of increasing importance in greenhouse gas emissions—it is not clear that this approach will work. Alternatives, including common measures (an agreement, say, on common levels of taxation), entailing fewer redistributive issues, should be explored.

There are some areas where new institutional arrangements are clearly needed. One, dealt with here, is sovereign debt restructurings, a topic (bankruptcy) that at the national level traditionally falls under the rubric of industrial organization and policy. And yet the issues are so central to global public finance that they rightly belong here.

One of the most important issues in both the old and the new public finance is how to provide assistance. The old public finance debated questions of matched grants or lump sum aid. The new public finance debates issues of development assistance, of loans or grants to developing countries, of how to enhance private sector participation, and of the role of conditionality, among others.

It is a rich landscape: redefining the vast subject of public finance in ways that respond to global challenges. It entails revisiting virtually every topic that has been discussed within the old public finance, plus some that have not. This book is a landmark—it provides the important beginnings of a field that will be tilled for years to come.

NOTES

1. Though the classic text of the mid-twentieth century, Musgrave and Musgrave (1989), did devote some attention to public goods.

2. Since I first developed the concept in 1995, the literature has blossomed. See, for instance, Kaul, Grunberg, and Stern (1999) and Kaul and others (2003). See also Stiglitz (1998).

REFERENCES

Kaul, Inge, Isabelle Grunberg, and Marc A. Stern, eds. 1999. *Global Public Goods: International Cooperation in the 21st Century.* New York: Oxford University Press.

Kaul, Inge, Pedro Conceição, Katell Le Goulven, and Ronald U. Mendoza, eds. 2003. *Providing Global Public Goods: Managing Globalization.* New York: Oxford University Press.

Musgrave, Richard A., and Peggy B. Musgrave. 1989. *Public Finance in Theory and Practice.* 5th edition. New York: McGraw-Hill.

Stiglitz, Joseph E. 1977. "Theory of Local Public Goods." In Martin S. Feldstein and Robert P. Inman, eds., *The Economics of Public Services.* New York: MacMillan Publishing Company. (Paper presented to the International Economics Association Conference, Turin, 1974).

———. 1983a."Public Goods in Open Economies with Heterogeneous Individuals." In Jacques-François Thisse and Henry G. Zoller, eds., *Locational Analysis of Public Facilities.* Amsterdam: North-Holland

———. 1983b."The Theory of Local Public Goods Twenty-Five Years after Tiebout: A Perspective." In George R. Zodrow, ed., *Local Provision of Public Services: The Tiebout Model After Twenty-Five Years.* New York: Academic Press.

———. 1986. *The Economics of the Public Sector.* 3rd edition. New York: W.W. Norton.

———. 1995. "The Theory of International Public Goods and the Architecture of International Organizations." Background Paper 7. Third Meeting, High Level Group on Development Strategy and Management of the Market Economy, United Nations University, World Institute for Development Economics Research, July 8–10, Helsinki.

———. 1998. "IFIs and the Provision of International Public Goods." *Cahiers Papers* 3 (2): 116–34.

Tiebout, Charles M. 1956."A Pure Theory of Local Public Expenditures." *Journal of Political Economy* 64 (5): 416–24.

ACKNOWLEDGMENTS

A great many people contributed to this book. Although too numerous to mention individually, we acknowledge with thanks and appreciation all those who shared with us their ideas and observations at seminars and workshops, during informal discussions, or in writing.

However, there are a number of people to whom we owe a special word of gratitude and without whom this book could not have been produced.

First, the book benefited from the leadership and support of Mark Malloch Brown, Administrator of the United Nations Development Programme (UNDP) and Chef de Cabinet of the United Nations Secretary-General. It also benefited from the advice and guidance of Zéphirin Diabré, Associate Administrator of UNDP. Their keen interest in the topics of this volume was an important source of inspiration for us.

Likewise, many of our UNDP colleagues gave of their time and effort to brainstorm with us and to comment as the book began to take shape. Our thanks go to the in-house readers group, especially to Chandrika Bahadur, Renata Lok Dessalien, Moez Doraid, Walter Franco, Bruce Jenks, Gabriele Koehler, Thierry Lemaresquier, Herbert McLeod, Christine McNab, Saraswathi Menon, Shoji Nishimoto, Robert Piper, Jordan Ryan, Cihan Sultanoglu, Mark Suzman, and Antonio Vigilante.

We are also greatly appreciative of the inputs we received from external peer reviewers of individual chapters or of the book manuscript as a whole: Will Acworth, Manuel Agosin, Dilip Ahuja, K.Y. Amoako, P.B. Anand, Gun-Britt Andersson, Brian Ardy, Ernest Aryeetey, Patrick Asea, Sir Anthony Atkinson, Suman Babbar, David Babbel, Stephen Bailey, Alicia Barcena, Thorsten Benner, Johannah Bernstein, Albert Breton, Nick Bridge, Jennifer Brinkerhoff, Henk-Jan Brinkman, Peter Brown, Ariel Buira, Naomi Caiden, Marshall Carter, Graciela Chichilnisky, Robert Chote, Richard Cooper, Dana Dalrymple, Oscar de Rojas, William de Vries, Bibek Debroy, Rahul Dhumale, James Dougherty, Jean Drèze, Jean-Pierre Dupuis, Mohamed El-Ashry, Paul Epstein, Philip Erquiaga, Daniel Esty, Gareth Evans, Robert Evenson, Frank Fabozzi, Marco Ferroni, David Fidler, Hani Findakly, Roger Gordon, Megan De Grandis, Paul Grout, Isabelle Grunberg-Filatov, Jörg Hartmann, Thomas Hertel, Arye Hillman, Otmar Issing, Saradha Iyer, Henry Jackelen, Raghbendra Jha, Yolanda Kakabadse, Patricia Kameri-Mbote, Charles Kenny, Monique Koning, Katell Le Goulven, Roberto Lenton, Steven Leslie, David Levi-Faur, Albert Link, Karin Lissakers, William Lyakurwa, John Marshall, Ajit Maru, Raechelle Mascarenhas, William Masters, Jörg Mayer, Norman Meade,

Rohinton Medhora, Nina V. Michaelis, Silvia Morgenroth, Agathi Moukouli, Dennis Mueller, Francis Mwega, Anant Nadkarni, Cristián Ossa, Rajendra Pachauri, Karl Pedersen, Robert Picciotto, Michael Pickhardt, Thomas Plümper, Dilip Ratha, Helmut Reisen, Nita Rudra, Stéphane Saussier, Frank Schroeder, Meinhard Schulz-Baldes, Gunnar Schuppert, Henry Schwalbenberg, Robert Sheppard, Elisabeth Sköns, Oliver Smoot, Bo Södersten, Michael Spackman, Christian Starck, Jonathan Stevenson, Kathryn Sturman, Elizabeth Sullivan, Robert Taanenwald, Kazuo Takahashi, Chawan Theungsang, Peter Utting, Shriti Vadera, Rick van der Ploeg, P.V. Venugopal, Ernst von Weizsäcker, Rob Ward, Thomas Weiss, Roy Widdus, James Winwood, Michael Wormser, Oran Young, and Simon Zadek.

We owe a special debt of gratitude to Lindsay Alexander, Meghnad Desai, Barry Herman, Jeffrey McNeely, Carol Medlin, Lyla Mehta, Layna Mosley, Kunibert Raffer, Andrew Sherriff, and Dan Smith for their contributions to the book's scope.

We also would like to thank the delegates to the permanent missions to the United Nations in New York, who offered their insight and advice throughout the book's production, and the governments of Canada and Switzerland, which provided financial support.

The staff members of the Office of Development Studies, who formed the in-house book-project team and provided valuable research assistance and management support, also need to be recognized: Romina Bandura, Ian Broadwater, Hana Haller, Ronald U. Mendoza, Sylvain Merlen, Balkissa Sidikou-Sow, and Nena Terrell. Our appreciation also goes to Fiorella Aller, Michael Hildebrand-Faust, and Jonathan Rose and to the interns of the Office of Development Studies: Sebastian Buckup, Dagmar Hertova, Ulrich Jacobi, Prerna Kapur, Alexander Kocks, Zezhong Li, Pachara Lochindaratn, Sahak Sargsyan, Silke Tabernik, Ayse Urganci, and Lying Zhou.

We would also like to thank Flora Aller and Maria Rocio Sieli for their years of valuable administrative support to our work.

Finally, we must praise the work of Terry Vaughn and Catherine Rae at Oxford University Press; Bruce Ross-Larson, Meta de Coquereaumont, Wendy Musco, Thomas Roncoli, Christopher Trott, and Timothy Walker of Communications Development Incorporated, for editing and production of the volume; and Gerald Quinn for design. Their inputs were a tremendous asset as the manuscript and book design were finalized.

While appreciating all these contributions, we wish to note that the views expressed in this volume are those of the authors and do not necessarily represent the views of the institutions with each they are affiliated.

Your comments on this publication are not only welcome but are very much solicited. Please send your observations and inquiries about the book to the Office of Development Studies, UNDP, Uganda House, 336 East 45th Street, 4th floor, New York, NY 10017, USA. Fax: (212) 906 3676. Email: ods@undp.org.

CONTRIBUTORS

YILMAZ AKYÜZ
University of Malaya

SCOTT BARRETT
Johns Hopkins University

NANCY BIRDSALL
Center for Global Development

PETER B. CLARK
International Monetary Fund

PAUL COLLIER
Oxford University

PEDRO CONCEIÇÃO
United Nations Development
Programme

BARRY EICHENGREEN
University of California, Berkeley

ANA TERESA FUZZO DE LIMA
Sussex University

STEPHANY GRIFFITH-JONES
Sussex University

PETER S. HELLER
International Monetary Fund

PHILIP JONES
University of Bath

INGE KAUL
United Nations Development
Programme

KENNETH KING
World Bank

MICHAEL KREMER
Harvard University

BRIGID LAFFAN
University College Dublin

RONALD U. MENDOZA
United Nations Development
Programme

C. WYN MORGAN
University of Nottingham

PEGGY B. MUSGRAVE
University of California, Santa Cruz

ALIX PETERSON ZWANE
University of California, Berkeley

JACQUES J. POLAK
International Monetary Fund

STEVEN RADELET
Center for Global Development

HARI RAJAN
JP Morgan Corsair Partners

TODD SANDLER
University of Southern California

RICHARD L. SANDOR
Chicago Climate Exchange

Rajiv Shah
Bill & Melinda Gates Foundation

Robert J. Shiller
Yale University

Vito Tanzi
Inter-American Development Bank

OVERVIEW

WHY REVISIT PUBLIC FINANCE TODAY?
WHAT THIS BOOK IS ABOUT
Inge Kaul and Pedro Conceição

•

THE CHANGES UNDER WAY
FINANCING GLOBAL CHALLENGES THROUGH
INTERNATIONAL COOPERATION BEHIND AND BEYOND BORDERS
Inge Kaul and Pedro Conceição

Public finance is undergoing a quiet revolution, responding to the greater porosity of the divide between the private and the public sectors and the greater openness of national policy domains.

Policymakers, no longer relying solely on raising and spending money and intervening directly in the economy to achieve policy objectives, are creating incentives for private actors, leveraging private finance, and drawing on markets to do what was once seen as the government's exclusive job. In this rebalancing of markets and states public and private finance are converging, and public-private partnering is more common.

And as national borders become more open, the divides between "domestic" and "foreign" are blurring as well. Policymakers face a lengthening agenda of global challenges—from cross-border integration of national markets and communication and transportation systems to global climate change, communicable diseases, terrorism, migration, and poverty reduction.

WHY REVISIT PUBLIC FINANCE TODAY?

WHAT THIS BOOK IS ABOUT

INGE KAUL AND PEDRO CONCEIÇÃO

The reengineering of public finance in response to the rebalancing of markets and states is well established worldwide, a process that has been researched and documented (see, for example, Salamon 2002b). Contracting out, private solutions to externalities, private financing of public sector projects, among others, are making their way into public finance textbooks (see, for example, Bailey [1995] 2002, 2004; Hillman 2003; and Rosen 2005).

The responses of public finance to the openness of national borders have been more tentative—but they do exist. National subsidy policies are the subject of heated international debate and intense diplomacy. Nations are urged to support each other in adjusting fiscal and monetary policies to avoid macroeconomic imbalances that may spell trouble for the world economy. The spotlight of the international community is also turned on national spending priorities—how much developing countries allocate to poverty reduction or industrial countries to foreign aid, and how well all countries observe fiscal discipline and debt sustainability.

Modes of public finance are also being subjected to outside scrutiny and international debate. Government performance is measured by the openness to market competition or the credibility of policy commitments. There is also discussion of when to keep policy responses national and when to centralize them internationally—and of whether to create more international funds to support intergovernmental action abroad. And there are questions about the role of intergovernmental organizations, about whether some of their traditional functions could now be performed more efficiently and effectively by global market actors or by public-private partnerships.

This volume takes stock of how public finance has responded to the policy challenges of greater openness. The focus is on how public finance has responded to the interlocking of national policy domains and the resultant globalization of its main "deliverables": public goods and equity in development, or fair life chances for all, including poverty reduction.

The findings corroborate the assertion that public finance has never stood still (Musgrave and Musgrave 1989). As realities have changed, public finance has evolved and adjusted its policies and tools to new circumstances—today in response to globalization.

Contrary to what might still be a widely held view, governments no longer merely act as aggregators of national policy preferences and national public policy is nested in global policy frameworks. And contrary to yet another perhaps still widely held view, the external policy expectations go far beyond promoting economic openness to promoting competitiveness, reducing negative cross-border spillovers, improving risk management, and sharing economic opportunities and gains more widely. The intended openness is to proceed, and the unintended (undesirable) openness is to be reined in.

The policy approaches and tools discussed in part 1 support this new policy function—the blending of domestic and external policy demands, or put differently, international cooperation *behind* national borders. Such cooperation is perhaps the preferred way of addressing global challenges today. But it cannot generate the desired policy outcome—say, the interoperability of national transportation systems. Meeting global challenges often calls for a "summation" of policy reforms in all or at least many countries. However, to ensure that the national policy reforms fit together and that all actors contribute their part—or to realize economies of scale or scope—it is frequently desirable for international cooperation behind national borders to be complemented by international cooperation *beyond* national borders.

Parts 2 to 4 examine international cooperation beyond national borders. They reveal that while global challenges have added a new function to the portfolio of national public finance—the blending of external and domestic policy demands—they have changed the rationales shaping international cooperation. Concerns about efficiency, often neglected, are taking their place next to the more conventional concerns of foreign policy, next to geopolitical and strategic military considerations and the moral and ethical concerns of foreign aid. Thinking about public finance is reaching into the realm of foreign policy.

International cooperation abroad, like national public policy, is relying more on public-private cooperation—and competition. The wave of market-state rebalancing that has swept across the world in recent decades and changed public finance practices nationally is now reaching the shores of intergovernmental organizations. And it is transforming international cooperation from an essentially intergovernmental process into a multiactor process. Investment thinking now shapes global public goods provision abroad (just as it generally does nationally). And efficiency-enhancing (rather than entitlement) thinking is reshaping foreign aid (as it did for domestic welfare and social insurance programs).

Why now? Globalization has brought with it a heightened awareness of its opportunities and its risks. The analyses in this volume suggest that globalization is entering a new phase. Among private and public actors demand is growing for a better managed, less volatile, and less crisis-prone process. One possible reason: the costs of not addressing some of today's problems are rapidly mounting, while the costs of taking corrective action are declining as new financing technology becomes available. Ever harder to ignore is that openness entails interdependence, which is best addressed through cooperation.

Once embarked on the path to economic openness, states find that one step leads to the next. They need to ensure that their jurisdiction is competitive in more integrated and more efficient markets. National policy alignment under these conditions is no longer an issue solely of power politics. It becomes a self-reinforcing systemic trend.

Many of the new financing mechanisms and tools discussed in this volume are recent innovations. Yet most have been tried and tested, and are ready to make the leap to the policy mainstream. If more widely adopted, they could generate significant cost savings and welfare gains.

THE NEW PUBLIC FINANCE—ANEW

Many issues raised in this volume require further debate, research, and testing. But one point seems clear: the policy approaches and tools of public finance tend to concentrate near the intersections of the public-private and the domestic-foreign policy axes. They form a distinct policy cluster: the new public finance 2. Why the "2"?

The responses of public finance to the porosity of borders between the private and the public sectors have just begun to be integrated into standard public finance theory. Still new, they are referred to here as the new public finance 1, because it breaks out of the statist mold of conventional public finance theory and practice (figure 1). It accepts the interaction of markets and states—and having public and private actors cooperating as well as competing.

New public finance 2, which incorporates modes of new public finance 1, is an emerging subfield of public finance, the financing of global challenges—or global public finance. New public finance 2 broadens the mainly national, single-economy focus of conventional public finance theory to cover the international and national aspects of global challenges (see figure 1). It is about how governments individually and collectively channel public and private financing to global public-policy challenges.[1]

Understanding how this channeling of resources works—and how it could work better—is important for fostering globalization that delivers on its promise of greater efficiency and a better life for all. But it is not the purpose here to recommend any particular financing approach or tool. Decisionmakers will have to choose the best financing package for the challenges they face on a case-by-case basis. This volume has a more limited purpose—to trace change and innovation in the practice of public finance.

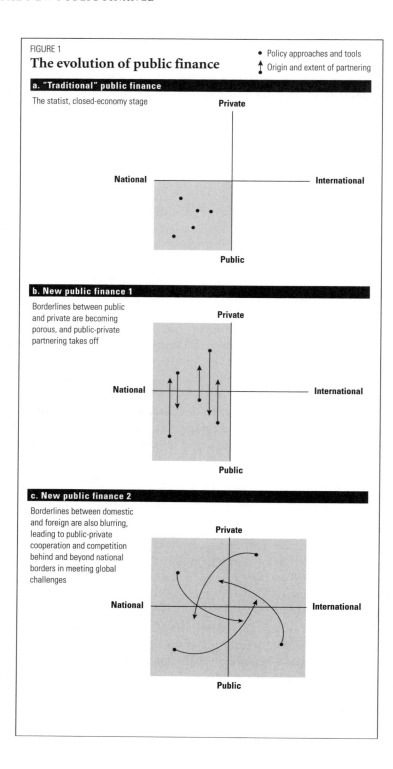

FIGURE 1

The evolution of public finance

● Policy approaches and tools
↕ Origin and extent of partnering

a. "Traditional" public finance

The statist, closed-economy stage

Private

National ——————————— International

Public

b. New public finance 1

Borderlines between public
and private are becoming
porous, and public-private
partnering takes off

Private

National ——————————— International

Public

c. New public finance 2

Borderlines between domestic
and foreign are also blurring,
leading to public-private
cooperation and competition
behind and beyond national
borders in meeting global
challenges

Private

National ——————————— International

Public

THE RESPONSE OF PUBLIC FINANCE TO THE REBALANCING OF MARKETS AND STATES: PUBLIC-PRIVATE PARTNERING

Public policy outcomes such as law and order, peace and security, public health, and poverty reduction are still often referred to as "state-provided." But few goods or services are provided—produced and financed—solely by the state. Many public policy outcomes now result from public-private partnering. The state's involvement may be direct or indirect. And in some instances public goods and services, including welfare programs, may even be undertaken voluntarily and financed with private money.

Referring to public goods and services as state-provided reflects common practice until about the 1980s, when policy began to shift toward public-private partnering. Between 1945 and the end of the 1970s the state played an important economic role in most countries, reflected in rising public spending (as Tanzi documents in this volume). This reflected a confidence in the state's ability and desire to correct market failures.[2]

As new research became available and new conditions emerged in the early 1970s, however, there was more awareness of distortions in political processes and of sources of government failure. The politicians and other policy advocates that advanced growth in public spending came under a more critical light. These new insights came from public choice theory, economic analysis of information asymmetry and agency, and incentives and game theory.[3] They led to a more cautious definition of the role of the state. And markets were seen to resolve problems when property rights are clearly defined (following on Coase's 1960 theorem).[4]

Market failure began to be viewed as merely a potential justification for state intervention, with the desirability of intervention needing to be assessed case by case, to avoid compounding market failure with public policy failure. More recently, greater understanding of the pervasiveness of market failure and of the comparative strengths and weaknesses of society's two major tools of coordination—governments and markets—has encouraged further rethinking. Markets and states are seen as an "interactive partnership" (Stiglitz 1998, p. 8), producing and financing various components of public policy outcomes in cooperation and in competition.

Taking public-private partnering even a step further, governments resort to outsourcing particular tasks (like the provision of meals for hospital patients or military personnel) or to contracting out whole public service lines (like the operation of a railway). The contracting arrangements are also known as private financing initiatives or public-private partnerships.[5]

Thus public finance today is about more than taxing and spending public revenue. It involves channeling resources to public policy goals, with the government using fiscal, regulatory, and monitoring tools to encourage and complement private activities and private spending on these goals. It also involves being open to private sector competition and sharing responsibility and risks with nonstate providers in the interest of enhanced efficiency and effectiveness.

This diversification and refurbishing of the public finance toolkit reflects what Salamon (2002a, p. 2) calls the emergence of "third-party government" and what is here called new public finance 1.

Whether based on full-scale third-party government or on more limited government incentives, many public policy outcomes are now multiactor products, often resulting from a close interlocking of markets and states and drawing on public and private finance. For example, while public investment is declining (figure 2.a), government regulation and norm and standard setting are increasing in many fields (figure 2.b). And while governments are scaling back direct ownership (figure 2.c), private cofinancing of public programs is rising (figure 2.d).

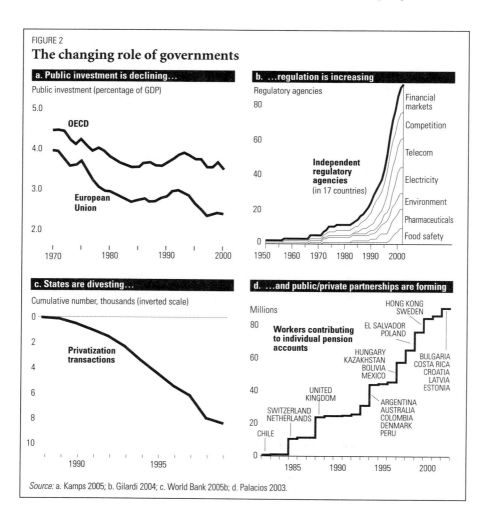

FIGURE 2

The changing role of governments

Source: a. Kamps 2005; b. Gilardi 2004; c. World Bank 2005b; d. Palacios 2003.

Civil society is also assuming a more active part in shaping public policy, and private corporations are more concerned about demonstrating their social responsibility.[6] The growing trend toward public-private partnering echoes changes in the roles of all these actor groups—a broadening consensus on the shared responsibility of state and nonstate actors for public policy concerns, the concerns that potentially affect all.

What makes a good or service public or private is its consumption properties—whether it affects all or is available for all to enjoy. If regulated and monitored well, and perhaps if subsidized to some extent, public goods and services can be produced by markets while still retaining their public consumption properties. While public support will have to be greater for goods or services destined to serve the poor, even poverty reduction programs can be implemented through public-private partnering and incentive schemes that allow private actors to take the extra step of adjusting their behavior to generate social (public) benefits as well as adequate private returns.

But what happens in the case of global challenges, when public policy outcomes are to be achieved under conditions of porous borders between the public and the private sectors and between the domestic and foreign policy realms?

GLOBAL PUBLIC GOODS AND DEVELOPMENT: THE NEW CHALLENGES CONFRONTING PUBLIC FINANCE

The list of global policy issues is long and growing longer. It includes a diverse set of concerns, including advancing international peace and security; fighting transnational terrorism; creating global communication and transportation systems; controlling global communicable diseases; averting and mitigating the risks of climate change; building an international financial architecture and fostering international financial stability; constructing a multilateral trade regime; establishing mechanisms to prevent intellectual piracy, money laundering, and drug trafficking; advancing the universalization of basic human rights and democracy; and reducing poverty and other forms of human deprivation.

These concerns require new policy approaches and new financing technology, presenting a challenge to public finance.

Traditional public finance has two distinguishing characteristics. It is largely state centered, on the assumption that public policy outcomes are state produced. This narrow perspective is now widening, both in practice and, to some extent, in theory, as new public finance 1 becomes more widely established and studied. And, especially important here, traditional public finance theory assumes a single economy, excluding from the analysis most of the outside world—external exigencies as well as opportunities. A recent survey of public finance and economics textbooks covering 170 titles found that few mention global or regional public goods or global equity concerns such as reducing world poverty (Sidikou-Sow

2005). Some of the textbooks address global challenges, especially greenhouse gases and chlorofluorocarbon emissions, but without discussing how dealing with them differs from internalizing externalities that stay within a local or national jurisdiction.[7] There is a wide—and perhaps widening—gap between the practice of public finance and the standard theory presented in public finance and economics textbooks.

Yet, policymakers are addressing global challenges. And in doing so, they have benefited from insightful new studies. Consider the voluminous literature on global warming, international finance and trade, and global poverty and foreign aid. These contributions are part of the new public finance puzzle. But the questions still to be answered are: What overall picture is emerging? How should the policy responses be interpreted?

Answering these questions (done later, when considering the findings of the analyses in this book) requires examining more closely the nature of the global challenges filling today's national and international policy agendas: What makes them global challenges? And why do they increase interdependence among countries?

Identifying the basic categories: global public goods and development

As currently viewed, public finance is expected to help provide public goods and to foster equity.[8] Promoting allocative efficiency is the main rationale for government interventions to support public goods provision—whether financial (subsidies or tax credits) or nonfinancial (regulation). Hence, the public goods-oriented branch of public finance is referred to as the efficiency or allocation branch, with a focus on issues and on particular goods.

The equity or distribution branch of public finance, seen to support society in realizing its goals of fairness and justice, may sometimes have to achieve its objectives through income redistribution and transfer payments. Its main focus is on actors, mainly groups of vulnerable actors such as poor people or people with disabilities.

The global issues on today's policy agendas can be grouped by these same two broad categories of public finance deliverables: global public goods and global equity in development. What is important to know about these two sets of concerns in the context of this volume? We look first at global public goods and then at development.

Global public goods: links to globalization and the required production path

Global public goods, a special class of public goods, share with all other public goods the basic characteristic of being public in consumption—available for all to consume—because they are goods in the public domain.[9] Some of these goods are "naturally" global and public—the moonlight or the warming rays of the sun, which are pure global public goods. Others are impure global public goods—the atmosphere and the ozone shield—available for all yet rival in consumption and are subject to overconsumption and depletion. The gas composition of the atmosphere, if overloaded by pollutants such as carbon dioxide, may change, which could lead to climate change with worldwide (although differentiated) impact.

But many global issues today are not natural global public goods but globalized (formerly essentially national) public goods.

The link between globalization and global public goods. Globalization can be said to result from two main processes, one deliberate and one unintended. Deliberate policy change aimed at openness is usually based on a strategy of removing at-the-border economic barriers (trade-related taxes, capital controls) and fostering policy harmonization behind national borders to promote cross-border market integration (property rights, port facilities, banking codes and standards, educational certificates). A country that removed economic barriers without harmonization behind borders might drive away foreign investors or trading partners who judged its institutions to be nontransparent and difficult to assess for risk. Countries with internationally harmonized institutions, and therefore with lower search and other transaction costs, would be more appealing. Intended globalization is thus typically an outcome of efforts by national policymakers to meet such expectations by fostering behind-the-border policy harmonization, including globalization of market-supporting public goods.

But a second process is also at play: unintended openness. This is for the most part the result of positive or negative spillovers of private or national public actions that are not taken into account by the agents who generate the spillovers when making consumption or production choices.[10] Examples are plant, animal, or human diseases that may hitch a ride with international freight shipments or airline crews and passengers. Thus, intended globalization—freer cross-border movements of goods and services, capital, and people—often generates unintended forms of globalization. But spillovers may occur whether borders are open or not. For example, greenhouse gas emissions have always risen, whether the world was in an era of more open or more closed borders, more extensive or more limited travel across countries and regions. However, their potential effects were not identified until these gases had accumulated heavily in the atmosphere and scientific and technological knowledge had advanced.

Globalization and global public goods are inextricably linked. Globalization, especially economic liberalization, is often perceived as entailing greater privateness—freer trade and other cross-border movements. While true, globalization is quintessentially about enhanced publicness—about more accessible and transparent national policy domains, public policy convergence, and greater interdependence as people experience the effects of others' management of cross-border spillovers.

The production path of global public goods. By choosing whether and how much to foster economic openness, states choose their international competitiveness. And they choose whether and how much to work to contain global pollution, terrorism, or the risk of a financial crisis. Often, then, it is a policy choice whether to provide a desired public good and whether to allow undesirable externalities to go unchecked, perhaps at high costs to other countries or to one's own country. Privateness and "nationalness" as well as publicness and "globalness" are in many instances not innate properties of a good but social constructs, a form conferred by society. This means that public goods can be produced. But how to envision their production path?

Figure 3 illustrates the production path of a national public good and figure 4 that of a global public good.

National building blocks. Many global public goods emerge from a summation of national public goods. Consider market integration. Markets are public goods,

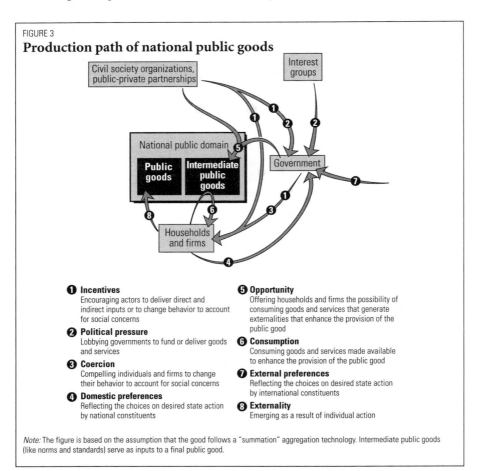

FIGURE 3

Production path of national public goods

❶ **Incentives**
Encouraging actors to deliver direct and indirect inputs or to change behavior to account for social concerns

❷ **Political pressure**
Lobbying governments to fund or deliver goods and services

❸ **Coercion**
Compelling individuals and firms to change their behavior to account for social concerns

❹ **Domestic preferences**
Reflecting the choices on desired state action by national constituents

❺ **Opportunity**
Offering households and firms the possibility of consuming goods and services that generate externalities that enhance the provision of the public good

❻ **Consumption**
Consuming goods and services made available to enhance the provision of the public good

❼ **External preferences**
Reflecting the choices on desired state action by international constituents

❽ **Externality**
Emerging as a result of individual action

Note: The figure is based on the assumption that the good follows a "summation" aggregation technology. Intermediate public goods (like norms and standards) serve as inputs to a final public good.

and integrating markets is a global public good. Integrated global markets could not emerge without country after country building up market-supporting national institutions and harmonizing them in a way that facilitates interoperability between national infrastructure systems and institutional frameworks.

While many global public goods follow such a summation process, important variations may occur.[11] The public effects of some goods or activities are perfectly substitutable and lend themselves to trading arrangements. Reductions in carbon dioxide emissions are a case in point. If actor B can reduce emissions more cheaply than actor A, actor A might pay actor B to provide A's contribution.

In other instances the public effects to be summed up are location specific and thus nonsubstitutable. For example, public health services might have to be improved everywhere to achieve effective global control of a communicable disease. If the goal is eradicating the disease, the smallest contribution will determine the overall provision level of the good. The same holds for terrorism control through improvements in aviation security. If such "weakest link" situations arise because an underproviding country lacks adequate resources, it might be in the enlightened self-interest of richer countries to financially support the poorer country. As Sandler (in this volume) argues, richer countries gain little from continuing to upgrade their airport screening facilities, for example, if other countries are not doing the same.

Thus, global public goods often emerge as countries move in the same direction nationally in public good provision. But sometimes effectiveness reasons suggest complementing national actions with international action—as in a weakest link situation—and sometimes cross-border cooperation is desirable for efficiency reasons, as with carbon dioxide emissions trading.

But before examining the production path of global public goods, it is helpful to look further at the actors engaged in producing national public goods.

Figure 3 clearly illustrates how public goods are multiactor products to which all groups might potentially contribute. For example, civil society and lobbyists might nudge the government into taking action (arrows 1 and 2) while also seeking to influence the general public through their advocacy activities (arrow 1). As a result, public demand for a certain public good, say smoke-free public spaces, may build (arrow 4). In response, the government might provide an intermediate public good such as an information campaign on the ill effects of smoking in public places (arrow 3), hoping to alter the behavior of individual actors (arrow 6). Coercive measures might also be needed, such as a ban on smoking in public places (arrow 3). Together, the positive externalities resulting from the changed behavior of individuals (voluntary and coerced) would then produce the desired public good, smoke-free public spaces (arrow 8). The government might also be influenced by external preferences (arrow 7), for example, by foreign visitors who demand smoke-free airports and hotel rooms or by international conventions such as the World Health Organization Framework Convention on Tobacco Control.[12]

International-level complements. National and global public goods are often closely linked (arrow 7 of figure 3). National public goods are the main building blocks of summation-type global public goods (figure 4). International cooperation of various types (arrows 1, 2, 4, and 5) may alter the behavior of individual states or private actors (arrows 3 and 6), generating the required national contributions (arrow 8) to the global public good.

An important difference between collective actions at the national and the international levels is that coercion is not available at the international level, where all interactions and choices are voluntary. This intensifies the importance of the incentive challenges that various goods present and of the distribution of their costs and benefits across actor groups: Who might be motivated, and how strongly, to enhance the provision of a good? And if preferences do not overlap, how could a better match of incentive structures be achieved? Perhaps simply by defining global rules of the game? Or by adding "carrots" such as money or "sticks" such as trade sanctions?

FIGURE 4

Production path of global public goods

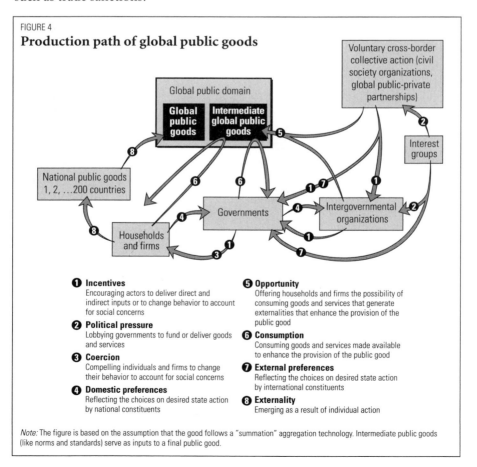

❶ **Incentives**
Encouraging actors to deliver direct and indirect inputs or to change behavior to account for social concerns

❷ **Political pressure**
Lobbying governments to fund or deliver goods and services

❸ **Coercion**
Compelling individuals and firms to change their behavior to account for social concerns

❹ **Domestic preferences**
Reflecting the choices on desired state action by national constituents

❺ **Opportunity**
Offering households and firms the possibility of consuming goods and services that generate externalities that enhance the provision of the public good

❻ **Consumption**
Consuming goods and services made available to enhance the provision of the public good

❼ **External preferences**
Reflecting the choices on desired state action by international constituents

❽ **Externality**
Emerging as a result of individual action

Note: The figure is based on the assumption that the good follows a "summation" aggregation technology. Intermediate public goods (like norms and standards) serve as inputs to a final public good.

Money—as compensatory financing—may also be required where a global public good follows the "best shot" aggregation technology. With scientific and technological knowledge, for example, a new technology need be invented only once to exist. One best shot suffices. A potential inventor may be able to finance the effort as long as the resources are available and there is an expectation that the research and development costs can be recovered. Where the individual returns will not cover expected costs, it may be necessary for other interested actors to share the costs.

International cooperation in sharing the costs of a joint international initiative always follows a summation process, whatever the aggregation technology of the goods' technical production path (Barrett in this volume). The group of financiers can be quite different from—and usually smaller than—the group of actors involved in the production process as a whole, however. This is especially so where money does not simply feed into cost-sharing arrangements but serves as an incentive or as compensation for services rendered.

Since the production of many global public goods requires interventions by different actor groups, questions arise about which actors to involve and at what level to undertake particular interventions. Using malaria control as an example, table 1 lists several rationales that could guide these selections—from fostering cross-border collective action and preventing free-riding to subsidiarity and other efficiency, equity, and effectiveness concerns. For implementation five main levels or actor groups could be involved: intergovernmental agencies, national governments, businesses, global public-private partnerships, and individual households and the general public. Table 1 also shows the building blocks that each group contributes.

Development: its global dimension and production path
Traditionally, development has been thought of as an essentially national public good. Foreign aid in support of development was motivated largely by moral and ethical concerns—empathy with those trapped in poverty. International support for development, notably official development assistance, fell squarely into the distribution or equity branch of public finance—representing the international arm of this branch.[13]

This perception of development is changing. While still viewed by many as a moral imperative, fostering global equity for development is acquiring an added global dimension: to support international peace and security.

The broadened global dimension of development. Experience has shown that where development is stagnating or reversing, the consequences may be felt worldwide: civil strife and conflict may worsen and spill violence and refugees across borders. Basic social services may falter and allow diseases long thought to be under control to resurface and cross borders.

TABLE 1

Rationales for identifying the appropriate actor and the level of policy interventions: the case of malaria control

Outcome to be produced	Level of intervention/ actor chosen	Rationale
• Agreements to act in a coordinated manner • International purchase commitment or other type of research and development (R&D) incentives • Bulk purchasing facility for medicines, bednets, and other inputs	Intergovernmental agencies	• To prevent free-riding by individual countries • To maximize efficiency by producing knowledge, a nonrival good, only once in a coordinated way, and by pooling national incentive resources to elicit pharmaceutical R&D • To unlock economies of scale and of scope
• Public health system services • Public awareness campaigns • Subsidies for local bednet production	National governments	• To adapt to country conditions for efficiency and equity reasons • To adapt to country conditions for efficiency and equity reasons • To align private and national social returns
• Development of vaccines and pharmaceutical products • Bednet production	Private firms	• To achieve efficiency and effectiveness (because much of the relevant expertise is in the private sector) • To achieve efficiency and effectiveness (because bednets are a private good and can be traded in markets if subsidies are available)
• Development of vaccines and pharmaceutical products	Global public-private partnerships	• To facilitate the linking of equity to efficiency and effectiveness considerations through such arrangements as differential patenting

TABLE 1 CONTINUED

Rationales for identifying the appropriate actor and the level of policy interventions: the case of malaria control

Outcome to be produced	Level of intervention/ actor chosen	Rationale
• Development of new ways to deliver vaccines to rural areas (for example, by including cold storage facilities in private distribution networks)		• To add equity to efficiency and effectiveness considerations
• Consumption of medicines and bednets; provision of policy feedback	Private households	• To foster efficiency
• Policy feedback		• To strengthen policy relevance and ownership

The vital role of development in achieving global security and stability is recognized in the report of the High-Level Panel on Threats, Challenges and Change (2004, p. viii) established by the United Nations Secretary-General: "extreme poverty and infectious diseases threaten many people directly, but they also provide fertile breeding-ground for threats, including civil conflict. Even people in rich countries will be more secure if their Governments help poor countries to defeat poverty and disease by meeting the Millennium Development Goals."

Beyond such direct costs for the international community, lack of development also entails opportunity costs. For example, the U.S. African Growth and Opportunity Act states that while forging stronger commercial ties between Africa and the United States "helps to integrate Africa into the world economy…U.S. firms may [also] find new opportunities in privatizations of African state-owned enterprises, or in partnership with African companies in infrastructure projects."[14]

Meanwhile, altruism is not waning either. Greater cross-border economic activity and connectivity have transformed the causes of misfortune in its many aspects—from crime and violence to hunger, disease, premature death, and natural disasters—from local into common global problems. Global communications and nearly instantaneous transmission of news now expose human rights violations, poverty, and disaster to the entire world, sometimes in real time, as in the tsunami disaster that hit several Asian and African countries in December 2004. The international community was "present" at the disaster, seeing it unfold.

Public opinion surveys show that in many parts of the world a majority of the public, politicians, and business leaders support poverty reduction efforts to enhance development—in part, because they consider it to be a moral or ethical imperative and in part because they view it to be in their enlightened political or economic self-interest.[15] One of the clearest reflections of the heightened global concern with inadequate progress in development is the Millennium Development Goals,[16] which emerged from the Millennium Declaration adopted by world leaders in 2000 (UN General Assembly 2000). These goals aim to bring about a real difference in people's lives: halving world poverty and reducing other targeted forms of human deprivation by 2015.

The production path of development. National factors—a country's location and size as well as its governance and policy choices—are key determinants of development (Sachs 2005; UN Millennium Project 2005). There is broad international consensus on this point and on the belief that external conditions also matter— the design of multilateral policy regimes, the policy choices of other countries, and the business strategies of market participants (Derviş 2005; UN 2002).

The main tool of external support for development has been official development assistance, bilateral and multilateral transfers from richer to poorer countries. More than 50 years of experience have shown that not only the level of foreign aid but also its timing and conditions are vitally important. Unpredictable aid flows may lead to costly disruptions in policy initiatives in developing countries (Bulíř and Hamann 2003; UN 2005). Tying foreign aid to purchases in donor countries also may do more harm than good to developing countries (OECD 2001; Jepma 1994).[17] And evidence is accumulating that in many instances the impact of foreign aid-financed initiatives was cancelled out by other international factors[18] and that adequately provided and fairly designed global public goods such as the multilateral trade regime and international financial architecture also matter. The same holds true for adequately provided regional public goods.[19]

Clearly, foreign aid for development must encompass more than financial transfers from governments of richer countries to governments of poorer countries. Besides the conventional government-to-government public resource transfers the major building blocks of foreign aid include adequately provided and fairly designed regional and global public goods and the coherence of industrial country policy objectives with global development—as also noted by the UK government-led Commission for Africa (2005) and the Group of Eight (G-8 2005).

Within this widened perspective on the production path of global development, foreign aid, like global public goods provision, involves national actions in recipient and donor countries and international collective action (figure 5). It also receives contributions from private actors through export earnings, foreign savings, and remittances.

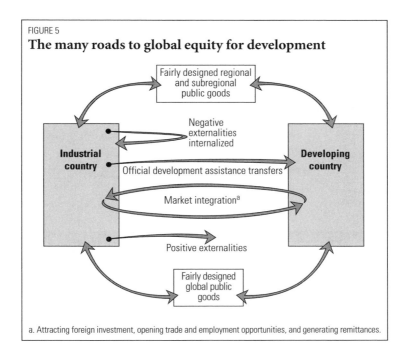

FIGURE 5

The many roads to global equity for development

Fairly designed regional and subregional public goods

Industrial country

Negative externalities internalized

Official development assistance transfers

Developing country

Market integration[a]

Positive externalities

Fairly designed global public goods

a. Attracting foreign investment, opening trade and employment opportunities, and generating remittances.

* * *

Globalization has changed the nature of the "deliverables" of public finance, both in how people experience them (consumption properties) and in what is required to achieve a policy result (production properties).

The rebalancing of markets and states led to an interlocking of the public and private sectors. Globalization has led to an interlocking of countries' national public domains—markets, public health conditions, law and order, security, and sociocultural conditions—and an increase in cross-border flows, both intended ones like trade and capital flows (figures 6.a and 6.b) and unintended ones like carbon dioxide emissions (figure 6.c) and the ill-effects of poverty, as reflected, for example, in the global resolve to step up poverty reduction (figure 6.d). And with greater openness (intended or not) and cross-border flows has come an intertwining of the public policy space of countries and the emergence of global challenges—problems and opportunities shared by all.

Has this growing importance of global challenges prompted changes in the policy approaches and tools of public finance, as happened with the rebalancing of the private and public sectors? That question is at the center of this volume. There is strong evidence that new public finance 2 is emerging, bringing new approaches and tools to bridge the foreign-domestic divide.

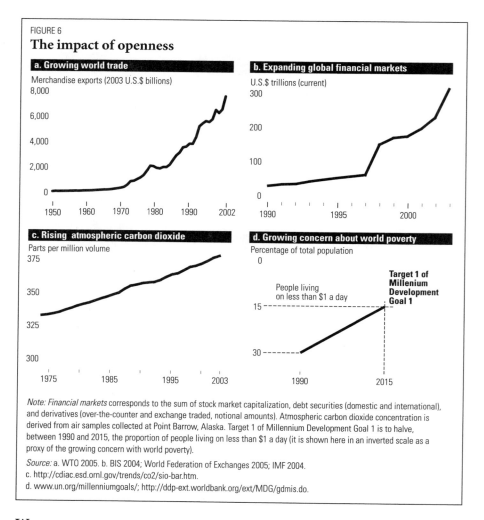

FIGURE 6
The impact of openness

a. Growing world trade

Merchandise exports (2003 U.S.$ billions)

b. Expanding global financial markets

U.S.$ trillions (current)

c. Rising atmospheric carbon dioxide

Parts per million volume

d. Growing concern about world poverty

Percentage of total population

People living
on less than $1 a day

Target 1 of
Millenium
Development
Goal 1

Note: *Financial markets* corresponds to the sum of stock market capitalization, debt securities (domestic and international), and derivatives (over-the-counter and exchange traded, notional amounts). Atmospheric carbon dioxide concentration is derived from air samples collected at Point Barrow, Alaska. Target 1 of Millennium Development Goal 1 is to halve, between 1990 and 2015, the proportion of people living on less than $1 a day (it is shown here in an inverted scale as a proxy of the growing concern with world poverty).

Source: a. WTO 2005. b. BIS 2004; World Federation of Exchanges 2005; IMF 2004.
c. http://cdiac.esd.ornl.gov/trends/co2/sio-bar.htm.
d. www.un.org/millenniumgoals/; http://ddp-ext.worldbank.org/ext/MDG/gdmis.do.

WHAT THE BOOK BUILDS ON

Above all, this book builds on the changing practice of public finance. The financing methods and tools discussed here are not untested or speculative. Most have been around for some time. They were selected for analysis precisely because they form part of a new emerging policy practice. These financing methods and tools are not about what "should" be done—but about what is being done.

The analyses in this book take their conceptual and analytical framework from the literature on public finance. But even a cursory look at the contents reveals that the chapters draw on a wide range of disciplines, from international economics and finance, financial markets, financial engineering and innovation, and environmental and health economics to international relations and cooperation theories and foreign aid studies. Contributors combine insights from behavioral, incentive, information, and institutional economics with those from public choice, principal-agent, and other theories. This multidisciplinarity reflects the nature of the global challenges—their position at the crossroads of the public-private and national-international policy axes.

While public finance and public economics textbooks tend to look inward from a microeconomic perspective, international economics and finance textbooks focus on macroeconomics, government policy action and conditions that affect—and are affected by—cross-border flows of goods, services, capital, and people.

Another strand of the literature looks at globalization and public finance from the outside in, examining such issues as how the lifting of at-the-border barriers to trade and capital flows affects national taxes and spending.[20] It examines mainly how globalization affects countries and domestic policy choices, not how state and nonstate actors reach out to each other to respond to and to shape globalization.

International relations studies examine collective action at the international level. These studies seek to explain how international, especially intergovernmental, negotiations work and why countries comply with or renege on agreements. Discussion of the financing of international cooperation tends to be limited to the foreign aid literature,[21] because much of the money required for cross-border cooperation on global public goods has so far been accommodated within the foreign aid portfolio.[22] The contributions to this literature focus mainly on the international dimension, leaving aside related issues of national public finance.

Thus strands of the literature contribute to an understanding of the financing of the global challenges discussed in this volume,[23] but none integrates its national and international and public and private perspectives. The added value of this volume is its integrated perspective on how public finance is adapting to the expanding globalizing nature of its main deliverables, public goods and equity, and reinventing itself along the way.

NOTES

1. Another body of literature that emerged in the 1970s was also referred to as the "new public finance." Its focus was on introducing more quantitative methods (see Boskin and Stiglitz 1977). Today, quantitative, including econometric, studies are at the core of empirical research in economics, including public finance. So the label "new public finance" is available again and is used here to denote recent changes in the practice of public finance.

2. Market failures, which impede the efficient allocation of resources that is assumed to take place in perfectly competitive markets, may emerge as a result of six factors: imperfect competition, public goods, externalities, incomplete markets,

imperfect information, and unemployment and other macroeconomic disturbances (Stiglitz 2000).

3. Jones (in this volume) describes aspects of the public choice critique. See Buchanan and Musgrave (1999) for a dialogue between the traditional public finance perspective and the public choice approach.

4. The Coase theorem states that efficient economic outcomes will emerge from market transactions after property rights have been assigned and exchange takes place in the presence of perfect competitive markets and without transaction costs; under these conditions the efficiency outcome is independent of the way in which property rights have been assigned (Coase 1960).

5. Public-private partnerships have many potential advantages. They can leverage private finance, transfer risk to the parties best suited to bear it, smooth the flow of public expenditures, and take advantage of each actor's comparative strength to improve results. These and other benefits help to realize public sector efficiency gains and provide scope for reducing public spending or for doing more with the same level of public resources, and so they have been the focus of much of the analysis of public-private partnering. Recent experience has also brought to light the potential risks. A rash of corporate scandals has underlined the need for stronger corporate governance, accountancy standards, and disclosure requirements. And while markets in most countries today are up to the task of mediating transactions in goods such as steel, soap, or matches, there is concern about contracting out such services as prisons, hospitals, defense, or airport security. These services are difficult to monitor and thus are at risk of "quality shading" (hospital rooms becoming more crowded, food portions less nutritious, security personnel less trained). Developing countries worry about the sudden withdrawal of foreign private capital from local projects, such as public-private partnerships in infrastructure provision. And investors in these countries worry about political risks, including governments reneging on contracts. See also Spackman (2002) and Harris (2003).

6. For a discussion of business responses to public policy concerns, see, for example, Froot (1999) and Labatt and White (2002).

7. Studies tracing the evolution of the changes in public finance scholarship over the past several decades reveal that the absence of such issues is characteristic not only of public finance textbooks but of the public finance field more generally. See, for example, Rosen (1997) and the special issue of the *Journal of Public Economics* (2002). A rare exception is the path-breaking 1969 book by Richard Musgrave, *Fiscal Systems*, which discusses a number of the topics referred to here as new public finance 2.

8. Earlier textbooks (such as Musgrave and Musgrave 1989) identified three branches of public finance, with the third being the stabilization branch. Its function was to correct the macroeconomic failure to ensure full employment with stable prices (Musgrave 1999). However, Rosen (1997) notes that this branch was not part of a representative public finance textbook of the late 1940s nor is it included in textbooks in the late 1990s.

9. More detailed definitions of public goods and global public goods are presented in the glossary in the annex to this volume. Interested readers may also wish to consult Barrett and Sandler (both in this volume) and Cornes and Sandler (1996); Ferroni and Mody (2002); Kanbur, Sandler, and Morrison (1999); Kaul, Grunberg, and Stern (1999); Kaul and others (2003); and Sandler (1997, 1998, 2004).

10. For a fuller definition of externalities, see the glossary in the annexes and the literature mentioned in note 9.

11. The concept of aggregation technology was introduced by Hirshleifer (1983) and by Cornes and Sandler (1984) and elaborated on by Cornes (1993).

12. This convention entered into force on February 27, 2005. For further information see www.who.int/tobacco/framework/en.

13. Of course, the motivation for development assistance or foreign aid has not always been based only on moral or ethical concerns. Only all too often commercial or geopolitical and strategic-military considerations also came into play. See, for example, Alesina and Dollar (2000).

14. The African Growth and Opportunity Act is Title 1 of the U.S. Trade and Development Act of 2000. See www.agoa.gov/faq/faq.html.

15. See, for example, Gallup International (2005) and McDonnell, Solignac Lecomte, and Wegimont (2003).

16. See www.un.org/millenniumgoals.

17. For more general assessments of the current shortcomings in the foreign aid system see Sachs (2005) and the analysis in UN Millennium Project (2005), among others.

18. Including, for example, lack of coherence in policymaking on the part of donor countries (see, for example, OECD 2003b).

19. See, for instance, Birdsall and Rojas-Suarez (2004).

20. See, for example, Cnossen and Sinn (2003); Kremer and Mehta (2000); Razin and Sadka (1999); Sinn (2002); and Sørensen (1998). See also the journal *International Tax and Public Finance.*

21. Important exceptions include Keohane and Levy (1996) and Sandler (1997, 2004).

22. See Atkinson (2004); Technical Group on Innovative Financing Mechanisms (2004), launched by the governments of Brazil, Chile, France, and Spain and joined by Algeria and Germany; Sagasti, Bezanson, and Prada (2005); and Working Group on New International Contributions to Finance Development (2004), known as "Landau report" for the chairman of the Working Group, Jean-Pierre Landau.

23. See also the Further Reading section in the annexes for additional literature consulted.

REFERENCES

Alesina, Alberto, and David Dollar. 2000. "Who Gives Foreign Aid to Whom and Why?" *Journal of Economic Growth* 5 (1): 33–63.

Atkinson, Anthony B., ed. 2004. *New Sources of Development Finance.* Oxford: Oxford University Press.

Bailey, Stephen J. [1995]. 2002. *Public Sector Economics: Theory, Policy, and Practice.* 2nd edition. Basingstoke, UK: Palgrave Macmillan.

———. 2004. *Strategic Public Finance.* Basingstoke, UK: Palgrave Macmillan.

Birdsall, Nancy, and Liliana Rojas-Suarez. 2004. *Financing Development: The Power of Regionalism.* Washington, D.C.: Center for Global Development.

BIS (Bank for International Settlements). 2004. *BIS Quarterly Review: International Banking and Financial Market Developments.* September. [www.bis.org/].

Boskin, Michael J., and Joseph E. Stiglitz. 1977. "Some Lessons from the New Public Finance." *American Economic Review* 67 (1): 295–301.

Buchanan, James M., and Richard A. Musgrave. 1999. *Public Finance and Public Choice: Two Contrasting Visions on the State.* Cambridge, Mass.: MIT Press.

Bulíř, Aleš, and Javier Hamann. 2003. "Aid Volatility: An Empirical Assessment." *IMF Staff Papers* 50 (1): 64–89.

Commission for Africa. 2005. *Our Common Interest: Report of the Commission for Africa.* London. [www.commissionforafrica.org/english/report/thereport/english/11-03-05 _cr_report.pdf].

Cnossen, Sijbren, and Hans-Werner Sinn, eds. 2003. *Public Finance and Public Policy in the New Century.* Cambridge, Mass.: MIT Press.

Coase, Ronald H. 1960. "The Problem of Social Cost." *Journal of Law and Economics* 3 (1): 1–44.

Cornes, Richard. 1993. "Dyke Maintenance and Other Stories: Some Neglected Types of Public Goods." *Quarterly Journal of Economics* 108 (1): 259–71.

Cornes, Richard, and Todd Sandler. 1984. "Easy Riders, Joint Production, and Public Goods." *Economic Journal* 94 (3): 580–98.

———. 1996. *The Theory of Externalities, Public Goods, and Club Goods.* Cambridge: Cambridge University Press.

Derviş, Kemal. 2005. *A Better Globalization: Legitimacy, Governance, and Reform.* Washington, D.C.: Center for Global Development.

Ferroni, Marco, and Ashoka Mody, eds. 2002. *International Public Goods: Incentives, Measurement, and Financing.* Washington, D.C.: Kluwer Academic Publishers and World Bank.

Froot, Kenneth A., ed. 1999. *The Financing of Catastrophe Risk.* Chicago, Ill.: Chicago University Press.

G-8 (Group of Eight). 2005. "Gleneagles Communiqué on Africa, Climate Change,

Energy, and Sustainable Development." [www.fco.gov.uk/Files/kfile/PostG8_Gleneagles_Communique.pdf].

Gallup International. 2005. *Voice of the People: Progress and Priorities for 2005.* Zurich, Switzerland.

Gilardi, Fabrizio. 2004. "Delegation in the Regulatory State: Origins and Diffusion of Independent Regulatory Agencies in Western Europe." Doctoral dissertation. University of Lausanne, Switzerland.

Harris, Clive. 2003. *Private Participation in Infrastructure in Developing Countries: Trends, Impacts, and Policy Lessons.* Washington, D.C.: World Bank.

High-Level Panel on Threats, Challenges, and Change. 2004. *A More Secure World: Our Shared Responsibility.* New York: United Nations.

Hillman, Arye L. 2003. *Public Finance and Public Policy: Responsibilities and Limitations of Government.* Cambridge: Cambridge University Press.

Hirshleifer, Jack. 1983. "From Weakest-Link to Best-Shot: The Voluntary Provision of Public Goods." *Public Choice* 41 (3): 371–86.

IMF (International Monetary Fund). 2004. "Sovereign Debt Structure for Crisis Prevention." Research Department, Washington, D.C. [www.imf.org/external/np/res/docs/2004/070204.pdf].

Jepma, Catrinus J. 1994. *Inter-Nation Policy Co-Ordination and Untying of Aid.* Brookfield, Vt.: Ashgate Publishing Company.

Journal of Public Economics. 2002. Special Issue on Public Finance and Economics. Volume 86, issue 3.

Kamps, Christophe. 2005. "Is There a Lack of Public Capital in the European Union?" Working Paper. Kiel Institute for World Economics, Kiel, Germany. [www.uni-kiel.de/ifw/staff/kampsc/paper_neu.pdf].

Kanbur, Ravi, Todd Sandler, and Kevin Morrison. 1999. "The Future of Development Assistance: Common Pools and International Public Goods." Policy Essay 25. Overseas Development Council, Washington, D.C.

Kaul, Inge, Isabelle Grunberg, and Marc A. Stern, eds. 1999. *Global Public Goods: International Cooperation in the 21st Century.* New York: Oxford University Press.

Kaul, Inge, Pedro Conceição, Katell Le Goulven, and Ronald U. Mendoza, eds. 2003. *Providing Global Public Goods: Managing Globalization.* New York: Oxford University Press.

Keohane, Robert O., and Marc A. Levy, eds. 1996. *Institutions for Environmental Aid.* Cambridge, Mass.: MIT Press.

Kremer, Michael, and Paras Mehta. 2000. *Globalization and International Public Finance.* NBER Working Paper 7575. Cambridge, Mass.: National Bureau of Economic Research.

Labatt, Sonia, and Rodney R. White. 2002. *Environmental Finance: A Guide to Environmental Risk Assessment and Financial Products.* New York: Wiley.

McDonnell, Ida, Henri-Bernard Solignac Lecomte, and Liam Wegimont. 2003. *Public Opinion and the Fight against Poverty.* Organisation for Economic Co-operation and Development, Paris.

Musgrave, Richard A. 1969. *Fiscal Systems.* New Haven, Conn.: Yale University Press.

————. 1999. "The Nature of the Fiscal State: The Roots of My Thinking." In James M. Buchanan and Richard A. Musgrave, eds., *Public Finance and Public Choice: Two Contrasting Visions on the State.* Cambridge, Mass.: MIT Press.

Musgrave, Richard A., and Peggy B. Musgrave. 1989. *Public Finance in Theory and Practice.* 5th edition. New York: McGraw-Hill.

OECD (Organisation for Economic Co-operation and Development). 2001. *Policy Brief: Untying Aid to Least Developing Countries.* Paris. [www.oecd.org/dataoecd/16/24/2002959.pdf].

————. 2003a. *Model Tax Convention on Income and on Capital: Condensed Version.* Paris.

————. 2003b. *Policy Brief: Policy Coherence—Vital for Global Development.* Paris. [www.oecd.org/dataoecd/11/35/20202515.pdf].

Palacios, Robert. 2003. "Privatizing National Social Security Schemes: The International Experience with Privatizing Pension Systems." International Social Security Association Meeting of Directors of Social Security Organizations in English-Speaking Africa, October 7–9, Banjul, The Gambia.

Razin, Assaf, and Efraim Sadka, eds. 1999. *The Economics of Globalization: Policy Perspectives from Public Economics.* Cambridge: Cambridge University Press.

Rosen, Harvey S. 1997. *The Way We Were (and Are): Changes in Public Finance and Its Textbooks.* NBER Working Paper 5972. Cambridge, Mass.: National Bureau of Economic Research.

————. 2005. *Public Finance.* 7th ed. New York: McGraw-Hill/Irwin.

Sachs, Jeffrey. 2005. *The End of Poverty: Economic Possibilities of Our Time.* New York: The Penguin Press.

Sagasti, Francisco, Keith Bezanson, and Fernando Prada. 2005. *The Future of Development Financing: Challenges and Strategic Choices.* Basingstoke: Palgrave Macmillan.

Salamon, Lester M. 2002a. "The New Governance and the Tools of Public Action: An Introduction." In Lester M. Salamon, ed., *The Tools of Government: A Guide to the New Governance.* New York: Oxford University Press.

————, ed. 2002b. *The Tools of Government: A Guide to the New Governance.* New York: Oxford University Press.

Sandler, Todd. 1997. *Global Challenges: An Approach to Environmental, Political, and Economic Problems.* Cambridge: Cambridge University Press.

————. 1998. "Global and Regional Public Goods: A Prognosis for Collective Action." *Fiscal Studies* 19 (3): 221–47.

————. 2004. *Global Collective Action.* Cambridge: Cambridge University Press.

Sidikou-Sow, Balkissa. 2005. "Has 'Globalization' As Yet Changed Standard Theory?

A Survey of Textbooks in Public Finance and Public Economics." UNDP/ODS Background Paper. United Nations Development Programme, Office of Development Studies, New York. [www.thenewpublicfinance.org].

Sinn, Hans-Werner. 2002. *The New Systems Competition.* NBER Working Paper 8747. Cambridge, Mass.: National Bureau of Economic Research.

Sørensen, Peter Birch, ed. 1998. *Public Finance in a Changing World.* Basingstoke, UK: Palgrave Macmillan.

Spackman, Michael. 2002. "Public-Private Partnerships: Lessons from the British Approach." *Economic Systems* 26 (3): 283–301.

Stiglitz, Joseph E. 1998. "Redefining the Role of the State: *What* Should It Do? *How* Should It Do It? And *How* Should These Decisions Be Made?" Paper presented on the Tenth Anniversary of the MITI Research Institute, March 17, Tokyo. [www.meti.go.jp/topic/mitilab/downloadfiles/m2012-1j.pdf].

————. 2000. *Economics of the Public Sector.* 3rd Edition. New York: W. W. Norton.

————. 2001. "Towards a New Paradigm for Development: Strategies, Policies, and Processes." 9th Raul Prebisch Lecture, delivered at the Palais des Nations, October 19, 1998, Geneva. In Ha-Joon Chang, ed., *The Rebel Within.* London: Wimbledon Publishing Company.

Technical Group on Innovative Financing Mechanisms. 2004. *Action against Poverty: Final Report of the Technical Group on Innovative Financing Mechanisms.* [www.mre. gov.br/ingles/politica_externa/temas_agenda/acfp/Report-final%20version.pdf].

UN (United Nations). 2002. *Report of the International Conference on Financing for Development.* A/CONF.198/11. New York.

————. 2005. *Resolution on Follow-up and Implementation of the Outcome of the International Conference on Financing for Development.* A/RES/59/225. New York.

UN General Assembly. 2000. *United Nations Millennium Declaration.* 55th session. Resolution adopted September 18. A/55/2. New York.

UN Millennium Project. 2005. *Investing in Development: A Practical Plan to Achieve the Millennium Development Goals.* London: Earthscan.

Working Group on New International Contributions to Finance Development. 2004. "Final Report of the Working Group on New International Contributions to Finance Development." [www.france.diplomatie.fr/actual/pdf/landau_report. pdf].

World Bank. 2005a. "Board Presentations of PRSP Documents as at May 31, 2005." Washington, D.C. [http://siteresources.worldbank.org/INTPRS1/Resources/boardlist.pdf].

————. 2005b. *Global Development Finance 2005: Mobilizing Finance and Managing Vulnerability.* Washington, D.C.

World Federation of Exchanges. 2005. "Time Series 1990–2003." [www.fibv.com/WFE/home.asp?menu=325].

WTO (World Trade Organization). 2005. *International Trade Statistics 2004.* Geneva. [www.wto.org/english/res_e/statis_e/its2004_e/its04_longterm_e.htm].

THE CHANGES UNDER WAY
FINANCING GLOBAL CHALLENGES THROUGH INTERNATIONAL COOPERATION BEHIND AND BEYOND BORDERS

INGE KAUL AND PEDRO CONCEIÇÃO

The world seems to be caught in a web of crises, risks, and uncertainties. International terrorist attacks are penetrating deep into countries. Competition between firms and states is intensifying, giving rise to fears about outsourcing, economic restructuring, unemployment, and thinning social safety nets. Financial and housing market bubbles—or collapses—are holding people in a state of near-permanent anxiety. Uncertainty about the availability of oil at low and stable prices is generating concern about meeting the world's future energy demands. Incidents of avian flu are triggering fears of an impending pandemic.

As this volume shows, the growing interdependence of countries and the accompanying volatility have prompted calls for managing globalization better, especially the downside—emerging global scarcities, negative cross-border spillovers, excess market swings, and world poverty. These persist in the midst of unprecedented wealth and rapid technological advance, undermining globalization's promise of a better life for all. Openness and competitiveness are now to be combined with sustainability and stability, including more broad-based development.

Public finance policy approaches and tools have responded to this widening of the policy focus with change and innovation. Nationally, public finance has taken on a new function: fostering a pattern of public and private spending to support the blending of external and domestic policy preferences or, put differently, international cooperation *behind* national borders. The objective is to provide the national building blocks that are crucial for meeting global challenges.

Internationally, economic rationales are becoming intertwined with foreign policy goals, engendering new modes of public finance 1 (see previous chapter) and transforming international cooperation *beyond* national borders from an

28

intergovernmental process into a multiactor process of public-private partnering and competition. Governments cooperate on these issues not—or at least not only—to strengthen their international position or to expand or firm up territorial borders. Rather, their goal is to correct the underprovision of policy goals that promise high global as well as national and social returns—and to do so cost-effectively.

INTERNATIONAL COOPERATION BEHIND NATIONAL BORDERS: INCORPORATING GLOBAL CHALLENGES INTO NATIONAL PUBLIC FINANCE

Public finance is intimately linked to the policy priorities that governments pursue and to their relationship with markets and civil society. Part 1 of this volume begins with an analysis of the new role of the state as intermediary between external and domestic policy preferences. It provides an overview of some of the reoriented traditional tasks and the newer, added tasks that are emerging and of how the pursuit of enhanced openness and competitiveness and, more recently, the emphasis on sustainability, stability, and a wider sharing of globalization's benefits have affected public finance at the national level (figure 1).

Subsequent chapters examine some of the newer national public finance tasks flowing from the state's role in blending external and domestic policy demands. These include maintaining fiscal discipline (preferably without jeopardizing prior

FIGURE 1

Public finance tasks of international cooperation behind borders

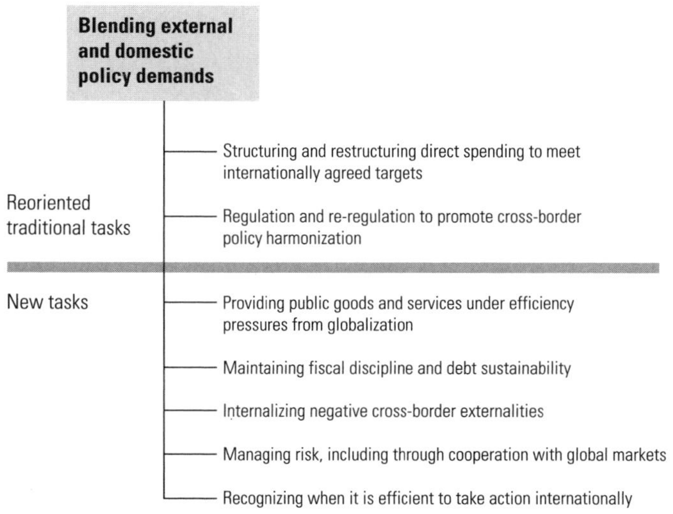

development gains or the provision of public services), managing cross-border externalities, using global markets to strengthen risk management, and knowing the limits to cooperation behind national borders or, put differently, knowing when it pays to seek the cooperation of others abroad.

A new function of public finance: blending external and domestic policy demands

States face a rapid increase in external expectations about desirable national policy that emanate from outside the domestic political process. As Kaul shows (in the chapter on the intermediary state), they arise from formal intergovernmental negotiations and, increasingly, from informal processes of norm and standard setting by nonstate actors, such as country credit rating agencies and other market analysts, global civil society networks, and international professional associations (accountants, lawyers, industry groups).

These external demands urge governments to pursue policies of sustainable globalization. Just as governments are encouraged to increase economic openness and enhance their country's competitiveness, so they are being asked to help people cope with the inevitable volatility that comes with economic openness and competitiveness, by managing cross-border externalities, including external risks to the economy. Worldwide, national public policies echo these expectations, in action as well as political rhetoric. Multiple influences, differing by country and issue, contribute to this alignment. Some are "push" factors, such as the political pressure one country or group of countries exerts on another. Others are "pull" factors, as with the prospects of reaping gains from participating in global networks such as those for international civil aviation or the multilateral trade regime.

Expectations of economic openness promote interaction between the public and private sectors and the adoption of new public finance 1 modalities. But such expectations also lead to a growing competitiveness among states. Once governments embrace openness, a gradual and self-propelling shift toward further policy alignment takes hold. With openness comes greater mobility of capital and, increasingly, of labor, while states remain shackled to their territory. A global "Tiebout effect" (Tiebout 1956) sets in, with mobile factors of production choosing the national jurisdiction that suits them best, pressuring governments to comply with what is expected of them if they wish to retain or attract those mobile factors. This pressure intensifies as more countries take the path of openness.

As states respond to these external pressures, goals from beyond the domestic arena move onto national policy agendas, shaping priorities and public and private resource allocation. Where once states may have insisted on exclusive policymaking sovereignty within their territory, today many states pursue a policy of responsive sovereignty, taking global concerns into account in formulating national policy. States are blending domestic and external policy demands.

Maintaining fiscal discipline and preventing negative cross-border externalities

National policy reforms to promote economic openness have strongly influenced the revenue side of public finance. In an important restructuring of national tax systems, states are shifting national tax bases away from at-the-border measures such as trade taxes toward domestic bases such as the value-added tax.[1] While these reforms are well advanced, some of the issues figuring prominently among the external expectations now directed toward governments suggest new forms of national closure: maintaining fiscal discipline and managing cross-border spillovers.

Is globalization pushing governments to spend more or to spend less? Analysts differ, but Tanzi concludes in his chapter that globalization is exerting efficiency pressures on governments, constraining public spending.

But important public policy concerns need not suffer. Governments can rely more on indirect measures of finance, leveraging private spending through tax expenditures (credits and deductions).[2] Where conditions are conducive, privatization is an option, with the government's contribution limited to regulation and oversight. Tanzi discusses these issues in a social welfare context (protection and insurance), an issue that ranks high on many international and national policy agendas since globalization and economic openness increase efficiency pressures on firms and workers as well as governments. Much the same logic applies to many other issues.[3]

The limits to increased public spending, as Heller shows, are compounded by growing pressures for fiscal discipline—which relate to demands for meeting global challenges and managing cross-border spillovers. He points out that many countries are facing longer term changes, such as aging populations and global climate change, that will heavily burden government budgets. Budgets may also feel the impact of many unpredictable events, such as outbreaks of communicable disease, terrorist attacks, or prolonged global recession. In Heller's (p. 131) words, "a slowly gathering fiscal storm" is on the horizon. If not managed in time, through improved internalization of externalities, these storms will lead to deep global fiscal crises.

To rein in negative cross-border spillovers, countries have used an array of policy measures such as regulation, fiscal incentives, national pollution trading schemes, and quota systems and are exploring other options. Countries are also initiating policy reforms for addressing predictable and unpredictable challenges. Heller identifies several as important for complying with fiscal discipline requirements: extended fiscal accounting, to promote longer term assessments of budget sustainability; balanced budgeting requirements, to create fiscal headroom to draw on as needed; and greater consideration of the political dimensions of the budget process, to avoid being taken by surprise by opposition to corrective measures such as a scaling back of current programs.

Cooperating with global markets to manage risk

Managing economic openness and volatility demands fiscal discipline. But stringent fiscal policies coupled with enhanced risk awareness can encourage excess precautionary public savings and depress economic growth and development. Following the financial crises of the 1990s, many developing countries (101 in a sample of 132) built up high foreign currency reserves ($292 billion in 2003 and $378 billion in 2004; World Bank 2005b, p. 2). With more effective ways to protect against shocks and reduce vulnerability, countries could free the resources tied up in reserves for more productive uses.[4]

Shiller (in this volume, p. 152) reminds us that the "finance and insurance industries were the source of much of the world's economic progress in the twentieth century." They foster productive risk taking by sharing risks across large numbers of market actors, thus blunting the impact that the possibility of an unfavorable outcome could have on any one actor's incentive to undertake promising ventures. With globalizing markets, countries are increasingly able to trade and to disperse country-specific risks across borders through international capital markets.

Governments, like firms and households, are exploiting such opportunities, for example, by hedging against commodity price volatility in futures and options markets on behalf of farmers or consumers, as Morgan discusses. Risk-management products such as the government bonds indexed to gross domestic product (GDP) mentioned by Shiller are an example of a market transaction extended by a collective action component. Against a modest insurance premium paid by the issuing government, the yearly coupon payments on these bonds are lowered when GDP growth is worse than expected and raised when GDP growth is better than expected. By holding the GDP to debt ratio to a narrower range, such arrangements help debt-issuing governments to smooth tax rates and expenditures over time and to reduce uncertainty and risk for firms and private households, enhancing welfare.[5]

GDP-indexed bonds are a precursor to the more encompassing risk management options proposed by Shiller, such as macro markets. By enabling trade in securities indexed to macroeconomic aggregates such as GDP, macro markets would allow national actors to hedge against the risk of a major recession by taking a short position on the security tied to the country's GDP.

As new technologies and opportunities emerge in risk management and other areas, global markets are assuming functions once reserved to governments—a further sign of the public-private rebalancing.

Shifting policy components from the national to the international level

Meeting global challenges often requires combining national building blocks and complementary inputs at the international level (see figures 3–5 in the previous chapter). But where does the production path start? The discussion so far has examined primarily national policy responses to global policy demands—the top-down side of the production path, with demand coming from "above" and action occurring nationally. International cooperation is an iterative, looping process, sometimes proceeding from the international to the national and sometimes from the national to the international.

Bottom-up international cooperation can result from global exigencies that emerge abruptly and force themselves on national policy agendas (as with international terrorism, examined by Sandler) or emerge more gradually (as with taxation of the income earned by mobile factors of production, at the center of Musgrave's chapter). The analyses show that the incentives of states to move from acting unilaterally to cooperating with other states vary with the issue and with the power of states to shape the international policy dialogue.

Following the terrorist attacks on the United States on September 11, 2001, many industrial countries toughened their internal security measures. Yet as Sandler stresses, unilateral efforts, while important, may simply shift terrorist activity to countries that lack the capacity, resources, or political will for similar security upgrades. Control of terrorism through enhanced protection against attacks is a global public good of the weakest link type: "everyone's participation is essential since the smallest provision level determines the amount of the public good that generates benefits" (Sandler, p. 199). Security in air travel or container shipping, for example, depends on adequate screening of cargo and passengers in every country. Once industrial countries have attained a certain level of national security, instead of spending more on upgrading national security, it can be in their self-interest to help poorer, weakest link countries contribute to global security—and to move the issue up to the international level for complementary collective action.

Although the threat posed by increasingly open borders has long been recognized, it took a major crisis to jolt the international community into action and a comprehensive reassessment of effective response measures (see, for example, High-Level Panel on Threats, Challenges, and Change 2004). In other areas, too, the challenges of globalization are increasingly recognized, but most are being dealt with bilaterally rather than multilaterally.

One issue is how to tax mobile actors. Taxpayers that reside and pay tax in one jurisdiction may earn income originating—and being taxed—in another jurisdiction. Musgrave explains how to determine which jurisdiction should be entitled to tax which part of that income. She finds strong efficiency and equity reasons for addressing this question multilaterally, suggesting two principles to guide a multilateral approach: capital-export neutrality and internation equity. However, multilateral agreement on this issue would mean transforming the national public good of tax systems into a common, globalized system. Many governments are reluctant to take such a step.

Currently, tax cooperation occurs primarily through bilateral negotiation: there are more than 2,000 bilateral double-taxation treaties (UNCTAD 2002). Yet many income streams find their way around current treaty arrangements and escape national tax authorities. Tax avoidance and evasion, transfer pricing, and tax competition cause high revenue losses for both industrial and developing countries.[6] Musgrave and others (Bird and Mintz 2003; Reinhold 2004) note that more global tax coordination may gradually evolve, as electronic commerce and other factors continue to undermine states' capacity to tax.

The first steps in this direction are already discernible. More bilateral tax agreements are being based on the model developed by the Organisation for Economic Co-operation and Development (OECD) and the United Nations.[7] By proceeding incrementally, governments may find, as Musgrave (p. 168) argues, that "harmonizing measures can be taken to neutralize the differences with respect to resource allocation across jurisdictions, while preserving the variations in fiscal choices." Policy harmonization behind borders, far from implying the erosion of national policymaking sovereignty, can be a tool for avoiding excess competition between states, making all better off.

INTERNATIONAL COOPERATION BEYOND NATIONAL BORDERS: BLENDING ECONOMIC RATIONALES WITH FOREIGN POLICY GOALS

International cooperation abroad has so far been essentially an intergovernmental process, focusing on rulemaking on between-country and at-the-border issues. Politics, not economics, has underpinned most intergovernmental negotiations. And security concerns, colonial ties, and national commercial interests, as well as moral and ethical concerns, have shaped foreign aid.

This is changing. Politics are not leaving international affairs, but economics is asserting itself more strongly. The economic principles and practices underlying public finance nationally are also shaping international cooperation beyond national borders.

The most visible sign of this shift is in the institutional landscape. Service providers and financing mechanisms and tools are diversifying and multiplying, with public-private cooperation and competition increasing at the international level just as at the national level. Part 2 shows how intergovernmental organizations, like national governments before them, are being reengineered.

Parts 3 and 4 deepen this analysis, examining collective action efforts to provide the international components of global public goods and development: the two deliverables of public finance.

Part 3 suggests that global public goods tend to be approached from a dual investment perspective: concern with allocating resources to collective action initiatives that promise relatively high social and global returns and concern with producing the desired cooperation with as little burden to national budgets and as little pooling of national public revenue in international funds as possible.

Efficiency concerns are also gaining prominence in foreign aid, with the mounting urgency of reducing poverty and the tight financial constraints in donor countries. As part 4 shows, this strategy depends on getting the incentives right and on recognizing the importance of adequately and fairly provided regional and global public goods.

And recognition seems to be growing that, with greater openness and interdependence, national public policy goals are often best pursued by enhancing global welfare gains and aiming at a higher national share of a more prosperous and secure world. Realizing this goal requires a focus on efficiency, nationally and internationally.

Figure 2 is an overview of the continuing, reoriented, and new tasks of public finance at the international level. Parts 2–4 of this volume address, in particular, the new tasks.

Relying on global public-private cooperation and competition

International cooperation beyond borders has been profoundly transformed, from an intergovernmental process to a multiactor process. Intergovernmental and nonstate actors (businesses and civil society), like their counterparts at the national level, are cooperating and competing to deliver both public goods and equity more efficiently and effectively.

One manifestation is the rapidly expanding universe of global public-private partnerships, contributing to global public goods provision and foreign aid (see the chapter by Kaul in part 2). Up from about 35 in 1990, there are now at least 400 such entities, most with an independent legal status (either for-profit or non-

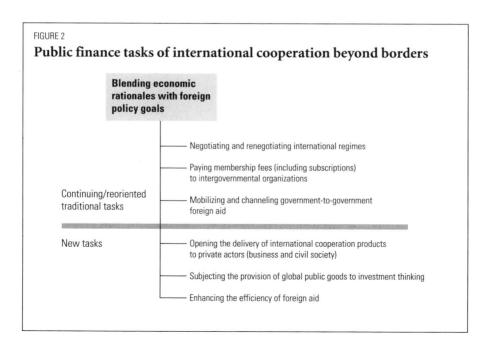

FIGURE 2

Public finance tasks of international cooperation beyond borders

Blending economic rationales with foreign policy goals

Continuing/reoriented traditional tasks
- Negotiating and renegotiating international regimes
- Paying membership fees (including subscriptions) to intergovernmental organizations
- Mobilizing and channeling government-to-government foreign aid

New tasks
- Opening the delivery of international cooperation products to private actors (business and civil society)
- Subjecting the provision of global public goods to investment thinking
- Enhancing the efficiency of foreign aid

profit), and the rest hosted by an intergovernmental or civil society organization.[8] Partners include intergovernmental organizations, national governments, civil society organizations, foundations, and businesses.

Another manifestation of the transformation of international cooperation into a multiactor process is the rapid increase in the number and diversity of international financing mechanisms, again especially since 1990. In volume of financial resources the traditional multilateral organizations (United Nations, World Bank) are still the major channels for multilateral cross-border cooperation. However, as Conceição points out, the picture changes dramatically when the focus is on the number of institutions mobilizing and channeling financial resources to global challenges. More than 30 of the roughly 60 identified in his chapter were created in the last decade. Twenty of these are no longer pure intergovernmental entities. Many are nonprofit organizations, and many involve public and private actors. If private foundations and investment funds that address global challenges are added to the count, the number of international financing mechanisms climbs into the 900 to 1,000 range (figure 3).

Several factors seem to be driving these changes: the international policy agenda, which calls for drawing on the comparative advantage of both the public and the private sectors; the fiscal constraints of governments, coupled with the opportunities presented by the growing depth and breadth of international financial markets; and public choice considerations, notably the growing concern about transnational nonstate actors and intergovernmental cooperation failure.

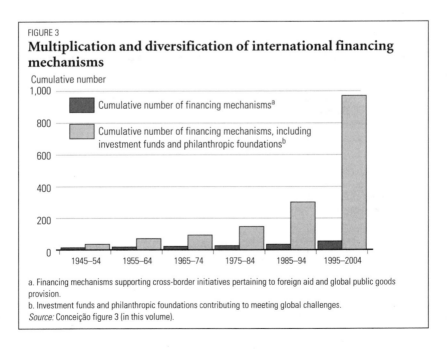

FIGURE 3

Multiplication and diversification of international financing mechanisms

Cumulative number

- Cumulative number of financing mechanisms[a]
- Cumulative number of financing mechanisms, including investment funds and philanthropic foundations[b]

a. Financing mechanisms supporting cross-border initiatives pertaining to foreign aid and global public goods provision.
b. Investment funds and philanthropic foundations contributing to meeting global challenges.
Source: Conceição figure 3 (in this volume).

Building on the comparative advantage of public and private actors. Policy issues often arrive on to the international policy agenda only after they have assumed crisis dimensions. Just think of global health challenges such as the HIV/AIDS pandemic. They evolved slowly but now demand urgent action: determined innovation (for new medicines and vaccines) combining public and private resources and entities capable of acting swiftly and flexibly. Many intergovernmental organizations have multiple mandates, making it difficult to pursue issues in the results-oriented way that many of today's challenges require. Public-private partnerships and single-issue financing mechanisms are stepping in and taking on some of these tasks.

Also, with market actors more involved in public policy delivery, market development is the subject of greater collective action abroad. Many global public-private partnerships engaged in market development involve both market participants and intergovernmental and governmental actors to ensure that evolving market institutions fit public as well as private purposes.

Overcoming resource constraints by turning to financial markets. Along with private actors, new financing technology is entering the international cooperation domain, including securitization and project finance, to allow responses motivated by economic rationales. Conceição, Rajan, and Shah show that projects are now designed to involve the private sector in resource mobilization as well as in the delivery of international cooperation products. To show these factors at play, the authors examine the proposal to establish an International Finance Facility to get around the budgetary constraints facing donor countries. Achieving the Millennium Development Goals on target would require huge investments now, whereas donor countries plan to increase foreign aid allocations only gradually. The International Finance Facility would enable the frontloading of foreign aid despite this constraint. It would back the issuance of bonds on international capital markets today by securitizing donor country promises of aid delivery in the future. These resources, otherwise available only over many years, could be used to finance the upfront costs of helping countries achieve the Millennium Development Goals. As a first step a planned International Finance Facility pilot project would raise resources to finance immunization projects in the world's poorest countries.[9]

Correcting intergovernmental cooperation failure. The growing involvement of nonprofit and for-profit firms in the provision of public services confirms expectations based on Jones's public choice analysis of international cooperation. If actors (voters, lobbyists, politicians, and bureaucrats) pursue their individual or organizational self-interests, there is no assurance that their policies will serve agreed-on public purposes. The failure of governments and intergovernmental organizations must also be reckoned with.

Involvement by market and civil society actors can counter some of this risk of failure. Part 2 shows that global market and civil society actors, including private foundations, often step in to correct public policy failures. They do so where global public policy outcomes that affect their interests are underprovided— because intergovernmental negotiations are bogged down in political stalemate or because national governments free ride and fail to contribute adequately to common international cooperation projects. Nonstate actors can correct failures of intergovernmental cooperation—which arise under conditions similar to those that make economic markets fail—by working through voluntary collective action and by prodding governments.[10]

Subjecting global public goods provision to investment thinking

Until recently, the foreign aid system has been the main operational system for international cooperation abroad. As global public goods issues moved to the fore and required operational activities at the international level, the public financing for such initiatives came largely from donor countries' foreign aid funds. Up to 30 percent of official development assistance may have gone into global public goods (World Bank 2001, p. 109).[11] Increasingly, however, foreign aid and global public goods provision are being disentangled, especially as businesses and markets play a larger role and demand sharper differentiation of purpose and approaches. Public goods provision at the international level is evolving as a distinct function—as the international arm of the allocation branch of public finance. And as this happens, public goods provision is increasingly shaped by investment thinking.

This new thinking is reflected in concerns to ensure that cooperation makes economic sense and in the emphasis on market-based solutions. Whether by design or by intuition, global public goods provision seems to be guided by the principle of subsidiarity.

Ensuring net gain. Does cooperation pay? Which interventions promise the highest returns?[12] Who will benefit? Questions such as these are being raised more frequently.[13] And data-driven policymaking, including cost-benefit analysis, is becoming more common (Esty and Porter forthcoming). Conceição and Mendoza build on this debate. Drawing on inputs from various studies (especially Barrett 2004 and Hertel 2004), they suggest a five-step methodology for determining the global welfare gains from more adequate provision of global public goods and the distribution of these gains across developing and industrial countries. The methodology for estimating net gains implies a goods-specific approach based on identifying the benefits of enhanced provision of the good and the costs of corrective action.

Applying the methodology to illustrative cases suggests that the global net gains would be huge—but also unevenly distributed.[14] Thus, some redistribution may be required to generate political support for the collective-action efforts required to unlock the potential gains. Barrett (in this volume) argues that such redistribution (in the form of transfers, for example) can bring on board countries that otherwise would not be net beneficiaries from the enhanced provision of the good or that would gain less than others. The Montreal Protocol Fund, an example mentioned by Barrett, has demonstrated the role of money as an incentive in international cooperation—making international cooperation work by allowing it to make economic sense for all concerned.

Emphasizing market approaches. King's chapter also highlights the incentive and compensation functions of financial transfers or, more concretely, of incremental cost payments between countries. These payments are intended to reimburse countries for the additional costs they incur when doing more than what they would need to do to address such global concerns as reductions in greenhouse gas emissions or preservation of biodiversity. Incremental cost payments, as employed by the Global Environment Facility, for example, can be viewed as a compensation or incentive tool. They can also be seen as signaling the emergence of a new market.

The Global Environment Facility is a precursor of today's emerging carbon markets. It facilitates trade between countries in the inputs to such global public goods as biodiversity preservation. On the demand side are the facility's donors, countries willing to financially support biodiversity preservation. On the supply side are the countries willing to offer this service within their jurisdiction. The Global Environment Facility acts as intermediary in this exchange.

When businesses become concerned about the adverse economic effects of global problems such as climate change mount or when a promising new trade opportunity emerges, market actors are likely to explore the creation of a "proper" new market. Sandor's chapter analyzes the development of the Chicago Climate Exchange.[15] He reveals that markets are constructs that demand deliberate steps, including the development of standardized products and a functioning trading platform. He also shows the importance of getting the word out about how the new arrangement work, lest it be ignored. All of this requires some public support, generally at the beginning before the market takes off. The Chicago Climate Exchange is set up as a public-private partnership.

Working with markets (engaging in public-private partnering) and helping to develop them (subsidizing exploratory activities or undertaking regulatory functions) are now an important focus of intergovernmental organizations. A third dimension of this market-related work is facilitating access to existing markets. Consider commodity futures markets, whose instruments for managing commodity risk can replace government-provided approaches such as buffer stocks and intergovernmental efforts such as international commodity agreements.[16] Commodity futures markets are difficult for producers in developing countries to access, depriving them of this tool for managing commodity price volatility. Facilitating their access, as Morgan discusses, would unlock unexploited efficiencies. One way is to establish national intermediaries in developing countries, and technical assistance and other services to help these intermediaries succeed.

Markets offer the double dividend of enhanced efficiency and reduced government involvement. Governments can limit their role to regulation and other complementary actions instead of tackling the task alone through conventional public finance. Governments might assign new property rights or quasi property rights such as pollution allowances and authorize and oversee trading arrangements, leaving the buying and selling and related financial transactions largely to private actors. Or they could provide financial incentives to private actors and assist them in overcoming market-access problems.

Even the challenging issue of the sovereign debt crises is now moving from a statutory and intergovernmental approach to a contractual and market-based solution. As Eichengreen discusses, sovereign bond issuance under New York law is beginning to follow the UK approach of incorporating collective action clauses into bond contracts, to permit more flexible responses to default. This shift was facilitated by limited but critical interventions by a few governments and the International Monetary Fund, aimed primarily at providing the model text for the clauses and demonstrating market acceptance.

Applying the subsidiarity principle. The basic policy choice in global public goods provision concerns which components of a good to provide nationally and which internationally. Part 1 suggests that many policy steps, even the responses to external policy expectations, are being taken nationally rather than through centralized reforms at the international level. Globalization appears to be more about cooperation behind than beyond national borders. Taking action nationally and addressing only selected components internationally (perhaps to exploit economies of scale or scope) is not only what technical and economic analysis of the production path of global public goods would suggest but also what is actually happening.

When interventions occur at the international level, a second choice arises: which instrument to employ. Until recently, the main instrument was pooled national public revenue executed through an intergovernmental agency. Today, there are other options, including markets and public-private partnering. And today a range of actors from (inter)governmental entities to businesses and civil society are selecting and applying these instruments.

Global public goods provision abroad can be seen to be guided by a five-tier hierarchy of preferences (figure 4), with each succeeding preference considered only if the preceding one is insufficient:

- *A preference for national action.* Taking corrective action at the national level and addressing only selected additional components at the international level (for example, to exploit economies of scale or scope).

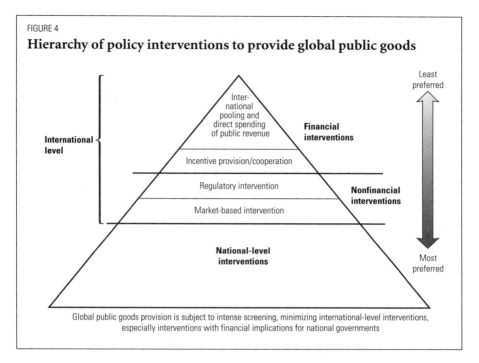

FIGURE 4

Hierarchy of policy interventions to provide global public goods

Global public goods provision is subject to intense screening, minimizing international-level interventions, especially interventions with financial implications for national governments

- *A preference for market-based intervention.* Relying on market-based provision, such as markets for carbon-related products to reverse global climate change and financial and insurance markets to improve risk management.

- *A preference for regulatory intervention.* Limiting government action to norm and standard setting and regulation, such as the assignment of pollution allowances, a regulatory measure that fosters the creation of new markets.

- *A preference for incentive provision.* Encouraging private actors to undertake projects that generate global social welfare gains (for example, by forming public-private partnerships or supporting guarantee instruments).

- *International pooling and direct spending of public revenue—the least preferred option.* Governments' reluctance to go this route is reflected in the institutional pattern of financing collective action abroad. While many new limited-purpose and temporary financing vehicles have emerged in the past 60 years, the international community has added only a few permanent entities to the system of multilateral organizations established in the 1940s and 1950s. Most international cooperation is funded through voluntary, short-term commitments.

The evolution of global public goods provision appears to be echoing the EU experience with regional public goods provision, as Laffan describes. Although the

European Union is politically more cohesive and socioeconomically less diverse than the international community as a whole, a preference for the same general principles—coalescing in the form of the subsidiarity principle—is discernible.

Enhancing the efficiency of foreign aid

While development depends on adequate levels of foreign aid (Sachs and others 2004; UN Millennium Project 2005), efficient allocation and deployment are also vital. Greater aid efficiency would reduce resource waste and could persuade donors to support foreign aid and other actors, notably business, to get involved.

Some obstacles to greater aid efficiency are being addressed, from enhanced donor coordination and harmonization (High-Level Forum on Aid Effectiveness 2005; High-Level Forum on Harmonization 2003) and greater coherence of donor aid and other policies (OECD 2003b) to measures that bring aid pro-gramming closer to the national level (such as poverty reduction strategies[17]).

Part 4 points to additional measures under debate or already under way to increase aid efficiency: using loans and grants more rationally. Benefiting from nonrival regional and global public goods and economies of scale. Reducing the risks to private actors from investing in development. And fostering coherence between global public goods and foreign aid. Incentive compatibility is a central concern in devising aid arrangements in such a way that "participants in the process would not find it advantageous to violate the rules of the process" (Ledyard 1989, p. 141).

Clarifying the rationales for grants and loans. Grants and loans are the main instruments for aid delivery. Collier addresses how to choose between them to ensure that aid is allocated most efficiently across countries. He argues that the "current pattern of using grants and loans has little economic rationale" (p. 471) and suggests that the choice should depend on a country's level of income and institutional development. The poorest countries with weak institutions should receive only grants. As a country's institutions strengthen and income rises, the share of loans relative to grants could increase until aid is delivered entirely through loans. The amount of aid received through grants and loans should peak at the same time, so that there is no suggestion that loans are being substituted for grants.

Choosing more rationally between grants and loans could also avert some debt sustainability problems. As Collier argues, under more rational selection, a country that reaches some debt sustainability ceiling would not be precluded from receiving aid but would receive it through grants instead of loans. Countries in a stronger position to service their debt could receive aid through loans.

Thus, both loans and grants play a role in aid delivery. But where should the loans come from? Are they still to come from the international financial institutions created more than five decades ago? Akyüz explores the rationales for continuing multilateral lending, concluding that the rationale for countercyclical lending is stronger than ever because of the greater vulnerability of developing countries to external shocks, that the rationale for development finance is weaker today than it was some 50 years ago but continues to be valid especially for low-income countries, and that the rationale for development grants rather than loans is stronger now, again primarily for low-income countries.

And what type of grants and for whom? In discussing these questions, Radelet, not unlike Collier, suggests that assistance strategies should vary with the countries' commitments to governance and development. The stronger that commitment, the more flexible and attractive the aid modalities should be and the larger, more predictable, and longer term the resource commitment by donors, to ensure that aid is used efficiently. Such differentiation in grant conditions would challenge developing countries to reform. Thus these instruments are called challenge grants.

Benefiting from nonrivalry and economies of scale. Unlocking efficiency gains goes beyond using aid delivery instruments more rationally. It can also involve identifying and exploiting economies of scale. A key finding by Birdsall is that regional public goods are a highly promising yet underfunded development opportunity. This inefficiency arises because of the "donors' strong country orientation and focus on country 'ownership'" (p. 529), which creates problems of coordination, attribution, and incentives. Coordination problems arise because multiple governments need to negotiate and agree on how much of the good to provide, how to provide it, and at what cost to whom. Attribution problems result from donor concerns with the transaction costs of dealing with multiple interlocutors and the difficulty of establishing accountability for the results. The coordination and attribution problems in turn lead to incentive problems. Both donors and recipients may view regional public goods as more complex and hence riskier than the simpler and more familiar country-based projects.

Unexploited opportunities for efficiency gains also exist at the global level. Polak and Clark show that a new Special Drawing Rights issuance could significantly reduce the costly foreign reserve holdings of many developing countries and do a better job of protecting them against financial crisis. This issuance would be efficient because it would be costless, but it would require global, rather than regional, coordination.

Birdsall's suggestion for overcoming the incentive problems at the regional level is similar to the answer to the question presented earlier on whether cooperation pays: to identify and demonstrate the potential net gains from investing in regional programs. The benefits of meeting the challenge of underfunded regionalism could be huge, especially in Sub-Saharan Africa, where political and geographic borders impose high costs on small and landlocked countries.

As the pressures to demonstrate aid results and achieve the Millennium Development Goals rise, industrial and developing countries alike may be willing to cross the coordination and attribution hurdles and to use cost-benefit analysis investment in setting priorities.[18]

Facilitating involvement by private actors in development. The efficiency of aid may also be increased by engaging the most appropriate actor. In the past private actors had little involvement in development, because of missing or incomplete markets in developing countries or lack of information about them and the perception of aid as charity. As circumstances changed, interest has grown in using aid resources to engage private actors in promoting development.

Public funds can cushion the risks that private actors take on when investing in developing countries. Intergovernmental organizations use guarantees for this purpose, as the Multilateral Investment Guarantee Agency does, or co-investment, as the International Finance Corporation does.[19]

Kremer and Peterson Zwane describe yet another tool, advanced purchase commitments, which provide incentives for private participation in generating and diffusing pro-poor knowledge. Through advanced purchase commitments, a group of donors promises to compensate innovators for the development of specific technologies to address problems of the poor. Kremer and Peterson Zwane illustrate the use of purchase commitments for technological innovation for tropical agriculture. An advanced purchase commitment is similar to a guarantee, in that it provides incentives for private investment without requiring immediate disbursements. However, whereas guarantees require disbursements for unfavorable outcomes, purchase commitments reward successful innovators—but only if they develop the product specified in the commitment.

An advantage of guarantees is that they strengthen incentives for investment without necessarily requiring a financial outlay by the guarantor. Griffith-Jones and Fuzzo de Lima suggest that currency-related risks for foreign investments in developing countries are inadequately covered and that new instruments are needed to help infrastructure projects withstand shocks that compromise borrowers' ability to repay debts incurred in foreign currency. They propose three guarantee-related instruments to complement existing political and partial credit guarantees: contingent liquidity facilities, countercyclical guarantees, and sovereign guarantee pools (which development agencies would extend to groups of developing countries engaged in a common project).

Phasing in the tools. Thus, there is growing recognition that an efficient use of foreign aid requires knowing which type of tool to use at what intensity to match a country's development stage and when to phase out the tool as the country advances.

A graphic depiction of the intensity with which various tools are being applied—individually and in combination—as development progresses might

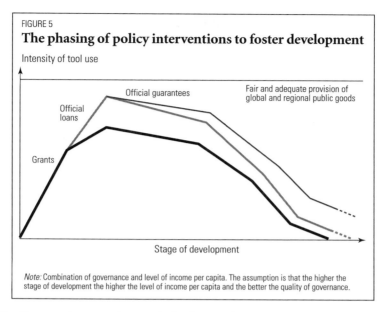

FIGURE 5

The phasing of policy interventions to foster development

Intensity of tool use

Official guarantees

Official loans

Fair and adequate provision of global and regional public goods

Grants

Stage of development

Note: Combination of governance and level of income per capita. The assumption is that the higher the stage of development the higher the level of income per capita and the better the quality of governance.

look like figure 5. Grant assistance is the first tool to come in and move out. Official loans arrive next and—in line with Collier's suggested strategy—peak and then decline together with grants. However, they are not being phased out completely because countries sometimes need to revert to official loan support (notably when experiencing external shocks to their economy). Guarantees from bilateral or multilateral aid agencies are the third tool in development assistance, progressively taking over from the other two. As developing countries find it easier to access markets, and market actors become more familiar with them, countries might need external support only in issuing guarantees—and this only initially and occasionally, as the dotted ending of the line marked "official guarantees" indicates.[20]

But recognition is also growing that both the efficient use of aid and development effectiveness depend on according a high and steady level of importance to a fair and adequate provision of regional and global public goods. The potential benefits to developing countries from the provision of these public goods can be substantial. For example, changes to the multilateral trade regime could generate benefits for developing countries estimated at nearly double current official development assistance.[21] And better ways for migrant workers to transfer remittances to developing countries could further increase benefits (remittances currently total nearly $130 billion; World Bank 2005b, p. 28).

Yet, despite the strength of this and other economic evidence, the link between fair and adequate global and regional public goods provision and development is still tenuous. This suggests that although economic rationales have a stronger influence now, politics has not left international cooperation—just as it has not left national public policymaking.

THE NEW PUBLIC FINANCE: COMBINING THE "BEHIND" AND THE "BEYOND"

The globalization of public goods and development concerns creates new tasks for public finance and requires new policy approaches and tools behind as well as beyond national borders. Increasingly, national and international initiatives on global concerns are progressing in tandem (figure 6), trying to avoid the Scylla of excessive centralization (tackling tasks intergovernmentally that are better left to individual governments or markets and civil society) and the Charybdis of excessive decentralization (trying to go it alone nationally where cooperation with other state and nonstate actors would be the better way to proceed).[22]

Globalization not only calls for new public finance tasks, like the internalization of cross-border spillovers, it also affords governments and intergovernmental agencies new means to tackle these tasks. Cooperation with global markets is one such means. Trade between governments in global public goods services such as carbon reduction credits is another. Governments have many possibilities for tapping into the pool of global resources—capital, expertise, or knowledge—to pursue public goals.

Just as the greater porosity of the borders between the public and the private sectors has led to new modes of public finance, new public finance 1, so the growing porosity of the borders between domestic and foreign has led to other new modes of public finance, new public finance 2. While new public finance 1 provides policies and tools for meshing the gears of public and private finance, new public finance 2 provides policies and tools for international cooperation behind and beyond borders.

The key issues in this new global public finance are essentially the same as those of traditional public finance. But they now reflect an active partnership between markets and states in a global—national and international—context (see figure 1 in the previous chapter). The key questions of global public finance are:

- *Which* global public policy goals are being—or should be—pursued?
- *What* production path is being—or should be—followed in each case?
- *Where* are public policy interventions being located—or where should they be located—to ensure efficient and fair provision of the desired outcome, nationally or internationally?
- *Who* is—or should be—receiving net benefits and how should the benefits be distributed?

While these issues are dominating policy dialogues nationally and internationally, current institutional frameworks—the way policymaking is organized and the concepts being used to analyze challenges and think about costs and benefits—are not well suited to finding the right answers, including making greater use of the innovative approaches discussed in this volume. What can be done to move forward?

MOVING FROM INNOVATION TO ADOPTION

Innovation usually happens by fits and starts (Shiller 2003). The new public finance—now a collection of measures being developed, tested, or applied sporadically—is no exception. Wider adoption will require adjustments in concepts and terms, ways of thinking, and institutional framework—from changes in laws and rules to new organizational structures. Policymakers and scholars have a role in this. Some changes would be minor, but still critical. Others would involve more fundamental policy issues and require deeper rethinking.

Advancing the new public finance will entail costs—for dialogue, public awareness building, financial product development, empirical and theoretical studies, and perhaps compensation for those who eventually lose out as the changes are introduced. Will the potential gains warrant the effort?

The potential gains

The thought experiment in box 1 shows what difference enhanced risk management could make to people's lives and ultimately to national economies and budgets and, if replicated across countries, to global welfare. Without adequate risk management the woman whose story is told in the box may not be able to pursue her career. She and her relatives could lose their jobs and become a burden on society instead of contributing to it.

Table 1 tells much the same story in quantitative terms for tools that include but go beyond risk management. It considers six applications of the new public finance tools discussed in this volume. It indicates who would gain how much from using each tool—either because the tool would make it possible to address the challenge or because it would do the job more efficiently than another tool. The total gains come to about $7 trillion in net present value terms—or $360 billion annually for the six tools.

Clearly, pursuing the public finance innovations already under way holds considerable promise of gains to many—and perhaps even to all.

So what can be done to enhance the conditions for change so that new financing policies and tools stand a better chance of becoming standard practice and so that globalization evolves, combining openness and competitiveness with enhanced stability, sustainability, and a wider sharing of its benefits.[23]

Next steps: decisionmakers' options

Laying the foundation for new approaches to the financing of global challenges requires national and international measures.

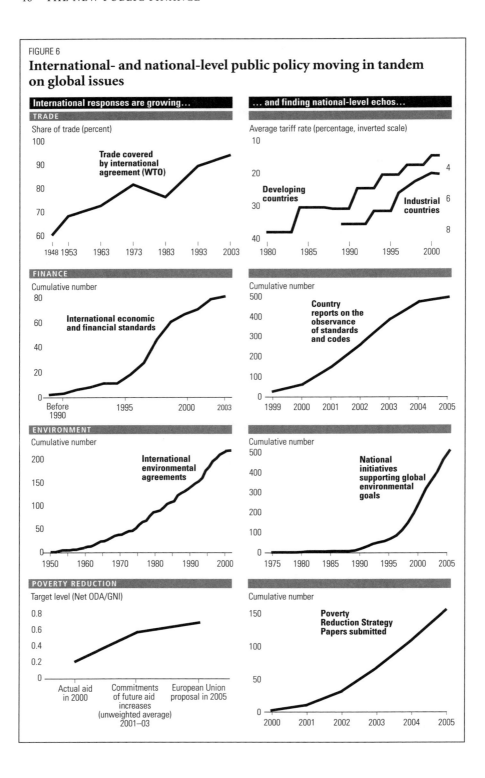

FIGURE 6

International- and national-level public policy moving in tandem on global issues

FIGURE 6 continued

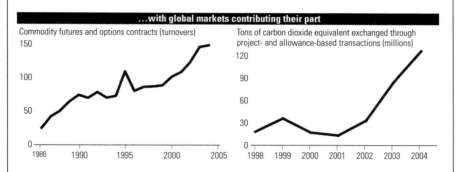

...with global markets contributing their part

Commodity futures and options contracts (turnovers)

Tons of carbon dioxide equivalent exchanged through project- and allowance-based transactions (millions)

Note: For trends in the four global issues, see figure 6 in the previous chapter.

Source: First panel, WTO 2005; UNCTAD 2004 (pp. 69 and 71). Second panel, Financial Stability Forum 2005; IMF 2005. Third panel, Barrett 2003; Merlen 2005. Fourth panel, EC 2005b; OECD 2004; UN 2003a; World Bank 2005a. Fifth panel, BIS 2005 (p. A105); Lecocq and Capoor 2005 (pp. 20 and 31).

Box 1

A NARRATIVE OF THE OPPORTUNITIES LOST WITHOUT ADEQUATE—AND FEASIBLE—RISK MANAGEMENT TOOLS

Consider a young woman from India, living in Chicago, Illinois, who wants to be a violinist. She finds it worrisome to borrow the money for her training because her future income as a musician is so uncertain. But new financial technology enables her to borrow money online that need not be fully repaid if an index of future income of violinists turns out to be disappointing. The loan makes it easier for her to pursue her favored career by limiting her risk. Her risk over time would be measured by indexes of occupational incomes maintained by computer networks. Most of the risk of her career is ultimately borne by portfolio investors all over the world rather than by her alone.

This same woman worries about members of her extended family in a small town in India, many of whom work in an industry in danger of closing and rendering their special skills obsolete. But their company buys a newly marketed livelihood insurance contract to protect its workers in the event of adverse economic developments. The insurance company then sells the risk on the international markets. Moreover, the Indian government makes an agreement with other countries to share economic risks, further protecting her family.

The young woman worries, too, about the neighborhood in a small industrial town in the United Kingdom where her parents live. The neighborhood is undergoing economic and social change, and she worries that

Box 1 Continued
A NARRATIVE OF THE OPPORTUNITIES LOST WITHOUT ADEQUATE—AND FEASIBLE—RISK MANAGEMENT TOOLS

her parents may lose their savings if their house loses value. But in a new financial order, her parents' mortgage comes with an attached home equity insurance policy that protects them against such an unfortunate outcome by paying a claim if the resale value of their home declines. Moreover, an intergenerational social security system and an inequality insurance system will further protect them.

New digital technology, with its millions of miles of fiber optic cable connections, can manage all these risks together, offsetting a risk in Chicago with another in Rio de Janeiro, a risk in the income of violinists with the risk in the income of wine producers in South Africa. The result will be the stabilization and enhancement of countries' economies and people's lives.

Most long-term economic risks are actually borne by individuals or families alone. Social welfare exists primarily for very poor people, but it is limited even for them. Today's world cannot insure against risk to people's paychecks over years and decades, cannot hedge against the economic risk that their neighborhoods will gradually decay, and cannot diversify away the risk that economic and societal changes will make old age difficult. Elderly people are left vulnerable to the risk that a stock market crash will wipe out their retirement savings, and many people live in relative poverty today because of a failure to control other risks.

To the extent that individuals are aware of these ever-present risks, they tend to be overcautious, sometimes avoiding opportunities because they justifiably fear having to bear the consequences of failure. They may tend to work cynically instead, treading water, staying in an unsatisfactory job, pretending to achieve, fearing to venture out into the rapids where real achievement is possible.

Under present conditions the woman in Chicago thus postpones her career as a violinist, waiting for some better time that may never come. She lacks information about the prospects for such a career and has no way to protect herself economically except to choose an uninspiring career.

Her uncle in India is laid off from his job and is unable to secure a comparable job. He goes into unwanted early retirement with only a meager income. Her parents in the United Kingdom see the value of their house fall as their neighborhood declines. At the same time the economy in their region slows, and the value of the UK stock market where they had stashed their other savings drops. As a result, they lack the wealth to support themselves well in their remaining years. Worrying about the risks to other members of her family can make the young woman's own life more difficult—and dreams of a career as a violinist even more remote.

Source: Shiller 2003 (pp. 6–8). Reprinted by permission of Princeton University Press.

TABLE 1

Six tools, $7 trillion gain
(billions of U.S. dollars)

Tool	Challenge addressed	Primary beneficiary	Annual gain	Net present value of gain[a]
Guarantees issued by aid agencies	Infrastructure investment	Developing countries	1.1	22
Securitization of future flow receivables	External borrowing	Developing countries	1.5	31
Advanced purchase commitments[b]	Malaria control	Malaria-endemic regions, especially Sub-Saharan Africa	1.4	47
GDP-indexed bonds	Public expenditure/ debt repayment smoothing	Developing countries	30.0	600
Macro markets[b]	Risk management	Group of Seven industrialized countries	145.1	2,902
International pollution permit trading	Reduction in greenhouse gas emissions	Industrialized countries	182.0	3,640
Total[c]			~360	~7,000

Note: For more details on the calculations, see the appendix to this chapter and the additional references mentioned there.

a. The sum of the gains is provided here for illustrative purposes only, since the methods used to estimate the gains refer to different base years.

b. The gains from these tools are expressed net of costs.

c. The discount rate is 5 percent for all the tools, except for advanced purchase commitments, where a discount rate of 3 percent is used in line with the common practice of using lower discount rates in health-related cost-benefit analyses.

Source: The estimates are based on data from Wormser and Babbar (2001); Kektar and Ratha (2001); Ratha (2002); Kremer and Glennerster (2004); Mills and Shillcutt (2004; 2005); Borensztein and Mauro (2004); Athanasoulis and Shiller (2001); and McKibben and Wilcoxen (1999).

Steps at the national level. Four measures at the national level seem especially important for realizing the policy potential of the new public finance:

- Strengthening demand for new financing technology, notably in risk management.
- Promoting the supply of such technology.
- Adjusting budgetary rules that stand in the way of meeting global challenges.
- Reaching more broad-based consensus on the role of the state as intermediary between external and domestic policy demands.

Paradoxical though it may sound, to increase demand for some of the new financing technology, especially the new risk management tools, policymakers should be more explicit about the risks of globalization while also demonstrating how the risks will no longer be allowed to unbalance, or even destroy, people's lives. The means to spread and share risk are at hand—such as bond indexation, commodity options, weather and terrorism insurance, guarantees, macro markets, and other income-smoothing technology. This new financing technology can better protect people against economic volatility and encourage productive risk taking, adding to an economy's dynamic efficiency.

One way to help people accept some of the newer finance and insurance instruments is to humanize the instruments (as in box 1) and to attach hard numbers to some of the potential gains (as in table 1). For Posner (2004, p. 139) cost-benefit analyses are "an indispensable step in rational decision-making." Such analysis could help persuade the general public and decisionmakers in the public and private sectors that investing in change, whether at home or abroad, can yield high social returns.

For policymakers in developing countries, where financial and insurance markets are usually less advanced and the potential gains are therefore especially large, the issue may be more one of letting their development partners and the markets know their interest in strengthening their finance and insurance systems (taken up again below, under next steps at the international level).[24]

Some of the new public finance instruments may need further testing and adaptation to the conditions in each country. Governments, in cooperation with industry and in consultation with the main stakeholders, may want to support research and development on new public finance instruments. The private sector has long recognized that finance is about more than money: it is a system and a craft. It would pay for governments to explore how to use more of the new technology for public policy purposes while safeguarding public benefits.

Some basic budgetary rules might also require revision. For example, in many countries line ministries may not financially support operational activities abroad, although ministries are increasingly involved in such activities. In industrial countries ministries often turn to foreign aid agencies to meet such objectives, contributing to the siphoning off of aid funds already noted. As a result, many countries not only underfund international cooperation abroad but also have no record of how much they actually spend on international concerns, at home or abroad. To avoid the type of fiscal illusion problems to which this gives rise and the consequences for resource availability (limiting what could be invested to supply new finance technology), legislators might consider redesigning budget laws and rules to make them more supportive of today's international cooperation requirements.[25]

But the importance of any one step may ultimately depend on how policymakers and the general public answer the most basic public finance question: what economic role for the state? If there is consensus that the role of the state in a globalized world is as intermediary between external and domestic policy demands, many of the other policy measures fall into place. This does not mean that they will be less controversial. They won't be, because they require change. And even when they result in enhanced national welfare, they may also entail redistribution of income and of other opportunities. Politics will not leave economics. But it is essential for society to gain a new common understanding of what role the state is to play, of when it is exercising responsive policymaking sovereignty that takes outside exigencies and opportunities into account to maximize national welfare.

Steps at the international level. Several measures could be undertaken at the international level to advance some of the new public finance practices:

- Reengineering intergovernmental organizations systematically and deliberately.
- Adopting a new approach to financing international cooperation, especially global public goods components.
- Strengthening demand for and supply of new financing technology, complementing the efforts of governments nationally.
- Creating an international high-level public-private finance council to foster and propel change along these lines.

National efforts to realign market-state relations have tended to reassess the government's role by exploring several questions (Stiglitz 1998). A similar battery of questions could be used to systematically review the role of intergovernmental organizations:

- Is there a role for public policy intervention at the international level (specifically, for intergovernmental organizations to complement national governments, markets, and civil society organizations)?
- If yes, what is it?
- What is the best way of performing that role?
- Do current policy practices reflect this best way?
- If not, what reforms are required?

Some intergovernmental organizations have begun to adjust to the new realities. Using a common set of criteria to examine these reforms across agencies could help to identify the new generic operational role of intergovernmental organizations. Such analysis could also help in formulating systematic criteria for the interaction between intergovernmental organizations and markets and public-private partnerships. A next step would be to develop methodologies for assessing how global public policy concerns would gain from such public-private interactions, which occupy a policy space between markets and governments. Preparing such assessments according to rigorous methodologies could allay many of the concerns that surround public-private partnering.[26]

Intergovernmental agencies (like governments nationally) also would benefit from a more dynamic view of what it means to correct market failure. They may need to do less about substituting for market imperfections and more about removing these imperfections and building capacity—within the private and the public sector—for market development.

It is common for intergovernmental organizations to mobilize resources based on a "business plan" sketched in broad strokes and only then to decide precisely how to use these resources. Encouraging greater use of modalities such as public-private partnerships could turn this practice around—bringing more specificity to the outputs to be produced and allowing financing packages to be structured on a product-by-product basis. This might imply a clearer differentiation between the financing provided to intergovernmental organizations to meet their regular budget costs and the financing intended for particular cooperation initiatives.

To encourage innovation, intergovernmental organizations could complement national research and development efforts, especially where the new financing technology involves products to be traded in global markets or the creation of a new international market. An example is the Prototype Carbon Fund, which is becoming a learning platform for the development of markets in carbon-related products.

But, as Jones points out, organizations are also guided by self-interest. Why assume that intergovernmental organizations would move along the new policy routes discussed here? Certainly, many international decisionmakers are fully committed to improving global conditions, achieving gains in efficiency and effectiveness, and promoting development wherever possible. One way to make the task of managing such change easier is to create an international high-level public-private finance council.

Composed of chief executive officers of private financial markets and finance ministers, the council could scan finance and insurance markets and the international public finance architecture for new developments, assess new financing needs, and advise intergovernmental organizations on how to promote more adequate financing of global challenges. Council members could hold consultations with concerned stakeholders, including civil society organizations, to gain new insights. The council's advice would be addressed to the operational agencies of the UN system and the international financial institutions, including the International Monetary Fund, World Bank, and regional development banks. In this way, intergovernmental organizations would be continuously prodded to innovate—something that may not come naturally to them (judging from the literature on the comparative advantage of public and private actors; see Shleifer and Vishny 2002).

Issues for further research
There is close interaction between policymaking and research. The concepts and analytical frameworks devised by scholars strongly influence how reality is described and interpreted. As Keynes (1936) cautioned, "Practical men, who believe themselves to be quite exempt from any intellectual influences, are usually the slaves of some defunct economist. Madmen in authority, who hear voices in the air, are distilling their frenzy from some academic scribbler of a few years back." Yet when faced with new realities, the "practical men" also deviate from standard theory. And, as is the case now in public finance, policymaking generates new insights that inform research and analysis and call for new research and "scribbling" to allow standard public finance theory to catch up with changed realities and the changed practice of public finance.

Public finance scholars will find a host of issues in this volume that require further research and study. Three issues in particular came up repeatedly during the preparation of this volume:
- Optimal provision of (global) public goods.
- Market failure and government failure.
- Transnational—global and regional—public goods.

At present, the "Samuelson condition" (Samuelson 1954, 1955) is the main criterion helping policymakers frame the determination of the efficient provision level of public goods. The condition is met when the marginal cost of providing the public good equals the sum of the marginal amount each person affected by the good is willing to pay. There are two main reasons why it may be useful to revisit the application of the Samuelson condition.

First, the state is no longer the sole producer or financier of public goods. Today, other actors provide many, if not most, public goods. Thus, in line with the changes characterizing new public finance 1, the relevant question is what types of public policy incentives are needed to ensure efficient provision as actors come together to provide the good. Is the government's input meant to cover the full cost of providing the good or only a fraction—say, the cost of a fiscal incentive?

The question of optimal provision becomes even more complicated for global public goods, where states may provide incentives nationally, intergovernmental organizations may offer additional incentives at the international level, and private actors respond to these public policy incentives with different private spending decisions. The usefulness of the Samuelson condition, as traditionally presented and applied, in answering these questions is limited. The issue to clarify is whose marginal willingness to pay for which input to the public good is to be aggregated; and whose costs are being taken into account on the other side of the equation?

Second, the blending function of the state also presents challenges. In the traditional analysis the Samuelson condition relates to the aggregation of national preferences. But today preferences for the provision of public goods often come from outside national borders as well as inside. If the external preferences demand a higher level of provision than domestic preferences suggest, and if the state aligns provision to the external demand, the Samuelson condition would not be met: the marginal cost of providing the good might exceed the sum of the marginal willingness to pay of the country's (tax-paying) residents. If the state ignores external demands, provision of the good would meet the Samuelson condition, leaving some of the domestic population content but, because provision falls short of external demand, costing the country internationally.

These analyses consider only the short run, but the time dimension may be crucial in both cases. For example, asking domestic constituencies to pay more than they are currently willing to pay could generate benefits for national actors in the longer run. Trade liberalization is an example. In other instances where external policy demand exceeds domestic demand, the state may justifiably seek compensation from the international community (incremental cost reimbursement) or suggest to the world community that time for adjustment is needed before outside demands are taken into account.

Thus, it seems that it might be useful to revisit the Samuelson condition and explore how it could be refined to better reflect the current reality that most public goods are provided by many actors rather than the state alone and that states are increasingly expected to blend external and domestic policy demands.

A further possible concern relates to optimal provision when information problems cause people to undervalue a particular public good (say, prevention against avian flu). Applying the Samuelson condition may lead to inadequate (over- or under-) provision. Global public goods—because of their complexity—are especially likely to generate such problems. The challenge thus is how to improve the availability of information about the costs and benefits of the current provision status of various global public goods and the net benefits to be derived from any enhancement measures. Might the concept of adequate provision and the assessment methodology suggested in the chapter by Conceição and Mendoza perhaps be a useful step forward?

Governments continue to have an important role in correcting market failure. But markets and civil society are also correcting state failure and failures of intergovernmental cooperation. With the globalization of markets and the increased mobility of factors of production and with states competing for these mobile factors, markets may exercise de facto coercive power over states. States, which remain shackled to their territory, may be tempted to free ride on global public goods provision, whereas the participants in globalizing markets and global civil society may want enhanced provision of various global public goods. Sometimes that interest is so strong that, as documented in Kaul's chapter on global public-private partnerships, these private actors may move ahead with voluntary provision rather than wait for the state to respond. And at times private actors may impose high penalties on noncompliant states, such as increased borrowing costs for states that do not offer what is generally perceived as a good business climate.

This, of course, raises the question of who is correcting whose failure.

Global public goods (perhaps more so than pure local, national, or even regional public goods) demonstrate that publicness in consumption does not imply that all enjoy the good in the same way. It only means that many, sometimes all, are affected by the good's costs or benefits. But they may be affected in different ways. The vast differences and disparities that exist in the world mean that preferences for global public goods are likely to vary considerably. This raises questions about the distributional consequences of the trend toward increased voluntary and private provision of these goods: whose preferences do global public goods reflect?

Preference aggregation at the intergovernmental level gives rise to related questions. A number of proposals for fairer decisionmaking on global issues are being considered.[27] Also important is understanding why agreements on global policy initiatives (like halving world poverty or reducing greenhouse gases) and agreements on how to share the costs of these initiatives are often negotiated separately, leading to many unfunded mandates (intergovernmental resolutions that lack financial backing) and many nonmandated funds (financing mechanisms linked to global concerns but created outside of intergovernmental processes).[28] This raises once again the question of how well global public policy and expenditure priorities are matched.

Another area requiring further study is the identification of the appropriate actor and level (local, national, or international) of policy intervention. In global communicable disease control the issues are how to ensure coherence between vertical, disease-specific interventions that are essentially international, and horizontal interventions (such as enhancing health systems), which are primarily national initiatives (see the example of malaria control in table 1 in the previous chapter). Empirical studies could draw on the experiences of global support initiatives such as the Global Fund to Fight AIDS, Tuberculosis, and Malaria to provide policy clues.

Many other questions can be raised, including how much the lessons from the fiscal equivalence principle apply internationally, how to conceptualize trade in public services between governments (like the ones brokered by the Global Environment Facility), and how to use aggregation technologies or the wider notion of the production path to identify which building blocks of the public good to assign to which actor or level.

The research outputs on such issues could ultimately lead to a comprehensive theory of the new public finance—a theory that combines international cooperation behind borders (the blending of domestic and external policy preferences) and international cooperation beyond national borders (the blending of economic and foreign policy goals).

Looking ahead

For centuries the world has been concerned with developing and strengthening the institutions of independent states and national policymaking sovereignty. Public finance has evolved to support these concerns. Today, however, globalization requires states to use their policymaking power more flexibly, taking actions nationally and internationally, wherever they can best be implemented. It challenges states to think in terms of "global public policy networks" (Reinicke 1998): international cooperation behind and beyond borders.

Governments are responding to this challenge, and public finance, as one of the major policy instruments of governments, is also changing as new issues and new policy avenues arise.

This volume is about how public finance is being reinvented to enable its policy measures and tools to cross public-private divides and domestic-foreign frontiers to meet the growing agenda of global challenges. It aspires to broaden and advance the debate on this emerging global public finance.

New issues can take a long time to be recognized. The new global public finance discussed in this volume is not as new as one might think. Richard A. Musgrave in his 1969 book *Fiscal Systems* raised many of the topics discussed here. He had already envisioned the challenges we are facing today with ever greater urgency. Now may be the time to take them on.

APPENDIX. CALCULATIONS BEHIND TABLE 1, SIX TOOLS, $7 TRILLION GAIN

New public finance tools are attractive because they allocate resources more efficiently than traditional tools do. The quantitative estimates of the efficiency gains—broadly understood—that are possible with the use of the new public finance tools presented in table 1 are described here in more detail.[29]

Since tools are generic and applicable to a wide range of situations, the efficiency gains are estimated in the context of concrete applications to specific policy tasks. Neither the size nor the scope (beneficiary range) of the gains is an inherent characteristic of the tool. Who gains and how much depends on its particular application.

The efficiency gains estimated here focus on the cost savings from achieving policy objectives more cheaply than is possible with conventional policy approaches. The following illustrations, presented in descending order of net present value gains, show that as few as six tools applied to six different issues could generate about $7 trillion in net present value gains. The annual gains from the six tools could be as high as $360 billion.[30]

- *Guarantees.* Guarantees provided by bilateral or multilateral aid agencies to reduce the risks to investors in developing countries can lower the cost of capital, as shown by the difference in interest spreads between U.S. Treasury bonds and long-term lending for infrastructure projects in selected developing countries with and without guarantees. Assuming annual private sector investment flows into developing country infrastructure of about $64 billion (based on the annual average for 1990–2003; Izaguirre 2004, p. 3) and a 170 basis point reduction in spread (based on the average of the actual reductions observed in a set of developing countries; Wormser and Babar 2001), the annual savings from guarantees to finance infrastructure in developing countries could reach $1.1 billion, or $22 billion in net present value.

- *Securitization of future flow receivables.* The amount of securitizable future flow receivables in hard currency available to developing countries is estimated to be at least $77 billion a year (Ratha 2002, p. 3). If these receivables were securitized (as, for example, discussed in the chapter by Conceição, Rajan, and Shah, in this volume), developing countries' borrowing cost would be about 200 basis points below that of an unsecured debt float (Kektar and Ratha 2001, p. 3). This implies yearly savings of about $1.5 billion, or $31 billion in net present value.

- *Advanced purchase commitments.* Advanced purchase commitments are a tool developed to encourage, among other things, pro-poor research and development, including the creation and diffusion of vaccines for neglected diseases. An estimated commitment of $3 billion (in net present value) would be required to encourage pharmaceutical companies to invest in a new vaccine—like a vaccine for malaria—that benefits primarily the poor (Kremer and Glennerster 2004, p. 89). An advanced purchase commitment of this type would bring forward the availability of a malaria vaccine by 10 years (Kremer and Glennerster 2004, p. 95). The vaccine would reduce the costs of the related annual disease burden by about half (Kremer 2001, pp. 50–51). The average annual net benefit of reducing the malaria burden by half in Sub-Saharan Africa would be about $3–$10 billion a year (Mills and Shillcutt 2004, 2005). Thus, taking the median, the vaccine would create gains of at least $6 billion a year, and bringing the vaccine's availability forward by 10 years would represent a net present value gain of $50 billion. Deducting the $3 billion needed to pay for the commitment leads to a gain in net present value terms of $47 billion, or $1.4 billion a year on an annualized basis.

- *GDP-indexed bonds.* GDP-indexed bonds link payments on sovereign debt to the issuing country's rate of economic growth. They act as automatic stabilizers of government resources, reducing the need for drastic public spending cuts when growth is slow and restraining new government spending when growth is rapid. Their advantage over unindexed bonds is that they limit the range of variation of the debt to GDP ratio. Although GDP-indexed bonds cannot compensate for unsustainable macro policies, they can help reduce the occurrence of debt defaults and financial crises in developing countries by stabilizing debt ratios. Econometric simulations suggest that an increase in the debt to GDP ratio of 10 percent is linked to a 20 percent increase in the probability of a crisis occurring (as indicated by Borensztein and Mauro 2004, pp. 168–69, based on empirical estimates by Detragiache and Spilimbergo 2001). Assuming that GDP-indexed bonds lower this probability by one-fifth and considering that the output costs of financial crises amounted to about $150 billion a year (based on a study of eight countries during 1995–2002 by Griffith-Jones and Gottschalk 2004, p. 5), growth-indexed bonds could yield annual cost savings of at least $30 billion, or $600 billion in net present value.
- *Macro markets.* Macro markets would enable the trading of securities linked to aggregated—"macro"—incomes like the GDP of a single country or a group of countries, or components of the national GDP, such as the income of particular occupational groups. Macro markets would allow public and private actors to "insure" against volatility in such income streams by buying securities that offset adverse swings. Simulations of such trading involving the Group of Seven industrial countries suggest that such trading could generate huge benefits. After subtracting the cost of paying for the securities, the annual net gain is estimated to reach $145.1 billion, or $2,902 billion in net present value (Athanasoulis and Shiller 2001, p. 1046).
- *International pollution permit trading.* Reduction of greenhouse gas emissions is a widely shared concern of the international community. There are several policy options for meeting emission targets such as those set forth in the Kyoto Protocol.[31] A frequently discussed set of alternatives is international permit trading and no international permit trading. Trading would be more efficient than if each country were to meet the targets through national-level measures alone. Countries where reductions are more costly could, for instance, buy permits from countries where reductions are less costly. In fact, through international permit trading the industrial countries (which, together with the transition economies, are required to reduce emissions under the Kyoto Protocol) could reduce their annual compliance cost by about $182 billion, or $3,640 billion in net present value (McKibben and Wilcoxen 1999, pp. 23–25).

NOTES

1. A vast literature has emerged on this topic. See, among others, Burgess and Stern (1993); Cnossen and Sinn (2003); Keen and Simone (2004); Schulze and Ursprung (1999); Slemrod (2004); Swank and Steinmo (2002); Tanzi (1994); and Zee (1996).

2. These measures can represent net savings by comparison with direct spending when they do not require the creation or expansion of government bureaucracies, as direct spending typically does.

3. The most desirable and feasible policy mix will vary across country groups. Tanzi suggests that developing countries still have room to increase public spending. Governments in industrial countries may have to scale back some programs and encourage people to assume more private responsibility for reducing their exposure to such risks as ill-health or temporary (business-cycle-related) unemployment.

4. As Caballero (2003, p. 4) puts it: "to do so, [countries] need access to hedging and insurance instruments to guard against the disastrous events caused by volatile capital flows. For now, [developing] economies are self-insuring through costly accumulation of large international reserves and stabilization funds. Most individuals would be underinsured if they had to leave a million dollars aside for a potential automobile collision and the liabilities that would follow, rather than buying insurance against such event; countries are no different. Underinsurance is what greatly amplifies these countries' recessions."

5. Bondholders would benefit as well. As Borensztein and Mauro (2004, p. 197) argue, "if low GDP growth renders a country's debt position unsustainable, the country will likely default. It is surely better for international investors to receive lower debt repayments through indexation that is agreed upon in a contract from the outset, rather than face uncertain recovery values through a chaotic default process." GDP-indexed bonds are receiving growing political attention (see, for example, IMF 2004; United Nations 2005; U.S. Council of Economic Advisers 2004). Other types of indexation might also be used. For example, countries that rely heavily on commodity exports are vulnerable to price volatility in commodity markets. A sudden drop in commodity prices could jeopardize a country's ability to meet its sovereign debt service obligations in hard currency—without any underlying change in domestic policy or other economic prospects. In these situations, bonds could be indexed to the price level of the key commodity (or basket of commodities). See, for example, Caballero (2003) and Atta-Mensah (2004).

6. By some estimates developing countries annually lose about $50 billion because of tax havens (Oxfam Great Britain 2000, p. 2). The U.S. Government Accountability Office estimates that the tax shelter services obtained by 61 companies during 1998–2003 resulted in tax revenue loss to the U.S. government of $3.4 billion (U.S. GAO 2005, p. 6). On possible future trends in tax avoidance and evasion, see Tanzi (2001).

7. Most bilateral tax treaties are drafted along the lines of the OECD model tax convention of 1997 (revised in 2003; OECD 2003a; www.oecd.org/dataoecd/52/34/

1914467.pdf) and the United Nations Model Double Taxation Convention between Developed and Developing Countries (UN 2001, 2003b). For a discussion, see UNCTAD (2000).

8. For more on the partnerships identified and analyzed, see the section on global public-private partnerships at www.thenewpublicfinance.org.

9. The UK government has pledged $1.8 billion over 15 years and the pilot is expected to raise an additional $4 billion over 10 years (UK DFID 2005).

10. Powerful nations may monopolize the international political dialogue and distort policy outcomes. Countries may try to free ride instead of contributing to the management of global externalities or providing inputs to global public goods (Sandler 2004). Information asymmetries also lead intergovernmental cooperation fail.

11. Various studies (Ferroni and Mody 2002; Kaul and Le Goulven 2003; Raffer 1999, 2004; Reisen, Soto, and Weithöner 2004; World Bank 2001) have shown that financing for international activities related to the provision of global public goods was often simply taken from the existing official development assistance envelope in industrial countries.

12. The persistent failure to provide information on the financing required to achieve internationally agreed goals is, at least in some instances, slowly being overcome. Major breakthroughs were achieved by the Commission on Macroeconomics and Health (CMH 2001) on control of communicable disease and subsequently by the UN Millennium Project (2005) on detailed estimates of the costs of achieving global goals. The UN Millennium Project (2005, p. 57) estimates that meeting the Millennium Development Goals would require annual increases in official development assistance of $70 billion in 2006, rising to $130 billion in 2015. It estimates that meeting the goals is likely to generate huge benefits, including lifting more than 500 million people out of poverty, saving millions of lives, giving millions of children an opportunity to attend school, reversing environmental degradation, and averting conflict, among other benefits (UN Millennium Project 2005, p. 60).

13. See, for example, Lomborg (2004), which also includes references to numerous other studies.

14. For example, Barrett (2004), as reported in Conceição and Mendoza (in this volume), shows the results of studies that indicate that most of the benefits of smallpox eradication are accruing to developing countries ($35 billion out of global net benefits of $47 billion), while polio eradication, according to one study, is likely to generate $72 billion in net benefits to industrial countries, with developing countries suffering a net loss of $11 billion.

15. Other schemes include the EU Emission Trading Scheme (EC 2005a), the UK Emission Trading Scheme (UK DEFRA 2001), and the New South Wales, Australia, trading scheme (New South Wales Government 2004).

16. On the issue of international commodity agreements, see, for example, Gilbert (1996).

17. See www.worldbank.org/poverty.

18. It is important to recognize that sometimes incentive structures are not easy to change, as debates on Special Drawing Right allocations show (see, for example, Mussa, Boughton, and Isard 1996).

19. For more detail on the activities of the Multilateral Investment Guarantee Agency, see www.miga.org, and the International Finance Corporation, see www.ifc.org.

20. Figure 5 could be refined further, for example, by indicating the evolution in the intensity of use with which the various types of grant assistance would be employed, as Radelet differentiates. In addition, one could reflect the continuum from peacekeeping support and humanitarian assistance to development aid. All these different types of aid are in figure 5 collapsed into the single tool "grants."

21. The costs to developing countries resulting from the multilateral trade regime as currently provided are estimated to be about $150 billion (see Hertel 2004, as reported in Conceição and Mendoza in this volume). And tariffs on agricultural imports in OECD countries cost the world more than $91 billion and developing countries about $12.5 billion a year (Tokarick 2005, p. 590).

22. For a related analysis of the balance between centralization and competition see Esty and Geradin (2001).

23. It should, of course, be kept in mind that country conditions and issues vary, and the question of which financing arrangement is best for which purpose can only be decided case by case. Wilensky (2002) discusses the diversity in approaches and pace of implementation of policies across countries, even when the policies address similar goals.

24. Domestic financial markets are an important ingredient of development (Levine 2004).

25. For more on the difficulties line ministries face as well as on what some countries have already done to improve this situation, see a series of country case studies available at www.thenewpublicfinance.org.

26. Kaul's chapter on global public-private partnerships provides some initial suggestions for developing such assessment criteria and methodologies; see also the reasons for participating in the UN Global Compact (www.unglobalcompact.org).

27. See, for example, Buira (2003) and Bradford and Linn (2004).

28. See again figure 3 in this chapter, and for more detail, the chapter by Conceição.

29. Estimates of the benefits associated with the enhanced provision of global public goods reported in Conceição and Mendoza describe courses of corrective action that do not necessarily explore the most efficient tool for the purpose. Thus, a further refinement of that exercise could consider first the determination of what is the most efficient tool— that is, the approach that would lead to the enhanced provision of the good at the least cost—before comparing the net benefits to be derived

from investing in alternative policy objectives. However, one of the tools considered here—international pollution permit trading—is the tool underlying the calculation of the net benefits of enhancing the provision of climate stability in Conceição and Mendoza—and, therefore, the benefits reported in that chapter include the efficiency gains of using this tool as opposed to the "no trading"option.

30. For details on the calculations see Mendoza, Merlen, and Conceição (2005), available at www.thenewpublicfinance.org. The totals are approximate and provided for illustrative purposes only, since the calculations for each application use different methods and do not use the same base year.

31. See http://unfccc.int/essential_background/kyoto_protocol/items/2830.php.

REFERENCES

Athanasoulis, Stefano G., and Robert J. Shiller. 2001. "World Income Components: Measuring and Exploiting Risk-Sharing Opportunities." *American Economic Review* 91 (4): 1031–54.

Atta-Mensah, Joseph. 2004. "Commodity-Linked Bonds: A Potential Means for Less-Developed Countries to Raise Foreign Capital." Bank of Canada Working Paper 2004/20. Ottawa.

Barrett, Scott. 2003. *Environment and Statecraft: the Strategy of Environmental Treaty-Making.* Oxford: Oxford University Press.

———. 2004. "The Provision Status of Disease Eradication." UNDP/ODS Background Paper. United Nations Development Programme, Office of Development Studies. [www.thenewpublicfinance.org].

Bird, Richard M., and Jack M. Mintz. 2003. "Sharing the International Tax Base in a Changing World." In Sijbren Cnossen and Hans-Werner Sinn, eds., *Public Finance and Public Policy in the New Century.* Cambridge, Mass.: MIT Press.

BIS (Bank for International Settlements). 2005. *BIS Quarterly Review: International Banking and Financial Market Developments.* Statistical Annex. June. [www.bis.org/].

Borensztein, Eduardo, and Paulo Mauro. 2004. "Reviving the Case for GDP-Indexed Bonds." *Economic Policy* 19 (38):165–216.

Bradford, Colin I., and Johannes F. Linn. 2004. "Global Economic Governance at a Crossroads: Replacing the G-7 with the G-20." Policy Brief 131. Brookings Institution, Washington, D.C.

Buira, Ariel. 2003. "The Governance of the International Monetary Fund." In Inge Kaul, Pedro Conceição, Katell Le Goulven, and Ronald U. Mendoza, eds., *Providing Global Public Goods: Managing Globalization.* New York: Oxford University Press.

Burgess, Robin, and Nicholas Stern. 1993. "Taxation and Development." *Journal of Economic Literature* 31 (2): 762–830.

Caballero, Ricardo J. 2003. *On the International Financial Architecture: Insuring Emerging Markets.* NBER Working Paper 9570. Cambridge, Mass.: National Bureau of Economic Research.

CMH (Commission on Macroeconomics and Health). 2001. *Macroeconomics and Health: Investing in Health for Economic Development. Report of the Commission on Macroeconomics and Health.* Geneva: World Health Organization.

Cnossen, Sijbren, and Hans-Werner Sinn, eds. 2003. *Public Finance and Public Policy in the New Century.* Cambridge, Mass.: MIT Press.

Detragiache, Enrica, and Antonio Spilimbergo. 2001. "Crises and Liquidity: Evidence and Interpretation." IMF Working Paper 01/2. Washington, D.C. [www.imf.org/external/pubs/ft/wp/2001/wp0102.pdf].

EC (European Commission). 2005a. *EU Emissions Trading. An Open Scheme Promoting Global Innovation to Combat Climate Change.* Brussels. [http://europa.eu.int/comm/environment/climat/pdf/emission_trading2_en.pdf].

———. 2005b. "Questions and Answers: The Commission's 'MDG Package' (Millennium Development Goals)." Brussels. [http://europa.eu.int/rapid/pressReleasesAction.do?reference=MEMO/05/124&format=HTML&aged=0&language=EN&guiLanguage=en].

Esty, Daniel C., and Damien Geradin, eds. 2001. *Regulatory Competition and Economic Integration: Comparative Perspectives.* New York: Oxford University Press.

Esty, Daniel C., and Michael E. Porter. Forthcoming. "National Environmental Performance: An Empirical Analysis of Policy Results and Determinants." *Journal of Environmental Development Economics.*

Ferroni, Marco, and Ashoka Mody, eds. 2002. *International Public Goods: Incentives, Measurement, and Financing.* Washington, D.C.: Kluwer Academic Publishers and World Bank.

Financial Stability Forum. 2005. "Compendium of Standards—Date." Basel, Switzerland. [www.fsforum.org/compendium/compendium_of_standards_date_2003.html].

Gilbert, Christopher L. 1996. "International Commodity Agreements: An Obituary Notice." *World Development* 24 (1): 1–19.

Griffith-Jones, Stephany, and Ricardo Gottschalk. 2004. "Costs of Currency Crises and Benefits of International Financial Reform." United Nations Development Programme, Office of Development Studies, New York. [www.thenewpublicfinance.org].

Hertel, Thomas. 2004. "Assessing the Provision of International Trade as a Global Public Good." UNDP/ODS Background Papers. United Nations Development Programme, Office of Development Studies, New York. [www.thenewpublicfinance.org].

High-Level Forum on Aid Effectiveness. 2005. *Paris Declaration on Aid Effectiveness: Ownership, Harmonisation, Alignment, Results and Mutual Accountability.* March 2,

Paris. [www1.worldbank.org/harmonization/Paris/FINALPARISDECLARATION. pdf].

High-Level Forum on Harmonization. 2003. *Rome Declaration on Harmonization.* February 25, Rome. [www1.worldbank.org/harmonization/romehlf/Documents/ RomeDeclaration.pdf].

High-Level Panel on Threats, Challenges, and Change. 2004. *A More Secure World: Our Shared Responsibilities.* New York: United Nations.

IMF (International Monetary Fund). 2004. "Sovereign Debt Structure for Crisis Prevention." Research Department, Washington, D.C. [www.imf.org/external/ np/res/docs/2004/070204.pdf].

————. 2005. "Reports on the Observance of Standards and Codes (ROSCs)—By Date." Washington, D.C. [www.imf.org/external/np/rosc/rosc.asp?sort=date#RR].

Izaguirre, Ada Karina. 2004. "Private Infrastructure: Activity Down by 13 Percent in 2003." Public Policy for the Private Sector Note 274. World Bank, Washington, D.C. [http://rru.worldbank.org/Documents/274izaguirre.pdf].

Kaul, Inge, and Katell Le Goulven. 2003. "Financing Global Public Goods: A New Frontier of Public Finance." In Inge Kaul, Pedro Conceição, Katell Le Goulven, and Ronald U. Mendoza, eds., *Providing Global Public Goods: Managing Globalization.* New York: Oxford University Press.

Keen, Michael, and Alejandro Simone. 2004. "Tax Policy in Developing Countries: Some Lessons from the 1990s and Some Challenges Ahead." In Sanjeev Gupta, Benedict Clements, and Gabriela Inchauste, eds., *Helping Countries Develop: The Role of Fiscal Policy.* Washington, D.C.: International Monetary Fund.

Ketkar, Suhas, and Dilip Ratha. 2001. "Securitization of Future Flow Receivables: A Useful Tool for Developing Countries." *Finance and Development* 38 (1). [Accessed December 22, 2004, www.imf.org/external/pubs/ft/fandd/2001/03/ ketkar.htm#author].

Keynes, John Maynard. 1936. *The General Theory of Employment, Interest, and Money.* New York: Harcourt Press.

Kremer, Michael. 2001. "Creating Markets for New Vaccines Part I: Rationale." In Adam B. Jaffe, Josh Lerner, and Scott Stern, eds., *Innovation Policy and the Economy.* Cambridge, Mass.: National Bureau of Economic Research and MIT Press.

Kremer, Michael, and Rachel Glennerster. 2004. *Strong Medicine: Creating Incentives for Pharmaceutical Research on Neglected Diseases.* Princeton, N.J.: Princton University Press.

Lecocq, Franck, and Karan Capoor. 2005. "State and Trends of the Carbon Market 2005." Washington D.C. [carbonfinance.org/docs/CarbonMarketStudy2005. pdf].

Ledyard, John O. 1989. "Incentive Compatibility." In John Eatwell, Murray Milgrave, and Peter Nenoman, eds., *Allocation, Information, and Markets.* New York: W. W. Norton.

Levine, Ross. 2004. *Finance and Growth: Theory and Evidence.* NBER Working Paper 10766. Cambridge, Mass.: National Bureau of Economic Research.

Lomborg, Bjørn, ed. 2004. *Global Crises, Global Solutions.* Cambridge: Cambridge University Press.

McKibbin, Warwick J., and Peter J. Wilcoxen. 1999. "Permit Trading under the Kyoto Protocol and Beyond." Brookings Discussion Papers in International Economics 150. Brookings Institution, Washington, D.C. [www.brook.edu/views/papers/bdp/bdp150/bdp150.pdf].

Mendoza, Ronald U., Sylvain Merlen, and Pedro Conceição. 2005. "Quantifying the Efficiency Gains from Financing Tools." United Nations Development Programme, Office of Development Studies, New York. [www.thenewpublicfinance.org].

Merlen, Sylvain. 2005. "International Cooperation Behind National Borders: An Inventory of Domestic Policy Measures Aimed at Internalizing Cross-Border Spillovers Adversely Affecting the Global Environment." UNDP/ODS Background Paper. United Nations Development Programme, Office of Development Studies, New York. [www.thenewpublicfinance.org].

Mills, Anne, and Sam Shillcutt. 2004. "Communicable Diseases." In Bjørn Lomborg, ed., *Global Crises, Global Solutions.* Cambridge: Cambridge University Press.

———. 2005. Email communication. August 19.

Mussa, Michael, James M. Boughton, and Peter Isard, eds. 1996. *The Future of the SDR in Light of Changes in the International Monetary System.* Washington, D.C.: International Monetary Fund.

New South Wales Government. 2004. "New South Wales Greenhouse Gas Abatement Scheme Fact Sheet: Summary of Scheme." [www.greenhousegas.nsw.gov.au/documents/Summary%20of%20scheme_GGAS-FS-01_v2_210704.pdf].

OECD (Organisation for Economic Co-operation and Development). 2003a. *Model Tax Convention on Income and on Capital: Condensed Version.* Paris.

———. 2003b. *Policy Brief: Policy Coherence—Vital for Global Development.* Paris. [www.oecd.org/dataoecd/11/35/20202515.pdf].

———. 2004. "Statistical Annex of the 2004 Development Cooperation Report." Paris. [www.oecd.org/dataoecd/52/9/1893143.xls].

Oxfam Great Britain. 2000. *Tax Havens: Releasing the Hidden Billions for Poverty Eradication.* [www.oxfam.org.uk/what_we_do/issues/debt_aid/tax_havens.htm].

Posner, Richard A. 2004. *Catastrophe: Risk and Response.* New York: Oxford University Press.

Raffer, Kunibert. 1999. *Official Development Assistance and Global Public Goods: A Trend Analysis of Past and Present Spending Patterns.* New York: United Nations Development Programme, Office of Development Studies.

———. 2004. "Applying Musgrave's Branches of Government Expenditures to ODA: Tentative Estimates." *Journal für Entwicklungspolitik* 20 (1): 104–19.

Ratha, Dilip. 2002. "Financing Development through Future-Flow Securitization." PREMnote 69. World Bank, Washington, D.C. [www1.worldbank.org/prem/PREMNotes/premnote69.pdf].

Reinicke, Wolfgang. 1998. *Global Public Policy: Governing without Government?* Washington, D.C.: Brookings Institution Press.

Reinhold, Richard L. 2004. "Some Things that Multilateral Tax Treaties Might Usefully Do." *The Tax Lawyer* 57 (3): 661–708.

Reisen, Helmut, Marcelo Soto, and Thomas Weithöner. 2004. "Financing Global and Regional Public Goods through ODA: Analysis and Evidence from the OECD Creditor Reporting System." OECD Development Centre Working Paper 232. Organisation for Economic Co-operation and Development, Paris.

Sachs, Jeffrey D., John W. McArthur, Guido Schmidt-Traub, Margaret Kruk, Chandrika Bahadur, Michael Faye, and Gordon McCord. 2004. "Ending Africa's Poverty Trap." *Brookings Papers on Economic Activity* 1: 117–240.

Samuelson, Paul A. 1954. "The Pure Theory of Public Expenditure." *Review of Economics and Statistics* 36 (4): 387–89.

———. 1955. "Diagrammatic Exposition of a Theory of Public Expenditure." *Review of Economics and Statistics* 37 (4): 350–56.

Sandler, Todd. 2004. *Global Collective Action.* Cambridge: Cambridge University Press.

Schulze, Günther G., and Heinrich W. Ursprung. 1999. "Globalisation of the Economy and the Nation State." *The World Economy* 22 (3): 295–352.

Shiller, Robert J. 2003. *The New Financial Order.* Princeton, N.J.: Princeton University Press.

Shleifer, Andrei, and Robert W. Vishny. 2002. *The Grabbing Hand: Government Pathologies and Their Cures.* Cambridge, Mass.: Harvard University Press.

Slemrod, Joel. 2004. "Are Corporate Taxes or Countries Converging?" *Journal of Public Economics* 88 (6): 1169–86.

Stiglitz, Joseph E. 1998. "Redefining the Role of the State: What Should It Do? How Should It Do It? And How Should These Decisions Be Made?" Paper presented on the Tenth Anniversary of the MITI Research Institute, March 17, Tokyo. [www.meti.go.jp/topic/mitilab/downloadfiles/m2012-1j.pdf].

Swank, Duane, and Sven Steinmo. 2002. "The New Political Economy of Taxation in Advanced Capitalist Democracies." *American Journal of Political Science* 46 (3): 642–55.

Tanzi, Vito. 1994. *Taxation in an Integrating World.* Washington, D.C.: Brookings Institution Press.

———. 2001. "Globalization, Technological Development, and the Work of Fiscal Termites." *Brooklyn Journal of International Law* 26 (4): 1261–84.

Tiebout, Charles M. 1956. "A Pure Theory of Local Public Expenditures." *Journal of Political Economy* 64 (3): 416–24.

Tokarick, Stephen. 2005. "Who Bears the Cost of Agricultural Support in OECD Countries?" *World Economy* 28 (4): 573–93.

UK DEFRA (Department for Environment, Food, and Rural Affairs). 2001. "Framework for the UK Emissions Trading Scheme." [www.defra.gov.uk/environment/climatechange/trading/uk/pdf/trading-full.pdf].

UK DFID (Department for International Development). 2005. "Hilary Benn Pledges £1 Billion to Boost Health Care in Developing Countries." Press release. January 26. [www.dfid.gov.uk/news/files/pressreleases/pr-bennhealthbostpledge26jan05.asp].

UN (United Nations). 2001. *United Nations Model Double Taxation Convention between Developed and Developing Countries.* New York.

———. 2003a. "Implementation of and Follow-up to Commitments and Agreements Made at the International Conference on Financing for Development: Report of the Secretary General." New York. [http://daccessdds.un.org/doc/UNDOC/GEN/N03/460/32/PDF/N0346032.pdf?OpenElement].

———. 2003b. *Manual for the Negotiation of Bilateral Tax Treaties between Developed and Developing Countries.* New York.

———. 2005. *World Economic and Social Survey.* New York.

UNCTAD (United Nations Conference on Trade and Development). 2000. "Taxation." UNCTAD Series on International Investment Agreements. Geneva. [www.unctad.org/en/docs/iteiit16_en.pdf].

———. 2002. "Quantitative Data on Bilateral Investment Treaties and Double Taxation Treaties." Geneva. [www.unctad.org/Templates/WebFlyer.asp?intItemID=3150&lang=1].

———. 2004. *Development and Globalization: Facts and Figures.* Geneva.

UN Millennium Project. 2005. *Investing in Development: A Practical Plan to Achieve the Millennium Development Goals.* London: Earthscan.

U.S. Council of Economic Advisers. 2004. "Growth-Indexed Bonds: A Primer." [www.whitehouse.gov/cea/growth-indexed-bonds-white-paper.pdf].

U.S. GAO (Government Accountability Office). 2005. *Tax Shelters: Services Provided by External Auditors.* GAO-05-171. Washington, D.C.

Wilensky, Harold L. 2002. *Rich Democracies: Political Economy, Public Policy, and Performance.* Berkeley, Calif.: California University Press.

World Bank. 2001. *Global Development Finance 2001: Building Coalitions for Effective Development Finance.* Washington, D.C.

———. 2005a. "Board Presentations of PRSP Documents as at May 31, 2005." Washington, D.C. [http://siteresources.worldbank.org/INTPRS1/Resources/boardlist.pdf].

———. 2005b. *Global Development Finance 2005: Mobilizing Finance and Managing Vulnerability.* Washington, D.C.

Wormser, Michel, and Suman Babbar. 2001. "Leveraging Private Finance in Frontier Markets." Paper presented at the World Bank Guarantee Program Infrastructure Forum, May 2–4, Washington, D.C.

WTO (World Trade Organization). 2005. *International Trade Statistics 2004.* Geneva. [wto.org/english/res_e/statis_e/its2004_e/its04_longterm_e.htm].

Zee, Howell H. 1996. "Empirics of Crosscountry Tax Revenue Comparisons." *World Development* 24 (10): 1659–71.

1

THE NEW NATIONAL PUBLIC FINANCE

TAKING THE OUTSIDE WORLD INTO ACCOUNT

BLENDING EXTERNAL AND DOMESTIC POLICY DEMANDS
THE RISE OF THE INTERMEDIARY STATE
Inge Kaul

•

MAKING POLICY UNDER EFFICIENCY PRESSURES
GLOBALIZATION, PUBLIC SPENDING, AND SOCIAL WELFARE
Vito Tanzi

•

INTERNALIZING CROSS-BORDER SPILLOVERS
POLICY OPTIONS FOR ADDRESSING LONG-TERM FISCAL CHALLENGES
Peter S. Heller

MANAGING RISKS TO NATIONAL ECONOMIES
THE ROLE OF MACRO MARKETS
Robert J. Shiller

•

COMBINING FISCAL SOVEREIGNTY AND COORDINATION
NATIONAL TAXATION IN A GLOBALIZING WORLD
Peggy B. Musgrave

•

RECOGNIZING THE LIMITS TO COOPERATION BEHIND NATIONAL BORDERS
FINANCING THE CONTROL OF TRANSNATIONAL TERRORISM
Todd Sandler

BLENDING EXTERNAL AND DOMESTIC POLICY DEMANDS
THE RISE OF THE INTERMEDIARY STATE

INGE KAUL

Public finance theory seems largely to assume the continued existence of the ideal-type Westphalian state with exclusive political authority within its geographic boundaries based on territorial and policymaking sovereignty. The state is an aggregator of national preferences concerning government interventions that are deemed to be potentially desirable, especially where market failure arises. To ensure that established policy priorities can be implemented, the state is also said to enjoy unique coercive powers.

This model of the state is increasingly at odds with reality. As states face an ever-denser network of external expectations too desirable or too costly to ignore, they respond with corresponding national policy reforms. As a result, their role has been changing. The Westphalian state has progressively transformed itself into an intermediary state—blending domestic and external policy preferences, correcting markets and standing corrected by nonstate actors (business and civil society), exerting coercive powers and being compelled to compete with other states for mobile resources (finance and skills). Exclusive national policymaking sovereignty has given way to responsive policymaking sovereignty.

This chapter explores the rise of the state as intermediary. Following a brief elaboration of the model of the state underpinning mainstream public finance theory, the chapter examines the external policy expectations facing the state: how and by whom they are formulated, what they require, and what their objectives are. States' responses to these expectations are then considered, setting the stage for a discussion of how states' acceptance of an intermediary role between external and domestic policy demands affects their role. The chapter points to discrepancies between the state's role in public finance theory and in actual policy practice and identifies areas in which public finance theory might need to better reflect the new, broadened role of the state.

The author thanks Romina Bandura for her excellent research assistance.

THE MODEL OF THE STATE IN PUBLIC FINANCE THEORY

As Desai (2003), Musgrave (1969, 1998), and others have noted, the role of the state has changed throughout history, and with it public finance and economics theory. During the twentieth century the state in most parts of the world played a strong role, still echoed in much of today's public finance theory. Especially in response to the Great Depression of 1929 and the devastation of World War II economic reality and theory emphasized active government intervention to accelerate reconstruction and stimulate economic growth. Keynesian ideas informed much of this policy approach in the Western industrial countries. A strong state and control of cross-border economic activity were also favored by many developing countries, for reasons of nation building, import substitution, and at times rent-seeking by the ruling elites. Of course, the state also reigned supreme in the former socialist, centrally planned economies.

The role of the state in both theory and practice started to change noticeably around the mid-1970s. The image of the state as a benign, paternalistic institution began to be queried (Chang 2003). Public choice theorists (such as Buchanan and Tullock 1962) developed a more nuanced concept of the state, depicting politicians and bureaucrats as self-interested actors pursuing private as well as public agendas. Principal-agent theories of bureaucracy (for example, Niskanen 1973) contributed to the debate, pointing to a growing state apparatus and arguing that state agents are more the masters of the public than their servants.

As markets deepened and expanded and gradually integrated across countries, and especially as the East-West divide vanished, the debate about market versus state gathered momentum. The policy pendulum swung toward markets, advocating privatization and economic liberalization.[1]

Mainstream public finance literature adapted. Textbooks typically identify three core elements of the state.[2] First, the state is the aggregator of national policy preferences. National political processes define the policy initiatives to be undertaken by the state and the corresponding budget. Many public finance textbooks devote considerable attention to preference revelation and other political economy issues, including voting rules and the incentives of politicians and bureaucrats, which may give rise to government failures. Although problems have been recognized (Arrow 1963), this parceling together of national policy demands is a recognized key role of the state.

Second, in line with the rebalancing of markets and states that began in the mid-1970s, leaving the provision of goods and services to the market has become the default scenario. The state's role is mainly to correct market failure and to promote desired levels of societal or intergenerational distribution where market outcomes deviate from those levels.[3] These roles are usually referred to as the state's allocation and distribution activities (Musgrave and Musgrave 1989).[4]

Third, the state enjoys unique coercive powers, including regulation and taxation. Drawing on its coercive powers, the state imposes taxes and collects other revenue to pay for planned public expenditures and puts in place other measures (typically regulatory) required for society to realize its established policy goals. These powers allow states to foster collective action by keeping free-riding in check and making all contribute their share to the costs of general administration and to the policy interventions defined under its role as aggregator of policy preferences (say, in support of a public good such as national security or a distributional effort such as social protection).

The underlying model described by these three core elements is still essentially that of the Westphalian state: a state enjoying *exclusive* political authority within its territorial boundaries. For the most part public finance and public economics textbooks still assume a closed economy. While some mention cross-border spillovers and global public goods issues (especially global environmental challenges), few treat these concerns systematically (Sidikou-Sow 2005).

Reality is increasingly at odds with this model. States are facing an ever-denser international network of external expectations about their national public policy, and they are, in large measure, complying with them, as the next two sections show.

EXTERNAL EXPECTATIONS ABOUT NATIONAL PUBLIC POLICY

Ideas about desirable state behavior are being discussed in numerous forums. Whether ultimately agreed on or not, many of these ideas become part of the pool of external expectations about desired national public policy and part of the international policy domain that Ruggie (2004, p. 519) describes as:

> constituted by interactions among non-state actors as well as states. It permits the direct expression and pursuit of a variety of human interests, not merely those mediated (filtered, interpreted, promoted) by states. It "exists" in transnational non-territorial spatial formations, and is anchored in norms and expectations as well as institutional networks and circuits within, across and beyond states....
>
> The effect...is not to replace states, but to embed systems of governance in broader global frameworks....

But what are these expectations? What are their origins and forms? And what is their purpose?

Origins and forms of external policy expectations

Policy expectations can be considered external when they emanate from outside the national political processes through which states ascertain and aggregate domestic policy demands. The origin (rather than the substance) matters when identifying a policy demand as external or domestic. External sources of policy expectations include intergovernmental forums, international business and civil society organizations, global media, and multiactor venues like the World Economic Forum.[5] Thus all actor groups—states (individually, as "clubs," or multilaterally), business, and civil society—are involved in formulating global policy visions and demands.

External policy expectations have proliferated since the 1990s so that it is now virtually impossible even to guess at their number. Undoubtedly, it is huge—and rising. Approximately 2,000 multilateral treaties are registered with the United Nations,[6] along with (perhaps thousands of) major international conference resolutions and plans of action that are not treaties but that demand follow-up. Add to this the more than 2,000 bilateral investment treaties (UNCTAD 2004), some 250 regional trade agreements (WTO 2005), and policy statements by the 60,000 or so international civil society organizations (Anheier, Glasius, and Kaldor 2004, p. 320), and the vast number and diversity of international expectations about national public policy become evident.

External policy expectations have also grown in the attention they command. The follow-up to global policy norms is ever more closely monitored, and many norms come with carrots and sticks. For instance, there are now more than 100 global reports prepared by intergovernmental, global business, or global civil society organizations that track major trends and policy achievements at the international as well as the national level (Haller 2005). In addition, numerous country reports review compliance with various global norms and standards. An example is the series of Reports on the Observance of Standards and Codes undertaken by the International Monetary Fund at countries' request.[7] Clearly, national public policy is subject to ever-closer scrutiny.

In addition, external expectations are increasingly taking the form of policy conditionality. For example, the number of conditions accompanying International Monetary Fund loan programs rose from 6 in the mid-1970s to 20 and more in recent years (Kapur 2001, p. 216).[8] Some stipulations touch on such policy issues as privatization and economic liberalization, which are not always directly linked to the borrowing government's repayment capacity. Foreign aid, too, is increasingly dependent on compliance with donor policy priorities, including respect for human rights, economic and financial liberalization, control of money laundering, and other political commitments (Raffer 2004). Similarly, credit rating agencies usually consider criteria that reflect external policy expectations and that have immediate financial implication, thereby enforcing the "discipline of the market" by determining the price at which national actors can borrow on financial markets.[9]

In addition to sovereign credit rating agencies there are approximately 130 composite indices and scorecards that measure and rank country performance and state behavior (Bandura 2005b). All actor groups are engaged in these "beauty competitions" among states—civil society organizations like Third World Network/Social Watch and Transparency International, policy think tanks like the Center for Global Development, private entities like the Economist Intelligence Unit and AT Kearney, and intergovernmental agencies like the United Nations Development Programme and the World Bank.

Thus, international public policymaking is an increasingly busy process, with multiple actors heaping layer upon layer on to the global stockpile of policy norms and, most important, expecting in ever more demanding terms that states will accept them as guideposts of national policymaking.

But what is all this ferment about? What are states actually expected to deliver in terms of national public policy reforms and outcomes?

The contents of external policy expectations

A pragmatic approach to answering these questions is to assume that all these indices and scorecards represent a codification of the most important external policy expectations and then to catalogue the dimensions of state behavior that they try to capture.[10] This exercise shows that external policy expectations fall into two main clusters, with two parts in each (figure 1)[11]:

- Cluster 1: Openness and competitiveness.
- Cluster 2: Development and security.

Cluster 1 reflects largely the interests of transnational business actors, while cluster 2 echoes the concerns of civil society and development advocates, including many bilateral and multilateral aid agencies. Yet there are no clear dividing lines between the clusters' constituencies. Individual firms and business associations can support basic education and public health services, because they recognize that such spending is a good investment in human capital and good for the company's reputation and, ultimately, its bottom line (Benioff and Southwick 2004; Dawkins 2002; Roman, Hayibor, and Agle 1999). And civil society and intergovernmental organizations increasingly stress the role of markets in pursuit of their aims, realizing that even such challenges as poverty reduction are often best met through private entrepreneurship (see, for example, Commission on the Private Sector and Development 2004 and World Bank 2004b).

Cluster 1: calls for economic openness and competitiveness. Cluster 1 expectations espouse a multilayered notion of economic openness plus the recognition that openness calls for a capacity by state and national nonstate actors to compete— lest the country fall behind others on the global competitiveness ladder (see box 1 for evidence on the dimensions under which openness and competitiveness are measured and monitored). To increase economic openness, recommended policy reforms call for: removing at-the-border policy barriers, treating foreign and

FIGURE 1

Clusters of external expectations about national public policy

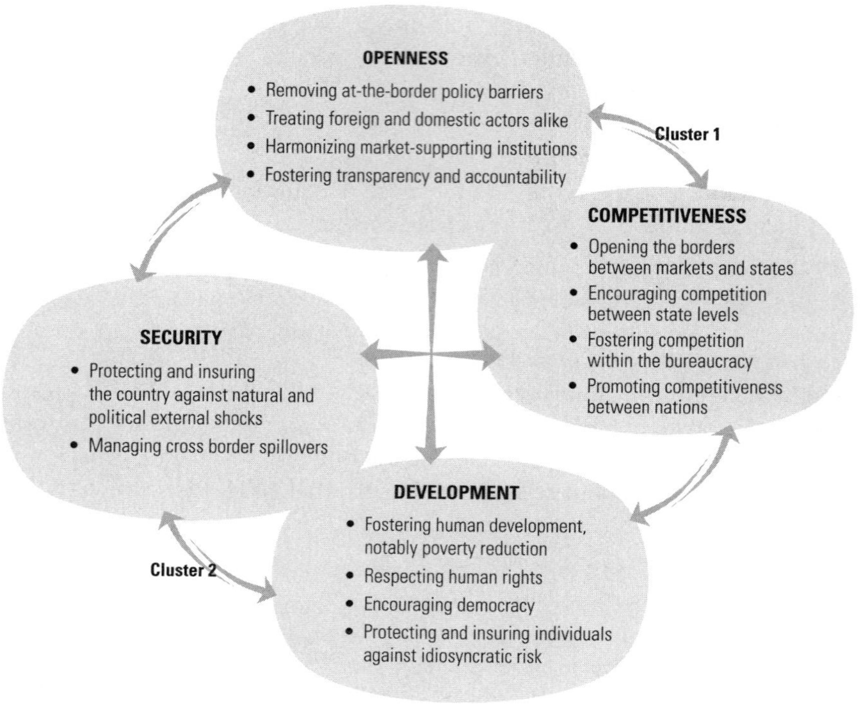

OPENNESS
- Removing at-the-border policy barriers
- Treating foreign and domestic actors alike
- Harmonizing market-supporting institutions
- Fostering transparency and accountability

Cluster 1

COMPETITIVENESS
- Opening the borders between markets and states
- Encouraging competition between state levels
- Fostering competition within the bureaucracy
- Promoting competitiveness between nations

SECURITY
- Protecting and insuring the country against natural and political external shocks
- Managing cross border spillovers

DEVELOPMENT
- Fostering human development, notably poverty reduction
- Respecting human rights
- Encouraging democracy
- Protecting and insuring individuals against idiosyncratic risk

Cluster 2

domestic actors alike, harmonizing market-supporting institutions, and fostering transparency and accountability. To boost competitiveness, reforms call for opening the borders between markets and states, encouraging competition between state levels, fostering competition within the bureaucracy, and promoting competitiveness between nations.

At-the-border issues related to improving global welfare, such as the removal of trade taxes and quotas and the lifting of capital controls, continue to be important concerns—witness the current Doha Round of multilateral trade negotiations.[12] A recent study estimates that without knowledge-related spillovers, world gross domestic product (GDP) would stand at only 6 percent of its current level—$3 trillion, the same as it was about 100 years ago—instead of $50 trillion (Klenow and Rodriguez-Clare 2004, p. 44).

However, the demands for economic openness also touch increasingly on behind-the-border issues. States are urged to abandon policies that interfere with market operations and prices by giving domestic actors an undue advantage over foreign competitors. The calls for removing export subsidies that support

Box 1

SELECT INDICES OF ECONOMIC OPENNESS AND COMPETITIVENESS

More than 60 indices seek to measure country performance and state behavior in terms of economic openness and competitiveness, as defined in this chapter. They measure the aspects of national public policy without which market integration, and so globalization, might not succeed. The following partial list of indices and their creators illustrates the range of topics they cover:

- Bribe Payers Index (Transparency International)
- Capital Access Index (Milken Institute)
- Corruption Perception Index (Transparency International)
- CSGR Globalisation Index (Warwick University)
- Ease of Doing Business (World Bank)
- Economic Freedom of the World Index (Fraser Institute)
- E-Government Index (World Markets Research Centre and Brown University)
- E-Government Readiness Index (United Nations Online Network in Public Finance and Administration)
- EIU Business Environment Rankings (Economist Intelligence Unit)
- Emerging Market Bond Indices (JPMorgan)
- E-readiness Ranking (Economist Intelligence Unit)
- Foreign Direct Investment Confidence Index (AT Kearney and Global Business Policy Council)
- Foreign Direct Investment Indices: Inward FDI Performance Index, Inward FDI Potential Index and Outward FDI Performance Index (United Nations Conference on Trade and Development)
- G-Index (Globalization index) (Foreign Policy and AT Kearney)
- G-Index (Globalization index) (World Markets Research Centre)
- Global Competitiveness Index (World Economic Forum)[a]
- Global Investment Prospects Assessment (United Nations Conference on Trade and Development)
- Global Retail Development Index (AT Kearney)
- Governance Indicators (World Bank)
- Index of Economic Freedom (Heritage Foundation and Wall Street Journal)
- Innovation Capacity Index (World Economic Forum)
- International Country Risk Guide Ratings (PRS Group)
- Networked Readiness Index (World Economic Forum)
- Offshore Location Attractiveness Index (AT Kearney)
- Opacity Index (Kurtzman Group and PriceWaterhouseCoopers)
- Overall Market Potential Index (Michigan State University)
- Quality of Workforce Index (Business Environment Risk Intelligence)

BOX 1 CONTINUED
SELECT INDICES OF ECONOMIC OPENNESS AND COMPETITIVENESS

- Sovereign Credit Ratings (Standard & Poor's)
- Sovereign Credit Ratings (Moody's)
- Sovereign Credit Ratings (FitchRatings)
- World Competitiveness Scoreboard (International Institute for Management Development)

a. The World Economic Forum has historically presented two indices in its annual *Global Competitiveness Report:* the Growth Competitiveness Index and the Business Competitiveness Index. Since *Global Competitiveness Report 2004–05,* however, the two indices have been consolidated into the more comprehensive Global Competitiveness Index.
Source: Bandura 2005b.

---

domestic producers in international markets are a case in point. In addition, states are being held to the principle of nondiscrimination between foreign and domestic market actors.[13]

Another dimension of behind-the-border economic openness is the expectation of harmonizing market-facilitating state institutions. Such ingredients of a good investment climate as a sound legal system that protects property rights (ensuring against expropriation), norms and standards for banking regulation and supervision, adequate accounting and auditing procedures, corruption control, and enforcement of competition and antitrust policy are expected to be strengthened and brought in line with international practices of good governance.[14]

Demands for harmonizing institutional infrastructure are complemented by demands for harmonizing physical infrastructure to facilitate international transport and communication. Harmonization lowers information and search costs. Similar concerns with reducing transaction costs prompt calls for transparency of government policy and government commitment to such policy principles as inflation targeting and currency convertibility.

There is broad recognition that once states increase economic openness, they need to enhance their capacity to compete along with the capacity of firms and workers residing in their territory. Thus, states are urged to foster innovation that improves productivity and economic competitiveness (Porter and others 2004a). And the indices and scorecards of state behavior and performance hold up a mirror to states, enabling governments and nonstate actors to see how well they meet expectations—relative to the performance of other states.

For the state apparatus itself external policy expectations suggest the erosion of conventional dividing lines between markets and states, private and public sectors, in search of enhanced economic efficiencies. This includes opening up the financing and delivery of government programs to competition from private for-profit or nonprofit firms and engaging in public-private partnering through, for example, outsourcing or contracting out. Governments are also expected to foster decentralization and competition among state agencies.[15]

Without the capacity to compete, countries are likely to jeopardize their economic growth and development. As Wolf (2004, p. 277) notes, "failed states, disorderly states, weak states and corrupt states are shunned states—they are the black holes of the global economic system." However, the inability of some countries to compete successfully also reflects negatively on globalization's claim to benefit all. Thus, being able to compete is not only important for each country individually but for the integrity of the world economic system. Not surprisingly, there are several competitiveness indices and country rankings, all spurring countries to enter, stay, and succeed in the global competitiveness game (see box 1).

Cluster 2: calls for development and security. Globalization's record is checkered. Many analysts agree that it has opened new opportunities. However, as Ocampo and Martin (2003) point out, what comes to mind in describing recent economic trends are such terms as "crisis," "volatility," "risk," "contagion," "inequity," and "insecurity." Cluster 2 expectations are intended to correct these failures, to provide development and security "cushions" (Kapstein and Milanovic 2002) that permit economic globalization to proceed (see box 2 for efforts to assess and monitor how countries fare in respect to these dimensions). To advance development, analysts recommend fostering human development (notably poverty reduction), respecting human rights, encouraging democracy, and protecting and insuring individuals against idiosyncratic risks. For improving security, they recommend protecting and insuring the country against natural and political external shocks and managing cross-border spillovers.

Democratic and participatory governance and the realization of basic human rights increasingly form part of the set of development-related expectations (see, for example, Amnesty International various years, Freedom House various years, Human Rights Watch various years). They are considered important ingredients of political openness and of people-centered public policy without which human development cannot take off or be sustained. Thus, states are increasingly pressed on their commitment to such issues as gender equality and equity, labor rights, elimination of the worst forms of child labor, and the rights to free speech and movement (see, among others, World Commission on the Social Dimension of Globalization 2004; UN 2005; UNICEF various years). Perhaps the most decisive call by the international community to make significant inroads into world poverty and other severe forms of human deprivation (such as preventable diseases and the looming challenge of water scarcity) is the Millennium Development Goals.[16]

But development advocates recognize that reversals of human development can easily occur, notably in times of economic downturn or crisis, when many

Box 2

SELECTED INDICES OF DEVELOPMENT AND SECURITY

The indices in the area of development and security are wide ranging. They assess country performance in meeting basic standards of human development and human rights; protection against such risks as unemployment, old age, and external shocks; and management of cross-border spillovers such as environmental pollution. Public policy promoting these concerns helps to advance globalization by providing a cushion for a country's residents.

The following selection of indices relating to development and security is drawn from approximately 70 such measures:

- Aging Vulnerability Index (Center for Strategic and International Studies and Watson Wyatt Worldwide)
- AIDS Program Effort Index (Joint United Nations Programme on HIV/AIDS, U.S. Agency for International Development, and POLICY Project)
- Assessing the Achievement of the Millennium Development Goals (United Nations Development Programme and World Bank)
- Bertelsmann Transformation Index (Bertelsmann Foundation)
- Climate Analysis Indicators Tool (World Resources Institute)
- Commitment to Development Index (Center for Global Development and Foreign Policy)
- Country Policy and Institutional Assessment (World Bank, International Development Association)
- Dashboard of Sustainability (International Institute for Sustainable Development)
- Democracy Score, Nations in Transit Ratings (Freedom House)
- Disaster Risk Index (United Nations Development Programme)
- Ecological Footprint and Living Planet Index (World Wildlife Fund)
- Education for All Development Index (United Nations Educational, Scientific and Cultural Organization)
- Environmental Performance Index and Environmental Sustainability Index (Columbia University and Yale University)
- Environmental Vulnerability Index (South Pacific Applied Geoscience Commission)
- Gender-related Development Index (United Nations Development Programme)
- Gender Empowerment Measure (United Nations Development Programme)
- Gender Gap (Population Action International)
- Global Natural Disasters Risks Hotspots (Columbia University)
- Global Terrorism Index (World Markets Research Centre)
- Governance Indicators (World Bank)

Box 2 Continued

SELECTED INDICES OF DEVELOPMENT AND SECURITY

- Human Development Index (United Nations Development Programme)
- Index of Social Vulnerability to Climate Change (Tyndall Centre for Climate Change Research)
- Mothers' Index and Early Motherhood Risk Ranking (Save the Children)
- National Biodiversity Index (United Nations Environment Programme)
- Overall Health System Achievement Index and Health System Performance Index (World Health Organization)
- Political Rights and Civil Liberties Ratings (Freedom House)
- Press Freedom Index (Freedom House)
- Reproductive Risk Index (Population Action International)
- Social Watch Scorecard (Social Watch)
- Sustainability Index (Zurich Cantonal Bank)
- Under Five Mortality Rank (United Nations Children's Fund)
- World Press Freedom Ranking (Reporters without Borders)

Source: Bandura 2005b.

poor people face a sudden income loss and, unable to fall back on their own savings, must rely on social protection. Thus, cluster 2 expectations also urge states to meet the triple challenge of satisfying increased demand for protection and insurance against the consequences of economic volatility, especially unemployment; satisfying the growing demand for old-age insurance, stemming from the aging of the population (as discussed by Heller in this volume); and observing established rules of monetary and fiscal prudence. States are encouraged to search for ways of complementing social security programs with increased (or even exclusive) private contributions and, in line with the cluster 1 expectations, to explore market-based insurance schemes. These topics have caught the attention of world leaders, among others, at summit meetings of the Group of Eight (G-8) and the World Economic Forum.[17]

In some instances individual insecurity is an outcome of personal circumstances or of the normal, competitive functioning of markets. In other instances, however, it is linked to a country's vulnerability—its exposure to external shocks such as international financial crises and their contagion effects, pollution spill-ins, spread of communicable diseases, natural catastrophes, or political violence, such as a terrorist attack. Therefore, the security component of cluster 2 urges states to do all they can to protect the country against external shocks, natural and human-caused. The report of the High-Level Panel of the United Nations Secretary-General on security challenges of the twenty-first century presents a comprehensive overview of the international policy recommendations on these aggregate threats to national security, which also bridge the span between security and development concerns (UN 2004).

Many external shocks result from negative cross-border spillovers from other countries. If all countries strive to reduce their negative cross-border spillovers, all countries will collectively experience fewer external shocks. Thus, the state is expected to increasingly observe certain limits to the global public "bads" that a country generates, particularly by reducing greenhouse gas emissions, controlling global communicable diseases, and fighting drug trafficking, international terrorism, money laundering, and web-based crime (UN 2004). In some areas new national allowances are being introduced to identify acceptable levels of border transgression, such as the carbon dioxide emission targets suggested under the Kyoto Protocol.[18] In other areas a list of expected reform measures may define what is in—or out of—bounds.[19]

Richer countries are encouraged to think not only about internalizing negative cross-border spillovers but also about generating positive ones, where this could contribute to solving global challenges. The Commitment to Development Index, for example, assesses donor country behavior from this dual perspective. It looks not only at the delivery of aid but also at how negative and positive spillovers from industrial country policies affect the development prospects of developing countries.[20]

The purpose of external policy expectations: a global framework for national policymaking

Taken together, external policy expectations seem to be calling on the state to foster globalization in two ways. States are to make globalization possible through national-level policy reforms along the lines suggested in cluster 1 and to make globalization politically feasible and sustainable by pursuing policy paths like those included in cluster 2 expectations. States are challenged to globalize particular national public goods as their contribution towards these two ends.

Cluster 1 expectations concern primarily the globalization of market-facilitating national public goods—goods that help markets emerge and function efficiently. The main suggested tools are open borders (so that national public policy domains can become interlocked), harmonized national policies and institutional and physical infrastructure (so that markets can integrate), and competitiveness (so that markets can expand and evolve).

Cluster 2 expectations focus on the globalization of market-embedding national public goods—goods that help people and countries cope with the normal volatility of markets as well as the tendency of some, especially financial markets, to generate boom and bust cycles. The main tools for this globalization are universalization (making select private goods, such as basic education, healthcare, and social protection, available for all or "public by policy design") and internalization of cross-border externalities (creating national public goods that prevent actions in one country from adversely affecting other jurisdictions).

A shared objective of the diverse external policy expectations seems to be to nudge individual nation states toward expanding their market failure–correcting role: from correcting the failure of domestic markets to also correcting the failures of integrating and progressively globalizing markets. Left to their own devices, individual states may underprovide essential market-facilitating and market-embedding public goods.[21] External policy demands may thus help tip national policy choices toward strengthening globalization and enhancing global welfare and development.

Do states meet these expectations?

NATIONAL POLICY ALIGNMENT: SIGNS AND DRIVING FORCES

Under the Westphalian model, states would likely reject all external interference with their internal affairs or at least would be highly selective in their response. But actual policy practice worldwide looks quite different. Most national policy agendas contain clear echoes of external policy demands. And most countries— industrial, transition, or developing—seem to be undergoing far-reaching policy reforms to achieve further alignments. So what is driving the recent spread to so many countries of what Rodrik (1996, p. 11) has called the "reform bug"? The conditions of national policymaking sovereignty have undergone incremental but fundamental transformation leading to significantly changed political realities. Exclusive policymaking sovereignty entails increasingly high costs for states, while more responsive sovereignty is either the least-cost policy option or the policy path promising a real gain in national welfare.

Signs of policy alignment

Even a cursory examination of recent major surveys of global trends reveals that national public policy clearly echoes cluster 1 and 2 expectations.[22] Country case studies confirm this impression (box 3), as do many issue-specific analyses.[23] Public spending on global challenges such as HIV/AIDS control has increased. Policy approaches are converging, including lifting at-the-border controls, increasing decentralization, reducing red tape, imposing fiscal discipline and taming inflation, expanding public-private partnering, and substituting incentive policies for control and command measures. States the world over are promoting labor market flexibility and reforming social security and other public programs (Bandura 2005a). Anecdotal evidence is presented in box 4 to illustrate some of the country-level policy initiatives that seem to echo the cluster elements reviewed above.

Box 3

COUNTRY STUDIES ON INTERNATIONAL COOPERATION BEHIND NATIONAL
BORDERS

As background for this chapter 19 case studies were conducted in developing and industrial countries (see list below). The studies examined international cooperation behind national borders, how countries adjust nationally to such global challenges as global warming, the policy norms used by sovereign credit rating agencies in assessing a country's creditworthiness, and newly emerging opportunities, such as new technology.

The studies reveal that global concerns are expressed in many different ways in national public finance policy. Sometimes budgetary allocations are adjusted to accommodate the provision of national-level inputs to various global public goods or aid concerns. Other times states change their delivery modalities, shifting, for example, from direct delivery of public programs to greater use of incentives, including guarantees and tax credits. Behind-the-border international cooperation is also reflected in national institutional reforms, such as new government structures for international terrorism control (especially in industrial countries) or management of the design and implementation of poverty reduction strategies. In brief, many of the concerns included in clusters 1 and 2 (see text) have found some traction at national levels.

The country case studies also indicate that while some industrial country interlocutors find the concept of international cooperation behind national borders slightly puzzling because they view international cooperation as an outgoing process, not an incoming demand, developing country interlocutors find the concept to be quite clear. This is especially evident in the least developed countries, where policymakers and government officials have to cope with a large number of donors—and their multiple requests.

Even where national policymakers and government officials intuitively understand the concept of international cooperation behind national borders, government machinery is not really set up to deal with global concerns. In most instances there is still a clear divide between "domestic" and "foreign" affairs. And although policies are adjusting to various external demands, it is often difficult to trace these changes in national budgets: new items are often conveniently "fitted" into existing budgets. There seems to be a growing awareness, however, that current government structures have to be revisited. In industrial countries reforms could usefully focus on developing the policy arm for incoming international cooperation demands. In developing countries the outgoing policy arm appears to need reinforcement.

Box 3 Continued

COUNTRY STUDIES ON INTERNATIONAL COOPERATION BEHIND NATIONAL BORDERS

Country studies and authors
Argentina, Humberto Petrei
Canada, François Vaillancourt
China, Ramgopal Agarwala
Egypt, Heba Handoussa, Nivine El Oraby, Mahmoud Mohieldin, and
    Doha Abdelhamid
Germany, Dirk Messner and Imme Scholz
India, Tarun Das
Japan, Toshihiro Ihori
Kenya, Francis M. Mwega
Republic of Korea, Joonook Choi
Netherlands, Harrie A. A. Verbon and Hanneke Wieland
Niger, Saidou Sidibe, Mahaman Sanoussi Tidjani Alou, and Joelle Bolho
Nigeria, Akpan H. Ekpo
Peru, Francisco Sagasti, Alvaro Espinoza, and Fernando Prada
Philippines, Cielito F. Habito
Russian Federation, Sergei Sinelnikov and Said Batkibekov
Sweden, Stefan Sjölander
Switzerland, Renate Schubert and Markus Ohndorf
United Kingdom, Alan Ingram, Graham Lister, and Malcolm Prowle
United States, Carol Lancaster

Note: These studies are available at www.thenewpublicfinance.org.

Drivers of policy alignment

How states respond to external policy demands depends in part on certain properties of the expectation: whether it is a more binding or a less binding norm, whether it is widely shared, and whether it comes with carrots or sticks attached. For example, Risse-Kappen (1995) argues that the more firmly entrenched and institutionalized an external policy demand is, the more difficult it is for a state to ignore it because demands for compliance become more difficult to suppress. Thus the passage of time may work in favor of more international cooperation. Yet that alone would not explain the growth in external policy expectations and the corresponding growth in national policy alignment, especially since the mid-1990s.

Four forces seem to propel these trends: waning political support for noninterference, increasing interdependence of states, growing political strength of transnational actors, and intensifying competitiveness between states.

Box 4
ECHOES OF EXTERNAL POLICY EXPECTATIONS IN NATIONAL PUBLIC POLICY

The following examples highlight a few national policy changes that appear to echo cluster 1 and 2 expectations.

Cluster 1: openness and competitiveness
- *Openness.* Trade and financial liberalization have progressed in the past decades and to that end states have even introduced changes in that most jealously guarded domain of national policymaking, the tax system. In many countries value-added taxes (VAT) have replaced trade taxes and other taxes on financial cross-border transactions (Cnossen 1998; Heady 2004; Keen and Simone 2004). As of 2001, more than 120 countries had adopted a VAT (Ebrill and others 2001, p. 8).
- *Competitive government.* States have also accepted competitiveness challenges. The indicators presented in the Overview of this volume show the increased porosity of the borders between the public and the private domains. Both privatization and public-private partnering are on the rise (Bangura 2000). Central bankers and finance ministers the world over strive to adhere to established rules of monetary and fiscal prudence, watching carefully how markets respond to their policy choices (Barlow and Radulescu 2002; Canova and Pappa 2005; de Ferranti and others 2000). Countries have also devolved fiscal, political, and administrative powers to lower levels of government. Some 95 percent of the world's 120 democracies have now elected subnational governments (Freedom House 2005; World Bank 2000, p. 107).
- *Fostering a conducive business environment.* Many developing countries are seeking to improve their business environment (Porter and others 2004a,b; World Bank 2004). Countries have sometimes created special economic zones that offer investors more advanced infrastructure and often more favorable investment conditions. As of 2002 there were some 3,000 export processing zones in 116 countries (World Bank 2004, p. 168). Moreover, regulatory restrictions have been removed, especially those that could impede foreign direct investment. Since 1995 some 60 countries have introduced regulatory changes considered favorable to foreign direct investment (World Bank 2004, pp. 111–12).
- *Innovation.* Innovation "hot spots" are emerging in developing countries, among them China, India, Israel, the Republic of Korea, the Russian Federation, Singapore, and Taiwan Province of China (Carey 2004). Industrial countries, feeling the pressure, are launching their own initiatives aimed at staying ahead in the technology and productivity game. For example, the Lisbon Strategy of the European Union is designed to make it the most dynamic and competitive

---

Box 4 Continued
ECHOES OF EXTERNAL POLICY EXPECTATIONS IN NATIONAL PUBLIC POLICY

knowledge-based economy in the world by 2010 (European Commission 2004).

Cluster 2: development and security

*   *Democracy and human rights.* The number of democratic states rose from 57 in 1985 to more than 120 in 2000 (Freedom House 2005, p. 5; UNDP 2002, p. 15). While there is still a long, unfinished agenda, recent decades have seen unprecedented advances in human rights. Nearly half the countries in the world had ratified all major international human rights instruments by 2000, up from 10 percent in 1990, laying the basis for national policy change (UNDP 2000, p. 3).
*   *Poverty reduction.* More than 50 of the poorest countries have prepared Poverty Reduction Strategy Papers (PRSPs), reconfirming their commitment to poverty reduction (World Bank 2005b). In return, the international donor community has promised to increase official development assistance and has stepped up measures to promote policy coherence for development (OECD/DAC 2005).
*   *Social security.* Social security reform is among the most hotly debated policy issues in many countries, industrial and developing alike (Blanchard 2004; de Ferranti and others 2000; Kapstein and Milanovic 2002; Södersten 2004). As of 2003 some 24 countries around the world had already incorporated private pillars to complement (or in some cases partially replace) their public pension schemes (Palacios 2003, p. 4). For many developing countries the main issue is introducing a system of protection and insurance or expanding a rudimentary one. For all countries a basic contested issue is the balance between a social, collective system and reliance on private responsibility, initiative, and choice, in line with cluster 1 expectations for enhanced competition between markets and states.
*   *Economic risk management.* The search for a better public-private mix also marks national policy discussions on aggregate risk management. Many countries have built up sizable savings and stabilization funds to protect against external economic shocks (Fasano 2000; Davis and others 2001). Other countries are increasingly using futures and options markets to hedge against commodity price risks and exchange rate volatility (Institute for Financial Markets 2005; Morgan in this volume).
*   *National security.* The terrorist attacks of September 11, 2001, raised new concerns about how to combine openness and national security. Many countries responded with increased public spending for international terrorism control (Bandura 2005a; Sandler in this

volume). By 2002 some 70 countries had raised or imposed new airport taxes (www.traveltax.msu.edu), and many proposed even
higher levies. Alarmed by the number of catastrophic events in
recent years, some states are encouraging markets for such new
products as terrorism insurance or catastrophe bonds (Michel-
Kerjan and Kunreuther 2004).

• *Management of cross-border externalities.* Countries have instituted
national-level measures to curb transborder environmental pollution (Merlen 2005; Ocampo and Martin 2003; UNDP, UNEP, World
Bank, and World Resources Institute 2003; World Watch Institute
various years), along with market-based policy approaches (IETA
2003; Stavins 2003). For instance, in January 2005 the EU
Greenhouse Gas Emission Trading Scheme commenced operations
as the largest multicountry, multisector greenhouse gas emission
trading scheme in the world. There is also evidence that spending
on global communicable disease control has increased in many
countries (UNAIDS 2003; U.S. GAO 2004).

As global surveys reveal only too clearly, wide diversity in policy outcomes and development remains between countries. But alongside such
diversity is evidence of growing similarity, as countries increasingly
adopt the same rules of the game.

Waning political support for noninterference. The norm of noninterference in the
internal affairs of states had strong support among rival superpowers during the
cold war era as a containment policy to keep states in the political bloc with which
they were aligned. Many developing countries also strongly endorsed this norm,
since it afforded them an opportunity to consolidate their recent status as independent countries, providing them with political breathing space and bargaining
power. As the East-West conflict waned, so did support for the norm of noninterference. International policy conditionality became more overt, more elaborate, and universal in nature and was often accompanied by more intensive
monitoring and heavier penalties for noncompliance.

Small, economically dependent countries in particular now feel that they have
no choice but to comply with common external expectations or risk losing needed
external assistance or other support (Addison and Roe 2004). They are the policy-takers in international relations, weighed down by multiple demands from
donors, civil society, and markets. For states that are policymakers, the need to
align is usually weaker because their government agencies, private business, and

civil society have the capacity and resources to shape external exigencies. As a result, it is often their policy approaches, norms, and standards that are rolled out through the channels of international policy formulation and advocacy. Through foreign aid and other means they can help finance—and push—reforms in poorer developing countries. Between the policy-takers and the policymakers are states that have some choice of policy paths and reform speed.

Increasing interdependence of states—and more opportunities for cooperation. Global public bads such as financial crises, faltering world economic growth, SARS, and computer viruses tend to affect countries and people indiscriminately. Left unchecked, their costs accumulate. Thus, international cooperation is often cheaper and more efficient than lack of cooperation, and it allows states to effectively play their role of public goods provider. To the extent that external policy expectations reflect real global exigencies, even economically and militarily powerful states are adjusting their national policies. Think how swiftly countries around the world upgraded border security after the September 11, 2001, terrorist attacks on the United States.

But international cooperation is a response not only to increased interdependence. Sometimes the underlying motivation is to exploit new economic opportunities, such as access to international capital or insurance markets. But greater openness and more transborder economic activity increase a country's vulnerability to outside shocks, calling for greater international cooperation and setting in motion an incremental process of policy alignment and globalization.

Growing political strength of transnational actors. Nonstate actors have become influential policymakers, with power that states are forced to reckon with. Public policy reforms aimed at economic and political openness have set nonstate actors "free," enabling them to become more globally involved. The state, meanwhile, remains shackled to its territory. As a result, in many issue areas the state is no longer the actor with the overarching public concern. Nonstate actors are increasingly adopting a more global, public viewpoint to avoid missing out on opportunities in an open and interdependent world. Being territorially constrained compels the state to take the demands of nonstate actors into account, lest market actors vote with their feet and civil society raise its voice, "naming and shaming" the state into living up to widely accepted international norms and standards.

Portfolio investors, for example, can threaten to exit a country whose business climate is not up to international standards. One response by states has been to recast their taxation systems in areas sensitive to international differentials, such as corporate tax rates. The 2004 KPMG Corporate Tax Rate Survey covering 69 countries finds that the average corporate tax rate in Organisation for Economic Co-operation and Development countries fell from about 37 percent in 1997 to 30 percent in 2004 (KPMG 2004, p. 2). Corporate tax rates on especially profitable investments have fallen even more (Devereux, Griffith, and Klemm 2002). Slemrod (2004) finds an inverse relation between countries' openness and corporate tax rates.[24] Thus states' immobility is another important factor in their compliance with external policy expectations.

While business actors strengthen their public policy demands by threatening to exit or to adjust their risk assessments (and thus prices), the power of civil society organizations lies in networking across borders and raising their voices in concert. Sometimes they do so in loud and spectacular ways, as in 2001 at the G-8 summit in Genoa or in 1999 at the World Trade Organization (WTO) ministerial meeting in Seattle. Modern communication technology bestows worldwide visibility on such events and on their political leaders. More often, however, civil society organizations insert their views and demands more subtly yet persistently wherever global issues are debated and negotiated (Edwards and Zadek 2003; Scholte 2001; Scholte and Schnabel 2002). Consider the role of Jubilee 2000 in making states address the issue of developing country debt.[25]

Intensifying competitiveness between states. While increasingly influential, business and civil society do not often exert pressure on states directly. Rather, states compel each other to take external expectations into account, with "rival states" (Stopford and Strange 1992) competing for mobile factors of production by delivering what is expected of them, including fiscal restraint, quality standards, investment regimes, and even competition rules (Sinn 2003).

Competition is intensified by the impermanence of a state's place on the international competitiveness ladder, with some countries moving down as others move up (see the chapter by Shiller in this volume for an example). As developing countries such as China and India are meeting the global competitiveness challenge, industrial country firms and workers are experiencing added competition in markets they have long dominated.[26] Bhagwati (2004) even senses the beginnings of a reversal in sentiments about globalization. Industrial countries seem to be increasingly concerned about how well their firms will withstand stronger competitive pressures from developing country firms, while the more advanced developing countries appear increasingly confident that globalization can work to their advantage. A clear expression of industrial country concern is the debate on outsourcing, the migration of jobs from industrial to developing countries (Bhagwati, Panagariya, and Srinivasan 2004). Reforms in industrial countries to improve labor market flexibility and restructure social security are motivated in part by the desire to stay competitive.[27]

Thus states align their national policies to external policy demands because of strong compulsions and incentives to do so. Some align because this is the least-cost policy option for them, others align to enhance national welfare, and yet others align to cater to the special interests of powerful political constituencies, domestic or foreign (including perhaps, their own state interests).

For now, the required degree of alignment seems to be higher for developing countries than for industrial countries, and the net benefits of reform appear more elusive.[28] However, this may be gradually changing. As some of the more advanced developing countries climb up the competitiveness ladder, they seem to pull more of globalization's opportunities toward them. This places today's industrial countries under increasing competitive pressure. In Friedman's (2005) words, the world is increasingly "flat": a level playing field for industrial and developing countries. Alignment may well become more of a compulsion for industrial countries and more of an opportunity for developing nations.

Reflecting both the growing demand for national public policy alignment and growing economic strength, developing country policymakers are seeking a stronger voice in the international policy arena. For them, deeper integration requires more participatory, competitive international decisionmaking. Seeking to achieve further integration, they often find that the international rules of the game either do not fit their circumstances or are stacked against them. The Group of 20 (G-20) developing countries has been formed to give developing countries more clout in WTO negotiations.[29] Proposals have also been made to adjust quotas and decisionmaking in the Bretton Woods institutions to today's economic realities (Buira 2003). Another sign of the strengthened political role of developing countries is their leadership in financing cooperation to achieve the Millennium Development Goals, as through the establishment of a trust fund by the members of the India-Brazil-South Africa Dialogue Forum.[30]

Industrial countries, too, are supporting enhanced participation in decisionmaking as an important step toward strengthened policy ownership by developing countries. For example, it is now standard practice for a selected group of developing country leaders (its composition varying with the issues under consideration) to participate in G-8 summit events.[31]

Thus, states' responses to external policy demands appear to be driven by both compulsion and opportunity. As a result, today's states have two arms of policy intermediation:

- *An inward-directed policy arm,* which blends external and domestic preferences in formulating national policy to improve domestic economic activities.
- *An outward-directed policy arm,* which weaves national policy concerns into the formulation of external policy expectations, projecting the country's strengths to outside actors and exploring new global opportunities.

REPLACING THE WESTPHALIAN STATE WITH THE INTERMEDIARY STATE: IMPLICATIONS FOR PUBLIC FINANCE

As Krasner (1995) shows, there have been compromises in the Westphalian state model from the beginning. Today, however, they appear to be the norm rather than the exception, a change rooted in new global realities. The time has come to reconceptualize the model of the state, to better reflect its actual role and to explore how such a reconceptualization might affect current mainstream public finance theory.

Key characteristics of the current role of the state

The three core elements of the state still apply, but as exclusive national policymaking sovereignty has evolved toward responsive policymaking sovereignty,[32] these core functions have been broadened:

- *From aggregating primarily national preferences to blending national and external policy demands.* A major role of states today is international cooperation behind national borders. By aligning national policies to external expectations, states achieve a matching of their policy framework with the global span of the goods that are typically at stake when policy alignment is expected of individual states.

- *From correcting market failure to also standing corrected by global business and civil society.* Business and civil society contribute in important measure to the pool of external policy expectations. In responding to the concerns of these actors, states in effect accept some correction of their policies by nonstate actors. Does this mean the capture of the state by particular private or civil society interests? Not necessarily, because nonstate actors—rather than states—often have the more global, public perspective. When they intervene in national public policymaking, it is often to promote global efficiency and equity.

- *From exerting coercive powers to being compelled to compete.* The state retains important coercive powers, notably in respect to less mobile domestic actors. However, when actors are mobile and network across borders, the state's coercive powers are blunted. To attract and retain mobile actors, states need to employ incentives that are at least as attractive as those offered by other states. States may align their policies and actively cooperate with external policy demands so as to compete more effectively with each other.

Thus, there is little evidence that the concept of the state as intermediary (box 5) means a hollowing out of the state (Ikenberry 2003; Kahler and Lake 2003; Sørensen 2001; Weiss 2003). States continue to play an important role. Yet how they play this role is significantly different from how they do so under the model of the Westphalian state.

Implications for public finance theory

Public finance and public economics textbooks give scant attention to issues of international cooperation. They tend to ignore issues of national-level policy alignment with external policy demands—issues of international cooperation behind national borders and issues of cooperation abroad. The concept of the intermediary state is important for its focus on the increasingly porous divide

Box 5

THE INTERMEDIARY STATE

In making national public policy, today's state takes into account external policy demands, constraints, and opportunities. All actors—states, business, civil society—contribute to the creation of the global pool of external policy expectations.

In exercising responsive national policymaking sovereignty, the state:
- Aggregates domestic policy preferences but also blends domestic and external policy demands.
- Corrects market failure but also stands corrected by global business and civil society, which intervene to correct public policy failure in the provision of national building blocks to global public goods or the management of cross-border spillovers.
- Exerts coercive powers, as in making and administering national law, but also recognizes that its coercive powers are blunted where nonstate actors can threaten exit or have a strong voice. While nonstate actors are increasingly mobile, states are bound to their territory—compelling them to compete with each other to attract mobile factors of production or to access global policy regimes, such as the multilateral trade regime or international financial markets.

In placing national public policy into the framework of external policy expectations, states engage in international cooperation behind national borders. As demand for such cooperation grows, so does demand by developing countries for more participatory cooperation beyond international borders. Thus, the intermediary state has two major policy arms: one for translating external expectations into national public policy and one for taking national concerns to the venues of international policy formulation so that the resulting expectations and norms fit a diverse range of national circumstances.

This actual role of the state differs in important ways from the model of the Westphalian state so often invoked in discussing the state's functions in public finance theory. In the Westphalian ideal type, the state exercises exclusive national policymaking sovereignty. The key characteristic of today's state in practice is responsive sovereignty—intermediation between domestic and external policy concerns.

between domestic and foreign policy matters, which calls into question the conventional division between domestically oriented public finance and international economics. Whereas public finance theory often assumes away the international economy, international economics focuses primarily on trade and finance issues, leaving aside many other public policy concerns that are increasingly global, such as health and the environment.[33]

New linkages between public finance theory and practice are one of the key themes of this book. This section simply alludes to some of the questions that the broadening of the three core elements of the state's role seems to raise. For example, how does the blending of domestic and external policy preferences affect what is considered an optimal provision of public goods? Textbooks suggest that a public good is optimally provided when the sum of the marginal willingness to pay of all the individuals who form a community (the citizenry of a country), for example, equals the marginal costs of providing an extra unit of the good. The intermediary state, however, may be expected to provide more or less of a good than is demanded domestically, by national taxpayers. It would be desirable for public finance theory to offer guidance to policymakers on how to assess and view such a situation.

Is it a case of the international community seeking to "buy" a global public service from a particular country or group of countries—say, biodiversity preservation—through an external policy demand? If so, the country facing the external policy demand might be justified in requesting some compensation for the incremental costs of providing the service (as discussed by King in this volume). Or is it a case of an external policy demand that seeks to encourage the state to internalize some negative cross-border spillover emanating from its jurisdiction, such as greenhouse gas emissions? If so, the state would be justified in expecting its citizens to bear the costs (especially if it were an industrial country with a record of high pollution).

Similarly, it might be useful to revisit the concepts of market failure and government failure. Nonstate actors sometimes intervene to pressure states into taking action to correct failures of globalizing markets. Are international markets failing under the same conditions as domestic markets? What should be the state's role in correcting international market failure? From an international perspective states are individual actors, and like other individual actors may be tempted to free-ride when it comes to providing global public goods or undertaking any other collective action needed to enhance the efficiency of global markets. International relations theory provides some answers. But still to be clarified is what predictions can be made about the role of nonstate actors in correcting both global market failure and related government failure.

Finally, an extensive literature deals with how states can use tax competition, tax incentives, and other persuasive measures to retain or attract transnational economic actors (see, for instance, Sinn 2003 and the chapter by Musgrave in this volume). Perhaps less well understood is the use and impact of incentive measures by mobile economic actors to encourage certain behavior by the state. For example, sovereign credit ratings can be seen as an incentive tool of market participants. Similarly, foreign aid donors move in and out of developing countries, responding, for example, to certain government behavior such as gross human rights violations. Such granting or withdrawing of aid could also be viewed as a tax measure.

While there are many more questions, those raised so far already demonstrate how substituting the model of the intermediary state for the model of the

Westphalian state would bring into focus a wide range of issues requiring research and policy debate to further illuminate the role of the state and public finance in today's world.

CONCLUSION

Comparing the actual role of the state and its role as depicted in public finance theory reveals three significant discrepancies: The state no longer merely aggregates national preferences but also seeks to blend domestic and external policy demands. The state still plays an important role in correcting market failure, but it also stands corrected by business and civil society actors who frequently intervene to correct public policy imperfections in the global (public) interest. The state still has coercive powers, but it also faces competitive pressures and has to compete with other states to attract mobile factors of production.

National policymaking sovereignty is no longer exclusive in the sense of shutting out external policy from business, civil society, or intergovernmental forums. Rather, it responds to these demands. As a result, the state resembles less and less the ideal-type Westphalian nation state that underpins much of public finance theory. A better reflection of reality is the concept of the state as intermediary. This discrepancy is apparent in public finance theory, which is based on this ideal type of the state rather than actual practice. Replacing the Westphalian state model with that of the intermediary state would thus require revisiting some of the basic concepts of mainstream public finance theory.

NOTES

1. For many developing countries the period from the early 1970s to the 1990s was marked by two opposing trends. While gaining political independence from the former colonial powers, they were simultaneously confronted with demands to open up freshly drawn national borders. Transition economies encountered a similar situation at the end of the 1990s, when they emerged as newly independent states after the break-up of the Soviet Union. Thus, during the 1970s to 1990s, while the current era of globalization was gathering greater momentum, the Westphalian nation state was at its high point.

2. For the list of textbooks of public finance and economics reviewed for this chapter, see "Background Papers" at www.thenewpublicfinance.org.

3. Stiglitz (2000), for example, lists six conditions under which markets are likely to generate suboptimal outcomes: imperfect competition, public goods, externalities, incomplete markets, imperfect information, and unemployment and other macroeconomic disturbances.

4. However, none of these challenges makes state intervention automatically desirable. The state should intervene only if that is likely to enhance efficiency—not to compound market failure by government failure. Similarly, its equity or transfer

role should improve not worsen the primary income distribution resulting from the functioning of markets.

5. Origin rather than content is emphasized in defining the external character of a policy expectation because most actors involved in its formulation are "at home" somewhere. For example, nonstate actors are likely to advocate their concerns both domestically and internationally, so a substantive overlap between domestic and external policy preferences is likely. However, an important objective of nonstate actors in networking across borders and engaging internationally is to join forces in support of shared global concerns on which they would like nation states to act more decisively. Similarly, government negotiating teams represent a particular country. They may support an intergovernmental agreement to strengthen the political leverage of the state nationally. Tying the state's hands through an international commitment can help policymakers implement difficult reforms by referring to the country's obligation to other governments, intergovernmental organizations, or markets that do not permit alternative policy paths and the country's obligation to act as a responsible global citizen. Also, as Abbott and Snidal (1998) point out, states have to grant international organizations a certain degree of independence so that the organizations can function in the relatively neutral, even-handed manner essential to their legitimacy and authority in the eyes of their member states.

6. See http://untreaty.un.org/English/overview.asp.

7. Other examples include the Trade Policy Reviews of the World Trade Organization, reports countries prepare in compliance with their membership in the Financial Action Task Force and related regional entities, country reports on progress in implementing national-level measures to control international terrorism called for by United Nations Security Council Resolution 1373 (UN 2001), and reports on progress toward the Millennium Development Goals prepared by countries in collaboration with various United Nations agencies. For details, see Haller (2005).

8. This refers to a narrow definition of conditionality that includes quantitative performance criteria. For a discussion of problems in measuring conditionality, see Kapur (2001, pp. 212–17). For other studies on conditionality see Goldstein (2000) and IMF (2001).

9. See, for example, Standard & Poor's at www.standardandpoors.com, Moody's at www.moodys.com, and Fitch Ratings at www.fitchratings.com.

10. The indices are of interest here only for what they try to measure and not for what measurements they produce or how they rank countries. For details on each index, including information on its constituent components, refer again to Bandura (2005b).

11. As indicated by the arrows in figure 1, which link the components of clusters 1 and 2, the four sets of policy expectations are not mutually exclusive. In fact, there is much debate about whether a goal such as poverty reduction is better achieved through direct social spending by the state in such areas as basic education and health care, through the promotion of enhanced economic openness and competitiveness, or through simultaneous policy efforts in all these areas. Many policy analysts would argue that an integrated approach is the most promising.

12. For an overview of the issues in the Doha Round of multilateral trade nego-tiations, see Guha-Khasnobis (2004) and the WTO Doha Agenda web site: www.wto.org/english/tratop_e/dda_e/dda_e.htm.

13. According to the World Bank (2003, p. 124): "The practice of placing foreign and domestic sellers on an equal competitive footing is a hallmark of trade agree-ments. This objective is no less important in investment agreements. Promoting lib-eralization in international investment essentially boils down to securing nondiscriminatory terms of entry and operation."

14. Besides the dimensions captured by the relevant indices, see also such initia-tives as the Revised International Capital Adequacy Framework, also known as Basel 2 (www.bis.org/publ/bcbsca.htm) and the work of the International Competition Network (www.internationalcompetitionnetwork.org).

15. For an elaboration of the theory of competitive government see, for exam-ple, Breton (1998), and for a discussion on how more competition within government could help meet current fiscal challenges see, among others, Dohrmann and Mendonca (2004). Decentralization has also been promoted for increasing competi-tiveness and for bringing the state closer to people; see, for example, the International Forum on Globalization (2002).

16. For the goals, see www.un.org/millenniumgoals. For reports on progress in achieving the goals in individual countries see www.undp.org/mdg/countryreports. html, for regional reports see www.undp.org/mdg/regionalreports.html, and for a worldwide overview see World Bank (2005a).

17. See, for example, WEF and Watson Wyatt Worldwide (2004), Federal Reserve Bank of Kansas City (2004), and G-8 (2003a).

18. See http://unfccc.int/resource/docs/convkp/kpeng.html.

19. The UN Security Council, for example, has adopted this approach for pro-moting follow-up to its Resolution 1373 against international terrorism.

20. For more detail on the Commitment to Development Index, see www.cgdev.org/rankingtherich/home.html.

21. It can be argued that not only are public goods one of the six cases of market failure listed by Stiglitz (2000) but that correcting the various conditions of market failure calls in most instances for the provision of a public good—such as enhanced information (to correct information asymmetries), a new property rights regime (to correct a problem of missing markets), or a reserve fund to provide protection against external shocks. Similarly, correcting various types of global or integrating market failure may require the provision of global(ized) public goods of a market-facilitating and market-embedding type.

22. For a comprehensive listing of these reports, see Haller (2005).

23. See, among others, Blanchard (2004); Bryant (2003); Drezner (2002); Hanson, Honohan, and Majnoni (2003); Held (2004); Kahler and Lake (2003); Keohane and Milner (1996); Mosley (2003); Rajan and Zingales (2003); Rodrik (1996); Schreurs and Economy (1997); Sinn (2003); Smith, Solinger, and Topik

(1999); Södersten (2004); Kapstein and Milanovic (2002); Underhill, Zhang, and Vines (2003); Weiss (2003); and Wijen, Zoeteman, and Pieters (2005).

24. So far, however, tax competition between states has occurred primarily within regions rather than across them (Ernst & Young and ZEW 2004; World Bank 2003). Because transnational corporations also compete with each other for "good" host countries (Chang 2003), states retain some room to maneuver.

25. There were Jubilee 2000 campaigns in more than 60 countries around the world. See, for instance, www.jubileeusa.org and www.jubilee2000uk.org.

26. For analyses of the potential of China and India to compete, see, for example, Basu (2004) and Virmani (2002a, b) on India, Shenkar (2005) on China, and Luce and McGregor (2005), Mallet and Merchant (2005), and Wolf (2005) for a comparative analysis of these two countries.

27. See, for example, the Hartz IV reforms in Germany at www.bundesregierung.de/en or the Social Security debate in the United States at www.whitehouse.gov/infocus/social-security.

28. In particular, the early structural adjustment programs in Sub-Saharan Africa often had high net costs for the countries concerned (Mkandawire and Soludo 1999; Cornia, Jolly, and Stewart 1987).

29. For details on the G-20 see www.g-20.mre.gov.br.

30. For details see www.dfa.gov.za/docs/2004/ibsa0305a.htm.

31. This practice began at the G-8 summit in Okinawa in 2000. For information on delegations at the most recent summits, see G-8 (2003b, 2004).

32. The notion of *responsive* sovereignty differs from that of *responsible* sovereignty as, for example, set forth by ICISS (2001). Responsive sovereignty is an objective concept. It neither judges the external expectations and norms (in terms of whether they are "good" or "bad" relative to certain higher order goals) nor implies that states must comply with them. Responsive sovereignty merely refers to the fact that states today take account of external expectations as well as constraints and opportunities when making national policy. Responsible sovereignty refers to states' responsibility to protect their communities from such atrocities as mass killing, systematic rape, and starvation. It is a normative concept.

33. Especially in the environment, new types of international trade in global public services have arisen, such as trade in carbon dioxide emissions (see the chapter by King in this volume).

REFERENCES

Abbott, Kenneth W., and Duncan Snidal. 1998. "Why States Act through Formal International Organizations." *Journal of Conflict Resolution* 42 (1): 3–32.

Addison, Anthony, and Alan Roe, eds. 2004. *Fiscal Policy for Development: Poverty, Reconstruction, and Growth.* Basingstoke, UK: Palgrave Macmillan.

Amnesty International. Various years. *Annual Report.* London.

Anheier, Helmut, Marlies Glasius, and Mary Kaldor, eds. 2004. *Global Civil Society 2004/05.* London: SAGE Publications.

Arrow, Kenneth J. 1963. *Social Choice and Individual Values.* New Haven, Conn., and London: Yale University Press.

Bandura, Romina. 2005a. "International Cooperation behind National Borders: Select Evidence." UNDP/ODS Background paper. United Nations Development Programme, Office of Development Studies. New York. [www.thenewpublic finance.org].

———. 2005b. "Measuring Country Performance and State Behavior: A Survey of Composite Indices." UNDP/ODS Background paper. United Nations Development Programme, Office of Development Studies. New York. [www. thenewpublicfinance.org].

Bangura, Yusuf. 2000. "Public Sector Restructuring: The Institutional and Social Effects of Fiscal, Managerial, and Capacity-Building Reforms." UNRISD Occasional Paper 3. United Nations Research Institute for Social Development, Geneva.

Barlow, David, and Roxana Radulescu. 2002. "The Dynamic Political Economy of Reform in Transition Economies: An Empirical Analysis." Economic and Policial Re-integration in an Enlarged EU (EPRIEE) Working Paper. New Castle upon Tyne, UK. [www.epriee.ncl.ac.uk/radules1.pdf].

Basu, Kaushik, ed. 2004. *India's Emerging Economy: Performance and Prospects in the 1990s and Beyond.* Cambridge, Mass: MIT Press.

Benioff, Marc, and Karen Southwick. 2004. *Compassionate Capitalism: How Corporations Can Make Doing Good an Integral Part of Doing Well.* Franklin Lakes, N.J.: Career Press.

Bhagwati, Jagdish. 2004. *In Defense of Globalization.* New York: Oxford University Press.

Bhagwati, Jagdish, Arvind Panagariya, and T. N. Srinivasan. 2004. "The Muddles over Outsourcing." *Journal of Economic Perspectives* 18 (4): 93–114.

Blanchard, Olivier. 2004. *The Economic Future of Europe.* NBER Working Paper 10310. Cambridge, Mass.: National Bureau of Economic Research.

Breton, Albert. 1998. *Competitive Governments: An Economic Theory of Politics and Public Finance.* Cambridge: Cambridge University Press.

Bryant, Ralph C. 2003. *Turbulent Waters: Cross-Border Finance and International Governance.* Washington, D.C.: Brookings Institution Press.

Buchanan, James M., and Gordon Tullock. 1962. *The Calculus of Consent: Logical Foundations of Constitutional Democracy.* Ann Arbor, Mich.: University of Michigan Press.

Buira, Ariel, ed. 2003. *Challenges to the World Bank and IMF: Developing Country Perspectives.* London: Anthem Press.

Canova, Fabio, and Evi Pappa. 2005. *Does It Cost to Be Virtuous? The Macroeconomic Effects of Fiscal Constraints.* NBER Working Paper 11065. Cambridge, Mass: National Bureau of Economic Research.

Carey, John. 2004. "Flying High?" *Business Week,* October 11. [www.businessweek.com/magazine/content/04_41/b3903413.htm].

Chang, Ha-Joong. 2003. *Globalisation, Economic Development, and the Role of the State.* Penang and New York: Third World Network and Zed Books Ltd.

Cnossen, Sijbren. 1998. "Global Trends and Issues in Value Added Taxation." *International Tax and Public Finance* 5 (3): 399–428.

Commission on the Private Sector and Development. 2004. *Unleashing Entrepreneurship: Making Business Work for the Poor.* New York: United Nations Development Programme. [www.undp.org/cpsd/report/index.html].

Cornia, Giovanni Andrea, Richard Jolly, and Frances Stewart. 1987. *Adjustment with a Human Face.* Vol. 1 and 2. Oxford: Clarendon Press.

Davis, Jeffrey, Rolando Ossowski, James Daniel, and Steven Barnett. 2001. "Stabilization and Savings Funds for Nonrenewable Resources Experience and Fiscal Policy Implications." IMF Occasional Paper 205. International Monetary Fund, Washington, D.C.

Dawkins, Cedric. 2002. "Corporate Welfare, Corporate Citizenship, and the Question of Accountability." *Business and Society* 41 (3): 269–91.

De Ferranti, David, Guillermo E. Perry, Indermit S. Gill, and Luis Servén. 2000. *Securing Our Future in a Global Economy.* Washington, D.C.: World Bank.

Desai, Meghnad. 2003. "Public Goods: A Historical Perspective." In Inge Kaul, Pedro Conceiçao, Katelle Le Gouven, and Ronald U. Mendoza, eds., *Providing Global Public Goods: Managing Globalization.* New York: Oxford University Press.

Devereux, Michael P., Rachel Griffith, and Alexander Klemm. 2002. "Corporate Income Tax Reforms and International Tax Competition." *Economic Policy* 17 (35): 451–95.

Dohrmann, Thomas, and Lenny T. Mendonca. 2004. "Boosting Government Productivity." *The McKinsey Quarterly,* Number 4 (December). [www.mckinseyquarterly.com/newsletters/2004_12-t.htm].

Drezner, Daniel W., ed. 2002. *Locating the Proper Authorities: The Interaction of Domestic and International Institutions.* Ann Arbor, Mich.: University of Michigan Press.

Ebrill, Liam, Michael Keen, Jean-Paul Bodin, and Victoria Summers. 2001. *The Modern VAT.* Washington, D.C.: International Monetary Fund.

Edwards, Michael, and Simon Zadek. 2003. "Governing the Provision of Global Public Goods: The Role and Legitimacy of Nonstate Actors." In Inge Kaul, Pedro Conceiçao, Katell Le Goulven, and Ronald U. Mendoza, eds. *Providing Global Public Goods: Managing Globalization.* New York: Oxford University Press.

Ernst & Young and ZEW (Centre for European Economic Research). 2004. "Company Taxation in the New EU Member States: Survey of the Tax Regimes and Effective Tax Burdens for Multinational Investors 2nd edition." [www.ey.com/global/download.nsf/International/EU_Tax_2004/$file/EU_Tax_2004.pdf].

European Commission. 2004. "Facing the Challenge: The Lisbon Strategy for Growth and Employment." Report from the high level group chaired by Wim Kok. Luxembourg: Office for Official Publications of the European Communities. [http://europa.eu.int/growthandjobs/pdf/2004-1866-EN-complet.pdf].

Fasano, Ugo. 2000. "Review of the Experience with Oil Stabilization and Savings Funds in Selected Countries." IMF Working Paper 112. International Monetary Fund, Washington, D.C.

Federal Reserve Bank of Kansas City. 2004. "Global Demographic Change: Economic Impacts and Policy Challenges." Symposium sponsored by the Federal Reserve Bank of Kansas City, August 26–28, Jackson Hole, Wyo. [www.kc.frb.org/PUBLICAT/SYMPOS/2004/sym04prg.htm].

Freedom House. Various years. *Freedom of the World: The Annual Survey of Political Rights and Civil Liberties.* Lanham, Md.: Rowman & Littlefield Publishers.

———. 2005. "Freedom in the World 2005: Selected Data from Freedom House's Annual Global Survey of Political Rights and Civil Liberties." Washington, D.C. [www.freedomhouse.org/research/freeworld/2005/charts2005.pdf].

Friedman, Thomas L. 2005. *The World Is Flat: A Brief History of the Twenty-first Century.* New York: Farrar, Straus, and Giroux.

G-8 (Group of Eight). 2003a. "2003 G8 Summit: Chair's Summary." June 3. [www.g8.fr/evian/english/navigation/2003_g8_summit/summit_documents/chair_s_summary.html].

———. 2003b. "2003 G8 Summit: Delegations." June 3. [www.g8.fr/evian/english/navigation/2003_g8_summit/delegations.html].

———. 2004. "Sea Island Summit 2004: G8 Extended Invitees." June 8–10. [www.g8usa.gov/extended.htm].

Goldstein, Morris. 2000. "IMF Structural Conditionality: How Much Is Too Much?" Revision of paper presented at National Bureau of Economic Research Conference on Economic and Financial Crises in Emerging Market Economies, October 19–21, Woodstock, Vt.

Guha-Khasnobis, Basudeb, ed. 2004. *The WTO, Developing Countries, and the Doha Development Agenda: Prospects and Challenges for Trade-led Growth.* Basingstoke, UK: Palgrave Macmillan.

Haller, Hana. 2005. "Global Reports: An Overview of their Evolution—2005 Update." United Nations Development Programme, Office of Development Studies, New York. [www.thenewpublicfinance.org].

Hanson, James A., Patrick Honohan, and Giovanni Majnoni. 2003. *Globalization and National Financial Systems.* Washington, D.C. and New York: World Bank and Oxford University Press.

Heady, Christopher. 2004. "Taxation Policy in Low-Income Countries." In Anthony Addison and Alan Roe, eds., *Fiscal Policy for Development: Poverty, Reconstruction, and Growth*. London: Palgrave Macmillan.

Held, David. 2004. *Global Covenant: The Social Democratic Alternative to the Washington Consensus*. Cambridge: Polity Press.

Human Rights Watch. Various years. *Human Rights Watch World Report*. New York.

ICISS (International Commission on Intervention and State Sovereignty). 2001. "The Responsibility to Protect." Ottawa: International Development Research Centre. [www.iciss.ca/pdf/Commission-Report.pdf].

IETA (International Emissions Trading Association). 2003. "Greenhouse Gas Market 2003: Emerging but Fragmented." Geneva.

Ikenberry, G. John. 2003. "What States Can Do Now." In T. V. Paul, G. John Ikenberry, and John A. Hall, eds., *The Nation-State in Question*. Princeton, N.J.: Princeton University Press.

Institute for Financial Markets. 2005. *Futures and Options Factbook*. Washington, D.C. [www.theifm.org/gfb].

International Forum on Globalization. 2002. *Alternatives to Economic Globalization*. San Francisco: Berrett-Koehler Publishers.

IMF (International Monetary Fund). 2001. "Structural Conditionality in Fund-Supported Programs." Policy Development and Review Department. Washington, D.C. [www.imf.org/external/np/pdr/cond/2001/eng/struct].

Kahler, Miles, and David A. Lake. 2003. "Globalization and Changing Patterns of Political Authority." In Miles Kahler and David A. Lake, eds., *Governance in a Global Economy: Political Authority in Transition*. Princeton, N.J.: Princeton University Press.

Kapstein, Ethan B., and Branko Milanovic, eds. 2002. *When Markets Fail: Social Policy and Economic Reform*. New York: Russell Sage Foundation Publications.

Kapur, Devesh. 2001. "Expansive Agendas and Weak Instruments: Governance Related Conditionalities of International Financial Institutions." *Journal of Policy Reform* 4 (3): 207–41.

Keen, Michael, and Alejandro Simone. 2004. "Tax Policy in Developing Countries: Some Lessons from the 1990s, and Some Challenges Ahead." In Sanjeev Gupta, Ben Clements, and Gabriela Inchauste, eds., *Helping Countries Develop: The Role of the Fiscal Policy*. Washington, D.C.: International Monetary Fund.

Keohane, Robert O., and Helen V. Milner, eds. 1996. *Internationalization and Domestic Politics*. Cambridge: Cambridge University Press.

Klenow, Peter J., and Andrés Rodriguez-Clare. 2004. *Externalities and Growth*. NBER Working Paper 11009. Cambridge, Mass.: National Bureau of Economic Research.

KPMG. 2004. "KPMG's Corporate Tax Rate Survey—January 2004." KPMG International Tax and Legal Center, Amsterdam. [www.us.kpmg.com/microsite/global%5Ftax/ctr%5Fsurvey/2004CTRS.pdf].

Krasner, Stephen D. 1995. "Compromising Westphalia." *International Security* 20 (3): 115–51.

Luce, Edward, and Richard McGregor. 2005. "A Share of Spoils: Beijing and New Delhi Get Mutual Benefits from Growing Trade." *Financial Times.* February 24.

Mallet, Victor, and Khozem Merchant. 2005. "Beijing and New Delhi Enter Foreign Deals to Bring Them Oil and Gas." *Financial Times.* February 25.

Merlen, Sylvain. 2005. "International Cooperation Behind National Borders: An Inventory of Domestic Policy Measures Aimed at Internalizing Cross-Border Spillovers Adversely Affecting the Global Environment." UNDP/ODS Background Paper. United Nations Development Programme, Office of Development Studies, New York. [www.thenewpublicfinance.org].

Michel-Kerjan, Erwann, and Howard Kunreuther. 2004. "Dealing with Extreme Events: New Challenges for Terrorism Risk Coverage in the US." Working Paper. University of Pennsylvania, Wharton School, Philadelphia. [http://grace. wharton.upenn.edu/risk/downloads/04-14-HK.pdf].

Mkandawire, Thandika, and Charles C. Soludo, eds. 1999. *Our Continent, Our Future: African Perspectives on Structural Adjustment.* Trenton, N.J., and Asmara: Africa World Press.

Mosley, Layna. 2003. *Global Capital and National Governments.* Cambridge: Cambridge University Press.

Musgrave, Richard A. 1969. *Fiscal Systems.* New Haven, Conn.: Yale University Press.

———. 1998. "The Role of the State in the Fiscal Theory." In Peter Birch Sørensen, ed., *Public Finance in a Changing World.* London: MacMillan Press.

Musgrave, Richard A., and Peggy B. Musgrave. 1989. *Public Finance in Theory and Practice.* 5th Edition. New York: McGraw-Hill.

Niskanen, William. 1973. *Bureaucracy: Servant or Master?* London: Institute of Economic Affairs.

Ocampo, Jose Antonio, and Juan Martin, eds. 2003. *A Decade of Light and Shadow: Latin America and the Caribbean in the 1990s.* Santiago, Chile: Economic Commission for Latin America and the Caribbean.

OECD/DAC (Organisation for Economic Co-operation and Development, Development Assistance Committee). 2005. *The DAC Journal: Development Cooperation 2004 Report—Efforts and Policies of the Members of the Development Assistance Committee* 6 (1): 1–243. Paris.

Palacios, Robert. 2003. "Privatizing National Social Security Schemes: The International Experience with Privatizing Pension Systems." International Social Security Association Meeting of Directors of Social Security Organizations in English-speaking Africa, October 7–9, Banjul, The Gambia.

Porter, Michael E., Klaus Schwab, Xavier Sala-i-Martin, and Augusto Lopez-Claros. 2004a. *The Global Competitiveness Report 2003–2004.* New York: Oxford University Press.

———. 2004b. *The Global Competitiveness Report 2004–2005*. Basingstoke, UK: Palgrave Macmillan.

Raffer, Kunibert. 2004. "Applying Musgrave's Branches of Government Expenditures to ODA: Tentative Estimates." *Journal für Entwicklungspolitik* 20 (1): 104–19.

Rajan, Raghuram G., and Luigi Zingales. 2003. *Saving Capitalism from the Capitalists: Unleashing the Power of Financial Markets to Create Wealth and Spread Opportunity*. New York: Crown Business.

Risse-Kappen, Thomas, ed. 1995. *Bringing Transnational Relations Back In: Non-State Actors, Domestic Structures and International Institutions*. Cambridge: Cambridge University Press.

Rodrik, Dani. 1996. "Understanding Economic Policy Reform." *Journal of Economic Literature* 34 (1): 9–41.

Roman, Ronald, Sefa Hayibor, and Bradley Agle. 1999. "The Relationship between Social and Financial Performance." *Business and Society* 38 (1): 109–25.

Ruggie, John Gerard. 2004. "Reconstituting the Global Public Domain—Issues, Actors, and Practices." *European Journal of International Relations* 10 (4): 499–531.

Scholte, Jan Aart. 2001. "The IMF and Civil Society: An Interim Progress Report." In Michael Edwards and John Gaventa, eds., *Global Citizen Action*. Boulder, Colo.: Lynne Rienner Publishers.

Scholte, Jan Aart, and Albrecht Schnabel, eds. 2002. *Civil Society and Global Finance*. London: Routledge.

Schreurs, Miranda A., and Elizabeth C. Economy, eds. 1997. *The Internationalization of Environmental Protection*. Cambridge: Cambridge University Press.

Shenkar, Oded. 2005. *The Chinese Century: The Rising Economy and Its Impact on the Global Economy, the Balance of Power, and Your Job*. Upper Saddle River, N.J.: University of Pennsylvania, Wharton School Publishing.

Sidikou-Sow, Balkissa. 2005. "Has 'Globalization' As Yet Changed Standard Theory? A Survey of Textbooks in Public Finance and Public Economics." Background Paper. United Nations Development Programme, Office of Development Studies, New York. [www.thenewpublicfinance.org].

Sinn, Hans Werner. 2003. *The New Systems Competition*. Oxford: Blackwell Publishers.

Slemrod, Joel. 2004. "Are Corporate Tax Rates, or Countries, Converging?" *Journal of Public Economics* 88 (6): 1169–86.

Smith, David A., Dorothy J. Solinger, and Steven C. Topik, eds. 1999. *States and Sovereignty in the Global Economy*. London: Routledge.

Södersten, Bo, ed. 2004. *Globalization and the Welfare State*. New York: Palgrave.

Sørensen, Georg. 2001. *Changes in Statehood: The Transformation of International Relations*. New York: Palgrave.

Stavins, Robert N. 2003. "Market-based Environmental Policy Instruments." In Karl-Göran Mäler and Jeffrey Vincent, eds., *Handbook of Environmental Economics*. Amsterdam: Elsevier Science.

Stiglitz, Joseph E. 2000. *Economics of the Public Sector*. New York: W. W. Norton & Company.

Stopford, John, and Susan Strange. 1992. *Rival States, Rival Firms: Competition for World Market Shares*. Cambridge: Cambridge University Press.

UN (United Nations). 2001. "Threats to International Peace and Security Caused by Terrorist Acts." Security Council Resolution 1377. New York. [www.un.org/Docs/scres/2001/sc2001.htm].

———. 2004. *Report of the High Level Panel on Threats, Challenges and Change*. New York. [www.un.org/secureworld/report2.pdf].

———. 2005. *Children and Armed Conflict: Report of the Secretary General*. Document A-59/695-S/2005/72. New York.

UNAIDS (Joint United Nations Programme on HIV/AIDS). 2003. *Follow Up to the 2001 United Nations General Assembly Special Session on HIV/AIDS, Progress Report on the Global Response to the HIV/AIDS Epidemic*. Geneva.

UNCTAD (United Nations Conference on Trade and Development). 2004. "Investment Instruments Online—UNCTAD Analysis of BITs." August 17. Geneva. [www.unctadxi.org/templates/Page____1007.aspx].

Underhill, Geoffrey R. D., Xiaoke Zhang, and David Vines, eds. 2003. *International Financial Governance under Stress: Global Structures versus National Imperatives*. Cambridge: Cambridge University Press.

UNDP (United Nations Development Programme). 2000. *Human Development Report 2000: Human Rights and Human Development*. New York: Oxford University Press.

———. 2002. *Human Development Report 2002: Deepening Democracy in a Fragmented World*. New York: Oxford University Press.

UNDP (UN Development Programme), UNEP (UN Environment Programme), World Bank, and World Resources Institute. 2003. *World Resources 2002–2004: Decisions for the Earth: Balance, Voice, and Power*. Washington, D.C.

UNICEF (United Nations Children's Fund). Various years. *The State of the World's Children*. New York.

U.S. GAO (General Accounting Office). 2004. "Emerging Infectious Diseases: Asian SARS Outbreak Challenged International and National Responses." GAO-04-564. Washington, D.C. [www.gao.gov/new.items/d04564.pdf].

Virmani, Arvind. 2002a. "India: A Potential Growth Star of the Next Decade." *The Financial Express*, June 11. [www.financialexpress.com/print.php?content_id=10892].

————. 2002b. "India and China Will Make 21st Century the Asian Century." *The Financial Express*, June 12. [www.financialexpress.com/fe_full_story.php?content_id=10964].

WEF (World Economic Forum) and Watson Wyatt Worldwide. 2004. "Living Happily Ever After: The Economic Implications of Aging Societies." Executive summary. Washington, D.C. [www.weforum.org/site/homepublic.nsf/Content/Pension+Reform+Task+Force%5CPension+Report+2004].

Weiss, Linda, ed. 2003. *States in the Global Economy: Bringing Domestic Institutions Back In.* Cambridge: Cambridge University Press.

Wijen, Frank, Kees Zoeteman, and Jan Pieters, eds. 2005. *A Handbook of Globalization and Environmental Policy: Interventions of National Government in a Global Arena.* Cheltenham, UK: Edward Elgar.

Wolf, Martin. 2004. *Why Globalization Works.* New Haven, Conn.: Yale University Press.

————. 2005. "On the Move: Asia's Giants Take Different Routes in Pursuit of Economic Greatness." *Financial Times*, February 23.

World Bank. 2000. *World Development Report 1999/2000: Entering the 21st Century.* Washington, D.C. and New York: World Bank and Oxford University Press.

————. 2003. *Global Economic Prospects and the Developing Countries 2003: Investing to Unlock Global Opportunities.* Washington, D.C.

————. 2004. *World Development Report 2005: A Better Investment Climate for Everyone.* Washington, D.C. and New York: World Bank and Oxford University Press.

————. 2005a. *Global Monitoring Report 2005—Millennium Development Goals: From Consensus to Momentum.* Washington, D.C. [http://siteresources.worldbank.org/GLOBALMONITORINGEXT/Resources/complete.pdf]

————. 2005b. "Board Presentations of PRSP Documents." [http://siteresources.worldbank.org/INTPRS1/Resources/boardlist.pdf].

World Commission on the Social Dimension of Globalization. 2004. *A Fair Globalization: Creating Opportunities for All.* Geneva: International Labour Office.

World Watch Institute. Various years. *State of the World.* New York: Norton.

WTO (World Trade Organization). 2005. "Regional Trade Agreements." [www.wto.org/english/tratop_e/region_e/region_e.htm].

MAKING POLICY UNDER EFFICIENCY PRESSURES
GLOBALIZATION, PUBLIC SPENDING, AND SOCIAL WELFARE

VITO TANZI

Recent academic studies on the link between globalization and public spending have advanced two hypotheses. The efficiency hypothesis predicts that increased economic integration is associated with declining public spending. The compensation hypothesis suggests that governments expand as economic openness increases.

While both public spending and economic openness have been rising since the late nineteenth century, the two phenomena are not necessarily associated. Matters have been more complex. For example, public spending has increased during periods when economies were relatively closed, and factors unrelated to globalization, such as the aging of populations or the availability of convenient "tax handles," have contributed to growth in public spending.

There is limited, if any, support for the compensation hypothesis today, but there is some empirical support for the efficiency hypothesis, especially in the more recent era. Growth in public spending appears static and in some instances is on the decline. And public social spending, often a contributor to rising levels of government spending, is being squeezed.

Does this imply, as many globalization critics fear, that social welfare is under pressure? This chapter suggests that this need not be so. Though important, public social spending is only one of several fiscal tools available to governments to help protect and insure people against such personal risks as ill-health, unemployment, and old age. Tax expenditures (credits and exemptions) and regulation are additional instruments that can replace or complement public spending. As the analysis in this chapter shows, different groups of countries are likely to use these measures to different degrees and in varying combinations.

GLOBALIZATION AND PUBLIC SPENDING: THEORETICAL PREDICTIONS AND EMPIRICAL EVIDENCE

Neither the efficiency hypothesis nor the compensation hypothesis adequately captures the link between globalization and public spending when the timeframe is extended to include earlier periods of expanding and reversing globalization and when the factors contributing to a rise in public spending are examined more closely.

The hypotheses

According to the efficiency hypothesis, Garrett (2001, pp. 5–6) explains,

> government spending—beyond minimal market friendly measures such as defense, securing property rights, and other fundamental public goods— reduces the competitiveness of national producers in international goods and services markets.... Income transfer programs and social services distort labor markets and bias intertemporal investment decisions. Moreover, government spending must be funded, often by borrowing in the short-term, and ultimately by higher taxes. Taxes on income and wealth directly erode the bottom lines of asset holders and distort their investment decisions, and this is exacerbated the more progressive tax systems are. Borrowing results in higher real interest rates, which further depresses investment. If this also leads to an appreciation in the real exchange rate, the competitiveness of national producers is decreased.

Given these relations, the efficiency hypothesis suggests that governments are likely to come under "lowest common denominator pressures" and that increasing globalization therefore goes hand in hand with declining public expenditures.

The compensation hypothesis, in contrast, points to the possibility of countervailing political forces that may outweigh downward pressures on public spending and create incentives for an expanded government role. This hypothesis was originally put forward by Ruggie (1982), confirming work by Cameron (1978).

More recently, Rodrik (1998, p. 997) argues that there is "a positive correlation between an economy's exposure to international trade and the size of its government" measured by the ratio of public spending to gross domestic product (GDP) as government expenditures are used to provide social insurance against external risk. Globalization, defined as increased trade openness, is expected to increase a country's exposure to external risks (such as instability in the terms of trade), leading to greater volatility in domestic income and consumption. This increased volatility can be reduced by increased government purchases of goods and services as a share of GDP.

Hence, the compensation hypothesis predicts that where democracy is well established and the losers from globalization are well organized, there may be strong public pressure for government spending to function as a shock absorber for the increased risks people face. Also, increased openness requires more public investment in human capital to retain or strengthen competitiveness in the global economy. Thus, increased public spending can both bolster political support for globalization and provide market-supporting public goods, such as a qualified and competitive labor force.

Thus, the efficiency and compensation hypotheses are to some extent competing predictions. Which appears to have more predictive value?

Some empirical evidence

The point of the discussion here is not to present detailed empirical tests of the two hypotheses but to suggest that a systematic study of the links between globalization and public spending requires a more comprehensive approach along three dimensions:

- Lengthening the timeframe and examining earlier periods of globalization and of reversed openness.
- Considering a wider range of factors affecting public spending.
- Assessing public spending against the capacity of governments to raise revenue (not just in terms of whether they were pressured into increasing or decreasing budgets).

The link between economic openness and public spending varies across periods and countries. Economic globalization has been going on for a long time—accelerating in some periods, when, for example, new technologies or a renewed policy emphasis on economic openness helped it along, and slowing or even reversing itself in periods when wars, plagues, or policy changes obstructed the free movement of goods, services, capital, or people. So, what has happened to public spending during periods of economic openness, and what when openness was reversed?

Scholars agree that from around 1870 to the beginning of World War I was a period of intense globalization. Technological advances in communications and transport made cross-border economic activity ever easier, and economic policies gave free rein to market forces. Moreover, the gold standard facilitated international payments, furthering economic globalization.[1] Many countries became more open to trade and to the movement of capital and even people. Indices of openness to trade and to capital movements for today's industrial countries were, at that time, broadly similar to those in recent years (Baldwin and Martin 1991).

Yet governments played a limited role in the economy during 1870–1914. The share of public spending in GDP in many of today's industrial countries was about 10 percent (Tanzi and Schuknecht 2000; Maddison 1997; and Lindert 2004). Spending on subsidies and transfers, later one of the main drivers of increased public spending, averaged about 1 percent of GDP (Tanzi and Schuknecht 2000, p.30).

Events after 1914 brought an end to these globalizing trends. World War I, the Great Depression, World War II, and autarkic policies in Germany, Italy, Russia, and other countries all contributed to the closing of economies. Economic policymakers lost their enthusiasm for openness, and the world went through a long period when borders were relatively closed to trade and very closed to capital and people.

However, it was in this period that the role of the state in the economy started
to change. Welfare states or mixed economies emerged, first slowly and then faster.
For a group of 14 industrial countries, public spending as a share of GDP more
than doubled between 1913 and 1960 and grew substantially between 1960 and
1980 (table 1). This phase lasted until the mid-1980s, when the current era of
globalization began and the rate of growth in public spending decelerated (table
2). Thus the growth of public spending had little relationship to globalization. It

TABLE 1

General government expenditures for 14 industrial countries, 1870–1980

Year[a]	Unweighted average (percent of GDP)
1870[b]	10.8
1913[b]	13.1
1920	19.6
1937	23.8
1960	28.0
1980	41.9

Note: Unless otherwise indicated, countries include Australia, Austria, Canada, France, Germany, Ireland, Italy, Japan, New Zealand, Norway, Sweden, Switzerland, United Kingdom, and United States. Pre–World War II data are sometimes on the basis of GNP or NNP instead of GDP.
a. Date shown or closest year available. Central government data for Sweden in 1870 and Austria for 1920. For New Zealand 1970 data are provided for 1960.
b. Canada, Ireland, and New Zealand not included in the data.
Source: Tanzi and Schuknecht 2000 (pp. 6–7).

TABLE 2

General government expenditures for OECD countries, 1987–2004

Year	Weighted average (percent of GDP)
1987[a]	40.4
1990[b]	40.3
1995	42.3
2000	39.2
2003	41.1
2004[c]	40.6

Note: Unless otherwise indicated, countries include all Organisation for Economic Co-operation and Development (OECD) members: Australia, Austria, Belgium, Canada, Czech Republic, Denmark, Finland, France, Germany, Greece, Hungary, Iceland, Ireland, Italy, Japan, Republic of Korea, Luxembourg, Mexico, Netherlands, New Zealand, Norway, Poland, Portugal, Slovak Republic, Spain, Sweden, Switzerland, Turkey, United Kingdom, and the United States.
a. Czech Republic, Hungary, Luxembourg, Poland, Slovak Republic, and Switzerland not included in the data.
b. Czech Republic, Hungary, Poland, and Slovak Republic not included in the data.
c. Estimate.
Source: OECD 2004b (p. 191).

took place before globalization in the contemporary sense and well before much of the recent discussion of globalization.

A similar pattern of events marked the history of some developing countries. During 1870–1914 Latin American countries had relatively closed economies, with the world's highest tariffs (Coatsworth and Williamson 2004). On the eve of World War I the unweighted average tariff (import duties as a share of total import values) for eight Latin American countries stood at more than 25 percent, while it was close to 20 percent for the United States, 10 percent for 10 Asian countries, and 5 percent for France, Germany, and the United Kingdom (Coatsworth and Williamson 2004, p. 39). Coatsworth and Williamson (2004) argue that these high tariffs were a result of an exceptionally high level of military conflicts that necessitated high public spending—and hence a higher taxation rate. Not globalization but conflicts contributed to increased public revenue collection and spending. Later, when economic openness increased in developing countries between 1980 and the end of the 1990s, public spending as a share of GDP declined (table 3).

Multiple drivers have contributed to changes in public spending. Studies have found that increased public spending depends on a variety of economic, demographic, social, and political factors, many with no link to economic openness.

One key factor influencing public spending has been income. As predicted by "Wagner's Law," the higher a country's income, the higher its public spending. Despite many ups and downs incomes have risen in industrial and developing countries, contributing to growth in public spending. To what extent this law will continue to hold as markets deepen, expand, and integrate, remains to be seen.

Alesina and Wacziarg (1997) point to country size as a determinant of public spending, arguing that smaller countries tend to be more open and to have higher public spending. Smaller countries also tend to be ethnically more homogeneous, which has a positive influence on public spending (Alesina, Glaeser, and Sacerdote 2001; Alesina and La Ferrara 2003). Democracy, political organization, or voice are

TABLE 3

Public expenditure for developing country regions, 1980–97
(percent of GDP)

Region	1980	1990	1997
Sub-Saharan Africa[a]	25.5	26.3	22.3
North Africa	39.0	29.4	30.4
Latin America	—	24.5	23.6
South East Asia	29.4	37.3	26.2[b]

— is not available.
a. Excludes South Africa.
b. Data are for 1996.
Source: UNRISD 2000 (p. 65).

highlighted by Adserà and Boix (2002), Garrett and Nickerson (2001), and Lindert (2002 and 2004). Schulze and Ursprung (1999) focus on fiscal decentralization and competition among jurisdictions and also on rent-seeking behavior.

Tanzi and Schuknecht (2000) and Tanzi (2002) show that the observed rise in public spending is related largely to the risks associated with becoming old or ill or with being illiterate and untrained. These risks do not derive from economic globalization, or only very indirectly. Advances in medical and pharmaceutical technology certainly generate spillover effects and contribute to rising life expectancy. And other factors, such as consumption habits, may also cross borders and affect people's health worldwide. Yet on the whole, people require social protection whether a country is globalized or not. Public spending on pensions in industrial countries rose enormously between 1920 and 1980 and continued to rise, at a slower rate, between 1985 and 2001 (tables 4 and 5). Some analysts forecast that government

TABLE 4

Public expenditure on pensions for 17 industrial countries, 1920–80

Year	Unweighted average (percent of GDP)
1920[a, b]	1.2
1937[a, c]	1.9
1960[d]	4.5
1980	8.4

Note: Unless otherwise indicated, the countries include Australia, Austria, Belgium, Canada, France, Germany, Ireland, Italy, Japan, Netherlands, New Zealand, Norway, Spain, Sweden, Switzerland, United Kingdom, and United States. Pension spending includes old-age cash benefits, disability pensions, and survivor pensions.
a. Central government only.
b. Australia, Canada, Ireland, Netherlands, New Zealand, and Switzerland not included in the data.
c. Canada, France, Germany, Ireland, Italy, Netherlands, Norway, Sweden, Switzerland, and the United States not included in the data.
d. Spain not included in the data.
Source: Tanzi and Schuknecht 2000 (p. 41).

TABLE 5

Public expenditure on pensions for OECD countries, 1985–2001

Year	Unweighted average (percent of GDP)
1985[a]	9.7
1990[b]	9.8
1995[c]	10.8
2001[d]	11.2

Note: Unless otherwise indicated, countries include all OECD member states. Pension spending includes old-age, survivor, and incapacity-related benefits.
a. Czech Republic, Hungary, Iceland, Korea, Poland, and Slovak Republic not included in the data.
b. Hungary and Slovak Republic not included in the data.
c. Hungary not included in the data.
d. Turkey not included in the data.
Source: Author's calculations based on OECD 2004a.

budgets in these countries will remain high because of population aging at least until 2020 or even later (Lindert 2004; Casey and others 2003). Public spending on pensions is also expected to rise in developing countries (Lindert 2002), where it now averages 1.4 percent of GDP in Africa, 3.0 percent of GDP in Asia, and 2.1 percent of GDP in Latin America and the Caribbean (table 6).

Changes in the political stance of a country or the international community are also important drivers of change in government spending. The pursuit of more pro-Keynesian policies in the wake of the Great Depression of the 1930s and World War II no doubt had an expansionary effect.[2] The subsequent shift toward more neoliberal policies and the call for limiting direct government involvement in the economy exerted a dampening effect, at least on the growth of public spending.

Public spending also depends on the availability of "tax handles." As the case of Latin American countries during 1870–1914 demonstrates, a high level of public spending is often associated with the availability of convenient "tax handles"—readily tapped sources of revenue. Foreign trade was the best tax handle for many countries. The larger the share of imports and exports, the easier it was for a country to raise revenue.[3] That makes it important to explore the actual scope that governments have for raising or maintaining revenue and expenditure levels when assessing trends in public spending.

In the 1960s and 1970s foreign trade taxes were an important source of revenue for many developing countries. Zee (1996, p. 1661) estimates that for 1975–79 trade taxes (unweighted) averaged just 4 percent of total tax revenues for Organisation for Economic Co-operation and Development (OECD) countries but 30 percent for non-OECD countries. During this time, increased openness to trade meant increased revenues and improved room for public spending. It was not, as scholars supporting the compensation hypothesis would argue, that spending was high because demands for social protection were high but that spending was high because revenue was high.

Trade liberalization has removed many of these tax handles. As a result, a number of developing countries that failed to build alternative tax bases have faced declining tax revenues (Abed 2000; Khattry and Rao 2002; Tanzi 2003).

TABLE 6

Public expenditure on pensions in developing country regions, 1990–96

Region	Public expenditure on pensions (percent of GDP)
Africa	1.4
Asia	3.0
Latin America and the Caribbean	2.1

Note: Pension spending includes old-age, disability, and survivors' pensions. Regional averages were calculated using 1996 and 1990 data. Averages are weighted by GNP in purchasing power parity dollars.
Source: ILO 2000.

Thus, the earlier positive relation between economic openness and revenue collection and public spending has turned negative. Today, for many developing countries more economic openness means (at least for now) lower revenue and curtailed spending possibilities or an increased need to take on debt.

In addition, other aspects of globalization have unleashed a set of "fiscal termites" (Tanzi 2001): forces that are progressively weakening national tax bases, making it more difficult for governments to maintain high tax levels. Among these corrosive forces are electronic commerce and transactions, electronic money, intracompany trade, off-shore financial centers and tax havens, unregulated or barely regulated derivatives and hedge funds, and a growing inability or unwillingness of governments to tax financial capital and the incomes of individuals with highly tradable skills.

Therefore, when examining changes in public spending it is important to explore to what extent these changes are due to efficiency pressures and to what extent to an erosion of the tax base. A third hypothesis could thus be added to the compensation and efficiency hypotheses: the fiscal termite hypothesis, which predicts that new global forces are weakening national tax bases, forcing a decline in government spending.

Which hypothesis holds?

There seems to be limited, if any, empirical evidence supporting the compensation hypothesis. As Garrett (2001) points out, scholars like Rodrik (1998) did not really explore how globalization affects public spending. They measured historic *levels* of market integration and spending—not how a *change* in the first variable causes a *change* in the second.

There is more evidence to support the efficiency hypothesis. The level of public spending did not grow during 1870–1913, when economies were particularly open. The political and intellectual winds that led to the expansion of government and produced the welfare state have been long in coming and became strong exactly in the years when economies became less open (Tanzi and Schuknecht 2000). The New Deal[4] and the Keynesian revolution were late products of the Great Depression, a period when economies that had been relatively closed became even more closed. And by the early 1950s, long before the current globalization process got under way, there was already support for the creation of welfare states in today's industrial countries (de Jouvenel 1952; Galbraith 1958).

So what findings emerge when *change* in economic openness is correlated with *change* in public spending? Garrett (2001, p. 3), who explores this link for more than a hundred industrial and developing countries, finds that "countries in which trade grew more quickly between the 1970–84 and 1985–95 periods witnessed slower growth in government spending between the two periods." This suggests that increased openness to trade indeed generates spending constraints.[5]

A comparison for 13 of the most open industrial countries of public spending at its highest level as a share of GDP and its level in 2002 shows that government expenditures are stagnant or declining, although economic openness clearly continues to be high (table 7). A scatter diagram supports this finding, linking change in openness to trade during 1987–2002 to change in public spending (figure 1). It shows a clear negative relationship (with a correlation coefficient of –0.67): the more open the economies became, the greater the downward pressure on spending.

Thus, there seems to be little if any empirical support for the compensation hypothesis and more for the efficiency hypothesis. The empirical evidence also seems to confirm the fiscal termite hypothesis, considering that public spending is likely to depend not only on political demand for certain expenditures but also on the government's capacity to collect revenue.

DIRECT PUBLIC SPENDING, TAX EXPENDITURES, AND REGULATION: PUBLIC POLICY INSTRUMENTS FOR SOCIAL PROTECTION AND INSURANCE

Protection and insurance against personal risks is required no matter how deeply integrated countries are. People grow old, suffer from disabilities and ill-health,

TABLE 7

Highest shares of public expenditures and shares in 2002 in selected economies, ranked by degree of openness in 2002
(percent of GDP)

Open economies	General government total outlays	
	Highest level (year)	2002 level
Belgium	57.0 (1987)	50.2
Slovak Republic	65.0 (1997)	51.0
Ireland	52.0 (1987)	33.8
Czech Republic	54.4 (1995)	46.9
Netherlands	58.4 (1987)	47.8
Hungary	63.4 (1994)	52.6
Austria	56.4 (1993)	50.6
Canada	53.3 (1992)	40.9
Korea, Rep. of	25.0 (2001)	24.8
Switzerland	36.1 (1998)	35.4
Denmark	61.7 (1993)	55.8
Sweden	72.9 (1993)	58.2
Finland	64.2 (1993)	50.1

Note: Openness is defined as exports plus imports divided by GDP in 2002. Peak figures for public spending are based on data for 1987–2002.
Source: Openness figures are from World Bank 2004 (pp. 306–09) and government spending figures are from OECD 2004b (p.191).

and are affected by economic downturns or natural disaster, requiring economic support and aid. Moreover, a more integrated world economy may generate more economic risk and insecurity, at least in the short run, with many studies point- ing to important associated short-term social costs, especially in developing coun- tries.[6] There is clearly a demand for risk mitigation and management. The question is how countries respond under current realities.

Many scholars equate public welfare with public social spending, notably transfer payments. And with the observed recent efficiency constraints on over- all public spending, they are concerned that economic welfare is suffering and that people's fate is being left to the vicissitudes of markets (see, for example, CEPAL 2002). However, public spending is only one of several measures that governments can employ to pursue policy objectives. Other instruments include tax expendi- tures and regulation.

Direct public social spending

Comparable data and time series on public social spending are unavailable for most non-OECD countries. Data come from country case studies or other ad hoc studies of select country groups and thus have to be interpreted with caution.

The data show that public social spending in today's industrial countries grew considerably during the twentieth century until the early 1980s: from an average of less than 1 percent of GDP around 1910 to about 20 percent of GDP in 1980 (Lindert 2004, vol. 1, pp. 12–13). Thereafter, growth in public social spending

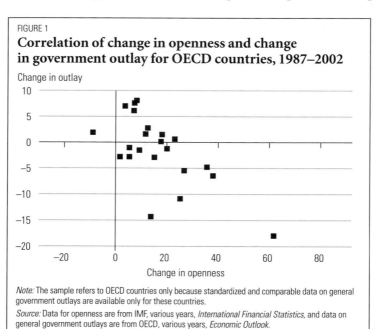

FIGURE 1

Correlation of change in openness and change in government outlay for OECD countries, 1987–2002

Note: The sample refers to OECD countries only because standardized and comparable data on general government outlays are available only for these countries.

Source: Data for openness are from IMF, various years, *International Financial Statistics*, and data on general government outlays are from OECD, various years, *Economic Outlook*.

TABLE 8

Public social expenditure in OECD countries, 1980–2001
(percent of GDP)

Country	1980	1985	1990	1995	2001
Australia	11.3	13.5	14.2	17.8	18.0
Austria	22.5	24.1	24.1	26.6	26.0
Belgium	24.1	26.9	26.9	28.1	27.2
Canada	14.3	17.4	18.6	19.6	17.8
Czech Republic	—	—	17.0	18.9	20.1
Denmark	29.1	27.9	29.3	32.4	29.2
Finland	18.5	23.0	24.8	31.1	24.8
France	21.1	26.6	26.6	29.2	28.5
Germany	23.0	23.6	22.8	27.5	27.4
Greece	11.5	17.9	20.9	21.4	24.3
Hungary	—	—	—	—	20.1
Iceland	—	—	16.4	19.0	19.8
Ireland	17.0	22.1	18.6	19.4	13.8
Italy	18.4	21.3	23.3	23.0	24.4
Japan	10.2	11.0	11.2	13.5	16.9
Korea, Rep. of	—	—	3.1	3.6	6.1
Luxembourg	23.5	23.0	21.9	23.8	20.8
Mexico	—	1.8	3.8	8.1	11.8
Netherlands	26.9	27.3	27.6	25.6	21.8
New Zealand	17.2	18.1	21.9	18.9	18.5
Norway	17.9	19.1	24.7	26.0	23.9
Poland	—	—	15.5	23.8	23.0
Portugal	10.9	11.1	13.9	18.0	21.1
Slovak Republic	—	—	—	19.2	17.9
Spain	15.9	18.2	19.5	21.4	19.6
Sweden	28.8	30.0	30.8	33.0	28.9
Switzerland	14.2	15.1	17.9	23.9	26.4
Turkey	4.3	4.2	7.6	7.5	13.2[a]
United Kingdom	17.9	21.1	19.5	23.0	21.8
United States	13.3	13.0	13.4	15.5	14.8
Unweighted average	17.9	19.1	19.1	21.3	20.9

— is not available.
a. Data are for 1999.
Source: OECD 2004a.

slowed and today is on the decline in several countries (table 8). While expenditures on pensions are still rising in many countries, spending on health and unemployment benefits and other transfers have stalled or declined (Lindert 2004; Adema 2001; and Tanzi and Schuknecht 2000).

In many developing countries social transfers were still relatively low in 1990 (0.9 percent of GDP in Syria, 1.9 percent of GDP in Ecuador and India, 1.1 percent in the Philippines), with only a few reaching a level higher than 10 percent of GDP, such as Costa Rica, Thailand, and Uruguay (Lindert 2004, vol. 2, app. F). Rudra (2002, 2004) points out that developing countries are at a lower spending level and have also often seen a decline in public social spending in recent years. Kaufman and Segura-Ubiergo (2000) and Dion (2004) reach similar conclusions, suggesting that, contrary to the trend in industrial countries, in developing countries transfer payments declined while investment in human capital (education, health) rose.

Tax expenditures

The tax system can be linked to social welfare through the generation of tax revenue, the tax structure, and targeted, implicit subsidies (referred to as "tax expenditures"). A high level of tax revenue can help finance a higher level of public social expenditure and is thus essential for a welfare state. A more progressive tax structure shifts the burden of taxation toward richer people, leaving poorer families with more resources to protect themselves against economic risks. For equity reasons progressive income taxes tend to be preferred over more regressive consumption taxes.

Targeted provisions of the tax system, especially tax credits and deductions to private agents for socially important purposes such as health, education, training, or housing are tax expenditures—"government spending in the form of a loss or deferment of tax revenue" (van den Ende, Haberham, and Boogert 2004, p. 135). Such tax provisions reduce the cost of these expenses for taxpayers, thus potentially helping them to cope with particular risks. In this way tax expenditures aim at achieving social protection or similar objectives to those produced through direct public spending. Governments often consider tax expenditures as direct substitutes for spending programs.

Tax expenditures are particularly relevant when connected with personal income taxes, high tax rates, and low personal exemptions. Their shortcomings are that they cannot be targeted precisely and that they are more valuable to individuals subjected to high tax rates than to individuals with low tax rates, especially when applied as tax deductions rather than credits. Individuals too poor to pay income taxes get no benefits from the tax expenditures, unless these are given through credits against taxes rather than credits against taxable income. Thus, tax expenditures may end up providing social protection to many individuals but not to those most in need.

A combination of public spending targeted to those at the lower end of the income distribution or, in the short run, to those most exposed to economic risks and well designed tax expenditures for the middle classes could significantly reduce both public spending and taxation. This combination would make it possible for the efficiency hypothesis to apply to countries during periods of accelerating globalization while still maintaining protection for those most in need. However, there are significant informational and political requirements in designing such a strategy. Targeting expenditures requires deciding who the beneficiaries should be, always a politically difficult question. It also requires specific information on the beneficiaries, which could be difficult to obtain. Politically and administratively it has been easier to enact universal programs than programs that benefit particular groups. Yet universal programs tend to be very expensive.[7]

Regulations

A third important instrument of social protection, in intention if not always in results, is regulation. Regulation at times substitutes for tax measures and expenditures. For example, the government can either provide subsidies to people with disabilities or require that a company's workforce include a given proportion of people with disabilities. Such regulations aim at protecting some categories of people against particular risks while implicitly taxing other groups (Tanzi 1998). Therefore, well targeted regulation can to some extent replace direct public spending and tax expenditures.

Regulation to achieve social goals was widely used in the formerly centrally planned economies. State enterprises were directed to absorb all workers who became available and to provide them with health care, retirement benefits, and often even food and housing. Prices for the output of these enterprises were controlled. These economies created a kind of regulatory welfare state. Of course, economies organized around these principles are far from efficient. However, if the main goal is not efficiency but social protection, the centrally planned economies broadly achieved that goal. They protected their citizens against many economic risks. A recurrent complaint from citizens of the economies in transition has been that the move to a market economy has made their lives more risky.

Many countries today rely on a large number of regulations, not to replace markets but to correct market failure (and enhance allocative efficiency) or to meet certain equity concerns.[8] Examples of protection through regulation include laws pertaining to minimum wage, parental leave, prohibition of child labor, rent controls and other restrictions on rental contracts, food safety and health-related environmental norms and standards, as well as licenses requiring say, firms to provide specified services to urban *and* rural areas. And examples of insurance through regulation include mandatory severance pay and health insurance and pension schemes to be funded either by the employer or by the employer and the workers (see, among others, Holzmann and Hinz 2005 and de Ferranti and others 2000).

These regulation-based protection and insurance measures are easy to criticize because of the economic inefficiencies they may generate. The protection they provide can be random and imperfect. The urban middle classes and those in the formal sector of the economy often end up receiving far more protection than the rural poor. Nevertheless, social regulation is an important measure where public revenue is scarce, government's scope for direct spending is limited, and tax expenditures would benefit a relatively thin segment of the population (those working in the formal sector of the economy).

Use of policy instruments by country groups
How much countries rely on each instrument depends on sociocultural preferences and on policymakers' access to these instruments, which is determined by such factors as government revenue and stage of market development, especially markets for risk management products. Such markets have become increasingly sophisticated in recent decades. Thus, governments experience globalization's efficiency pressures at a time when many of them are progressively able, as shown in box 1, to point individuals to alternative, private services, substituting for or complementing scaled-down government programs.

Industrial countries, which benefit from the most developed markets, usually have all three social welfare instruments at their disposal. However, closer observation reveals that some industrial countries have evidently used certain measures more than others. For example, direct social spending has traditionally been significantly higher in Scandinavian countries than in Anglo-Saxon countries (figure 2). But these differences narrow when both direct spending and indirect spending (loss of revenue to governments resulting from the use of tax expenditures) are considered. Tax expenditure budgets are not easy to calculate and compare across countries.[9] Yet, when such calculations and comparisons are attempted, as by Adema (2001), it becomes evident that the Anglo-Saxon countries apparently did with tax expenditures what they did not do with direct public spending. Put differently, Anglo-Saxon countries have had a preference for tax expenditures that encourage private spending whereas the Scandinavian countries have had a preference for direct social spending.

Other OECD countries, including France, Germany, and Italy, have relied more evenly on all three measures. However, the differences in preferences within the group of industrial countries are beginning to shrink (see figure 2).

Given fiscal constraints and many competing purposes, developing countries generally have limited scope for direct social spending. The second measure, tax expenditures, is often also not available to many developing countries. This instrument works best when a country has a personal income tax with high rates that generates high tax revenue. However, when tax expenditures are defined also to include exonerations from value-added taxes and traditional tax incentives for enterprises, tax expenditures in some developing countries are relatively high. For example,

Box 1

MANAGING PERSONAL RISK: THE ROLE OF GOVERNMENTS AND MARKETS

In the period following World War II, when, for a variety of reasons, markets were not well developed in many countries, the concept of a "mixed economy," with a large role for the state, became popular. At the time it must have seemed natural for governments to take on many new responsibilities, including that of producing private goods like insurance products or private savings accounts.

Over the years markets have developed and increasingly removed the presumption that governments should be involved in the allocation of private savings, credit, and other products that people might want to buy for their protection and insurance against various personal risks.

As shown in the figure, if R represents the role of the state (identified here with the level of public social spending) and D represents the degree of development and the sophistication of markets, then it can be postulated that R is negative function of D and that governments can progressively reduce their social spending as D increases.

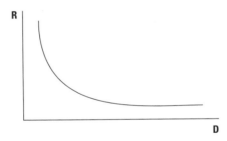

However, this does not imply that governments can leave everything to the market. Rather, government intervention through tax expenditures or regulation can provide important impetus to the development of markets offering products for individuals to protect or insure themselves against such risks as unemployment, ill-health, and old age—in most instances, perhaps, complementing rather than substituting for what the state offers in social security.

Source: Tanzi 2004.

Simonit (2002, p. 129) reports tax expenditures of about 3 percent of GDP for Argentina in 2001, 1.5 percent of GDP for Brazil in the same year, 3.8 percent of GDP for Chile in 1998, and a remarkable 9.2 percent of GDP for Colombia in 1999.[10]

Thus, most developing countries have been left with the alternative of the regulatory instrument. However, many developing countries have scope for improving their tax collection and increasing public social spending in the future. If their

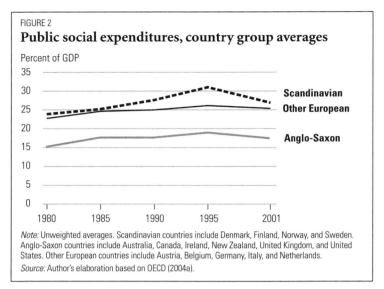

FIGURE 2
Public social expenditures, country group averages

Note: Unweighted averages. Scandinavian countries include Denmark, Finland, Norway, and Sweden. Anglo-Saxon countries include Australia, Canada, Ireland, New Zealand, United Kingdom, and United States. Other European countries include Austria, Belgium, Germany, Italy, and Netherlands.
Source: Author's elaboration based on OECD (2004a).

social programs were well targeted and made to reach beyond the urban middle class (whom the programs have often benefited in the past), these countries could achieve significant social progress through increased social spending and, as some already do, increased use of tax expenditures.

Some transition economies (like those in Central Europe) can potentially use all three measures and some (like those in central Asia) have more limited policy options because of revenue, public management, and market constraints (Barr 2002). Yet all transition economies have to address the challenge of redesigning their various instruments to respond to the risks of a market economy (such as unemployment) and to increased income inequality (Barr 2002).

This is a very broad-brush description. Determining which instruments— and in which combination—are best for which country requires a case-by-case assessment. Even more difficult is predicting what combination of instruments will be best in the future. Yet assuming that globalization continues, international economic competition and downward pressures on public spending, including social spending, may increase. At the same time countries face the challenge of aging populations and other problems that may, as discussed by Heller (in this volume), place new demands on government budgets. These pressures will also limit the availability of such measures as tax expenditures or redistributive regulations, although these will remain important for some time to come to leverage private spending on social protection. Industrial countries will perhaps be the first to feel this pressure, and regulatory authorities may increasingly use their powers to foster economic efficiency rather than to pursue redistributive goals.

Further—and bolder—policy reforms have to be sought if social protection is not to suffer in the longer run and weaken political support for economic openness.

CONCLUSION

The analysis in this chapter led to five main conclusions. First, many of the factors that have contributed to the growth in public spending over the past 150 years were not related to globalization. In fact, public spending has often increased when economies were relatively closed.

Second, in the more recent past the correlation of change in the rate of economic openness and change in the growth of public spending suggests that the faster a country's integration in the world economy, notably through trade, the slower its growth in public spending. Globalization in its current phase evidently constrains public spending. Possible reasons are growing economic competitiveness among countries and the weakening of countries' tax bases, stemming from the loss of earlier, trade-related tax handles and the emergence of "fiscal termites."

Third, since the 1980s public social spending shows signs of decline. In some developing countries overall public social spending is down; in others social transfers are affected more than other spending. In industrial countries various categories of public spending for social protection are stagnant or in decline, while pension-related expenditures continue to grow.

Fourth, spending on social protection cannot be equated with public spending. More governments are resorting to complementary measures such as tax expenditures, which should also be taken into account when assessing the overall fiscal effort. And more governments are making use of regulatory measures to encourage or enforce private spending on personal risk protection and insurance, so that when assessing the overall level of spending on these purposes, it is important to consider public and private expenditures.

Fifth, the extent to which governments can resort to the three types of measures depends on the country's policy management capacity and especially on the existence of a well functioning market for insurance and other social protection products.

In light of these findings, it might be useful for developing countries and their international development partners to explore ways to facilitate access to risk management and insurance markets, at least for their economically better-off population groups, and to target their public social spending programs on those who most need that support.

However, assuming that globalization continues, industrial countries may be the first to realize that public policy incentive measures such as social regulation and tax expenditures may also come under pressure from the forces of international economic competition. The time may be ripe to begin to think about the next round of policy reforms, to ensure that globalization delivers on its promise of development by all and for all.

Notes

1. For more than a quarter of a century before World War I and during part of the interwar period, the gold standard underpinned the system for international monetary relations. Currencies could be converted into gold, based on an internationally recognized rate of exchange. For more details on the operation of the gold standard before World War I and during the interwar years, until its demise in 1936, see Eichengreen (1995).

2. For further discussion see Keynes (1926).

3. See Musgrave (1969) for a discussion of tax handles and Tanzi (1973) for a description of the related general theory of tax structure change.

4. In his first 100 days of office, U.S. President Franklin D. Roosevelt proposed a sweeping program—known as the New Deal—to bring recovery to business and agriculture and relief to the unemployed and to those in danger of losing farms and homes (see www.whitehouse.gov/history/presidents/fr32.html).

5. Garrett (2001) did not find that changes in capital mobility affected government spending.

6. In terms of financial openness for instance, Honohan and Klingebiel (2003) discuss the fiscal implications of policies to mitigate a banking crisis. In addition, some estimates of the fiscal and output costs of currency and banking crises are discussed in IMF (1998). Krebs, Krishna, and Maloney (2004) study the effects of trade policy changes on income risk using data for Mexico.

7. For an assessment of the instrument of tax expenditures in such terms as efficiency, effectiveness, and equity, see Howard (2002).

8. For an assessment of the tool of social regulations, see May (2002).

9. Due to the methodological and conceptual difficulties involved in calculating tax expenditure budgets, the OECD abandoned publishing comparable data on this item for individual member countries. However, several industrial countries do prepare national tax expenditure budgets (see Swift, Brixi, and Valenduc 2004). And to the extent that tax expenditures become more widely used, including in developing countries, it would be important to develop proper procedures for calculating the costs of these measures to government (in forgone revenue). See, on this point, the recommendations in Brixi, Valenduc, and Swift (2004).

10. The definitional problems of these estimates must be kept in mind.

References

Abed, George. 2000. "Trade Liberalization and Tax Reform in the Southern Mediterranean Region." In Bernard M. Hoekman and Hana Khayr-El-Din, eds., *Trade Policy Developments in the Middle East and North Africa.* Washington, D.C.: World Bank.

Adema, Willem. 2001. "Net Social Expenditure." 2nd edition. Labour Market and Social Policy Occasional Paper 52. DEELSA/ELSA/WD(2001)5. Organisation for Economic Co-operation and Development, Directorate for Education, Employment, Labour and Social Affairs, Paris.

Adserà, Alícia, and Charles Boix. 2002. "Trade, Democracy, and the Size of the Public Sector: The Political Underpinnings of Openness." *International Organization* 56 (2): 229–62.

Alesina, Alberto, and Eliana La Ferrara. 2003. "Ethnic Diversity and Economic Performance." Discussion Paper 2028. Harvard University, Economics Department, Harvard Institute of Economic Research, Cambridge, Mass.

Alesina, Alberto, and Romain Wacziarg. 1997. *Openness, Country Size, and the Government.* NBER Working Paper 6042. Cambridge, Mass.: National Bureau of Economic Research.

Alesina, Alberto, Edward Glaeser, and Bruce Sacerdote. 2001. "Why Doesn't the U.S. Have a European Style Welfare State?" *Brookings Papers on Economic Activity* 2001 (2): 187–278.

Barr, Nicholas. 2002. "Welfare States in Central and Eastern Europe." In Ethan B. Kapstein and Branko Milanovic, eds., *When Markets Fail: Social Policy and Economic Reform.* New York: Russell Sage Foundation.

Baldwin, Richard E., and Philippe Martin. 1991. "Two Waves of Globalization: Superficial Similarity, Fundamental Differences." In Horst Siebert, ed., *Globalization and Labor.* Tubingen, Germany: Mohr Siedeck.

Brixi, Hana Polackova, Christian M. A. Valenduc, and Zhicheng Li Swift, eds. 2004. *Tax Expenditures—Shedding Light on Government Spending through the Tax System.* Washington, D.C.: World Bank.

Cameron, David. 1978. "The Expansion of the Public Economy: A Comparative Analysis." *American Political Science Review* 72 (4): 1243–61.

Casey, Bernard, Howard Oxley, Edward Whitehouse, Pablo Antolin, Romain Duval, and Willi Leibfritz. 2003. "Policies for an Ageing Society: Recent Measures and Areas for Further Reform." Economics Department Working Paper 369. Organisation for Economic Co-operation and Development, Paris.

CEPAL (Comisión Económica para América Latina y el Caribe). 2002. *Globalizacion y Desarrollo.* Santiago.

Coatsworth, John H., and Jeffrey G. Williamson. 2004. "The Roots of Latin American Protectionism: Looking before the Great Depression." In Antoni Estevadeordal, Dani Rodrik, Alan M. Taylor, and Andres Velasco, eds., *Integrating the Americas: FTAA and Beyond.* Cambridge Mass.: Harvard University Press.

De Ferranti, David, Guillermo Perry, Indermit S. Gill, and Luis Serven. 2000. *Securing Our Future in a Global Economy.* Washington, D.C.: World Bank.

De Jouvenel, Bertrand. 1952. *The Ethics of Redistribution.* Cambridge: Cambridge University Press.

Dion, Michelle. 2004. "Globalization, Political Institutions, and Social Spending Change in Middle Income Countries, 1980–1999." Paper prepared for the 2004 Annual Meeting of the American Political Science Association Meeting, September 1–5, Chicago, Ill.

Eichengreen, Barry. 1995. *Golden Fetters: The Gold Standard and the Great Depression.* New York: Oxford University Press.

Galbraith, John Kenneth. 1958. *The Affluent Society.* Boston, Mass.: Houghton Mifflin.

Garrett, Geoffrey. 2001. "Globalization and Government Spending around the World." *Studies in Comparative International Development* 35 (4): 3–29.

Garrett, Geoffrey, and David Nickerson. 2001. "Globalization, Democratization, and Government Spending in Middle Income Countries." Working Paper. Yale University, New Haven, Conn. [www.international.ucla.edu/profile/ggarrett/papers.asp].

Holzmann, Robert, and Richard Hinz. 2005. *Old-Age Income Support in the Twenty-First Century: An International Perspective on Pension Systems and Reform.* Washington, D.C.: World Bank. [http://www1.worldbank.org/sp/incomesupport.asp].

Honohan, Patrick, and Daniela Klingebiel. 2003. "The Fiscal Implications of an Accommodating Approach to Banking Crises." *Journal of Banking and Finance* 28 (8): 1539–60.

Howard, Christopher. 2002. "Tax Expenditures." In Lester M. Salamon, ed., *The Tools of Government: A Guide to the New Governance.* New York: Oxford University Press.

ILO (International Labour Organization). 2000. "Public Social Security Expenditure." [www.ilo.org/public/english/protection/socsec/publ/css/table14.htm].

IMF (International Monetary Fund). Various years. *International Financial Statistics.* Washington, D.C.

———. 1998. *World Economic Outlook. May 1998.* Washington, D.C.

Kaufman, Robert R., and Alex Segura-Ubiergo. 2000. "Globalization, Domestic Politics, and Welfare Spending in Latin America: A Time-Series Cross-Section Analysis, 1973–1997." Working paper. Columbia University, Institute for Latin American Studies, New York.

Keynes, John Maynard. 1926. *The End of Laissez-Faire.* London: Hogarth Press.

Khattry, Barsha, and J. Mohan Rao. 2002. "Fiscal Faux Pas?: An Analysis of the Revenue Implications of Trade Liberalization." *World Development* 30 (8): 1431–44.

Krebs, Tom, Pravin Krishna, and William Maloney. 2004. "Trade Policy, Income Risks, and Welfare." Brown University, Department of Economics, Providence, R.I. [www.brown.edu/Departments/Economics/Papers/2004/2004-09_paper.pdf].

Lindert, Peter H. 2002. "What Drives Social Spending? 1780 to 2020." In Ethan B. Kapstein and Branko Milanovic, eds., *When Markets Fail: Social Policy and Economic Reform.* New York: Russell Sage Foundation.

————. 2004. *Growing Public. Vol 1 and 2.* Cambridge: Cambridge University Press.

Maddison, Angus. 1997. "Economic Policy and Performance in Capitalist Europe." In Louis Emmerig, ed., *Economic and Social Development into the XXI Century.* Washington, D.C.: Inter-American Development Bank.

May, Peter. 2002. "Social Regulation." In Lester M. Salamon, ed., *The Tools of Government: A Guide to the New Governance.* New York: Oxford University Press.

Musgrave, Richard. 1969. *Fiscal Systems.* New Haven, Conn.: Yale University Press.

OECD (Organisation for Economic Co-operation and Development). Various years. *Economic Outlook.* Paris.

————. 2004a. "Total Public Social Expenditure (1980–2001) by Main Category, as a Percentage of GDP." Social Expenditure database (SOCX), 1980–2001. [www.oecd.org/dataoecd/56/37/31613113.xls].

————. 2004b. *OECD Economic Outlook.* Volume 2004/2, number 76. Paris.

Rodrik, Dani. 1998. "Why Do More Open Economies Have Bigger Government?" *Journal of Political Economy* 106 (5): 997–1032.

Rudra, Nita. 2002. "Globalization and the Decline of the Welfare State in Less-Developed Countries." *International Organization* 56 (2): 411–45.

————. 2004. "Openness, Welfare Spending, and Inequality in the Developing World." *International Studies Quarterly* 48 (3): 683–709.

Ruggie, John Gerard. 1982. "International Regimes, Transactions, and Change: Embedded Liberalism in the Postwar Economic Order." *International Organization* 36 (2): 379–415.

Schulze, Günther G., and Heinrich W. Ursprung. 1999. "Globalisation of the Economy and the Nation State." *World Economy* 22 (3): 295–352.

Simonit, Silvia. 2002. "Los gastos tributarios y las renuncias tributarias en América Latina." [Tax Expenditures and Tax Surrenders in Latin America]. In Economic Commission for Latin America and the Caribbean, *Compendio de documentos XIV Seminario de política fiscal* [Collected Documents of the XIV Fiscal Policy Seminar]. Santiago de Chile.

Swift, Zhicheng Li, Hana Polackova Brixi, and Christian Valenduc. 2004. "Tax Expenditures: General Concept, Measurement, and Overview of Country Practices." In Hana Polackova Brixi, Christian M. A. Valenduc, and Zhicheng Li Swift, eds., *Tax Expenditures—Shedding Light on Government Spending through the Tax System.* Washington, D.C.: World Bank.

Tanzi, Vito. 1973. "The Theory of Tax Structure Change during Economic Development: A Critical Survey." *Rivista di Diritto Finanziario e Scienza delle Finanze* (1): 199.

————. 1998. "Government Role and the Efficiency of Policy Instruments." In Peter Birch Sorensen, ed., *Public Finance in a Changing World.* London: MacMillan Press Ltd.

————. 2001. "Globalization, Technological Development, and the Work of Fiscal Termites." *Brooklyn Journal of International Law* 26 (4): 1261–84.

————. 2002. "Globalization and the Future of Social Protection." *Scottish Journal of Political Economy* 49 (1): 116–27.

————. 2003. "Globalization and the Need for Fiscal Reform in Developing Countries." Revised version of a paper presented at the International Conference on Globalization and Economic Growth, October 8–9, Mexico City.

————. 2004. "A Lower Tax Future? The Economic Role of the State in the 21st Century." Politeia Policy Series 44. Cambridge, UK: Politeia.

Tanzi, Vito, and Ludger Schuknecht. 2000. *Public Spending in the 20th Century: A Global Perspective.* Cambridge: Cambridge University Press.

UNRISD (United Nations Research Institute for Social Development). 2000. *Visible Hands: Taking Responsibility for Social Development.* Geneva.

Van den Ende, Leo, Amir Haberham, and Kees den Boogert. 2004. "Tax Expenditure in the Netherlands." In Hana Polackova Brixi, Christian M. A. Valenduc, and Zhicheng Li Swift, eds., *Tax Expenditures—Shedding Light on Government Spending through the Tax System.* Washington, D.C.: World Bank.

World Bank. 2004. *World Development Indicators 2004.* Washington, D.C.

Zee, Howell H. 1996. "Empirics of Crosscountry Tax Revenue Comparisons." *World Development* 24 (10): 1659–71.

INTERNALIZING CROSS-BORDER SPILLOVERS

POLICY OPTIONS FOR ADDRESSING LONG-TERM FISCAL CHALLENGES

PETER S. HELLER

Many countries are confronting a slowly gathering fiscal storm. For some the consequences are years, possibly decades away. For others the fiscal threats are much closer. Some of the threats reflect structural trends arising from a country's demographics, sociology, location, or economic profile. Others reflect the way in which a country's policies or economic situation is influenced by its interdependence with the world economy or by the forces of globalization. But the concatenation of the underlying structural trends already apparent today suggests that policymakers must confront and anticipate these long-term challenges. How they do so will depend on the country, the preferences and capacities of its people and institutions, its policy commitments, and the challenges it faces.

This chapter surveys some of these long-term challenges and examines how policymakers could begin to address their fiscal implications. Its main message is that governments have an important domestic responsibility to take account of long-term risks by considering both the current aggregative fiscal policy stance and the specifics of policy and transfer programs. Governments also need to leave adequate fiscal leeway to deal with predictable and unpredictable developments over the next several decades.

These steps are important preconditions for exploring mutually beneficial cooperation at the international level. To the extent that these challenges are shared, governments need to work together internationally to understand how these common problems will influence the economic context and the assumptions on which they make decisions. Especially when countries' needs are complementary, there is scope for cooperation—both behind national borders through concerted domestic action and at the international level through regional and multilateral efforts—to find common solutions and avoid undesirable cross-border spillover effects.

This chapter introduces some of the principal transformative issues of the next several decades, examining two with global significance: population aging and climate change. It outlines possible policy responses and the likely fiscal implications and considers how governments can better take account of long-term issues in their fiscal policymaking through changes in analytic methods. It examines some policy reforms that address both the aggregate fiscal situation and the content of specific government policies viewed from a long-term perspective, and proposes several concrete steps in response to political economy considerations. The chapter then considers how governments, through strengthened multilateral policy coordination, can develop mutually beneficial solutions to many long-term fiscal challenges.

PRINCIPAL TRANSFORMATIVE ISSUES OF THE TWENTY-FIRST CENTURY

Several social, economic, and environmental developments can be expected over the next few decades. They include the aging populations in many countries; outbreaks of diseases, both new and resurgent; climate change; natural resource scarcities, including increasing limits on the world's oil reserves; "technology revolutions" that create bursts of productivity growth but also pose new risks; greater tax competition; and various cultural and political challenges, including international terrorism and tensions and conflicts associated with globalization. Many of these trends are already well under way and likely to affect many countries in the same rough time frame (appendix box A.1 provides a more detailed overview of these trends). Most are likely to have significant structural economic effects across industrial and developing countries. Some may have substantial global effects. Many will have significant fiscal implications, even if their magnitude is uncertain. Besides these identifiable, if not wholly predictable, developments, other less foreseeable disruptive trends and events are likely to emerge, as they have throughout history. Governments, as responsible stewards, need to be prepared for both kinds of challenges.

To get a clearer sense of the intergenerational and international dimensions of these trends and their potentially significant fiscal ramifications over the long horizon, two issues are examined in more detail—population aging and the possible effects of climate change.

Population aging
Perhaps the most important emerging long-term issue that governments face is also the most predictable: the aging of populations, particularly in industrial countries, reflecting rising life expectancies and sharp declines in fertility (the demographic effects of which are illustrated in figure 1). Emerging market and developing countries will experience a comparable aging phenomenon, albeit with a lag of about a decade or so during which some will initially see a substantial increase in their productive labor force. For many developing countries, however, the more immediate demographic challenge will be a growing young and working-age population urgently seeking jobs (see figure 1). If those jobs are lacking, the result would be high unemployment rates that could provoke social and

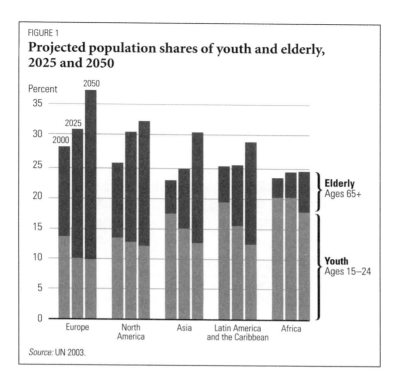

FIGURE 1

Projected population shares of youth and elderly, 2025 and 2050

Source: UN 2003.

political instability, which could easily spill across borders. Pressures for migration to the aging, more developed areas of the world will be intense. The challenge is whether these pressures can be productive for both source and receiving countries, or whether they lead to destabilizing conflict and brain drain.

Graying populations will have their most profound and immediate implications for government budgets in most industrial countries. Social insurance programs oriented to the elderly, including guaranteed public pensions, health care (either insured or directly provided by the state), and long-term nursing care already command a large share of government budgets. That share will grow in the next few decades—and it will grow even faster if escalating medical costs are not restrained. A study of 12 industrial countries estimates that the cost of public benefits for the elderly could double on average, from about 12 percent to 24 percent of gross domestic product (GDP) between 2000 and 2040 (Jackson and Howe 2003) (figure 2).

The effects of aging populations in the industrial countries will be felt worldwide. The simultaneous graying of countries that now account for a substantial share of the world's output can be expected to put pressure on global interest rates: downward at first, as relatively prosperous middle-age workers increase their retirement savings, and then upward, as they consume their accumulated savings in retirement. These trends may make it harder for these workers to save enough

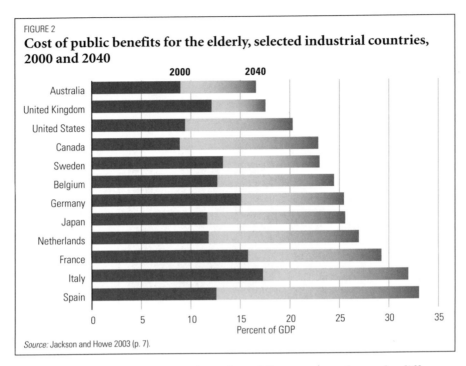

FIGURE 2

Cost of public benefits for the elderly, selected industrial countries, 2000 and 2040

Source: Jackson and Howe 2003 (p. 7).

for retirement, leading to demands on the public purse to make up the difference. Depending on how countries respond, these trends could affect global capital markets, with impacts on industrial and developing countries alike.

Climate change

While there is greater uncertainty about the extent of future climate change and its physical and economic effects than there is about population aging, there is little scientific doubt that climate change will occur. Greenhouse gases are projected to raise average global temperatures by 1.4–5.8 degrees Celsius over this century (IPCC 2001b, p. 8). Warming of this magnitude will have substantial effects on the world's natural resources, primarily its arable land area and biodiversity.

Other impacts will arise from the greater frequency and severity of hurricanes and other extreme weather events, which are projected to result in substantial economic losses and pressure on insurance systems (figure 3). In the last 50 years, global economic losses due to extreme weather events have increased tenfold, from an average of $4 billion a year in the 1950s to roughly $40 billion a year in the 1990s. The insured portion of those losses increased from negligible levels to about $9.2 billion a year. In view of changing risk patterns the global insurance industry will need to reevaluate what risks it can realistically cover and what premiums it will need to charge. The role of government, as the ultimate reinsurer, will likely become the subject of pressing debate.

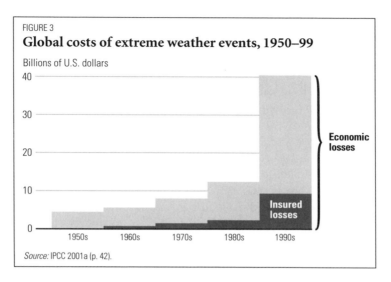

FIGURE 3
Global costs of extreme weather events, 1950–99

Billions of U.S. dollars

Source: IPCC 2001a (p. 42).

What are the potential fiscal implications of climate change? First, the rate of change will likely be gradual, allowing countries to adapt if they act soon. Second, like population aging, climate change will affect countries differently. Some, such as the United States and Canada, may even benefit in net terms. However, developing countries will suffer disproportionately because they tend to be located in the tropics and along the equator, where climate change is likely to do the most damage. Furthermore, their economies depend heavily on agriculture and their large cities lie mostly in coastal areas, which are vulnerable to rising sea levels, flooding, and other effects of extreme weather events. One estimate suggests that when the concentration of carbon dioxide in the atmosphere reaches twice the pre-industrial level—now projected to occur sometime in the second half of the twenty-first century—the aggregate global costs will be significant, equaling $269.5 billion (in 1998 dollars), with $180.4 billion falling on Organisation for Economic Co-operation and Development (OECD) countries and $89.1 billion on non-OECD countries. This suggests costs of about 1.3 percent of OECD countries' gross national product (GNP), and about 1.6 percent of non-OECD countries' combined GNP (Frankhauser 1995, p. 55, tables 3.15 and 3.16).

Much of the worldwide burden of climate change will fall on the private sector. But governments are also likely to bear some costs, including those of adapting public infrastructure, preventing and dealing with the spread of tropical diseases, conducting agricultural research, resettling populations from low-lying areas, and providing emergency assistance when extreme weather events or other catastrophes occur.

Meanwhile, both governments and private firms face the costs of preventing further climate change by taking actions to stabilize or reduce greenhouse gas concentrations. Reducing greenhouse gases by an average of 5 percent below 1990 levels by 2008–12, as called for by the Kyoto Protocol, is expected to cost about $125 billion a year (IPCC 2001b, p. 25).[1] And even with the Kyoto Protocol in force, the world still faces the challenge of how to induce developing countries— particularly some of the large, faster growing emerging market countries, notably India and China—to invest in production and consumption technologies that foster reduced greenhouse gas emissions.

THE WAY FORWARD

There are no silver bullets for resolving the long-run challenges. Policymakers not only confront large prospective aggregate deficits. They must also deal with con- siderable uncertainty about the deficit size, a multiplicity of underlying factors, and political institutions prone to myopia. And they must do so in a global mar- ket environment, where their policy decisions are affected by the actions of other countries. A multipronged strategy is thus required.

The broad task will include at least four critical steps, three at the national level and one requiring international cooperation. The first step is to place bud- get analysis and decisionmaking within a long-term perspective. The second is to identify fiscal policy areas for concrete domestic actions. The third responds to political economy considerations by developing sound national institutional processes for framing budget policy decisions that address long-term concerns and by building on independent or international surveillance functions. The fourth focuses on possible cooperation with other countries, as appropriate and justified by clear national benefits.

Taking a long-term analytical perspective
Before the impact of new developments on the horizon can be taken into account, a country needs to determine whether the budget is on a sustainable path. Such assessments judge whether the current primary fiscal balance (the balance— surplus or deficit—exclusive of interest payments), if maintained, would increase the ratio of public debt to GDP. Countries also need to broaden their analysis to include the implicit debt arising from long-term policy commitments that can be identified but does not yet appear on a government's books. For example, the con- tributions that workers make to a public pension program or medical insurance that entitle them to receive benefits at retirement are recorded now as current gov- ernment revenue on its income statement, but the corresponding obligations to provide future benefits are not shown as a liability on a government's balance sheet.

The latitude that a government has to vary the scope of these obligations needs to be entered into the analysis. Obvious uncertainties make estimating implicit obligations an unwieldy exercise, but without some accounting for them, the government's fiscal picture is dangerously incomplete and misleading. Account also needs to be taken of potential liabilities—areas where a government

---

Box 1

EXAMPLES OF EXTENDED FISCAL ACCOUNTING PRACTICES

Several industrial countries practice various forms of long-term fiscal accounting. Among them:

The *United Kingdom's "Code for Fiscal Sustainability"* requires the government to publish illustrative long-term projections covering a period of at least 10 years. In recent years it has published 30-year projections.

New Zealand's "Fiscal Responsibility Act" mandates that the government take long-term factors into consideration in its annual Fiscal Strategy Report. Explicit consideration is given to projections of at least 10 years, to demonstrate that the overall budget framework is consistent with long-term policy objectives.

Australia's "Charter of Budget Honesty" requires the government to present a medium-term fiscal strategy with each budget. Also required is a longer term intergenerational report that evaluates the long-term sustainability of current government policies over the 40 years following the release of the report. This evaluation is also intended to take account of the financial implications of demographic changes.

The *United States' 75-year "Analytical Perspectives,"* although not explicitly required by law, includes the president's budget projections in the stewardship section of the volume. These projections assume continuation of current policies as well as a discussion of the government's balance sheet, including some liabilities not yet included in the primary budget data.

Source: United Kingdom, Her Majesty's Treasury 2000, 2001; New Zealand Treasury 1995, 2001; Australia Treasury 2002; U.S. GAO 2003 (p. 28).

---

has no obligations today but may be compelled to take them on in the future. For example, contingent liabilities may arise from government guarantees of state enterprise debt or of the deposit insurance system. More problematic are contingencies for which the government has no explicit commitment but on which it may be expected to intervene nonetheless. Identifying these requires an honest and comprehensive assessment of the government's role in society (without creating too much of a moral hazard).

Such extended fiscal accounting can be structured as a balance sheet summarizing the government's assets and liabilities, including accrued and contingent liabilities, discounted to the present. Or it can be accomplished through long-term projections. Many governments (and the International Monetary Fund) already construct fiscal projections for the medium term. Several industrial countries make 10–30 year (if not longer) projections of their fiscal balance, at least for certain parts of the budget such as the major social insurance schemes. (See box 1 for examples.)

Such projections are valuable despite the many uncertainties. They can inform policymakers of the resources available for public investment and of the implied fiscal leeway for new policy initiatives or contingencies. Fiscal gap indicators can be used to estimate the amount of fiscal adjustment needed to restore sustainability and to calculate a revised time path indicating whether the adjustment will cause debt to fall or assets to accumulate.

The use of long-term forecasts could be extended in several ways. The most desirable extension would be stochastic estimates that yield a sense of how wide the range of likely error is around a given outcome. Assessments are also needed of the scope for change in the structure of a country's budget, to indicate how much give there may be in various areas of the budget. For understanding the international dimensions of structural change, a multiregional general equilibrium approach (as, for example, used by Conceição and Mendoza for their analysis of trade in this volume) to long-term forecasting and policy analysis might be especially valuable, given that many industrial and emerging market economies are facing similar long-term developments. This approach could also be used to measure the impact of convergent policy approaches and behavioral patterns— as societies respond in their savings and investment decisions—on world interest rates and other global macroeconomic variables.

Changing government programs to promote fiscal sustainability

Domestically, governments can enhance fiscal sustainability in two ways. They can explore aggregative approaches that focus on the level of the budget as a whole, responding to conjunctural fiscal pressures by increasing taxes or reducing other expenditures, or alternatively by freeing budgetary room through fiscal consolidation that reduces public debt (and thus the associated interest costs) or builds up assets (prefunding). And they can take specific policy reforms to reduce future spending commitments at the program level.

Higher taxes or prefunding. Some governments are already applying aggregative approaches. Denmark has set targets through 2010 for the budget balance and growth in public consumption (Denmark, Ministry of Finance 2003). Sweden's multiyear budget framework explicitly includes binding ceilings on expenditures for three years on a rolling basis (Sweden, Ministry of Finance 2003). Over time, balanced budgets or surpluses can reduce public debt, creating room to accommodate future spending commitments. The government may even be able to retire its debt and accumulate assets, in effect prefunding future outlays. These approaches often rely on fiscal rules (discussed later) that require governments to stay within preset fiscal bounds.

A rules-based aggregative approach can be an effective strategy, but it has its limitations. Government actions to reduce the overall deficit or debt can induce reactions by households and businesses that can offset the intended boost in national saving. Taxpayers may respond to increased government saving by reducing their own saving in the belief that taxes will be lower in the future. If an aggregative approach results in regular budget surpluses, political pressures may build to spend the growing assets. A large fiscal nest egg may also reduce the will of governments to reform policies and programs in ways that would support long-term fiscal health.

An aggregative approach may require an increased tax burden that is inefficient or politically insupportable. For some industrial countries (notably the United States), a larger tax burden might be a reasonable solution, since tax shares are notably lower than in the past and lower than those in many other industrial countries (IMF 2003a). For many European countries, however, where the ratio of total taxes to GDP is higher, there may be less room for raising the tax ratio without undermining incentives to work or inducing growth in the shadow economy to avoid taxation.

Spending cutbacks may also be hard to sustain beyond a certain point. Governments may have little room to trim their outlays on public goods outside of defense—doing so might worsen existing biases against physical investment. While subsidies could be a good candidate for further rationalization in some countries, in most they are already quite a small share of total spending. More broadly, an aggregative approach that relies on spending cuts may sharply reduce a government's room to maneuver in the economy, leaving the government as no more than a vehicle for redistributing income. There would thus be scant remaining capacity to use the budget for macroeconomic stabilization, to provide public goods, to address the challenges of globalization, or to formulate initiatives in response to new risks and external shocks.

Various institutional mechanisms can support an aggregative approach in addition to fiscal rules. Some countries have relied on earmarking—placing funds in a "lockbox"—to forestall attempts to raid the funds for current spending.[2] An example is the New Zealand Superannuation Fund, which is intended to build up a pool of assets separate from the gross debt target of the government to prefund part of the public pension scheme. The fund is not expected to be drawn on for at least 20 years.[3] Norway's Government Petroleum Fund, established in 1990, invests oil and gas royalties in external financial assets to accumulate resources to finance in part the large anticipated outlays associated with an aging population and to prevent the country's currency from appreciating.[4]

Reform of specific policies and programs. Whereas the aggregative approach to achieving long-term fiscal sustainability in essence raises the present fiscal balance more or less directly, reform of specific policies and programs indirectly raises the future fiscal balance by reducing the nature and extent of future commitments or increasing future revenues. Reforms may reduce explicit commitments to future beneficiaries or may specify a previously vague commitment at a lower level than might otherwise have prevailed. Some broad categories of policy reforms can be identified.

First, the aggregate financing parameters of a specific program can be adjusted without altering the program's benefit structure. For example, the contribution rate for a public pension program might be raised. Or discrete adjustments can be made to the benefit parameters without any change in contribution rates. Benefits could accrue more slowly, they could be taxed or tax rates could be raised, minimum benefit levels could be lowered, copayments and deductibles on government health insurance could be raised, or the way future benefits are determined could be changed, for example, by altering the benefit indexation formula or tying the age of eligibility to changes in life expectancy. Both financing and benefit parameters can be subject to mandatory periodic review of their financial sustainability.

Reforms can also change the quality or quantity of benefits or reduce their coverage. In medical insurance programs, for example, the quality of services may be reduced, coverage of some services may be dropped, or rationing or longer queues for service may be allowed. Financial incentives could make households more proactive about their health through greater prevention efforts (such as diet and exercise) or their demands for more competitive alternatives for medical services and pharmaceuticals.

Reforms may totally revamp a program or substitute a new one. Examples are shifting a medical insurance program's financing from fee for service to some form of managed care or medical savings account and replacing a public pay as you go, defined benefit pension system with a private, funded, defined contribution system.[5]

Policy reform may also involve regulations requiring preventive actions: curbs on smoking might lower the government's future health care spending; tighter restrictions on building in low-lying coastal areas may lower future fiscal costs of responding to climate change. Some reforms might involve increased spending today to avoid larger spending tomorrow. For example, funding research on technologies to reduce greenhouse gas emissions or facilitate capture and storage of carbon dioxide could lower the future cost of addressing the effects of climate change.

Governments may also revisit specific policy commitments as risks change and as new risks emerge, such as new diseases, climate change, terrorism, and dangers accompanying new technologies (such as computer viruses). Globalization is likely to intensify these risks and introduce new ones. The private insurance industry will cover some of these risks, but it may set limits on that coverage. Where important risks go uncovered, government may need to provide some minimal coverage or some support for private insurers. It may need to act as a financial backstop for catastrophic situations through reinsurance, or it may require private insurers to provide coverage and then share part of the burden.

And it can promote the development of insurance markets through more effective regulation and dissemination of information to consumers.[6]

In all these situations moral hazard is a consideration. If the perception becomes widespread that the government will step in to cover losses, that might weaken the incentive to obtain coverage in the market and induce more risky behavior. Insurers might see the government's potential intervention as an opportunity to shift the burden of a costly area of coverage. Part of the answer to moral hazard is to communicate clearly to the public what government will not cover.

The government can reduce its exposure to risk through regulation and infrastructure investment. Urban planning standards, building codes, and land-use restrictions can be expanded to address risks on the horizon, such as the effects of a rising sea level caused by climate change. Through infrastructure investment, government can facilitate adaptation or reduce the fiscal risks associated with extreme weather events. Additional outlays on research, for example, into ways of adapting to climate change, may be necessary to support the policy response to some risks, especially the less predictable ones.

Responding to political economy considerations by improving the budget process

The political and economic challenges of such program changes, especially reductions in a government's potential future expenditure commitments, should not be underestimated. Even modest changes can have profound distributional consequences, within or across generations, that will generate political resistance. Those who will be affected by the changes should be told that the changes are coming and have sufficient time to adapt. When a narrower targeting of benefits is accomplished through means testing, concerns about moral hazard and allocative efficiency inevitably arise. Also, scaling back in one area, such as public pensions, may increase the burden of commitments in another, such as assistance for the poor. Finally, some reforms, such as indexing the minimum age for pension benefits to life expectancy, shift risk from the government to the benefit recipient. Recipients must be informed well in advance of the increased risk.

Addressing long-term fiscal challenges thus also needs to take account of the political economy issues that underpin policymaking. As Jones discusses (in this volume), politicians tend to be short-term oriented and focused on "their" country (or even "their" local constituency). Encouraging them to adopt a broader (sometimes cross-border) and longer term perspective is an enormous challenge.

The best way to begin is probably with important reforms to the budgetary process that introduce more broad-based consideration of long-term issues. Four main elements are involved: providing transparent and comprehensive information, establishing an independent mechanism for assessing the fiscal dimensions of long-term trends, establishing a mechanism for public debate on the central long-term questions, and ensuring that the interests of future generations are adequately considered.

Transparent and comprehensive information. Integrating the long term into the annual budget process is not a simple matter of extending detailed budget projections from the current 3–5 years to 10 years or more. That would only lend a false accuracy to the projections. Rather, the objective should be to provide more information more transparently and to highlight how current policy decisions influence the long-term fiscal position, and vice versa. The key question is what types of information and assessments to provide.

Essential elements are an assessment of whether fiscal policy under the present budgetary regime is sustainable over at least the next 25–40 years and a projection of what surpluses or deficits are likely to emerge at different periods during that time frame. Long-term assessments should be sufficiently disaggregated to clarify how much each major program contributes to the projected growth of total spending, with a range of scenarios under alternative assumptions. The long-term implications of any new budget initiative should be quantified, including the likely time path of expenditure.

The accounting framework adopted in the budget should adhere to the transparency codes of the International Monetary Fund (IMF) and the OECD, especially with respect to accrual accounting for explicit liabilities.[7] The fiscal consequences of fiscal commitments should be explicitly disclosed. Implicit liabilities, contingent liabilities, and guarantees should probably be included as memorandum items, with or without quantitative estimates (Brixi and Mody 2002).

Key uncertainties in the budget projections and the principal downside risks to fiscal sustainability should be reported, along with any strategies for attenuating those risks or reducing the degree of uncertainty about them. The costs associated with realization of any contingent liabilities should be reported, as well as any contingency provisions or reserves against those liabilities.

Independent and competent assessments. Having an independent body that provides its own forecasts and assessments of the long-term fiscal situation can help to maintain public confidence by providing an independent perspective on government budgeting. This entity could be located within the government but administratively separated from the executive function, or it could be a private or quasi-public institution. Unlike a corporate auditor, an independent budget review agency should also stimulate public debate on key budget issues, including long-term issues, and call attention to (if the executive does not) the major risks to the budget and their implications.

There is also an important place for international surveillance of countries' long-term budget positions, not least because fiscal recklessness in one country can affect neighbors and trading partners and even the global economy. The large private credit rating agencies (such as Moody's, Standard & Poor's, and Fitch Ratings) perform this function to some extent since their sovereign risk assessments take fiscal sustainability issues into account. The IMF, through its annual surveillance discussions with its member countries, plays the lead role in international fiscal surveillance.[8] International surveillance by market actors or international agencies could also facilitate more broad-based transparency.

Mechanism for public debate on long-term issues. For transparency to contribute to sound policymaking, governments need to foster public awareness and debate on the key long-term issues confronting public decisionmakers. In many countries the legislature is the natural forum for ventilating the key long-term issues raised by the executive's budget proposals. If such debate does not arise spontaneously, a mechanism should be introduced in the budget process that fosters debate. Some countries might want to establish an independent fiscal commission, charged with highlighting key long-term fiscal issues for the electorate before each national election.

Regardless of the institutional approach taken, what is fundamental is that there be a mechanism for informing the electorate of the principal long-term risks confronting the country and their potential consequences, including the costs of failing to address them. The same mechanism could be used to examine cross-border policy implications and to explore cooperative solutions, as appropriate.

Safeguarding the interests of future generations. Even with transparent information, an independent perspective, and adequate public debate, the problem remains that political leaders have an incentive to underestimate—and often the ability to circumvent—any fiscal sustainability concerns. Possible solutions include constitutionally established ceilings or targets for the allowable tax burden or the debt to GDP ratio or an independent fiscal agency with constitutional authority to force adjustments in aggregate expenditure or in the overall tax bill.

Fiscal rules, which can foster discipline supportive of aggregative fiscal policies that contribute to addressing long-term fiscal disequilibria, are another possible solution (box 2). Fiscal rules have been written into national fiscal responsibility laws. They are also a requirement of some economic and monetary unions.

Experience suggests some clear prerequisites for the use of fiscal rules. The rules must be realistic in their expectations for tax burdens and expenditure provision over the long term. They must be comprehensive, so that, for example, central government surpluses are not offset by deficits elsewhere in the public sector. And they must be based on an accrual concept that takes full account of policy reforms with longer term financial implications.

Engaging in international cooperation to foster national fiscal sustainability

In addition to national policy changes that countries undertake individually, there are international cooperative efforts that can ease looming fiscal burdens and

---

Box 2

EXAMPLES OF FISCAL RULES

The *EU Stability and Growth Pact* calls on member countries to achieve balanced budgets or surpluses over the medium term, with a maximum allowable overall deficit of 3 percent in any given year. Over time, adherence to this rule would lead to the steady diminution of net public debt to GDP ratios (assuming a comprehensive measurement of public sector fiscal operations), thus creating additional budgetary room for social insurance expenditures associated with a rising old-age dependency ratio (ratio of the elderly to the working age population).

The *Golden Rule of the United Kingdom* requires that current government consumption be at least matched, if not exceeded, by current revenue. It seeks to achieve intergenerational fairness by requiring each generation to leave an unchanged level of resources to the next generation.

Source: EU 2005; United Kingdom Office for National Statistics 2002.

---

increase the prospects of success for all. Other chapters in this volume discuss the possibilities for cooperation—both behind national borders through concerted domestic action and internationally through regional and multilateral efforts. This chapter offers a few examples.

One important opportunity for cooperation arises from differences in the future demographics of the world's industrial and developing countries. Industrial countries need to increase their saving to prepare for the retirement of their aging baby boomers, but if they channel savings into investments only within that same group of countries, interest rates could fall, making the prefunding of retirement benefits all the harder. But if the increased retirement saving were channeled into investments in the rest of the world, this could improve prospects for all.

The rub is to match those savings with productive investments. Wasteful investments were behind the East Asian financial crisis and its aftershocks elsewhere, and investors in industrial countries have been cautious about reentering the arena. Merely pipelining money from industrial to developing countries does not guarantee its productive absorption. Much remains to be done to build the capacity of emerging markets and developing countries to absorb large inflows of foreign capital.

A key step is to reform and strengthen financial institutions and capital markets in these countries so that incoming capital is allocated to worthwhile projects. Corporate governance reform, strengthened accounting practices, and greater transparency are all needed. There is great scope for international cooperation to make this process work better. The danger is that governments on both sides may be too overwhelmed by their own demographic and other fiscal challenges to cooperate effectively. Countries can enhance their potential for exploring and undertaking mutually beneficial cooperation by pursuing the important changes at the national level discussed above—taking a long-term analytical perspective and changing programs to promote fiscal sustainability.

Similarly urgent is the need to develop an international framework for "productive" migration. Aging industrial countries can benefit from immigration from the overpopulated, young countries of the world, which can provide labor for many activities through actual and virtual migration. Virtual migration includes different forms of outsourcing and the direct provision of services within developing countries (medical treatment in the more advanced centers of emerging and developing countries, for example). While migration from developing to industrial countries cannot solve the fiscal problems of rising elderly dependency rates, it can be an important part of the solution. Migration is also an important source of remittances to the developing world. The problems of migration also need to be considered, from brain drain, which reduces the growth potential of developing countries, to the social challenges of assimilation into industrial countries (particularly given underlying cultural differences). The pressures for immigration will be great—the question is whether immigration can occur in a coordinated, rational way or whether it will lead to undesirable unplanned outcomes.

Climate change is another area that would benefit from international cooperation. Any international effort aimed at controlling greenhouse gas emissions will have little impact if the most rapidly developing countries are excluded. But these countries are unlikely to be willing or able to contribute to this effort without significant financial assistance from industrial countries. A global bargain that distributes the burden fairly between industrial and developing countries would benefit both. Cooperative efforts on research on climate change are also needed, and the results need to be widely shared if developing countries are to participate effectively in adaptation and mitigation efforts. In addition, the creation of new markets for emissions trading (see the chapter by Sandor in this volume) would contribute to a more efficient global response to climate change, and success will hinge crucially on cooperative efforts.

Finally, it is hard to imagine that the smoldering geopolitical tensions arising from the huge international disparities in income and power, from natural resource scarcities and environmental concerns, and, not least, from religious differences and strained ethnic relations can be resolved by any means other than international cooperation. Resolution of these tensions would go far toward easing the burdens on government budgets and reducing uncertainties worldwide. Some of the proposed solutions, such as increased aid transfers from industrial to developing countries, would be costly to budgets as well, but the future dividends could be enormous.

CONCLUSION

Future uncertainties are enormous for governments everywhere. Making fiscal policy in the face of these uncertainties is a dauntingly complex undertaking, presenting different challenges from fiscal policymaking in the short to medium term. But uncertainty does not absolve fiscal policymakers from the need to address issues of the long term, because what they do or fail to do will critically influence the welfare of current and future generations and the role and capacity of the state.

And while there is much we do not know about the future, there is also much that we do know. We know that important structural changes will occur in the coming decades, both in human societies and in the natural environment. We know that these changes will have important fiscal consequences, both because of the heavy overhang of existing government commitments, explicit and implicit, and because of unavoidable new commitments. We know further that these changes will not proceed along straight, predictable paths but rather will evolve dynamically and will interact, and thus can emerge explosively. And we know that delay in addressing these changes will increase their costs, some of which will be borne by those living today.

Governments and the societies they represent need to account much more explicitly for the potential fiscal consequences of these long-term developments and take direct actions to address them. They must do so despite the inadequacies of current analytical forecasting techniques and despite the political turbulence that will arise. And they must start doing these things now, because the long term has already begun.

With the way forward so uncertain, this chapter provides not a map of the rough fiscal terrain ahead but a compass and a toolkit with many useful instruments and insights. Reform must proceed on many fronts, both because multiple reforms are needed and because together they establish a necessary symbiosis. Countries can take some key steps individually. They could improve analytical techniques, so that debate can proceed on an informed basis and so that the right actions are identified. They could implement detailed reforms of specific policies and programs, so that aggregate tax and spending reductions can close the remaining budget gap, while still leaving governments with adequate fiscal leeway to address unexpected policy challenges. They could create effective institutions to monitor budget trends and force debate on emerging dangers.

These steps will also enhance the prospects for international cooperation, likely to be a critical step in addressing long-term fiscal challenges. Countries could work collectively to identify and take advantage of complementarities in their fiscal needs, so that individual efforts at fiscal reform and rationalization do not work at cross-purposes. This last point is especially important. Although the issues to be faced, the strategies that will work, and the aspirations to be achieved may differ by country, the gathering force of this century's long-term developments is worldwide in scope. It is a force that the world, as a community, can no longer ignore.

APPENDIX BOX A.1

THE RANGE OF LONG-TERM FISCAL CHALLENGES

The list of long-term fiscal challenges facing countries is long and broad.[1]

Demographic challenges
- For industrial and many emerging market economies, increasing population share of the elderly and very elderly, declining population size for some, very high elderly dependency ratios.
- For many developing countries, increasing population size, continuing high youth dependency rates, increasing elderly share (albeit from low levels), high unemployment rates.
- Further urbanization, with growth of megacities and large urban centers, significant shortfalls in urban water and sewage infrastructure.
- Significant likelihood of high levels of internal regional migration and international migration, with cultural tensions emerging; brain drain affecting the poorest countries.
- Continuing high burdens in some countries of HIV/AIDS, tuberculosis, and malaria; dramatic growth in burden of chronic diseases (cardiovascular, obesity, cancer) in emerging market and developing economies.

Climate change
- Rise in average temperature levels; significant change in precipitation rates, resulting in increased risk of flooding in some areas and drought in others; increased intensity and frequency of extreme weather events (hurricanes, flooding, landslides); higher risks of flooding in major river valleys.
- Rise in average sea level, reflecting intensified polar warming.
- Some possibility of abrupt climate change (shift in thermohaline circulation and El Niño Southern Oscillation).[2]
- Increasing risk of vector-borne diseases

Economic growth, development, and globalization
- Pressures on the availability of critical natural resources (sources of energy and clean water).
- In many industrial and emerging market economies, pressures for delayed retirement.
- Rising public debt ratios, reflecting high current debt to GDP ratios and rising fiscal burdens associated with social insurance obligations and rising cost of medical care.
- Pressures to adapt social welfare systems in response to forced cutbacks of social insurance benefits.

THE RANGE OF LONG-TERM FISCAL CHALLENGES

- High tax rate environments associated with rising fiscal burdens, resulting in reduced incentive for labor force participation.
- Increasing tax competition, limiting capacity of governments to tax capital; pressures for harmonization of approaches to international accounting practices and social insurance systems.
- A core set of countries fall further behind industrial, emerging market, and some developing economies; continuing significant inequalities in income and wealth in many industrial and developing countries.
- Intensified pressure for some common consumption patterns (reflecting rapid information flows).
- Potential for unanticipated market volatility, reflecting large pools of investment capital (associated with institutional savings vehicles for retirement), immediacy of information flows, and effects of unanticipated events arising from security risks and resource shocks; potential for large price swings.
- Shifts in locus of many sectors (in agriculture and tourism particularly), reflecting climate change.
- Inadequate risk insurance affecting financial viability of many companies.

Political and cultural issues
- Heightened security risks (terrorist incidents, including possible use of weapons of mass destruction; technology and bioterrorism viruses; cyberterrorism).
- Potential for conflict over rights to critical natural resources (water, energy, forests).
- Cultural tensions associated with significant immigration into aging industrial countries.
- Tensions and conflicts associated with religion, particularly in Middle Eastern and South Asian regions.
- Backlash against globalization, adversely affecting economic potential of some developing countries.
- Risks of regional breakdown in some high population countries (India and China) should regional inequalities not diminish.

Scientific and technological developments
- Potential innovations in nanotechnology, information technology, biogenetics.
- Potential for the occasional "technology revolution," creating bursts of productivity growth.
- Technological innovations engendering advances in health and life expectancy but also creating cost pressures in the medical care sector.

THE RANGE OF LONG-TERM FISCAL CHALLENGES

- Risks to security, risks to civil liberties.
- Potential for heightened economic vulnerability of long-established sectors.

1. An extensive list of possible sources of long-term fiscal pressure for various countries and regions is available in Heller (2003).

2. The thermohaline circulation is a global ocean circulation driven by differences in the density of the sea water, in turn controlled by temperature (thermal) and salinity (haline). With the Gulf Stream it contributes to the comparatively warm sea surface temperature along the coast of Western Europe and the mild European winters (see Broecker 1995 for additional detail). El Niño is the phenomenon of the major warming of the equatorial waters in the Pacific Ocean, typically occurring every 3–7 years. El Niño events are characterized by shifts in "normal" weather patterns (see www.elnino.noaa.gov).

NOTES

1. This is just one estimate of the cost of implementing the Kyoto Protocol. Estimated costs vary by study and region, depending strongly on the assumptions on the use of the Kyoto mechanisms, such as emissions trading, and their interactions with domestic measures. For a further elaboration on how these costs were calculated, see IPCC (2001b).

2. Accrual accounting can be a useful presentational tool in such an environment by exposing the true size of a government's unfunded liabilities.

3. See www.nzsuperfund.co.nz/.

4. See odin.dep.no/fin/engelsk/dep/p10001829/p10001837/bn.html.

5. Pay as you go defined benefit programs rely on the young today to pay for the pensions of the old today. Thus, sustainability becomes suspect with declining population growth—fewer young people will be contributing to finance the pensions of more old people. Prefunded defined contribution (investment based) systems, on the other hand, rely on contributions from the young for their own pensions when they become old. For further discussion, see Feldstein and Liebman (2002).

6. For a discussion on this issue, see Morgan on commodity risk insurance markets and Shiller on macromarkets, both in this volume.

7. The IMF's "Code of Good Practices on Fiscal Transparency" calls on governments to provide a statement of fiscal risks and, if possible, to quantify the potential fiscal cost of such risks in their annual budgets (www.imf.org/external/np/fad/trans/). The OECD code on budget transparency calls on governments to provide a long-term report at least every five years, with more frequent assessments if there are major revenue or expenditure changes. The code advocates that policy commitments with significant future financial impacts, including unfunded public pension liabilities, be taken into account in any budgeting exercise. (OECD 2001).

8. Usually undertaken once a year, these discussions—referred to as "Article IV consultations"—assess member countries on a range of economic policies (exchange rate, monetary and fiscal policies); structural policies (international trade, labor market issues, power sector reform); financial sector issues and institutional issues (central bank independence, financial sector regulation, corporate governance, policy transparency and accountability); and assessment of risks and vulnerabilities (focusing on the current account position, external debt sustainability, vulnerabilities stemming from large and volatile capital flows). For further information, see IMF (2003b).

References

Australia, Treasury. 2002. "Intergenerational Report 2002–2003." 2002–2003 Budget Paper 5. Canberra.

Brixi, Hana Polackova, and Ashoka Mody. 2002. "Dealing with Government Fiscal Risk: An Overview." In Hana Polackova Brixi and Allen Schick, eds., *Government at Risk: Contingent Liabilities and Fiscal Risk.* New York and Washington: Oxford University Press and the World Bank.

Broecker, Wallace S. 1995. "Chaotic Climate." *Scientific American* 273 (5): 62–69.

Denmark, Ministry of Finance. 2003. "Convergence Program for Denmark: Updated Program for the Period 2003-2010." Copenhagen. [europa.eu.int/comm/economy_finance/about/activities/sgp/country/countryfiles/dk/dk20032004_en.pdf].

EU (European Union). 2005. "Economic and Financial Affairs." [http://europa.eu.int/comm/economy_finance/].

Feldstein, Martin, and Jeffrey Liebman. 2002. "Social Security." In Allan J. Auerbach, and Martin Feldstein, eds., *Handbook of Public Economics.* Vol. 4. Amsterdam: North Holland.

Frankhauser, Samuel. 1995. *Valuing Climate Change.* London: Earthscan.

Heller, Peter S. 2003. *Who Will Pay? Coping with Aging Societies, Climate Change, and Other Long-Term Fiscal Challenges.* Washington, D.C.: International Monetary Fund.

IPCC (Intergovernmental Panel on Climate Change). 2001a. "Climate Change 2001: Impacts, Adaption, and Vulnerability." Report of Working Group 2 of the Intergovernmental Panel on Climate Change. Geneva. [www.grida.no/climate/ipcc_tar/wg2/pdf/wg2TARtechsum.pdf].

———. 2001b. "Climate Change 2001: Synthesis Report, Summary for Policymakers." Geneva. [www.grida.no/climate/ipcc_tar/vol4/english/pdf/spm.pdf].

IMF (International Monetary Fund). 2003a. *Government Finance Statistics Yearbook 2003.* Washington, D.C.

———. 2003b. "IMF Surveillance: A Factsheet." Washington, D.C. [www.imf.org/external/np/exr/facts/surv.htm].

Jackson, Richard, and Neil Howe. 2003. "The 2003 Aging Vulnerability Index." Center for Strategic and International Studies and Watson Wyatt Worldwide, Washington, D.C. [www.csis.org/gai/aging_index.pdf].

New Zealand, Treasury. 2001. *Budget 2001*. Wellington.

————. 1995. "Fiscal Responsibility Act of 1994: An Explanation." Wellington.

OECD (Organisation for Economic Co-operation and Development). 2001. "OECD Best Practices for Budget Transparency." Paris. [www.oecd.org/dataoecd/33/13/1905258.pdf].

Sweden, Ministry of Finance. 2003. "Updated Swedish Convergence Program." Stockholm. [www.sweden.gov.se/content/1/c4/26/52/db1b61b7.pdf].

United Kingdom, Her Majesty's Treasury. 2001. "Illustrative Long-Term Fiscal Projections." In *The Budget 2001*. London.

————. 2000. "Long-Term Fiscal Projections." In *The Budget 2000*. London.

United Kingdom, Office for National Statistics. 2002. "Public Sector Accounts." National Statistics Online. [www.statistics.gov.uk/CCI/nugget.asp?ID=172].

UN (United Nations). 2003. *World Population Prospects: The 2002 Revision*. New York: United Nations. [esa.un.org/unpp/].

U.S. GAO (General Accounting Office). 2003. *Fiscal Exposures: Improving the Budget Focus on Long-Term Costs and Uncertainties*. Washington, D.C.

MANAGING RISKS TO NATIONAL ECONOMIES

THE ROLE OF MACRO MARKETS

ROBERT J. SHILLER

The finance and insurance industries were the source of much of the world's economic progress in the twentieth century. All of the industrial countries of the world have well developed financial sectors. This is no coincidence: the financial and insurance sectors have fostered productive risk-taking behavior (Levine 2003; Zingales 2003). Finance and insurance enable the sharing of risks across large numbers of people, blunting the impact in a way that promotes good incentives for productive work.

Despite these achievements, the finance and insurance industries have yet to tackle the biggest risks of today. Most of the income streams that people rely on for their sustenance are not represented in securities markets or covered by insurance institutions. The inability to control these risks leaves countries exposed to economic catastrophes and stands as a major barrier to economic progress, which by its nature involves taking risks.

The costs of this inability to manage risks are especially high for developing countries, where the margin for error in economic outcomes is much lower. But even industrial economies could make much more economic progress if risk management were better. Thus the costs of inadequate risk management are substantial for all countries.

Labor income accounts for most of a country's gross domestic product (GDP), but its risks are not hedgeable on any organized markets. By contrast, risk management institutions are very good at managing lesser risks, such as capital risks, even though after-tax corporate profits account for a much lower share of a country's GDP (about 10 percent in the United States; U.S. Department of Commerce 2004). Claims on the income of corporations are traded on stock markets. Not only are stock markets small relative to their economies, but changes in stock prices do not correlate very well with changes in measures of the aggregate economy.[1] But the news media, ever attracted by grand and simple stories, have created the impression that a country's stock market is an index of the country's performance. They create the impression that forecasting the stock market is like forecasting the economic future and that being mindful of one's investment portfolio is the essence of good risk management.

There is also very little risk sharing across countries. Countries enter into numerous trade agreements, which lower tariff barriers that inhibit commerce, but these pacts do not include explicit provisions to share economic risks. Foreign aid serves to manage some risks. A poor country with an extremely bad economic outcome can expect to receive some international relief. But the foreign aid that has been offered by industrial countries to developing countries in economic distress has been very limited, ranging from about 0.1 percent to close to 1 percent of donor countries' GDP. To make a significant impact, transfers of income might have to be much larger.

Moreover, foreign aid today tends to be directed toward a country's former colonies or to be motivated by political interests. There is no system for giving substantial aid to countries that have suffered most in their economic progress (Alesina and Dollar 2000). This chapter proposes such a system.[2] It considers how risk-sharing agreements between governments could better manage national risk and then describes how the same objective could be achieved by relying on private actors and decentralized markets. Finally, it discusses concrete steps to create a better system for national risk management.

BETTER NATIONAL RISK MANAGEMENT THROUGH INTERNATIONAL RISK-SHARING AGREEMENTS BETWEEN GOVERNMENTS

The failure to manage country risks has had striking consequences. Human suffering is deep and widespread in many developing countries whose economies have had disastrous outcomes. There is a lack of opportunity for fulfillment and self-actualization in many other countries that have experienced no economic disaster but merely disappointing economic progress. But workable proposals to deal with these problems are in short supply.

The Jubilee Debt Campaign of 2000, represented most visibly by the rock star Bono but also championed by economists such as Jeffrey Sachs and Lawrence Summers, made a moral case for economic justice. The campaign's goal was an international agreement to forgive the foreign debt of a troubled group of least developed countries. Bono pressed his campaign with visits to heads of state and religious leaders.

Certainly, humanitarian reasons prompt consideration of such forgiveness; some of these countries whose economies have collapsed are suffering enormously. But canceling their debts today at the expense of lenders raises questions about the future. What would the effect be on willingness to lend to such countries in the future? What level of uncertainty does such a policy introduce into all future debt contracts, and will investors be pleased with such fundamental uncertainty?

It would be better to prevent such dilemmas from arising by including debt forgiveness clauses in the initial debt contracts or, analogously, in international risk-sharing agreements. Countries that experience difficulties would automatically find their "debt" substantially forgiven.

These are risk management plans, not welfare. In effect, the risk sharing agreements would be creating the same kind of humanitarian relief that the Jubilee Debt Campaign called for, but in advance, before the outcome was known, not after. Moreover, had such a plan been in place, it would have worked. In contrast, the Jubilee Debt Campaign, despite statements of good intentions from governments, had limited success.[3]

Setting up risk management treaties between governments

Between 1965 and 1990 two countries on opposite sides of the globe experienced sharp reversals in economic fortunes—Argentina and the Republic of Korea. In 1965 real GDP per capita was $1,803 in Korea and $8,235 in Argentina, nearly five times as high. Twenty-five years later, Korea's real GDP per capita had risen to $9,952, while Argentina's had fallen to $7,219.[4] No one had expected this severe reversal of fortunes.

Things could have been different had Korea been able in 1965, presumably with the help of an international agency, to share its development risks through financial arrangements with another country or countries, including Argentina. Korea would pay the other countries if its GDP did better than expected relative to their performance during the contract period, and they would pay Korea if its economy did less well than theirs did. The international agency that arranged the deal might well make such arrangements among countries that are far from each other since distance is more likely to mean that countries would have different economic experiences. Perhaps such a deal might best be arranged not directly between the two countries but as a pair of contracts, one between Argentina and the international agency and the other between Korea and the international agency, or one between Argentina and a major country and the other between Korea and that same country. If appropriately matched, such a pair of contracts could amount to the same thing in economic terms as a contract between the two countries, differing only in political ramifications.

We now know that the outcome of such a contract would have had Korea paying Argentina a large sum of money, substantially mitigating the economic disaster in Argentina. Korea could easily afford to pay large sums to support Argentina, given Korea's great fortune. This outcome goes against expectations, but that is what would have happened. Of course, Korea's fortunes could have gone the other way, with GDP per capita not rising substantially, and Argentina could have had the economic success. In that case, Korea could have been saved decades of hardship by Argentina.

In 1965 no one knew which eventuality would prevail. Either way, had such a deal been made, substantial help could have been sent from one country to the other, depending on relative economic performance. Viewed in advance, from 1965, the contract clearly benefits both countries.

Moreover, had such a deal been made in 1965, higher standards of living might have prevailed in both countries. This would be possible because the risk management agreement would have permitted both countries to take calculated risks, to seize opportunities that would have been impossible for either country to take advantage of otherwise.

A risk management treaty could also be made between a single emerging market economy and a large group of industrial countries. Such a deal could be very appealing to all parties, since it would impose slight risks on the individual industrial country and yet be a godsend to the emerging market economy.

Shiller and Athanasoulis (1995) sought to define a contract that is, in a well defined sense, optimal from the standpoint of utility maximization for all countries. They presented a very ambitious example of such risk sharing. They considered India, an emerging market economy, against 11 other economies in 1990: Brazil, Canada, China, France, Germany, Italy, Japan, Mexico, the United Kingdom, the United States, and the Commonwealth of Independent States. India's per capita income in 1990 was far below that of any of the others. Athanasoulis and Shiller found that the optimal 40-year risk management arrangement was very nearly a simple GDP swap between India and the other economies as a group. In this agreement only China was given a substantially smaller burden of bearing India's risk since China had a substantially lower per capita income than the others, though still much higher than India's.

The study estimated that the benefit to India would have been enormous, with an estimated welfare gain (present value of consumer surplus) to India of 47 percent of annual GDP per capita. This welfare benefit is so large because the risk management contract relieves India of the risk that an economic downturn would thrust hundreds of millions more people into poverty, which would be very painful with the already low living standards (and correspondingly high marginal utility of income).

Remarkably, providing this risk management to India would have cost the other countries less than nothing in terms of economic welfare. Because India's GDP shows very low correlation (in fact, negative correlation) with the GDPs of the other countries, they all benefit from the risk management deal, though less than India does since the deal was designed to help India. They benefit in just the same way that India does, in having made a contract that swaps some of their GDP risk with another country. This optimal contract has a welfare benefit (present value of consumer-surplus as a fraction of annual GDP) ranging from 4 percent for the United States to 0.01 percent for Brazil.

Economists are fond of saying that "there is no free lunch." But taking advantage of unexploited risk management opportunities is in effect a free lunch for every country on an ex ante basis in terms of utility, even though the exploitation of these risk management opportunities generates no new aggregate resources for the world.

Making risk sharing part of the language of international agreements
Why have such agreements not emerged? Part of the problem is that economic risks and their management through international risk-sharing agreements have

not been part of the vocabulary and toolkits of the diplomats who make the international agreements. There is little awareness of the kind of slowly evolving risks to national standards of living that add up to substantial changes over many years. There also is little awareness that measures exist in GDP accounts that can identify the combined effects of numerous heterogeneous risks on the well-being of countries and could be the basis of risk management contracts. And there is almost no awareness that contractual arrangements could help offset such risks.

It is hard to find clear examples of international risk sharing. Because the principle of risk sharing is not widely recognized, any risk-sharing agreements tend to be incidental to other arrangements or described in terms other than risk management. The European Union has some explicit provisions for effective risk sharing among member countries. It collects a share of value added taxes assessed by member countries and has other revenues that give it a budget of about 1 percent of member countries' GDP. About a third of this revenue is used for Structural Funds to help poorer regions in Europe, and a smaller Cohesion Fund is used for the same purpose (see the chapter by Laffan in this volume). While this arrangement provides risk sharing, it is not described in the language of risk sharing. The European Commission describes the funds' purpose as mobilizing unused resources, as represented by unemployment and lagging regional development, thus contributing to faster and more sustainable growth.[5] The language describes the objectives of risk management but not the technology for achieving it.

It may be politically difficult to describe risk management openly. A mutually advantageous agreement between countries would have to acknowledge the current economic superiority of the richer country, as well as the likelihood that the superiority will persist for many decades, if not indefinitely. Richer countries will not find the contract advantageous if the contract taxes away their current advantage with certainty. The contract has to be about future changes relative to expectations, so defined that they really could go either way for either country.

It is generally advantageous for wealthy countries to make risk management contracts with poorer countries rather than with other wealthy countries, because there are likely to be more differences in economic outcomes and hence more idiosyncratic risk to share. Risk sharing is generally more potent among dissimilar parties. And yet it is just such risk-sharing contracts that appear difficult to make, since they look only at the future risks and not at the inequality in place today, which is already likely to be a source of resentment.

BETTER NATIONAL RISK MANAGEMENT THROUGH DECENTRALIZED, MARKET-BASED APPROACHES

The discussion so far has assumed that risk management arrangements are made by governments, since they already negotiate treaties that represent the interests of the country. But such risk management could also be arranged for privately by

individuals and firms. It could arise gradually from small beginnings and eventually grow to large proportions as more and more individuals and firms reach the
decision to manage these risks.

Private market responses to national risks

The entire economy of a country could participate in managing national risks
through the creation of a market for a security that pays, say, a quarterly dividend
equal to a specified fraction of that quarter's GDP. Each shareholder would receive
this dividend indefinitely. The government or private corporations could contract
to issue the securities and pay the dividends.

Suppose that the United States issued these securities, with a quarterly dividend equal to one-trillionth of that quarter's GDP. Based on the current U.S. economy, with a GDP of about $10 trillion, the dividend on one share would be $10 a
year. The dividend would rise and fall with the U.S. economy. If the economy did
well over the next five years, the dividend per share would rise, say to $12 a year.
If the economy slipped into a serious economic crisis, the dividend could fall, say
to $8 a share.

Potential investors would want to predict the likely future dividends, so the
valuation placed on the security, and hence its market price, would represent the
value of a claim on GDP. In the U.S. example, if the investors expected the economy to grow roughly in line with growth in the past, and if they behave as stock
market investors have in the past, they might value this share at $200, so that the
annual dividend yield is 5 percent. At this price the market would be placing a
value on the entire U.S. economy (multiplying by the inverse of the fraction, that
is, by a trillion) of $200 trillion, on the order of 20 times the value of the U.S. stock
market. This figure is just illustrative. The market would have to be created before
the valuation it would place on the U.S. economy could be known.

These securities could be designed to value other economic features, such as
incomes by educational category, occupation, or other personal characteristics, or
indexes of the price of single-family homes by city or of commercial real estate by
type. These securities would pay regular dividends proportional to these income
flows or proportional to the prices of major assets. The prices that these securities
would command would represent the market's estimated long-term valuation of
these income flows or real estate investments.

Creation of a macro market of this type (box 1) would allow trading of enormous risks that have never been traded before. The securities tied to a country's
GDP would allow investors around the world to invest directly in the economy of
the United States. They would be able to diversify their portfolios much more
broadly than is possible now, to include the entire national economy, not just the
stock market. For example, those who represent the economic interests of
Americans could issue the U.S. GDP securities to foreigners to reduce the economic risks that Americans share.

Box 1
MACRO MARKETS FOR NATIONAL RISK MANAGEMENT

Macro markets, as originally proposed by Shiller (1993a), would expand the realm of possible financial transactions by creating new international markets for trading claims on aggregate national incomes. Macro markets would work like stock markets, which trade claims on corporate incomes (dividends). In addition to claims on overall national income, macro markets could trade claims on components of GDP or on the incomes of various population groups organized by occupation, education, or other criteria.

Macro markets would allow public and private agents to "insure" their income, and thus, also, their level of well-being by hedging, that is, by making off-setting bets to balance the bets that people necessarily and involuntary have to make because they live in a certain country, work in a certain occupation, and have a certain level of education.

Thus, the level of well-being of someone who lives in, say, Brazil is intrinsically tied to the economic prospects of the Brazilian economy. This person has made a bet (most certainly unintentionally) on the future growth and economic prosperity of the economy. If the economy suffers a severe recession, the person is not insured against the hardships that come if the downturn reduces the person's income or leads to a job loss. With a macro market to trade claims on income, however, individuals, firms, or even government agents in Brazil could have bought claims on the income of another country that would be likely to offset the downward shift of national income. With this "insurance policy" people living in Brazil would not be adversely affected by the recession, since they could be compensated through the positive evolution in income in the other country.

Today, there is no liquid market for long-term claims on the aggregate output of a country. There is no market for claims on components of GDP either or for claims on occupational or personal incomes.[6] Trading these big risks allows the most massive risk sharing, making possible all kinds of risk management products that can help individuals. Creation of a macro market thus contributes to the kind of risk management infrastructure that is needed for the effective democratization of finance, even if most individuals never buy or sell on the macro markets. Those who issue the risk management products to individuals can do the buying and selling on these markets.

Creating macro markets
In a path-breaking development Citibank N. A. arranged a loan of $1.865 billion to Bulgaria in 1994 with an interest rate tied to the growth rate of its economy, in

Box 2

GDP-INDEXED BONDS

The main purpose of GDP-indexed bonds is to align a country's sovereign debt service obligations to its economic growth rate, and thus to lower the risk of default should its economic growth falter. Growth-indexed bonds are particularly advantageous for countries that are vulnerable to external shocks, such as slower growth in major export markets or natural disasters. Such events may cause a steep decline in export income. Tying the interest rate to be paid to bond holders to the GDP growth rate offers the bond-issuing country some respite during such episodes of exceptional volatility.

However, this breathing space comes at a cost. When economic growth rates rise, the bonds' interest rates rise too.

Variants of GDP-indexed bonds have been issued by Bulgaria, Bosnia and Herzegovina, and Costa Rica. They are increasingly seen as a risk management tool from which both borrowers and lenders in international debt markets might benefit (see, for example, Borensztein and Mauro 2002).

the form of a GDP-indexed bond (box 2). These bonds were part of the refinancing of Bulgaria's foreign debt following its request for debt restructuring in 1994. The bonds pay out as additional interest each year one half of the growth rate of real GDP if Bulgarian real GDP (as reported by the World Bank) rises more than 25 percent above the 1993 level. The higher the economic growth rate in Bulgaria, the more Bulgaria pays as interest.

This bond has served its risk management function for Bulgaria well: Bulgaria's economic growth since 1994 has been disappointing and so Bulgaria has not had to pay much interest. But Bulgaria successfully transferred some of its national risks to diversified investors, an especially important step for this transition economy. The investors who lent the money to Bulgaria are of course not happy to have received less interest than they had hoped, but these are presumably portfolio investors whose diversified holdings can manage this risk.

The possibility of a substantial extension of GDP-indexed bonds was heightened at the annual meetings of the International Monetary Fund and the World Bank in Dubai in the fall of 2003 when Argentina presented a proposal to introduce GDP indexing as part of the restructuring of its debt. This proposal launched discussion among governments about the risk structure of international lending institutions.

In January 2004 at the Summit of the Americas in Monterrey, Mexico, 34 Western Hemisphere heads of state issued a declaration suggesting the possibility of governmental support for GDP-indexed bonds, a possible precursor to macro markets. The declaration states: "We take note with satisfaction that governments in the Hemisphere are implementing the Monterrey Consensus by exploring innovative ways to mobilize financing for private and public investment and to strengthen debt management by considering financial instruments, such as growth-indexed bonds and others, to promote macroeconomic stability and reduce financial vulnerability" (OAS 2004, p. 11).

GDP-indexed bonds are government-issued instruments. However, one could also imagine that private, nonstate actors could develop vehicles for hedging against such risks as changes in a country's income.

One alternative instrument, proposed by Shiller (1993a,b), is perpetual futures (box 3). These futures would differ from conventional futures in their time horizon. Conventional futures are of limited duration, covering perhaps only a few months into the future. Their contract price can be thought of as approximating the expected value of the underlying asset or index on the defined, final settlement date. Perpetual futures have a long term horizon, reflecting that countries will have an income well into the future—that is to say, perpetually. Their contract price represents the expected present discounted value of the long term flow of a country's income. Perpetual futures would thus provide an important opportunity for trading long-term risks.

However, perpetual futures may be too complex for many actors. Macro securities are another product that could be supplied by private actors for hedging against such risks as change in a country's income. Because these securities pay regular dividends, they may be more familiar and acceptable to market participants, including institutional investors (box 4). Weiss and Shiller (1999) have worked this instrument into a patentable invention, secured in the United States in 1999,[7] and formed an alliance with the American Stock Exchange. Most of the legal work to allow such securities to be created has been completed.

MAKING BETTER NATIONAL RISK MANAGEMENT HAPPEN

Making effective risk management happen calls for creating an infrastructure for proper risk management, a formidable, though by no means impossible task. Perhaps the greatest obstacle is psychological. The public is unaware of its biggest risks and tends to focus on inconsequential risks that seem more salient. It is not enough for researchers and analysts to identify major risks statistically. If people at large do not recognize these risks, they will neither take steps to deal with them nor give full support to the institutions that do.

Persuading the public of the bigger, long-term economic risks that remain unmanaged today will take some work. There seems to be no public recognition of the risk of a major change in countries' economic status. The focus among business commentators is exclusively on predicting whether the business situation will

Box 3
Perpetual Futures

Similar to GDP-indexed bonds (see box 2), perpetual futures can be used for hedging against change in a country's income, with the important difference that they do not depend on the government's willingness to issue the bonds. Thus perpetual futures would be a way to provide to anyone the possibility to hedge against the harmful consequences of a drop in a country's GDP. They could be bought and sold in futures markets, by private as well as public agents. Yet their design would differ from that of conventional futures.

Conventional futures are used mainly for hedging shorter term risks. Someone wishing to protect against a drop in an index or in the price of an asset can take a short position in a futures contract. For example, a farmer might want to lock in a certain price for a crop by entering into a futures contract guaranteeing a certain price at harvest time. The price of the futures contract is related to the expected value of the index or the price of the asset at a prespecified date (know as the futures contract settlement date).

Perpetual futures, in contrast, would have no expiration date, effectively making the contract open ended or perpetual. The price of the contract would reflect the expected long-term future flow of national income. An economic agent taking a short position in this perpetual futures contract would be hedging (or insuring) against a drop in GDP, and the one taking the long position would be speculating on the income's rise.

The Economic Derivatives market created in 2002 by Goldman Sachs in the United States and Deutsche Bank in Europe is an antecedent of the perpetual futures proposal. This market creates options—rather than futures—for such macroeconomic variables as nonfarm payroll, retail sales, and confidence indexes. These options are not directly tied to a country's GDP, but the macroeconomic variables they chose have some correlation with it.

Source: Shiller 1993a,b.

improve in the next six months to a year, as if this were the only concern. Public leaders must be willing to talk about the longer term risks that we all face. They should address the long-term uncertainties that really matter and do so within the context of risk management instruments that can be realistically implemented— thus helping to alleviate such risk.

Financial innovators, to be really effective, need to think about what kind of reframing of basic standards and institutions they should encourage, so that the

Box 4

MACRO SECURITIES

Macro securities are issued in pairs—an "up macro," whose price moves up when a country's GDP index moves up, and a "down macro," whose price moves down when the index moves up. Each member of a pair has a cash account that is adjusted according to the index by reallocating across accounts. Each macro security pays dividends equal to interest on its cash account.

Suppose a pair of securities is issued for $200 when the index is 100. The accounts of the up and down macros are each credited with $100. If the index rises to 102, the custodian of the cash accounts takes $2 from the down macro, reducing the account to $98, and puts them in the up macro account, so that the balance in that account again equals the index at $102. Thereafter, dividends on the down macro security will be lower, and the holder of the up security will be rewarded through subsequent dividends by the rise in the index. Because investors can anticipate these higher dividends now that the account balance is higher, investors should bid up the price of the long security (the one betting on an increase in the index) immediately, even before any of the new higher dividends are paid. Responding quickly to new information, the price of the security will likely be rather volatile, just as prices are in the stock market.

Since dividends are tied to the index value, the up macro is really a claim on the flow of index values extending into the indefinite future and therefore resembles a stock, which is a claim on corporate earnings extending into the indefinite future. The price of the up macro should in equilibrium reflect market valuation of a claim on the cash flow represented by the index. The price of the down macro security will move opposite that of the up macro, since the value of the two together sums to the value in the combined accounts, in this case $200.

People who want to invest in the index can buy the up macro security, while those who want to protect themselves at a preexisting risk related to the index can buy the down macro security.

Source: Weiss and Shiller 1999.

innovations can achieve their full potential. Innovators need to get past the mind-set of incremental thinking, creating only small improvements in products that will immediately succeed in the current environment. They must try to envision major changes that are outside consumers' habitual frame of reference, plan a new psychological framing, and have the patience to promote the new ideas for as long as it takes for them to become a part of public thinking.

No matter how extensive the research, risk management instruments cannot be adequately designed based on abstract principles alone. No one has a theoretical model of risks and moral hazard that is so well defined that it can be used to build risk management instruments that work perfectly the first time. Over the years businesses have experimented and their observations of the outcome have helped them to shape and reshape their business models. The same process must take place with radical financial innovations that can transform economies. We must begin with multiple small experiments.

People cannot anticipate the full consequences of economic inventions. But many countries, many local governments, many stock exchanges, many banks, and many insurance companies can all try somewhat different experiments. Experimenting with new financial ideas whose stated and explicit goal is to result in fundamental changes must become a priority. Of necessity, this will include many experiments whose probability of success is low.

The methods that will one day be used to make possible the sharing of major economic risks are under active development today. Table 1 summarizes the proposals discussed in this chapter, along with their antecedents or work in progress toward their implementation. These methods will provide price discovery for the present values of income flows, such as of GDP, that are not represented in any market today. Experimentation will be necessary, to find the institutional framework that will allow better risk management.

Ensuring that risk sharing proceeds on a massive scale will require public advocacy. Society cannot just create exchanges to trade new risks and hope that people start trading. There has to be a human force behind the use of new risk management instruments. The benefits of such risk sharing are not so obvious to most people. Opinion leaders will have to take steps to make these ideas compelling.

Good public advocacy of fundamental risk sharing would involve many institutions in society beyond the government. Of course, the major institutions for

TABLE 1

Major proposed risk management vehicles and their antecedents

Proposed vehicle	Antecedent
Risk management agreements among countries	EU Structural Funds, 1958
GDP-linked bonds	Bulgarian GDP warrants attached to 30-year discount bonds, 1994
Perpetual futures	Economic derivatives market for nonfarm payroll, Deutsche Bank and Goldman Sachs, 2002
Macro securities tied to macroeconomic aggregates	Macro Securities Research, LLC; collaboration with American Stock Exchange, 2003

Source: Author's compilation.

risk management—insurance, securities, and banking industries—must play a key role. These institutions have an enormous body of knowledge and experience that can help them lead the way to more pervasive risk management. They should view promoting better risk management as the largest part of their benevolent activities, as well as of their profit making activities.

The news media can help by resisting the temptation to dwell too much on eye-catching news ("Dow Crosses 10,000") and to focus on the slowly evolving and still poorly measured risks that really matter. Academic researchers can help by focusing more on the nature of long-term risks. Labor unions and professional societies can help by serving as advocates for their members on the all-important role of proper risk management tailored to their interests.

We have seen radical innovation in risk management practice in the past, as whole new categories of risks became amenable to scientific risk management. We can see such radical innovation in the future as well, to deal with the all-important issue of the risks of nations.

NOTES

1. Stock market dividends or returns do not correlate well enough with the risks that countries face for stock markets to hedge these larger risks. Evidence can be found in Bottazzi, Pesenti, and van Wincoop (1996). See also Shiller (1993a).

2. This chapter draws on Shiller (2003).

3. By some accounts, the Jubilee 2000 campaign secured a reduction of $18 billion out of $300 billion in debt for these countries. But these reductions might have happened anyway. See Mathiason (2001).

4. These real GDP numbers, in 1996 U.S. dollars, are from Heston, Summers, and Aten 2002. (The Penn World Table, Mark 6.1, is available at http://pwt.econ.upenn.edu/php_site/pwt61_form.php.) By 1998, Korean real GDP per capita had risen to $13,444, while Argentina's had risen to $11,639, closing some of the gap. A severe economic crisis in Argentina starting in 2001, however, is reopening the gap.

5. For further information see EU (2002) and http://europa.eu.int/comm/regional_policy/index_en.htm.

6. For evidence that risks are not fully shared around the world today, see Baxter and Jermann (1997), Obstfeld (1994), Sala-i-Martin and Sachs (1992), Tesar (1995), and Tesar and Werner (1995).

7. Allan Weiss, when he first arrived at this idea, originally called them proxy assets; later, they were called *macro securities*. Note the fundamental distinction between macro markets based on income indexes, such as national income, and macro markets based on price indexes, such as real estate. Macro markets based on price indexes have somewhat different properties and economic functions. The macro markets based on indexes of prices of illiquid assets such as real estate serve the

purpose of discovering something closer to the true market price of these assets, if the market were not so illiquid. For further discussion, see Shiller (1993a).

REFERENCES

Alesina, Alberto, and David Dollar. 2000. "Who Gives Foreign Aid to Whom and Why?" *Jouranl of Economic Growth* 5 (1): 33–63.

Baxter, Marianne, and Urban Jermann. 1997. "The International Diversification Puzzle Is Worse Than You Think." *American Economic Review* 87 (1): 170–80.

Borensztein, Eduardo, and Paolo Mauro. 2002. "Reviving the Case for GDP-Indexed Bonds." IMF Policy Discussion Paper PDP/02/10. Washington, D.C.: International Monetary Fund.

Bottazzi, Laura, Paolo Pesanti, and Eric van Wincoop. 1996. "Wages, Profits, and the International Portfolio Puzzle." *European Economic Review* 40 (2): 219–54.

EU (European Union). 2002. "At the Service of the Regions: Facts and Figures." [http://europa.eu.int/comm/regional_policy/intro/regions2_en.htm].

Heston, Alan, Robert Summers, and Bettina Aten. 2002. "Penn World Table Version 6.1." University of Pennsylvania, Center for International Comparisons, Philadelphia. [http://pwt.econ.upenn.edu/php_site/pwt61_form.php].

Levine, Ross. 2003. "More on Finance and Growth: More Finance, More Growth?" *Federal Reserve Bank of St. Louis Review* 65 (4): 31–37.

Mathiason, Nick. 2001. "G-7's Debt Relief Plan a 'Cruel Joke.'" *The Guardian.* December 30.

OAS (Organization of American States). 2004. "Declaration of Nuevo León." [www.oas.org/documents/SpecialSummitMexico/DeclaracionLeon_eng.pdf].

Obstfeld, Maurice. 1994. "Risk-Taking, Global Diversification, and Growth." *American Economic Review* 84 (5): 1310–29.

Sala-i-Martin, Xavier, and Jeffrey Sachs. 1992. "Fiscal Federalism and Optimum Currency Areas: Evidence for Europe and the United States." In Matthew B. Canzoneri, Vittorio Grilli, Paul R. Masson, eds., *Establishing a Central Bank: Issues in Europe and Lessons from the US.* Cambridge: Cambridge University Press.

Shiller, Robert J. 1993a. *Macro Markets: Creating Institutions for Managing Society's Largest Economic Risks.* Oxford: Oxford University Press.

———. 1993b. "Measuring Asset Value for Cash Settlement in Derivative Markets: Hedonic Repeated Measures Indices and Perpetual Futures." *Journal of Finance* 68 (July): 911–31.

———. 2003. *The New Financial Order: Risk in the 21st Century.* Princeton, N.J.: Princeton University Press.

Shiller, Robert J., and Stefano Athanasoulis. 1995. *World Income Components: Measuring and Exploiting International Risk Sharing Opportunities.* NBER Working Paper 5095. Cambridge, Mass.: National Bureau of Economic Research.

Tesar, Linda L. 1995. "Evaluating the Gains from International Risksharing." *Carnegie-Rochester Conference Series on Public Policy* 42 (June): 95–103.

Tesar, Linda L., and Ingrid Werner. 1995. "Home Bias and High Turnover." *Journal of International Money and Finance* 14 (4): 467–92.

U.S. Department of Commerce, Bureau of Economic Analysis. 2004. "Table 1.12 National Income by Type of Income." Interactive National Income and Product Account Tables. Washington, D.C. [www.bea.gov/bea/dn/nipaweb/index.asp].

Weiss, Allan N., and Robert J. Shiller. 1999. "Proxy Asset Data Processor." U.S. Patent 5,987,435. [www.uspto.gov/patft/].

Zingales, Luigi. 2003. "The Weak Links." *Federal Reserve Bank of St. Louis Review* 85 (4): 48–52.

COMBINING FISCAL SOVEREIGNTY AND COORDINATION
NATIONAL TAXATION IN A GLOBALIZING WORLD

PEGGY B. MUSGRAVE

Tax systems should be designed to yield the needed revenue in an equitable and efficient fashion. Most people will agree with these basic goals, but they will differ once they take a closer look. As taxes are imposed, taxpayers respond by adjusting their behavior. Consumption, work, saving, and investment will be affected, as will the distribution of the tax burden and the economy's overall performance. Moreover, administrative constraints limit what can be done, as may diverging interests of fiscal politics. No wonder then that tax design has long been a difficult and controversial issue.

Along with the rising complexity of economies and their financial institutions, taxation has posed increasingly complex problems. The ongoing globalization of economic activity now adds a challenging new chapter to that process. Traditionally, tax systems were viewed largely in the context of single and sovereign jurisdictions, unaffected by tax systems outside their borders. Some allowance was made for multiple subjurisdictions in federal systems and for local finance, but the major focus was on the tax design of central governments operating independently of others. With increasing globalization this narrow perspective is no longer adequate. Economic activity frequently crosses national boundaries, and international trade has been rising in importance, as have international capital, labor, and income flows.

Taxpayers who reside and pay tax in one jurisdiction may receive income originating and taxed in another, as is particularly the case of corporations that invest and have been taxed on their profits abroad. Issues of overlapping taxation must be resolved. Consumers purchase imported products that may already have been taxed in the country of origin. How should tax bases be divided? Which jurisdictions should be entitled to tax what part of the base and at what rate? How is internation equity to be determined (Musgrave and Musgrave 1972)? Should these issues be resolved through the policy choices of single jurisdictions, should they be settled by tax competition, or will coordinating measures secured through cooperative agreements be needed to attain equitable and efficient results? How compatible will such rules be with the freedom of jurisdictions to choose their own tax systems, or will uniformity be required?

This chapter discusses the rationale behind the design of cooperative rules across tax jurisdictions and the issues involved. Coordination of different national tax systems and rates may require uniformity in some instances, but it need not in others. Rather, harmonizing measures can be taken to neutralize the differences with respect to resource allocation across jurisdictions, while preserving the variations in fiscal choices.

Problems differ by type of tax, but primary concern, not surprisingly, has been with the corporate profits tax and its treatment of income and capital flows across national borders, the focus of the first part of this chapter. A brief discussion follows of how recent reforms or proposed reforms of corporate and personal income taxation may change that scene. The chapter then revisits, in the context of consumption taxation, the principles suggested earlier and finally summarizes the main suggestions.[1]

ENTITLEMENTS TO TAX INCOME

There are two universally recognized and widely practiced national entitlements to tax income in an open economy setting: one to the country of residence of the income recipient and one to the country of the source of the income.[2] The economic consequences of the interaction of these entitlements will differ in settings of conflict and cooperation.

Tax entitlement of the residence country

So long as there are countries serving populations with common purposes and interests, such countries will wish to retain a degree of sovereignty over the tax treatment of the income-earning activities abroad of their residents. This has been discussed in connection with the principle of "subsidiarity" in the European Union.[3] The national right to tax the global income of residents is recognized in international law (Kaufman 1998). Residents are held to owe tax allegiance in return for the rights and privileges that they receive as residents (commonly referred to as the "residence principle").

Exercise of tax sovereignty over foreign source income is also necessary to achieve equitable tax treatment of resident taxpayers by making all income, wherever earned, subject to tax, consistent with the accretion principle.[4] It also provides a policy instrument for affecting the outflow of capital in line with national policy objectives. It may also be justified in benefit terms, as a payment for productivity-enhancing benefits provided by the country of residence to its own factors of production prior to transfer abroad and for the rights and privileges afforded the corporation by its country of registration. What is important is that the country of residence, as the residual taxing authority, has control over the total tax burden on the foreign-source income of its resident taxpayers.

Policy options in absence of cooperation. The home or residence country then has various choices for treatment of the source or host country's tax on that income:

1. It may make no allowance for such tax, applying its own tax on foreign income gross of foreign tax.

2. It may apply its tax on foreign income net of the foreign tax, treating the foreign tax as a deduction from taxable income.

3. It may allow full or limited crediting of the foreign tax, treating the foreign tax as its own.

4. It may surrender its tax sovereignty over the foreign income of its residents, exempting the foreign income from its own tax.

Often taxation is deferred until foreign earnings are repatriated as dividends.[5]

Each of these rules has very different tax consequences for taxpayers, affecting their behavior and in turn the amount and direction of capital outflow.[6] An extensive literature deals with the theoretical and empirical aspects of these effects (for instance, Hartman 1985; Sinn 1993; Hines 1994; Grubert 1998). These are not discussed further in this chapter, the focus of which is on the derivation of appropriate tax rules. Suffice it to say that rule 1 would serve as a strong deterrent to capital outflow. Rule 2 would ensure that the national return to investment abroad (net of foreign tax) will not fall below the gross rate of return on domestic investment (Richman [Musgrave] 1963; Feldstein and Hartman 1979; Devereux 2004). Rule 3 would promote the efficient international allocation of investment (Slemrod 1995), even though the national return to foreign investment (net of foreign tax) may fall short of the national return to domestic investment (gross of domestic tax) (Musgrave 1969). Put another way, the foreign tax credit implies a substantial revenue sacrifice by the country of residence to satisfy an international efficiency standard. Exemption of foreign income under rule 4 leaves capital flows exposed to various incentives related to the pattern of effective tax rate differentials between countries of residence and source and further encourages capital-importing countries to engage in tax competition.

The choice by the country of residence of how to exercise its tax sovereignty is, therefore, largely a choice of how its own tax rules treat the tax imposed by the country of source. In the absence of cooperation the principal considerations in making that choice are equitable tax treatment for its residents and citizens and national economic interests. Such interests include the level and growth of national income and its distribution and the country's balance of payments, with bearing on its exchange rate and terms of trade (OECD 1991; U.S. Department of the Treasury 1993).

Taxpayer equity. The basic consideration for the residence country is to preserve the integrity of its comprehensive income tax. Integrity requires the inclusion in the tax base of all income earned abroad by its residents and subjection of that income to national standards of tax equity. Without that basic provision standards of both horizontal and vertical equity are violated. For individuals the exercise of the residence entitlement suggests the use of a personalized income tax—in contrast, as discussed later, to an impersonal tax called for in the exercise of source entitlement.

However, a rule for the equitable treatment of foreign income taxes paid on that income is not clear-cut, since a case may be made for crediting, deducting, or disregarding the foreign tax (Musgrave 2001). Full crediting for the foreign tax (refundable, if necessary) is called for if an "international" view of taxpayer equity is taken, with the foreign tax regarded as equivalent to the domestic tax. The country of residence might define taxpayer equity in "national" terms, however. In that case the source country tax would be viewed as a cost to the taxpayer and therefore deducted from taxable foreign income, just as lower level (state and local) domestic taxes are usually treated. Finally, the definition of "national" taxpayer equity might well disregard the foreign tax entirely, with the residence country's tax applied to foreign income with no allowance for the foreign tax, on the grounds that the standard of taxpayer equity is applicable only to the residence country tax and that the foreign tax is irrelevant. Which rule is followed, as in most other equity issues, has to be a matter of judgment by national consensus.

Although the concept of equity is usually applied to individual taxpayers, the corporation is an essential halfway house for foreign income flowing to resident individual shareholders, and it can be argued that similar principles should apply to its taxation. For resident corporations equity principles would again call for an income tax that includes all income, both domestic and foreign.[7] For reasons familiar in the context of domestic taxation, both efficiency and equity call for taxation of corporations on an accrual basis, without deferral until distribution. This applies to income earned abroad by the resident corporation, whether arising in a foreign affiliate or branch, or by a foreign-incorporated subsidiary form. But again on equity grounds there is no definitive rule for treatment of foreign tax.

National economic interests. The transfer of economic activity abroad may have a profound effect on the national economic interests of the residence country. None looms larger than overseas investment, which may affect the level and distribution of national income within the capital-exporting country. Consequently, tax policies that affect capital outflows are an important instrument of economic policy. Countries of residence can shape their tax policy to manipulate the size and type of capital outflow to their own advantage rather than contribute to the worldwide gains obtained through a neutral tax policy that promotes the efficient international allocation of capital (Slemrod 1995; Hines 1997) or to international redistributional considerations calling for investment in low-income countries.

Viewing the treatment of foreign taxes in national efficiency terms, it will be to the residence country's advantage to maximize the contribution of investment made abroad to the national welfare. The residence country may seek to ensure that the national returns to such investment are at least equal to the returns had the investment been made at home. Since the foreign tax may be regarded as a subtraction from the national return, this goal of national efficiency is secured by allowing foreign income taxes as deductions from taxable income rather than as credits against the home country tax. Under this regime investors will be inclined to invest abroad only if returns after foreign tax are equal to or greater than those obtainable before tax in the domestic economy. In this way investment abroad will be less than that called for on worldwide efficiency grounds but will be consistent with a standard of national efficiency imposed by the residence country.

The residence country can make a further national economic argument for the deduction treatment of foreign taxes. Provided that the combined effective tax rate of the residence country and the source country on investment made in the source country is similar to the effective tax rate on domestic investment in the residence country, the net result will be an overall increase in the combined national income of both the residence and the source countries.[8] However, the general assumption of neoclassical economics is that the decision of investors resident in one country to invest their savings in another country rather than at home will raise the income of investors in the residence country and of labor in the source country, while lowering the income of investors in the source country and labor in the residence country.

Thus, even if tax neutrality ensures efficiency with respect to global income, there will be redistributive effects in both residence and source countries (presumably equalizing in the source country and the reverse in the residence country). Furthermore, allowing for the tax take of the source country in foreign investment earnings, there may well be a net income loss to the capital-exporting residence country, with the presumption of larger income gains to the source country. Since foreign investment has powerful redistributive effects within and among participating countries through capital and labor earnings as well as in the shares of tax revenue, the residence country would be expected to want to exercise some control over such investment. This is particularly the case if government budgets have no means of correcting redistributive effects. Short-run effects of capital outflow on the balance of payments may be a further concern for the residence country, especially if the investment abroad displaces its exports and implements the familiar "outsourcing" of labor.

Thus, just as it is generally accepted that a country has the right to assert sovereignty over labor immigration, it is logical that a country should exercise sovereignty over the outflow of capital. In the absence of direct capital controls, taxation is the favored instrument, in particular the corporate income tax.

Tax entitlement of the source country

While countries do not always exercise their full sovereignty as countries of residence, choosing instead to exempt foreign income or to tax it only when repatriated, most countries claim their entitlement to tax income arising within their borders, including that accruing to foreign investors. This entitlement to tax at source is the bedrock of most international tax treaties, which recognize as a fundamental entitlement the right of a jurisdiction to tax all income arising within its borders. This permits a country to share in the gains of foreign-owned factors of production operating within its borders, gains that are generated in cooperation with its own inputs, whether they be natural resources, an educated or low-cost workforce, or proximity to a market.

The tax revenue may be thought of as a national return to the leasing of these complementary factors to nonresident investors or temporary workers. In broader terms, such taxation may also be thought of in benefit terms, as a quid pro quo payment for cost-reducing, profit-enhancing services provided by the source country. The source country's entitlement to share in the taxation of income earned by nonresidents thus expresses a norm of internation equity distinct from that pertaining to the equitable taxation of taxpayers within their country of residence (Musgrave and Musgrave 1972).

Policy options in the absence of cooperation. In exercising this tax entitlement, the source country requires an *in rem* or impersonal form of taxation, since a personal form of income taxation is not appropriate for a situation in which only part of the taxpayer's global income is to be taxed and the taxing authority's entitlement extends only to income earned within its own borders. Source taxation of income is therefore appropriately implemented by a corporate income tax, a payroll tax (in the case of labor income), withholding taxes, or an income-type value-added tax based on the origin principle. The source country has two primary instruments for exercising its entitlement to tax income accruing to nonresidents. One is its definition of source, which determines its share of the tax base, and the other is the tax rate that it applies to that share of the base. In the absence of international treaty rules, each source country will tend to choose policy options to serve its own interests with respect to each aspect.

- *Division of tax base.* Corporations resident in one country and investing in another usually derive income not only from operations in that one source country, but also from other source countries, including the residence country. Consequently, each source country has to determine what share of the worldwide profits of the multinational corporation it can claim for tax purposes. The current international practice of assigning profits to source countries by means of unilateral separate accounting is proving to be increasingly arbitrary as international business operations become more intertwined, with shared costs and overheads and other interdependencies (McLure 1984; Bird and Mintz 2003). Variability in accounting rules add a further complication. In the absence of international agreements each source country will adopt accounting rules and permit transfer pricing that assign to it as large a share of the base as possible. With each country following its own source rules, both gaps and overlaps in the assignment of tax base may result.

- Rate of tax. The tax claim of the source country is a product of the rate of tax that it applies and its claim to the tax base. The tax rate involves both the corporate tax on basic profits and the withholding tax applied to remitted dividends. In the absence of treaty agreements the choice of rates may be subject to conflicting purposes: the desires to capture as large a tax share of profits and dividends as possible and to attract as large an inflow of capital as possible by offering tax incentives. This tradeoff can be avoided to some extent by offering profits tax incentives to attract incoming investment, while applying relatively high withholding tax rates to recoup revenue losses and encourage reinvestment of earnings. Countries that depend heavily on investment inflow from a single capital-exporting country that offers a foreign tax credit often adopt "soak up" tax rates that are sufficient to absorb the maximum allowable credit.

This pattern of tax behavior by source countries can lead to tax competition among capital-importing countries, with the result that no one country obtains enough additional investment from abroad to justify the lower tax. This especially will be the case where the residence country either exempts its foreign income from tax or treats foreign income taxes as deductible costs, thus leaving foreign investment flows open to variations in tax rates of the source countries. Furthermore, such tax competition may have damaging effects on domestic tax equity and possibly on the conduct of the public sector if the tax incentives offered to nonresident investors have to be extended to domestic investors (Musgrave 1991; Avi-Yonah 2000). These are highly relevant problems for developing countries, which need foreign capital for development but also need to create the infrastructure to support that development.

Need for cooperative rules

In the absence of international agreements taxation of foreign income earned by residents and of domestic income earned by nonresidents can raise problems of inefficiency in the allocation of foreign investment and predatory inequities in the tax shares of the income therefrom. Cooperative rules are needed for both economic efficiency and internation equity. Cooperation is also essential for administrative reasons, in particular for reporting purposes.

Cooperation may take various forms. It may be represented by the current network of bilateral treaties between countries of residence and source, which broadly follow an internationally accepted model tax treaty format (OECD 2003). It would be desirable to supplement such treaties with multilateral agreements, particularly among source countries, to prescribe rules for the division of the tax base and for rates of taxation. Finally, for reasons discussed below, a higher degree of international cooperation may ultimately be needed that assigns certain taxes, such as the corporation income tax, to an international tax authority (see section below on "Higher degrees of cooperation").

Tax competition or coordination. While the case for tax competition seems compelling as analogous to the case for competition in the private sector, it has been highly controversial (see Oates 2001 for a review of the literature). Extended too far, it may endanger the freedom of jurisdictions to form their own tax systems, thereby conflicting with the principle of subsidiarity as established by the European Union. Not surprisingly, coordination is of primary importance for the taxation of capital income, the most mobile and complex tax base. The same focus holds for tax competition, an alternative and contrary perspective on tax policy in the international setting. A word, therefore, might be added on how tax competition differs from cooperative coordination.

TAX COMPETITION TO ATTRACT CAPITAL. Tax competition does not involve competition for the most equitable and efficient way to finance the required level of public services. Instead, it uses taxation as an instrument for attracting capital by offering preferences that raise net returns over those available in higher tax jurisdictions (Wilson 1999; Zodrow 2003). As investment from abroad increases, so do the productivity of labor and economic growth. These gains come at the cost of efficient global capital allocation, however, and of equitable and efficient taxation. The spirit of tax competition thus runs counter to that of coordination, the principal purpose of which is to neutralize the impact of taxation on capital flows.

Tax competition tends to be self-defeating. In the context of game theory tax competition differs from the simple prisoner's dilemma, in which two players may reach an equilibrium, though not necessarily an efficient one, in a once-for-all agreement. Instead, numerous players and successive moves are involved. As any one jurisdiction offers a tax incentive, others follow suit. Successive moves are followed by further diversion of capital to the haven with highest net return, eventually leading to a "race to the bottom" or zero taxation of capital income. The resulting shrinkage of the tax base will increase the cost of taxation and, as the literature on tax competition concludes, will lead to a suboptimal budget size and an inequitable distribution of the tax burden. As tax competition expands to include high-skilled labor, now increasingly mobile, the tax base shrinks further, leaving only unskilled labor and rental income to be taxed. The race to the very bottom, to be sure, rests on some unrealistic assumptions, such as large numbers, perfect markets, and balanced budgets, but the extensive literature on tax competition generally agrees that a suboptimal budget size will result (Oates 2001; Razin and Sadka 1991; OECD 1998).

COMPETITION AS FISCAL DISCIPLINE. There is, however, a more basic critique to be met. Tax competition, far from being harmful, is asserted to be a useful instrument of fiscal discipline (Borcherding 1977), holding down the size of budgets and the role of the public sector, the familiar "Leviathan" argument (Edwards and

Keen 1996). The problem is not how to improve tax design, but how to reduce taxation. While bureaucrats find it in their interest to overexpand budgets, the argument goes, they are kept from doing so out of fear that tax bases will move to lower tax jurisdictions. Tax competition is seen as a positive force, curtailing the size of the budget and securing an efficient fiscal system. With capital the most mobile part of the tax base, this view again focuses on capital income taxation.

But consider the underlying premise, that bureaucrats generate undue budget expansion. Some such tendency may exist, but other factors enter as well. Bureaucrats working for a tax-hostile executive may gain from supporting tax reduction, and voters may undervalue the benefits of public goods. Moreover, even if tax competition prevents excessive budgets, it may open the way to inequitable undertaxation of mobile factors such as capital income. There may well be preferable ways to build an efficient fiscal system involving broad issues of social and political theory. This is not the place to examine whether budgets are too large or too small, but tax competition is hardly the appropriate way to apply any needed correction.[9]

Tax coordination: equalization or harmonization. Tax coordination seeks to avoid the inefficiencies and inequities that arise as economic activity flows across borders and is exposed to multiple tax jurisdictions. Coordination does not necessarily require a commonality of tax bases and rates. Rather, it may call for harmonization of tax systems, leaving jurisdictions free to choose their own tax design. While coordination may be implemented through equalization, as with the recent adoption by the Nordic countries of a similar corporate tax rate and as proposed for the European Union, equalization offends the subsidiarity rule. Tax harmonization, an alternative form of coordination, far from requiring uniformity is a handmaiden of the subsidiarity rule.

The spirit of tax coordination runs counter to that of tax competition. Coordination is designed to improve the quality of tax systems across jurisdictions, whereas tax competition seeks to achieve nonfiscal objectives at the cost of fair and efficient taxation. Most inefficiencies and inequities in an uncoordinated setting can be corrected by well designed coordination, but international agreement to do so requires that the procedure promise mutual gains. Few empirical studies have measured the welfare gains from coordination (or the losses from tax competition), and all are sensitive to assumptions in the models, but most tentatively suggest that the gains are modest (Zodrow 2003).

Internation equity. The share of the tax base and the tax rate applied by source countries to income accruing to others should be viewed as a matter of internation equity, calling for international cooperation (Musgrave 2000b).

Share of tax base. In current practice the division of the tax base at the international level is generally determined unilaterally by the process of separate accounting applied to separate business entities, with the profits derived from the actual or notional arm's-length pricing and accounting practices of one country often in conflict with those of others (OECD 1991). With business operations integrated in various ways across borders, the untangling of profits and their assignment to different source jurisdictions becomes an artificial exercise, and rule of thumb measures often have to be adopted. Furthermore, this practice lends itself to profit shifting by the taxpayer to lower tax jurisdictions. Most fundamentally, rules are needed to assign equitable shares to the source countries in the income accruing to multinational corporations. Common source rules employing unitary combination and uniform formula apportionment are needed to avoid arbitrary and predatory practices for determining source (Musgrave 1984).

With the prevalence of interconnected business operations, no single formula based on economic theory alone can be claimed to correctly assign profits to source countries. Consequently, to achieve mutual international agreement, it is necessary to adopt a formula that is generally acceptable for reasons of fairness. One possible formula among many might contain elements that on the supply side measure each country's share of the firm's factors of production, such as labor and capital, and on the demand side measure each country's contribution to the firm's sales. Whatever the formula, it is critical that there be international agreement on its general form.[10]

RATE OF TAX. The rate of tax applied at source should also be a matter of international agreement based on standards of internation equity. An obvious rule would be based on reciprocity, or internationally equal rates of tax on income accruing to nonresidents. Bilateral tax treaties usually call for reciprocally equal rates to be applied to withholding taxes, while profits are subject to a rule of nondiscrimination between resident and nonresident taxpayers. For the standard of internation equity as proposed here, however, reciprocity should apply to such taxes in combination with withholding taxes. The rates applied to resident corporations are governed by domestic tax policy considerations, such as taxpayer equity and economic growth, whereas the rates applied to nonresidents should be determined by the appropriate share of their income earned at source, a share that should be set by international agreement and apply equally to all source countries.

Clearly, the usual treaty requirements of nondiscrimination in corporate income tax combined with reciprocity in withholding tax rates is unsatisfactory with respect to internation equity. If for administrative or other reasons the nondiscrimination rule must apply to the corporate income tax rate, then withholding tax rates on the remitted income might be adjusted to yield, in combination with the corporate income tax rate, a common and internally agreed rate. Thus, if the internationally agreed tax share is 30 percent and the source country's corporate income tax rate is 25 percent, then the source country's permitted withholding tax rate (wt) would be:

$$\{.30 = .25 + wt(1.0 - .25)\} \text{ or } wt = 6.7 \text{ percent.}$$

If the source country's corporate profits tax rate is 40 percent, its withholding tax rate would be negative, calling for a refund of 1.7 percent. In all cases the withholding rate would be applied to the remitted income grossed up by the profits tax.

Neutrality. While the exercise of source entitlement involves the claim by the source country on the income accruing to nonresidents and is a matter of internation equity, to be resolved by international agreement, the exercise of residence entitlement determines the ultimate tax burden borne by corporations in the residence country with investments in the source country. Allocative efficiency with respect to foreign investment requires a regime of international tax neutrality such that investors in the residence country face the same effective tax rate whether they invest at home or abroad. Once the source country's tax is paid, the ultimate effective tax rate on that income is determined by the residence country.

Ensuring international tax neutrality is thus in the hands of the residence country. It can attain international neutrality by applying its tax to foreign income grossed up by the tax paid to the source country and applying a full credit for that tax, with a refund if the credit exceeds the resident country's tax on the same income. Thus, if the source country's combined (corporate and withholding) tax rate is 30 percent and the residence country's is 40 percent, the residence country should impose a tax rate of 10 percent on dividends grossed up by the source country's combined rate. Additionally, the residence country should tax such profits as they are earned, without deferral until repatriation.

While this situation of "capital-export neutrality" as it has been termed (Musgrave 1959) is needed for allocative efficiency, it requires some sacrifice of tax revenue by the residence country in the interests of international efficiency.[11] Capital outflow will be larger and the tax take will be less than if the residence country pursues a tax policy that serves only its national economic interests. The practice of taxing foreign income and providing a foreign tax credit will render tax competition unattractive to the capital-importing source countries and protect them from the ensuing loss of revenue. Cooperation is thus required of the residence countries in the interest of international welfare, just as cooperation is required of the source countries in the interest of internation equity.

Individual taxpayer equity. While cooperative agreements among countries are necessary to secure internation equity and the efficient allocation of international capital, there is no reason why countries should have to surrender their ability to apply their own standards of taxpayer equity in the process. As noted, it is possible to take different views of individual taxpayer equity (insofar as it applies to those receiving foreign income), each calling for different treatment of the foreign tax.

The standard of what might be called an "international" view of equity would call for treating the foreign tax the same as the domestic tax, a view consistent with the foreign tax credit approach. The same treatment for corporations receiving income from abroad is necessary not only to secure neutral tax treatment for corporate investment but also to preserve equity for individual shareholders by equalizing the underlying corporate tax on shareholders' dividends. In the same spirit, if dividends are distributed directly from a corporation in a source country to a resident shareholder in the residence country, the residence country's corporate tax should be interposed with a credit for the foreign tax before shareholders' dividends are taxed.[12] Alternatively, under what may be called a "national" view of taxpayer equity the foreign tax is treated as a deduction from foreign-source income (in effect, a cost of doing business), and the residence country's corporate tax is applied to foreign earnings net of foreign tax. This treatment of the foreign tax is similar to the central government's treatment of state and local taxes in the United States and other federal systems. Finally, under a third view, taxpayer equity can be said to apply only to the domestic tax, and so no adjustment (either credit or deduction) for the foreign tax is called for. Only the international view of taxpayer equity is consistent with capital-export neutrality.

Administrative cooperation. It goes without saying that there are considerable administrative difficulties in implementing such a model. Cooperation among national tax administrations is vital to its success, particularly cooperation on the exchange of information needed to ensure compliance (Mintz 2004).[13]

INCOME TAX REFORMS

The discussion thus far has been within the traditional framework that treats corporate income tax as a separate tax. In recent years interest has grown in reforms that would remove the tax or integrate it with the personal income tax on shareholders. These reforms are motivated by a desire to improve the efficiency of capital allocation by reducing the disincentives to save and invest and to distribute corporate earnings and by reducing the incentives to debt finance and to operate in the unincorporated form. One reform would eliminate the corporate income tax, substituting either accrual taxation of capital gains or imputation of retained corporate earnings to the shareholder, to be taxed along with dividends under the personal income tax.

Another reform sees the corporate tax not as an extra tax but as a withholding tax against the personal income taxation of dividends. The corporate tax would be credited against the personal income tax on dividends, thereby integrating the two taxes and eliminating the so-called "double taxation" of dividend income.[14] The dividend-credit approach is administratively more feasible, especially in the international context (Boadway and Bruce 1992) and is one of the two types of reform evaluated below.

Yet another approach, applied recently by the Nordic countries, is the dual income tax with separate rates on capital and wage income. Finally, and diverging most fundamentally from past practice, is a shift from an income- to a consumption-based tax.

Integration of personal and corporate income taxes

There are two ways to integrate corporate and individual income taxes, a long-standing proposal for removing "double taxation" of dividends (U.S. Department of the Treasury 1992). The dividend-received credit method avoids double taxation by applying the personal income tax to dividends grossed up by the underlying corporate tax and crediting the corporate tax. The dividend-paid credit method relieves dividends of the corporate tax when they are paid out and taxes them fully at the individual level.[15] Sometimes integration is partial, with a lower tax rate applied to dividends than to retained earnings. It is assumed for this discussion that all countries adopt the same approach. In the international context each approach can have different implications for residence and source countries.

Dividend-received credit. This approach has implications for internation equity, capital-export neutrality, and taxpayer equity.

INTERNATION EQUITY. The ability of the source country to exercise its entitlement to an appropriate tax share of the earnings accruing to a nonresident corporation is not disturbed since internation equity may be served by adjusting the withholding tax on the remitted dividends. Nor is there any interference with the entitlement of the residence country to tax all the capital income of its residents under the personal income tax. However, the residence country has to decide whether the foreign corporate tax on income earned abroad should be integrated with its own personal income tax on shareholders.

CAPITAL-EXPORT NEUTRALITY. To meet the standard of neutrality, the source country's corporate and withholding taxes on profits must again be credited against the residence country's corporate tax and the combined taxes must then be credited against the personal income tax on dividends. In this way shareholders are subject to the same combined effective tax rate whether the dividends emanate from investment abroad or at home. This implies, however, that the foreign taxes are passed through (via the residence country's corporate tax) as credits against the resident country's personal income tax. As will be evident, this suggests a larger loss of revenue in the interest of capital-export neutrality by the residence country than in the case of integration by the dividends-paid credit.

TAXPAYER EQUITY. The domestic corporate tax could act not only as a withholding agent but also as a pass-through agent for any crediting of foreign taxes on dividends from foreign corporate earnings. If the residence country accepts an international concept of taxpayer equity, the foreign tax would first be credited against the residence country's corporate tax on foreign earnings, and then the combined tax would be credited against shareholders' personal income tax. A national concept of taxpayer equity would deduct the foreign tax from foreign earnings, with the resident country's corporate tax applied to net foreign earnings and then credited against shareholders' personal income tax on dividends. Finally, if taxpayer equity is construed to call for no allowance for foreign tax, there would be no pass-through of the foreign corporate tax by crediting or deduction against the residence country's corporate tax before crediting to individual shareholders.

ADMINISTRATIVE PROBLEMS. Administrative problems would be somewhat increased for the country of residence of shareholders if rules to secure capital-export neutrality and taxpayer equity were implemented with the dividends-received form of integration. This would especially be the case if a shareholder were to invest directly in a foreign corporation and would then need to report foreign taxes on the profits underlying the dividend.[16] Again, cooperation among tax authorities would be necessary.

Dividends-paid credit. The dividends-paid credit seeks to integrate corporate and personal income taxes at the corporate level by relieving dividends, either fully or partially, from the profits tax. Assuming dividends to be fully free of tax, this raises the question of whether dividends paid to foreign investors should also be free of tax.

INTERNATION EQUITY. Clearly a regime of tax-free dividends would interfere with internation equity unless an appropriate compensatory withholding tax is applied on dividends paid abroad. In the absence of an international agreement to do so, from a revenue perspective the country that is a net payer of dividends abroad might prefer the dividends-received credit form of integration, while the country that is a net recipient of dividends from abroad would prefer the dividends-paid method.

CAPITAL-EXPORT NEUTRALITY. Attaining capital-export neutrality is in the hands of the residence country, which must achieve the same effective tax rate for the total tax on dividends from abroad as on dividends from domestic investment. If a dividends-paid credit is the rule, dividends must be relieved of corporate tax when paid. If both residence and source countries adopt this practice of integration, no further adjustment is needed when the foreign dividends are received in the residence country. But if the source country imposes a withholding tax on dividends paid to the residence country (in line with internation equity), the tax must be credited against the corporate tax in the residence country, which must in turn be credited against individual shareholders' personal income tax. Alternatively, the source country's withholding tax might be refunded to the corporation by the residence country before dividends are distributed to individual shareholders.

ADMINISTRATIVE PROBLEMS. Many other scenarios may be postulated, in which residence and source countries follow different modes of integration or in which one country integrates and the other does not. This brief outline gives a sense of how integration of corporate and personal income taxes further complicates coordination in the interests of taxpayer equity, internation equity, and capital-export neutrality.

The dual income tax. The Nordic countries have recently taken a novel approach to income tax reform, breaking the link between corporate and individual income taxes by moving to a dual income tax with separate rates on capital and labor income (Sørenson 1998; Cnossen 2000). Capital income is taxed at a low, flat rate, while progressive rates are applied to other income at the personal level. General adoption of the low, flat corporate rate permits personal income tax rates to differ, preserving a degree of tax sovereignty for the residence country and maintaining consistency with the principle of subsidiarity. The issues underlying the quest for personal and corporate tax integration disappear, and taxation of capital income is simplified. Although countries may differ in how they apply the dual income tax (such as point of collection and treatment of capital gains, interest, and royalties), the focus here is on taxation of corporate profits and dividends.

INTERNATION EQUITY. The source country's entitlement to share in the profit base of nonresident investors is preserved so long as the tax on corporate profits is collected at the source rather than at the recipient level. As applied in the Nordic countries, the tax on capital income has been imposed at uniform rates which, along with largely equal withholding rates on dividends, meet the standard of reciprocity. If corporate profits tax rates were unequal, compensatory withholding taxes (either positive or negative, as the case may be) would need to be applied to dividends paid abroad to maintain reciprocity, which is the sine qua non of internation equity.

CAPITAL-EXPORT NEUTRALITY. If all countries adopted uniform rates on corporate income, capital-export neutrality would be attained with pure source-based taxation. If such tax rates differ, however, source-based taxation alone leaves capital flows open to international tax differentials and the standard of capital-export neutrality is not met. When such differentials are present, capital-export neutrality requires a residence-based system, whereby corporate investors face the same rate of tax whether they invest at home or abroad. Double taxation might then be avoided either by the source country exempting the income accruing to nonresident corporations or, more realistically, by the residence country providing a full credit for the source country's tax against its own tax on the foreign income. In the case of an economic union or association with each member country applying a uniform rate, the criterion of capital-export neutrality would be met within the union without the need for residence-based taxation applied to internal investments, but it would not be met for investments made outside that area (where tax rates would likely differ). Member countries should then apply the residence principle to such investments, taxing income earned outside the union and giving full credit given for external taxes paid at source.

TAXPAYER EQUITY. While such a dual or schedular approach would simplify tax administration and compliance, it would come at the cost of excluding capital income from a uniform pattern of progressive rates at the shareholder level. If rates on capital income are variable among countries, this might be especially damaging to taxpayer equity in the international setting.

Higher degrees of cooperation

In the absence of cooperative agreements it is likely that both source and residence countries will exercise their entitlements in a way that serves their national interests, which may conflict with each other and with standards of internation equity and allocative efficiency. The current international tax regime is deficient in these respects despite an extensive network of treaties. A higher degree of cooperation is necessary to achieve an orderly, just, and efficient international tax regime that comes closer to meeting these criteria.

Whereas the question of internation equity has to be resolved among countries in their role as source countries, international efficiency in resource allocation is a standard determined by countries in their role as residence countries, unless all source countries adopt similar effective tax rates. Creating an international tax order of the kind outlined calls for a high degree of cooperation and an institutional structure analogous to that for implementing international agreements on trade. This process might begin with the design of an improved model tax treaty to replace outdated treaties that do not adequately address internation equity and capital-export neutrality.

The immense administrative and political difficulties inherent in such an undertaking might be lessened if responsibility for the corporate income tax were assigned to central authorities of groups of countries forming free trade areas or economic unions, with responsibility to negotiate agreements setting source rules and common tax rates. The tax revenue might then be allocated to member countries in line with mutually agreed source rules. Member countries would be free to set their own rules on the relation between their personal income taxes on resident shareholders and the corporate income tax on profits, whether earned within or outside the union (Musgrave 2000b).

Looking ahead, it can be expected that corporations will become ever more globalized, with interlocking relationships in both operations and ownership. Electronic commerce and the rapid transfer of funds across borders will further complicate tax administration and enforcement. Many of the problems associated with the establishment of a reasonable international tax order may well call for international administration of the corporate income tax, imposed at a uniform effective rate. This would help meet the efficiency criterion, although the primary task would be the distribution of the tax revenue among countries according to a source rule based on a single mutually acceptable formula, as broadly followed in some federal systems today, including Canada and Germany.

INTERNATIONAL ASPECTS OF CONSUMPTION TAXATION

The leading tax debate in recent years, especially in the United States, has concerned the merits of broad-based consumption taxes over traditional income taxes (Bradford and U.S. Treasury Policy Staff 1984; Rose 1990). Whatever the taxpayer equity properties of consumption taxes, the issue of concern here is the unilateral policies and multilateral agreements that would be needed to make such taxes consistent with the criteria outlined above: internation equity, international efficiency, and maintenance of entitlement by the residence country (Musgrave 2000a).

Consumption taxes take several forms, the principal distinction being between *in rem* types, such as retail sales and value-added taxes, and personal types, such as the personal expenditure tax. Numerous hybrids of consumption taxes have been proposed in the United States (McLure and Zodrow 1995). They usually involve a business cash-flow tax combined with a personal tax on wages or consumption expenditures and have been variously named the individual pre-payment tax, the unlimited savings allowance tax (Alliance USA 1995), and the flat rate tax (Hall and Rabushka 1995), creating a complex and sometimes confusing pattern.

Nature of entitlements with consumption taxation
Under a consumption tax the entitlement to tax by source and residence countries is defined in terms of consumption rather than income. The tax entitlement of the residence country applies to the total consumption of its residents or citizens. The origin of consumption goods substitutes for the source of income as the geographic-based tax entitlement. Analogous to the income tax entitlements, entitlements for the residence country of consumers call for a personal consumption or expenditure tax and entitlements for the source country call for a source-based *in rem* tax on consumption.

The two major consumption taxes considered here are the value-added tax and the personal expenditure tax, with some attention to a cash-flow business tax. Each is evaluated for its role in an international setting with cross-border capital and trade mobility.

Value-added tax (VAT). The two most commonly discussed VATs are of the consumption type (in general use in the European Union and elsewhere) and the income type. With both, the firm's base equals its sales minus purchases of inputs from other firms. The consumption type also allows for the deduction of capital equipment expenditures, while the income type permits only the deduction of depreciation. With both, if the tax is aimed at value added at origin, the base includes exports and excludes imports, while if the tax is directed to value added at destination the reverse applies.

As *in rem* taxes, origin-type VATs are appropriate instruments for exercising the tax entitlement of the country where the value added originates. But of course only the origin-consumption VAT conforms to the origin-consumption entitlement, while a destination-consumption VAT (or a retail sales tax) is consistent with residence entitlement, or a country's sovereignty over the consumption of its residents. As an *in rem* tax, however, it does not afford the residence country sovereignty over personal taxation with the aim of achieving individual taxpayer equity.

Personal expenditure tax. The base of the personal expenditure tax is the total income of the taxpayer minus net saving measured as the change in net worth (Kaldor 1965; Slemrod and Bakija 1996, pp. 203–04). Abstracting from various adjustments, the base should thus be similar to that of the destination-consumption VAT. If a country is to be assigned sovereignty over the total consumption of its residents as called for by residence entitlement, taxpayer equity is an important consideration and the personal rather than *in rem* form of consumption tax is preferable (Musgrave 1990). The residence country may thus choose an average level of tax to meet its revenue requirements and choose its own standard of taxpayer equity through the appropriate degree of progressivity of tax rates. Administrative and compliance costs are greater under the expenditure tax than under the VAT. For example, identifying and reporting foreign asset acquisition and withdrawal present substantial challenges for tax enforcement in the residence country.

Provided the tax base is comprehensive, including consumption abroad (for example, through foreign travel and tourism), the efficiency effects of tax rate differentials are relatively minor, since individuals are hardly likely to change their country of residence in response to these differentials. Thus tax competition might be blocked by replacing income with consumption as the tax base. Differential consumption taxes may still leave some scope for tax competition (now aimed to attract or retain high-income consumers), but its scope would be greatly reduced.

Business cash-flow tax. A business cash-flow tax has been proposed in conjunction with either a consumption or a wage tax on individuals, referred to here as cash-flow tax types 1 and 2. In type 1 the tax base is derived from the firm's cash receipts minus the cost of inputs other than wages. It allows for the deduction of investment cost when the investment is made rather than by accretion or depreciation of capital, as under the traditional definition of the corporate income tax base. With this instantaneous depreciation the "normal" return on investment is exempt from tax so that only "excess" returns and wages remain in the tax base. Cash-flow tax type 2 further excludes wages from the business cash-flow base, transferring them to the tax base at the individual level and taxing the remaining "excess" returns in the business tax base at a flat rate while permitting progressive rates to be applied at the personal level.

Neither type fits neatly into either the income- or consumption-based form of entitlements. Assuming that cash receipts and input costs from foreign operations of the firm are allowed for in the bases of both taxes, type 1 includes foreign wages and excludes all normal returns and therefore does not meet the requirement for income-based residence entitlement. With wages and "excess" profits included in the base, only a partial income-source entitlement requirement would be met. At the same time, if combined with a personal expenditure tax, the package would meet the consumption-residence entitlement requirement, providing that the personal expenditure tax has a comprehensive base.

In isolation the type 2 cash-flow tax would also not meet the income-based entitlements standards since only abnormal or "excess" profits are left in the base. A personal tax on wages, with which the type 2 cash-flow tax is usually combined, also fails to meet the income-residence requirement since capital income is excluded. With regard to the consumption-based standards of entitlement, neither the type 2 cash-flow tax nor the personal wage tax meet the residence entitlement, even if the necessary assumptions are made to render wages equivalent to consumption. Neither can the tax package be said to apply to consumption goods at origin, the requirement to meet the consumption-at-origin entitlement.

Cooperative coordination of consumption taxes

While the "residence entitlement" is fulfilled by the personal expenditure tax and the "origin entitlement" by the origin-consumption VAT, without certain cooperative measures these consumption taxes, like income taxes, may not comply with the criteria of international efficiency and internation equity.

It has been suggested that the tax base of this VAT is consistent with the requirement of the origin-based consumption entitlement. However, internation equity would further require a reciprocally equal tax rate on exports. Thus, unless the rates of all VATs are equal, a tax adjustment (either plus or minus) at the border would be needed.

On the requirement of international efficiency there has been considerable dispute regarding the distortion in patterns of trade caused by differential rates of a VAT of the origin type. It is usually argued that to avoid such distortions, VATs should be of the destination type, with exports subtracted from the base and imports included. Another argument suggests that adjustments through flexible exchange rates can resolve the problem (Feldstein and Krugman 1990).

CONCLUSION

The suggestions in this chapter on the conformance of various business profits taxes and consumption taxes with the requirements of entitlement to tax of the residence and source countries in a world of cross-border capital and trade flows are summarized in tables 1 and 2. The tables also show what adjustments source countries need to make to comply with a standard of internation equity—to take a reciprocally equal tax share in income or consumption attributable to others—and what adjustments residence countries need to make to ensure international neutrality with respect to the taxation of business income and commodity trade (Musgrave 1990; Grubert and Newlon 1999).

TABLE 1

Entitlements, international equity, and efficiency for business income taxes

	Corporate income tax (absolute)	Integrated corporate-personal			Cash-flow tax	
		Dividends-received credit	Dividends-paid credit	Dual or schedular	Wages included	Wages excluded
Conformity with entitlements						
Residence entitlement, consumption based	Not applicable	Not applicable	Not applicable	Not applicable	No	No
Origin entitlement, consumption based	Not applicable	Not applicable	Not applicable	Not applicable	Perhaps	No
Residence entitlement, income based	Yes, if base includes foreign income	No	Yes	Yes, if base includes foreign income	Partial	No
Source entitlement, income based	Yes	Yes	No	Yes	Partial	No
International coordination required						
International equity	Reciprocity in (profits tax + withholding tax on dividends) tax rate or adjustable withholding tax on dividends rates/ rebates on dividends	Reciprocity in (profits tax + withholding tax on dividends) tax rate or adjustable withholding tax on dividends rates/ rebates on dividends	Reciprocity in withholding tax on dividends tax rate on dividends	Reciprocity in (profits tax + withholding tax on dividends) tax rate or adjustable withholding tax on dividends rates/ rebates on dividends	Not applicable	Not applicable

| International efficiency | Tax foreign profits grossed up by foreign (profits tax + witholding tax on dividends) wtih foreign tax credit and no deferral | Credit foreign profits tax underlying dividends against profits tax of recipient firm | Credit foreign profits tax | Tax foreign profits grossed up by foreign (profits tax + withholding tax on dividends) with foreign tax credit and no deferral | Tax foreign profits grossed up by foreign (profits tax + withholding tax on dividends) with foreign tax credit and no deferral | Tax foreign profits grossed up by foreign (profits tax + withholding tax on dividends) with foreign tax credit and no deferral | Tax foreign profits grossed up by foreign (profits tax + withholding tax on dividends) with foreign tax credit and no deferral |

Source: Author's analysis and compilation.

TABLE 2

Entitlements, international equity, and efficiency for consumption taxes

	Value-added tax				Personal expenditure tax
	Consumption type		Income type		
	Origin type	Destination type	Origin type	Destination type	
Conformity with entitlements					
Residence entitlement, consumption based	No	Yes	Not applicable	Not applicable	Yes
Origin entitlement, consumption based	Yes	No	Not applicable	Not applicable	No
Residence entitlement, income based	Not applicable	Not applicable	No	No	Not applicable
Source entitlement, income based	Not applicable	Not applicable	Yes	No	Not applicable
International coordination required					
Internation equity	Equal rates on exports	Not applicable	Equal rates on exports	Not applicable	Not applicable
International efficiency	Equal rates or exchange rate adjustments	No adjustments needed	Equal rates or exchange rate adjustments	No adjustments needed	Tax allegiance based on citizenship as well as residence

Source: Author's analysis and compilation.

It is not surprising that no single tax fulfills all the conditions without the application of internationally accepted rules. Thus, while the corporate income tax (whether traditional or schedular) satisfies source entitlement, it does not meet residence entitlement unless foreign income is included in the base. Further, unless tax rates are equalized across countries, the residence country needs to bring the foreign income of its firms into its tax base by crediting foreign taxes (see table 1). At the same time, to accommodate internation equity, which suggests that a country should take reciprocally equal tax shares of income or consumption accruing to another, the withholding tax on dividends paid abroad should be adapted to the profits tax rate to yield an internationally agreed total tax share.

If the corporate tax is integrated with the individual income tax, much depends on the method of integration. Where the method is one of relieving dividends of tax to the shareholder (dividends-received credit), the tax conforms with source entitlement but not with residence entitlement. The reverse is true of the dividends-paid credit method, which is, however, more amenable to coordination measures to achieve internation equity and international efficiency. The cash-flow tax does not perform well on any count, particularly if wages are excluded from the base.

With respect to consumption taxes, the VAT of the consumption-origin type conforms with origin-consumption entitlement but requires an international agreement to equalize the tax on exports at a rate that may lie above or below the country's normal VAT rate. Yet what is needed to achieve tax neutrality with respect to trade, and in the absence of flexible exchange rates, is the destination-type VAT that taxes imports but relieves exports of tax. The personal expenditure tax, on the other hand, meets residence-consumption entitlement but not origin-consumption entitlement and also performs well on efficiency.

All this suggests that for a fair and efficient international tax order, countries should adopt combinations of taxes, as, for instance, the personal expenditure tax with a schedular corporate tax, or a VAT of the origin type together with an integrated corporate-individual income tax. This, of course, depends on whether international rules, where necessary, are applied.

Notes

1. For a more extended discussion of the issues discussed in this chapter, see Musgrave (1990, 2001).

2. The United States includes citizenship as well as residence as a basis for the right to tax individuals. See note 7 for the conditions establishing the residency of the corporation.

3. Subsidiarity is used to denote the degree of independence of member countries permissible within the rules of harmonization, in the spirit of allowing a maximum degree of tax diversity among member states consistent with the goals of tax harmonization.

4. The principle by which income should be taxable to the shareholder when accrued regardless of whether it has been realized as dividends.

5. This is common practice. The U.S. defers tax, with certain restrictions, for undistributed earnings of foreign-incorporated subsidiaries of U.S. corporations, but not for unincorporated branches of U.S. firms.

6. In a 1993 report the U.S. Treasury (1993) proposed five international tax policy objectives: simplicity of compliance and administration, preservation of the U.S. tax base, and consistency with international standards, economic efficiency, and competitiveness. There are likely to be inherent conflicts among these national objectives, requiring tradeoffs among them.

7. The question arises, how is "residency" of the corporation to be defined? Is it country of registration, of principal management, or of majority shareholder residence? For example, U.S. rules define residency as the country where the corporation is registered or incorporated, whereas the UK defines it as the location of principal management.

8. Effective tax rate is defined as the actual tax paid as a percentage of the true economic base in the absence of special deductions and allowing for economic depreciation. Thus, comparison of the corporate tax bases for tax purposes is as important as comparison of statutory tax rates.

9. For a discussion of the deleterious effects of tax competition on redistributive policies in the European Union, see Sinn (1990).

10. Experience with attempts to reach uniformity of formula apportionment among the states in the United States is not encouraging.

11. See Grubert and Mutti (1995), in which an efficiency-based defense of the policy of capital-export neutrality is critiqued.

12. This procedure is followed in the French precompte system.

13. Going further, a World Tax Organization to parallel the World Trade Organization might be called for in an economically linked world (Tanzi 1998).

14. This treatment falls short of complete integration when profits are retained rather than fully distributed, thus delaying tax payment until realization. Complete integration would require taxation of capital gains when they are accrued.

15. See note 12.

16. This presents particular problems for value-added and other sales taxes (McLure 2003).

References

Alliance USA. 1995. "USA Tax System, Description, and Explanation of the Unlimited Savings Allowance Income Tax System." *Tax Notes* 66 (March): 1483–1575.

Avi-Yonah, Reuven S. 2000 "Globalization, Tax Competition, and the Fiscal Crisis of the Welfare State." *Harvard Law Review* 113: 1573–1603.

Bird, Richard M., and Jack M. Mintz. 2003. "Sharing the International Tax Base in a Changing World." In Sijbern Cnossen and Hans Werner Sinn, eds., *Public Finance and Public Policy in the New Century*. Cambridge, Mass.: MIT Press.

Boadway, Robin, and Neil Bruce. 1992. "Problems with Integrating Corporate and Personal Income Taxes in an Open Economy." *Journal of Public Economics* 48 (1): 39–66.

Borcherding, Thomas E. 1977. *Budgets and Bureaucrats*. Durham, N.C.: Duke University Press.

Bradford, David F., and U.S. Treasury Policy Staff. 1984. *Blueprints for Basic Tax Reform*. 2nd edition. Arlington, Va.: Tax Analysts.

Cnossen, Sijbren. 2000. "Taxing Capital Income in the Nordic Countries: A Model for the European Union?" In Sijbren Cnossen, ed., *Tax Policy in the European Union*. Oxford: Oxford University Press.

Devereux, Michael P. 2004. "Some Optimal Tax Rules for International Portfolio and Direct Investment." *FinanzArchiv* 60 (1): 1–23.

Devereux, Michael, and Mark Pearson. 1989. *Corporate Tax Harmonisation and Economic Efficiency*. London: Institute for Fiscal Studies.

Edwards, Jeremy, and Michael Keen. 1996. "Tax Competition and Leviathan." *European Economic Review* 40 (1): 113–34.

Feldstein, Martin S., and David G. Hartman. 1979. "The Optimal Taxation of Foreign Source Investment Income." *Quarterly Journal of Economics* 93 (4): 613–29.

Feldstein, Martin S., and Paul Krugman. 1990. "International Trade Effects of Value-Added Taxation." In Assaf Razin and Joel Slemrod, eds., *Taxation in the Global Economy*. Chicago, Ill.: University of Chicago Press.

Grubert, Harry. 1998. "Taxes and the Division of Foreign Operating Income among Royalties, Interest, Dividends, and Retained Earnings." *Journal of Public Economics* 68 (2): 269–90.

Grubert, Harry, and John Mutti. 1995. "Taxing Multinationals with Portfolio Flows and R&D: Is Capital Export Neutrality Obsolete?" *International Tax and Public Finance* 2 (3): 439–57.

Grubert, Harry, and T. Scott Newlon. 1999. "The International Implications of Consumption Tax Proposals." In Joel Slemrod, ed., *Tax Policy in the Real World*. Cambridge: Cambridge University Press.

Hall, Robert E., and Alvin Rabushka. 1995. *The Flat Tax*. 2nd edition. Stanford, Calif.: Hoover Institution Press.

Hartman, David G. 1985. "Tax Policy and Foreign Direct Investment." *Journal of Public Economics* 26 (1): 107–21.

Hines, James R. Jr. 1994. "Credit and Deferral as International Investment Incentives." *Journal of Public Economics* 55 (2): 323–47.

————. 1997. "Tax Policy and the Activities of Multinational Corporations." In Alan J. Auerbach, ed., *Fiscal Policy: Lessons from Economic Research*. Cambridge, Mass.: MIT Press.

Kaldor, Nicholas. 1965. *An Expenditure Tax*. 4th edition. London: Irwin University Books.

Kaufman, Nancy H. 1998. "Fairness and the Taxation of International Income." *Law and Policy in International Business* 29 (2): 145–203.

McLure, Charles E., Jr. 1984. "Defining a Unitary Business: An Economist's View." In Charles. E. McLure Jr., ed., *The State Corporation Income Tax: Issues in Worldwide Unitary Combination*. Stanford, Calif.: Hoover Institution Press.

————. 2003. "The Value-Added Tax on Electronic Commerce in the European Union." *International Tax and Public Finance* 10 (6): 753–62.

McLure, Charles E., Jr., and George Zodrow. 1995. "Advantages of a Hybrid Direct Tax on Consumption." In National Tax Association, *Proceedings of the 88th Annual Conference on Taxation*. San Diego, Calif.

Mintz, Jack. 2004. "Corporate Tax Harmonization in Europe: It's All about Compliance." *International Tax and Public Finance* 11 (2): 221–34.

Musgrave, Peggy B. 1969. *United States Taxation of Foreign Investment Income: Issues and Arguments*. Cambridge, Mass.: Harvard Law School, International Tax Program.

————. 1984. "Principles for Dividing the State Corporate Tax Base." In Charles E. McLure, Jr., ed., *The State Corporation Income Tax: Issues in Worldwide Unitary Combination*. Stanford, Calif.: Hoover Institution Press.

————. 1990. "International Coordination Problems of Substituting Consumption for Income Taxation." In Manfred Rose, ed., *Heidelberg Congress on Taxing Consumption*. New York: Springer-Verlag.

————. 1991. "Merits and Demerits of Fiscal Competition." In Remy Prud'homme, ed., *Public Finance with Several Levels of Government*. Detroit, Mich.: Wayne University Press.

————. 2000a. "Consumption Tax Proposals in an International Setting." *Tax Law Review* 54: 77–100.

————. 2000b. "Interjurisdictional Equity in Company Taxation: Principles and Application to the European Union." In Sijbren Cnossen, ed., *Tax Policy in the European Union*. Oxford: Oxford University Press.

————. 2001. "Sovereignty, Entitlement, and Cooperation in International Taxation." *Brooklyn Journal of International Law* 26 (4): 1335–56.

Musgrave, Richard A. 1959. "Criteria for Foreign Tax Credit." In *Taxation and Operations Abroad*. Princeton: Tax Institute Inc. Tax Institute Symposium.

Musgrave, Richard A., and Peggy B. Musgrave. 1972. "Internation Equity." In Richard M. Bird and John G. Head, eds., *Modern Fiscal Issues*. Toronto: University of Toronto Press.

Oates, Wallace E. 2001. "Fiscal Competition and European Union: Contrasting Perspectives." *Regional Science and Urban Economics* 31 (2–3): 133–45.

OECD (Organisation for Economic Co-operation and Development). 1991. *Taxing Profits in a Global Economy—Domestic and International Issues.* Paris.

———. 1998. *Harmful Tax Competition: An Emerging Global Issue.* Paris.

———. 2003. *Model Tax Convention on Income and Capital.* Committee on Fiscal Affairs. Paris.

Razin, Assaf, and Efraim Sadka. 1991. "International Tax Competition and the Gains from Tax Harmonization." *Economics Letters* 37 (1): 69–76.

Richman [Musgrave], Peggy B. 1963. *Taxation of Foreign Investment Income: An Economic Analysis.* Baltimore, Md.: Johns Hopkins University Press.

Rose, Manfred. 1990. "The Superiority of a Consumption-Based Tax System." In Manfred Rose, ed., *Heidelberg Congress on Taxing Consumption.* New York: Springer-Verlag.

Sinn, Hans-Werner. 1990. "Tax Harmonisation and Tax Competition in Europe." *European Economic Review* 34: 489–504.

———. 1993. "Taxation and the Birth of Foreign Subsidiaries." In Horst Herberg and Ngo Van Long, eds., *Trade, Welfare, and Economic Policies.* Ann Arbor, Mich.: University of Michigan Press.

Slemrod, Joel. 1995. "Free Trade Taxation and Protectionist Taxation." *International Tax and Public Finance* 2 (3): 471–89.

Slemrod, Joel, and Jon Bakija. 1996. *Taxing Ourselves.* Cambridge, Mass.: MIT Press.

Sørenson, Peter, ed. 1998. *Tax Policy in the Nordic Countries.* New York: MacMillan.

Tanzi, Vito. 1998. "The Need for Tax Coordination in an Economically Integrated World." In Paolo Roberti, ed., *Financial Markets and Capital Income Taxation in a Global Economy.* New York: Elsevier.

U.S. Department of the Treasury. 1992. *Report on Integration of the Individual and Corporate Tax Systems.* Washington, D.C.: U.S. Government Printing Office.

———. 1993. "Treasury Report on International Tax Reform." *Tax Notes International* 6 (2): 269.

Wilson, John Douglas. 1999. "Theories of Tax Competition." *National Tax Journal* 52 (2): 269–304.

Zodrow, George. 2003. "Tax Competition and Tax Coordination in the European Union." *International Tax and Public Finance* 10 (5): 626–51.

Recognizing the Limits to Cooperation behind National Borders

Financing the Control of Transnational Terrorism

Todd Sandler

In a globalized world transnational terrorism is a global public bad, while actions to control it are a quintessential global public good. Globalization means that even the most impregnable national border may afford little security to a targeted country, because its citizens can be massacred in a tourist attraction abroad and its property can be bombed in a foreign capital. As terrorist attacks usually cause collateral damage to the host country and affect innocent passers-by, the global community gains from limiting transnational terrorism. Just consider how many Turkish and non-Turkish people were killed or wounded in the two car bombings aimed against British interests in Istanbul on November 20, 2003.[1]

Because of the sheer volume of cross-border flows of all kinds today, only a small fraction can be monitored, so terrorists can move personnel and equipment with relative ease. Terrorists weigh comparative risks when identifying the least secure venue at which to stage their attacks against a targeted country's assets. The transnationalization of terrorism means that one country's antiterrorism decisions are highly dependent on those of other countries. This interdependency implies that greater policy effectiveness can be achieved only if some antiterrorist decisions are made in concert with other countries.

Yet in response to the attacks on September 11, 2001 (called 9/11 after this), many industrial countries have greatly augmented their internal protective security efforts on their own. While critically important, these efforts can have counterproductive results. They may drive terrorists into developing countries that lack the capacity, funds, or political will to achieve an acceptable standard of security, which makes them an opportune host venue for terrorist activity. Recall the simultaneous terrorist attacks in Kenya on November

28, 2002.[2] Even though most countries have an incentive to enhance national security, developing countries may lack the resources to do so, threatening the security of all. Therefore, national action aimed at enhancing security must be complemented by international cooperation efforts to assist such vulnerable countries—the weakest links in the global chain of transnational terrorism control.

This chapter first discusses some characteristics of, and trends in, transnational terrorism. Next, it examines the cooperation challenges in controlling this phenomenon, differentiating between preemption (weakening or destroying terrorist capacity) and protection (augmenting protective security). The analysis shows that preemption has the properties of a pure public good and that protection often has the characteristics of what economists call a weakest link public good, with the overall level of security depending on the lowest level of control provided by any actor in the control chain, nationally and internationally. The discussion focuses on protection and on how to overcome related weakest link problems. The chapter also examines relevant country-level strategies, selecting the United States as a case study. The focus then shifts to the international level. The concluding section summarizes the findings and policy recommendations.

The analysis shows that nationally, the weakest link problems involved in enhancing national security can be overcome through the special powers entrusted in the central government. These include enforcing harmonized countrywide security standards and, where necessary, enabling all key actors to comply through interjurisdictional transfers or public to private incentive schemes. Providing such weakest link support nationally is one of the major functions of the U.S. Department of Homeland Security, established in 2003.

Although countries may realize that their security level depends on the level provided by the weakest international link, they may try to free ride when it comes to financing international cooperative action. A way forward could be to adopt a common pool approach and to introduce assessed contributions, such as those used to finance UN peacekeeping missions since the mid-1970s, combining, for example, such criteria as a country's income and the share of international attacks against its interests abroad.

But why would countries agree to such a pooled, assessment-based financing arrangement? Their incentive to do so might flow from fuller recognition of the evidence that even as governments remain extremely reluctant to cooperate on security matters (Sandler 2003; Sandler and Enders 2004), terrorists have cooperated in networks since the onset of modern-day terrorism in the late 1960s (Alexander and Pluchinsky 1992; Hoffman 1998). This cooperation asymmetry not only undermines antiterrorism policy but also provides a strategic advantage to terrorist networks. Effective control of transnational terrorism requires that governments cooperate across borders.

TRANSNATIONAL TERRORISM: CONCEPTS AND TRENDS

There are two types of terrorism, domestic and transnational. Domestic terror-ism is home grown and has consequences largely for the host country, its institu-tions, citizens, property, and policies. In a domestic terrorist incident perpetrators and targets are from the same country. Many ethnonationalist conflicts are asso-ciated only with domestic terrorism unless the rebels use transnational events to publicize their cause to the world. In recent years domestic incidents have out-numbered transnational incidents by about eight to one (MIPT 2003). Reflecting the topic of this volume, the focus here is on transnational terrorism.

Transnational terrorism involves more than one country, usually through the victims, targets, institutions, supporters, terrorists, and other implications. For example, the toppling of the World Trade Center towers was a transnational incident because the victims were from many different countries, the mission had been planned abroad, the terrorists were foreigners, and the implications of the event (financial repercussions, for example) were global. Transnational ter-rorist attacks often entail transboundary externalities: actions conducted by ter-rorists or authorities in one country impose uncompensated costs or benefits on people or property in another country. An attack against a multilateral organi-zation is a transnational incident owing to its multicountry impact, as in the case of the suicide car bombing of the UN headquarters in Baghdad on August 19, 2003.

The number of transnational terrorist incidents has declined in the post–cold war period compared with past decades, but the number of casualties has not fallen, meaning that events since 1992 have been more likely to end with deaths and injuries (table 1).[3] In an average year just under 40 percent of the attacks are directed against U.S. interests. Since very few transnational incidents take place on U.S. soil—9/11 being a noteworthy exception—one must conclude that the United States has been effective at deflecting the attacks abroad.[4] Excluding 2001, the average annual death toll from terrorist attacks is 329 people, a tiny fraction of the 40,000 or so people who die on U.S. highways annually. The death toll from the four hijackings on 9/11 is about equal to all transnational terrorism-related deaths during 1988–2000. Except for 2001, far more people are wounded than are killed in any year. Statistical analysis indicates that the attacks are cyclical (Enders, Parise, and Sandler 1992). Obviously, there is no way to know how many terror-ist events would have occurred had governments not taken protective and proac-tive policies, including invading Afghanistan (October 2001), collecting intelligence, infiltrating groups, freezing assets, and capturing terrorists.

Much of the terrorism that concerns the industrial world is transnational and has two primary motives: grievances against these countries' foreign policies and a desire to capture the world's attention. Efforts by industrial countries to secure their borders often deflect attacks to insecure targets abroad, as the U.S. experi-

TABLE 1

Transnational terrorism events, 1968–2003

Year	Number of events	Deaths	Wounded	Attacks on U.S. interests
2003	208	625	3,646	60
2002	199	725	2,013	77
2001	355	3,296	2,283	219
2000	426	405	791	200
1999	395	233	706	169
1998	274	741	5,952	111
1997	304	221	693	123
1996	296	314	2,652	73
1995	440	163	6,291	90
1994	322	314	663	66
1993	431	109	1,393	88
1992	363	93	636	142
1991	565	102	233	308
1990	437	200	675	197
1989	375	193	397	193
1988	605	407	1,131	185
1987	665	612	2,272	149
1986	612	604	1,717	204
1985	635	825	1,217	170
1984	565	312	967	133
1983	497	637	1,267	199
1982	487	128	755	208
1981	489	168	804	159
1980	499	507	1,062	169
1979	434	697	542	157
1978	530	435	629	215
1977	419	230	404	158
1976	457	409	806	164
1975	382	266	516	139
1974	394	311	879	151
1973	345	121	199	152
1972	558	151	390	177
1971	264	36	225	190
1970	309	127	209	202

TABLE 1 CONTINUED

Transnational terrorism events, 1968–2003

Year	Number of events	Deaths	Wounded	Attacks on U.S. interests
1969	193	56	190	110
1968	125	34	207	57

Source: U.S. Department of State various years; tables provided to the author in 1988 by the U.S. Department of State, Office of the Ambassador at Large for Counterterrorism.

ence demonstrates. At times, targeted nations may work at cross-purposes by engaging in a deterrence race in an attempt to make the attacks occur elsewhere (Sandler and Siqueira 2003). These efforts may be counterproductive if they result in the deflector's citizens being targeted in a country that has less ability to inhibit attacks or to bring terrorists to justice. As terrorists look for an opportune location, some of the grievances against industrial countries' policies are transferred to developing countries, whose less secure environments make them an attractive staging place for terrorist events.

Thus, the security policies of industrial countries may have unintended negative externalities for developing countries whose security capacity may already be compromised owing to domestic terrorism and nearby conflicts. The globalization of terrorism poses a collective action question: in whose interest is it to improve security in developing countries, plagued in some cases by both domestic terrorism and imported transnational terrorism?

CONTROL OF TRANSNATIONAL TERRORIST THREATS: THE COOPERATION CHALLENGES

Terrorism control can be achieved in different ways. Two important strategies are preemption (active measures to weaken a terrorist group, for example, by attacking its training camps and infrastructure) and enhanced security (for example, improved screening arrangements for passengers, luggage, and freight at airports and seaports). Each strategy achieves a different outcome, with different public benefits and underlying incentive structures.

Preemption or enhanced security?

Preemption is a pure public good, because it makes it difficult for terrorists to launch subsequent attacks. Assume two actors. The preemption benefits achieved depend on the actors' cumulative efforts—identical inputs by each provide twice the benefits of each one acting alone. Thus, preemption abides by a summation aggregator where the overall level of the good consumed equals the sum of the amounts provided.[5] If each actor contributes two units of a pure public good, both derive benefits from the four aggregate units. For these public goods, contributions are perfect substitutes so that a unit supplied by one actor offers the same collective benefits as a unit supplied by any other actor. Because only aggregate contributions matter, a pure public good is associated with free-riding, as potential contributors wait for others to provide the good. As long as the good is supplied, other actors benefit whether they participated in supplying it or not.

By contrast, promoting security, say, against bombs in checked bags aboard planes, depends on the least vigilant connecting airport's scanning techniques, especially because transferred bags are typically not reexamined (Heal and Kunreuther 2003). Thus, security—or protection—is a weakest link public good. That means that everyone's participation is essential since the smallest provision level determines the amount of the public good that generates benefits. If, for example, one actor supplies three units of the weakest link public good and the other provides nothing, then both effectively consume zero units of the good. Thus, the incentive to free ride is absent. The anticipated (and rational) behavior is to match the smallest provision level because to supply more uses a country's scarce resources without gaining additional benefits.

To illustrate the strategic implications of these two different public goods, the appendix presents simple 2 × 2 game representations in which two players—the United States and the European Union—must jointly decide between preemption and security upgrades to counter terrorism.

Although these games are simple and stylized, they illustrate important points about international incentives to control terrorism. The first game corresponds to a situation where the two players decide whether to preempt, with the benefits of preemption being the same for both players (Sandler and Arce M. 2003). This game represents a prisoner's dilemma whose low-level equilibrium corresponds to a situation where each player acting individually is better off not preempting, a situation that can be improved only if both agree to act in concert.[6] The incentives to preempt change if the distribution of benefits is asymmetric. Since the United States is the target of the greatest share of transnational attacks, one can assume that it obtains a larger benefit from acting to preempt than the European Union does. In this case the dominant strategies are asymmetric: the United States has a dominant strategy to preempt, while the European Union has a dominant strategy to free ride. The Nash equilibrium (a position from which neither player would unilaterally want to change its choice if given the opportunity) corresponds to the situation where the United States preempts alone.

Because terrorists do not target countries equally, favorite targets derive greater benefits from acting alone, and this motivates their efforts (as shown in the appendix). If terrorists target all countries equally, no country may perceive sufficient gains to resort to proactive measures such as preemption. Terrorists bring about strong antiterrorist responses by favoring some targets over others. While a case can be made that countries such as the United States ought to assume more of the burden of global antiterrorist efforts because their policies give rise to more terrorism, there is no need to make this case. The United States is motivated to do more because it gains disproportionately from proactive measures. Clearly, perceived U.S. gains following 9/11 motivated its leadership role in Afghanistan. Thus, asymmetric benefits can induce action.

Next, consider upgrading security at vulnerable venues, which is a weakest link public good. The lower level of protection determines the level of protection afforded to all. If just one player upgrades security, the risks of a terrorist incident remain unchanged. As explained in the appendix, there is no dominant strategy for this weakest link scenario. There are, however, two Nash equilibriums in which either both players act or none of them acts. If each player has several provision options—to supply up to a set number of units in one-unit increments—for a weakest link public good such as security upgrades, then all of the Nash equilibriums correspond to situations where players' effort levels are the same (Sandler 1998). Which equilibrium applies is a matter of relative resource capacity. If one player has less capacity to provide because of income, the outcome will be determined by that player. Thus, each player may contribute two units, because this is the maximum level that the poorer one can afford.

Further reflections on protection against transnational terrorism as a weakest link public good

Weakest link scenarios apply to a number of antiterrorist policies including eliminating safe havens, freezing terrorist assets, and maintaining security standards. They can relate to national strategies as well as to international strategies.

Problems arise for weakest link antiterrorist policies when one or more players do not have the income or capacity to achieve an acceptable standard of action. For example, even one safe haven can jeopardize everyone's safety and completely negate the collective efforts of others to eliminate safe havens. In such cases a prime target country may gain significantly by helping a weakest link country achieve an acceptable level of national security.

In the case of transnational terrorism appropriate levels of weakest link measures of control are achieved when agents within targeted countries have similar capabilities and derive similar benefits from action and when similar conditions apply across countries. In other scenarios some type of centralized effort is required by a capable federal or central government (for national-level action) or a country (for international cooperation efforts) or another collective that raises low provision levels to an acceptable standard.

NATIONAL RESPONSES TO CONTROLLING TRANSNATIONAL TERRORISM

This section examines how some of the weakest link challenges involved in terrorism control have been addressed at the national level. Although the events of

9/11 unleashed a flurry of activities in many countries,[7] the discussion here focuses on the United States. As a federal country the United States confronts its own intergovernmental (federal, state, local authority) cooperation challenges. This permits viewing not only the need for complementary national and international cooperation strategies but also the difference in the functioning of cooperation within and across countries.

The situation before 9/11

As various post-9/11 investigations and reports have pointed out, a major weakness of the preceding years was that responsibility for preventing and responding to terrorist attacks was spread across many state and nonstate agencies.[8] Communication and coordination between them was weak, and the capacity and incentive of individual agents to contribute differed.

For example, state and local governments had responsibility in their jurisdictions for protecting buildings, public places, and cities. Various federal agencies had responsibility at home for protecting federal buildings, national parks, border crossings, and the nation's capital. The federal government was in charge of gathering intelligence on terrorism and sharing information with state and local jurisdictions. And it was responsible for any overseas action, including the use of military force, against terrorists or their supporters.

Security at U.S. airports was provided primarily by airlines, airport authorities, and local authorities. The airlines used money from a security surcharge on tickets to pay for private sector screeners and other security activities. There were virtually no guidelines on screeners' qualification or training, and screeners often had little training and received low wages. Thus, airlines may have had a perverse incentive to minimize their expenditures on security. And local authorities, too, may not always have had the right motivation. They had to pay for airport police from "their" taxes.[9]

Many of these problems continued in the initial months after 9/11. Thus, U.S. state and local governments had to continue covering much of the cost associated with preventing terrorist acts in their jurisdiction or responding to elevated terrorist alert levels issued by the federal government. The National Governors Association estimated added antiterrorism expense of $650 million for 2001, while the U.S. Conference of Mayors estimated added expense of $525 million (Bush 2002; U.S. Conference of Mayors 2002). The Conference of Mayors predicted added costs of $2.1 billion in 2002 unless the federal government came to the assistance of cities.

Clearly, the pre-9/11 situation was a mosaic of different preferences, measures, and security outcomes.

Policy reforms after 9/11

The creation in 2003 of the U.S. Department of Homeland Security (DHS) was intended to address these and many other problems. The department is headed by a cabinet-level secretary to coordinate efforts to prevent, respond to, and recover from terrorist acts (U.S. Congress 2002; U.S. DHS 2004c). It brings together into a single organization 180,000 employees from 22 separate government agencies. With homeland security now centralized, the department can draw on the enforcement powers and the tax-raising ability of the federal government. Thus, it has the means to raise security standards at all jurisdictional levels, for example, by providing funding to lower level jurisdictions, including small townships, that otherwise would be unable to prepare for or respond to a biological or chemical terrorist attack. In principle, the establishment of the DHS addresses the weakest link problem by achieving security standards countrywide.

The DHS provides this assistance through a number of programs. The grant-sharing formula for first responders and other aid is geared to the likely threat, which ideally equates to the threat at the margin, thereby minimizing the weakest link problem. For example, the Office for Domestic Preparedness instituted a first-responder program that gives grants to states to assist their efforts to protect against and respond to terrorist attacks.[10] These grants pay for local public safety and law enforcement personnel training, wages (including overtime pay during alerts), equipment, and exercises. States are required to distribute 80 percent to the local level (cities, towns, counties). Some of this money is earmarked to protect critical infrastructure and high-threat urban areas. Distribution of the first-responder grants is based on population density, vulnerabilities, and gathered risk-assessment intelligence. For 2005 about $3.5 billion in grants was allocated to the states (the allocations were $1.96 billion in 2003 and $4.36 billion in 2004).

The Federal Law Enforcement Training Center provides basic and advanced counterterrorism training for federal, state, and local officials. Its budget was $170 million in 2003, $191 million in 2004, and was anticipated to be $196 million in 2005 (table 2). Entities whose activities fall under the heading Preparedness and Recovery transfer resources to states and local jurisdictions to prepare for and respond to bioterrorism attacks. In 2003 some $1.6 billion of the total $5.2 billion budget of the Emergency Preparedness and Response Division was set aside for states and local jurisdictions (Bush 2002). And the Information Analysis and Infrastructure Protection Directorate integrates the collection and dissemination of intelligence on terrorism, to foster improved links among jurisdictional levels. Its budget was slated to grow from $185 million in 2003 to $834 million in 2004 and is expected to reach $864 million in 2005.

To improve airport security, DHS implemented a "federalization" process, training and deploying professional screeners at all U.S. airports. These federal employees must meet a higher standard of training than their private counterparts. In addition, improved equipment was installed at airports to screen passengers, hand baggage, and checked luggage. In line with this the 2005 budget request allocates $50 million for improved screening devices (U.S. DHS 2004a, p. 7).

TABLE 2

Budgets for Department of Homeland Security by Organization as of January 31, 2004, fiscal 2003–05
(millions of U.S. dollars)

Organization	2003	2004[a]	2005[b]
Security Enforcement and Investigation	21,566	22,606	24,691
Border and Transportation Security Under Secretary	0	8	10
U.S. VISIT Program	380	328	340
Bureau of Customs and Border Protection	5,887	5,942	6,199
Bureau of Immigration and Customs Enforcement	3,262	3,654	4,011
Transportation Security Administration	4,648	4,405	5,297
United States Coast Guard	6,196	6,935	7,471
United States Secret Service	1,193	1,334	1,363
Preparedness and Recovery	5,175	5,493	7,372
Emergency Preparedness and Response, Federal Emergency Management Agency (excluding Biodefense)[c]	5,175	4,608	4,844
Biodefense	0	885	2,528
Research, Development, Training, Assessments, and Services	2,330	3,591	3,810
Bureau of Citizenship and Immigration Services	1,422	1,653	1,711
Federal Law Enforcement Training Center	170	191	196
Information Analysis and Infrastructure Protection Directorate	185	834	864
Science and Technology Directorate	553	913	1,039
Departmental Management and Operations	2,111	4,851	4,294
Departmental Operations	22	211	405
Technology Investments	47	184	226
Counterterrorism Fund	10	10	20
Office for Domestic Preparedness	1,961	4,366	3,561
Inspector General	71	80	82
Total	31,182	36,541	40,167

a. Estimated. Total excludes war supplemental funding.
b. Requested amounts. The actual enacted budget for 2005 was $40.7 billion (U.S. DHS 2004b).
c. Fiscal 2003 includes supplemental funding for Emergency Preparedness and Response, Federal Emergency Management Agency ($1.4 billion); all other supplemental funding has been excluded.
Source: U.S. DHS 2004a (p. 13).

Among the organizations of the DHS, those whose activites fall under the heading Security, Enforcement, and Investigation (which includes border and transportation security) have taken up the largest portion of the DHS budget (see table 2). The Bureau of Customs and Border Protection has a significant antiterrorism component to keep terrorists and their weapons from entering the country, while the Bureau of Immigration and Customs Enforcement has less to do with antiterrorism. The Transportation Security Administration deals in large part with securing the country's airports and funding the federal screeners and equipment. It also compensates airlines for security upgrades (for example, $100 million in 2003 to reinforce cockpit doors[11]).

Other DHS divisions include the Coast Guard, which protects against terrorism by guarding the nation's coastline and ports while providing many other benefits, such as drug interdiction and protection of coastal resources. The Science and Technology Directorate addresses terrorist threats from weapons of mass destruction, including biological, chemical, radiological, and nuclear. The remaining DHS units have little to do with fighting terrorism.

From fiscal 2002 to fiscal 2004 the DHS budget grew by more than 60 percent, to more than $36 billion (U.S. DHS 2003), and it has grown to $40.7 billion in fiscal 2005 (U.S. DHS 2004b). Some $24 billion, or 66 percent, of the 2004 budget is truly for homeland security; the rest supports nonsecurity activities in some of the 22 DHS agencies (U.S. DHS 2003, p. 4). However, DHS expenditures represent only part of the money spent in the United States on antiterrorism measures. More than $40 billion was allocated for this purpose during fiscal 2004, including allocations for the Departments of Justice and Health and Human Services and a variety of other agencies and institutions (U.S. GAO 2004).

In addition to these allocations for within-country spending (homeland security, of which the DHS budget represents half), the overall U.S. budget for terrorism control includes allocations for spending abroad. Called funding for the overseas combating of terrorism, requested allocations in 2004 amounted to $11.4 billion, bringing the total request for funding in 2004 for combating terrorism to $52.7 billion (U.S. OMB 2003, pp. 9–10, 14).

Like other industrial countries, the United States funds most of these activities out of federal tax revenues, notably general-fund revenues (from income taxes and value-added taxes). Some initiatives, such as airport security, are funded out of earmarked taxes (surcharges on tickets or other airport fees). Allocative efficiency is served by having the people whose activity puts them in harm's way underwrite the associated enhanced security. Similar taxes can be used for cruise ship tickets or admissions to high-profile venues (monuments and other tourist attractions). The operating authorities of these potential targets can thus pass on some of the extra security costs to customers through higher admission fees, without the need to draw on tax revenues. The operating authorities, too, must choose security levels so as to balance security cost at the margin with insurance fees, since less security entails greater insurance premiums. Other private spending actions also have a role to play in hardening targets against terrorist attacks. For example, companies often maintain their own security guards and facilities.

Unlike industrial countries, many developing countries have only limited capacity to curb terrorism owing to budgetary and technological constraints. And it is this difference in capacity, resources, and sometimes also political willingness that may give rise to weakest link situations in the international realm and undermine higher national-level efforts in industrial countries. Where such a situation arises, domestic security efforts may need to be complemented by cross-border cooperation to achieve desired levels of protection.

INTERNATIONAL COOPERATION TO CONTROL TRANSNATIONAL TERRORISM

There are thus two important elements to national terrorism control strategies: national security standards (and their enforcement) and measures enabling all agents to contribute to the security strategy (sometimes requiring assistance programs and financial transfers). At the international level numerous conventions and resolutions perform a norm and standard-setting function. While declaring certain terrorist activities illegal, they have usually provided neither an effective enforcement mechanism nor financial support for possible weakest links. This section investigates why this occurs and what could be done to improve the situation.

Conventions alone do not suffice
Global and regional antiterrorism conventions and treaties (listed in table 3) differ from international resolutions (not listed in table 3). A convention indicates a mandated, but usually unenforced response while a resolution expresses a declared position or intended action. There are 13 international conventions that forbid terrorist attacks against diplomatic missions, aircrafts, ocean platforms, nuclear power plants, and ships. One convention makes terrorism more difficult by tagging plastic explosives for later identification, and another seeks to suppress terrorist financing. The most recent convention (adopted on April 13, 2005) makes possessing nuclear weapons and threatening to use them a crime. It also strengthens the legal framework against terrorism (UN 2005). Unlike their global counterparts, the seven regional conventions outlaw all forms of terrorism that meet the convention-approved definition.

Most of these conventions have been reactive, responding only after a spate of attacks. For example, the International Civil Aviation Organization (ICAO) conventions followed numerous hijackings and bombing of commercial airlines in the 1960s. The UN convention outlawing crimes against diplomats and other protected persons came about only after many such attacks in the late 1960s and early 1970s. All conventions rely on the ratifying countries to implement the stipulated prohibition or institute the required action. Thus, the global public goods stemming from each convention derive from national efforts.

These conventions are a means of bolstering antiterrorist policy by coordinating national action through set guidelines. Varied adherence is consequently anticipated, especially since none of these conventions has an enforcement mechanism[12] and the resulting global public good can be compromised by inadequate responses by nonratifiers as terrorists take advantage of vulnerabilities. For example, plastic explosives may not be traced following a bombing if some countries do not implement or ratify the treaty on tagging plastic explosives and the terrorists acquire their explosives there. For many conventions a single compliance failure can jeopardize the safety of everyone in a globalized world. Universal ratification and implementation are necessary but never achieved owing to the weakest link nature of the associated public good.

To examine the effectiveness of some of these international conventions, Enders, Sandler, and Cauley (1990) applied time-series analysis to various terrorist events. For crimes against diplomats and other protected persons, they compared the pre-convention mean of the series for such attacks with its post-convention mean and found no significant differences, suggesting that the convention was ineffective. They performed the same test for the UN convention and other antihijacking resolutions and again uncovered no significant impact on average number of hijackings. Even a cursory examination of the time series for bombings shows that the recent International Convention for the Suppression of Terrorist Bombings has had no real effect: bombing as a proportion of terrorist events has been higher since this convention went into force in April 2002 (U.S. Department of State 2003). Simply condemning a type of terrorist event is not going to hold much sway over individuals who see no legitimate avenue for inducing the political change that they crave and are willing to make the ultimate sacrifice to achieve it.

Financing assistance programs for weakest link nations: a common pool approach with assessed contribution

The game-theoretic analysis in this chapter indicates that most countries will protect against terrorist attacks through enhanced security rather than preemption. Each nation is responsible for financing its own antiterrorism measures through tax revenues. Industrial countries are able to centralize counterterrorism measures to achieve a more equal standard of protection throughout the country, similar to the U.S. efforts. In reaction to 9/11 most industrial countries have greatly augmented their protective efforts, which has had a cumulative influence on shifting terrorist incidents to less secure countries with more limited resources and capabilities. There has consequently been an enhanced transference of terrorist attacks to the developing world—a pattern consistent with experience since 9/11 with attacks in Afghanistan, Indonesia, Kenya, Morocco, Saudi Arabia, Tunisia, Turkey, and elsewhere.

TABLE 3

Global and regional conventions and treaties relating to controlling international terrorism

Convention or treaty	Supporting institution	Date/place signed	Entry into force
Global conventions			
Convention on Offences and Certain Other Acts Committed on Board Aircraft	International Civil Aviation Organization	September 14, 1963 Tokyo	December 4, 1969
Convention for the Suppression of Unlawful Seizure of Aircraft	International Civil Aviation Organization	December 16, 1970 The Hague	October 14, 1971
Convention for the Suppression of Unlawful Acts against the Safety of Civil Aviation	International Civil Aviation Organization	September 23, 1971 Montreal	January 26, 1973
Convention on the Prevention and Punishment of Crimes against International Protected Persons, including Diplomatic Agents	UN General Assembly	December 14, 1973 New York	February 20, 1977
International Convention against Taking of Hostages	UN General Assembly	December 17, 1979 New York	June 3, 1983
Convention on the Physical Protection of Nuclear Material	International Atomic Energy Agency	March 3, 1980 Vienna and New York	February 8, 1987
Protocol for the Suppression of Unlawful Acts of Violence at Airports Serving International Civil Aviation	International Civil Aviation Organization	February 24, 1988 Montreal	August 6, 1989
Convention for the Suppression of Unlawful Acts against the Safety of Maritime Navigation	International Maritime Organization	March 10, 1988 Rome	March 1, 1992
Protocol for the Suppression of Unlawful Acts against the Safety of Fixed Platforms Located on the Continental Shelf	International Maritime Organization	March 10, 1988 Rome	March 1, 1992
Convention on the Marking of Plastic Explosives for the Purpose of Detection	International Civil Aviation Organization	March 1, 1991 Montreal	June 21, 1998

TABLE 3 CONTINUED

Global and regional conventions and treaties relating to controlling international terrorism

Convention or treaty	Supporting institution	Date/place signed	Entry into force
International Convention for the Suppression of Terrorist Bombings	UN General Assembly	December 15, 1997 New York	May 23, 2001
International Convention on the Suppression of Financing of Terrorism	UN General Assembly	December 9, 1999 New York	April 10, 2002
International Convention for the Suppression of Acts of Nuclear Terrorism	UN General Assembly	Open for signature September 14, 2005– December 2006	Not yet in force
Regional conventions			
Arab Convention on the Suppression of Terrorism	League of Arab States	April 22, 1998 Cairo	May 7, 1999
Convention on Combating International Terrorism	Organization of the Islamic Conference	July 1, 1999 Ouagadougo	Not yet in force
European Convention on the Suppression of Terrorism	Council of Europe	January 27, 1977 Strasbourg	August 4, 1978
Convention to Prevent and Punish the Acts of Terrorism Taking the Form of Crimes against Persons and Related Extortion That Are of International Significance	Organization of American States	February 2, 1971 Washington, DC	October 16, 1973
Convention on the Prevention and Combating of Terrorism	African Union	July 14, 1999 Algiers	Not yet in force
Regional Convention on Suppression of Terrorism	South Asian Association for Regional Cooperation	November 4, 1987 Kathmandu	August 22, 1988
Treaty on Cooperation among the States Members of the Commonwealth of Independent States in Combating Terrorism	Commonwealth of Independent States	June 4, 1999 Minsk	Not yet in force

Source: UN 2002 (pp. 17–18), 2003, 2005.

This disturbing trend means that industrial countries must shore up the weakest links by assisting them in financing counterterrorism. Clearly, the United States has a direct incentive to support the weakest links, because U.S. citizens and property can be attacked in these countries. U.S. efforts in 2001 to train the Philippine military to root out Abu Sayyaf is an example where such assistance was offered and accepted (U.S. Department of State 2002, 2003). Reliance on U.S. assistance to bolster the defenses of weakest links will not be adequate, however, because the United States does not have the resources to bring all countries' security up to an acceptable standard. Additionally, many countries may not want U.S. support since this assistance may make them a more likely target.

One means for addressing the weakest link concern is to resort to a common pool, with industrial countries contributing to a fund for augmenting security where it is weakest yet critical. Multilateral, common pool approaches have often been used to finance international cooperation. An example is the Global Fund to Fight AIDS, Tuberculosis, and Malaria, which pools resources mostly from industrial countries and private actors to assist primarily low-income developing countries in implementing strategies to control these diseases.[13] The Nuclear Security Fund of the International Atomic Energy Agency mobilizes resources from industrial countries to support activities for preventing the spread of nuclear and radioactive materials.[14] The International Financial Facility for Aviation Safety provides financial support to developing countries for projects aimed at improving aviation safety.[15] Funding comes mostly from voluntary contributions. Similarly, the Global Programme on Maritime and Port Security funds training and other technical cooperation to help developing countries meet new port safety regulations.[16]

While such initiatives are steps in the right direction, they are voluntarily financed and their combined funding is well below that required to achieve globally acceptable standards of security and financial safeguards against terrorism. If the provision of a weakest link public good is supported by a common pool, the sum of the contributions determines the associated level of security (Vicary 1990; Vicary and Sandler 2002). Each country's contribution is a perfect substitute for the contributions of others. The free-riding incentive, reduced by a weakest link aggregator, resurfaces through the collective funding mechanism required to lift provision levels to an acceptable standard. An effective common pool must confront this free-rider problem.

International cooperation experience, especially with funding UN peacekeeping missions, suggests that free-riding can be best addressed with an assessment scheme that clearly defines the criteria for sharing international cooperation costs among countries. For antiterrorism efforts the assessment shares could be based on two criteria: a country's income and the share of international attacks against its interests abroad. There is a certain fairness behind this arrangement, because the prime-target countries are likely to be (or are seen to be) most responsible for the grievances behind attacks.

Yet why would countries agree to such an assessment formula? A disturbing asymmetry characterizes the terrorists and the adversaries of terrorism (Sandler 2003; Sandler and Enders 2004). Since the onset of modern-day terrorism in the late 1960s, terrorist groups have cooperated in networks, sharing personnel, intelligence, logistics, training camps, and resources (Alexander and Pluchinsky 1992; Hoffman 1998). Through common training camps, shared funding, similar logistics, communication links, and common grievances, they forge loosely linked networks (Arquilla and Ronfeldt 2001; Hoffman 1998, 2003). In contrast, governments are often reluctant to sacrifice their autonomy over security matters and so severely limit their cooperation. An exigency such as 9/11 fosters more cooperation, but cooperation fades over time because most countries do not view themselves as prime targets.

This cooperation asymmetry not only hampers effective antiterrorism policy, but also provides a significant strategic advantage to terrorist networks that exploit the uncoordinated policies of targeted governments. Failure of governments to cooperate not only creates a target-rich environment, but also provides ready routes along which to dispatch terrorists to their targets since some borders are more porous than others.

Concluding remarks

Networked terrorists present a formidable threat to a globalized and technologically sophisticated world where targets still act largely independently to curb transnational terrorism. The sheer volume of money, people, resources, and goods that cross borders offers cover for terrorist operations. Much of the fight against terrorism is conducted at the national level through security upgrades financed from tax revenues. As industrial countries responded to 9/11 with enhanced security and some augmented cooperation, terrorists diverted their attacks to less-secure developing countries with more limited capacity to protect against attacks. If security levels are to attain acceptable standards, industrial countries must devise a way to raise safeguards worldwide. Countries must cooperate in eliminating the terrorist threat.

Both security upgrades in developing countries and proactive measures against terrorists present free-riding problems. Efforts to raise the security of weakest link venues should ideally be funded by a common pool, financed by the industrial countries whose people and property draw most of the attacks. An assessment account, like the one for UN peacekeeping, can overcome the free-riding problem associated with a common pool to shore up soft targets in developing countries.

Country-financed actions in the fight against terrorism do achieve some global public benefits. By favoring some countries as targets, terrorists provide these prime targets with an incentive to curb transnational terrorism—the proposed common pool approach taps into this incentive. An essential concern is that these prime targets are also creating a serious global public bad by unintentionally deflecting attacks to developing countries, which lack capacity to act. The solutions involve enhancing security in these countries, rooting out terrorists, and limiting grievances fueling terrorism. All solutions require collective action by industrial countries.

APPENDIX. PREEMPTION AND SECURITY ENHANCEMENTS: INCENTIVES TO COOPERATE

The prisoner's dilemma matrix in figure A.1 depicts a symmetric scenario in which a country[17] incurs costs of 8 from preempting. Now suppose that preemption confers a public benefit of 5 on both countries regardless of which one acts to limit terrorism. In the matrices the left-hand payoff in each cell is that of the United States and the right-hand payoff is that of the European Union. When only one country preempts, this country nets -3 ($= 5 - 8$) as costs are deducted from its benefits, while the inactive country obtains a free-riding gain of 5 (see the off-diagonal payoffs). If both countries preempt, then each receives a net gain of 2 [= $(2 \times 5) - 8$] as benefits of 10 (received from the two units of the public good) are reduced by the costs of 8. The payoffs are 0 when neither country acts.

From either country's viewpoint there is a dominant strategy that gives a greater payoff regardless of the other country's action. For example, the United States is better off not preempting, since its payoffs of 5 and 0 are greater than the payoffs of 2 and -3 for preempting. The same holds for the European Union owing to the assumed symmetry. Because each player exercises its dominant strategy, neither acts. This outcome is a Nash equilibrium. At the Nash equilibrium, each player would lower its payoff from 0 to -3 by acting alone and preempting. This game represents a prisoner's dilemma whose low-level equilibrium can be improved only if the two could agree to act in concert.

Next, consider upgrading security at vulnerable venues, which is a weakest link public good. If these upgrades involve screening passengers at international airports in the United States and the European Union, then the lower standard of monitoring determines the level of protection afforded to the flying public. For illustration, suppose that both the United States and the European Union receive benefits of 10 only when both upgrade their airport security. If just one of them upgrades, the risks of a terrorist incident for citizens in both the United States and the European Union remain unchanged owing to the unsecured airport, so there is no gain from isolated upgrades. Suppose that the upgrade costs 8. In the weakest link matrix of figure A.1, mutual security upgrades and mutual inaction result in payoffs of 2 and 0, respectively, for both the United States and the European Union. If just one of them upgrades, the weakest link level is 0 units so there is no gain for either: the upgrader incurs costs of 8 with no benefits and the free-rider gains nothing for payoff combinations of –8 and 0 and 0 and –8. There is no dominant strategy for this weakest link scenario: from either side's vantage, upgrading security gives payoffs of 2 and –8, where 2 > 0 but –8 $\not> 0$. There are, however, two Nash equilibriums where either both sides act or neither side acts. A hallmark of a weakest link public good is this matching behavior.

If two countries have, say, five provision options each—to supply up to four units in one-unit increments—of a weakest link public good such as security upgrades, then all of the Nash equilibriums are along the diagonal of the associated 5 x 5 game matrix (not shown) where countries' effort levels are the same (Sandler 1998). Which of these equilibriums applies is a matter of relative resource capacity. If one country has less capacity to provide because of income, the outcome will be determined by the poorer country; thus, each country may contribute two units, because this is the maximum level that the poorer country can afford.

Even greater relative income differences may result in an equilibrium in which no one contributes to the weakest link public good owing to the poorer country's inability to contribute anything. If the capacity of the poorer country results in a level of the public good unacceptable to the wealthier country, the wealthier coun-

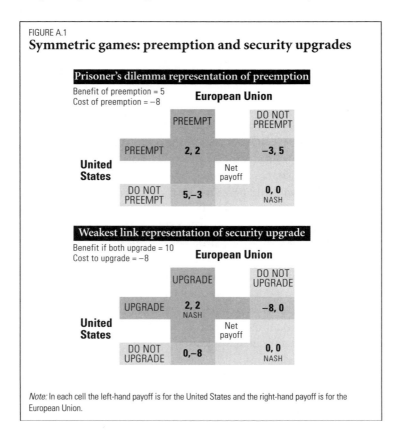

FIGURE A.1
Symmetric games: preemption and security upgrades

Prisoner's dilemma representation of preemption

Benefit of preemption = 5
Cost of preemption = –8

European Union

		PREEMPT	DO NOT PREEMPT
United States	PREEMPT	2, 2	–3, 5
	DO NOT PREEMPT	5, –3	0, 0 NASH

Net payoff

Weakest link representation of security upgrade

Benefit if both upgrade = 10
Cost to upgrade = –8

European Union

		UPGRADE	DO NOT UPGRADE
United States	UPGRADE	2, 2 NASH	–8, 0
	DO NOT UPGRADE	0, –8	0, 0 NASH

Net payoff

Note: In each cell the left-hand payoff is for the United States and the right-hand payoff is for the European Union.

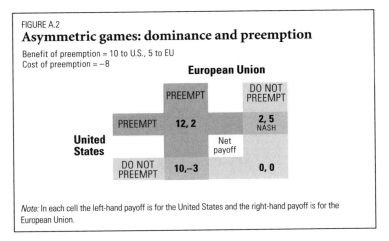

FIGURE A.2
Asymmetric games: dominance and preemption

Benefit of preemption = 10 to U.S., 5 to EU
Cost of preemption = −8

Note: In each cell the left-hand payoff is for the United States and the right-hand payoff is for the European Union.

try may have no choice but to provide the good on the soil of the poorer country (Vicary and Sandler 2002). The willingness of the United States to bolster antiterrorist efforts in other countries is an example of raising another country's level of a weakest link public good to an acceptable standard (U.S. Department of State 2002).

A final example of asymmetric benefits from preemption is especially instructive. The difference between figure A.2 and the prisoner's dilemma matrix of figure A.1 concerns U.S. benefits derived from U.S. or EU preemption. Because the United States is the target of the greatest share of transnational attacks, it obtains a larger benefit of 10 from either its action or that of the European Union to preempt terrorist attacks, while the European Union obtains a smaller benefit of 5 from its action or that of the United States. Costs for taking steps remain at 8. If just the United States preempts, it nets 2 (= 10 − 8) as benefits of 10 are reduced by the associated costs, while the European Union gains the free-rider reward of 5. When the roles are reversed the United States gets a free-rider gain of 10 and the European Union receives −3 as before. If both preempt, then the United States profits by 12 [= (2 × 10) − 8] and the European Union profits by 2 [= (2 × 5) − 8]. Now the dominant strategies are asymmetric: the United States has a dominant strategy to preempt since 12 > 10 and 2 > 0, while the European Union has a dominant strategy to free ride since 5 > 2 and 0 > −3. The Nash equilibrium is in the upper right-hand cell where the United States preempts alone.

NOTES

1. This incident is different from the near-simultaneous suicide truck bombings outside two Istanbul synagogues on November 15, 2003. Of the 25 people killed, 6 were Jews and the rest were Muslims in the vicinity.

2. On this date, three suicide bombers crashed an explosive-laden vehicle into the Israeli-owned Paradise Hotel in Mombasa. On the same day a surface-to-air

missile was fired at an Israeli charter jet with 271 people aboard that was taking off from Mombasa. The hotel attack killed 13, while the missile missed the airliner.

3. Enders and Sandler (2000) show that the likelihood of death or injury for each event is 17 percentage points greater in the post–cold war era.

4. In 1998 and 2000 there were no such events, while in 1999 there was just a single event (U.S. Department of State 1999–2001). In most years the U.S. Department of State records only a few, if any, transnational terrorist incidents in the United States (U.S. Department of State various years).

5. On aggregator technologies and their importance, see Hirshleifer (1983), Sandler (1998), and Vicary (1990).

6. On the properties of the prisoner's dilemma, see Sandler (1997, ch. 2).

7. For examples of country activities after September 11, 2001, see van de Linde and others (2002), the counterterrorism page of the Asia-Pacific Economic Cooperation (APEC) web site (www.apecsec.org.sg/apec/apec_groups/som_special_task_groups/counter_terrorism.html), and a list of the Group of 8 (G-8) activities immediately after 9/11 (www.g8.gc.ca/2002Kananaskis/counterterrorism-en.asp).

8. See, for example, U.S. National Commission on Terrorist Attacks upon the United States (2004), and U.S. Senate Select Committee on Intelligence and U.S. House Permanent Select Committee on Intelligence (2002).

9. See U.S. GAO (2000, 2001), for a description of the pre-9/11 airport security situation and the challenges it presented.

10. The information in this paragraph is derived from U.S. DHS (2003).

11. See www.tsa.gov/public/display?theme=44&content=0900051980056949.

12. An enforcement mechanism is a public good with its own free-riding concerns.

13. See www.theglobalfund.org.

14. See www.iaea.org.

15. See www.icao.int/iffas.

16. See www.imo.org.

17. For ease of exposition, the European Union is referred to as a country in this appendix.

REFERENCES

Alexander, Yonah, and Dennis Pluchinsky. 1992. *Europe's Red Terrorists: The Fighting Communist Organizations.* London: Frank Cass.

Arquilla, John, and David Ronfeldt. 2001. *Networks and Netwars.* Santa Monica, Calif.: RAND.

Bush, George W. 2002. *Securing the Homeland: Strengthening the Nation.* Washington, D.C.: White House.

Enders, Walter, and Todd Sandler. 2000. "Is Transnational Terrorism Becoming More Threatening? A Time-Series Investigation." *Journal of Conflict Resolution* 44 (3): 307–32.

Enders, Walter, Gerald Parise, and Todd Sandler. 1992. "A Time-Series Analysis of Transnational Terrorism: Trends and Cycles." *Defence Economics* 3 (4): 305–20.

Enders, Walter, Todd Sandler, and Jon Cauley. 1990. "UN Conventions, Technology, and Retaliation in the Fight against Terrorism: An Econometric Evaluation." *Terrorism and Political Violence* 2 (1): 83–105.

Heal, Geoffrey, and Howard Kunreuther. 2003. *You Only Die Once: Managing Discrete Interdependent Risks.* NBER Working Paper 9885. Cambridge, Mass.: National Bureau of Economic Research. [http://papers.nber.org/papers/w9885].

Hirshleifer, Jack. 1983. "From Weakest-Link to Best-Shot: The Voluntary Provision of Public Goods." *Public Choice* 41 (3): 371–86.

Hoffman, Bruce. 1998. *Inside Terrorism.* New York: Columbia University Press.

———. 2003. "Al Qaeda, Trends in Terrorism, and Future Potentialities: An Assessment." *Studies in Conflict and Terrorism* 26 (1): 429–42.

MIPT (National Memorial Institute for the Prevention of Terrorism). 2003. "MIPT Terrorism Database." Oklahoma City, Okla. [www.mipt.org].

Sandler, Todd. 1997. *Global Challenges: An Approach to Environmental, Political, and Economic Problems.* Cambridge, UK: Cambridge University Press.

———. 1998. "Global and Regional Public Goods: A Prognosis for Collective Action." *Fiscal Studies* 19 (3): 221–47.

———. 2003. "Collective Action and Transnational Terrorism." *World Economy* 26 (6): 779–802.

Sandler, Todd, and Daniel G. Arce M. 2003. "Terrorism and Game Theory." *Simulation and Gaming* 34 (3): 313–37.

Sandler, Todd, and Walter Enders. 2004. "An Economic Perspective on Transnational Terrorism." *European Journal of Political Economy* 20 (2): 301–16.

Sandler, Todd, and Kevin Siqueira. 2003. "Global Terrorism: Deterrence versus Preemption." University of Southern California, School of International Relations, Los Angeles, Calif.

UN (United Nations). 2002. "Report of the Policy Working Group on the United Nations and Terrorism." A/57/273-S/2002/875. New York. [www.un.org/terrorism/a57273.htm].

———. 2003. "United Nations: Treaty Collection: Conventions on Terrorism." New York. [http://untreaty.un.org/English/Terrorism.asp].

———. 2005. "General Assembly Adopts Convention on Nuclear Terrorism; Will Open for Signature at Headquarters 14 September." Press Release GA/10340. New York. [www.un.org/News/Press/docs/2005/ga10340.doc.htm].

U.S. Conference of Mayors. 2002. *The Cost of Heightened Security in America's Cities: A 192-City Survey.* Washington, D.C.: City Policy Associates.

U.S. Congress. 2002. Homeland Security Act of 2002. Public Law 107-296. 107th Congress. November 25. [http://frwebgate.access.gpo.gov/cgi-bin/getdoc.cgi?dbname= 107_cong_public_laws&docid=f:publ296.107.pdf].

U.S. Department of State. Various years. *Patterns of Global Terrorism*. Washington, D.C.

U.S. DHS (Department of Homeland Security). 2003. "Budget in Brief." Fiscal 2004 DHS Budget. Washington, D.C. [www.dhs.gov/dhspublic/display?theme=12].

————. 2004a. "Budget in Brief." Fiscal 2005 DHS Budget. Washington, D.C. [www.dhs.gov/dhspublic/display?theme=12].

————. 2004b. "Fact Sheet: Department of Homeland Security Appropriations Act of 2005." Washington, D.C. [www.dhs.gov/dhspublic/display?theme=12].

————. 2004c. *Securing Our Homeland: U.S. Department of Homeland Security Strategic Plan.* Washington, D.C.

U.S. GAO (General Accounting Office). 2000. "Aviation Security: Long-Standing Problems Impair Airport Screeners' Performance." GAO/RCED-00-75. Washington, D.C.

————. 2001. "Aviation Security: Weaknesses in Airport Security and Options for Assigning Screening Responsibilities." GAO-01-1165T. Washington, D.C.

————. 2004. "Combating Terrorism: Evaluation of Selected Characteristics in National Strategies Related to Terrorism." GAO-04-408T. Washington, D.C.

U.S. National Commission on Terrorist Attacks upon the United States. 2004. *The 9/11 Commission Report: Final Report of the National Commission on Terrorist Attacks upon the United States.* New York: W.W. Norton & Company.

U.S. OMB (Office of Management and Budget). 2003. *2003 Report to Congress on Combating Terrorism.* Washington, D.C.: Executive Office of the President. [www.whitehouse.gov/omb/inforeg/2003_combat_terr.pdf].

U.S. Senate Select Committee on Intelligence and U.S. House Permanent Select Committee on Intelligence. 2002. "Joint Inquiry into Intelligence Community Activities Before and After the Terrorist Attacks of September 11, 2001." Senate Report 107-351 and House Report 107-792. 107th Congress. Washington, D.C.

Van de Linde, Erik, Kevin O'Brien, Gustav Lindstrom, Stephan de Spiegeleire, Mikko Vayrynen, and Hans de Vries. 2002. *Quick Scan of Post 9/11 National Counter-Terrorism Policymaking and Implementation in Selected European Countries.* Research Project for the Netherlands Ministry of Justice. Leiden, The Netherlands: RAND Europe.

Vicary, Simon. 1990. "Transfers and the Weakest-Link: An Extension of Hirshleifer's Analysis." *Journal of Public Economics* 43 (3): 375–94.

Vicary, Simon, and Todd Sandler. 2002. "Weakest-Link Public Goods: Giving In-Kind of Transferring Money." *European Economic Review* 46 (8): 1501–20.

2

THE NEW INTERNATIONAL PUBLIC FINANCE

RELYING ON PUBLIC-PRIVATE

COOPERATION AND COMPETITION

EXPLORING THE POLICY SPACE BETWEEN MARKETS AND STATES
GLOBAL PUBLIC-PRIVATE PARTNERSHIPS
Inge Kaul

•

ACCOMMODATING NEW ACTORS AND NEW PURPOSES
IN INTERNATIONAL COOPERATION
THE GROWING DIVERSIFICATION OF FINANCING MECHANISMS
Pedro Conceição

•

MAKING THE RIGHT MONEY AVAILABLE AT THE RIGHT TIME
FOR INTERNATIONAL COOPERATION
NEW FINANCING TECHNOLOGIES
Pedro Conceição, Hari Rajan, and Rajiv Shah

Taking Self-Interest into Account
A Public Choice Analysis of International Cooperation
Philip Jones

EXPLORING THE POLICY SPACE BETWEEN MARKETS AND STATES
GLOBAL PUBLIC-PRIVATE PARTNERSHIPS

INGE KAUL

Public-private partnerships have emerged in many countries, both industrial and developing. These partnerships straddle the conventional divide between state and nonstate actors. They often involve partners from government, business, and civil society. These public-private partnerships go beyond mere contracting across actor lines. They typically entail some joint decisionmaking and sharing of responsibilities, opportunities, and risks. They are, as the name suggests, about partnering.

Nationally, public-private partnering has been on the rise in recent decades. More and more projects, such as the construction and operation of airports, hospitals, roads, and water systems, are set up in this hybrid form. Similarly, norm and standard setting, such as devising and monitoring environmental standards, is increasingly being undertaken by public-private partnerships. And the same holds true for research and development in many areas.[1]

More recently, there has also been rapid growth in the number of public-private partnerships that address global concerns, such as climate stability, control of communicable diseases, and the fight against world poverty and hunger. Some of these global partnerships, like the World Water Council, function as advocates, contributing to international policy dialogue and outreach.[2] They are concerned primarily with the negotiating and policymaking side of international cooperation. Others, like the Global Fund to Fight AIDS, Tuberculosis, and Malaria (the Global Fund), are more operational.[3] They act on the policy implementation side of international cooperation. This second group is the focus of this chapter.

By some estimates the number of these global operational partnerships has risen from some 50 initiatives in the mid-1980s to at least 400 today (Broadwater and Kaul 2005). It thus seems timely and important to take stock and gain a more structured understanding of this growing phenomenon—of what these

The author wishes to thank Ian Broadwater for excellent research assistance.

partnerships intend to do, how they are organized, and how they fit into the landscape of international cooperation.

This chapter provides an overview of global public-private partnering today. Based on a sample of initiatives, it develops a typology of partnerships, followed by in-depth profiles of the main classes and types. It also examines why global public-private partnerships have grown in prominence and how likely this trend is to continue.

From this discussion three main findings emerge. One, global public-private partnerships come in many forms—driven by different motivations, pursuing a variety of purposes, and following different modes of partnering, depending on the outcome they seek.

Two, global public-private partnerships seem to be here to stay. They occupy an increasingly open middle ground between markets and states, permitting more nuanced and potentially more effective policymaking. They demonstrate that when markets fail, the policy response does not have to be government intervention alone. It can also be partnering. And where governments fail, the response is not necessarily to turn to the market. Again, it could also be public-private partnering.

Three, the implications of global public-private partnerships for the conventional system of international cooperation are potentially far-reaching and mixed. Designed to be nimble, single-focused, results-oriented, innovative, and risk-taking, the partnerships can do many things that the typically larger intergovernmental organizations find difficult to accomplish. Thus they complement the conventional system in important ways. Global public-private partnerships can sometimes also present a challenge to intergovernmental organizations by competing for financial resources. And sometimes resource-constrained intergovernmental organizations enter into private sector-initiated partnerships that generate low global social returns.

Thus there is the possibility of a discrepancy between multilateral policy and operational priorities. To the extent that ad hoc partnerships assume the role of delivering international cooperation projects, only some policy priorities—those that reflect the priority concerns of the financiers—may get implemented, while others languish, starved of necessary funding.

In light of these findings, the chapter discusses how the suggested typology of partnerships could guide a more systematic approach to global public-private partnering, notably on the part of intergovernmental organizations. It suggests that the typology can be used to analyze, design, and manage partnerships; evaluate them; and foster their accountability to stakeholders.

The main conclusion: the wave of government reengineering and market-state rebalancing that has swept across many countries in recent decades has now reached the arena of international cooperation. Global public-private partnerships are an expression of this change and contributors to it. This makes it all the more important to develop a more systematic understanding of partnering—to benefit from its opportunities and avoid its pitfalls.

The reflections here are preliminary. This chapter examines the intended or stated purposes of partnerships, not their actual performance and effectiveness; their organizational design, not their actual governance or management processes. As a result, the goal of the chapter is limited: to see more clearly what global public-private partnerships intend to accomplish, where they are headed, and what their contribution might be to meeting global challenges. It is left to future research to examine whether these partnerships are accomplishing what they set out to do—and how they affect international cooperation. And future research and policy debate will also have to revisit and further test and refine the typology of partnerships suggested here.

AN OVERVIEW OF THE LANDSCAPE OF GLOBAL PUBLIC-PRIVATE PARTNERSHIPS

Gaining an overview of the current landscape of global public-private partnerships requires understanding their defining characteristics. This section presents a working definition of global public-private partnerships and uses it to scan the domain of international cooperation for qualifying initiatives and to develop a typology of global public-private partnerships.

The typology that emerges reveals that global public-private partnerships differ widely, depending on what motivates them, what goal they pursue, and the nature of the partnership product or intended outcome (whether it has the properties of a private, club, merit, or public good).[4] While the diversity might at first seem puzzling and difficult to absorb, it shows that public-private partnering can be a highly versatile, flexible, and therefore potentially very useful organizational form.

Defining global public-private partnerships

The current literature offers multiple definitions of public-private partnerships.[5] This is not surprising for such a recent phenomenon, with many dimensions still to be fully recognized. For some analysts partnerships are about shared agendas as well as combined resources, risks, and rewards (UN Foundation and WEF 2003). For others they are a form of governance (Boerzel and Risse-Kappen forthcoming). Yet others see them simply as a collaborative effort for creating the conditions to improve performance (North 2004). As shown later, partnerships can be found that exhibit all these and other properties. The challenge is to formulate a definition that is wide enough to capture the broad gamut of partnerships yet precise enough for analytical as well as policy purposes.

A definition highlighting five characteristics of global public-private partnerships seems to meet these criteria (box 1). The first three characteristics are

---

Box 1

THE FIVE DEFINING CHARACTERISTICS OF GLOBAL PUBLIC-PRIVATE PARTNERSHIPS

- *Voluntary.* Arising from the partners' self-interest.
- *Horizontally organized.* Maintaining the partners' autonomy.
- *Participatory.* Involving joint governance and specifying the issues on which partners will consult or decide jointly.
- *Multiactor-based.* Bringing together different actor groups, such as government and intergovernmental organizations, business, academia, civil society, and charitable or philanthropic foundations.
- *Global.* Addressing issues or involving activities of worldwide reach and sometimes of multigenerational scope.

---

common to all partnerships: a voluntary collaborative effort by multiple agents, an organizational structure that maintains the agents' autonomy and identity, and a governance structure that allows sharing control rights and decisionmaking powers. Partnerships can be formed by agents of a single actor group. Examples include the professional partnerships common in law and medicine (Levin and Tadelis 2004) and joint ventures between businesses, such as those between large manufacturing companies and small research and development firms (Stiglitz and Wallsten 2000). Governments also enter into partnerships with each other, as in the New Partnership for African Development.

Public-private partnerships also involve agents from different actor groups. Thus they have a fourth characteristic, that of being multiactor-based, involving government agents, business, academia, civil society, and charitable or philanthropic organizations in varying compositions and roles. And to qualify as a global public-private partnership, a partnership should also have a fifth characteristic, that of addressing issues or activities affecting several regions—and sometimes several generations.

At least 400 initiatives were found to exhibit these five characteristics and to perform primarily an operational role, based on a screening of databases, reports, and other studies.[6] They exist in virtually all realms of activity, with the greatest number in the health and environment sectors, which each account for about a fourth of the total.[7] Initiatives addressing finance, investment, and enterprise development, with a focus on extending relevant markets and products to developing countries and to underserved communities such as the rural poor, account for about a 15 percent share. The remaining global public-private partnerships cover concerns ranging from agriculture and food security to communication and transport, peace and security, multisector development, and governance, including corruption control.

A typology for global public-private partnerships

From this (no doubt incomplete) universe of global public-private partnerships, a sample of 100 was chosen using two criteria: the sample should roughly mirror the sectoral distribution of partnerships in the universe, and the information needed to construct a typology of partnerships should be available. Information was collected on seven variables (listed as the headings of columns 2–8 of table 1), using published sources, including self-assessments (mission statements, activity reports) and external assessments (evaluation reports and other literature). Because the analysis is based on published materials only, many of the findings are preliminary, and further research is needed to ascertain their robustness.[8]

Three venture classes and seven functional types

Clearly, many forms of global public-private partnerships exist. But so do many configurations of firms, government agencies, and civil society organizations. Reality is often complex, something that tends to be noticed more when encountering a still unfamiliar phenomenon. Therefore, it might be useful to examine table 1 step by step. Column 2 suggests three basic classes of global public-private partnerships:

* *Business ventures,* seeking mainly private gain that would accrue to at least one partner.[9]
* *Double bottom-line ventures,* seeking to combine private returns on investment with such social or public-interest goals as enhanced energy or water provision in poorer countries.
* *Social ventures,* pursuing as a primary objective such public-interest concerns as poverty reduction, communicable disease control, and sustainable development.

Business ventures and social ventures each include three types of partnership (column 3), distinguished by functional purpose, while double bottom-line ventures include just one type, together making seven partnership types (see also box 2).

The functional types highlight the pioneering character of many global public-private partnerships. The partnerships try to accomplish something out of the ordinary by trading comparative advantage (type 1);[10] exploring new products and markets (type 2); improving market inefficiencies by developing and disseminating new norms and standards (type 3); expanding markets into new countries and to new consumer groups, including the rural poor (type 4); brokering special market deals (type 5); encouraging actors to innovate and undertake research and development (type 6); or pulling together all available forces and resources to respond to a pressing global challenge (type 7).

Business ventures occur where the good or service to be produced by the partnership has the properties of a private good or club good and can therefore be relatively easily appropriated (see table 1, column 4). The products of double bottom-line ventures are typically of a mixed nature, offering private bene-

TABLE 1

Typology of global public-private partnerships

Type	Venture class	Partnership purpose	Nature of partnership product
1	Business venture (private interest)	Trading comparative advantage	Private good
2		Pioneering new institutions (notably new markets)	Private good/club good
3		Defining rules/ setting standards	Club good
4	Double bottom-line venture	Advancing the frontiers of markets	Private good/ national public good
5	Social venture	Brokering "affordable price" deals	Merit good[b]
6		Leveraging research and development	Merit good[b]/private good
7		Managing for strategic results	Merit good[b]

a. M+ refers to market transaction complemented by a joint governance component; CA– refers to collective action occurring voluntarily, without government coercion or any other constraints.
b. Denotes a private good that society chooses, for efficiency, equity, or other reasons, to make available for all.

fits to the business partners and public benefits to a third party, often an emerging market economy or a particular group within these economies, such as small or medium-scale entrepreneurs. Social venture partnerships are concerned primarily with producing merit goods. They often aim at making an essentially private good, such as a vaccine, universally available and thus quasi public in consumption.

Judging from their stated goals, all global public-private partnership types, and so all venture classes, ultimately seek to contribute to a global public concern, even if only through spillover effects (see table 1, column 5). For example, several type 2 partnerships are exploratory investment initiatives linked to projects that contribute to reductions in greenhouse gas emissions and to the larger goal of climate stability, among other goals. They generate both direct private benefits, such as financial returns and the possibility of learning by doing, and global public bene-

Partnership product contributes to	Partnership mode[a]	Legal status of partnership agency	Main sources of financing
Global public good	M+	For-profit/nonprofit	Payments for services, reassignment of right to collect revenue
Global public good	M+/CA−	For-profit	Cost-sharing contributions from partners
Global public good	CA−	Nonprofit	Fees, charges
Global public good	M+	For-profit	Equity and other capital, guarantees
Global public good	M+	Nonprofit	Differential contracting/ patenting, purchase guarantees
Global public good	CA−/M+	Nonprofit	Donations, differential patenting
Global public good	CA−	Nonprofit/unit of intergovernmental organization	Donations

fits. The fact that the world may derive some benefit from the partnership, even when the partners are the primary beneficiaries, is often the basic justification for the involvement of a public actor. And where a third party is the primary beneficiary, such as the poor in developing countries, the spillover effects may ensure that at least in some diffuse and indirect way, the partners also gain something, say, enhanced international peace and security or improved global health conditions.

Two basic modes of partnering

There are two basic modes of partnering (see table 1, column 6). Partnering can be an extended form of a market transaction (labeled M+). Or it can take the form of a voluntary collective-action initiative (labeled CA−, with the minus sign indicating the voluntary nature of partnering—its occurrence without government coercion).

Box 2
SEVEN MAIN TYPES OF GLOBAL PUBLIC-PRIVATE PARTNERSHIPS

Global public-private partnerships operate in many sectors and address a wide variety of concerns. When grouped by their main purpose, they fall into one of seven types of partnership:

- *Type 1.* Trading comparative advantage, so that the trade-initiating (purchasing) partner can benefit from the strengths of the provider partner or so that each side can benefit from the other's special competencies and assets.
- *Type 2.* Pioneering new institutions (especially for missing markets) to test their desirability and feasibility, learn by doing, acquire expertise, and perhaps eventually enjoy a first-mover advantage.
- *Type 3.* Designing rules and setting standards to facilitate interactions, notably in technical areas, and ensure that emerging rules match each partner's circumstances and interests.
- *Type 4.* Advancing the frontiers of markets to open up new business opportunities and reduce poverty or advance sustainable development.
- *Type 5.* Brokering affordable-price deals to make critically important private goods more broadly available in poor countries.
- *Type 6.* Leveraging research and development, especially in areas of concern to the world's poor.
- *Type 7.* Managing for strategic results, in particular where problems require urgent attention.

Market transaction "plus" mode. Institutional economics, notably the theories of transaction costs and incomplete contracting, helps to elucidate why market-based partnerships occur.[11] The literature on partnerships compares them with the standard, on-the-spot form of market transaction, seeking to identify why agents sometimes choose other arrangements, like a firm or partnership. Under certain conditions closer, more frequent, and prolonged contact between transacting parties may be cheaper than an on-the-spot complete transaction. This can be the case where the good to be exchanged is complex or difficult to observe or where the contract spans a long period, making it infeasible or undesirable to specify all eventualities up front and to draw up a complete contract. Leaving certain issues open and agreeing on a governance procedure for settling them later (incomplete contracting) may enable purchasers and suppliers to better manage risks and uncertainties. Williamson (1985) refers to these transactions as "relational contracting." Here, they are called market transaction plus arrangements, or M+. The plus indicates that they are essentially market transactions—but with a governance component.

Collective action "minus" mode. Public goods theory helps explain the second form of partnering, the voluntary collective action mode—collective action minus state coercion. Theory predicts that public goods, including externalities generated by private consumption or production activities, are important sources of market failure. Agents may try to free ride on a public good by hiding their true preference and letting someone else provide it. If all or many agents act this way, public goods will be suboptimally provided, thus justifying government intervention, including use of the state's coercive powers of taxation, regulation, and enforcement.

However, several studies have shown that reality sometimes deviates from this state-centered concept of public goods provision. At the national level voluntary collective action is most likely when a good is highly valued and the actors who must cooperate to ensure adequate provision are homogeneous and small in number and so can be relatively easily organized.[12] Some partnerships engage in such voluntary collective action and so can be described as collective action minus, or CA–, by comparison with the standard form of public goods provision. The minus indicates that collective action occurs voluntarily, free of the compulsion or special inducements (such as tax credits) that tend to accompany government-based collective action.

Some people would argue that all cases of intergovernmental cooperation are voluntary acts among sovereign nation states. What then sets global public-private partnerships apart? For one, they are not just intergovernmental but also multi-actor. For another, multilateral negotiations have become large-number events, and agreement is usually more difficult in large groups than in smaller groups. Thus, actors with "minority" views and interests may at times feel overwhelmed by the majority concerns and pressured into a decision that they may not fully endorse. For a third, multilateral negotiations are more formalized and embedded in prior policy agreements. As a result, multilateral collective action is often less voluntary than it appears. Therefore, actors who want to effect a particular change may form partnerships (which tend to be composed of a limited number of actors). They may even help finance them to make this change happen.[13]

There is no set link between partnering mode and venture class. The M+ mode, which is a market mechanism, finds uses in both business and social ventures. The CA– mode also occurs in both these venture classes. Double bottom-line ventures seem to use only the M+ mode. Partnerships are "middlings"—organizational forms between markets and states—and so partnership modes can be of two different types, either an expanded market transaction or a curtailed, compulsion-free collective action (figure 1). The choice of the partnering mode reflects the type of partnership product to be produced. If the product has private-good properties, the partnering mode will be M+; if the product has the characteristics of a club, merit, or proper public good, the mode will be CA–. Some partnerships produce a mixed bundle of goods, and therefore they employ multiple partnering modes, M+ and CA– (see table 1, column 6).

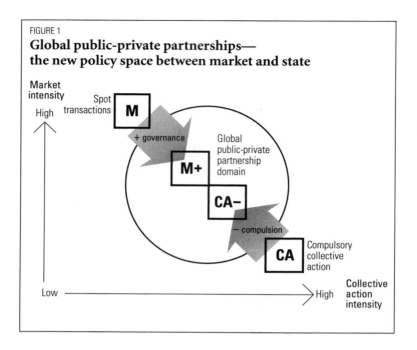

FIGURE 1

Global public-private partnerships—
the new policy space between market and state

Partnering as cogovernance, cofunding, and coproduction

By the definition used in this chapter, partnerships provide for a sharing of decisionmaking rights among partners. And judging from the sample of partnerships surveyed in this chapter, most if not all have a joint decisionmaking mechanism such as a governing board. Since partnerships are voluntary, they are unlikely to succeed—or at least unlikely to function smoothly—where partners disagree seriously about decisionmaking arrangements. Whether partnering is of the M+ or CA– form, agents are likely to expect an effective voice or—to use Hirschman's (1970) phrase—exit.

So, is partnering primarily a matter of cogovernance and power sharing? Yes, in many instances it is. Most partnership types are implemented by an agency that has either a for-profit or nonprofit legal status (see table 1, column 7). While the public and private members of governing boards provide overall guidance, day-to-day operations are usually left to a chief executive officer. In some instances the partnership agency's funders may include both public and private members. In other instances both public and private providers may be contracted to deliver inputs into the partnership product.[14] Partnering can thus be a one-, two-, or three-layer process, reaching from joint governance to cofinancing of partnership activities and co-implementation—with several variants in between.[15]

Financing through donations, capital, and other payments

With partnering happening for multiple reasons and in various forms, financing patterns also differ. Social ventures function primarily as nonprofit organizations and, accordingly, rely on donations for financing (see table 1, column 8). Thus, it is not surprising that social ventures often benefit from financial inputs by charitable and philanthropic foundations. Donations take many forms—financial and in-kind contributions and willingness to engage in differential pricing or patenting, as, for example, in type 5 partnerships. Double bottom-line ventures are mostly for-profit investment funds, pooling different types of capital, including that from public partners such as aid agencies. Sometimes such partnerships also benefit from public sector guarantees. Business ventures rely on a variety of financing arrangements, ranging from payments for services rendered to mutual investment funds and membership fees.[16]

A growing literature has examined why entrepreneurs sometimes prefer nonprofit organizations over for-profit enterprises. The argument is similar to that advanced by Williamson (1985) and others in support of relational contracting: provision of a difficult-to-monitor good.[17] As Hansmann (1980) argues, the fact that nonprofit organizations usually operate under a "distribution constraint" reassures donors and clients that they take their mission seriously and that profit considerations (by governing partners or management) will not interfere with the quality of the product being produced.[18]

Despite these considerations, partnerships of the double bottom-line type (type 4) with the status of a for-profit enterprise have been increasing. Some analysts (for example, Hansmann 1987) attribute this trend to the limited capacity of nonprofit organizations to tap private capital markets. As private capital markets expand and more governments experience a fiscal squeeze, initiatives trying to meet a double bottom line are attracting growing attention. Public investors usually try to limit their involvement to risk sharing, and they expect the bulk of the investment funds to come from private financiers.

PROFILES OF PARTNERSHIP TYPES

This section examines the venture classes and partnership types, providing examples of each. All the case descriptions seek to answer one question: why public-private partnering?

The discussion reinforces the finding, mentioned previously, that global public-private partnerships pursue ambitious missions—goals aimed at breaking new ground and reaching higher levels of achievement. Partnerships capitalize on the differences between public and private actors—differences in incentive structures, competencies, and assets. They trade, pool, and match in often innovative ways the comparative advantage that partners offer. This also is why global public-private partnerships deserve to be called "ventures."

Business ventures

The motivating force behind all business ventures is private gain. Accordingly, markets play an important role. Type 1 partnerships use existing markets to trade comparative advantage between actor groups.[19] Type 2 partnerships explore new products and new markets, typically mixing and matching partners with different interests and competencies in risk bearing, different roles (purchaser, provider, regulator) in the new market, and so on. And type 3 initiatives aim at reducing market imperfections, again bringing together different actor groups to negotiate jointly and if possible to reach consensus on norms and standards.

Partners may expect quite different things from the partnership. In type 1 partnerships often only one partner derives a partnership-specific benefit, like cost saving (frequently sought by public agents) or a "social license to operate" (which may motivate private actors). For the other actor the partnership may be simply another opportunity to get access to resources or earn an income. In type 2 and type 3 initiatives each partner may walk away with a gain that it may not even have communicated to the other partners, lest that weaken its bargaining power.

Type 1: Trading comparative advantage. The impetus for type 1 partnerships is that actors see agents on the other side of the public-private spectrum as better equipped to implement a particular task or project. They may perceive the other as being better at resource mobilization, risk bearing, efficient management, or product quality. By contracting out "their job" to the other actor group, purchasers hope to realize such benefits as financial gains (cost savings), improved results and impact, and enhanced reputation. Partnering thus takes the form of trading comparative advantage. In many instances it involves an exchange of comparative advantages—special competencies or assets—against money. This means that a partnership-specific benefit accrues only to the purchasers. For the provider partnering often has little more to offer than an increase in profit potential or project funding.

However, because a difficult matter is at stake (such as the private provision of a public good or a public input to a private firm's reputation), the trade between the partners is typically not of a spot nature, conducted at arm's length. Rather, it tends to involve—as the definition of partnership requires—joint governance by the purchasing and supplying parties.

In a national context government agencies are usually the initiating agent in a contracting-out arrangement, often following the private finance initiative model developed in the United Kingdom.[20] The reverse holds true internationally, where the number of private to public contracting-out arrangements is large and growing and there are few initiatives in which a public agent is the purchaser and a private business the provider.[21]

The Galileo satellite navigation system, an international public to private contracting-out arrangement, is one of the few exceptions (appendix box A.2).

Through partnering, the public project owners, the European Commission and the European Space Agency, have shifted major responsibility for financing to the private sector. This allows the commission to undertake the project without unduly burdening its budget. But why partner? Why choose contracting out rather than a standard market transaction such as outsourcing, which turns complete control of implementation over to an alternative agent but lacks the joint governance aspect of partnerships? The answer: to benefit from incomplete contracting and shared decisionmaking (through the project's governing body, the supervisory authority), which the commission considers critical for safeguarding the public-interest dimension of the project. The project is thus an example of an M+ arrangement.[22]

Examples of private sector-initiated contracting out abound, in particular the many—and rapidly proliferating—projects financed by businesses, often transnational corporations, with implementation delegated to a bilateral or multilateral aid agency or group of agencies, often involving the participation of civil society organizations. These initiatives form part of the philanthropy or corporate social responsibility programs that often accompany a company's outreach to foreign markets. The objectives span a wide range of concerns—from poverty reduction and human rights to global health, disaster management, and sustainable development (appendix box A.3).

The benefit sought by the private actor can be economies of scale to be achieved by joining a campaign that has already secured other funding and promises to generate visible impact with which the company can be associated. Companies can also benefit from economies of scope, by handing implementation over to an aid agency or other public organization that has a delivery network in place and that is often a more qualified provider of public services. Delegated implementation can protect the company against the potential risks entailed by a philanthropic or corporate social responsibility initiative.[23]

Partnering with a public agent may also confer a social license to operate on the private corporation. This motivation undoubtedly explains the increase in private to public contracting out of projects in which private agents lack the support of local communities, as is the case with many oil companies and other corporations in the extractive industries.[24] Being seen as an accepted peer of a respected public actor in a sustained partnership is an effective, relatively low-cost way of signaling social or environmental concern. A standard, on-the-spot market transaction is unlikely to generate the same reputation spillover.

For intergovernmental organizations the potential for resource mobilization has led many to reach out to private corporations and to supply project ideas for partnering. However, few of these supply-driven offers have attracted funding. Evidently, they did not speak to the range of interests and comparative advantages of the private actors solicited.[25] The prospect of resources also attracts public scientists to research partnerships funded and led by private industry, especially in the life sciences. Such partnerships usually facilitate bridge building between academic and commercially oriented research and between global technology development and local field-testing.[26]

Type 2: Pioneering institutional innovation, notably new markets. Whereas type 1 partnerships involve trading between partners in existing markets, type 2 initiatives are essentially about pooling differences—bringing affected parties together to jointly test new products and markets under conditions that replicate reality as closely as possible. And replicating reality means involving all potentially concerned actors. Often, the primary product to be produced is experience: learning by doing and perhaps acquiring a first-mover advantage on which to cash in, should the market take off. Each partner will draw particular lessons (a private good) from the joint experience of pilot trading (a club good) and perhaps will also enjoy a further private good, such as earned carbon credits or simply returns on investment. The Prototype Carbon Fund is illustrative of type 2 initiatives (appendix box A.4).

At present, market-exploring global public-private partnerships are mostly environmentally oriented, linked to such products as reduced greenhouse gases and the sustainable use of biodiversity in the face of new and pressing scarcities. For such partnerships to be effective, contributions must come from both potential providers and potential purchasers of the new product. Only when all parties are represented can the desirability and feasibility of the new good be determined and the trading mechanism be created. For carbon emissions-related markets such as the Prototype Carbon Fund, this means bringing in industrial country governments and concerned industries as the likely main purchasers, and developing countries, including their governments, industries, and local communities, as the likely main providers.

The Chicago Climate Exchange, which explores trading in greenhouse gas emission allowances, is another type 2 global public-private partnership (for a detailed discussion, see the chapter by Sandor in this volume). Another is the Climate Investment Partnership, which aims to familiarize public and private investors with carbon markets. It facilitates investor access to high-quality projects that generate carbon reduction credits, and it helps investors put together risk-sharing arrangements. The partners include an array of government environmental agencies, development finance agencies, private banks and investment funds, accountancy firms, and associations such as the Earth Council and the World Economic Forum.

An example of a partnership testing the nascent market for biodiversity products and services is that between Costa Rica's National Biodiversity Institute (INBio) and Merck & Co., Inc. INBio provides biodiversity samples to Merck & Co. for an annual fee. The partnership gives Merck & Co. lawful access to Costa Rica's rich biodiversity pool, while Costa Rica benefits from sharing any commercial gains that may flow from samples provided by INBio, as well as from the annual payment to INBio. Another trading arrangement for biodiversity, still under development, is the Multilateral System of Access and Benefit-Sharing, which is to be established under the International Treaty on Plant Genetic Resources for Food and Agriculture.[27]

Type 3: Designing and strengthening norms and standards. Type 3 partnerships are usually formed by concerned professional communities, public and private, to develop global norms and standards or to certify compliance with them. Some agents consider these partnerships to be so important to their private goals and objectives that they are willing to pay to participate (to influence rulemaking or obtain the club's seal of approval). Recognizing this willingness to pay, some providers of negotiating venues charge entrance or participation fees, used to finance club operations. Participants may also volunteer additional time and effort. Since norms and standards have public goods properties, type 3 partnerships employ the CA– mode: cooperation among concerned parties with a view to aligning different points of view and shaping the norms or standards under negotiation, to make them workable for all partners.

Many type 3 partnerships deal with highly technical matters and communicate with an audience of specialists (which is not to imply that they are distribution neutral or free of political ramifications). An example of an influential type 3 partnership is the International Organization for Standardization (appendix box A.5). Other examples are the Open GIS Consortium, Inc., established to resolve interoperability problems linked to the geographic specifications used in various information systems, and the Unicode Consortium, which seeks to standardize the way characters are referred to in software products. Another is the Internet Corporation for Assigned Names and Numbers, which oversees and manages the Internet's domain name system and its unique identifiers.[28]

A second set of type 3 partnerships promotes norms and standards that address a wider public. Among these are the Global Reporting Initiative, the Marine Stewardship Council, the Ethical Trading Initiative, the Fair Trade Labeling Organization, and Green Dot. These partnerships develop corporate social responsibility norms and standards and provide firms with a platform (such as being listed in a report) or a seal of approval to demonstrate their compliance with the defined norms and standards. They form part of, and are a response to, the growing trend toward self-regulation (Andrews 1998; Cutler, Haufler, and Porter 1999; Khanna 2001; Murphy and Bendell 1997). The argument behind self-regulation is that private agents come to recognize that norms and standards can be good for business as well as for society. Norms and standards thus become self-enforcing, obviating the need for compliance monitoring and enforcement by government.

A prominent global public-private partnership furthering self-regulation is the Global Compact of the United Nations Secretary-General. It invites businesses to sign on to 10 principles of human rights, labor conditions, environmental responsibility, and good governance, including the promotion of a corruption-free environment.[29] Some 1,300 companies from more than 50 countries have joined thus far (UN 2003). Commitment to the principles is spreading from large corporations to the firms in their supply chains, reducing risk and uncertainty for the provider of the final product (Calder 2003; McKinsey & Co. 2004). Transparency International, itself a global public-private partnership, collaborates with the Global Compact in the fight against corruption.

Double bottom-line ventures—type 4 partnerships

The principal aim of type 4 double bottom-line ventures is to promote social goals such as poverty reduction, health, and environmental sustainability in developing countries through private sector development activities and with the help of private actors. The focus is on extending the frontiers of existing markets to new countries, areas, and consumer groups, such as the rural poor. Double bottom-line ventures invest primarily in small and medium-scale enterprises.

For many private investors, developing countries and rural small and medium-scale enterprises are unfamiliar clients. Public agents help to cushion the risks that might otherwise deter private investors. Sometimes the public agent is an aid agency, providing equity or other start-up capital for a private investment fund willing to meet the challenge. However, the private partner manages the actual investment activity, picking promising investment opportunities. Double bottom-line ventures are typically supported by a board composed of all shareholders.

Often set up as development venture capital funds, type 4 partnerships use equity and equity-like instruments, along with intensive technical and managerial assistance (Gibson 1999). Among the expanding array of global public-private partnerships of this type is NetMark Plus, a partnership that seeks through joint investment with international companies and local business promotion to ensure an adequate supply of insecticide-treated bednets throughout Sub-Saharan Africa to protect against mosquitoes that transmit malaria. Yet other examples are the African Trade Insurance Agency (appendix box A.6), AIG African Infrastructure Fund L.L.C., CleanTech Fund, Emerging Africa Infrastructure Fund (Emerging Africa), E7 Fund for Sustainable Energy Development, Patient Capital Initiative, Terra Capital Fund, Triodos Renewable Energy for Development Fund, and Small Enterprise Assistance Funds.

The International Finance Corporation of the World Bank Group has long facilitated investment for private sector development in developing countries, often arranging public-private financing packages. Although not a partnership itself, it has demonstrated the value of public-private partnering, and its project portfolio fits the pattern of double bottom-line ventures (IFC 2003). So does that of the World Bank Group's Multilateral Investment Guarantee Agency (MIGA

2003). Many newer funds benefit from the path that these organizations helped chart.

As are so many other partnerships, these initiatives are still in the experimental stage. And what is typical of venture capital in the national context also holds for these international endeavors: not all succeed. But when they do, they generate good returns for their investors and create an important national public good for the host developing country—a stronger, often larger domestic market system.

Social ventures

Social ventures are oriented toward public service. Frequently, they are about exceptionalism—mobilizing contributions from all actors to accelerate change or offering incentives to encourage actors to look beyond private returns to enhance social welfare. Some set themselves the challenge of turning select private goods into merit goods with a view to reducing extreme poverty and its social ill-effects, such as the spread of communicable diseases, environmental degradation, and social unrest and civil strife. Others seek to enhance the provision of a public good, such as precommercial knowledge, that no single actor would be willing to provide.

The impetus for solving a seemingly intractable problem in many instances comes not from an intergovernmental organization but from private foundations or businesses that have the money required to act. Another reason is the dilemma of international cooperation: governance without government. Nation states tend to act internationally as private actors do nationally—in their own national self-interest. This causes a double jeopardy for the world's poor, whose concerns suffer from both market failure and international (intergovernmental) cooperation failure. Social venture partnerships often come in where these two failures coincide and threaten to lead to a global crisis.

Type 5: Brokering affordable price deals. Type 5 partnerships facilitate market transactions in which developing country governments are the purchaser and private firms the supplier. Brokers weave a partnership between the two sides. The main tool is the political clout and persuasiveness of the key mediator. The outcome is differential contracting and differential patenting—to make critical goods affordable for poor countries and poor people.

An example of differential contracting is the agreement negotiated by the Clinton Foundation, in collaboration with the Global Fund to Fight AIDS, Tuberculosis, and Malaria, the World Bank, and the United Nations Children Fund, under which developing country governments purchasing AIDS drugs and diagnostics commit themselves to longer term purchase contracts. In return, pharmaceutical companies offer the goods at their lowest possible price (appendix box A.7). The multilateral agencies provide financing guarantees, while the Clinton Foundation bundles demand.

Differential patenting is the approach chosen by Médecins sans Frontières for a deal involving Yale University and Bristol-Myers Squibb. Under the mediated deal Yale licensed an AIDS drug patent to Bristol-Myers Squibb, and Bristol-Myers Squibb permitted relicensing to a South African manufacturer. The result has been a thirtyfold reduction in the price of the patented drug.[30]

The African Agricultural Technology Foundation plays a similar intermediary role between resource-poor farmers in Sub-Saharan Africa and owners of proprietary biotechnology innovations. The foundation is not just a one-time arrangement but an institutionalized operation, and it plays an active intermediation role. With support from the Rockefeller Foundation and others it obtains technology licenses on a royalty-free basis, mostly from industrial country businesses, and sublicenses them to public and private actors in developing countries for adaptation to smallholder farming conditions.

Voluntary drug donations and price reductions by pharmaceutical companies probably also belong in this category of type 5 partnerships. Some of these contributions are made in response to public pressure from civil society. Civil society has acted as a powerful broker of market transactions, to make goods both more affordable and safer for people and the environment, helping to change the policy context and to ease the way for similar arrangements in the future.[31]

Type 6: Leveraging research and development. Both knowledge with commercial potential and noncommercial knowledge (such as knowing that hand-washing reduces exposure to infection) are key ingredients in development (Sachs 2003).

Private firms have a major role in research and development (R&D), with smaller companies often working on leading-edge issues and larger companies focusing on commercializing new technologies and products (Kettler, White, and Jordan 2003), while universities and other state-funded institutions tend to engage in basic science and research. Private firms have to overcome many technical screening barriers and institutional hurdles to bring a new product to the market. Thus an agent must have a strong incentive to see the process through. That incentive is usually the promise of a high market value for the product.

Products that respond to the needs of poor people do not hold this same promise, so R&D and product-development initiatives are often stunted. Especially neglected is pro-poor knowledge that is completely noncommercial, such as knowledge about hygiene and nutrition.[32] Type 6 global public-private partnerships try to correct these shortcomings by targeting incentives, mostly financial support, to R&D providers.

Given the many health challenges facing the poor and, through spillover effects, the world as a whole, several health-related pro-poor R&D and product-development partnerships have sprung up, including Aeras Global TB Vaccine Foundation, Global Alliance for Tuberculosis Drug Development, Hookworm Vaccine Initiative, International AIDS Vaccine Initiative, Medicines for Malaria

Venture (appendix box A.8), and Institute for OneWorld Health.[33] Other type 6 partnerships foster knowledge generation on critical environment issues, such as the Global Climate and Energy Project and the Global Water Partnership.

Some of these global public-private partnerships are akin in their functioning to the public-private R&D partnerships that have become common in the national context. Such partnerships began to emerge as governments found that R&D promotion often requires going beyond an arm's-length approach—going beyond tax credits, subsidies, or prizes. To ensure that public policy incentives generate more than company-specific private gains and benefit society more broadly, close interaction between researchers and their sponsors may be needed. This realization has given rise to several national public-private research partnerships (Audretsch, Link, and Scott 2002). Global R&D partnerships are similar, emerging in particular where there is a need to incentivize private industry to explore urgently needed knowledge products for which there is no readily available market and to ensure, through close public-private interaction, that the end product is of high quality and appropriately priced.

Thus type 6 partnerships are incentive vehicles. For many of the participating private actors, however, they constitute normal business operations. As Kettler, White, and Jordan (2003) note, smaller R&D companies, with their thin profit margins, cannot afford to engage in charity. They need effective financial incentives that let them clear their private investment hurdle—and make involvement in a partnership a meaningful business proposition.[34] Larger participating companies may offer in-kind contributions, such as use of laboratory facilities. But they may also gain from the partnership. For example, they may be offered the patent rights to the partnership product in industrial countries, while the partnership itself has the right to determine product use in developing country markets. Thus, partnering may provide a real incentive and net benefit even for larger companies.

An example of a global public-private partnership that seeks to generate new noncommercial knowledge or know-how is the African Comprehensive HIV/ AIDS Partnership (its partners include the government of Botswana, the Bill & Melinda Gates Foundation, the Merck Company Foundation, and Merck & Co., Inc.). Its objective is to develop a model for a national public-private partnership to support effective and efficient implementation of health programs, analyzing and documenting its experiences and sharing the lessons learned. Strategies for Enhancing Access to Medicines for Health is also funded by the Bill & Melinda Gates Foundation and implemented by Management Science, a nonprofit firm, in collaboration with the World Health Organization (WHO), the United Nations Children's Fund (UNICEF), and national ministries of health in a number of developing countries. Its aim is to develop and test a franchise system for distributing essential medicines and vaccines through private retail outlets in underserved areas of developing countries.

Type 7: Managing for strategic results. Economic activity is usually organized along sectors (agriculture, health, finance, industry, trade), geographic lines (local, national, regional), or actor groups (civil society, firms, private households, the state). Yet many of today's policy challenges call for multisectoral, multilevel, and multiactor interventions. This discrepancy between the nature of the policy challenges and the institutions set up to respond to them causes many problems to be inadequately addressed and allows social costs to accumulate and assume crisis proportions.

To illustrate, intergovernmental organizations are well equipped to handle multilevel initiatives linking the international and national levels. But they find it difficult to tackle multiactor and multisectoral problems because of their intergovernmental nature and their usually limited, sector-specific mandate (Kaul and Le Goulven 2003). Business is better equipped to organize multidimensional production processes, but it often lacks the legitimacy and the incentives to do what type 7 global public-private partnerships do: to act as issues managers, orchestrating comprehensive change-delivery networks. Type 7 partnerships bring together public and private, national and international agents. By assembling inputs from all relevant economic sectors, type 7 partnerships increase the international community's overall problem-solving capacity. They follow issues through all the necessary steps, soliciting and combining inputs strategically to produce a clear result and make a noticeable difference. But they do so based not on coercion but on persuasion, in a CA– mode.

If the challenge is to achieve an important targeted result such as polio eradication rather than to deal with an acute crisis, the management partnership is likely to take a concerted but decentralized form. In the Global Polio Eradication Initiative, for example, partnering takes the form of agreeing on a common framework for action but pursuing follow-up initiatives independently. The lead partners are Rotary International, the U.S. Centers for Disease Control and Prevention, UNICEF, and WHO, which also serves as the initiative's secretariat.[35] Secretariats coordinate partnership activities and may also foster mutual accountability through meetings and reports that enable partners to learn how each is following through on its promises. Such secretariat services are usually performed by an intergovernmental organization on behalf of the partnership.

Issues management initiatives assume a more organized character and partnership offices become more proactive where concerns are more urgent and tasks more complex, with potentially far-reaching and serious consequences. The World Economic Forum's Disaster Resource Network illustrates such an initiative. It fosters collaboration among businesses, national governmental agencies, intergovernmental organizations, and civil society organizations to promote a more effective and coordinated response by all parties when disaster strikes.

The Global Fund to Fight AIDS, Tuberculosis, and Malaria perhaps best illustrates the type of strategic issues management that is the hallmark of type 7 global public-private partnerships (appendix box A.9). The Global Fund, with a governing board representing stakeholder groups, acts as the nodal point of the international community's efforts to control these three major global diseases. It looks to ensure that all necessary inputs are brought together internationally, channels support mostly to governments of developing countries and to other key actors, and helps build partnership-based initiatives for change at the country level. Among the activities that it supports at the country level are efforts to extend workplace-based health initiatives to the wider community. In this activity the fund collaborates, among others, with the Global Business Coalition on HIV/AIDS, a private sector-led public-private partnership. As issue manager the fund also encourages and draws on the work of other health-related global public-private partnerships, including several of those mentioned in this chapter, notably when discussing type 5 and type 6 partnerships.

In the future, mechanisms such as the Global Environment Facility might be reoriented along lines similar to those of the Global Fund to Fight AIDS, Tuberculosis, and Malaria in the event that such global environmental challenges as global climate change, depletion of oil reserves, or loss of biodiversity assume more threatening dimensions.[36]

IMPLICATIONS FOR THE CURRENT SYSTEM OF INTERNATIONAL COOPERATION

Although diverse in purpose and rationale, global public-private partnerships share a common characteristic: they are increasingly chosen in cases where some actors are ready to move and pay for exploring new avenues or averting a crisis. But why are they happening? Are they just a fad, a temporary shift in policy mood? Or are they here to stay? And if they are to become a fixture, how will they fit into the current system of international cooperation?

Much of the evidence presented below points to an enduring role for global public-private partnerships, with further growth in their number and importance. They are poised to change the current system of international cooperation from being primarily intergovernmental to being tripartite, drawing in all actor groups—state, business, and civil society.

Fad or fixture?

An important driver of the growth in global public-private partnerships is the increased prevalence of national public-private partnerships and thus national actors' greater familiarity with this modality. The changes that have opened up space for such partnering nationally are structural in nature and thus likely to endure and shape economic activity and policymaking for some time to come.

For example, notions of market-state and public-private divides are closely linked to the former East-West conflict and the political rivalry between centrally planned and market-based economies. This conflict has vanished. Its demise has opened up opportunities for enhanced policy flexibility and for a more realistic assessment of the comparative strengths of different actor groups. Following an initial surge toward privatization and economic liberalization during the 1980s and early 1990s, recognition has grown of the importance to market efficiency of institutions and a well designed and managed public policy framework. These and other changes have contributed to less ideological, more mutually supportive relations between market and state and public and private agents.

Further, states have become more sophisticated in reaching out to markets, and markets have broadened and deepened so that they can now handle many more types of goods, including goods for the poor, thanks in part to innovative types of securitization and other advances in financial intermediation. The type 4 and type 5 partnerships in particular speak to this fact.

Also, partnering and networking have become important in many areas, flourishing in an environment of enhanced political and economic freedoms. These range from political alliance building among civil society organizations to the formation of joint ventures and alliances among firms. Public-private partnerships both emerge from and express these trends. Type 7 partnerships, for example, reflect this trend toward networked production.

Another driving force behind the growth in public-private partnering nationally and internationally is the increasing importance attached to corporate social responsibility. With more information becoming available on such issues as the environmental effects of various pollutants or the health hazards of materials used in manufacturing processes, stakeholders, especially civil society activists, are increasingly holding corporations accountable for the public effects of their production activities (Christian Aid 2004; GlobeScan Inc. 2002; Hopkins 2002; UNRISD 2004). Therefore, especially when operating in countries with lax labor or environmental standards, transnational corporations are concerned about supply chain management in the interest of protecting their brand and safeguarding their global corporate reputation. As noted, a number of the type 1 global public-private partnerships have been born of this concern.

A further impetus for public-private partnering internationally comes from the growing volume of common norms and standards and international law, including international agreements on intellectual property rights. To enable these rules to be applicable to a highly diverse world, exceptions are sometimes required. As was noted when discussing type 5 and type 6 partnerships, this need for exceptions is especially relevant in the health area today.

Finally, a large number of current global public-private partnerships, again notably in the health area, are linked to the tremendous increase in private wealth and in charitable and philanthropic foundations devoted to furthering public policy (Ferris and Minstrom 2002; Schervish 2000). Foundations are often the key promoters of social venture partnerships (types 5–7). Foundation funds and other private resources, such as those motivated by corporate social responsibility, are particularly attractive to intergovernmental organizations. It is important to consider, however, that this increased involvement of private resources may reflect current taxation policies and practices, and so may be less durable than the other forces driving the growth in public-private partnering.

Several recent policy documents call for greater use of public-private partnering, among them the report of the Commission on the Private Sector and Development (2004) convened by the United Nations Secretary-General and the report of the World Panel on Financing Water Infrastructure (Winpenny 2003). Facilitating partnering has become a new "business," both nationally and internationally. Organizations have been created specifically to promote this objective. They include, among others, the Global Business Coalition on HIV/AIDS, the Seed Initiative, the United Nations Fund for International Partnerships, and the World Economic Forum's Global Institute for Partnership and Governance.[37] Driving this promotion of public-private partnerships is the awareness of the daunting magnitude of the challenges facing the international community in the years ahead. If the world is to meet such objectives as the Millennium Development Goals, avert the risk of global warming, and reduce dependence on fossil fuels, extraordinary effort and innovation will be required for many years to come.

Global public-private partnerships and intergovernmental organizations—competition or complementarity?

Global public-private partnerships often compete with each other for scarce resources. For example, some 12 global public-private partnerships are addressing the challenge of developing antimalarial medicines and vaccines. Similarly, multiple global public-private partnerships are working to support many other issues, including alternative energy technologies. Global public-private partnerships also compete with intergovernmental organizations for funding, as they increasingly engage in activities that only a few years ago would have been viewed as classical intergovernmental organization tasks, such as norms and standards setting and supporting pro-poor R&D. Today, intergovernmental organizations working on the operational side of international cooperation increasingly see others running with "their" mandate and "their" resources, because many donors prefer to support global public-private partnerships.

Competition between intergovernmental organizations and global public-private partnerships can be desirable. However, it also can be a source of distortion. These global partnerships may reflect agreed-on multilateral priorities, as shown before (see table 1, column 5). The link may be very loose, however. In addition, agents with money can set up partnerships for international cooperation in areas of their own interest. As Utting (2000) asks, "Whose agenda counts?" Also, when intergovernmental organizations are implementing projects financed by private partners who find it important for business reasons to do "well and good," they too may shift their attention away from where it can best enhance social welfare to where the private partner wants to focus to maximize private gains. This does not suggest staying away from public-private partnering. Rather it underlines the importance of being clear about when—and for whom—partnering is desirable and of generating net benefits.

If approached systematically, global public-private partnerships have certain comparative advantages over intergovernmental organizations. They tend to be more product focused, with greater operational flexibility, and since they often face more competition, they are challenged to function effectively and efficiently. Set up as enterprises, they are run and managed by an entrepreneur, a chief executive officer who is likely to be familiar with both the private business side and the public service side of the venture.

These characteristics distinguish global public-private partnerships from intergovernmental organizations, while also complementing them. As large bureaucracies, intergovernmental organizations are set up to facilitate continuity and rule-based behavior—not the exceptionalism, innovation, focus, and risk taking often expected of global public-private partnerships. Thus some partnerships step in where intergovernmental organizations are unable to advance, an important complementarity that ought to be fostered.

Recognizing this, some intergovernmental organizations have begun to deliberately encourage partnerships.[38] For example, it would be difficult for an organization such as the WHO to strike the type of patent deals with private pharmaceutical companies that the Medicines for Malaria Venture promotes. And it would be difficult for an intergovernmental institution such as the World Bank to directly undertake the carbon-credit trading being arranged by the Prototype Carbon Fund. Realizing this, the WHO and the World Bank became leading partners in these global public-private partnerships, hoping to take advantage of the ability of such partnerships to accomplish previously unattainable goals. In today's world of expanding and deepening markets the types of tools used by these partnerships may be among the best for the purpose, or at least more appropriate than the conventional instruments at the disposal of intergovernmental organizations, notably the traditional government-to-government foreign aid modality.

"SO WHAT?"—CONCLUSIONS AND POLICY IMPLICATIONS

Global public-private partnerships, more numerous than ever, are likely to be here to stay and to form an important part of international cooperation in the future. This makes it imperative to understand what these partnerships are about: what forms they can take, how to match form and function, when they are desirable, and how to assess whether they are effective in achieving their goals.

What has the discussion here contributed to enhancing understanding of global public-private partnerships? How could these insights help to approach global public-private partnering more deliberately and systematically? In particular, how can the suggested typology of partnerships be of use?

Three major conclusions emerge from the discussion and point toward concrete ways to improve public-private partnering.

Conclusion 1: Global public-private partnerships come in many forms, driven by different motivations and pursuing different purposes

This conclusion is important because it emphasizes that partnerships can be used for a wide variety of purposes. Policymakers and actors interested in partnering can choose a number of avenues. The typology developed in this chapter could guide them in choosing the most appropriate approach.

Similarly, by showing that partnerships differ, the typology can be a useful tool for those who wish to assess how one type of partnership functions in practice—in terms of achievement of stated goals (effectiveness), distribution of net benefits (equity), legitimacy, and accountability.[39] Obviously, a type 1 partnership, designed for trading comparative advantage between private and public actors, should be judged by different criteria than a partnership of the social venture class. Enhanced efficiency would be an important aspect of a type 1 partnership and improved equity an expected outcome of the social venture class of partnerships.

Conclusion 2: Global public-private partnerships occupy an increasingly open middle ground between markets and states

The policy response to market failure need no longer be simply government intervention. Nor should the response to government failure simply be to assign the production of a particular good or service straight to the market—to privatize. In both instances public-private partnering can be a desirable and feasible policy option, providing valuable opportunities for more nuanced policymaking.

For partnerships to succeed, it is important to distinguish between what has been referred to here as the market plus governance (M+) mode of partnering and the voluntary (not state-coerced) collective action (CA–) mode of partnering. In the M+ mode the partners essentially engage in an exchange transaction of private goods, a quid pro quo. In the CA– mode the issue at stake is jointly producing a club good or global public good (as shown in table 1, column 4). No one can provide the desired good unilaterally, and therefore the parties need to cooperate by pooling their interests and resources. To ignore this link between intended product and partnering mode would result in partnership failure, because it would mean ignoring the incentives that bring partners together.

The M+ mode of partnering demands sophisticated contracting arrangements. The CA– mode works only for those who are not only prepared to reveal their willingness to pay but are also able to pay.

As Zadek (2004) stresses, the question thus is not only how to foster good governance within partnerships but also whether partnerships are a new form of governance. Since they aim at being participatory, they may reduce some current democracy deficits. But many tend to have a relatively small number of partners. So are they generating new participation gaps? Do they give a stronger voice to those who can afford to pay for a voluntary initiative than to others? Under what circumstances may cooperation within smaller "clubs" be more desirable than negotiations between a large number of parties? Judging from existing club-type partnerships (type 3), they seem to be focused on highly technical issues.

Conclusion 3: Global public-private partnerships have sprung up primarily in an ad hoc way, without a well founded policy framework and clear desirability criteria

Given such ad hoc origins, there is likely considerable scope for improving the relation between intergovernmental organizations, the cornerstones of the conventional system of international cooperation, and the new "players on the ground"—global public-private partnerships.

Two steps could help to achieve that. First, intergovernmental organizations could review their mandates to determine which functions could best be delivered through global public-private partnerships, with funding or cofunding by the intergovernmental organization. Second, they could conduct desirability studies to clarify whether public support is needed and in what form.

On the first step, how should intergovernmental organizations identify the qualifying tasks? Judging from table 1 and the types of partnerships it identifies, public-private partnering might be a preferred way for intergovernmental organizations to proceed under the following conditions:

- Desired competencies (such as managing risk and picking promising investment opportunities) are perceived to reside with the other actor groups (suggesting, respectively, a type 1 and type 4 partnership arrangement).

- New public policy mechanisms need to be developed (indicating the desirability of a type 2 partnership if the issue is testing the mechanism and gauging the response of nonstate actors, or a type 3 arrangement if the issue is reaching consensus with nonstate actors).

- Accomplishing a desired goal requires innovation and perhaps also ownership and management of intellectual property (making a type 6 partnership appear preferable).

- Reaching a particular objective calls for exceptionalism, reaching beyond organizational mandates, and speed that cannot easily be aligned with the organization's governance and oversight procedures and requirements (suggesting a partnership arrangement along the lines of type 5 or 7).

A further question arises in this context, especially in light of the discussion of type 1 partnerships and the competition for scarce resources between intergovernmental agencies and global public-private partnerships. Do intergovernmental organizations, such as funds and programs or the specialized agencies of the United Nations system, have the financial means to proactively pursue the partnership modality? The answer is that if they hesitate to use this modality where it would be the better approach, they may find that partnerships emerge anyhow and attract resources away from intergovernmental organizations, perhaps to the detriment of effective implementation of multilateral policy priorities. A deliberate and active policy of public-private partnering could perhaps allow intergovernmental organizations to avoid such an outcome.

The second step for fostering enhanced complementarity would be to require that intergovernmental organizations undertake desirability studies, demonstrating that partnering not only provides a windfall profit for the private partner but also enhances global social welfare. Desirability studies, common for national public-private partnerships, could clarify whether public support is needed at all and if so in what form.

Figure 2 illustrates how to assess the desirability of public support for a national R&D project. For project C no public intervention is required. Because the expected rate of return exceeds the private hurdle rate, the private actor is likely to undertake the project on its own. For project B, an arm's-length intervention might suffice. In the national context this could mean a tax credit or subsidy. In the international context, where such instruments are unavailable, a simple partnership may be required, along the lines, say, of type 5 or 6. For project A, however, where large or multiple incentive gaps have to be overcome, a type 7 partnership might be warranted.

Enhanced complementarity also has a longer term dimension related to the question of whether public-private partnering is likely to continue along its current path of hundreds of limited and often overlapping initiatives. Or will it perhaps evolve into a more mainstream way of performing certain tasks. The 2004 Group of Eight summit agreed to establish a Global HIV Vaccine Enterprise, a virtual consortium facilitating closer coordination and cooperation among public and private actors around the world to accelerate HIV vaccine development.[40] Similarly, the recently created Global Crop Diversity Trust—its goal to increase food security through crop diversity—was organized as a global public-private partnership.[41] These initiatives may be the beginning of institutionalization and consolidation of current type 6 and type 7 partnerships into more regular, longer term service provision organizations.

Other partnership types may also evolve from being an exceptional approach when problems are on the verge of becoming a crisis to being a more routine method of policy implementation. Following in the footsteps of some existing type 4 partnerships, for example, public-private partnerships could tackle problems of commodity price and farm income volatility, discussed in the chapter by Morgan in this volume. Public-private partnering could make risk management more affordable for all. Similarly, differential contracting and patenting (type 5

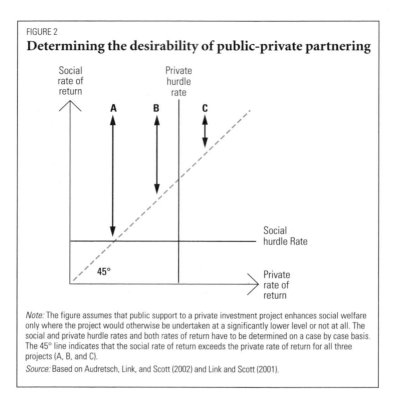

FIGURE 2

Determining the desirability of public-private partnering

Note: The figure assumes that public support to a private investment project enhances social welfare only where the project would otherwise be undertaken at a significantly lower level or not at all. The social and private hurdle rates and both rates of return have to be determined on a case by case basis. The 45° line indicates that the social rate of return exceeds the private rate of return for all three projects (A, B, and C).

Source: Based on Audretsch, Link, and Scott (2002) and Link and Scott (2001).

public-private partnering) could be applied to meeting the challenge of disseminating critical energy technology. And as Kremer and Peterson Zwane (in this volume) argue, there is much to learn from the health-related type 6 partnerships for fostering agricultural R&D.

The WHO, the International Labour Organization, and the International Telecommunication Union, which already pursue partnership approaches, are rare exceptions in the current multilateral system of international organizations. Perhaps today's global public-private partnerships are the forerunners of change, of the emergence of a more partnership-based multilateral system.

*   *   *

Most countries have been redefining and rebalancing the roles of states and markets. This wave of policy change has now reached the system of international cooperation. A growing number of global public-private partnerships are challenging a system that still relies primarily on intergovernmental participation. This chapter has provided an overview of the current landscape of global public-private partnerships and has explored the different motivations that drive them, what they intend to accomplish, and how they are organized.

The typology of partnerships developed in the chapter reveals that partnerships can take a variety of such forms, depending primarily on their motivation and the outcomes they seek. The full scale of current partnership arrangements reveals that public-private partnering has opened up an important middle ground between markets and states and contributed to an important differentiation in policy approaches and tools. Instead of state intervention alone, the answer to market failure can also be an M+ partnership, a market transaction complemented by a joint governance component. And instead of just assigning goods to the market, the response to state failure can also be a CA– partnership of voluntary collective action without government coercion.

Again, the suggested typology provides criteria for policymakers to determine when public-private partnering may be desirable and what type to choose. The discussion highlights ways of fostering complementarity between intergovernmental organizations, the cornerstones of the conventional system of international cooperation, and the newer players, the global public-private partnerships. Similarly, analysts wishing to evaluate the effectiveness, efficiency, equity, or other aspects of these partnerships could be guided by the differentiation of partnership types that the typology offers.

Improving the understanding of public-private partnering and avoiding its drawbacks are important for preserving and nurturing these new policy opportunities.

GLOBAL PUBLIC-PRIVATE PARTNERSHIPS MENTIONED IN THE CHAPTER

Action TB Programme [www.gsk.com/community]
Aeras Global TB Vaccine Foundation [www.aeras.org]
African Agricultural Technology Foundation [www.aftechfound.org]
African Comprehensive HIV/AIDS Partnership [www.achap.org]
African Trade Insurance Agency [www.ati-aca.com]
AIG African Infrastructure Fund L.L.C.
    [www.empwdc.com/EMP_Africa.htm]
Chicago Climate Exchange [www.chicagoclimatex.com]
CleanTech Fund [www.econergy.net/cleantech_fund.html]
Climate Investment Partnership [www.climateinvestors.com]
Clinton Foundation AIDS Initiative [www.clintonfoundation.org/
    aids-initiative5.htm]
E7 Fund for Sustainable Energy Development [www.e7.org/Pages/
    O-Fund.html]
Emerging Africa Infrastructure Fund [www.emergingafricafund.com]
Ethical Trading Initiative [www.ethicaltrade.org]
Fair Trade Labeling Organization [www.fairtrade.net]
Galileo [http://europa.eu.int/comm/dgs/energy_transport/galileo/
    index_en.htm]
Global Alliance for TB Drug Development [www.tballiance.org]
Global Business Coalition on HIV/AIDS [www.businessfightsaids.org]
Global Climate and Energy Project [http://gcep.Stanford.edu]
Global Compact [www.unglobalcompact.org]
Global Crop Diversity Trust [www.startwithaseed.org]
Global Fund to Fight Aids, Tuberculosis, and Malaria
    [www.theglobalfund.org]
Global HIV Vaccine Enterprise [www.g8usa.gov/f_061004b.htm]
Global Polio Eradication Initiative [www.polioeradication.org]
Global Reporting Initiative [www.globalreporting.org]
Global Water Partnership [www.gwpforum.org]
Green Dot [www.green-dot.de]
Hookworm Vaccine Initiative [www.sabin.org/hookworm.htm]
IKEA Social Responsibility Initiatives [www.ikea-usa.com/ms/en_US/
    about_ikea/social_environmental/projects.html]
INBio/Merck Bio-prospecting [www.inbio.ac.cr]
Intelsat [www.intelsat.com]
International AIDS Vaccine Initiative [www.iavi.org]
International Labour Organization [www.ilo.org]
International Organization for Standardization [www.iso.org]
International Telecommunications Union [www.itu.int]

GLOBAL PUBLIC-PRIVATE PARTNERSHIPS MENTIONED IN THE CHAPTER

Internet Corporation for Assigned Names and Numbers
   [www.icann.org]
JSTOR [www.jstor.org]
Marine Stewardship Council [www.msc.org]
Medicines for Malaria Venture [www.mmv.org]
Médicins Sans Frontières AIDS drug deal with Yale University and
   Bristol-Myers Squibb [www.newsmax.com/archives/articles/
   2001/3/13/60623.shtml]
NetMark Plus [www.netmarkafrica.org]
Onchocerciasis Control Programme [www.worldbank.org/afr/gper/
   ocp.htm or www.who.int/ocp]
Open GIS Consortium [www.opengis.org]
Patient Capital Initiative [www.energy-base.org/sef_bonn/pub/
   sef_presentations/PPP_rossbach.pdf]
Prototype Carbon Fund [http://prototypecarbonfund.org]
Secure the Future [www.securethefuture.com]
Seed Initiative [www.seedawards.org]
Small Enterprise Assistance Funds [www.seaf.com]
Strategies for Enhancing Access to Medicines for Health
   [www.msh.org/seam]
Terra Capital Fund [http://ifcln1.ifc.org/ifcext/enviro.nsf/
   Content/TerraCapital]
Transparency International [www.transparency.org]
Triodos Renewable Energy for Development Fund [www.triodos.com/
   com/whats_new/latest_news/press_releases/60888?lang]
Unicode Consortium [www.unicode.org/consortium/consort.html]
Universal Flour Fortification Initiative [http://webapps01.un.org/dsd/
   partnerships/search/partnerships/205.html]
World Economic Forum Disaster Resource Network
   [www.weforum.org/drn]

GALILEO: A PRIVATELY PROVIDED GLOBAL PUBLIC SERVICE

Galileo, a European satellite radio navigation program, is an example of a type 1 global public-private partnership. It is intended to complement the U.S. Global Positioning System and the Russian Global Navigation Satellite System, both funded and controlled by military authorities. Galileo, however, will be partially managed and controlled by civilians. It thus offers the guarantee of continuity of service, critical for many potential applications. It is expected that users will be willing to pay for this greater reliability and that demand for Galileo's global services will be high and growing.

With this prospect of profitability Galileo's founding members—the European Commission and the European Space Agency—decided to contract out management and operation to a private sector concessionaire. The concessionaire is to contribute two-thirds of the program's deployment costs (an estimated €2.2 billion) and assume all risks of time and cost overruns in return for the right to the operating revenues for a set number of years. A public body, the Supervisory Authority, will oversee the concessionaire's work and manage the public interests relating to the Galileo system and its implementation. Now composed of the founding members, it will include any other parties that join the undertaking by subscribing to Galileo's initial funding.

Private sector involvement in the deployment and operation of Galileo were considered desirable to attract private funding, to shift risk to the private sector, to benefit from efficient private sector management, and to draw on the private sector's commercial orientation to improve revenue generation. Without the opportunity to contract out, the European Commission might have considered the program too costly. And without the commission's input into the development phase, private sector agents might not have participated. So public-private partnering helped to overcome both market failure and intergovernmental failure.

Source: http://europa.eu.int/comm/dgs/energy_transport/galileo/index_en.htm.

Appendix Box A.3
The IKEA Group: worldwide business—worldwide social and environmental responsibility

Contracting out at the national level consists mainly of a public agent delegating project implementation to a private sector actor. Internationally, most contracting out (type 1 global public-private partnerships) runs the other way, with a private agent purchasing the services of a public agent, frequently an intergovernmental organization. Partnerships of this type usually form part of a corporation's philanthropy or social responsibility initiatives.

The operational social responsibility initiatives of the IKEA Group provide an example of this large subgroup of type 1 global public-private partnerships. Much of the raw material for IKEA's products is wood or wood fibers. To ensure longer term sustainability, the company sources its wood from forests that are managed responsibly. And because child labor is a reality in many countries in which IKEA purchases labor and products, the company supports projects that go to the root cause of the problem: quality education. Its initiatives span large parts of the globe— from Africa to Asia and Eastern Europe.

In each of its key areas of social and environmental responsibility IKEA has established relationships with recognized international and national organizations, including among others, the United Nations Children's Fund, the United Nations Development Programme, the World Health Organization, the World Resources Institute, and the World Wide Fund for Nature. Partnering with agencies such as these allows IKEA to use its philanthropic and social responsibility money more efficiently and effectively. Partnering provides immediate access to expertise and experience, access to national and local government authorities, and an established project-delivery system.

What makes such deals attractive for intergovernmental organizations and nongovernmental organizations is both the added income and the promise of working with some of the world's most powerful players. And the incentive for national government agencies to support or even join such initiatives can be to be seen as making sure that foreign direct investment also generates benefits for the local communities concerned.

Thus, partnerships can be a means to quite different ends for each partner.

Source: www.ikea-usa.com/ms/en_US/about_ikea/social_environmental/projects.html.

APPENDIX BOX A.4
THE PROTOTYPE CARBON FUND: PIONEERING A NEW MARKET

The Prototype Carbon Fund (PCF), a type 2 global public-private partnership, is a pioneer in the market for project-based greenhouse gas emission reductions within the framework of the Kyoto Protocol. A closed mutual fund, it invests on a pilot basis, primarily in transition economies and developing countries. Its contributors are 6 industrial countries and 17 private companies, including power and oil companies and global banks. The World Bank provided the seed money.

Overall, the PCF expects to purchase some 30 million metric tons of carbon dioxide equivalent, about a third of the volume generated by the projects it supports. The emission reduction credits thus obtained will be distributed to PCF participants in line with their contributions. PCF's trading partners—transition economies and developing countries—will benefit from generating and selling emission reductions and opening up a new income stream. Negotiating with the PCF will also build their institutional capacity and expertise in climate issues, strengthening their position in future intergovernmental negotiations and transactions in carbon-related markets.

Development of new markets works best when potential purchasers and providers collaborate and reach a common understanding on desirability and feasibility. An effective, joint governance mechanism, such as the PCF's partnership trilogy (contributors, project owners, and the World Bank), is therefore an essential component of market-pioneering initiatives.

Source: Lecocq 2003; PCF 2003.

APPENDIX BOX A.5
THE INTERNATIONAL ORGANIZATION FOR STANDARDIZATION: PROMOTING GLOBAL TECHNICAL STANDARDS

The International Organization for Standardization (ISO), a type 3 global public-private partnership, is a nongovernmental organization whose members are drawn from national standards institutes in more than 140 countries and private sector agencies, often set up by industry associations. Its main role is to facilitate the development of technical standards, including those related to the environment (the ISO 14000 family) and social responsibility.

ISO's work is demand driven. Industries report standards gaps to their national-level standardization organization, which then reports them to the appropriate ISO technical committee, which is sometimes joined by representatives of government agencies, testing laboratories, consumer organizations, or environmental groups.

ISO standards are voluntary. Their adoption is a sovereign policy choice of national governments. The ISO has no legal authority to enforce implementation. However, standards often become a market requirement and thus are self-implementing and self-enforcing.

ISO is governed by its members, who meet at the annual General Assembly. Member subscriptions pay for the organization's Secretariat. The development of individual standards, accounting for four-fifths of the operational costs of the ISO, is made possible by the contributions of individual standardization organizations and by the willingness of business organizations to lend experts to conduct the technical work. Recognizing that standards can affect the economic and social well-being of many stakeholder groups, many ISO members have public review procedures for making draft standards available for comment to interested parties, including the general public. In this way ISO acknowledges that a participatory development process is more likely than a narrow, club-based one to yield standards that are globally useful.

Source: www.iso.org.

APPENDIX BOX A.6
THE AFRICAN TRADE INSURANCE AGENCY: ADVANCING THE FRONTIERS OF THE INSURANCE MARKET

The African Trade Insurance Agency (ATI) was set up to reverse the perception that Africa is a high-risk region for investment, a belief that has been contributing to the continent's limited access to private capital. ATI's objective is to alleviate this constraint on development by extending the trade insurance market into Africa.

Drawing on experience acquired in several Eastern European countries, the Common Market for Eastern and Southern Africa (COMESA) worked with the International Development Association (IDA) of the World Bank Group to develop a design for the ATI. The ATI was set up at the regional rather than the national level to enhance its credibility to the private sector. A regional approach would facilitate pooling and diversification of risk and benefit from economies of scale.

ATI was supported by a number of public sponsors, including the European Union, the government of Japan, and the World Bank's Institutional Development Fund, as well as IDA. ATI's private sector partner is a leading global insurance company, Atradius. The world's second-largest credit insurer, Atradius offers political risk insurance and trade credit insurance to protect exporters against a buyer's credit risk. A type 4 global public-private partnership, the ATI thus serves as a one-stop shop for comprehensive trade insurance within Eastern and Southern Africa.

Source: World Bank 2003.

APPENDIX BOX A.7
BROKERING LOWEST PRICE DEALS: MAKING ESSENTIAL PRIVATE GOODS AFFORDABLE FOR ALL

In the spring of 2004 the Clinton Foundation brought together the Global Fund to Fight AIDS, Tuberculosis, and Malaria (the Global Fund), the United Nations Children's Fund (UNICEF), the World Bank, and pharmaceutical companies in India and South Africa to reach agreement on distributing critically needed AIDS drugs and diagnostics at greatly reduced prices in developing countries. This type 5 global public-private partnership has lowered the price of medicines by one-third to one-half and the price of diagnostics by more than three-quarters.

The Clinton Foundation, as broker, overcame a critical barrier to the purchase of AIDS drugs and diagnostics: the lack of credible purchasing power of some of the most HIV/AIDS-affected countries in Sub-Saharan Africa and the Caribbean. This obstacle was overcome by bundling country demands to allow bulk purchasing. National HIV/AIDS programs contact the Clinton Foundation to express their interest in becoming a Member Purchaser. Countries must secure a letter of credit or other guarantee (including from the participating funding organizations, if appropriate) certifying the availability of funds to buy drugs and tests. Further, they must demonstrate that they have sufficient national capacity to securely store and administer the drugs and reagents. And they must tender for extended periods. This change in incentive structures has made it possible for participating pharmaceutical companies to reduce prices.

Other manufacturers, including patent-holding companies, are invited to join the agreement. Measures are in place to prevent these low-price drugs and tests from entering industrial country markets. All the actors involved in the Clinton Foundation initiative support intellectual property rights. However, they also recognize that only a small portion of the pharmaceutical industry's income comes from the countries that will benefit from this low-price deal. So this initiative will not adversely affect their business or their research and development activities. If anything, it could have a positive effect, affording them an important opportunity to demonstrate social responsibility—at no cost.

Source: www.aidspan.org/gfo/archives/newsletter and www.clintonfoundation.org/aids-initiative5.htm.

APPENDIX BOX A.8
THE MEDICINES FOR MALARIA VENTURE: PROMOTING PRO-POOR
RESEARCH AND DEVELOPMENT

Malaria kills more than 1 million people each year. Some 300–500 million new clinical cases occur annually, mainly among poor people and mainly among children and pregnant women. More than 90 percent of the malaria burden falls on Sub-Saharan Africa. Drug resistance is a serious challenge, calling for continuous research and development (R&D) and requiring a new antimalarial drug to be commercialized every five years on average.

But because most people threatened by malaria are poor, market incentives for R&D are weak. The Medicines for Malaria Venture (MMV), a type 6 global public-private partnership, seeks to provide the missing incentives to encourage the private pharmaceutical industry to focus on affordable antimalarial drugs.

The MMV has a two-part strategy for building new incentives. First, it uses the financial contributions of its donor group (private foundations, intergovernmental organizations, national aid agencies, and the International Federation of Pharmaceutical Manufacturers Associations) and the in-kind contributions (such as free use of laboratory facilities) of its business partners to support research by private companies. Second, the MMV negotiates differential patenting agreements with its private sector partners. The MMV's intellectual property rights usually cover the disease-endemic countries and its private partners, the richer, industrial countries (the "travelers' market").

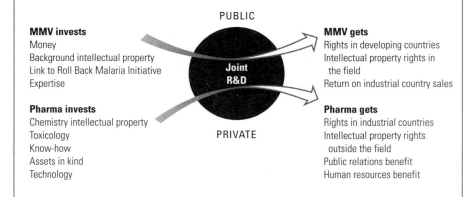

PUBLIC

MMV invests
Money
Background intellectual property
Link to Roll Back Malaria Initiative
Expertise

Joint
R&D

MMV gets
Rights in developing countries
Intellectual property rights in
   the field
Return on industrial country sales

Pharma invests
Chemistry intellectual property
Toxicology
Know-how
Assets in kind
Technology

PRIVATE

Pharma gets
Rights in industrial countries
Intellectual property rights
   outside the field
Public relations benefit
Human resources benefit

Source: www.mmv.org; Mattock 2002; and Ridley 2000.

APPENDIX BOX A.9

THE GLOBAL FUND TO FIGHT AIDS, TUBERCULOSIS, AND MALARIA:
MANAGING FOR STRATEGIC RESULTS

The Global Fund to Fight AIDS, Tuberculosis, and Malaria is the principal funding mechanism for efforts to control these communicable diseases. It is challenged to seek and support partnerships by its mandate—which is to facilitate the mobilization and channeling of resources—not to develop or deliver assistance to projects. Controlling three of the world's major communicable diseases is too vast a task for one actor. That requires inputs and active collaboration from many public and private actors; initiatives at all levels of development, from the local to the international; and contributions from multiple sectors, from medical and pharmaceutical research to health sector management, global knowledge management, and international trade. Implementing the Global Fund's mandate thus calls for a comprehensive approach to strategic issues management—a clear vision and focus on what is to be achieved, backed by financial resources.

The complexity of the Global Fund's mission is reflected in its governance structures. Both its governing board and its country-level coordinating mechanisms show its public-private partnership character. These participatory governance structures reflect a broad-based but targeted resource-mobilization strategy. The Global Fund reveals how resource mobilization can be a highly diversified activity that goes well beyond mobilizing contributions in cash. The Global Fund has been a party to the Clinton Foundation-initiated arrangement for low-price drugs (appendix box A.6). It collaborates with the Global Business Coalition for HIV/AIDS to create synergies between firm-based health programs and government-run health initiatives. And it keenly follows, and draws on, the work of such initiatives as the Medicines for Malaria Venture (appendix box A.8) and other drug development initiatives.

Source: www.theglobalfund.org and www.businessfightsaids.org.

NOTES

1. For studies on national public-private partnerships, see, among others, EC (2003); Gabriel (2004); Gunningham and Sinclair (2002); Harris (2003); Kelly (2000); NCPPP (2000); Osborne (2000); Social Watch (2003); and Spackman (2002).

2. See www.worldwatercouncil.org.

3. See www.theglobalfund.org. For the web sites of other global public-private partnerships mentioned in this chapter, see appendix box A.1.

4. For simplicity, the term *good* is used in this chapter to refer to both goods and services. The glossary at the end of the volume defines the types of goods referred to in this chapter, including merit goods, club goods, public goods, and global public goods.

5. See, for example, Andersen and Mailand (2002); Liebenthal, Feinstein, and Ingram (2004); Linder (1999); Ridley (2000); McQuaid (2000); Nelson (2002); Rosenau (2000); UN Foundation and WEF (2003); Witte, Benner, and Streck (2003); and Zadek (2004).

6. The most comprehensive database is that of health-related global public-private partnerships, which was launched by the Initiative on Public-Private Partnerships for Health (www.ippph.org). It contains more than 80 partnerships. The United Nations maintains a list of public-private partnerships engaged in sustainable development activities, including about 90 global ones that fit the criteria set forth in this chapter (www.un.org/esa/sustdev/partnerships/partnerships.htm). The United Nations Fund for International Partnerships also maintains a list of partnerships in such diverse fields as children's health, population and women, environment, peace and security, and human rights (www.un.org/unfip/). Its catalogue of projects over-laps in part with other data sets and other UN-related data sources. Leads to global public-private partnerships can furthermore be found in various studies, including Brinkerhoff (2002); Malena (2004); Nelson (2002); Spielman and von Grebmer (2004); Rausser, Simon, and Ameden (2000); Tessner and Kell (2000); and UN (2004). Company web sites are another important data source, notably reports on corporate social responsibility. For a list of the approximately 400 initiatives identi-fied based on these and other data sources, see Broadwater and Kaul (2005) and www.thenewpublicfinance.org.

7. This fact already shows what can be seen repeatedly later, namely the critical role that global public-private partnerships play in responding to urgent challenges and situations for which conventional single-actor responses would be inadequate. These include, among others, the concerns on which global public-private partner-ships appear to be focused.

8. For a more complete methodological note on how the sample was con-structed, see Broadwater and Kaul (2005) and the page on "Global Public-Private Partnerships" at www.thenewpublicfinance.org.

9. The term *private gain,* when accruing to a public partner such as a govern-ment agency, refers to organizational benefits, such as cost savings, not (or not only) to the personal gains of bureaucrats or politicians.

10. The term *trading comparative advantage* (also referred to as *contracting out*) refers to the fact that different actors (private firms, government bureaucracies) tend to have different strengths. Hence, it can sometimes be desirable for an actor (say, a government agency) to implement a particular task by involving another actor (a private firm). However, as discussed in more detail later, such a "trade" needs to be distinguished from outsourcing. Assuming that a government agency is the initiating party, outsourcing may involve the procurement from a private sector supplier of inputs into an otherwise government-managed process. In the case of trading comparative advantage the government hands management responsibility over to a nonstate actor.

11. For an overview of the literature on institutional economics, see Furubotn and Richter (2000). For the concept of incomplete contracting, see Hart (1995); Hart, Shleifer, and Vishny (1997); and Williamson (1985).

12. For a discussion of voluntary provision and refinements of the arguments presented here, see Bergstrom, Blume, and Varian (1986); Cornes and Sandler (1996); Dougherty (2003); Olson (1965); Ostrom (1990); and Sandler and Tschirhart (1997).

13. This of course raises the fundamental issue of how global public-private partnership initiatives are linked to multilateral priorities, an issue covered later in the chapter. From the perspective of purported goals and intended activities, as applied here, most global public-private partnerships try to link themselves to an agreed-on global goal (see table 1, column 5). An interesting question, however, is whether some goals are more likely than others to be "picked" for implementation by a partnership.

14. These implementation arrangements sometimes also take the form of partnering, notably type 1 partnership. As discussed later, such partnerships within partnerships can be found in initiatives that are involved in research and development, such as the type 6 partnerships.

15. For an empirical analysis of the functioning of governance in select global public-private partnerships, see Buse (2004).

16. For more details on the financiers of the 100 partnerships included in the study sample, see "Global Public-Private Partnerships" at www.thenewpublicfinance.org.

17. See, for example, Cordes, Steuerle, and Twombly (2004); Rose-Ackerman (1986); and Weisbrod (1977, 1998).

18. While nonprofit organizations can generate a surplus, they cannot distribute it as profit to their contributors. Laws usually require that any surplus be reinvested. Therefore, the money contributed to a nonprofit organization cannot be an investment but only a donation.

19. There is an extensive literature on the comparative advantage of different actor groups, including Acemoglu, Kremer, and Mian (2003); Besley and Ghatak (2001); Brinkerhoff and Brinkerhoff (2002); Dixit (2000); Francois (2003); and Shleifer (1998). Such studies show that the institutional context in which agents operate, such as the market, for-profit firm, nonprofit firm, government bureau-

cracy, or civil society organization, presents agents with different incentive structures, and that each type of incentive structure encourages different patterns of economic behavior.

20. For more detail on the private finance initiative model, see Arthur Andersen and Enterprise LSE (2000); PricewaterhouseCoopers Corporate Finance (2002); and Spackman (2002).

21. One reason that public to private contracting out is relatively rare internationally is that most intergovernmental organizations depend on voluntary contributions for operational programs. Where international cooperation initiatives offer opportunities for public to private contracting out, two things may happen. Governments may prefer to divide up the tasks among themselves for decentralized, national implementation so that they can involve corporations of their choice in implementing them (the model of the International Space Station project). Or "social entrepreneurs" may move in, forming a global public-private partnership and attracting available funding. As a result, resources are diverted before they reach intergovernmental organizations.

22. Another interesting case is Intelsat Ltd. Originally an intergovernmental organization paid for by its member states, Intelsat was privatized in 2001. Similar to the Galileo project, member states decided to create a supervisory agency, the International Telecommunications Satellite Organization.

23. According to Frost, Reich, and Fujisaki (2002), such considerations motivated Merck & Co., Inc. to channel its donation of Ivermectin® to the Onchocerciasis Control Programme through the Task Force for Child Survival and Development, a U.S.-based nonprofit organization. Before approving country requests for the drug, the task force obtains advice from its expert advisory body, creating further distance between Merck and the project.

24. For an independent assessment of the impact of extractive industries on development in developing countries, see the *Extractive Industry Review* commissioned by the World Bank, at www.eireview.org.

25. Many of the more than 260 public-private partnerships announced at the World Summit on Sustainable Development in Johannesburg in 2002 were of a supply-driven nature. According to a recent progress report, only a few are fully funded, and less than 6 percent have secured any private sector resources (UN 2004). See also Andanova and Levy (2003).

26. For industry-led biotechnology partnerships that cover several countries and involve publicly funded researchers and institutes in developing countries, see Kameri-Mbote, Wafula, and Clarke (2001); Rausser, Simon, and Ameden (2000); and Spielman and von Grebmer (2004). Examples of health-related initiatives include the Action TB Programme, led by GlaxoSmithKline, and Secure the Future, led by the Bristol-Myers Squibb Company and Foundation.

27. See www.fao.org/ag/cgrfa.

28. Even organizations that were formerly purely intergovernmental, such as the International Telecommunication Union (ITU), are increasingly employing public-

private partnering. For example, the ITU's study groups are composed of experts from the public and private sectors working together to develop technical specifications and operating parameters for equipment and systems (www.itu.int/aboutitu/overview/o-s.html).

29. The Global Compact takes a learning approach to corporate change, rather than a regulatory bureaucratic one. In the words of Ruggie (2002, p. 32) this means: "Companies submit case studies of what they have done to translate their commitment to the...principles into concrete corporate practices. This occasions a dialogue among...UN, business, labour, and civil society organizations...to reach broader, consensus-based definitions of what constitutes good practices than any of the parties could achieve alone. Those definitions, together with illustrative case studies, are then publicized in an online information bank.... The hope and expectation is that good practices will help to drive out bad ones through the power of dialogue, transparency, advocacy, and competition."

30. For more detailed information, see http://info.med.yale.edu/eph/pdf/SCIENCE%20Editorial%20Final%209.16.03.pdf.

31. A similar point can be made about the norm and standard setting initiatives of type 3 global public-private partnerships, notably those pertaining to social, governance, and environmental issues (Florini 2000, 2003).

32. The importance of according more attention to noncommercial or tacit knowledge is just beginning to be realized. See, for example, the World Bank's Global Conference on Scaling Up Poverty Reduction in Shanghai (www.worldbank.org/wbi/reducingpoverty/Conference.html).

33. For a comprehensive discussion of health-related type 6 partnerships, see Buse and Waxman (2001); Sander and Widdus (2004); Wheeler and Berkley (2001); and Widdus (2001).

34. In some cases, smaller R&D companies may, in effect, require full payment for the services they render to a partnership. In such a case the partnership would shift from a type 6 to a type 1, a contracting-out initiative. Also, some partnerships may have a primary form, say, that of type 6. Yet for certain activities partnership managers may also employ other forms, notably a type 1 relation.

35. The Universal Flour Fortification initiative is organized along similar lines, but where the polio initiative is binary (it either accomplishes its goal of eradication or it does not), flour fortification is a more continuous, less targeted effort, which often receives less attention (see the chapter by Barrett in this volume).

36. For the current structure and functioning of the Global Environment Facility, see www.gefweb.org/participants/council/council.html.

37. For a more complete list of public-private partnership facilitators and promoters, see the "Global Public-Private Partnerships" page at www.thenewpublicfinance.org.

38. The 100 partnership profiles presented on the "Global Public-Private Partnerships" page at www.thenewpublicfinance.org list the names or types of partners involved for each initiative.

39. On the issue of the legitimacy of nonstate actors such as public-private part-nerships, see Bernstein and Cashore (2004). For a discussion on accountability and how the notion of accountability may have to change when it is applied to entities such as global public-private partnerships, see, for example, Benner, Reinicke, and Witte (2004) and Raynard and Cohen (2003).

40. See www.g8usa.gov/d_061004d.htm.

41. For further information, see www.startwithaseed.org/pages/trust.htm.

References

Acemoglu, Daron, Michael Kremer, and Atif Mian. 2003. *Incentives in Markets, Firms, and Governments*. NBER Working Paper 9802. Cambridge, Mass.: National Bureau of Economic Research.

Andanova, Liliana, and Marc Levy. 2003. "Franchising Global Governance: Making Sense of the Johannesburg Type II Partnerships." In Olav Stokke and Oystein Thommessn, eds., *Yearbook of International Co-operation on Environment and Development 2003/2004*. London: Earthscan.

Andersen, Søren Kaj, and Mikkel Mailand. 2002. *Multipartite Social Partnerships—A New Role for Employers and Trade Unions*. Copenhagen: Copenhagen Centre.

Andrews, Richard N. 1998. "Environmental Regulation and Business 'Self-Regulation.'" *Policy Sciences* 31 (3): 177–97.

Arthur Andersen and Enterprise LSE. 2000. *Value for Money Drivers in the Private Finance Initiative*. London: Treasury Taskforce.

Audretsch, David, Albert Link, and John Scott. 2002. "Public/Private Technology Partnerships: Evaluating SBIR-Supported Research." *Research Policy* 31 (1): 145–58.

Benner, Thorsten, Wolfgang H. Reinicke, and Jan Martin Witte. 2004. "Multisectoral Networks in Global Governance: Towards a Pluralistic System of Accountability." *Government and Opposition* 39 (2): 191–210.

Bergstrom, Theodore, Lawrence Blume, and Hal Varian. 1986. "On the Private Provision of Public Goods." *Journal of Public Economics* 29 (1): 25–59.

Bernstein, Steven, and Benjamin Cashore. 2004. "The Two-Level Logic of Non-State Global Governance." Yale University, New Haven, Conn. [www.yale.edu/environment/cashore].

Besley, Timothy, and Matreesh Ghatak. 2001. "Government versus Private Ownership of Public Goods." *Quarterly Journal of Economics* 116 (4): 1343–72.

Boerzel, Tanja A., and Thomas Risse-Kappen. Forthcoming. "Public-Private Partnerships: Effective and Legitimate Tools of Transnational Governance?" In Edgar Grande and Louis W. Pauly, eds., *Reconstituting Political Authority in the 21st Century*. Toronto: Toronto University Press.

Brinkerhoff, Jennifer M. 2002. *Partnership for International Development: Rhetoric or Results?* London: Lynne Rienner Publishers.

Brinkerhoff, Jennifer, and Derick Brinkerhoff. 2002. "Government-Nonprofit Relations in Comparative Perspective: Evolution, Themes, and New Directions." *Public Administration and Development* 22 (1): 3–18.

Broadwater, Ian, and Inge Kaul. 2005. "Global Public Private Partnerships: The Current Landscape." [www.thenewpublicfinance.org].

Buse, Kent. 2004. "Governing Public-Private Infectious Disease Partnerships." *Brown Journal of World Affairs* 10 (2): 225–42.

Buse, Kent, and Amalia Waxman. 2001. "Public-Private Health Partnerships: A Strategy for WHO." *Bulletin of the World Health Organization* 79 (8): 748–54.

Calder, Fanny. 2003. "Summary Report of Partnership Sessions." Paper prepared for the Global Compact Policy Dialogue, "Supply Chain Management and Partnerships," June 12–13, United Nations, New York.

Christian Aid. 2004. *Behind the Mask: The Real Face of Corporate Social Responsibility.* London.

Commission on the Private Sector and Development. 2004. *Unleashing Entrepreneurship: Making Business Work for the Poor.* Report to the Secretary-General of the United Nations. New York: United Nations Development Programme.

Cordes, Joseph J., C. Eugene Steuerle, and Eric Twombly. 2004. "Dimensions of Nonprofit Entrepreneurship: An Exploratory Essay." In Douglas Holtz-Eakin and Harvey S. Rosen, eds., *Public Policy and the Economics of Entrepreneurship.* Cambridge, Mass.: MIT Press.

Cornes, Richard, and Todd Sandler. 1996. *The Theory of Externalities, Public Goods, and Club Goods.* Cambridge: Cambridge University Press.

Cutler, Claire A., Virginia Haufler, and Tony Porter, eds. 1999. *Private Authority and International Affairs.* Albany, N.Y.: State University of New York Press.

Dixit, Avinash. 2000. "Incentives and Organization in the Public Sector: An Interpretive Review." *Journal of Human Resources* 37 (4): 696–727.

Dougherty, Keith. 2003. "Public Goods Theory: From Eighteenth Century Political Theory to Twentieth Century Economics." *Public Choice* 117: 239–53.

EC (European Commission). 2003. "Guidelines for Successful Public-Private Partnerships." Directorate-General Regional Policy, Brussels.

Ferris, James, and Michael Minstrom. 2002. "Foundations and Public Policymaking: A Conceptual Framework." Research Report 10. University of Southern California, Center on Philanthropy and Public Policy, Los Angeles.

Florini, Ann. 2000. *The Third Force: The Rise of Transnational Civil Society.* Washington, D.C.: Carnegie Endowment for International Peace.

———. 2003. *The Coming Democracy: New Rules for Running a New World.* Washington, D.C.: Island Press.

Francois, Patrick. 2003. "Not-for-Profit Provision of Public Services." *Economic Journal* 113 (486): C53–C61.

Frost, Laura, Michael R. Reich, and Tomoko Fujisaki. 2002. "A Partnership for Ivermectin: Social Worlds and Boundary Objects." In Michael R. Reich, ed., *Public-Private Partnerships for Public Health*. Cambridge, Mass.: Harvard University Press [www.hsph.harvard.edu/hcpds/partnerbook/chap5.PDF].

Furubotn, Eirik G., and Rudolf Richter. 2000. *Institutions and Economic Theory: The Contribution of the New Institutional Economics*. Ann Arbor, Mich.: University of Michigan Press.

Gabriel, Omoh. 2004. "PPP, New Vehicle for Infrastructural Provision (1)." [http://allafrica.com/stories/printable/200406180136.html].

Gibson, Tom. 1999. *Equity Investment for Small and Medium Enterprises in the Newly Independent States*. Washington, D.C.: Eurasia Foundation.

GlobeScan Inc. [formerly Environics International]. 2002. *Corporate Social Responsibility Monitor 2002*. Executive Brief. London.

Gunningham, Niel, and Darren Sinclair. 2002. *Environmental Partnerships: Combining Sustainability and Commercial Advantage in the Agricultural Sector*. Canberra: Rural Industries Research Development Corporation.

Hansmann, Henry. 1980. "The Role of the Nonprofit Enterprise." *Yale Law Journal* 89: 835–901.

———. 1987. "Economic Theories of the Nonprofit Sector." In Walter Powell, ed., *The Nonprofit Sector*. New Haven, Conn.: Yale University Press.

Harris, Clive. 2003. "Private Participation in Infrastructure in Developing Countries: Trends, Impacts, and Policy Lessons." Working Paper 5. World Bank, Washington, D.C.

Hart, Oliver. 1995. *Firms, Contracts, and Financial Structure*. Oxford: Clarendon Press.

Hart, Oliver, Andrei Shleifer, and Robert Vishny. 1997. "The Proper Scope of Government: Theory and Application to Prisons." *Quarterly Journal of Economics* 112 (4): 1127–61.

Hirschman, Albert. 1970. *Exit, Voice, and Loyalty: Responses to Decline in Firms, Organizations, and States*. Cambridge, Mass.: Harvard University Press.

Hopkins, Michael. 2002. *The Planetary Bargain: Corporate Social Responsibility Matters*. London: Earthscan.

IFC (International Finance Corporation). 2003. *Annual Report: Innovation, Impact, Sustainability: IFC's Commitment*. Washington, D.C.

Kameri-Mbote, Patricia, David Wafula, and Norman Clarke. 2001. "Public/Private Partnerships for Biotechnology in Africa: The Future Agenda." Working Paper. African Centre for Technology Studies, Nairobi.

Kaul, Inge, and Katell Le Goulven. 2003. "Institutional Options for Producing Global Public Goods." In Inge Kaul, Pedro Conceição, Katell Le Goulven, and Ronald

U. Mendoza, eds., *Providing Global Public Goods: Managing Globalization.* New York: Oxford University Press.

Kelly, Gavin. 2000. "Providing Public Services: How Great a Role for PPPs?" *New Economy* 7 (3): 132–37.

Kettler, Hannah, Karen White, and Scott Jordan. 2003. *Valuing Industry Contributions to Public-Private Partnerships for Health Product Development.* Geneva: Initiative on Public-Private Partnerships for Health.

Khanna, Madhu. 2001. "Non-Mandatory Approaches to Environmental Protection." *Journal of Economic Surveys* 15 (3): 291–324.

Lecocq, Frank. 2003. "Pioneering Transactions, Catalyzing Markets, and Building Capacity: The Prototype Carbon Fund Contributions to Climate Policies." *American Journal of Agricultural Economy* 85 (3): 703–7.

Levin, Jonathan D., and Steven Tadelis. 2004. "Profit Sharing and the Role of Professional Partnerships." Stanford University, Department of Economics, Stanford, Calif.

Liebenthal, Andres, Osvaldo N. Feinstein, and Gregory K. Ingram, eds. 2004. *Evaluation and Development: The Partnership Dimension.* London: Transaction Publishers.

Linder, Stephen. 1999. "Coming to Terms with the Public-Private Partnership: A Grammar of Multiple Meanings." *American Behavioral Scientist* 43 (1): 35–51.

Link, Albert N., and John T. Scott. 2001. "Public/Private Partnerships: Stimulating Competition in a Dynamic Market." *International Journal of Industrial Organization* 19 (5): 763–94.

Malena, Carmen. 2004. "Strategic Partnership: Challenges and Best Practices in the Management and Governance of Multi-Stakeholder Partnerships Involving UN and Civil Society Actors." Presented at the Multi-Stakeholder Workshop on Partnerships and UN-Civil Society Relations, February 10–12, New York.

Mattock, Nina. 2002. "New Ventures for Malaria: A Suitable Venture for Public-Private Partnership." Sustainable Development International Issue 7. [www.sustdev.org].

McKinsey & Co. 2004. "Assessing the Global Compact's Impact." Commissioned Report. [www.unglobalcompact.org].

McQuaid, Ronald W. 2000. "The Theory of Partnerships: Why Have Partnerships?" In Stephen P. Osborne, ed., *Public-Private Partnerships: Theory and Practice in International Perspective.* London: Routledge.

MIGA (Multilateral Investment Guarantee Agency). 2003. *Annual Report 2003.* Washington, D.C.

Murphy, David, and Jemm Bendell. 1997. *In the Company of Partners: Business, Environmental Groups, and Sustainable Development Post-Rio.* Bristol, UK: The Policy Press.

NCPPP (National Council for Public-Private Partnerships). 2002. "For the Good of the People: Using Public-Private Partnerships to Meet America's Essential Needs." [www.ncppp.org/presskit/ncpppwhitepaper.pdf].

Nelson, Jane. 2002. *Building Partnerships: Cooperation between the United Nations System and the Private Sector.* New York: United Nations Department of Public Information.

North, Douglass. 2004. "Partnership as a Means to Improve Economic Performance." In Andres Liebenthal, Osvaldo Feinstein, and Gregory Ingram, eds., *Evaluation and Development: The Partnership Dimension.* London: Transaction Publishers.

Olson, Mancur. 1965. *The Logic of Collective Action: Public Goods and the Theory of Groups.* Cambridge, Mass.: Harvard University Press.

Osborne, Steven, ed. 2000. *Public-Private Partnerships: Theory and Practice in International Perspective.* London: Routledge.

Ostrom, Elinor. 1990. *Governing the Commons: The Evolution of Institutions for Collective Action.* Cambridge: Cambridge University Press.

PCF (Prototype Carbon Fund). 2003. *Annual Report.* Washington, D.C. [http://carbonfinance.org].

PricewaterhouseCoopers Corporate Finance. 2002. "Financing and Risk Issues Associated with Not for Profit Models Applied to the UK Public Private Partnerships." Discussion paper prepared for the Institute for Public Policy Research. [www.ippr.org.uk/].

Rausser, Gordon, Leo Simon, and Holly Ameden. 2000. "Public-Private Alliances in Biotechnology: Can They Narrow the Knowledge Gaps between Rich and Poor?" *Food Policy* 25 (4): 499–513.

Raynard, Peter, and Jonathan Cohen. 2003. "Dimensions of Partnership Accountability." *AccountAbility Quarterly* 20:49.

Ridley, Robert C. 2000. "A New Public/Private Approach to Develop Affordable Medicines: Medicines for Malaria Venture." *Bulletin Medicus Mundi* 78. [www.medicusmundi.ch/bulletin/bulletin7809.htm].

Rose-Ackerman, Susan, ed. 1986. *The Economics of Nonprofit Institutions: Studies in Structure and Policy.* New York: Oxford University Press.

Rosenau, Pauline Vaillancourt, ed. 2000. *Public-Private Policy Partnerships.* Cambridge, Mass.: MIT Press.

Ruggie, John Gerard. 2002. "The Theory and Practice of Learning Networks: Corporate Social Responsibility and the Global Compact." *Journal of Corporate Citizenship* 5 (spring): 27–36.

Sachs, Jeffrey. 2003. "The Global Innovation Divide." In Adam B. Jaffe, Josh Lerner, and Scott Stern, eds., *Innovation Policy and the Economy.* Vol. 3. Cambridge, Mass.: MIT Press.

Sander, Alison, and Roy Widdus. 2004. "The Emerging Landscape of Public-Private Partnerships for Product Development." Presented at the Initiative on

Public-Private Partnerships for Health (IPPPH) conference "Combating Diseases Associated with Poverty: Financing Strategies for Product Development and the Potential Role of Public-Private Partnerships," April 15–16, London.

Sandler, Todd, and John Tschirhart. 1997. "Club Theory: Thirty Years Later." *Public Choice* 93 (3–4): 335–55.

Schervish, Paul G. 2000. "The Modern Medici: Patterns, Motivations, and Giving Strategies of the Wealthy." Research Report 5. The Center on Philanthropy and Public Policy, Los Angeles, Calif.

Shleifer, Andrei. 1998. "State versus Private Ownership." *Journal of Economic Perspectives* 12 (4): 133–50.

Social Watch. 2003. *Social Watch Annual Report 2003.* Montevideo: The Third World Institute-Social Watch.

Spackman, Michael. 2002. "Public-Private Partnerships: Lessons from the British Approach." *Economic Systems* 26 (3): 283–301.

Spielman, David, and Klaus von Grebmer. 2004. "Public-Private Partnerships in Agricultural Research: An Analysis of Challenges Facing Industry and the Consultative Group on International Agricultural Research." EPTD Discussion Paper 113. International Food Policy Research Institute, Environment and Production Technology Division, Washington, D.C.

Stiglitz, Joseph, and Scott Wallsten. 2000. "Public-Private Technology Partnerships: Promises and Pitfalls." In Pauline Vaillancourt Rosenau, ed., *Public-Private Policy Partnerships.* Cambridge, Mass.: MIT Press.

Tessner, Sandrine, and Georg Kell. 2000. *United Nations and Business: A Partnership Recovered.* New York: St. Martin's Press.

UN (United Nations). 2003. *The Global Compact: Report on Progress and Activities: July 2002–July 2003.* New York.

———. 2004. "Partnerships for Sustainable Development. Report of the Secretary-General to the Economic and Social Council." Document E/CN.17/2004/16. New York.

UN Foundation and WEF (World Economic Forum). 2003. "Public-Private Partnerships: Meeting in the Middle." [www.weforum.org/pdf/Initiatives/GHI_2003_Meeting_in_the_middle.pdf].

UNRISD (United Nations Research Institute for Social Development). 2004. "Corporate Social Responsibility and Development: Towards a New Agenda?" Report of the UNRISD Conference, November 17–18, 2003, Geneva.

Utting, Peter. 2000. "UN Business Partnerships: Whose Agenda Counts?" United Nations Research Institute for Social Development, Geneva.

Weisbrod, Burton A. 1977. *The Voluntary Nonprofit Sector: An Economic Analysis.* Lexington, Mass.: Lexington Books.

Wheeler, Craig, and Seth Berkley. 2001. "Initial Lessons from Public-Private Partnerships in Drug and Vaccine Development." *Bulletin of the World Health Organization* 79 (8): 728–34.

Widdus, Roy. 2001. "Public-Private Partnerships for Health: Their Main Targets, Their Diversity, and Their Future Directions." *Bulletin of the World Health Organization* 79 (8): 713–20.

Williamson, Oliver E. 1985. *The Economic Institutions of Capitalism.* New York: Free Press.

Winpenny, James. 2003. "Financing Water for All: Report of the World Panel on Financing Water Infrastructure." World Water Council, Third Water Forum, and Global Water Partnership, Marseille, France. [www.worldwatercouncil.org/download/CamdessusReport.pdf].

Witte, Jan Martin, Thorsten Benner, and Charlotte Streck. 2003. *Progress or Peril? Partnerships and Networks in Global Environmental Governance: The Post-Johannesburg Agenda.* Washington, D.C.: Global Public Policy Institute.

World Bank. 2003. "Agreement Establishing the African Trade Insurance Agency." In Rudolf V. Van Puymbroeck, ed., *World Bank Legal Review: Law and Justice for Development.* The Hague, Netherlands: Kluwer Law International.

Zadek, Simon. 2004. "Civil Partnerships, Governance, and the UN." Paper prepared for the Secretary-General's Panel of Eminent Persons on Civil Society and UN Relationships. New York.

Accommodating New Actors and New Purposes in International Cooperation

The Growing Diversification of Financing Mechanisms

Pedro Conceição

Since the mid-1990s the number and type of international financing mechanisms have multiplied rapidly. Of some 60 international financing mechanisms in operation today, more than half were created in the last decade. Once equated with funds and programs of intergovernmental entities like the United Nations or the World Bank, the term *international financing mechanism* now has a much broader compass. True, in value terms these agencies still account for most international cooperation financing. But in number of institutions involved in mobilizing and channeling finance for international cooperation, the picture changes. A growing number of issue-specific mechanisms are taking their place alongside the traditional multipurpose intergovernmental financing mechanisms. Some two-thirds of these newer financing mechanisms are not pure intergovernmental entities. Many are nonprofit organizations, and many involve global public-private partnerships.

This chapter's overview of the growth in international financing mechanisms and their increasing diversity suggests that the proliferation is due to the broadened international policy agenda, which now includes concerns related to the provision of global public goods as well as development assistance. It is also due to the involvement of many new actors in the public policy arena, with business and civil society organizations, including private philanthropic foundations, joining governments and intergovernmental entities.

The analysis draws on a detailed inventory of financing mechanisms and tools for international cooperation, prepared as part of the background analysis for this

Sylvain Merlen's contribution to the research underlying this chapter is deeply appreciated.

volume. To be included, financing mechanisms had to meet three criteria: their primary purpose is to help finance a global public policy goal, the resources are typically collected from a variety of private and public donors, and the resources are channeled to recipients (state and nonstate actors) in line with established operating procedures.[1]

THE EVOLUTION OF INTERNATIONAL FINANCING MECHANISMS

Up to the mid-1990s intergovernmental entities dominated the institutional context, notably the United Nations system and the Bretton Woods institutions. Since the mid-1990s, however, the institutional landscape has clearly been changing. Intergovernmental entities remain important, and they have even grown more rapidly over the last decade than before (table 1). But the overall picture is now much more diversified. An increasing number of international financing mechanisms are nonprofit organizations (such as the International AIDS Vaccine Initiative),[2] investment funds (such as the Prototype Carbon Fund),[3] and other self-standing organizational arrangements (such as the African Programme for the Control of Onchocerciasis) that are not separate legal entities but have their own statutes, governance structures, and operating procedures, including their own fund raising and disbursement modalities. Sometimes, these alliances involve several international financing mechanisms and additional funders, including bilateral donors and philanthropic foundations.[4]

Philanthropic foundations have much in common with the entities listed in table 1. Both old-line foundations such as the Rockefeller Foundation (established in 1913) and the Ford Foundation (1936) and the younger generation of foundations such as the Turner Foundation (1990) and the Bill & Melinda Gates Foundation (2000) are also increasingly involved in international cooperation. However, foundations differ from the financing mechanisms presented in table 1 in that they typically have a single donor who endows the foundation by leaving a bequest or transferring assets over time.[5] In a way, foundations are financing mechanisms without a resource mobilization arm (figure 1).

Another important type of financing mechanism that shares some features with the financing mechanisms listed in table 1 is the for-profit private investment fund that mobilizes money from various sources (predominantly private) and channels it to ventures that not only generate private returns but also contribute to global public policy purposes. These double bottom-line ventures include funds that invest in renewable energy schemes or in commercial pollution-reduction initiatives. The investments create social returns, but there are usually also private gains that the investors appropriate. Through the investment fund the flow of resources goes from the funding sources (the investors) to the recipients, from the recipients back to the investment fund, and finally back to the investors in the form of financial returns on the investments (see figure 1).

TABLE 1

Selected financing mechanisms supporting international cooperation, 1930–present

Intergovernmental entities	Date established	Other mechanisms[a]
Bank for International Settlements	1930	
International Monetary Fund	1945	
International Bank for Reconstruction and Development/World Bank	1945	
United Nations Children's Fund	1946	
Office of the United Nations High Commissioner for Refugees	1950	
International Organization for Migration	1951	
International Finance Corporation/World Bank	1956	
European Development Fund	1957	
International Development Association/ World Bank	1960	
	1961	World Wildlife Fund
United Nations Capital Development Fund	1966	
United Nations Development Programme	1966	
United Nations Population Fund	1969	
	1971	Consultative Group on International Agricultural Research
World Heritage Fund/United Nations Educational, Scientific and Cultural Organization	1972	
	1972	International Foundation for Science
Special Programme for Research and Training in Tropical Diseases	1975	
United Nations Development Fund for Women	1976	
Organization of the Petroleum Exporting Countries Fund for International Development	1976	
International Fund for Agricultural Development	1977	
International Oil Pollution Compensation Funds	1978	

TABLE 1 CONTINUED

Selected financing mechanisms supporting international cooperation, 1930–present

Intergovernmental entities	Date established	Other mechanisms[a]
Multilateral Investment Guarantee Agency/ World Bank	1988	
Common Fund for Commodities	1989	
Multilateral Fund for the Implementation of the Montreal Protocol	1991	
Global Environment Facility	1991	
International Seabed Authority	1994	
	1996	African Programme for the Control of Onchocerciasis
	1996	International AIDS Vaccine Initiative
	1997	Aeras Global TB Vaccine Foundation
	1999	e7 Fund For Sustainable Energy Development
Basel Convention Emergency Trust Fund	1999	
Universal Postal Union Quality of Service Fund	1999	
	1999	Vaccine Fund
	1999	Malaria Vaccine Initiative
	1999	Medicines for Malaria Venture
	1999	Global Development Network
	1999	Prototype Carbon Fund
	2000	Alliance For Health Policy and System Research
	2000	Critical Ecosystem Partnership Fund
	2000	Global Alliance for TB Drug Development
	2000	Institute for OneWorld Health
Least Developed Countries Fund	2001	
Special Climate Change Fund	2001	
Kyoto Adaptation Fund	2001	
European and Developing Countries Clinical Trials Partnership	2001	

TABLE 1 CONTINUED

Selected financing mechanisms supporting international cooperation, 1930–present

Intergovernmental entities	Date established	Other mechanisms[a]
Nuclear Security Fund/International Atomic Energy Agency	2002	
World Solidarity Fund	2002	
	2002	Global Fund to Fight AIDS, Tuberculosis, and Malaria
	2002	International Partnership for Microbicides
International Financial Facility for Aviation Safety	2003	BioCarbon Fund
	2003	Community Development Carbon Fund
	2003	Drugs for Neglected Diseases Initiative
	2003	Foundation for Innovative New Diagnostics
	2003	Global Alliance for Improved Nutrition
Codex Trust Fund	2003	
	2004	Grand Challenges in Global Health
	2004	Digital Solidarity Fund
Global Crop Diversity Trust	2004	
India-Brazil-South Africa Facility for Hunger and Poverty Alleviation	2004	
	Proposed	International Finance Facility
International Treaty on Plant Genetic Resources for Food and Agriculture Specially Designated Fund	Proposed	
	Proposed	Global Lottery Fund
	Proposed	Global Vaccine Enterprise
	Proposed	Patient Capital Initiative

Note: For a description of the financing mechanisms listed here, see www.thenewpublicfinance.org.
a. This category includes primarily nonprofit organizations.

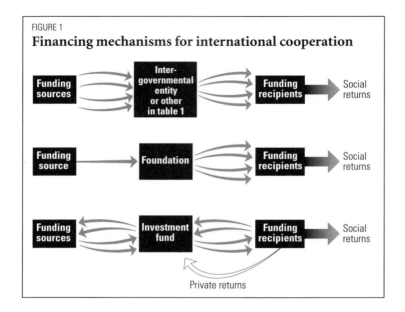

FIGURE 1

Financing mechanisms for international cooperation

While the financing mechanisms listed in table 1 have expanded significantly, the number of philanthropic foundations that finance international cooperation has expanded even faster, followed by the double bottom-line investment funds. There are now more than 500 philanthropic foundations involved in international cooperation and about 75 investments funds with an international cooperation purpose.[6] Yet it remains difficult to identify these entities and establish their exact number. They often have to be found and tracked individually, and many of them come and go, entering into and out of financing international cooperation.

If all of those mechanisms are taken into account, the institutional landscape becomes even more dynamic and complex. First consider only the financing mechanisms included in table 1. They grew steadily until 1994, when the number of new mechanisms began to proliferate—almost seven times as many new mechanisms were created between 1995 and 2004 (34) as in each of the preceding seven decades (figure 2). Now consider the growth in the number of financing mechanisms when foundations and investments funds are included and place this side by side with the growth in the financing mechanisms included in table 1 (figure 3). This institutional landscape is considerably more complex than is suggested by table 1 alone. Clearly, the financing of international cooperation occurs through an increasingly diverse and varied range of mechanisms.

Adding foundations and investment funds to the mix does not substantially change the evolutionary trend. Once again, growth accelerates rapidly only after 1995. What happened after the mid-1990s that led to this proliferation and diversity of financing mechanisms?

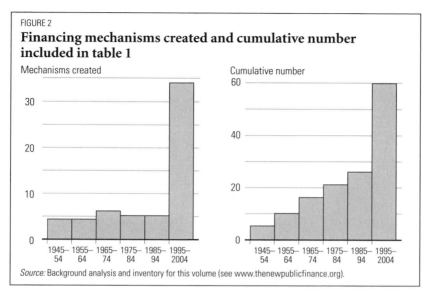

FIGURE 2

Financing mechanisms created and cumulative number included in table 1

Source: Background analysis and inventory for this volume (see www.thenewpublicfinance.org).

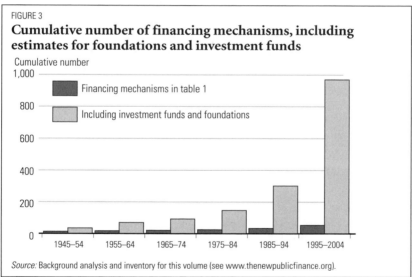

FIGURE 3

Cumulative number of financing mechanisms, including estimates for foundations and investment funds

Source: Background analysis and inventory for this volume (see www.thenewpublicfinance.org).

THE DRIVING FORCES BEHIND THE GROWING INSTITUTIONAL
DIFFERENTIATION: NEW CONCERNS AND NEW ACTORS

Among contributing factors two seem to have been particularly important in driving the emergence of the diversified and complex institutional landscape that exists today. One is the new concern on the international cooperation agenda with global public goods provision. Another is the involvement in international cooperation of new actors, especially private actors. These drivers often work in mutually reinforcing ways, as new concerns attract or require the involvement of new actors and as new actors are able to engage in international cooperation only through new (other than intergovernmental) institutional arrangements.

New concerns

As measured by volume of financing, aid (including humanitarian assistance) still accounts for most financing for international cooperation—and most of the non-bilateral aid is still implemented through intergovernmental entities. However, most financing mechanisms created since the 1970s have focused on global public goods provision. Consider, for example, on the intergovernmental side of table 1, the World Heritage Fund, International Oil Pollution Compensation Fund, Global Environment Facility, Universal Postal Union Quality of Service Fund, or Nuclear Security Fund of the International Atomic Energy Agency. Even older funds such as that of the Office of the United Nations High Commissioner for Refugees, established in 1950, and the United Nations Population Fund, established in 1969, have brought a global public goods focus to the financing of international cooperation. The Office of the United Nations High Commissioner for Refugees provides resources to help the international community deal with the aftermath of natural disasters and conflicts, while the United Nations Population Fund addresses issues related to global demographic transitions.

Still, it has been largely through the financing mechanisms established in the 1990s, notably those on the right side of table 1 dealing with global health and environmental issues, that the focus on the provision of global public goods has become more pronounced. Some of the global public goods being financed are of special importance to poor countries and poor people. Why then the creation of these special funds? Why not deliver support through country-focused established aid channels? One reason is the very nature of public goods. Since they are public in consumption, one person's or one country's consumption of, say, a pharmaceutical technology does not diminish its availability to others. Thus it makes economic sense for donors and recipient countries to organize a special joint initiative for producing a good that several developing countries desire. This allows aid efforts to exploit economies of scale and thus enhances aid efficiency. Several issue-specific financing arrangements fall in this category (for example, the Medicines for Malaria Venture or the Malaria Vaccine Initiative).

Another reason is that the global public goods–focused or issue-specific mechanisms often address urgent issues such as control of HIV/AIDS. This brings into play an important difference between financing mechanisms on the left and right sides of table 1. The issue-specific financing mechanisms on the intergovernmental side of table 1 differ from those of other financing mechanisms (the right side) in their focus on such steady, continuous services as the provision of compensatory financing by the International Oil Pollution Compensation Fund and the payment of incremental costs by the Global Environment Facility. Many of the other financing mechanisms seek to produce a particular product for which the requisite expertise and equipment may reside in the private sector. And that leads directly to the second driver behind the growing number and diversity of financing mechanisms, the new actors involved in international cooperation.

New actors

Along with governments, business and civil society actors are increasingly participating as financiers in international cooperation efforts (figure 4). There has been a steady decrease in the share of new financing mechanisms financed exclusively by public resources, with the greatest decline during 1995–2004. During that decade only half the newly created financing mechanisms drew their money exclusively from public funding sources. The rest were funded through private sources or through mixed public and private sources. Public resources had financed about 75 percent of all new mechanisms that emerged in the preceding three decades, and about 80 percent in both 1945–54 and 1955–64.

So who are these new actors who are funding international cooperation in place of public resources? Foundations, for one. In health the Bill & Melinda Gates Foundation has played a large role in launching and supporting a number of initiatives, from the Vaccine Fund to the Grand Challenges in Global Health. Social entrepreneurs have also been important, frequently taking the lead in establishing and managing new mechanisms and convincing donors that they know how to spot high-return investments. Finally, business firms have also come on board as funders, as with the e7 Fund for Sustainable Energy Development.

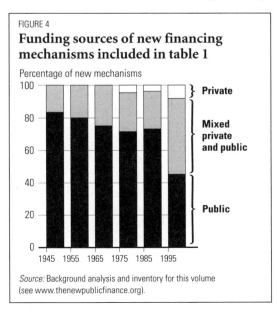

FIGURE 4

Funding sources of new financing mechanisms included in table 1

Percentage of new mechanisms

Source: Background analysis and inventory for this volume (see www.thenewpublicfinance.org).

But the new actors provide more than money. Often their unique expertise and skills are essential. For example, business firms are key actors in several stages of pharmaceutical research and product development. To attract them, financing mechanisms may go beyond providing funds and use new tools to pay them in kind. For example, the Medicines for Malaria Venture provides not only financial support for private research and product development, but also grants firms certain patent rights on the intellectual property developed with the support of the financing mechanism (see the chapter by Kaul on global public-private partnerships in this volume). Businesses often also contribute as copromoters and implementers of public-private partnerships.

This illustrates two important features of the new financing mechanisms that have engaged new actors over the last decade. First, the new actors, particularly private ones, are attracted to international cooperation in part because there are market opportunities to be exploited—in the Medicines for Malaria Venture the possible sharing of new intellectual property may be as much an incentive as the grants provided by the funding mechanism. Second, more sophisticated financing tools are now available that allow public and private contributors to join forces. New and proposed financing mechanisms often experiment with new tools (see the chapter by Conceição, Rajan, and Shah in this volume). Among recent proposals for new mechanisms that are under active consideration are entities that would use tools such as debt issuance through asset-backed securitization types of structures (the International Finance Facility) and royalty payments (the International Treaty on Plant Genetic Resources for Food and Agriculture Specially Designated Fund).

CONCLUSION

This overview of the institutional landscape of financing mechanisms for international cooperation has identified several characteristics of that landscape:

- Since the mid-1990s there has been unprecedented growth in the number of new financing mechanisms to support international cooperation.
- Since 1995 the new mechanisms have adopted a variety of organizational forms beyond the more traditional intergovernmental arrangements, although the rate of growth in intergovernmental entities has been greater than ever.
- Many of these new financing mechanisms address global public goods issues, including some that finance pro-poor global public goods, such as new pharmaceutical technologies for malaria vaccines.
- There has been a shift from public to private and mixed public-private funding sources, in part reflecting the appearance of new actors, including private charitable foundations, social entrepreneurs, and businesses.

- Financing mechanisms have developed a growing diversity of tools to mobilize and disburse resources.

As table 1 shows, institutional innovation continues: just consider the number of active proposals for the creation of new financing mechanisms that are listed there. The diversification of financing mechanisms to support international cooperation, therefore, is a trend that is likely to continue.

NOTES

1. The study methodology is described in detail in the full inventory report available at www.thenewpublicfinance.org. The inventory includes international financing mechanisms (but not national or regional ones) created over the past eight decades and still in existence. (Excluded are mechanisms that collapsed for lack of effectiveness or political and financial support; that were merged into other organizations, such as the United Nations Expanded Programme of Technical Assistance and the United Nations Special Fund, which fused to form the United Nations Development Programme; or that successfully completed their task, such as the Onchocerciasis Control Programme.) While this approach may give undue weight to more recent mechanisms, the number of financing mechanisms that have ceased to exist appears to be relatively small. Nevertheless, the change in the overall institutional landscape is so profound that the conclusions are likely to hold, even accounting for some possible distortion in the data for a bias toward more recent mechanisms.

2. Nonprofit international financing organizations are defined as organizations that mobilize and channel resources for public policy purposes and that use any net earnings for the purposes for which they were established and not for the benefit of any private shareholder or individual.

3. An investment fund is a for-profit arrangement that allows return flows to investors. In the case of the Prototype Carbon Fund, the investment aspect is paired with the fund's objective of testing carbon-credit trading and learning by doing. Thus the fund seeks to generate both private and social returns.

4. Such alliances and partnerships are distinguished from the trust funds that intergovernmental entities have established in growing numbers to channel resources to particular issues, often on the request of their donors. These trust funds are usually an integral part of the entities' funding operations, without their own governance, resource mobilization, and operational procedures. Similarly, intergovernmental entities have established some other types of organizational arrangements for resource allocation or disbursement purposes—such as the International Monetary Fund's Compensatory Financing Facility or Extended Fund Facility. These are also considered internal to the organization and are not covered here.

5. While a large number of nonprofit organizations use charitable and philanthropic giving for international cooperation purposes (including a wide range of development-oriented nongovernmental organizations), they typically do not work as funding mechanisms that channel resources but instead consume these resources

internally or in the acquisition of goods and services (for a general review of the theory and international data on philanthropy see Andreoni 2004; for a study focused on international cooperation aspects see Micklewright and Wright 2003). Thus, they are excluded from the inventory.

6. These estimates are based on Foundation Center (2004a,b) and OECD (2003).

REFERENCES

Andreoni, James. 2004. "Philanthropy." Working Paper. University of Wisconsin, Madison. [www.ssc.wisc.edu/~andreoni/WorkingPapers/Philanthropy.pdf].

Foundation Center. 2004a. *International Grantmaking III: An Update on U.S. Foundation Trends.* New York.

———. 2004b. *Foundation Growth and Giving Estimates.* New York.

Micklewright, John, and Anna Wright. 2003. "Private Donations for International Development." WIDER Discussion Paper 2003/82. United Nations University, World Institute for Development Economics Research, Helsinki.

OECD (Organisation for Economic Co-operation and Development). 2003. "Philanthropic Foundations and Development Cooperation." *DAC Journal* 4 (3): 74–149.

MAKING THE RIGHT MONEY AVAILABLE AT THE RIGHT TIME FOR INTERNATIONAL COOPERATION

NEW FINANCING TECHNOLOGIES

PEDRO CONCEIÇÃO, HARI RAJAN, AND RAJIV SHAH

Resource shortages are a pervasive concern in international cooperation debates and a frequently cited reason for failing to follow up on international resolutions. These concerns are puzzling in light of world gross domestic product (GDP) of more than $40.7 trillion[1] and a tripling of world income per capita over the last five decades. Why should it be so difficult to mobilize the estimated additional $100 billion[2] or so needed annually for foreign aid and global public goods, especially considering that delay often makes matters worse—and more costly to remedy?

As the analysis in this chapter suggests, a basic problem may be an over-reliance on the conventional approach to financing international cooperation: channeling public revenue directly from one group of (contributing) governments to another group of (receiving) governments. A related problem is that such transfers are often seen as a spot transaction to settle an outstanding bill in full. However, international cooperation initiatives such as meeting the Millennium Development Goals require levels of resources that potential donors may find difficult to accommodate in their immediate annual budgets. As a result, some worthwhile investments are not made or are made in a piecemeal fashion that falls short of achieving the desired outcome.

Drawing on the experiences of governments that have tried to resolve resource constraints nationally, the chapter extracts three main lessons. One is to make greater use of modern financing technology, such as securitization and project finance, and to tap financial markets, so that funding is available in the right amount at the right time. A second lesson is to create special-purpose facilities—government-related but independent entities with a for-profit or nonprofit legal status—to mobilize private financing rather than have governments handle directly these new financial tools themselves. The third lesson is that financing arrangements are often made on an issue-specific basis rather than for general and nonearmarked budgetary allocations, with governments reassigning responsibility for financing and implementation to private actors.

These special-purpose facilities are beginning to find application in the international cooperation domain, where they are a natural fit. Since donor-recipient transactions almost always involve the sovereign or semisovereign obligations or commitments of wealthy industrial countries, these transactions can access financial markets that are among the deepest and most liquid in the global financial system. The benefits of these financial and institutional innovations in enhanced global efficiency, economic growth, and human development are great and clear to many. But there are a number of technical feasibility and transparency and accountability issues that need to be resolved before the potential gains can be realized.

PERCEPTIONS OF A RESOURCE SHORTAGE FOR INTERNATIONAL COOPERATION PURPOSES

Perceptions of a lack of financial resources for even the most urgent and worthwhile international cooperation purposes are pervasive. Current resource levels are seen as falling short of long-agreed funding targets and identified resource needs. Governments, facing demands for fiscal discipline coupled with looming resource requirements for such domestic concerns as pension programs (see the chapter by Heller in this volume), find it difficult to raise expenditures to the levels required to achieve funding targets for international cooperation.

The real questions though are: Why this strong focus on what government budgets can accommodate for international cooperation? Why are the financing and implementation of international cooperation projects still seen as a task to be undertaken directly by governments or intergovernmental agencies?

Commonly cited reasons for perceptions of resource shortages

Several reasons are often cited for the inadequate availability of resources for international cooperation.

Available resources fall short of commitments. It is rare for any international conference to pass without at least one delegation deploring the continuing failure of donor countries to meet the long-standing target of allocating 0.7 percent of their gross national income (GNI) to official development assistance. At the 2002 International Conference on Financing for Development in Monterrey, Mexico, the industrial countries recommitted themselves to taking steps to meet the 0.7 percent target (UN 2002, 2004). So far only 5 of 22 donor countries have met this goal (although others have announced a timetable for moving toward it), with the result that aid allocations represent only 0.25 percent of their combined GNI (OECD 2005).[3]

International cooperation needs exceed available resources. Perceptions of shortages also arise from the large gap between identified needs and currently available resources. Recent estimates indicate that an additional $70 billion a year would be required by 2006 and as much as $130 billion a year by 2015 to meet the Millennium Development Goals (UN General Assembly 2000; UN Millennium Project 2005). And there are many other urgent needs, such as rebuilding war-ravaged or disaster-stricken societies or controlling drug trafficking and other global public bads.

Resource allocation is often out of sync with resource requirements. The timing of resource allocations also contributes to the perception of lack of resources. Heavy up-front investments are often required to ensure aid effectiveness (Sachs and others 2004; UK Her Majesty's Treasury and DFID 2003). Effective water systems, for example, cannot be built by dribbling small amounts of money toward their construction over many years (Winpenny 2003). And some investments, like those in education, health, and water, are best made concurrently, to benefit from synergies and to maximize results. However, current resource allocation processes often do not permit such expenditure spikes.

Resource flows are haphazard and unpredictable. Volatile aid flows also add to perceptions of resource inadequacy. Low-income developing countries most frequently experience volatile aid flows (Bulíř and Hamann 2003; Arellano and others 2005), with especially severe effects (Pallage and Robe 2003).

Formal and informal ceilings on government spending. Industrial and developing countries alike are expected (by credit rating agencies and other monitors of good public policy) to strictly observe monetary and fiscal discipline (Bryant 2004; Setty and Dodd 2003). This often means that public expenditures are capped, while demand for funding continues to expand, from the looming pension crisis to natural disaster relief, security-related demands (see the chapter by Sandler in this volume), and other policy aims.

The deeper cause: the conventional notion of financing for international cooperation

While plausible, all these explanations pale next to the world's enormous wealth. In 2003 global GDP totaled $40.7 trillion, international bank lending and bond issuance reached $3.4 trillion (World Bank 2004, p. 161), and international financial markets reached 3–10 times the size of global GDP.[4] So why does this perception of inadequate resources coexist with this abundance of resources? The answer may lie in current approaches to the financing of international cooperation.

Many people in industrial and developing countries alike view global challenges of all sorts as involving issues that are removed from people's daily life.

Foreign aid is considered a second-order priority, a charity to which people contribute when their resources permit or when the demands come from highly visible human tragedies. Global public goods are considered remote until the ill-effects of underprovision cause a local crisis—a disease outbreak, a terrorist attack, devastation from a tsunami. However, in an open and globalized world these challenges are neither remote nor a matter of charity alone. The underprovision of global public goods has clear and direct consequences locally and is highly inefficient globally (Kaul and others 2003). Financing the provision of global public goods and efforts to meet such development targets as the Millennium Development Goals are important investments in global and national security and cohesion. They have the potential to generate high social returns for the world as a whole and for individual countries (Conceição and Mendoza in this volume; UN Millennium Project 2005).

Thus a first step toward overcoming current perceptions of resource shortages would be a shift in perspective. International cooperation needs to be seen for what it is: a worthwhile investment—not a charity.

A complementary step would be to expand the pool of revenue sources to include private finance as well as public revenue, which is so often constrained by annual budget procedures and formal and informal spending limits. Distributing the costs of international cooperation to governments more evenly over time would make it possible for governments to accommodate smaller annual increases that fall within their expenditure ceilings.

But expenditure smoothing solves only one problem. For projects that need the full amount of money up front, the answer lies in more private finance. Governments and intergovernmental agencies need to find ways to make participation in international cooperation a worthwhile and attractive (meaning profitable) proposition for private investors.

From this it follows that governments and intergovernmental agencies would need to abandon the notion that they must be the direct financiers and implementers of international cooperation projects. Rather, their task could be making sure that the needed money flows to the desired purposes. For example, governments could provide incentives to private actors, including guarantees, rather than making the investments themselves. Or, where a project generates a future income stream, governments could grant investors the right to capture the income stream in return for making the resources to pay for the project available now. Or governments could contract to reimburse investors and others involved in project implementation and operation for the services they will render in fixed annual installments. The role of governments in international cooperation would shift from direct resource provider to incentive provider.

Table 1 summarizes the required changes in perspective on international cooperation. These proposed shifts outline fine principles, but are they feasible? The next section looks at national experiences that illustrate some of the

TABLE 1

Widening the focus: a new perspective on financing international cooperation

Widening the focus:	
From...	To...
Public revenue	Private finance
Direct spending by governments and intergovernmental agencies	Provision of public-policy incentives to private investors
Payment now and in full	Payment for services when they become available
International cooperation as charity	International cooperation as an investment

approaches adopted by sovereign and subsovereign government agencies to overcome resource shortages similar to those that impede international cooperation.

NATIONAL EXPERIENCES WITH LOOSENING RESOURCE CONSTRAINTS

Government authorities have long looked beyond immediately available public revenue to finance public projects, from national defense and public infrastructure to housing and education. Whether by borrowing from public and private banks, issuing debt securities nationally and internationally, or other means, many governments have mobilized the right amount of money, at the right time, and for the right period, while avoiding sudden expenditure and tax hikes. More recently, stricter demands on fiscal discipline (including limits on public debt) and the expanding scale of some financing requirements have made it necessary to explore additional means of financing, notably to apply to public policy purposes, as appropriate, some of the more recent financing technology often initially developed by market actors for private investment purposes.

Sovereign and subsovereign debt securities to raise capital for government spending

Borrowing permits governments to access private capital and enhance their spending flexibility. When governments need to borrow to finance programs, bank loans are not always suitable because of the large volume required and the long-term repayment schedule needed. Thus both industrial and developing country governments borrow on domestic[5] and international financial markets by selling debt securities.[6] This gives them the flexibility to borrow the amount and type of resources needed when they are required. And it dilutes the fiscal impact by spreading it out over time, with public revenue being used to pay only the interest until the security reaches maturity.

Issuing government debt securities has a long history. Cities and towns in Europe have engaged in this practice since the Middle Ages (Kohn 1999). Today, subsovereign bonds (state and municipal bonds) are an important source of finance for states and municipalities in the United States.[7] When these securities are backed by the general taxation power of the issuing government and by general revenue, they are known as general obligation bonds. When they are backed by dedicated revenues from a state venture, such as a power plant or a toll road, they are called revenue bonds (Lamb and Rappaport 1980).

Ultimately, however, the ability of governments to borrow is bounded. To be sustainable, borrowing has to remain aligned with government revenue. This constraint has driven governments to consider other possibilities, including the use of guarantees.

Public guarantees to leverage private finance for public policy purposes

Governments have begun to shift from direct spending to reassignment of responsibility for resource mobilization and investment to private actors. For that to work, private investors needed proper incentives, such as government guarantees. As Griffith-Jones and Fuzzo de Lima (in this volume) explain, government guarantees mitigate the risks that loans or bonds will not be repaid.

The U.S. government used guarantees to overcome bottlenecks in the housing loan market, enabling the creation of mortgage-backed securities (see the chapter by Sandor in this volume).[8] Facing the challenge of an inadequate supply of housing finance, the U.S. government had several options. It could invest huge sums of money into directly providing new housing units, allocate substantial revenue to subsidy schemes for private home construction, or design a guarantee scheme that would enable individual households to borrow in the financial market.

The government chose the last option. It recognized that one reason for the housing loan shortages was that originators of mortgage loans were left for extended periods with illiquid assets on their books (Fabozzi and others 2002), limiting the amount of additional credit they could provide. There were no secondary markets where loan originators could sell mortgages to third parties, refreshing their ability to extend new credit.

To overcome this constraint, several government-sponsored agencies were created to purchase and pool mortgages and to issue securities using the pool of mortgages as collateral—the Federal National Mortgage Association (Fannie Mae), the Federal Home Loan Mortgage Corporation (Freddie Mac), and the Government National Mortgage Association (Ginnie Mae).[9] These mortgage-backed securities, which were serviced using interest proceeds and principal payments on the underlying mortgages, allowed a secondary market to develop, spreading the risks and pulling resources from a dispersed set of investors.

Making all this possible were U.S. government guarantees. The government promised to step in in case of mortgage defaults, ensuring that the securities issued by the new agencies would be serviced at least in part. Ginnie Mae, as part of the U.S. government, provides guarantees that carry the full faith and credit of the government. Freddie Mac and Fannie Mae are government-sponsored enterprises, but not part of the government. Their guarantees do not carry the full faith and credit of the U.S. government. Still, most market participants view these agencies' guarantees as close in creditworthiness to government securities.

Securitization and project finance: relying on the private sector to manage adequate resource mobilization

Today, many mortgage-backed securities are issued entirely by private actors, using insurance or other credit enhancements in place of government guarantees. In addition, loans other than mortgages are now used as collateral for issuing securities through a process called securitization. Examples are credit card receivables, automobile loans, and student loans. These securities are referred to as asset-backed securities (Fabozzi and others 2002), because they are backed by the receivables from loans or other types of financial assets.

Other future-flow receivables that are not linked to formal financial assets have also been securitized, ranging from intellectual property revenues (starting with the David Bowie bonds collateralized by future record sales) to migrant remittances and revenues from exports of commodities such as oil (Ketkar and Ratha 2004). Developing country governments have used securitization of future-flow receivables to improve their borrowing conditions (Chalk 2002).

Securitization thus expands the range of assets against which new funds can be raised. Also, it makes long-term funding available in the near term.

Future-flow receivables also play a critical role in project finance arrangements, in which future flows are directly related to the operations of the project being financed. One example is the Private Financing Initiative set up by the UK government (UK Her Majesty's Treasury 2003). The initiative encourages the establishment of public-private partnerships to undertake such diverse projects as building and operating hospitals, schools, prisons, and telecommunications, transport, and power infrastructure; renovating government buildings; and implementing defense contracts.[10] The partnerships, both for-profit and nonprofit entities, are typically called project companies in the context of project finance.

Through the project company private partners typically mobilize the required investment funds (from project financiers, who provide either equity or debt financing) and often manage the construction and even the operation of the public project, which is also implemented by private contractors. To finance the project, the project company can also use future income receivables (projected income from the sale of the project's goods and services) as an asset to back borrowing through loans or the issuance of debt instruments.

To enable the project company to collect cash flows to compensate the private sector partners (financiers and contractors), the government can either agree to pay an annual fee for the services the project delivers over a set number of years or it can grant the project company the right to collect part or all of the income that the project generates. With the annual fee option the use of Private Financing Initiative–type public-private partnerships facilitates expenditure smoothing. By distributing project costs more evenly over a number of years, the government avoids the need to increase taxes or cancel existing programs, both politically difficult. With the right to the project's income flow option, the cost to the budget is a revenue loss rather than a direct expenditure.

The project finance modality offers several advantages. Where governments face budgetary and borrowing constraints, the project finance approach, by making the right amount of money available at the right time, can allow the government to launch—and finance in full—initiatives that might otherwise have languished. It also offers other overall efficiency (value for money) and efficacy gains to the government. Spackman (2002), for example, stresses the following advantages over standard public execution or contracting:

- *More effective monitoring by private financiers.* The monitoring pressures for efficient use of resources and appropriate delivery of goods or services by the contractors come from the private financiers and so may be stronger than they would be coming from the public sector clients under conventional contracts.
- *The contractual benefits of long-term capital at risk.* Tying contractors into a long-term commitment, with their own capital at risk, keeps them from building and walking away and gives them a stake in ensuring good performance in order to generate the requisite cash flow.
- *Enforcement of whole-life costing.*[11] Whole-life costing forces both the government and the contractor to consider the interaction between design changes at the construction stage and long-term performance.

The financing arrangements underlying project finance can be quite complex, involving many different actors, a great diversity of tools, and contracts that span many years (sometimes up to 30 years). At the hub of this complex network of arrangements and contracts is the project company, a special-purpose facility that structures the roles of different actors, with contracts specifying all the commitments and claims involved. It may be accompanied also by one or more special-purpose vehicles that undertake designated functions, such as a finance vehicle used to issue debt or an entity used to serve as a holding company of the project sponsors.[12] Box 1 describes a typical project finance arrangement, illustrating the role that the special-purpose facility—in this case a project company—plays in mobilizing private finance.

Special-purpose facilities, often consisting of not much more than a finance vehicle, are also an important institutional go-between when developing coun-

Box 1

SPECIAL-PURPOSE FACILITIES IN PROJECT FINANCE: THE ROLE OF PROJECT COMPANIES

Project companies are legally independent entities, with a for-profit or a nonprofit status, created to structure a complex network of contractual agreements among multiple parties. Many project companies are set up as public-private partnerships, because one of their objectives is to facilitate greater involvement in the project by the private sector, especially private investors.

The figure illustrates the role of a project company and the ways that the government enables the project company to collect revenue. In the first approach the project generates its own future income stream, such as user fees, based on a government concession. In the second approach the project benefits from a government commitment to make future contributions to the project. The project company's revenues can also come through offtake agreements between the project company and a buyer who agrees in advance to purchase the output of the project. The buyer can be the government, a government-owned company, or a private company. Similarly, there are often symmetric contracts with suppliers to lock in a price for the purchase of inputs.

The role of a project company

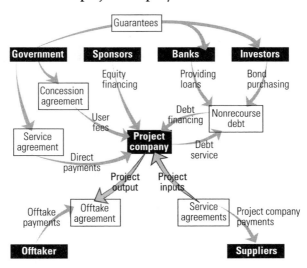

Those who propose the project (such as a government) are the project originators. Those who make an equity investment are the project sponsors. And those who provide debt financing are the project investors.

Source: Based on Buljevich and Park 1999 and Sorge and Gadanecz 2004.

try governments seek to borrow against such future-flow receivables from abroad as revenues from oil sales. Investors want to be assured that the receivables will stay abroad, never entering the country. The special-purpose finance vehicle can be set up abroad to issue securities backed by the future flows (which become "assets" of the vehicle), collect receivables, make debt service and other related payments, and channel proceeds from the sales of the securities to the government. (See box 2 for an example of such a financing arrangement.) Similar arrangements have been made for securitizing future remittances from workers abroad.[13]

New financing technology may require institutional innovation

Three main lessons emerge from experience with new financing technology. First, governments are increasingly using new financing technology rather than relying on direct spending under annual budgets. Governments have issued sovereign bonds, offered guarantees to private investors, reassigned (temporarily) rights to levy user fees and other charges, securitized future receivables such as revenue from sales abroad or workers' remittances, and created new asset classes, such as government commitments to buy specified services or to make specified payments at a future date.

Second, governments have often created new organizational entities, or special-purpose facilities, to handle these financing tools. For example, the U.S. government created Ginnie Mae, Fannie Mae, and Freddie Mac to encourage a secondary mortgage market. Other organizational entities, such as project companies in Private Financing Initiative—project finance—types of undertaking, are typically a step further removed from the government, as are simpler finance vehicles such as those used in the securitization of future-flow receivables. These new institutional mechanisms and tools have provided new financing opportunities and helped to overcome many types of resource constraints. They have broken through the lines dividing the public and private sectors, reassigning risks and responsibilities in line with comparative advantage. The private sector can quickly mobilize large amounts of money—when it is needed—and is able to readily manage many types of risks. Governments can more easily and efficiently accommodate large investments by spreading them over a longer period of time so as to avoid (politically sensitive) tax hikes and often new and perhaps excessive borrowing.

Third, financing arrangements are often made on an issue-specific basis. Governments are not issuing bonds only to raise money for general budgets and direct-spending activities. Rather, they are also raising money for specific purposes for which they often reassign responsibility for financing and implementation to private actors. Governments limit their role to ensuring that the public good or service is being provided, leaving most of the provision, including resource mobilization, to others.

Box 2
SPECIAL-PURPOSE FACILITIES IN SECURITIZATION: THE ROLE OF FINANCE VEHICLES

Pemex Finance Ltd., Mexico's state-owned oil and gas company, illustrates the role of finance vehicles in securitization. Pemex has exclusive authority over the production and sale of gas and oil in the country. In the late 1990s Pemex created an offshore finance vehicle, Pemex Finance, that issued debt securities against future receivables from exports of crude oil to Canada and the United States. Proceeds from sales to designated customers abroad were irrevocably directed to the finance vehicle. In turn, the finance vehicle used the proceeds to service its debt, channeling any remaining funds back to Pemex in Mexico (see figure).

Pemex use of a finance vehicle

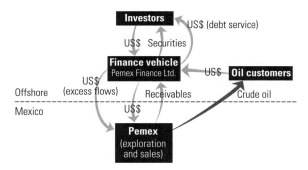

Pemex sold $2.6 billion in securities through the finance vehicle, at spreads of 125–412 basis points over U.S. Treasuries. Mexico's sovereign unsecured debt at the time was 570 basis points over the same benchmark. The cost of borrowing through the finance vehicle was lower because all cash flow transactions were offshore and so were effectively isolated from sovereign action by the Mexican government. This enabled the decoupling of the transaction from the government's sovereign credit rating.

Still, several risks (other than sovereign intervention) remain. A drop in crude oil prices could result in inadequate revenues to cover interest and principal owed to investors. To mitigate this risk, the securities were overcollaterized, with a coverage ratio of three times the amount needed for payment of interest and principal. In addition, Pemex bought commercial insurance and other commercial guarantees to further enhance the credit standing of the transaction.

Source: Based on Chalk 2002 and Ketkar and Ratha 2004.

What these lessons imply is that overcoming public sector resource constraints requires institutional innovation: creating the right type of organizational entity to handle the new technologies, straddling the public-private divide. No doubt, as the borders between the public and private sectors have become less distinct, effective contracting and contract supervision are important for safeguarding against private interests overtaking public interests (or public interests overtaking private interests, perhaps as damaging to both private and public partners). But when used effectively, the new financing mechanisms can significantly improve financing for public policy purposes, both quantitatively and qualitatively.

Can these institutional innovations and lessons of national experience be applied to the financing of international cooperation? And if so, how?

ENHANCING RESOURCE MOBILIZATION FOR INTERNATIONAL COOPERATION THROUGH INSTITUTIONAL INNOVATION: SPECIAL-PURPOSE FACILITIES

Some of the institutional innovations at the national level are already making their way into the international arena. Their feasibility and desirability are being tested in two quite different types of international cooperation efforts. Type 1 includes international cooperation endeavors that generate both social returns and easy-to-capture private returns that can be passed on to potential private investors. This is the easier type for mobilizing private finance for public purposes. An example is Galileo, the European Union's international satellite navigation system (discussed in more detail below; see also the chapter by Kaul on global public-private partnerships). Type 2 projects include international cooperation challenges such as achieving the Millennium Development Goals, which may generate high social returns but yield few direct private returns that can be captured by private financiers. Achieving these goals by the set target dates would require large up-front investments. And while donor countries are committed to increasing official development assistance, they find it difficult to accommodate such increases in the short term in their foreign aid budgets. Could donors use some of the new financing mechanisms to deliver on their commitments?

For type 1 projects with both social returns and easy-to-capture private returns, responsibility for resource mobilization can be reassigned to the private sector, in line, for example, with the project finance model discussed earlier. For the more complex case of type 2 projects that yield few direct private returns, financial markets could be brought in by creating a new asset class, through government commitments to pay later, as in the context of Private Financing Initiative–type public-private partnerships. In the first case the overall burden on donor budgets is reduced. In the second case financial markets can help donors with expenditure smoothing. Donors will ultimately have to pay, but with the added benefit (shown below) of enhanced project efficiency and efficacy.

Type 1 projects: borrowing against the project's own future income streams
Projects that produce goods and services that are valued by individual actors can sell their output. If the proceeds are sufficiently attractive, private actors may agree to implement the project, in full or in part, including taking on responsibility for financing it.

In such situations the public project initiators arrange for the creation of a special-purpose facility, which is entitled to some or all of the future revenues, usually for a defined period. With this backing the project company can then attract debt and equity capital to finance the project and can contract with suppliers and other actors engaged in the design, implementation, and operation of the project. Although the projects attract private investors, it is important to keep in mind that the projects are being developed to serve a public policy purpose. Therefore, public actors (governments or intergovernmental organizations) also have a key role in setting up the project structure and ensuring that the generation of project revenues does not interfere with its public purpose.

Project revenue streams can come from the sale of goods and services that the project produces or from assets created by the project, such as intellectual property rights.

Project revenue streams resulting from direct sales of private goods and services. The Galileo satellite navigation system is an example of a revenue stream in the international context arising from sales of private services.[14] Galileo will provide services that are of high value to a wide range of businesses and thus are likely to generate a large volume of sales proceeds. Recognizing this income potential, the European Commission and the European Space Agency, the public project promoters, arranged for a project company concession, allowing the company to collect the income generated through Galileo's commercial use in exchange for responsibility for partially financing and building and operating the project for a set period.

Project revenue streams from nonmonetary assets created by the project. The Medicines for Malaria Venture draws on nonmonetary assets to attract private investors.[15] A public-private partnership organized as a nonprofit foundation under Swiss law, it partners with pharmaceutical firms in developing new malaria medicines. The firms' contributions are mostly in kind. The partnership products are new drug formulations that can be codified and patented. While the Medicines for Malaria Venture usually retains the patent rights for developing countries, the partnering firms have the right to use the new inventions in industrial countries.

This differential patenting attracts private sector resources to the project. The venture is an important reminder that money is only one of many assets against which to borrow or issue debt. Many private actors also highly value other assets, such as intellectual property rights, under the proviso, of course, that they can ultimately be used to generate cash flows.

Type 2 projects: borrowing against donor promises to pay in the future

For projects that generate few, if any, direct financial returns for their investors, the key concern is how to use donor commitments of future financial contributions to motivate private actors to invest now so that project activities can start and produce results on time, in the most efficient and effective way. The following two examples suggest how this challenge could be met.

Project revenue streams resulting from up-front donor purchase commitments. Potential market size is an important criterion for investors contemplating whether to fund a particular research and development (R&D) project. Likely market size and expected sales proceeds determine to what extent a potential project can recover some of its R&D costs and generate profits. No surprise, then, that pro-poor R&D is largely lacking.

A way to overcome this obstacle is through up-front donor purchase commitments. Donors agree to purchase a certain quantity of a specified new product (such as a new vaccine or seed variety) at a defined price when it becomes available (Kremer and Glennerster 2004; Kremer and Petterson Zwane in this volume).

Donors thus absorb the risk that a potential investor is unwilling to bear. No up-front cash is required from either the donor or the potential beneficiaries, apart from the purchase commitment, which is essentially a guarantee. The R&D effort would be financed entirely by the firms or by other institutions developing the desired new product.

The purchase commitment could be implemented through an offtake agreement, typical in project finance (see box 1). The special-purpose facility could take the form of a finance vehicle. Donors could enter into a credible offtake agreement with the finance vehicle, promising to buy the product at a preset price once it becomes available. The finance vehicle could then raise the debt or equity finance in capital markets, based on the strength of the offtake agreement.

Project revenue streams resulting from untied, up-front donor commitments. The International Finance Facility, a mechanism proposed to improve the timing of financing for the Millennium Development Goals, illustrates this approach well.[16] The facility's "assets" would be commitments by donor countries to make defined annual contributions over a set period to enable the facility to issue bonds and facilitate the front-loading of aid resources. This would enable investments in meeting the Millennium Development Goals to start as soon as possible, increasing the likelihood of achieving the goals on time (2015 for most of them). The facility would function only as a resource mobilization vehicle, not as an operational agency. It would disburse funds through bilateral and multilateral aid agencies. Disbursements would extend over a period of about 15 years, and repayment activities would continue for another 15 years, after which operations would be closed down (figure 1).

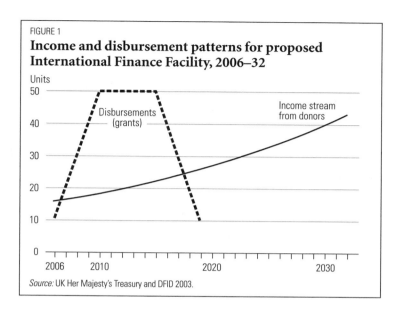

FIGURE 1

Income and disbursement patterns for proposed International Finance Facility, 2006–32

Source: UK Her Majesty's Treasury and DFID 2003.

The special-purpose facility could be set up as a nonprofit public-private partnership, with an accompanying finance vehicle whose assets would consist of the pledged contributions from donors. Securities (bonds) could then be issued against donor pledges, turning the long-term income stream from donors into capital available for more immediate disbursement. Borrowing costs would be minimized by securing the highest possible rating for the securities. Several strategies for credit enhancement could be considered. For example, some donors might want to contribute directly while others might prefer to provide guarantees.

As the organizational design indicates, all stakeholders, including aid recipients, would participate in the facility's governance structure (figure 2). From the design it is also clear, however, that the proposed International Finance Facility is a complex financing arrangement, with high transaction costs. Whether the benefits outweigh the costs to all ultimately depends on a number of details still being worked out, but at least in principle the answer appears to be yes.[17]

Donor countries would benefit as well as recipient countries because the International Finance Facility would permit them to honor their aid commitments while avoiding undesirable public expenditure hikes. Their citizens would enjoy other public benefits—a world freed of the worst forms of poverty, with enhanced economic growth and global development.

Another question is why not let each donor do its own borrowing? Why establish a special project facility and a special financing vehicle? There are several reasons for taking the multilateral, project facility approach rather than a bilateral route:

- *Less risk of free-riding nationally.* If borrowing is left to individual governments, international cooperation agencies and ministries may have to

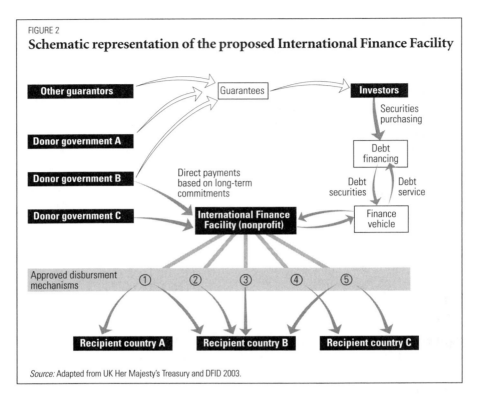

FIGURE 2

Schematic representation of the proposed International Finance Facility

Source: Adapted from UK Her Majesty's Treasury and DFID 2003.

compete for the additional resources with other government entities that may not be willing to reveal their true preferences for reduced global poverty or more sustainable development. So the world could be back to square one, the type of resource constraints discussed at the beginning of this chapter.

- *Less risk of free-riding internationally.* A special project facility such as the International Finance Facility increases transparency and accountability in financing international cooperation. It makes evident who is promising what, so that private market pressure is likely to be brought to bear on donors trying to renege on their commitments.

- *Lower transaction costs.* Although the proposed arrangement for the International Finance Facility appears complicated, it looks much less complicated when compared with the arrangements that would have to be made in, say, 20 or so donor countries individually to mobilize resources for achievement of the Millennium Development Goals.

Thus, for donor and recipient countries alike the International Finance Facility could mean much improved aid effectiveness. It could help make money available in the right amount and at the right time—predictably and reliably.

The next question is how to make the issuance of debt both viable and cost-effective. From an investor's perspective the International Finance Facility is borrowing funds in excess of its current resources (the first year, or funded portion, of donor commitments) based on a sovereign promise to contribute additional resources in subsequent years. These promises are not fully fledged sovereign obligations; if that were the case the donor would bear the full budgetary impact in the current year and the benefit of this structure would be compromised.[18] Rather, the commitments are a unique "asset" of the International Finance Facility (or, more precisely, of the finance vehicle) that capital markets will need to evaluate carefully in determining the cost of debt for the facility.

Some donors are concerned about committing future budgets. But many national public-private partnerships do that routinely. And governments precommit future budgets every time they establish new schools or hospitals nationally, because such public services cannot be opened one day and closed the next—or only at the risk of political turmoil and public outcry. In this sense, governments are not themselves the borrowers but rather the providers of some form of budget-neutral support that the independent project financier (the facility) must then leverage to secure additional financing.

But would private investors feel confident about such an arrangement? Despite the conceptual appeal, such structures have not yet been attempted. Borrowings secured by donor commitments to international cooperation (as opposed to true sovereign obligations) do not yet exist as an asset class. But governments are free to enhance the credit value of their commitments in any way that does not render them sovereign obligations or compromise their exclusion from current fiscal expenditures. The scope of such potential enhancement will vary based on each country's budgetary regime.

But perhaps the question should be turned around. Why shouldn't private investors feel confident? International cooperation represents a long-term but high-return investment for donors—not charity, which investors might view as being more easily subordinated to changing political and fiscal conditions. Most important, the underlying asset class would be based on legally binding government commitments with the International Finance Facility. A failure to honor those commitments would risk the government's reputation and perhaps even its credit risk rating. Moreover, because donors would be acting as a group, peer pressure could help to prevent any one party from failing to live up to its commitment and thereby potentially damaging the reputation of all the others. Repayment of bondholders would not be contingent on actual success in meeting the Millennium Development Goals. It would depend only on the firmness and reliability of the donors' commitments.

Private investors and their financial instruments have become very sophisticated in recent decades, and they have addressed issues with greater complexity and risks than an International Finance Facility-type arrangement might present. With some effort to explain the new asset class of untied government commitments to pay in the future, and to overcome information problems that make this new asset class look unusual, it should become quite an attractive instrument.

Thus, there is much to recommend an International Finance Facility-type approach. One way to test the modality is to launch a pilot initiative. The international community is moving in that direction with suggestions for implementing the International Finance Facility for Immunization pilot project.[19]

CONCLUSION

In reviewing the resource constraints facing policymakers in the international cooperation domain today, this chapter has explored how governments have overcome similar constraints and how that experience can be applied to the financing of international cooperation. For newer financing technologies such as guarantees or asset-backed securitization to be used internationally, one lesson of national experience is especially important: financing innovation often has to be accompanied by institutional innovation. Governments have responded to particular challenges by encouraging the creation of special-purpose facilities to handle these tools and attract private actors to take responsibility for resource mobilization—and its risks.

Private actors become involved because the private rewards are adequate. The potential benefits for governments and intergovernmental organizations are substantial as well: better risk management, expenditure smoothing, lower transaction costs, less risk of free-riding by other donors, and enhanced efficiency and efficacy of international cooperation.

As does any innovation, the new modalities have to be assessed in terms of both potential benefits and costs. Many of the innovations discussed here are still in an exploratory state—being tested, and no doubt, requiring further improvements. Yet today's international cooperation challenges, whether they concern meeting the Millennium Development Goals or enhancing the provision of global public goods, are too urgent and too costly in human, environmental, and economic terms for the international community not to try to overcome some of the operational obstacles.

World economic growth and sustainable development cannot succeed through government spending alone. Governments, intergovernmental organizations, and private foundations must find ways and the means to tap the wealth of financial markets, structuring deals that would make all actors better off—private investors, donors, and especially developing countries and the world's poor. The new financing modalities discussed here do not call for charity or philanthropic considerations. They propose looking at financing international cooperation as a worthwhile, high-value activity—that pays private and social returns.

Notes

1. IMF World Economic Outlook www.imf.org/external/pubs/ft/weo/2005/01/pdf/statappx.pdf.

2. The UN Millennium Project estimates that meeting the Millennium Development Goals would require annual increases in official development assistance of $70 billion in 2006, rising to $130 billion in 2015 (UN Millennium Project 2005, p. 57).

3. The 22 countries are the members of the OECD Development Assistance Committee (DAC); the countries that have met the target are Denmark, Luxembourg, the Netherlands, Norway, and Sweden.

4. The amount depends on what is included in the estimate. In 2003 equities, debt securities (including bonds, notes, bills, and other money market instruments, both domestic and international), and bank assets totaled about $125 trillion, or about 3.5 times global GDP (IMF 2004, p. 179). Adding to this the $250 trillion in notional value of derivative contracts (both exchange traded and over the counter; BIS 2004) brings the total in financial markets to $375 trillion, or more than 10 times world GDP.

5. Well developed domestic financial markets are important in themselves for development (King and Levine 1993; Levine 1997, 2004; Wolf 2004).

6. See World Bank (2004) for the volume of bond issuance by national governments.

7. While U.S. municipal bonds dominate the market (issuance in 2003 totaled $453 billion; www.bondmarkets.com), the practice is spreading to other countries. Daniels and Vijayakumar (2002) review recent developments and note that during the last decade of the twentieth century more than 400 local and state entities in 29 countries other than the United States issued municipal bonds totaling $270 billion.

8. For a more detailed analysis of the evolution of securitization's role in housing finance in the United States, see, for example, Brendsel (1996) and Ranieri (1996).

9. For further details, see www.fanniemae.com, www.freddiemac.com, and www.ginniemae.gov.

10. For assessments of experiences with Private Financing Initiative-type projects, see Spackman (2002); UK Her Majesty's Treasury (2003); and Fitch Ratings (2003).

11. Whole-life costing systematically considers all costs and revenues associated with the design, implementation, and operation of a project. It enables comparison of different options, including their associated cost (including initial capital, procurement costs, and opportunity costs) and income streams over the life of the project.

12. For more information on special-purpose vehicles, see Gorton and Souleles (forthcoming). Special-purpose vehicles have become the subject of much controversy, notably in connection with the legal difficulties of Enron Corporation (see, again, Gorton and Souleles forthcoming). However, the use of these vehicles within public-private partnerships is typically subject to extensive public scrutiny, so that there is less risk of potential misuse.

13. See, for example, the securitization by Banco do Brasil (a government-owned Brazilian bank with a dominant market position) of future remittance receivables from Brazilian workers in Japan (Ketkar and Ratha 2004).

14. See http://europa.eu.int/comm/dgs/energy_transport/galileo/index_en.htm.

15. See www.mmv.org and the chapter by Kaul in this volume on global public-private partnerships, box A.8.

16. For a description of this proposed facility, see UK Her Majesty's Treasury and DFID (2003).

17. Mavrotas (2005) provides a more detailed assessment. For technical details and the implications of different options, see World Bank and IMF (2004). The International Finance Facility is also described in the Technical Group on Innovative Financing Mechanisms (2004), which resulted from an initiative led by the governments of Brazil, Chile, Spain, and France, and in the Working Group on New International Contributions to Finance Development (2004), also known as the "Landau Report." For some concerns expressed by potential donor countries, see, for example, Giles, Balls, and Daneshkhu (2005).

18. The way borrowing under the International Finance Facility would be accounted for in donor governments' public accounts (in the case of European Union members, not only by their national statistical offices, but also by Eurostat, the European Commission statistical office) is still being worked out. This is largely a statistical and accounting issue, but relevant because if borrowing under the International Finance Facility is counted toward the government's budgetary deficit or public debt, then expenditure smoothing could be difficult—or impossible—to achieve. But there is a more substantive tradeoff to be considered: the level of explicitness and the volume of the pledges that appear on government books have to balance the demands for assurance of capital markets (the stronger the assurances, the larger the volume and level of explicitness of the commitments on government books) and the desire of governments to benefit from intertemporal expenditure smoothing (which implies having as much as possible off the balance sheet).

19. The pilot would follow the principles and approaches of the International Finance Facility but would focus on immunizing children and adults in the world's poorest countries. The UK government has pledged $1.8 billion over 15 years. Backed by this and other pledges the pilot is expected to raise an additional $4 billion over the next 10 years (www.dfid.gov.uk/news/files/pressreleases/pr-bennhealth bostpledge26jan05.asp). The Group of Seven finance ministers has also included the International Finance Facility and the International Finance Facility for Immunization among the options they are exploring to enhance the availability of finance for development (www.hm-treasury.gov.uk/otherhmtsites/g7/news/g7_statement_conclusions050205.cfm).

REFERENCES

Arellano, Cristina, Aleš Bulíř, Timothy Lane, and Leslie Lipschitz. 2005. "The Dynamic Implications of Foreign Aid and Its Variability." IMF Working Paper WP/05/119. Washington, D.C.

BIS (Bank for International Settlements). 2004. *BIS Quarterly Review.* September. Basel, Switzerland. [www.bis.org/statistics/index.htm].

Brendsel, Leland C. 1996. "Securitization's Role in Housing Finance: The Special Contributions of the Government-Sponsored Enterprises." In Leon T. Kendall and Michael J. Fishman, eds., *A Primer on Securitization.* Cambridge, Mass.: MIT Press.

Bryant, Ralph C. 2004. *Crisis Prevention and Prosperity Management for the World Economy.* Washington, D.C.: Brookings Institution Press.

Bulíř, Aleš, and Javier Hamann. 2003. "Aid Volatility: An Empirical Assessment." *IMF Staff Papers* 50 (1): 64–89.

Buljevich, Esteban C., and Yoon S. Park. 1999. *Project Finance and the International Financial Markets.* Dordrecht, Netherlands: Kluwer Academic Publishers.

Chalk, Nigel A. 2002. "The Potential Role for Securitizing Public Sector Revenue Flows: An Application to the Philippines." IMF Working Paper WP/02/106. International Monetary Fund, Washington, D.C.

Daniels, Kenneth N., and Jayaraman Vijayakumar. 2002. "Municipal Bonds— International and Not Just U.S. Anymore." *Public Fund Digest* 2 (1): 60–67.

Fabozzi, Frank J., Fracon Modigliani, Frank J. Jones, and Michael G. Ferri. 2002. *Foundations of Financial Markets and Institutions.* 3rd edition. Upper Saddle River, N.J.: Prentice Hall.

Fitch Ratings. 2003. *PPP-PFI: UK Market Trends and Fitch Rating Criteria for European PPP Transactions.* New York.

Giles, Chris, Andrew Balls, and Scheherazade Daneshkhu. 2005. "G-7 Nations Still Split on Debt Relief for Africa." *Financial Times.* February 7.

Gorton, Gary, and Nicholas S. Souleles. Forthcoming. "Special Purpose Vehicles and Securitization." In René Stulz and Mark Carey, eds., *The Risks of Financial Institutions.* Chicago, Ill.: Chicago University Press.

IMF (International Monetary Fund). 2004. *Global Financial Stability Report.* Washington, D.C. [www.imf.org/External/Pubs/FT/GFSR/2004/02/pdf/statappx.pdf].

Kaul, Inge, Pedro Conceição, Katell Le Goulven, and Ronald U. Mendoza, eds. 2003. *Providing Global Public Goods: Managing Globalization.* New York: Oxford University Press.

Ketkar, Suhas, and Dilip Ratha. 2004. "Recent Advances in Future-Flow Securitization." Paper presented at Annual Finance and Accounting International Conference on Managing Securitization for Lebanon and the MENA Region, American University of Beirut School of Business, December 3–4, Beirut.

King, Robert G., and Ross Levine. 1993. "Finance and Growth: Schumpeter Might Be Right." *Quarterly Journal of Economics* 108 (3): 717–37.

Kohn, Meir. 1999. "The Capital Market before 1600." Dartmouth College, Department of Economics, Hanover, N.H. [www.dartmouth.edu/~mkohn/99-06.pdf].

Kremer, Michael and Rachel Glennerster. 2004. *Strong Medicine: Creating Incentives for Pharmaceutical Research on Neglected Diseases.* Princeton, N.J.: Princeton University Press.

Lamb, Robert, and Stephen P. Rappaport. 1980. *Municipal Bonds.* New York: McGraw-Hill.

Levine, Ross. 1997. "Financial Development and Economic Growth: Views and Agenda." *Journal of Economic Literature* 35 (2): 688–726.

———. 2004. *Finance and Growth: Theory and Evidence.* NBER Working Paper 10766. Cambridge, Mass.: National Bureau of Economic Research.

Mavrotas, George. 2005. "The International Finance Facility." In Anthony B. Atkinson, ed., *New Sources of Development Finance.* Oxford: Oxford University Press.

OECD (Organisation for Economic Co-operation and Development). 2005. "Official Development Assistance Increases Further - but 2006 Targets Still a Challenge." Paris. [www.oecd.org/document/3/0,2340,en_2649_33721_34700611_1_1_1_1,00.html].

Pallage, Stéphane, and Michel A. Robe. 2003. "On the Welfare Cost of Economic Fluctuations in Developing Countries." *International Economic Review* 44 (2): 677–98.

Ranieri, Lewis S. 1996. "The Origins of Securitization, Sources of Its Growth, and Its Future Potential." In Leon T. Kendall and Michael J. Fishman, eds., *A Primer on Securitization.* Cambridge, Mass.: MIT Press.

Sachs, Jeffrey, John W. McArthur, Guido Schmidt-Traub, Margaret Kruk, Chandrika Bahadur, Michael Faye, and Gordon McCord. 2004. "Ending Africa's Poverty Trap." *Brookings Papers on Economic Activity* 1: 117–240.

Setty, Gautam, and Randall Dodd. 2003. "Credit Rating Agencies: Their Impact on Capital Flows to Developing Countries." Special Policy Report 6. Financial Policy Forum, Derivates Study Center, Washington, D.C. [www.financialpolicy.org/FPFSPR6.pdf].

Sorge, Marco, and Blaise Gadanecz. 2004. "The Term Structure of Credit Spreads in Project Finance." BIS Working Paper 159. Bank for International Settlements, Basel, Switzerland.

Spackman, Michael. 2002. "Public-Private Partnerships: Lessons from the British Approach." *Economic Systems* 26 (3): 283–301.

Technical Group on Innovative Financing Mechanisms. 2004. *Action against Hunger and Poverty: Report of the Technical Group on Innovative Financing Mechanisms.*

Brasília. [www.mre.gov.br/ingles/politica_externa/temas_agenda/acfp/Report-final%20version.pdf].

UK Her Majesty's Treasury. 2003. *PFI: Meeting the Investment Challenge.* London.

UK Her Majesty's Treasury and DFID (UK Department for International Development). 2003. *International Finance Facility.* London. [www.dfid.gov.uk/pubs/files/International-Finance-Facility2003.pdf].

UN (United Nations). 2002. *Report of the International Conference on Financing for Development.* A/CONF.198/11. New York.

————. 2004. *Follow-up and Implementation of the Outcome of the International Conference on Financing for Development.* A/59/150. New York.

UN (United Nations) General Assembly. 2000. *United Nations Millennium Declaration.* 55th session. Resolution adopted September 18. A/55/2. New York.

UN Millennium Project. 2005. *Investing in Development: A Practical Plan to Achieve the Millennium Development Goals.* London: Earthscan.

Winpenny, James. 2003. *Financing Water for All: Report of the World Panel on Financing Water Infrastructure.* Marseilles: World Water Council, 3rd World Water Forum, and Global Water Partnership.

Wolf, Martin. 2004. *Why Globalization Works.* New Haven, Conn.: Yale University Press.

Working Group on New International Contributions to Finance Development. 2004. "Final Report of the Working Group on New International Contributions to Finance Development." ("Landau Report"). [www.france.diplomatie.fr/actual/pdf/landau_report.pdf].

World Bank. 2004. *Global Development Finance 2004: Harnessing Cyclical Gains for Development.* Washington D.C.

World Bank and IMF (International Monetary Fund). 2004. "Aid Effectiveness and Financing Modalities." Background paper for the Development Committee Meeting of the World Bank and IMF, October 2, Washington, D.C.

TAKING SELF-INTEREST INTO ACCOUNT

A PUBLIC CHOICE ANALYSIS OF INTERNATIONAL COOPERATION

PHILIP JONES

Two complementary ways to analyze international collective action can be considered. One is normative and considers the rationale for collective action. The other is positive, based on public choice analysis, and explores what is politically feasible.

Normative analysis identifies a rationale for international cooperation and offers prescriptions for its design and finance framed with reference to welfare criteria (efficiency and equity). But are governments motivated to act on such advice? This chapter focuses on a positive analysis, looking at willingness to finance international cooperation. Public choice analysis yields predictions with reference to the interests of those who participate in democratic processes. Are voters prepared to support policies to finance international cooperation? Are politicians disposed to advocate such finance? Will lobbyists press for international cooperation? Will bureaucrats influence finance for international agencies? The focus is on individuals' preferences and on how these are aggregated within collective decisionmaking processes. A normative analysis furnishes welfare prescriptions; a public choice perspective questions motivation.

International cooperation is often commended as a means of supplying global public goods, such as global security and economic stability (Stiglitz 2002, p. 240). Unilateral action fails because each country has an incentive to under-reveal demand for a nonexcludable good (Buchanan 1968). Even within alliances there is undersupply of public goods if each member state reduces expenditures as allies increase theirs (Olson and Zeckhauser 1966). The provision of global public goods is at stake when there are externalities, that is, if one country's action affects its neighbors. Environmental damage may spill over to neighbors (Heal 1999); the negative consequences of a country's financial mistakes can be transmitted to other countries (Wyplosz 1999). Market failure also occurs if exploitation of common international resources remains unabated (creating "the tragedy of the commons"; Hardin 1968) and if economies of scale remain unexploited (Vaubel 1986).

Such normative analysis is premised on the assumption that countries act as rational, utility-maximizing actors (Snidal 2002). But is there an entity that is "the state," an entity independent of the individuals who constitute it? If not, the behavior of countries depends on the preferences and political influence of individuals. Some might argue that countries strive to maximize their citizens' welfare, but this simply begs the question of how individuals' preferences are articulated. Individuals' welfare might increase if a corrective response to market failure allows "states to reach the Pareto frontiers" (Martin 1999, p. 54), but the pursuit of efficiency is unlikely to be the sole motive of government. Analysts may ponder "whether international institutions reflect…a move to the Pareto frontier or a movement along the frontier" (Richards 1999, p. 4), but governments have a broader agenda. If countries frequently eschew corrective prescriptions in domestic policy (Cullis and Jones 1998), why would they behave differently in international relations?

Normative analysis focuses on comparisons of efficient and inefficient outcomes. Public choice analysis focuses on decisionmaking processes that change outcomes. Predictions of countries' willingness to cooperate are more informative if premised on analysis of individuals' participation in collective decisionmaking processes. Action chosen by decisionmakers can be distinguished from action that countries "should" adopt.

This chapter successively examines the preferences of voters, lobbyists, politicians, and bureaucrats. Each section identifies a received public choice critique and considers how it informs predictions about international cooperation. Adequacy and mode of finance are of central importance. As "government failure" is easily identified, there are policy implications to consider. Both market failure in the global economy and government failure are relevant when assessing policy to finance international cooperation.

The voter's perspective: willingness to finance international cooperation

A public choice analysis of voters' behavior yields the prediction that finance for international cooperation will be inadequate to redress failure in the global economy. Voters' perceptions are distorted (fiscal illusion), and reliance on specific voting rules exacerbates the impact of such distortion (through majority voting bias). Voters systematically underestimate the benefits of expenditure on international programs, particularly by comparison with expenditure on domestic programs. However, even if voters had full information, incentives inherent in a simple-majority voting rule (50 percent +1) create a preference for domestic expenditure over expenditure on global public goods—leading to majority voting bias.

Fiscal illusion
Fiscal illusion exists when individuals are not fully informed about "tax prices" and the benefits of government programs. Debate ensues as to whether govern-

ment budgets are too small or too large. While the debate concerning overall levels of public spending remains moot, the more specific prediction regarding insufficient finance for international programs is far more robust.

Voters have no incentive to become fully informed. The probability that an individual's vote will alter an electoral outcome is minuscule (Downs 1957). Voting incurs costs, and the net expected utility of such instrumental action is almost certainly negative. Why incur costs to assimilate information? Downs predicted apathy and "rational ignorance." But, of course, individuals turn out in large numbers (Aldrich 1993); they behave as if they derive satisfaction from expressing personal preference and performing a civic duty.[1] They manage information costs by relying on low-cost signals.[2] Voters participate, but with bounded rationality, with incomplete information.

Some argue that in the absence of complete information overall government spending is too small. Downs (1960) argues that "rational ignorance" means that the benefits of public expenditure are underestimated. Similarly, Galbraith (1962) argues that public spending is less than optimal and notes that advertising and marketing are greater in the private sector. Voters are also better informed about prices in the private sector than in the public sector (Kemp and Burt 2001). There is a tendency to overestimate the price of technology-intensive public sector services, such as defense (Jones 1993). The implication is that overall government spending is too small. If so, finance for international cooperation is likely to be grossly inadequate, because national public spending is by far the most important source of finance for international cooperation (Kaul and Le Goulven 2003).

The proposition that overall levels of public spending are too small has been contested. A "Leviathan school" blames fiscal illusion for "excessive" public spending; taxpayer-voters are said to underestimate the taxes they pay. Oates (1988) reviews this literature and finds the evidence mixed. Gemell, Morrissey, and Pinar (2004, p. F134) analyze questionnaire responses in the United Kingdom to conclude that "voters' perceptions of their income tax and value added tax liabilities are systematically biased towards *over*-estimation" (emphasis added). The proposition that public spending is excessive because voters are not fully informed about their tax payments is less than robust. But even if that were the case, fears about adequate funding of international cooperation are far from allayed. Fiscal illusion is asymmetric. Within overall government budgets, domestic programs are very likely to crowd out international programs.

Downs' (1960) discussion of "rational ignorance" is illustrated with reference to international expenditure. The benefits of such programs are perceived to be remote from day-to-day concerns, appearing less tangible than benefits from domestic spending (education, medical care, transport) and expected much further in the future. Voters' preferences may respond to events (for example, terrorist activity), but assessments of the benefits of expenditure on international programs are difficult. Downs (1960, p. 562) refers to defense expenditure, international relations, and overseas aid, noting that "this tendency is most obvious in international affairs, where economic and technical progress have spread a web of interdependency over the whole world."

Evidence supports the prediction that voters are far less concerned with elections that focus on international concerns (Vaubel 1994; Lord 1998). Asymmetric fiscal illusion is also evident in questionnaire responses on public expenditure priorities. In the British Social Attitudes Survey (an annual representative survey of some 3,400 households) health care and education are invariably considered first or second priority for additional expenditure. Overseas aid has remained at the bottom, with defense expenditure just a little higher (table 1). Even when confronted with the prospect of higher taxation, nearly two-thirds of respondents persistently (since the 1980s) favor higher spending for health, education, and social benefits (Hills 2002).

Such asymmetry is not peculiar to the United Kingdom. In the United States a 1994 Program on International Policy Attitudes poll reported that 64 percent of respondents favored cutting foreign aid. Voters continue to overestimate public expenditure on foreign aid. Even in February 2001, when those favoring reduction in spending on foreign aid had fallen to 40 percent, voters believed that 20 percent of the federal budget had been spent on foreign aid (more than 20 times the actual amount). In 1997 respondents ranked foreign aid as the largest area of spending in the federal budget. When presented with accurate information, voters approve of the levels of expenditure on foreign aid.[3]

Asymmetry is magnified by the incentives that face career-conscious politicians. Vaubel (1986, p. 48) argues that "national politicians...try to get rid of unpleasant activities" by delegating to international agencies. If the agencies' activities damage electoral support, they are inclined to blame international agencies, as "fewer votes are lost...if the costs are widely dispersed." Frey (1997, p. 116) refers to "the 'political dustbin' theory whereby an international organisation serves as an alibi or scapegoat for local politicians undertaking measures undesired by the local voters." Griffith-Jones (2003) and Drehr and Vaubel (2001) refer to the blame that politicians place on international financial institutions when adopting unpopular monetary policies. Little surprise, then, if voters question the benefits of international cooperation.

While the relative benefits of international programs are underestimated, the relative costs are exaggerated. Consider the presentation of tax prices. National government grants are provided for local provision of domestic services (education, local transport, street lighting, refuse management). Voters underestimate the cost of locally provided services (Oates 1979). Indeed, it is sometimes argued that voters are deliberately presented with choices loaded in favor of greater domestic expenditure (Romer and Rosenthal 1980). The result is the "flypaper effect": receipt of a lump sum grant from the national government results in a greater increase in public spending on local services than if local residents' income

TABLE 1

First or second priority for extra public spending, results of British Social Attitudes Survey, 1983–2001
(percent)

Expenditure	1983	1987	1991	1995	1999	2001	Change 1983 to 2001
Health	63	79	74	76	79	83	20
Education	50	56	62	66	69	67	17
Public transport	3	1	5	7	10	11	8
Police and prisons	8	8	6	9	8	11	3
Housing	21	24	21	14	11	8	−13
Social security	12	12	11	11	7	6	−6
Roads	5	3	5	3	7	5	nc
Help for industry	29	12	10	9	6	4	−25
Defense	8	4	4	3	2	3	−5
Overseas aid	1	1	1	*	1	1	nc
Number of responses	1,761	2,847	2,918	1,234	3,143	3,287	

* Not ranked by respondents in 1995.
nc is no change.
Note: As the table adds together first and second priorities for extra spending, columns sum to 200 percent.
Source: Taylor-Gooby and Hastie 2002.

had increased by the same value (Cullis and Jones 1998; Bailey and Connolly 1995). The flypaper effect increases spending on domestic programs at the expense of national spending on international public goods. Hewitt (1986, pp. 478–79) notes that as grants as a proportion of U.S. federal spending rose from 6.7 percent in 1963 to 17.1 percent in 1973 and then fell to 12.1 percent in 1982, voters' demand for defense fell and rose. He concludes that "the shifts in demand are therefore entirely consistent with the fiscal illusion thesis."

With asymmetric fiscal illusion voters underestimate the benefits and overestimate the costs of international cooperation. Politicians have little incentive to correct this illusion. Their incentive is to spend more on public investment projects that pay off within a four- to five-year electoral cycle (Downs 1957). Because returns to international programs are of long gestation, "problems arise because of the short decision-making horizons of government officials, who may greatly discount future consequences" (Sandler 1998, p. 225).

Majority voting bias
Voters' fiscal illusion is just part of the problem. Biases would occur even if voters had full information. A public choice critique of the simple-majority voting rule predicts that voters will have an incentive to focus on programs that facili-

tate domestic transfers. While this may not harm support to official development assistance directly (because it is based on international transfers), if domestic transfers are more easily achieved through public sector provision of private goods than of public goods, finance for global public goods appears to be prejudiced.

It has long been recognized that a majority decisionmaking rule can yield a "tyranny of the majority" (de Tocqueville [1835] 2002). Tullock (1959) illustrates this with reference to a community of five farmers. A majority of farmers vote for public expenditure programs to construct roads linking their farms with the public highway. As construction is financed by a tax on each member of the community, each member of the majority acquires the good at three-fifths its cost. Since costs to a majority are reduced by taxation across the whole community, there is always a price effect. Musgrave (1981) questions why private goods should be tax financed (surely they can be supplied in the market). Tax financing is attractive in Tullock's example because it facilitates transfers to a majority.

Public finance texts classify goods and services by degree of publicness (Cullis and Jones 1998; Hyman 2002; Rosen 2002). With reference to table 1, it is impossible to ignore an inverse correlation between degree of publicness (for example, in defense and overseas aid) and voters' priorities (for more private services such as education and medical care). Both finance for international agencies and finance for national public goods (such as national environmental projects) are prejudiced. Since the financing of national public goods is often seen as an important contribution to the provision of global public goods (Ferroni and Mody 2002; Kaul and Le Goulven 2003), the financing of global public goods would appear to suffer.

Evidence supports the proposition that majorities favor such redistribution. Stigler (1970) argues that, by Director's Law, the middle-income cohort is likely to be the main beneficiary of redistribution.[4] In the United Kingdom redistribution to a middle-income cohort is achieved by the provision of more private services, such as medical care and education, since members of the middle class are the primary beneficiaries of the National Health Service and university education (see, for example, Le Grand 1982; Dixon and others 2003).

The tendency to focus on programs that supply such private services is exacerbated in federal structures. Mueller (2003) shows how representatives press for federal taxes to finance domestic projects in their own local jurisdiction. The net effect is increased demand for federal revenue, and with the increasing marginal cost of public funds this crowds out federal expenditure that would deliver public goods, nationally and internationally. Mueller (2003) notes the European Union's preoccupation with finance for programs that redistribute, rather than finance for international public goods.

So with or without fiscal illusion, there is reason for concern. Voters are preoccupied with tax-financed private services, rather than support for international cooperation. There is irony in Rodrik's (1997) prediction that, because globalization increases uncertainty, demand for *domestic* public expenditure on social security will increase. In a normative approach governments benignly equate marginal benefit per dollar spent across programs (by reference to the well-being of all members of society) and paternally correct choices if voters are misinformed (for example, by providing "merit wants"; Musgrave 1957). In a positive analysis politicians respond to the impact of public opinion on an electoral calculus. In the United Kingdom changes in the relative importance of public spending programs have reflected the priorities reported in table 1.

THE LOBBYIST'S PERSPECTIVE: ASSESSING POLITICIANS' RESPONSE TO POLITICAL PRESSURE

So where is the motivation for international cooperation? While voters appear indifferent, small coalitions press for international collaboration. A public choice critique of lobbying reveals that small (producer) groups are more effective lobbyists than large (consumer) groups (Olson 1965). Producers lobby for change that creates profitable prospects. Profitable prospects can be created by international cooperation. Politicians are more responsive to interest group pressure when the design of international cooperation minimizes electoral risk. The mode of finance for international cooperation will reflect a political compromise, brokered between producer group pressure and electoral sensitivity.

While political scientists have long extolled the virtues of a plural society (see, for example, Bentley 1908), public choice scholars express concern. Olson (1965) argues that members of a large group have little incentive to contribute to the provision of a collective good; if a lobby successfully presses for changes in legislation, nonmembers cannot be excluded. At the same time, consumers have little incentive to appraise legislation on any particular product (consumers spend money on a range of products). By contrast, producers are organized as small groups (through trade associations) and are conscious of the importance of legislation (livelihoods are at stake). Public choice analysis predicts that small producer groups will prove more effective. Producers' incentive is to press for government legislation that delivers rent (payment in excess of earnings under competitive conditions) (Tullock 1967).

While international cooperation has the potential to deliver rent, politicians are wary that excessive indulgence might invoke voter disenchantment (Peltzman 1976). So, if international cooperation is premised on a domestic political compromise brokered by politicians, what are the implications for mode of finance? What conditions make international cooperation more attractive?

The answer depends on a domestic political compromise brokered by politicians (rather than on normative diagnosis of efficiency and equity). The pursuit of profitable prospects might motivate international cooperation, formally or informally.[5] But it is unlikely to motivate efficient international cooperation because political costs and benefits prove the main consideration. International cooperation becomes more attractive in three circumstances:

- It is implemented through regulation (avoiding explicit taxation, relying on implicit costs of regulation).
- Its costs can be passed on to other countries.
- It includes subsidy, or price support mechanisms, to earmark gains for producer groups.

There are a number of policy implications. First, estimates of financial transfers and public expenditure contributions prove misleading measures of commitment to international cooperation: estimates of both explicit and implicit costs are required. Second, while prospects for international cooperation are said to depend on considerations such as public goods technologies, this simply reflects the extent to which different technologies imply different public choice appeal. Reflecting on weakest link technology, Sandler (2002, p. 98) argues that "it is an easy political sell to the rich country's constituency that foreign assistance to improve, say, the fight against infectious disease, provides safety at home." Jayaraman and Kanbur (1999) argue that if a donor country has both funds and a comparative advantage in providing a public good, assistance should be in kind rather than in cash. The political sell is easier if the electorate can be persuaded and if domestic producers have prospects of profitable contracts (through in-kind provision in recipient countries).

International cooperation is more attractive if implemented through regulation

Progress with international cooperation is more likely when taxation can be avoided and when domestic producers can be advantaged. In fact, finance arrangements differ systematically from those commended by neoclassical normative analysis, which prescribes taxation as a means of revenue generation or internalization of externalities. In contrast with this approach, the willingness to engage in international cooperation may be motivated by prospective gains for producer groups and so can be achieved through regulatory measures.

Consider the Basel Accord on the International Convergence of Capital Measures and Capital Standards of 1987. While Kapstein (1994) argues that it was designed to provide international financial stability as a public good, Oatley and Nabors (1998) argue that its design was premised on a political compromise. In response to financial problems created by debt in developing countries, the United States first proposed that additional resources be transferred to developing countries through the International Monetary Fund. Congress expressed concern about the tax implications (if society as a whole were to bear the risk of default), and political support atrophied.

The solution was an international agreement that changed the relative competitiveness of U.S., European, and Japanese banks and compensated U.S. banks for the cost of regulation. Oatley and Nabors (1998, pp. 42 and 44) argue that "international agreement on capital adequacy offered U.S. politicians a way to satisfy both demands; the voters would get regulations and commercial banks would be compensated by reducing the regulatory advantage enjoyed by foreign commercial banks." The Basel Accord "corresponds more to a rent seeking than to a market failure logic." It also corresponds to a regulatory solution to an international cooperation challenge.

More generally, public choice analysis predicts a predilection for regulation over taxation (even when less efficient) because regulatory costs are less visible (Buchanan and Tullock 1975). Prest (1985) refers to "implicit taxation" when regulation leads to higher prices for consumers. Researchers observe that international cooperation is frequently based on regulation (Kaul and Le Goulven 2003).

Richards (1999, p. 2) argues that "the fundamental commodity at stake in international regulation is the transfer of wealth, with constituents demanding regulation favorable to their interests and politicians supplying regulations designed to secure electoral success." He argues that the creation of the International Air Transport Association can be explained as a desire to restrain licensed aircraft travel and ensure prices on international flights sufficient to cross-subsidize domestic carriers. If costs must be borne at home, they are better borne less visibly and by those least likely to withdraw electoral support.

Commitment to international regulation depends on political constraints; politicians will not willingly relinquish low-cost options to accommodate lobby groups. A multilateral trade regime promoting free trade might be rationalized as a global public good (Mendoza 2003), but motivation is important. With reference to the General Agreement on Tariffs and Trade (GATT) Rowley (2001, p. 671) comments: "the conventional wisdom of international economics is that free trade [was] preserved and protected by the GATT.... The wisdom is misplaced. From the outset the GATT was always an instrument of managed rather than of free trade." The extent of trade liberalization through the GATT has been determined by the willingness to relinquish more visible forms of protection such as trade taxes. Politicians insist on retaining less visible, more informal instruments (thus, for example, voluntary export restraints were permissible under the GATT; Finger 1994).

International cooperation is more attractive if costs can be passed to citizens in other nations

The electoral risks of responding to pressure groups are mitigated if the costs can be passed on to citizens in other countries. In recent years commentators have remarked on the rapid growth of preferential regional trade agreements. Neoclassical trade theory presents a rationale in terms of resource allocation gains (trade creation) relative to losses (trade diversion). Public choice analysis explains motivation in terms of the implicit potential in this form of cooperation to satisfy political pressures. Exporters press for trade liberalization (Thorbecke 1997), and import-competing producers press for protection (Baldwin 1976). Both can be accommodated if preferential trade agreements pass costs on to citizens of nonmember states (Mansfield and Milner 1999).

Of course, there is even more harmony domestically if there is a moral defense for imposing costs abroad. Consider trade sanctions. Empirical studies demonstrate that "sanctions seldom achieve their goals" (van den Berg 2003, p. 242). One explanation is that politicians' primary concern is to deploy sanctions to restrain imports (rather than to best effect change in targeted regimes). Kaempfer and Lowenbourg (1988) refer to pressure by U.S. sugar producers for sanctions on imports of Cuban sugar and to lobbying by U.S. producers of steel and textiles for sanctions against South Africa.

In general, willingness to engage in international cooperation is greater if the design of cooperation accommodates domestic producers and electorates. Consider U.S. measures in 1990 to advance the international goal of protecting dolphins. The timing of this policy change can be explained in terms of the relocation of U.S. producers of canned tuna in the 1980s, which reduced their reliance on the supply of tuna from waters where tuna fishing was harmful to dolphins. It was now the case that both environmentalists and producers of canned tuna in the United States welcomed such international concern. European governments recognized the cost implications for their producers of canned tuna (Körber 1998).

International cooperation is more attractive if gains to domestic producers can be earmarked

If taxes are to be levied, there is greater incentive to earmark gains for domestic producers. While voters are reluctant to increase overseas aid, domestic producer groups are active advocates of tied aid (requiring recipient countries to purchase products or services from the donor country). The United Kingdom has experienced vigorous support for the government's Aid and Trade Provision (Burnell 1991; Morrisey, Smith, and Horesh 1992), offering concessional loans to developing countries to enable them to purchase British exports. Tied aid is inefficient because it reduces recipients' choices and leads to far higher procurement prices, with producers appropriating much of the subsidy.[6] Thus tied aid is attractive for earmarking gains for domestic producers (Jones 1996).

Similarly, an EU member state is more likely to support financial transfers to the EU budget if disbursement arrangements benefit its farmers. Historically, the main purpose of the EU budget has been to purchase "excess" supply to regulate available output (Bowles and Jones 1992). With ease of entry and exit, agricultural output is difficult to regulate by license. Such intervention can be interpreted as the provision of a regional public good (price stability for consumers), but again it is impossible to ignore the vested interests of farmers (Mueller 2003).

BUREAUCRATS IN INTERNATIONAL AGENCIES: AN EXAMPLE OF BUDGET-MAXIMIZING?

Attention has concentrated on individuals (rather than on countries as distinct entities). Similarly, public choice analysis of international agencies focuses on individuals' preferences rather than on the presumed interests of institutions.

In this context what effect might those employed in international agencies exert on funding? Niskanen (1971) argues that bureaucrats' emoluments depend on departmental budgets, creating an incentive to budget maximize. Politicians might be conscious of the demand for publicly provided services, but they are unfamiliar with the costs of supplying services. Niskanen (1971) predicts that bureaucrats take advantage of asymmetric information in requesting annual budgets greater than optimal from a taxpayer perspective.

This critique seems particularly apposite for international agencies. As the number of sponsors increases, there is less incentive for any one sponsor to monitor funding carefully. In an analysis of changes in staff numbers and funding at the International Monetary Fund (IMF), Vaubel (1994) argues that had budgets been premised on public interest, indicators of need for funding (as measured by the deflated reserve losses of current account deficits of low-reserve member states) would have proven statistically significant. Instead, Vaubel (1994) reports that the greater the quota share of the 10 member countries with the largest quotas, the lower the staff numbers at the IMF.

However, the proposition that bureaucrats always budget maximize is open to question. While Vaubel (1996, p. 195) argues that bureaucrats in international agencies "try to maximize their budget, their staff, and their independence," Frey (1997, p. 21) suggests that international bureaucrats pursue policies that "give them most prestige and influence." Willett (2001) argues that prestige is far more pertinent at the IMF (see also Banaian, Burdekin, and Willett 1995). Vaubel (1996) finds evidence of IMF hurry-up lending ahead of reviews of quota increases (an activity consistent with criticism that failure to spend makes it difficult to increase budgets), but Willet questions its significance. While Vaubel (1996) argues that staff growth was higher at the IMF than at the Bank for International Settlements, Willett (2001, p. 329) argues that it is "not clear a priori...whether any of these growth rates are too high or too low." A common criticism of the Leviathan school is that "excess" is difficult to gauge in the absence of a clear statement of optimal provision (Cullis and Jones 1998).

Moreover, are sponsors really so disinterested? Taxation is a politically costly option, and there is an incentive to divert international agencies' disbursement to substitute for direct spending by sponsors' own (national) departments. Finance is often substitutive, rather than additive. Frey and Schneider (1986) demonstrate that disbursement of aid by the World Bank was not motivated simply by recipient need but was targeted to countries that would otherwise have been assisted independently by the larger World Bank donor countries. Similarly, Perman, Ma, and McGilvray (1996, p. 317) note for the Global Environment Facility (GEF) that "funds are intended to be new, additional contributions. However, controversy has plagued the GEF from the outset in terms of the extent to which GEF funding has in fact been additional rather than a redirection of existing commitments."

The influence of bureaucrats cannot be ignored. Willett (2001, p. 322) concedes that Vaubel's critique might apply to the World Bank because as "[a]ll but the top World Bank officials are likely to have much less visibility," prestige may be less relevant than budget maximizing. However, its impact in terms of "excessive" funding can be questioned. With reluctance by leading sponsor countries to fulfill their financial obligations to international agencies (Chalmers 2001), it is far from obvious that finance is easily available.

LEARNING FROM PUBLIC CHOICE: BARRIERS AND OPPORTUNITIES IN ENHANCING THE FINANCING OF INTERNATIONAL COOPERATION

Public choice analysis reveals possible reasons for underfinancing international cooperation. Voters are preoccupied with the more immediate benefits of domestic programs, which appear less costly when supported by intergovernmental grants, and politicians have little incentive to correct such asymmetric fiscal illusion. Reliance on a simple-majority voting rule exacerbates this asymmetry. The degree of publicness of services proves important. Incentive structures in collective decisionmaking processes are such that the more private the service, the more popular. Again, the incentive is to focus on programs that deliver domestic services to voters. Such distortion is evident in analysis of voter turnout and of questionnaire responses. The degree to which such distortion is acute is reflected in the remarkably high rates of return that remain possible from further investment in international collaboration (Kaul and others 2003).[7]

Such analysis of perceptions and incentives adds weight to proposals already in the policy domain. Kaul and Le Goulven (2003, p. 337) would "enhance the public's and politicians' awareness of interdependence and of the need to cooperate." This policy recommendation can be justified in terms of efficiency (a "corrective" to fiscal illusion and collective choice bias).

Analysis of fiscal illusion highlights the importance of perceptions. Thus, for example, tax relief for private donations to international charities will be perceived quite differently from increased taxation to fund official charitable transfers.[8] Ferroni and Mody (2002) would place greater emphasis on leverage of private finance.

To be effective, policy must focus on individuals' perceptions and responses. An "implementation deficit" occurs in the European Union when policy directives are leveled at countries (Hassan 1999, p. 247). The response of individuals, in markets and political processes, is the important policy consideration.[9] This suggests that there is scope for policies that better inform voters and that mitigate distortion related to willingness to pay.

Turning to mode of finance, it is impossible to ignore the interplay between pressure from producer lobbies and electoral risk. Political momentum relies on prospective gains for domestic producers and ability to avoid explicit taxation. Growth of regional cooperation can be explained by pressure from producer groups and ability to shift the costs to individuals in nonmember states. When costs must be borne domestically, there is a predilection for regulation, for implicit rather than explicit taxation as the mode of finance. When explicit taxation cannot be avoided (for example, to regulate output), there is greater pressure to ensure that finance includes subsidies, or price support mechanisms, to earmark profitable opportunities for domestic producers. Export producers and civil groups (environmentalists, advocates of human rights and overseas aid; see Kaul and others 2003) might press for more liberal international collaboration. However, the interaction of different political pressures within collective decisionmaking processes is unlikely to ensure an efficient and equitable mode of finance.

Such analysis invites policy reappraisal of the design and mode of finance of a multitude of international agreements. It also highlights a policy distinction between explicit and implicit taxation. A country that appears to make generous monetary provision for overseas aid may in reality be acting far more parsimoniously if, for example, informal import restraints deny recipient countries access to its market. Focusing only on financial transfers is shortsighted. If contributions of different countries are considered and if policy reform is intended to alter incentives to cooperation, it is important to broaden policy analysis of the costs of international cooperation.[10]

While there is no room for complacency about the "supply side" influence of bureaucrats, it is easy to exaggerate its importance. Again, the interplay between the interests of different political actors is important. If there is pressure for finance from bureaucrats, there is resistance at the ballot box. There are incentives for vote-maximizing politicians to divert disbursements by international agencies, to substitute for expenditure by sponsor countries' government departments. Finance through international agencies is, in part, substitutive rather than additive.

Finally, the overarching conclusion is that both market failure and government failure are relevant when assessing supranational architecture.[11] For example, the design of mutual alliances such as the North Atlantic Treaty Organization has been criticized because member states' contributions are crowded out (Olson and Zeckhauser 1966), but crowding out can mitigate bureaucratic excesses if there is pressure to maximize budgets in defense departments (Jones 1992). A public choice perspective will give greater weight to design features that permit adjustment, competition, and (ultimately) exit (Buchanan 1990); each option permits a response to government failure.[12]

Normative analysis delivers a rationale to act; public choice analysis questions motivation. A public choice analysis yields the disturbing conclusions that finance for international cooperation appears less than adequate and that mode of finance appears less than efficient.

NOTES

1. With reference to a consumption gain from the act of expressing preference see Fiorina (1976) and Brennan and Lomasky (1993), and from performing a civic duty see Riker and Ordeshook (1968).

2. For example, Downs (1957) suggests that "party signal" (position on a left wing–right wing spectrum) provides low-cost information of the policy position of affiliated political candidates (for empirical analysis see Jones and Hudson 2000).

3. See www.pipa.org/OnlineReports/BFW/finding1.html.

4. Stigler (1970) attributes the law to Aaron Director; the middle-income cohort will be wooed by the poor to support redistribution and by the rich to resist.

5. As an example of informal coordination consider the reaction to standardization (in the case of fitting catalytic converters to automobiles in the United States). This might have served as a measure of import restraint for U.S. producers, but economies of scale and network externalities created incentives to foreign producers to supply the same environmental design to models in home markets as for exports to the United States (Barrett 2003).

6. Jepma (1991) suggests that tied-aid prices are some 10–15 percent higher than competitive world prices. Hayter and Watson (1985, pp. 15–16) go further, calculating that the price of goods financed by aid exceeds world market prices by an average of 25–30 percent. They argue that "such price disadvantages may cancel out the advantages of concessional terms, when the aid is in the form of a loan or a grant associated with export credits."

7. While undersupply of public goods is also predicted by a nation state rational actor model (see, for example, Olson and Zeckhauser 1966), behavior is better explained by public choice analysis. "Whether states are able to play tit-for-tat, employ side payments, or use force depends very much on domestic factors. Strategies may be suggested by a state's structural position but the nature of its political system, bureaucratic politics, the influence of special interests, and public opinion may ultimately determine which strategies states can pursue internationally" (Milner 1992, p. 493).

8. For a survey of evidence on the relationship between tax framing and tax evasion, see Hasseldine (1999).

9. Policy response relies on the impact of changes on consumers, producers, taxpayers, voters, lobbyists, and bureaucrats. For example, Barrett (2003) explains the

greater effectiveness of the Montreal Protocol over the Kyoto Protocol in terms of the fears of producers that they will risk loss of exports.

10. For example, countries that offer preferential access to imports from developing countries may be imposing an implicit tax on consumers that is as relevant as direct taxation that finances international transfers to developing countries.

11. For example, rent-seeking activity is regarded as wasteful (resources are dissipated to win transfers), but rent-seeking can provide some redress if market failure causes undersupply (Lee 1990; Jones 1999).

12. There are signs of awareness of government failure, but are they sufficient and evenhanded? For example, it is argued that international aid should be conditional on good governance by recipient countries (Burnside and Dollar 2000), but what of good governance in terms of design of international cooperation between donor countries?

References

Aldrich, John. 1993. "Rational Choice and Turnout." *American Journal of Political Science* 37 (1): 246–78.

Bailey, Stephen. J., and Stephen Connolly. 1995. "The Flypaper Effect: Identifying Areas for Further Research." *Public Choice* 95 (3–4): 335–61.

Baldwin, Robert E. 1976. "The Political Economy of Postwar U.S. Trade Policy." *Bulletin.* New York University, Graduate School of Business Administration, New York.

Banaian, King, Richard C. K. Burdekin, and Thomas D. Willett. 1995. "On the Political Economy of Central Bank Independence." In Kevin D. Hoover and Steven M. Sheffrin, eds., *Monetarism and the Methodology of Economics: Essays in Honour of Thomas Mayer.* Brookfield, Vt.: Edward Elgar.

Barrett, Scott. 2003. "Creating Incentives for Co-operation: Strategic Choices." In Inge Kaul, Pedro Conceição, Katell Le Goulven, and Ronald U. Mendoza, eds., *Global Public Goods: Managing Globalization.* New York: Oxford University Press.

Bentley, Arthur. 1908. *The Process of Government.* Evanston Ill.: Principia Press.

Bowles, Roger, and Philip Jones. 1992. "Equity and the EC Budget: A Pooled Cross-Section Time Series Analysis." *European Journal of Social Policy* 2 (2): 87–106.

Brennan, Geoffrey, and Loren Lomasky. 1993. *Democracy and Decision: The Pure Theory of Electoral Preference.* Cambridge: Cambridge University Press.

Buchanan, James M. 1968. *The Demand and Supply of Public Goods.* Chicago, Ill.: Rand McNally.

———. 1990. "Europe's Constitutional Opportunity." In James M. Buchanan, Karl O. Pöhl, Victoria C. Price, and Frank Vibert, eds., *Europe's Constitutional Future.* London: Institute of Economic Affairs.

Buchanan, James M., and Gordon Tullock. 1975. "Polluters' Profits and Political Response: Direct Controls versus Taxes." *American Economic Review* 65 (1): 139–47.

Burnell, Peter. 1991. *Charity, Politics and the Third World.* London: Harvester Wheatsheaf.

Burnside, Craig, and David Dollar. 2000. "Aid Policies and Growth." *American Economic Review* 90 (4): 847–68.

Chalmers, Malcolm. 2001. "The Atlantic Burden Sharing Debate—Widening or Fragmenting." *International Affairs* 77 (3): 569–85.

Cullis, John G., and Philip R. Jones. 1998. *Public Finance and Public Choice.* 2nd edition. Oxford: Oxford University Press.

de Tocqueville, Alexis. [1835] 2002. *Democracy in America.* Reprint. Chicago, Ill.: Chicago University Press.

Dixon, Anna, Julian Le Grand, John Henderson, Richard Murray, and Emmi Poteliakhoff. 2003. *Is the NHS Equitable? A Review of Evidence.* Health and Social Care Discussion Paper 11. London School of Economics.

Downs, Anthony. 1957. *An Economic Theory of Democracy.* New York: Harper and Row.

———. 1960. "Why the Government Is 'Too Small' in a Democracy." *World Politics* 12 (4): 541–63.

Drehr, Axel, and Roland Vaubel. 2001. "Does the IMF Cause Moral Hazard and Political Business Cycles? Evidence from Panel Data." Working Paper 598-01. University of Mannheim, Institut für Volkswirtschaftslehre und Statistik, Germany.

Ferroni, Marco, and Ashoka Mody. 2002. "Global Incentives for International Public Goods: Introduction and Overview." In Marco Ferroni and Ashoka Mody, eds., *International Public Goods: Incentives Measuring and Financing.* Dordrecht, the Netherlands: Kluwer Publishers.

Finger, J. Michael. 1994. "The GATT As an International Discipline Over Trade Restrictions: A Public Choice Approach." In Roland Vaubel and Thomas D. Willett, eds., *The Political Economy of International Organization: A Public Choice Approach.* Boulder, Colo.: Westview.

Fiorina, Morris P. 1976. "The Voting Decision: Instrumental and Expressive Aspects." *Journal of Politics* 38 (2): 390–415.

Frey, Bruno S. 1984. *International Political Economics.* Oxford: Basil Blackwell.

———. 1997. "The Public Choice of International Organizations." In Dennis C. Mueller, ed., *Perspectives on Public Choice: A Handbook.* Cambridge: Cambridge University Press.

Frey, Bruno S., and Friedrich Schneider. 1986. "Competing Models of International Lending Activity." *Journal of Development Economics* 20 (2): 225–45.

Galbraith, John K. 1962. *The Affluent Society.* Harmondsworth, UK: Penguin.

Gemmell, Norman, Oliver Morrissey, and Abuzer Pinar. 2004. "Tax Perceptions and Preferences over Tax Structures in the United Kingdom." *Economic Journal* 114 (493): F117–F138.

Griffith-Jones, Stephany. 2003. "International Financial Stability and Market Efficiency as a Global Public Good." In Inge Kaul, Pedro Conceição, Kattell Le Goulven, and Ronald U. Mendoza, eds., *Global Public Goods: Managing Globalization.* New York: Oxford University Press.

Hardin, Garrett. 1968. "The Tragedy of the Commons." *Science* 162 (3859): 1243–48.

Hassan, John. 1999. "Environmental Policy." In Frank MacDonald and Stephen Dearden, eds., *European Economic Integration.* 3rd edition. Harlow, UK: Longman.

Hasseldine, John. 1999. "Prospect Theory and Tax Reporting Decisions: Implication for Administrators." *Bulletin for Fiscal International Documentation* 52 (11): 501–05.

Hayter, Teresa, and Catherine Watson. 1985. *Aid Rhetoric and Reality.* London: Pluto Press.

Heal, Geoffrey. 1999. "New Strategies for the Provision of Global Public Goods: Learning from International Environmental Challenges." In Inge Kaul, Isabelle Grunberg, and Marc. A. Stern, eds., *Global Public Goods International Cooperation in the 21st Century.* New York: Oxford University Press.

Hewitt, Daniel. 1986. "Fiscal Illusion from Grants and the Level of State and Federal Expenditures." *National Tax Journal* 39 (4): 471–83.

Hills, John. 2002. "Following or Leading Public Opinion: Social Security Policy and Attitudes since 1997." *Fiscal Studies* 23 (4): 539–58.

Hyman, David. 2002. *Public Finance: A Contemporary Application of Theory to Policy.* 7th edition. Fort Worth, Tex.: Harcourt.

Jayaraman, Rajshri, and Ravi Kanbur. 1999. "International Public Goods and the Case for Foreign Aid." In Inge Kaul, Isabelle Grunberg, and Marc A. Stern, eds., *Global Public Goods International Cooperation in the 21st Century.* New York: Oxford University Press.

Jepma, Caterinus. 1991. *The Tying of Aid.* Paris: Organisation for Economic Co-operation and Development.

Jones, Philip. 1992. "International Alliances and the Economics of Bureaucracy." *Defence Economics* 3 (2): 127–33.

———. 1993. "Preferences for Private Goods: A Public Choice Critique of the Political Process." *Political Studies* 29 (3): 492–505.

———. 1996. "Rents from In-kind Subsidy: 'Charity' in the Public Sector." *Public Choice* 86 (3–4): 359–87.

———. 1999. "Rent Seeking and Defence Expenditure." *Defence and Peace Economics* 10 (2): 117–224.

Jones, Philip, and John Hudson. 2000. "Civic Duty and Expressive Voting: Is Virtue Its Own Reward?" *Kyklos* 53 (1): 3–16.

Kaempfer, William H., and Anton D. Lowenbourg. 1988. "The Theory of International Economic Sanctions: A Public Choice Approach." *American Economic Review* 78 (4): 786–93.

Kapstein, Ethan. 1994. *Governing the Global Economy: International Finance and the State.* Cambridge, Mass: Harvard University Press.

Kaul, Inge, and Kattell Le Goulven. 2003. "Financing Public Goods: A New Frontier of Public Finance." In Inge Kaul, Pedro Conceição, Kattell Le Goulven, and Ronald U. Mendoza, eds., *Global Public Goods: Managing Globalization.* New York: Oxford University Press.

Kaul, Inge, Pedro Conceição, Kattell Le Goulven, and Ronald U. Mendoza, eds. 2003. *Global Public Goods: Managing Globalization.* New York: Oxford University Press.

Kemp, Simon, and Christopher D. Burt. 2001. "Estimation of the Value and Cost of Government and Market Supplied Goods." *Public Choice* 107 (3–4): 235–52.

Körber, Achim. 1998. "Why Everybody Loves Flipper: The Political Economy of the U.S. Dolphin Safe Laws." *European Journal of Political Economy* 14 (3): 475–509.

Lee, Dwight L. 1990. "The Politics and Pitfalls of Reducing Waste in the Military." *Defence Economics* 1 (2): 129–139.

Le Grand, Julian. 1982. *The Strategy of Equality.* London: Allen and Unwin.

Lord, Christopher. 1998. *Democracy in the European Union.* Sheffield, UK: Sheffield Academic Press.

Mansfield, Edward D., and Helen V. Milner. 1999. "The New Wave of Regionalism." *International Organization* 53 (3): 589–627.

Martin, Lisa L. 1999. "The Political Economy of International Co-operation." In Inge Kaul, Isabelle Grunberg, and Marc A. Stern, eds., *Global Public Goods: International Cooperation in the 21st Century.* New York: Oxford University Press.

Mendoza, Ronald U. 2003. "The Multilateral Trade Regime: A Public Good for All?" In Inge Kaul, Pedro Conceição, Kattell Le Goulven, and Ronald U. Mendoza, eds., *Global Public Goods: Managing Globalization.* New York: Oxford University Press.

Milner, Helen. 1992. "International Theories of Co-operation among Nations: A Review Essay." *World Politics* 44 (3): 466–96.

Morrisey, Oliver, Brian Smith, and Edward Horesh. 1992. *British Aid and International Trade.* Buckingham, UK: Open University Press.

Mueller, Dennis. 2003. *Public Choice III.* Cambridge: Cambridge University Press.

Musgrave, Richard A. 1957. *The Theory of Public Finance.* New York: McGraw Hill.

———. 1981. "Leviathan Cometh—Or Does He?" In Helen Ladd and Nicholas Tideman, eds., *Tax and Expenditure Limitations.* Washington, D.C.: Urban Institute.

Niskanen, William A. 1971. *Bureaucracy and Representative Government.* Chicago, Ill.: Aldine.

Oately, Thomas, and Robert Nabors. 1998. "Redistributive Cooperation: Market Failure, Wealth Transfers, and the Basle Accord." *International Organization* 52 (1): 35–54.

Oates, Wallace E. 1979. "Lump Sum Intergovernmental Grants Have Price Effects." In Peter Mieszkowski and William H. Oakland, eds., *Fiscal Federalism and Grants in Aid.* Washington, D.C.: Urban Institute.

———. 1988. "On the Nature and Measurement of Fiscal Illusion: A Survey." In Geoffrey Brennan, Bhajan. S. Grewal, and Peter Groenwegan, eds., *Taxation and Fiscal Federalism: Essays in Honour of Russel Matthews.* Rushcutters Bay, Australia: Australian National Press.

Olson, Mancur Jr. 1965. *The Logic of Collective Action.* Cambridge, Mass.: Harvard University Press.

Olson, Mancur Jr., and Richard Zeckhauser. 1966. "An Economic Theory of Alliances." *Review of Economics and Statistics* 48 (3): 266–79.

Peltzman, Sam. 1976. "Towards a More General Theory of Regulation." *Journal of Law and Economics* 19: 211–40.

Perman, Roger, Yue Ma, and James McGilvray. 1996. *Natural Resource and Environmental Economics.* London: Longman.

Prest, Alan R. 1985. "Implicit Taxes." *Royal Bank of Scotland Review* 147 (September): 10–26.

Richards, John E. 1999. "Towards a Positive Theory of International Institutions: Regulating International Aviation Markets." *International Organization* 53 (3): 1–37.

Riker, William H., and Peter C. Ordeshook. 1968. "A Theory of the Calculus of Voting." *American Political Science Review* 62 (1): 25–42.

Rodrik, Dani. 1997. *Has Globalization Gone Too Far?* Washington, D.C.: Institute for International Economics.

Romer, Thomas, and Howard Rosenthal. 1980. "An Institutional Theory of the Effect of Intergovernmental Grants." *National Tax Journal* 33 (December): 451–58.

Rosen, Harvey S. 2002. *Public Finance.* 6th edition. New York: McGraw Hill.

Rowley, Charles K. 2001. "The International Economy in Public Choice Perspective." In William Shughgart II and Laura Razzolini, eds., *The Elgar Companion to Public Choice.* Cheltenham, UK: Edward Elgar Publishing.

Sandler, Todd. 1998. "Global and Regional Public Goods: A Prognosis for Collective Action." *Fiscal Studies* 19 (3): 221–47.

———. 2002. "Financing International Public Goods." In Marco Ferroni and Ashoka Mody, eds., *International Public Goods: Incentives Measuring and Financing.* Dordrecht, the Netherlands: Kluwer Publishers.

Snidal, Duncan. 2002. "Rational Choice and International Relations." In Walter Carlsnaes, Thomas Risse, and Beth A. Simmons, eds., *Handbook of International*

Relations. London: Sage.

Stigler, George. 1970. "Director's Law of Public Income Redistribution." *Journal of Law and Economics* 13 (1): 1–10.

Stiglitz, Joseph. 2002. "Globalization and the Logic of International Collective Action: Re-examining the Bretton Woods Institutions." In Deepak Nayyar, ed., *Governing Globalization: Issues and Institutions.* New York: Oxford University Press.

Taylor-Gooby, Peter, and Charlotte Hastie. 2002. "Support for State Spending: Has New Labour Got It Right?" In Alison Park, John Curtice, Katarina Thomson, Lindsay Jarvis, and Catherine Bromley, eds., *British Social Attitudes: The 19th Report.* London: Sage.

Thorbecke, Willem. 1997. "Explaining House Voting on the North American Free Trade Agreement." *Public Choice* 92 (3–4): 231–42.

Tullock, Gordon. 1959. "Some Problems of Majority Voting." *Journal of Political Economy* 67(6): 571–79.

————. 1967. "The Welfare Costs of Tariffs, Monopolies, and Theft." *Western Economic Journal* 5 (3): 224–32.

Van den Berg, Hendrik. 2003. *International Economics.* Boston, Mass.: McGraw Hill.

Vaubel, Roland. 1986. "A Public Choice View of International Organisation." *Public Choice* 51 (1): 39–57.

————. 1994. "The Political Economy of the International Monetary Fund: A Public Choice Analysis." In Roland Vaubel and Thomas D. Willett, eds., *The Political Economy of International Organization: A Public Choice Approach.* Boulder, Colo.: Westview.

————. 1996. "Bureaucracy at the IMF and the World Bank: A Comparison of the Evidence." *World Economy* 19 (2): 195–210.

Willett, Thomas, D. 2001. "Upping the Ante for Political Economy: Analysis of International Financial Institutions." *World Economy* 24 (3): 317–32.

Wyploz, Charles. 1999. "International Financial Instability." In Inge Kaul, Isabelle Grunberg, and Marc A. Stern, eds., *Global Public Goods: International Cooperation in the 21st Century.* New York: Oxford University Press.

3

THE NEW INTERNATIONAL PUBLIC FINANCE

INVESTING IN GLOBAL PUBLIC GOODS

PROVISION ABROAD

IDENTIFYING HIGH-RETURN INVESTMENTS
A METHODOLOGY FOR ASSESSING WHEN INTERNATIONAL COOPERATION PAYS—
AND FOR WHOM
Pedro Conceição and Ronald U. Mendoza

•

MAKING INTERNATIONAL COOPERATION PAY
FINANCING AS A STRATEGIC INCENTIVE
Scott Barrett

•

COMPENSATING COUNTRIES FOR THE PROVISION OF GLOBAL PUBLIC SERVICES
THE TOOL OF INCREMENTAL COSTS
Kenneth King

CREATING NEW MARKETS
THE CHICAGO CLIMATE EXCHANGE
Richard L. Sandor

•

USING MARKETS MORE EFFECTIVELY
DEVELOPING COUNTRY ACCESS TO COMMODITY FUTURES MARKETS
C. Wyn Morgan

•

ASSESSING CONTRACTUAL AND STATUTORY APPROACHES
POLICY PROPOSALS FOR RESTRUCTURING UNSUSTAINABLE SOVEREIGN DEBT
Barry Eichengreen

•

PLACING THE EMPHASIS ON REGULATION
LESSONS FROM PUBLIC FINANCE IN THE EUROPEAN UNION
Brigid Laffan

IDENTIFYING HIGH-RETURN INVESTMENTS

INVESTMENTS

A METHODOLOGY FOR ASSESSING WHEN INTERNATIONAL COOPERATION PAYS—AND FOR WHOM

PEDRO CONCEIÇÃO AND RONALD U. MENDOZA

Every day, the media report on global challenges that inflict huge losses on the world. For example, the tsunami catastrophe that struck Asia and Africa in December 2004 claimed more than 200,000 lives, devastating wide stretches of land and destroying local economies. Its effects might have been less severe had an early-warning system been in place—at an investment cost of just $20 million to install.[1]

The outbreak of severe acute respiratory syndrome (SARS) in 2002 has cost the world as much as $140 billion—this, despite the disease having been contained relatively quickly (WHO 2004, p. 2). The threat of terrorist attacks imposes annual costs of about $75 billion in increased trade friction alone (Walkenhorst and Dihel 2002, table 1, p. 16). Computer hacking adds another $200 billion a year in productivity losses, forgone business opportunities, and higher insurance premiums.[2] Counterfeiting costs the world an additional $450 billion annually,[3] and corrupt transactions—which undermine economic efficiency and productive investments—cost yet another $1 trillion a year (World Bank 2004). Continuing inaction on international trade reforms imposes an estimated global opportunity cost of up to $300 billion a year, as is shown later in the chapter. The list of global costs goes on and on.

Why, despite the high costs, are more decisive corrective actions not taken? Many factors come into play. Sometimes, one crisis follows on the heels of another, shifting world attention. Other times, the technology for an effective policy response may not be available—such as an effective vaccine.

But in many instances a key delaying factor is that different actor groups have different consumption preferences. Addressing global challenges often involves cross-border international cooperation—concerted provision of global public goods, such as control of communicable diseases or corruption. Effective international cooperation depends largely on countries agreeing to join forces and to make financial resources available as necessary. If preferences vary substantially—which they tend to do in a world of wide socioeconomic disparities and geographic and cultural diversity—consensus is often difficult to achieve on which global public goods to provide, in what quantity, and at what net benefit to whom. This is especially so when detailed empirically founded information on the distribution of net benefits of corrective action is not easily available, if at all.

Improving the availability of information on what the world stands to gain from taking specific corrective actions—and how the gains would be distributed—would be a step toward reducing the risk of global crises and the accompanying loss of global welfare. This information could also shed light on the scope for achieving win-win situations, including transfers from winners to losers so that in the end all parties would derive significant and fair net benefits from international cooperation.

This chapter suggests the beginnings of a methodology for such assessments. The objective is to identify potentially high-return investments in global public goods and to show how the gains would be distributed across major actor groups, notably different groups of countries.

UNDERSTANDING ADEQUATE PROVISION OF GLOBAL PUBLIC GOODS

Key to identifying high-return investments in global public goods is a clear understanding of when provision is adequate. Clear adequacy criteria can help determine the type and magnitude of the corrective action required. This section first sets out the types of provision problems that plague public goods, including global public goods, and then offers an operational—pragmatic and practical—approach to determining full provision.

Establishing a taxonomy of provision problems

Public goods are goods or services in the public domain that can—and often even must—be consumed by all (Kaul and Mendoza 2003). This "publicness" often leads to problems of provision. Economic theory identifies public goods as a potential case of market failure. From the individual actor's viewpoint it appears rational not to reveal true preferences for the good and to enjoy it free of charge by letting others step forward and provide the good.[4] The resulting underprovision of the public good can take several forms. From Conceição (2003), three main types of provision problems can be distinguished: underuse on the consumption side and underprovision and overprovision on the supply side (figure 1).

Underuse. Underuse means that a global public good exists but that some actors cannot consume it, either in full or in part. Some global public goods are underused because of access problems or because the nature of these goods' production makes consumption difficult or impossible. Access problems may result from a lack of

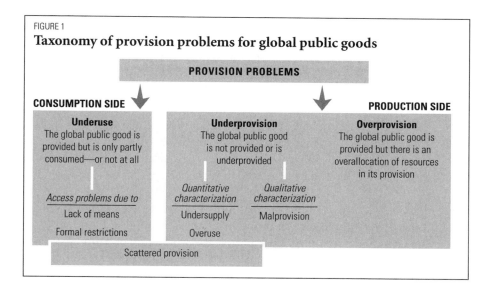

FIGURE 1

Taxonomy of provision problems for global public goods

(often private) means needed to consume a good (such as a computer to access the Internet) or from formal restrictions (such as patents that limit access to pharmaceutical technology).

Underprovision. Underprovision means that a good does not exist or is not fully or adequately provided, for any of several reasons:

- *Undersupply,* which results when a good is not provided or is only partially provided. This shortfall can be characterized quantitatively. For example, if some—but not all—countries ensure airport security, the public good may not exist as a global public good (see the chapter by Sandler in this volume). If a disease surveillance system covers only 100 countries, the public good exists in an incomplete way.

- *Malprovision,* which results in distorted provision, thus generating benefits (or costs) that are systematically biased against groups of countries or people. The characterization of malprovision is predominantly qualitative. For example, the multilateral trade regime systematically benefits industrial countries far more than it does developing countries. The provision problem is not a matter of access, as with underused global public goods, or (or not only) a matter of undersupply. Rather, some countries derive considerable utility from consuming the good and others derive very little utility or even incur net costs. Thus, the provision problem has to be solved on the supply side: it calls for redesigning and reshaping the good.

- *Overuse or destruction,* which results from excessive use of goods such as the global natural commons. For example, climate stability is an underprovided global public good because the global atmosphere is overused as an outlet for pollution.

When provision of a global public good is scattered, the outcome may be both underuse and underprovision. As noted, underuse can result from the way in which a good is produced. For example, the global stock of knowledge—including practical and other unprotected knowledge—is often so scattered that consuming it is difficult or impossible. Thus the good exists, but in an inadequately packaged form. Supply is incomplete, and extra steps may be needed to make the good accessible. For example, noncommercial knowledge about how to undertake effective policy reform may have to be systematically collected, analyzed, categorized, and referenced so that interested users can locate and benefit from it. New knowledge may have to be produced to make scattered knowledge useful.

Overprovision. Overprovision means that more resources are allocated to a public good than are required for full provision. A clear example is a nuclear arms race. From an individual country's perspective the production of national defense could be realized through an international agreement to ban nuclear arms or, failing that, by the provision of a nuclear counterstrike capability as a deterrent to nuclear attack. However, from a global perspective national defense is overprovided if countries enter into an arms race, with overprovision resulting in a global public bad—the increased global risk of nuclear war. As with underprovision, collective action is often required to correct overprovision.[5]

Table 1 lists examples of global public goods and the main provision problem that affects each good.

Determining full provision

Underlying this taxonomy of provision problems is, of course, a notion of "full provision." But when is a public good considered fully provided?

Paul Samuelson employed the criterion of Pareto optimality in his pathbreaking contributions of 1954 and 1955. He showed that optimality is achieved in the provision of public goods when the sum of the marginal willingness to pay for the public good of all concerned actors equals the marginal cost of the good's provision.[6] But how to make this criterion operational?

If the public good under consideration is, say, a local school, policymakers may be able to determine a community's willingness to pay through referendums or town meetings. Trying to ascertain this information worldwide for a global public good, such as ensuring international financial stability or preserving climate stability, is another matter. Global public opinion polls might seem to be an answer. But the literature on contingent valuation shows that although survey-based approaches can generate important insights, they are hard to implement.[7] Moreover, preferences are difficult to identify and difficult, if not impossible, to aggregate. In addition, people may express preferences without having full information—a particular risk for global public goods, which are often complex and hard to understand.

TABLE 1

Global public goods and their main provision problems

Global public good	Main provision problem
Climate stability	Underprovision (overuse)[a]
Global communications network and the Internet	Underuse (access problems)[b]
International financial stability	Underprovision (undersupply)[b]
Multilateral trade regime	Underprovision (malprovision)[a]
Peace and security	Underprovision (undersupply)[b]
Polio eradication	Underprovision (undersupply)[a]
Smallpox eradication	Underprovision (undersupply)[a, c]

a. See appendix for full assessment.
b. See Conceição (2003) for full assessment.
c. Before the eradication of smallpox.

Are there criteria other than optimality that could more easily be made operational and guide public policymaking, including international negotiations? Instead of people's preferences for a good, the focus could be on the physical or technical properties of the good itself. These properties are usually easier to observe and measure. One approach would be to determine innate physical or technical characteristics of full provision for each public good.[8] From this perspective, public goods consist of two main types: binary goods and moving-target goods.

- *Binary goods* have properties that enable the unambiguous determination of whether the goods are fully provided or not. They either exist at a full provision level or they do not. Consider the public good of disease eradication. For example, smallpox is either eradicated (100 percent provided) or not eradicated (not provided).
- *Moving-target goods* are goods whose provision level could always be enhanced. For example, the global public goods of international financial stability and climate stability do not have a unique target for full provision. Provision could always be enhanced, depending on improvements in the world's knowledge of these challenges and in the technologies used to address them.

For the technical approach to determining full provision that is suggested in this chapter, binary goods are a clear-cut case. But what could be an objective measure of full provision for moving-target public goods? There are at least two ways to proceed: to use already politically agreed on goals as benchmarks or to rely on expert opinions about feasible levels and benchmarks of full provision.

For many global public goods society has already established some desirable goals through political processes. Consider the case of preventing climate change. Through the United Nations Framework Convention on Climate Change the international community has identified as a target level of provision the reduction in carbon dioxide emissions by an average of 5 percent below 1990 levels by 2008–12.[9] Or consider the case of Millennium Development Goal 1, which aims to reduce hunger and poverty levels by half by 2015. "Excessive" poverty generates many cross-border externalities, from global health risks to psychological externalities, illegal migration pressures, and risks to peace and security prompting moral and ethical concerns. So, excessive poverty has global public bad dimensions. Thus, Millennium Development Goal 1 establishes a target for provision that can be used for the type of assessment discussed in this chapter. Many international conferences have contributed to this type of goal setting.

Where such targets do not yet exist, experts can be called on to suggest benchmark figures. For example, experts could advise on how the duration of patent protection influences innovation and productivity. This type of information could help establish benchmarks for an international intellectual property rights regime that seeks to attain two—possibly conflicting—policy objectives. One objective is to maximize the dynamic benefits from new inventions by providing innovators with the incentive of monopoly use of their innovation for a specified time. The other objective is to maximize static benefits from the more widespread consumption of an existing invention by allowing its wider adoption by manufacturers. Full provision could thus be identified as a regime that balances these two goals. Expert opinions on the form of the regime that strikes the most desirable (and feasible) balance would then need to draw on empirical evidence (see, for example, Lerner 2002 and Maskus 2000).

Even for knowledge—the quintessential moving-target good—experts could help identify next frontiers and milestones. Sending a mission to Titan, one of Saturn's moons, is such a milestone.[10] This type of observable, next-step goal can be assigned to moving-target public goods, making the determination of their full provision similar to that of binary goods.

These two approaches—using political goals and relying on expert opinion—are not mutually exclusive. Political goal setting often draws on expert opinions, and expert opinions shape views about what constitutes politically desirable objectives (Parson 2003).[11]

This discussion leads to the following proposed definition of full provision that would meet the criterion set of being focused on objective and easy to observe properties of the public good itself:

Definition: Full provision is the level from which no further enhancements are feasible, given the good's innate or defined (physical) properties and the current state of knowledge and technology.

How does this definition of full provision differ from the notion of optimal provision in the Samuelson tradition? Studies that use Samuelson's optimal provision as an adequacy criterion typically focus on whether the resources allo-cated to a good align with the public's marginal willingness to pay (see Cornes and Sandler 1996). By contrast, the approach suggested here places the good itself at the center of the analysis, thus making it possible to set an objective benchmark or target for full provision.

Full provision is not necessarily equivalent to optimal provision (the provision level for which marginal cost equals marginal benefit). But that does not imply that society should not try to achieve full provision based on the technical criterion. Aggregate net benefits—that is, the social rate of return on an investment—may still be positive. As noted earlier, a discrepancy between optimal and full provision could arise because of information problems, for example.

Thus, for both binary and moving-target types of public goods, each incre-mental contribution to enhanced provision ought to be justified in terms of the aggregate net benefits it would yield. Various assessments of costs and benefits can show society the potential gains, with varying degrees of certainty. These types of assessments cannot resolve all uncertainties and eliminate all challenges of risk taking, however. Policymakers will still have to make choices. The methodology developed here merely provides a better information base for decisionmaking.

ASSESSING THE POTENTIAL GLOBAL NET BENEFITS OF INVESTING IN GLOBAL PUBLIC GOODS

Armed with a taxonomy of the provision problems that might need to be cor-rected and a criterion for determining full provision, it is now possible to deter-mine the net benefits of enhancing the provision of global public goods. The discussion begins with global net benefits, leaving to the next section the question of why and how to make the global assessment distribution sensitive. A five-step framework is recommended for assessing net benefits.

Step 1: characterize current provision
The first step is to set an objective benchmark for full provision and to compare current provision with this benchmark. Consider eradicating a communicable disease. The technical criterion that defines its full provision is elimination of the infectious agent from nature, reflected in part in the absence of cases of the dis-ease. Eradication could thus be viewed in a binary way: it has either been achieved or not been achieved. The profile could nevertheless consider progress over time: if the world is 90 percent free of a certain infection (expressed as the reduction in the number of cases since the eradication program started), the shortfall from full provision is 10 percent.

Not all global public goods lend themselves to such simple percentage quan-tifications of provision status. Alternative benchmarks could be required. In the case of achieving climate stability, emissions of greenhouse gases in a particular year serve as the benchmark, with reductions in emission levels assessed against the benchmark level. In the case of the multilateral trade regime, enhancing trade facilitation based on some measure of the average global level of trade could serve as the benchmark, with trade facilitation assessed on the basis of bringing all countries currently under this average up to that level. Setting these targets for "full" provision defines in a very technical way what is required to move from current to full provision.

Step 2: establish the global costs (or benefits) of current provision
It is not always possible to assess the full costs of underprovision, but it is usually possible to estimate some of the costs. Extensive databases have been developed as a result of growth in global reporting initiatives and other influences.[12] To stay with the example of communicable disease control, the number of cases that correspond to the 10 percent shortfall from eradication can be translated into a burden measured by the years of healthy life or productive time lost to disability and early death. This burden can then be converted into economic costs.

Step 3: assess the global costs of corrective actions
The actions needed to improve the provision of a global public good—to the extent that they can be known—are associated with the good's production path. The data required to estimate the costs of these actions, and thus their resource implications, are available for very few global public goods, but estimates are possible for some.

Step 4: evaluate the global benefits of corrective action
The cost reductions (including opportunity cost reductions) derived in step 2 are one measure of benefits. For example, opening up to international trade could eliminate the opportunity costs of repressed markets (the nonrealized welfare gains). The benefits of controlling contagious diseases could be derived from eliminating the real costs that arise from underproviding this global public good.

Step 5: indicate the likely global net benefits of enhanced provision
Enhancing the provision of a global public good eliminates or substantially reduces the costs associated with its underprovision. Comparing the costs of corrective actions with the savings from eliminating those costs provides a rough estimate of direct net benefits. But enhancing the provision of a global public good often generates indirect benefits as well. For example, reducing the burden of a disease produces spillovers that range from enhancing people's ability to learn to improving participation and performance in the workforce—these changes generate substantial indirect social and economic benefits. In certain cases there are estimates of these broader, indirect benefits. However, in general, these indirect benefits remain largely unaccounted for.

Other studies

With some slight variations, the methodology just described has been applied in several studies.[13] For instance, Conceição (2003, p. 159) estimates the aggregate global net benefits from enhanced provision of several global public goods at some $2 trillion a year.[14]

The expert studies undertaken by the Copenhagen Consensus, a research initiative that examined various global crises, offer further examples.[15] Working from the belief that public dissemination of the results of academic studies enhances democratic decisionmaking, the Copenhagen Consensus asked: where should the world invest, say, $50 billion of extra resources during the next four years to do the most good? Where possible, the studies presented benefit–cost ratios of promising investment opportunities in key areas of international policy.[16] A group of eminent economists was then asked to rank the investment opportunities based on these benefit–cost ratios and other information from benefit–cost analyses. The objective was to achieve a final priority ranking of global projects to address global crises.

MAKING THE GLOBAL ASSESSMENT OF NET BENEFITS DISTRIBUTION SENSITIVE

Although measuring aggregate net benefits from the enhanced provision of specific global public goods is a useful first step, it is also important to assess the distribution of these gains across groups. The international relations literature suggests that international cooperation is facilitated when all actors perceive that the likely outcome provides them with significant and fair net benefits.

Noting earlier work by Nash (1950), Sen (2005, p. 6) explains that "in the presence of gains from cooperation, the central issue is not whether a particular arrangement is better for all than no cooperation (there are many such alternatives), but whether that was a fair division of the benefits." Thus, knowing that the outcome will be win-win may not be enough. The parties typically want to know what the bargain offers each party and how the gains of each party compare with those of the others. If the same party always gains a lot while others gain significantly less, global inequality could increase (see also Albin 2003 and Rao 1999).

How do differences in preferences affect the distribution of benefits? A country's net benefits from participation in an international cooperation initiative undoubtedly influence its preferences for global public goods and thus its decision to support a particular initiative. Although this is only one factor influencing preferences for private and public goods (others include climate, geography, level of income, and sociocultural traditions[17]), it is precisely because countries differ in such respects that the monetary gains from international cooperation often serve as a way of aligning their respective policy priorities. And that is why the distribution of the net benefits from participating in an international cooperation initiative is often so important to achieving consensus on global issues.

Net benefit calculus is clearly not equivalent to a full assessment of preferences, but it is a pragmatic and practical approach for reflecting what are likely to be diverse preferences for different global public goods. Identifying and aggregating individual preferences—often impossible or undesirably time-consuming—are replaced by measuring social net benefits (or costs) based on concrete factors linked to the provision of the good itself, such as lives saved (or extended), consumer or producer welfare gained, poverty reduced, and economic losses averted.

Each country could enter international negotiations knowing, at a minimum, the likely net benefits (or costs) that may result from a particular agreement. Industrial countries and developing countries with strong research and policy analysis capacity can readily undertake such studies. However, many developing countries lack the national capacity. It would thus be useful to prepare information about the distribution of net benefits across broad groups of countries, thus providing an approximate idea of what each group stands to gain or lose from a particular international cooperation effort.

To generate this information, the methodology outlined earlier in this chapter could be further refined—notably, steps 2, 3, 4, and 5 could be made more distribution sensitive. Each cost and benefit calculation would be broken down by major actor groups (box 1). The fineness of disaggregation will depend on the availability of data, but disaggregation between industrial and developing

---

Box 1

DESIGN OF A DISTRIBUTION-SENSITIVE GLOBAL PUBLIC GOODS ASSESSMENT

Step1:   Characterize current provision.

Step 2a: Establish the global costs of underprovision or underuse.

Step 2b: Identify the distribution of costs of underprovision or underuse.

Step 3a: Assess the global costs of corrective action.

Step 3b: Identify the distribution of costs of corrective action.

Step 4a: Evaluate the global benefits from corrective action.

Step 4b: Identify the distribution of benefits from corrective action.

Step 5a: Indicate the likely global net benefits of enhanced provision.

Step 5b: Identify the likely distribution of net benefits of enhanced provision.

countries would be a first step. If the countries in these two groups express fairly similar preferences for certain global public goods (many studies show that income is a key factor driving preferences), this disaggregation could prove informative. However, if preferences within these groups are highly divergent—as, for example, on various aspects of the multilateral trade regime (discussed in the next section)—further disaggregation is indispensable for more informed policy analysis—and perhaps more effective international cooperation.

APPLICATION OF A DISTRIBUTION-SENSITIVE ASSESSMENT METHODOLOGY TO SELECTED GLOBAL PUBLIC GOODS

The methodology suggested here was applied to four global public goods: the multilateral trade regime, smallpox eradication, polio eradication, and climate stability. (The appendix contains profiles of these assessments.)

Application to four global public goods

Table 2 presents estimates that illustrate how the assessment methodology could be applied and interpreted. The estimates (further detailed and sourced in appendix boxes 1–4) are by no means the final word on these issues, but they do illustrate the kinds of results that can be achieved with the methodology.[18] Examination of table 2 shows the following:

Multilateral trade regime. Enhancing provision of the multilateral trade regime could bring global net benefits of well over $5 trillion (in net present value terms in 2001 dollars). The benefits are fairly evenly distributed, at $2.9 trillion in welfare gains for industrial countries and $2.5 trillion for developing countries. Enhancements to the trade regime include not only changes in national trade policy but also improvements in infrastructure for trade facilitation.

However, the costs of corrective action could fall much more heavily on developing countries, which are expected to pay a one-time cost of about $23 billion and annual costs of $20 billion, while industrial countries incur only a one-time cost of about $6 billion. Thus, even though developing countries could benefit, they may not be able to pay for the costs of corrective action. The large potential benefits that could accrue to them—and to the world—from enhancing the provision status of the multilateral trade regime would therefore not be realized.

Smallpox eradication. Using as a point of reference interventions beginning in 1966, estimates of the global net benefit of smallpox eradication (a fully provided global public good) are $47 billion globally (in net present value terms in 1967 dollars), with developing countries gaining $35 billion and industrial countries gaining $12 billion. Developing countries gain more because the disease had already been eliminated in industrial countries when the eradication effort began.

TABLE 2

Summary of results from distribution-sensitive global public good assessments
(billions of U.S. dollars in net present value terms unless otherwise stated)

Step 1	Step 2		Step 3		Step 4		Step 5	
	Estimate costs (or benefits) of current provision[a]		Estimate costs of corrective action		Estimate benefits from enhanced provision		Calculate net benefits and costs of enhanced provision	
Identify full provision	*2a* *Overall*	*2b* *Disaggregated*	*3a* *Overall*	*3b* *Disaggregated*	*4a* *Overall*	*4b* *Disaggregated*	*5a* *Overall*	*5b* *Disaggregated*
Multilateral trade regime Tariff and subsidy reduction and trade facilitation (see appendix box A.1 for specific package of policy reforms) Base year: 2001 Discount rate: 5 percent	−$293 (annual)	• Developing countries: −$147 (annual) • Industrial countries: −$146 (annual)	$20 (annual) $29 (one time)	• Developing countries: $20 (annual) $23 (one time) • Industrial countries: $6 (one time)	$293 (annual)	• Developing countries: $147 (annual) • Industrial countries: $146 (annual)	$5,422	• Developing countries: $2,530 • Industrial countries: $2,892
Smallpox eradication[b] Complete (100 percent) eradication in the "wild" (see appendix box A.2) Base year: 1967 Discount rate: 3 percent	$1.42 (annual)	• Developing countries: $1.07 (annual) • Industrial countries: $0.35 (annual)	$0.30 (one time)	• Developing countries: $0.20 (one time) • Industrial countries: $0.10 (one time)	$1.42 (annual)	• Developing countries: $1.07 (annual) • Industrial countries: $0.35 (annual)	$47	• Developing countries: $35 • Industrial countries: $12

Polio eradication Complete (100 percent) eradication in the "wild" (see appendix box A.3) Base year: 2000 Discount rate: 5 percent	—	$67	• Developing countries: $24 • Industrial countries: $43	$128	• Developing countries: $13 • Industrial countries: $115	$61	• Developing countries: –$11 • Industrial countries: $72
Climate stability United Nations Framework Convention on Climate Change target reduction (see appendix box A.4 for a description of this target) Base year: 1990 Discount rate: 1.5 percent	—	$94,000	• Developing countries: $0 • Industrial countries: $94,000	$166,000	• Developing countries: $111,000 • Industrial countries: $55,000	$72,000	• Developing countries: $111,000 • Industrial countries: –$39,000

— is not available in the study used to complete steps 3 through 5. The appendix boxes provide estimates based on other studies.

a. Costs expressed in negative terms; benefits (when the good is fully provided) expressed in positive terms.

b. Smallpox eradication in the wild has been achieved, so the benefits of current provision are the same as that of enhanced provision.

Source: See appendix boxes A.1–A.4.

Industrial country gains are therefore limited to the savings from not having to vaccinate once the disease is eradicated.

Polio eradication. For polio eradication enhanced provision could bring global net benefits of more than $60 billion (in net present value terms in 2000 dollars). However, the benefits would likely be unevenly distributed: industrial countries experience a net benefit of $72 billion, and developing countries experience a net cost of about $11 billion. This uneven distribution does not mean that polio eradication would not be in the self-interest of developing countries, but only that within the assumptions of the study used to derive the estimates presented in table 2 it would be costly to developing countries, while industrial countries would achieve net savings. Polio eradication would still be a good global investment.

Climate stability. Global net benefits from enhanced provision of climate stability are estimated at $72 trillion (in net present value terms in 1990 dollars). Since all the costs associated with enhancing climate stability would fall on industrial countries, these countries would benefit from enhanced provision, but not enough to cover their costs. It is important to note that these results do not take into consideration which countries were the primary polluters up to the point of the hypothetical intervention, nor the historical costs and benefits that have accumulated as a result of that pollution.

What value added?
Table 2, together with the information in appendix boxes A.1–A.4 shows the importance of a distribution-sensitive analysis. It can help to identify high-return investments in global public goods from both global and country-specific viewpoints in three ways. It can establish the scope for possible Pareto-optimal transfers (compensation that changes win-lose situations to win-win outcomes). It can clarify fairness and equity considerations that may even apply in win-win situations. And it can be used to develop guideposts for selecting burden-sharing formulas in international cooperation.

Identifying high-return investments from global and country-specific perspectives. The global perspective helps flag possible global efficiency gains and thus directs the attention of the international community to potential investment opportunities for enhancing the provision of global public goods. This perspective can help to establish a list of global challenges that could potentially benefit from welfare-enhancing international cooperation and corrective action.

The list then needs to be refined by identifying which countries or groups of countries are most affected and stand to gain (or lose) the most from such cooperation. The disaggregated net benefit calculus shows that although global public goods usually affect everyone (they are public in consumption), they are not necessarily "good" for everyone (they are not necessarily public in utility). The assessments of the four global public goods in this chapter suggest high-return investments, promising global net gains in the billions and even trillions of dollars. But the results in table 2 also show how unevenly distributed these benefits could be.

Establishing the scope for Pareto-optimal transfers. A reallocation of resources that results from an international cooperation initiative would be a Pareto improvement if it made at least one party better off without making any other party worse off. So what should be done if some parties believe that they have been made worse off, even if only because they gained less than another party?

In that case redistributing some of the global gains from the winners to the losers could make the outcome truly welfare enhancing by making the public good public in both consumption and utility. One way to do this would be to facilitate a "fair" compensation of net losers. Without such Pareto transfers, it is unlikely that investments in global public goods that are not perceived as public in utility will find the needed political support. Such transfers could make both winners and losers better off in many cases, because without the transfers there might not be any cooperative venture. This is a pragmatic application of the Pareto decision rule, which—as many scholars note—requires compensation in many instances.[19] Thus, the distribution-sensitive assessment methodology developed here could also shed light on whether compensation is required to ensure fairness in international cooperation and what scope exists for redistribution from winners to losers.

Clarifying fairness and equity. Distribution-sensitive assessments of global public goods provision also can shed light on fairness and equity considerations, even when all parties stand to make net gains. Fairness would call for compensating any net losers. Equity might call for rebalancing gains that are skewed in favor of some countries over others.

To flesh out the information needed to make such a determination, the assessment could further disaggregate net benefits. For example, figure 2 draws on the same model of the multilateral trade regime used earlier to show the different welfare impacts on countries and regions of enhanced provision of the multilateral trade regime.

Two key pieces of information are of interest here. First, countries in Sub-Saharan Africa could experience a net yearly loss of $811 million as a result of the proposed multilateral trade measures because of the erosion of the trade preferences they already enjoy.[20] For the reasons explained earlier, compensation would be required to ensure a win-win outcome for all.

Second, the impact of the proposed multilateral trade measures is higher for many middle-income countries relative to the size of their economies. For example, countries that were part of the former Soviet Union have net gains (as a share of national income) roughly three times those of countries in the Central American and Caribbean region. Because enhanced provision of global public goods with skewed net benefits could exacerbate global inequity, it would be critical to analyze whether these goods are malprovided. In the current form of provision, do the global public goods generate benefits and costs that are systematically skewed in favor of some countries over others? Do they generate skewed benefits in their enhanced provision? Earlier research on the multilateral trade regime (see, for example, Mendoza 2003 and Bahadur and Mendoza 2002) found this global public good to be heavily malprovided; the evidence presented in figure 2 appears to support those studies.

What should be the response to such malprovision of global public goods? Economists have grappled with the issues of compensation and equity within the context of cost–benefit analyses. Some economists support using greater weights for net benefits to poor people (Drèze 1998; Stiglitz 2000). Others suggest con-

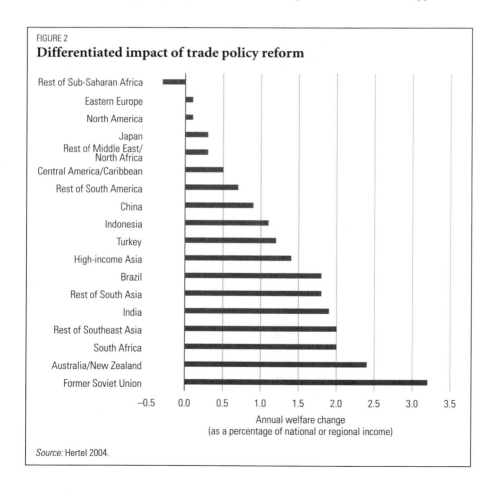

FIGURE 2

Differentiated impact of trade policy reform

Annual welfare change
(as a percentage of national or regional income)

Source: Hertel 2004.

ducting distribution-sensitive cost–benefit analyses and then incorporating mechanisms for transfers or compensation to those who lose (Cernea 2000, 2003). Although this point remains largely unsettled, the distribution-sensitive approach developed here is a pragmatic step that advances the discussion on the most appropriate assessment methodology and enriches international policy discussions of fairness and equity.[21]

Developing guideposts for international burden sharing. The assessment methodology presented here reveals that the burden- (or cost-) sharing principle in international cooperation can no longer be identified solely on the basis of who picks up the costs of corrective action. The parties who pay are usually referred to as "donors"—in most cases, industrial countries. Relying on this single dimension of "Who pays?" could suggest that the ability-to-pay principle almost always applies—that industrial countries, out of altruistic or equity considerations, always pay most (if not all) of the international cooperation bill. The assessment approach developed here exposes the weakness of this position in many cases. Net benefit seems to be a more appropriate measure for determining what burden-sharing principle applies—ability to pay or beneficiary pays.

In cases where industrial countries meet the investment costs and are also the primary beneficiaries, the burden formula would be beneficiary pays.[22] For example, industrial countries' share of the cost of corrective action for polio eradication is higher ($43 billion in 2000 dollars) than developing countries' share ($24 billion), which seems to suggest a burden-sharing arrangement based on ability to pay, with industrial countries paying more. However, a calculation of net benefits reveals that the global net benefits accrue to industrial countries ($72 billion), suggesting that a beneficiary-pays burden-sharing principle is actually in place. Developing countries could end up being net losers. Thus, the distribution-sensitive assessment methodology presented in this chapter could reveal a switch from an ability-to-pay principle to a beneficiary-pays principle in many cases of international cooperation. This switch could refine how policymakers and, more important, the general public (notably in donor countries) think about burden-sharing arrangements in international cooperation.

CONCLUSION

This chapter has suggested a methodology for preparing provision profiles of global public goods that shows how different countries are affected by the current provision status of the good and what net benefits (or costs) they could expect to derive from enhanced provision of the good. The original steps developed by Conceição (2003) help identify good investments in global public goods from a global perspective. The additional steps suggested in this chapter disaggregate the information to reveal how global benefits and costs are distributed across countries.

The underlying logic of the analysis of global net gains from different invest-ment opportunities in global public goods is clear: the international community would like to invest in goods that bring high social returns for the world. Yet because preferences for global public goods differ, the distribution of net benefits also needs to be considered. Voluntary cooperation to provide global public goods could be more effective and more sustainable if this information were available. Information on the distribution of net benefits could thus improve policy analy-sis, facilitate international negotiations, and encourage followup actions—now so often lacking—to global crises and other inadequate provision of global public goods.

In the land of the blind, so the saying goes, the one-eyed man is king. But the world needs clearer vision than that if international cooperation is to succeed and crises are to be prevented. Policymakers will need 20/20 vision to make good investments—seeing not only the efficiency gains but also the impact on equity.

APPENDIX. DISTRIBUTION-SENSITIVE ASSESSMENTS OF THE NET
BENEFITS OF INVESTING IN SELECT GLOBAL PUBLIC GOODS

These profiles draw on assessments prepared by Barrett (2004) and Hertel (2004). The full text of their studies and others on assessing the provision status of global public goods—including such issues as financial stability, invasive species control, and peace and security—are available at www.thenewpublicfinance.org.

APPENDIX BOX A.1
PROVISION ASSESSMENT FOR THE MULTILATERAL TRADE REGIME

The global public good. The multilateral trade regime is a global public good. The effects of its rules and institutions likely go beyond its 148 member countries.

Characterizing current provision. Full provision of this global public good is an example of a moving-target good—there is no final adequacy threshold of 100 percent provision. Nevertheless, packages of additional rules and their implied policy reforms could be evaluated as incremental additions to the regime. To the extent that free trade could still be enhanced, the multilateral trade regime is underprovided.

There are two areas of interest in enhancing provision: trade policy and trade facilitation. Both trade policies (tariffs and subsidies) and non-policy barriers (inadequate port facilities, outmoded or corrupt customs clearance procedures, unharmonized standards) impede free trade. The metric used to indicate full provision in trade policy is complete trade liberalization (abolition of all tariffs and export subsidies). The metric considered for enhanced trade facilitation is a move halfway to the global average for all countries that are below average in four dimensions of trade facilitation (port efficiency, customs environments, regulatory environment, and electronic commerce).

The costs of underprovision are substantial. Export subsidies and tariffs impose significant welfare costs on consumers and taxpayers in the countries that apply them as well as on potential trading partners that are denied access to these markets. The annual global gross opportunity costs of trade policy distortions are $176 billion (in 2001 dollars)—$121 billion borne by industrial (or Organisation for Economic Co-operation and Development—OECD—member countries), and $55 billion borne by developing (non-OECD) countries (Hertel 2004, table 5). Various nonpolicy barriers cost the world approximately $117 billion—$92 billion in developing countries and $25 billion in industrial countries (Hertel 2004, p. 19).

Costs of corrective action. Underprovision is corrected by reforming trade policy (eliminating protectionist tariffs and export subsidies), which

Provision assessment for the multilateral trade regime

requires no outlay of funds, and by improving trade facilitation, which does. All calculations are net of the tax replacement needed to compensate for revenue losses from abolishing tariffs. The main cost associated with trade policy reform is the adjustment cost of workers and capital once protection is removed. A reasonable guesstimate of the costs of adjustment is a one-time 5 percent share of the annual gains (Matusz and Tarr 2000), or about $9 billion globally—$3 billion for developing countries and $6 billion for industrial countries (Hertel 2004, p. 22).

The costs associated with corrective actions for trade facilitation (bringing below-average countries halfway to the global average) are likely significant and will fall almost entirely on developing countries. From evidence on individual components (customs automization, capacity-building, the physical infrastructure underpinning international trade), there will likely be one-time costs for each developing country of about $150 million (Finger and Schuler 2001, p. 129), totaling about $20 billion (these costs are added to the $3 billion in one-time adjustment costs to get the total one-time cost for developing countries). There will also be aggregate recurring costs for all developing countries of another $20 billion, including those incurred from maintaining improved physical infrastructure (Hertel 2004, p. 23).

Benefits. The global gross benefits of trade policy reforms stemming from elimination of the opportunity costs would total $176 billion annually—$121 billion of it accruing to industrial countries and $55 billion to developing countries. Improvement in trade facilitation would annually bring $117 billion globally—$92 billion to developing countries and $25 billion to industrial countries.

Global net benefits. Reforming trade policy would thus bring global net present benefits of $3.5 trillion (in 2001 dollars discounted at 5 percent). Improvements in trade facilitation would generate global net present benefits of $1.9 trillion. Enhancing the provision of multilateral trade would thus generate total global net present benefits of $5.4 trillion (Hertel 2004, p. 24).

Distribution of net benefits. About 70 percent of global net benefits from trade policy reforms would accrue to industrial countries, while more than 70 percent of global net benefits from trade facilitation would go to developing countries. Taken together, these reforms are expected to generate about $2.9 trillion for industrial countries and $2.5 trillion for developing countries (in 2001 dollars in net present value terms).

PROVISION ASSESSMENT FOR SMALLPOX ERADICATION

The global public good. The eradication of an infectious disease such as smallpox is a global public good. No country can be excluded from the benefits of smallpox eradication, and no country's consumption of that benefit diminishes the amounts available to other countries.

Characterizing current provision. The full level of provision of eradication corresponds to the permanent reduction to zero of the worldwide incidence of infection caused by a specific agent. Once eradication is achieved, it is expected that no further intervention measures are needed. The World Health Assembly declared smallpox eradicated in 1980 (Barrett 2004, p. 3), so this global public good is currently fully (100 percent) provided.

Costs of corrective action. The costs of corrective action are measured retrospectively. Included are the costs of the deliberate actions taken to eradicate the disease starting in 1966, when the World Health Assembly voted to support an intensified program to eradicate smallpox. The costs incurred by both industrial countries and developing countries were for interventions that took place only in developing countries, where the disease was endemic at the time; the disease had already been eliminated in industrial countries (Fenner and others 1988, pp. 393–94). The total global cost of eradication was $300 million (in 1967 dollars), with developing countries contributing $200 million and industrial countries contributing $100 million (Barrett 2004, table 1).

Benefits. The annual flow of global benefits since 1980 is $1.42 billion (in 1967 dollars), with $350 million going to industrial countries and $1.07 billion to developing countries (Barrett 2004, table 1). The baseline reference is the situation at the time the eradication effort began. In industrial countries the benefits are limited to elimination of the need for vaccination. In developing countries the benefits also include the deaths and disability averted after eradication started.

Global net benefits. Smallpox eradication generates global net present value benefits of about $47 billion (in 1967 dollars discounted at 3 percent).

Distribution of net benefits. About 75 percent of the net benefits flow to developing countries ($35 billion), and about 25 percent to industrial countries ($12 billion).

APPENDIX BOX A.3
PROVISION ASSESSMENT FOR POLIO ERADICATION

The global public good. The eradication of an infectious disease such as polio is a global public good. No country can be excluded from the benefits of polio eradication, and no country's consumption of that benefit diminishes the amounts available to other countries.

Characterizing current provision. Polio eradication is underprovided. It is about 99.7 percent provided (expressed as the reduction in the number of cases since the eradication program started), with 1,263 new cases of polio virus in the "wild" in 2004 (there were 350,000 in 1988, when the eradication effort was officially launched through a World Health Assembly resolution; www.polioeradication.org/progress.asp).

Costs of corrective action. The global direct costs of eradicating polio over the expected duration of the campaign (1988–2006) are estimated at more than $6 billion (in 2003 dollars). Of this total, external sources (industrial countries, foundations, and other private sources) are expected to contribute about $4 billion (WHO 2005, p. 7), and volunteers the equivalent of $2.35 billion in polio-endemic (mostly developing) countries during 1998–2002 (WHO 2005, p. 8). An alternative estimate of the global cost of corrective action by Khan and Ehreth (2003, table 3, p. 704) is $67 billion in present value terms. Of this, $24 billion accrues to developing countries and $43 billion to industrial countries.

Benefits. The prospective benefits from eradicating polio are still uncertain, because of ambiguity about the most effective strategy to follow once eradication has been certified. Key questions are whether vaccination needs to continue and for how long and, if continued, which type of vaccine should be used—the oral vaccine, which is cheap and easy to administer but has the risk of reverting to wild polio, or the inactivated polio vaccine, which cannot cause infection but is more difficult and expensive to administer (Barrett 2004, p. 7). One approach to estimating benefits draws on the fact that vaccination costs in industrial countries, at about $1.5 billion a year (2000 prices; Aylward and others 2000, table 2, p. 1516), could be stopped if vaccination ends completely—thus generating global net present benefits of about $50 billion (in 2000 prices, using a 3 percent discount rate), flowing mostly to industrial countries.

Khan and Ehreth (2003) estimate benefits taking a different approach, based on the following assumptions. Benefits include only savings in medical costs (derived through historical analysis of costs back to 1970 and projected into 2040)—costs that would be avoided through immunization and eradication assessed against the baseline scenario of no immunization—and the cessation of vaccination after 2010. Together, these factors suggest global present benefits of $128 billion (in 2000 dollars discounted at

PROVISION ASSESSMENT FOR POLIO ERADICATION

5 percent; Khan and Ehreth 2003, table 3, p. 704). Most of the benefits ($115 billion) flow to the largely industrial and middle-income countries of Europe and the Americas (World Health Organization regions), with the remaining benefits ($13 billion) flowing mostly to developing countries (Khan and Ehreth 2003, table 3, p. 704).

Global net benefits. Global net present benefits for 1970–2005 are estimated at $61 billion (in 2000 dollars discounted at 5 percent), after subtracting the present global costs of $67 billion (Khan and Ehreth 2003, table 3, p. 704). It remains unclear, however, whether vaccination can cease after eradication, even after 2010.

Distribution of net benefits. About $72 billion in global net present benefits would flow entirely to the mostly industrial countries of Europe and the Americas (after subtracting $43 billion in present costs), with the other regions (mostly developing countries) incurring net losses of $11 billion (benefits are not sufficient to cover costs of $24 billion; Khan and Ehreth 2003, table 3, p. 704).

PROVISION ASSESSMENT FOR CLIMATE STABILITY

The global public good. Climate stability is a global public good. No country can be excluded from its provision and no country's consumption of it diminishes the amounts available to other countries.

Characterizing current provision. For global climate stability full provision would be stabilization of greenhouse gas concentrations in the atmosphere at a level that would prevent dangerous anthropogenic interference with the climate system (as set out in the United Nations Framework Convention on Climate Change). By this measure climate stability is likely to be underprovided. By one current estimate the damages that result from a doubling of carbon dioxide in the atmosphere (if no corrective action is taken) would imply global costs of $270 billion (in 1988 dollars). Industrial countries (OECD countries) would bear $180 billion, or about 1.3 percent of their gross national product (GNP) in 1988, and developing countries (non-OECD countries) would bear $89 billion, or about 1.6 percent of their combined GNP (Fankhauser 1995, table 3.15, p. 55). Thus, relative to GNP, the costs of underprovision are likely to fall more heavily on developing countries.

Costs of corrective action. Corrective actions to enhance the provision of climate stability include emission reductions and, possibly, carbon sequestration. Costs are estimated using a "Kyoto Forever" model, which assumes that the emission limits for industrial countries (Annex I countries in the study) hold indefinitely, and a global permit trading scenario, which assumes that the emission limits imposed on Annex I countries are implemented at least cost globally. The discounted present costs of emission abatement could reach $94 trillion and are concentrated exclusively in industrial countries (Cline 2004, table 1.3, p. 37).

Benefits. The discounted present value of global abatement benefits in the Kyoto Forever model are $166 trillion (Cline 2004, table 1.3, p. 37). Industrial countries enjoy a discounted present value of $55 trillion, and developing countries, $111 trillion (Cline 2004, p. 31).

Global net benefits. Enhanced climate stability is expected to provide about $72 trillion (in 1990 dollars discounted at 1.5 percent) in global net present benefits.

Distribution of net benefits. The costs of corrective action under this scenario are borne entirely by industrial countries. Developing countries would accrue net benefits of $111 trillion and industrial countries net losses of $39 trillion (Cline 2004, p. 31). However, it is important to emphasize that these figures do not reflect the fact that historically industrial countries have been the primary polluters and thus ignore the historical costs and benefits and their distributions.

NOTES

1. See www.unisdr.org/eng/media-room/media-room.htm.

2. Mid-range estimate for 2004 drawn from mi2g Intelligence Unit (www.mi2g.com). Other estimates range from $50 billion at the lower end (Laudsburg 2004) to $1.6 trillion at the upper end (Knight 2000).

3. The global aggregated costs of counterfeiting range between 5 percent and 7 percent of global trade (OECD 1998, p. 23). Since global trade in 2003 reached about $7,600 billion, and considering the mid-range estimate (6 percent), the estimated global cost due to counterfeiting is $456 billion.

4. For a detailed discussion on the incentive structures that underlie public goods and collective action problems such as free-riding, see, among others, Cornes and Sandler (1996).

5. An example is the Strategic Arms Limitations Talks (SALT) in the 1970s between the United States and the Soviet Union.

6. Contrast this instance with the case of a private good, in which optimal consumption is achieved when an individual agent's marginal willingness to pay equals the marginal cost of obtaining a further unit of the good. Determining an actor's willingness to pay corresponds to translating that willingness into a dollar figure (monetizing) the benefits that the enhanced provision will bring to the actor. For further discussion, see Cornes and Sandler (1996).

7. For a discussion of the issues surrounding contingent valuation and its applications, see Berrens and others (1998); Carson, Flores, and Meade (2001); and Diamond and Hausman (1994).

8. Because of the difficulties in measuring preferences, many studies have already turned to this approach in cost-benefit analysis. The methodology suggested here merely formalizes the approach and clarifies its key features.

9. The specific targets for each country (or set of countries) can be viewed at: http://unfccc.int/essential_background/kyoto_protocol/items/3145.php.

10. Information about the Huygens probe and the data it was sent to accumulate is available at www.nasa.gov/mission_pages/cassini/whycassini/30dec_titan.html.

11. An example of this interplay is the international negotiations on mitigating global climate change, in which the scientific community—in the form of the Intergovernmental Panel on Climate Change (IPCC)—contributed significantly to advancing the political debate. For further information on the IPCC, see www.ipcc.ch.

12. See, for example, UNDP, ODS (2004) and Haller (2005) for surveys of global reporting initiatives.

13. For a discussion of the standard technical methods applied in these studies—including estimating social discount rates, measuring consumer surplus, estimating welfare under general equilibrium, and accounting for nonmarket welfare effects—see Just, Hueth, and Schmitz (2005).

14. The global public goods assessed were climate stability, international financial stability, the multilateral trade regime, peace and security, and a reduction in disease burden.

15. These studies, called "challenge papers," were written by renowned experts in the areas of climate change, communicable diseases, conflict and arms proliferation, access to education, financial instability, governance and corruption, malnutrition and hunger, migration, sanitation and access to clean water, and subsidies and trade barriers. For details on the methodologies and results of these studies, and on the final ranking of investment opportunities, see Lomborg (2004) and www.copenhagenconsensus.com.

16. For each project the benefit–cost ratio is simply the benefits divided by the costs, both expressed in a common currency. Higher ratios imply more promising investment returns.

17. See, for example, Grossman and Krueger (1994); Maddison (2003); Rehdanz and Maddison (2005); WMO (2004); and Yandle, Bhattarai, and Vijayaraghavan (2004).

18. For each global public good considered, several studies present different estimates, so a future improvement in the methodology could include using intervals of estimates. The studies also use different methodological approaches, and the estimates are conditioned by the underlying methodology and prevailing scientific knowledge. As the underlying methodologies and scientific knowledge change, so would the results. Consensus on the assumptions and the type of methodology used will also be a factor to consider in improving the methodology.

19. Pareto optimality implies that there is no longer an opportunity to enhance the welfare of a certain individual (or group) without harming another individual (or group). Yet welfare-enhancing investments that strictly satisfy this criterion are rare. Hence, compensation is a pragmatic response. See, for example, Just, Hueth, and Schmitz (2005); Kanbur (2003); and Sen (2000).

20. Because the proposed reforms would eliminate tariffs and subsidies, they would likely erode demand for Sub-Saharan countries' food products in favor of exports from more competitive countries such as Brazil and China.

21. A discussion of these issues is beyond the scope of this chapter. Kanbur (2003) presents a historical perspective on this debate.

22. It is also for this reason that Kaul, Grunberg, and Stern (1999) and Kaul and Le Goulven (2003) suggest a distinction between international cooperation to support global public goods and international cooperation aimed at delivering foreign aid. See also Jayaraman and Kanbur (1999) and Sandmo (2003).

REFERENCES

Albin, Cecilia. 2003. "Getting to Fairness: Negotiations over Global Public Goods." In Inge Kaul, Pedro Conceição, Katell Le Goulven, and Ronald U. Mendoza, eds., *Providing Global Public Goods: Managing Globalization*. New York: Oxford University Press.

Aylward, Bruce R., Karen A. Hennessy, Nevio Zagaria, Jean-Marc Olivé, and Stephen L. Cochi. 2000. "When Is a Disease Eradicable? 100 Years of Lessons Learned." *American Journal of Public Health* 90 (10): 1515–20.

Bahadur, Chandrika, and Ronald U. Mendoza. 2002. "Towards Free and Fair Trade: A Global Public Good Perspective" *Challenge* 45 (5): 21–62.

Barrett, Scott. 2004. "The Provision Status of Disease Eradication." UNDP/ODS Background paper. United Nations Development Programme, Office of Development Studies, New York. [www.thenewpublicfinance.org].

Berrens, Robert P., David Brookshire, Philip Ganderton, and Mike McKee. 1998. "Exploring Nonmarket Values for the Social Impacts of Environmental Policy Change." *Resource and Energy Economics* 20 (2): 117–37.

Carson, Richard T., Nicholas E. Flores, and Norman F. Meade. 2001. "Contingent Valuation: Controversies and Evidence." *Environmental and Resource Economics* 19 (2): 173–210.

Cernea, Michael. 2000. "Risks, Safeguards, and Reconstruction: A Model for Population Displacement and Resettlement." In Michael Cernea and C. McDowell, eds., *Risks and Reconstruction: Experiences of Resettlers and Refugees*. Washington, D.C.: World Bank.

———. 2003. "For a New Economics of Resettlement: A Sociological Critique of the Compensation Principle." *International Social Science Journal* 55 (175): 37–45.

Cline, William R. 2004. "Climate Change." In Bjørn Lomborg, ed., *Global Crises, Global Solutions*. Cambridge: Cambridge University Press.

Conceição, Pedro. 2003. "Assessing the Provision Status of Global Public Goods." In Inge Kaul, Pedro Conceição, Katell Le Goulven, and Ronald U. Mendoza, eds., *Providing Global Public Goods: Managing Globalization*. New York: Oxford University Press.

Cornes, Richard, and Todd Sandler. 1996. *The Theory of Externalities, Public Goods, and Club Goods*. Cambridge: Cambridge University Press.

Diamond, Peter A., and Jerry A. Hausman. 1994. "Contingent Valuation: Is Some Number Better Than No Number?" *Journal of Economic Perspectives* 8 (4): 45–64.

Drèze, Jean. 1998. "Distribution Matters in Cost-Benefit Analysis." *Journal of Public Economics* 70 (3): 485–88.

Fankhauser, Samuel. 1995. *Valuing Climate Change*. London: Earthscan.

Fenner, Frank, Donald A. Henderson, Isao Arita, Zdenek Ježek, and, Ivan Danilovich Ladnyi. 1988. *Smallpox and Its Eradication.* Geneva: World Health Organization.

Finger, J. Michael, and Philip Schuler. 2001. "Implementation of Uruguay Round Commitments: The Development Challenge." In Bernard Hoekman and Will Martin, eds., *Developing Countries and the WTO: A Pro-active Agenda.* Oxford and Malden, Mass.: Blackwell Publishers.

Grossman, Gene M., and Alan B. Krueger. 1994. "Environmental Impacts of a North American Free Trade Agreement." In Peter Garber, ed., *The Mexico-U.S. Trade Agreement.* Cambridge, Mass.: MIT Press.

Haller, Hana. 2005. "Global Reports: An Overview of Their Evolution—2005 Update." United Nations Development Programme, Office of Development Studies, New York. [www.thenewpublicfinance.org].

Hertel, Thomas. 2004. "Assessing the Provision of International Trade as a Global Public Good." UNDP/ODS Background paper. United Nations Development Programme, Office of Development Studies, New York. [www.thenewpublic finance.org].

Jayaraman, Rajshri, and Ravi Kanbur. 1999. "International Public Goods and the Case for Foreign Aid." In Inge Kaul, Isabelle Grunberg, and Marc A. Stern, eds., *Global Public Goods: International Cooperation in the 21st Century.* New York: Oxford University Press.

Just, Richard E., Darrell L. Hueth, and Andrew Schmitz. 2005. *The Welfare Economics of Public Policy: A Practical Approach to Project and Policy Evaluation.* London: Edward Elgar.

Kanbur, Ravi. 2003. "Development Economics and the Compensation Principle." *International Social Science Journal* 55 (175): 27–35.

Kaul, Inge, and Katell Le Goulven. 2003. "Financing Global Public Goods: A New Frontier of Public Finance." In Inge Kaul, Pedro Conceição, Katell Le Goulven, and Ronald U. Mendoza, eds., *Providing Global Public Goods: Responding to Global Challenges.* New York: Oxford University Press.

Kaul, Inge, and Ronald U. Mendoza. 2003. "Advancing the Concept of Public Goods." In Inge Kaul, Pedro Conceição, Katell Le Goulven, and Ronald U. Mendoza, eds., *Providing Global Public Goods: Managing Globalization.* New York: Oxford University Press.

Kaul, Inge, Isabelle Grunberg, and Marc A. Stern. 1999. *Global Public Goods: International Cooperation in the 21st Century.* New York: Oxford University Press.

Knight, Will. 2000. "Hacking Will Cost World $1.6 Trillion This Year." *ZDNet UK.* July 11. [http://news.zdnet.co.uk/internet/security/0,39020375,2080075,00.htm].

Khan, M. Mahmud, and Jennifer Ehreth. 2003. "Costs and Benefits of Polio Eradication: A Long-Run Global Perspective." *Vaccine* 21 (7-8): 702–05.

Laudsburg, Steven E. 2004. "Feed the Worms Who Write Worms to the Worms." *Slate,* May 26. [http://slate.msn.com/id/2101297].

Lerner, Josh. 2002. *Patent Protection and Innovation over 150 Years.* NBER Working Paper 8977. Cambridge, Mass.: National Bureau of Economic Research.

Lomborg, Bjørn, ed. 2004. *Global Crises, Global Solutions.* Cambridge: Cambridge University Press.

Maddison, David. 2003. "The Amenity Value of the Climate: The Household Production Function Approach." *Resource and Energy Economics* 25 (2): 155–75.

Maskus, Keith. 2000. *Intellectual Property Rights in the Global Economy.* Washington, D.C.: Institute for International Economics.

Matusz, Steven, and David Tarr. 2000. "Adjusting to Trade Policy Reform." In Anne Krueger, ed., *Economic Policy Reform: The Second Stage.* Chicago, Ill.: Chicago University Press.

Mendoza, Ronald U. 2003. "The Multilateral Trade Regime: A Global Public Good for All?" In Inge Kaul, Pedro Conceição, Katell Le Goulven, and Ronald U. Mendoza, eds., *Providing Global Public Goods: Managing Globalization.* New York: Oxford University Press.

Nash, John. 1950. "The Bargaining Problem." *Econometrica* 18 (2): 155–62.

OECD (Organisation for Economic Co-operation and Development). 1998. *The Economic Impact of Counterfeiting.* Paris. [www.oecd.org/dataoecd/11/112090589.pdf].

Parson, Edward A. 2003. *Protecting the Ozone Layer: Science and Strategy.* New York: Oxford University Press.

Rao, J. Mohan. 1999. "Equity in Global Public Goods Framework." In Inge Kaul, Isabelle Grunberg, and Marc A. Stern, eds., *Global Public Goods: International Cooperation in the 21st Century.* New York: Oxford University Press.

Rehdanz, Katrin, and David Maddison. 2005. "Climate and Happiness." *Ecological Economics* 52 (1): 111–25.

Samuelson, Paul A. 1954. "The Pure Theory of Public Expenditure." *Review of Economics and Statistics* 36 (4): 387–89.

———. 1955. "Diagrammatic Exposition of a Theory of Public Expenditure." *Review of Economics and Statistics* 37 (4): 350–56.

Sandmo, Agnar. 2003. "International Aspects of Public Goods Provision." In Inge Kaul, Pedro Conceição, Katell Le Goulven, and Ronald U. Mendoza, eds., *Providing Global Public Goods: Managing Globalization.* New York: Oxford University Press.

Sen, Amartya. 2000. "The Discipline of Cost-Benefit Analysis." *Journal of Legal Studies* 29 (2): 931–52.

———. 2005. "What Is It Like to Be a Human Being?" Speech delivered at the 3rd Forum on Human Development, January 17, Paris.

Stiglitz, Joseph. 2000. *Economics of the Public Sector.* New York: W.W. Norton.

UNDP, ODS (United Nations Development Programme, Office of Development Studies). 2004. "Global Reports: An Overview of Their Evolution." Staff Paper. New York.

Walkenhorst, Peter, and Nora Dihel. 2002. "Trade Impacts of the Terrorist Attacks of 11 September 2001: A Quantitative Assessment." Deutsches Institut für Wirtschaftsforschung. Paper prepared for the Workshop on "The Economic Consequences of Global Terrorism," June 14–15, Berlin.

WHO (World Health Organization). 2004. *Severe Acute Respiratory Syndrome (SARS): Report by the Secretariat.* EB113/33. Geneva.

———. 2005. *Global Polio Eradication Initiative: Financial Resource Requirements 2005–2008.* Geneva.

WMO (World Meteorological Organization). 2004. "Natural Disaster Prevention and Mitigation: Role and Contribution of the WMO and National Meteorological and Hydrological Services." WMO Discussion Paper. Geneva.

World Bank. 2004. "The Costs of Corruption." Washington, D.C. [http://web.world bank.org/WBSITE/EXTERNAL/NEWS/0,,contentMDK:20190187~menuPK:34457 ~pagePK:34370~piPK:34424~theSitePK:4607,00.html].

Yandle, Bruce, Madhusudan Bhattarai, and Maya Vijayaraghavan. 2004. "Environmental Kuznets Curves: A Review of Findings, Methods, and Policy Implications." PERC Research Study 02-1. Property and Environment Research Center, Montana, Mo. [www.perc.org/pdf/rs02_1a.pdf].

MAKING INTERNATIONAL COOPERATION PAY

FINANCING AS A STRATEGIC INCENTIVE

SCOTT BARRETT

An important characteristic of public goods is that they are public in consumption: available for all to consume. This presents a problem: If no one can be excluded from their consumption, how can public goods be financed? Wouldn't self-interest dictate that it is better to free ride? And why should anyone pay when others do not? Wouldn't that be unfair?

These fundamental questions apply to all public goods—local, national, and transnational.[1] They hint at two facts: that public goods will tend to be undersupplied and that there are gains to be obtained from putting in place institutions and policy measures for overcoming these incentive problems. Indeed, individual countries have developed a variety of such instruments. But transnational public goods pose special challenges. Many require for their adequate provision some international cooperation among states. Yet the principle of state sovereignty essentially means that such international cooperation can only happen voluntarily. This chapter shows how voluntary intergovernmental cooperation works—when it might work spontaneously and when it might require some strategic manipulation, notably an injection of financing.

International cooperation suffers from free riding, both during the negotiation of international agreements and during implementation, when international commitments are translated into national-level action. It is also challenged at both stages by another factor: asymmetry among countries. This chapter focuses especially on overcoming the lack of international cooperation due to asymmetry. For example, smallpox eradication might not have been realized without international financial support to assist national eradication efforts in poorer developing countries. The case is similar for protection of the ozone layer.

Incentives for fostering international cooperation can be positive (offers of financial support) or negative (threats of trade restrictions). This chapter focuses on positive financial incentives. Such incentives are likely to be provided by a subgroup of countries that are parties to the main international agreement, such as the Montreal Protocol. This implies that in addition to negotiations on the overall agreement, there will likely be negotiations among funders about how to share the burden of mobilizing resources for the financing arrangement associated with this agreement. As this chapter will show, the "game" by which these burden-sharing arrangements are agreed can be quite different from the cooperation that underlies negotiation of the main agreements.

What makes international cooperation succeed?

Why are some attempts to supply transnational public goods more successful than others, given the constraints imposed by sovereignty? One reason is that coercion is not always needed; volunteerism is sometimes sufficient. Another reason is that strategic manipulation can change incentives, making volunteerism more effective. Strategic manipulation is the horizontal equivalent of coercion, a power invested in every domestic government but unavailable to the international community.

Success in the supply of transnational public goods depends on several factors: the nature of the public good itself, the motivation countries have to supply the public good, and the incentives used to facilitate supply. These, in turn, differ for the three main types of public goods—best shot, weakest link, and summation.[2] Sometimes financing is necessary for adequate provision.

Best shot public goods
In 1908 a meteoroid perhaps 50–70 meters in diameter exploded in the atmosphere over Siberia, devastating an area the size of Manhattan. According to some experts, there is a 10 percent probability of another such encounter in this century (Milani 2003; Schweickart and others 2003). Larger space debris would obviously cause more damage. Asteroids a kilometer or more in diameter are likely to strike the earth's surface eventually, perhaps with the potential to wipe out human civilization, just as a 10 kilometer-wide asteroid that hit Earth 65 million years ago coincided with the extinction of dinosaurs. By one calculation the chance is about 1 in 5,000 that such a strike will occur in this century (Schweickart and others 2003).

Several options are being investigated for protecting humanity against such an event. One is to launch a "space tug" that could attach itself to an approaching asteroid and gently nudge it off a collision course with Earth (if the asteroid is far enough away, a nudge is enough). This kind of protection against an asteroid collision is an example of a "best shot" technology: only one (successful) intervention is needed to supply the good.

Provision. Protecting the Earth by developing and deploying such a technology would be a global public good. Could we expect it to be provided? The answer is likely to be yes, since global benefits would clearly outweigh global costs. However, who would be willing to pay the cost?

Consider some calculations. Schweickart and others (2003) suggest that a space tug would cost about $1 billion. According to Milani (2003), a catastrophic collision would cause the equivalent of about 1,000 deaths a year. Investment in the tug would be worthwhile if the benefit in lives saved exceeded the cost. Denote the benefit per life saved by b and let the discount rate be 3 percent, so that the present value of future benefits would be approximately equal to $1,000b/0.03$. Under reasonable assumptions the investment is worthwhile if $b > \$30,000$. The average value of a statistical life for the whole world exceeds this value, and so protection from asteroid collision appears to be a sound global investment.[3] In fact, the economics of asteroid protection are so strong that it would pay for the United States to finance the entire protection program by itself.[4]

For such best shot transnational public goods, the amount supplied is equal to the largest amount supplied by any country. Other examples include discrete forms of knowledge, such as the knowledge of how to stimulate the human immune system to defend against infection. Here, again, a single country will sometimes have an incentive unilaterally to supply the public good of basic vaccine research because it is in its national interest to do so. The two widely used polio vaccines, for example, were both developed in the United States, with U.S. financing, for the purpose of protecting the U.S. population from an epidemic.

Provision with international financing. Suppose it is not in the interests of any one country to supply a best shot public good unilaterally but that all countries would be better off if the good were supplied. If the United States did not benefit enough from asteroid protection, would countries cooperate to finance this global public good?

Plainly, if other countries contribute enough, it may be in the interests of each country to contribute something, whereas if others do not contribute enough, it may pay each country to contribute nothing.

Assume that every country derives a benefit of $10 million from the provision of a public good. Assume as well that the cost of supplying the public good is $25 million. Then, if no other country contributes, each country has an incentive not to contribute because any money contributed would be wasted.[5] Similarly, if some countries together contribute $25 million, the others have no incentive to contribute any more. Suppose however, that countries have contributed $21 million, so that only $4 million more is needed to supply the public good. Each of the noncontributors would then have an incentive to contribute the last $4 million.[6] Why? Because doing so would cause the public good to be supplied, yielding the last contributor a net benefit of $6 million.

In analytical game theory, situations like this have two equilibria: one in which the public good is not supplied, and one in which it is. Since all countries are better off in the second equilibrium, there should be incentives for countries to coordinate their contributions to ensure that the public good is supplied.

Experiments by Cadsby and Maynes (1999), however, suggest that coordination is not so easy. In their experiments the public good was supplied only about 20 percent of the time. However, in their experiments cooperation was implicit;

communication was forbidden, and no agreements could be negotiated. It seems likely that if countries were able to negotiate cofinancing, the public good would be supplied.

An example is research in high-energy particle physics, which requires huge and costly facilities, such as the European Organization for Nuclear Research (CERN) laboratory. Even the larger European countries could not justify constructing a laboratory as big as CERN's unilaterally, and a single nation could not supply the human resources to run it (CERN 2002). Experiments using accelerators like CERN's have led to the development of a number of new technologies, such as positron emission tomography (the PET scan), used for cancer diagnosis; lithography, used in the design of computer chips; synchrotron radiation, used for the study of very small objects like viruses; and mass spectrometry, used for dating materials. None of these inventions would have been possible without collective provision of this public good—and cofinancing of the facility by participating countries.

Weakest link public goods

Weakest link public goods require that all countries contribute, and the smallest provision by any country determines the total amount supplied. An example is eradication of an infectious disease. Diseases easily cross borders. As long as a disease exists anywhere in nature, it poses a risk to every country. Eradication requires that the disease be eliminated in every country. If even one country fails to eliminate the disease, it will not be eradicated.

Provision. For eradication to be feasible, several demanding conditions— biological, technical, economic, and political—must be satisfied (Lederberg 2002). To date, only one disease, smallpox, has been eradicated. Attempts to eradicate other diseases, such as malaria, have failed. Currently, the world is attempting to eradicate poliomyelitis, a global disease, and Guinea worm, a tropical disease. Many other candidates are being considered for eradication. One of the most challenging is measles, which kills more than 600,000 children a year in developing countries.

What incentives do countries have to supply the global public good of disease eradication? Barrett (2003b) points to four possible situations. First, the costs of eradication may exceed the benefits for the whole world, so that eradication is not achieved, but the world is no worse off. Second, the benefits of elimination may exceed the costs for every country, so that every country eliminates the disease unilaterally, and the disease is eradicated, with all countries gaining. For these two situations, there is no welfare loss associated with unilateral behavior.

Third, each country may have an incentive to eliminate the disease at home only if all other countries have already eliminated the disease within their borders. Put differently, each country may have an incentive to eliminate the disease only if assured that all others will eliminate the disease. In this situation disease eradication requires international coordination—a commitment by all to act nationally. And, finally, the benefits of eradication for all countries may exceed the costs, but the benefits of eradication for at least one country may fall short of the costs of eliminating the disease at home. Alternatively, at least one country may be unable, say, for lack of resources, to eliminate the disease. In both these situations there is a need for international incentives. And in the last case, in particular, international financing may be the most appropriate incentive.

Provision with international financing. In the case of weakest link global public goods, international financial support may be necessary if countries are asymmetric.

Suppose first that there are N symmetric countries. Each incurs cost c in contributing to supply the weakest link good, and each receives benefit b if the good is supplied (and a benefit of zero if it is not supplied). With a weakest link good, supply requires that every country contribute. No country will contribute if others do not contribute, provided $c > 0$, but each can gain from universal contribution provided $b > c$. Aggregate supply is efficient provided that the aggregate benefit of supply exceeds the aggregate cost—that is, provided $bN > cN$ or $b > c$. Put differently, all countries gain from supply only if each gains. Under these circumstances cost sharing is not needed.

Now assume that countries are asymmetric. Some countries may gain a lot from the provision of a particular good, and some may benefit very little. Under these circumstances it may not be in the interest of each country to contribute, even if all others contributed. Assurance would not suffice to supply the public good.

Smallpox eradication is a case in point. Industrial countries eliminated smallpox by the mid-twentieth century, whereas many developing countries did not. The eradication challenge was thus to eliminate smallpox from the developing countries where the disease remained endemic. All countries had strong incentives to achieve eradication. The developing countries would avoid the costs of infection—at the start of the eradication campaign 1–2 million people died every year from the disease in poor countries—while the industrial countries would avoid the costs of vaccination to protect against imports of smallpox. Many developing countries lacked the resources to eliminate smallpox on their own. Eradication thus required providing financial and other support to a number of developing countries—something that the industrial countries were willing to do because they would still come out ahead, with a net benefit.

This game of financing resembles that for the best shot public good discussed previously. In both cases the public good has a "threshold." In the best shot case a certain amount of money is needed to build a particle collider of particular dimensions, and in the weakest link case a certain amount of money is needed to finance an eradication program. If too little money is raised, neither public good can be supplied. Indeed, the value of coming close to raising the required amount of money may be zero.

The main difference between the particle collider and the smallpox example is that in the disease eradication case one group of countries paid for activities to be undertaken in another group of countries. A large-scale research project, as a best shot public good, must be located in a single place—and so will be located in one of the countries contributing toward its supply. Eradication, as a weakest link public good, must achieve elimination in every country, including every country unable to eliminate the disease on its own.

The returns to investment in smallpox eradication have been huge. By some estimates the total cost of international financing was about $100 million, while the annual global benefit has been about $1.35 billion (Fenner and others 1988).[7] The United States alone might have saved about $150 million a year because of eradication. Theoretically, it would have made economic sense for the United States to finance the whole eradication campaign alone, if necessary.[8]

And yet despite the overwhelming economics of smallpox eradication, financing of this program was miserly. The reasons may be related to the fact that the motivations for countries to have the good provided are different from the "game" that countries face when it comes to financing the good's provision. The reason cannot have been a concern about the ultimate success of eradication, because financing proved hard to obtain even after the disease had been eliminated everywhere except the horn of Africa. The reason might have been that each potential donor wanted the other potential donors to pay as well, reflecting the difference between the primary cooperation game (the decision to aim at disease eradication) and the financing game (how to share the costs of any required financing arrangement).

Summation public goods

The supply of some public goods is equal to the sum of the amounts supplied by individual countries. Supply of the global public good protection of the ozone layer, for example, depends on the aggregate reduction in the release of ozone-destroying chemicals. Similarly, mitigating the risk of global climate change depends on reducing global levels of greenhouse gas emissions.

Provision. Many times, one country's contribution can substitute for another country's contribution. But of course the reverse also holds true. In the example of greenhouse gases one country's emissions can nullify the reduction efforts of others, so that, despite cuts by some parties, worldwide emission levels stay the same. This is an important reason why those interested in controlling a global public bad have a keen interest in bringing all concerned actors into an international agreement.

Provision with international financing. As with weakest link public goods, the issue of supplemental financing to enhance the provision of a summation public good is likely to arise only under conditions of asymmetry. When countries are highly asymmetric—say, in terms of income or development—some countries may hesitate to commit to contributing to the supply of a summation public good. Developing countries may be concerned about not being able to live up to their international commitment, given national resource constraints. Or they may elect not to contribute because the costs of doing so exceed the benefits they receive individually. Or they may be unwilling to make the commitment because industrial countries will benefit more than they will—a question of fairness. In such cases international financial support may be in the interests of all, allowing countries initially unable or unwilling to join the agreement to do so.

An example is the Montreal Protocol for supplying the global public good of ozone layer protection.[9] As originally negotiated, the Montreal Protocol required all industrial country parties to reduce their production and consumption of ozone-damaging substances by half (from the 1986 level) by 1999. Each party had to pay its own way, with no provisions for cost sharing.

The industrial countries had a strong incentive to supply the global public good of ozone layer protection, but developing countries had much less incentive. This was partly because depletion would be less severe near the equator, partly because depletion would be less harmful to darker skinned people, and partly because poorer countries had different priorities. Moreover, the industrial countries were responsible for the depletion to date; the developing countries would affect the ozone layer mainly over the longer term.

For all of these reasons developing countries were essentially committed not to supply the public good, while the industrial countries would gain from provision by developing countries. The industrial countries thus had a strong incentive to offer compensatory payments to encourage developing countries to participate in the treaty. Three years after the original treaty was signed, compensatory financing—based on the principle of agreed incremental costs—was incorporated in an amendment to the Montreal Protocol negotiated in London in 1990.

At first glance this situation appears reminiscent of the smallpox experience. In both cases industrial countries financed activities undertaken in developing countries. But there is an important difference: Financing of smallpox eradication had to reach a threshold sufficient to eliminate the disease everywhere. Otherwise, the industrial countries would not have derived any benefit from their contributions. For ozone depletion there is no such threshold. Every ton of ozone-destroying chemicals abated benefits every industrial country. And so every dollar spent on abatement also benefits every industrial country.

Enforcement
So far, the analysis has focused on how positive (notably, financial) incentives can foster international cooperation and thus promote the provision of transnational public goods. But is there a role also for negative incentives?

In the case of ozone depletion the offer of compensation was complemented by a threat to restrict trade between parties to the agreement and nonparties. The promise to compensate was the "carrot." The threat to restrict trade was the "stick." It was this combination that made the Montreal Protocol a stunning success (Barrett 2003a).

To see how disincentives might work, suppose that only a few countries participate in the treaty. Country X then has two reasons not to accede: it can free ride and yet continue to trade with the rest of the world—almost all countries. Now suppose every country but X is in the treaty. Then X can still free ride on the provision efforts of others, but it cannot trade (in the ozone-destroying substances and the products containing such materials) with the rest of the world. Provided the trade losses were large enough, nonparticipation by any country would not pay given a high level of participation by others. Inclusion in this agreement of the threat to restrict trade was thus strategic, intended to increase participation. And it has had the desired effect. Today, participation in the Montreal Protocol is virtually universal. Moreover, the trade restrictions have not had to be applied. It is the credible threat of imposing them that promoted participation (Barrett 2003a).

From a narrow perspective of self-interest the trade restrictions may have induced developing countries to participate, but the agreement might then have been perceived as being unfair or lacking in legitimacy. Substantial experimental evidence shows that people will often reject unfair offers, even when doing so is not in their self-interest (Fehr and Gächter 2000). Financing may thus have been needed to make the threat to restrict trade not only credible but also politically acceptable.

Table 1 summarizes the main findings of this section.

TABLE 1

Providing transnational public goods: which goods require strategic manipulation?

Type of public good	Tendency for efficient provision?	Strategic financing needed?	Additional strategic manipulation needed?
Best shot	Yes	Yes, if it does not pay any country to supply unilaterally	No
Weakest link	Yes	Yes, if countries are strongly asymmetric	No
Summation	No	Yes, if countries are strongly asymmetric	Yes, in some cases

THE SUPPLEMENTAL INTERNATIONAL COOPERATION GAME:
NEGOTIATING COST-SHARING ARRANGEMENTS

If enhancing the supply of a transnational public good calls for the provision of financial incentives by some countries to other countries, potential donors face the question of how to share the burden of mobilizing the requisite funds. This means that they must agree (implicitly, if not explicitly) on a principle or formula for dividing costs.

Clearly, international financing arrangements also have public goods characteristics. They benefit all those who benefit from adequate provision of the public good—say, climate stability or communicable disease control. In the terminology of Kaul and Le Goulven (2003), financial contributions are an "intermediate" transnational public good.

More specifically, each freely convertible money unit contributed by one potential donor is a substitute for contributions by others. Put differently, international financing arrangements have the characteristics—and problems—of a summation public good. They are thus prone to free riding. This holds true for the financing of all types of public goods, whether best shot, weakest link, or summation.

Negotiating a burden-sharing formula is essential when financing is integral to an international agreement. However, it may also be desirable to consider cost sharing when no special international financing facility is being set up. As noted previously, a best shot transnational public good could be self-financed when the benefit of unilateral provision exceeds the cost of supply. However, this cost-benefit condition is not sufficient for self-financing. Though failing to supply the public good would be economically irrational for the potential best shot provider, a desire to punish nonproviders might outweigh concerns for the country's more narrow self-interest in being able to enjoy the good. Indeed, such considerations could also explain why issues of international burden sharing arise in situations where unilateral provision would be both technically and economically possible. Burden sharing is less a technical necessity than an expression of the acceptance of shared responsibility.

But how exactly is burden sharing determined?

There is no simple answer. Formal game theory provides little help. Reconsider the example given for best shot provision with international support financing. Assuming that all countries are identical, there would be a symmetric equilibrium in which each country financed an equal share of the cost. With 100 countries and a total cost of $25 million, each country would pay $250,000. This burden-sharing arrangement would be an equilibrium in the sense that, given the payments made by every other country, none has an incentive to deviate. Paying more would not change the outcome and so would only be self-damaging. Paying less would mean that the transnational public good would not be provided, given that no other country will make up for the shortfall. So this, too, would be a self-damaging course of action (and damaging to others as well).

The problem is that many other equilibria can also be sustained. For example, if one country simply refuses to contribute, the remaining 99 countries might share the burden equally among themselves, with each paying $253,525. Another possible burden-sharing formula could be three countries each paying $8,333,333, with the remaining 97 countries paying nothing. Though an equilibrium in the formal sense, this situation may seem implausible. The three financiers might feel that they had been taken advantage of. Why should they pay when so many others free ride?

Thus, even when self-interest favors provision, countries may fail to contribute if they feel that the burden sharing is unfair. The experiment analyzed by Cadsby and Maynes (1999) offers some support for this hypothesis. In their experiment players were symmetric, and so the obvious fair burden-sharing arrangement was for each of the N players to contribute $1/N$th of the total cost of supplying the public good. What they found was that when the public good was provided first, a number of players did offer the symmetric equilibrium amounts, and others offered contributions close to these amounts. By contrast, when players were asked to contribute first, before the good was available, they tended to deviate more from these symmetric values.

So when countries are symmetric, sharing costs equally may be one arrangement that could be perceived as being "fair" by the parties concerned. However, in most instances, countries are not, or may not perceive themselves to be, truly and fully equal in all respects. That is when concerns for fairness and justice surface (see, for example, Albin 2003). So, how to arrange burden sharing when countries are asymmetric?

There is no standard formula. Contributions of member states to the UN regular budget essentially follow the principle of ability to pay (UN General Assembly 2004). In some other international organizations, such as the International Telecommunication Union[10] and the Universal Postal Union, members share costs according to ability to pay and benefits received. Countries contribute voluntarily to the two organizations, under a system of indicative contribution classes determined on the basis of gross domestic product per capita. There is a principle of free choice of contribution class, and the approach is based on "the importance of services rendered" (UPU 2000). The International Civil Aviation Organization also applies a mixed system, with a country's assessed contribution based on both its ability to pay and its interest and importance in civil aviation.[11] Members of the International Maritime Organization (IMO), by contrast, share costs primarily in proportion to the size of each country's fleet of merchant ships—an expression of the beneficiary paying. Since Panama and Liberia operate the biggest fleets, they pay the biggest share of IMO's budget.[12]

CONCLUSION

This chapter has examined the provision of transnational public goods, with a special focus on identifying when these goods require international cooperation, when voluntary international cooperation is likely to suffice, and when strategic manipulation of incentive structures is needed to motivate provision. The emphasis has been on how positive incentives, such as financial payments, can encourage international cooperation. This is not to deny the usefulness of negative incentives, such as trade restrictions. But to be perceived as being legitimate, trade restrictions may have to be paired with positive incentives. Of course, efficiency may also demand the offer of carrots.

Three main findings stand out. First, best shot and weakest link public goods are less likely than summation public goods to be underprovided. Nevertheless, all three types of goods may, for a variety of reasons, require financial incentives to foster successful international cooperation.

Second, the cooperation strategy required for adequate provision of the transnational good may vary from that required for decisions about how to share the costs of pooled international incentive mechanisms. Whatever the aggregation technology of the (final) transnational good (whether best shot, weakest link, or summation good), cost-sharing arrangements have the character of a (intermediate) summation public good. The reason is that each unit of money contributed by one country is a substitute for the contributions of other countries.

Third, when countries are symmetric, equal cost sharing will seem especially compelling. However, when they are asymmetric, fairness and justice may call for a distribution of costs according to countries' ability to pay or according to the amount of net benefits they are likely to derive from a particular international agreement. There may even exist a burden sharing formula that deviates from these rules because it happens to be "focal" in a particular situation.

In practice, many different arrangements exist—and seem to be sustainable—suggesting that international cooperation is shaped by more than economic rationality. Nevertheless, understanding when international cooperation is likely to be successful on a purely voluntary basis and when it requires strategic manipulation and international financing can facilitate countries' decisionmaking—and should be a consideration in the analysis of international policy, even if other factors also determine the choices that are eventually made.

NOTES

1. The term *transnational public goods* is used to denote both regional and global public goods.

2. These classifications were developed by Hirshleifer (1983) and further elaborated by Sandler (1992, 1997).

3. Estimates of the value of a statistical life in industrial countries are typically in the millions of dollars; see Viscusi and Aldy (2003). Few estimates exist for developing countries, but a study of willingness to pay for a reduction in mortality linked to air pollution in Santiago, Chile, yielded estimated values of more than $0.5 million per life (Bowland and Beghin 2001; for other countries see also Cropper and Simon 1996). In any case, the population of industrial countries makes up a large enough proportion of the total that the average value of a statistical life for the world as a whole would be many times greater than $30,000, regardless of the value of a statistical life in developing countries.

4. Suppose that each person on Earth has an equal chance of dying from an asteroid collision. The U.S. share of global population is about 4.6 percent (World Bank 2005, table 2.1). Since the tug is estimated to avert about 1,000 deaths a year, it could be expected to save about 1,000 x 0.046 U.S. lives a year. The value of a statistical life for the United States is between $4 million and $9 million (Viscusi and Aldy 2003). For the lower value, the annual benefit of avoiding an asteroid collision would be about $4 million x 1,000 x 0.046 = $184 million. For a discount rate of 3 percent, the present value of all future deaths avoided would be $184 million / 0.03 = $6.1 billion. Since the cost of a space tug is just $1 billion, even the United States acting alone would have an incentive to supply the asteroid protection.

5. Each country is only willing to pay up to $10 million, and yet it costs $25 million to supply the good.

6. Even the countries that contributed previously may have an incentive to contribute more. Much depends on how much each contributed earlier and on whether those contributions were sunk.

7. Taking the cost to be a one-time expenditure, and assuming a 3 percent discount rate, the benefit of smallpox eradication would be about $1.35 billion/0.03 = $45 billion in present value terms. The cost of international financing was $100 million. Hence, the benefit cost ratio was about $45 billion to $100 million, or 450:1.

8. Again, assuming a 3 percent discount rate, the present value benefit of smallpox eradication for the United States would be about $150 million / 0.03 = $5 billion, or about 50 times the cost of international finance.

9. See www.unep.org/ozone/pdfs/Montreal-Protocol2000.pdf.

10. See www.itu.int/aboutitu/basic-texts/constitution.html.

11. See www.icao.int/icao/en/res/a21_33.htm.

12. See www.imo.org/home.asp.

REFERENCES

Albin, Cecilia. 2003. "Getting to Fairness: Negotiations over Global Public Goods." In Inge Kaul, Pedro Conceição, Katell Le Goulven, and Ronald U. Mendoza, eds., *Providing Global Public Goods: Managing Globalization*. New York: Oxford University Press.

Barrett, Scott. 2003a. *Environment and Statecraft: The Strategy of Environmental Treaty Making.* Oxford: Oxford University Press.

———. 2003b. "Global Disease Eradication." *Journal of the European Economic Association* 1 (2–3): 591–600.

Bowland, Bradley J., and John C. Beghin. 2001. "Robust Estimates of Value of a Statistical Life for Developing Economies." *Journal of Policy Modeling* 23 (4): 385–96.

Cadsby, C. Bram, and Elizabeth Maynes. 1999. "Voluntary Provision of Threshold Public Goods with Continuous Contributions: Experimental Evidence." *Journal of Public Economics* 71 (1): 53–73.

CERN (European Organization for Nuclear Research). 2002. "Why Do We Need CERN?" [http://public.web.cern.ch/Public/Content/Chapters/AboutCERN/WhatIsCERN/NeedCERN/NeedCERN-en.html].

Cropper, Maureen L., and Nathalie B. Simon. 1996. "Valuing the Health Effects of Air Pollution." DEC Notes 7, April. World Bank, Washington, D.C.

Fehr, Ernst, and Simon Gächter. 2000. "Cooperation and Punishment in Public Goods Experiments." *American Economic Review* 90 (4): 980–94.

Fenner, Frank, Donald A. Henderson, Isao Arita, Zdenek Jezek, and Ivan D. Ladnyi. 1988. *Smallpox and Its Eradication.* Geneva: World Health Organization.

Hirshleifer, Jack. 1983. "From Weakest-Link to Best-Shot: The Voluntary Provision of Public Goods." *Public Choice* 41 (3): 371–86.

Kaul, Inge, and Katell Le Goulven. 2003. "Financing Global Public Goods: A New Frontier of Public Finance." In Inge Kaul, Pedro Conceição, Katell Le Goulven, and Ronald U. Mendoza, eds., *Providing Global Public Goods: Managing Globalization.* New York: Oxford University Press.

Lederberg, Joshua. 2002. "Summary and Assessment." In Stacey Knobler, Joshua Lederberg, and Leslie A. Pray, eds., *Considerations for Viral Disease Eradication: Lessons Learned and Future Strategies.* Washington, D.C.: National Academy Press.

Milani, Andrea. 2003. "Extraterrestrial Material—Virtual or Real Hazards?" *Science* 300 (5627): 1882–83.

Sandler, Todd. 1992. *Collective Action: Theory and Applications.* Ann Arbor, Mich.: University of Michigan Press.

———. 1997. *Global Challenges: An Approach to Environmental, Political, and Economic Problems.* Cambridge: Cambridge University Press.

Schweickart, Russell L., Edward T. Lu, Piet Hut, and Clark R. Chapman. 2003. "The Asteroid Tugboat." *Scientific American* 289 (5): 54–61.

UN General Assembly. 2004. *Scale of Assessments for the Apportionment of the Expenses of the United Nations.* A/RES/58/1 B. New York.

UPU (Universal Postal Union). 2000. *Constitution General Regulations: Resolutions and Decisions, Rules of Procedure, Legal Status of the UPU. With the Commentary by the International Bureau of the UPU.* Berne. [www.upu.int/acts/en/1_constitution_en.pdf].

Viscusi, W. Kip, and Joseph E. Aldy. 2003. "The Value of a Statistical Life: A Critical Review of Market Estimates throughout the World." *Journal of Risk and Uncertainty* 27 (1): 5–76

World Bank. 2005. *World Development Indicators 2005.* Washington, D.C.

COMPENSATING COUNTRIES FOR THE PROVISION OF GLOBAL PUBLIC SERVICES

THE TOOL OF INCREMENTAL COSTS

KENNETH KING

The notion of incremental cost dates to the 1920s. Yet not until the 1980s and early 1990s did it achieve wide use in international cooperation, in the context of the international debate on global environment issues. When introduced, it was intended to help decisionmakers choose among alternative courses of action. More recently, it has become an important tool for determining the extra cost that a country incurs when contributing to a global public good in an amount greater than it would have contributed (or would have been expected to contribute by the international community) had it been guided solely by criteria of national interest and responsibility.

This chapter clarifies the concept of incremental cost and shows how it applies in different policy areas. It discusses the technical and political-economy issues of estimating incremental cost and illustrates two basic models for sharing incremental cost between a national provider and the international consumers of the added benefits.

The discussion suggests that the concept of incremental cost is important for at least two reasons. First, it provides the country that undertakes an extra effort in the global common interest an opportunity to make its contribution visible and measurable. And the prospect of compensation can act as a powerful incentive for potential providers. This is critical to any discussion of possible compensation. Second, for the country or countries requesting the extra effort, it clarifies that the payments made to compensate the providing nation are not conventional aid but an investment in the requesters' self-interest or at least in the mutual interest of all concerned. Thus the concept of incremental cost is important for making international cooperation more incentive compatible.

EVOLUTION AND USES OF THE CONCEPT OF INCREMENTAL COST

As Johnson and Kaplan (1987) note, the concept of incremental cost emerged in the early 1920s within the academic discipline of managerial cost accounting. One of the first academics to write influentially on this topic was John Maurice Clark (1923a, pp. xiv, 502; 1923b, pp. 50–59; Jackson 1925), who sought to determine when it is desirable to put unused plant or infrastructure capacity to work. He noted that in answering this question it was not necessary to calculate all costs twice—those of the baseline scenario and those of the possible alternative. To the extent that certain costs could be considered fixed whatever the level of capacity utilization chosen, it would suffice to identify and measure only the additional, variable cost—the incremental cost, or as Clark called it, "the differential cost," between the alternatives considered. Then incremental cost can be compared with incremental revenue. As long as incremental revenue is higher, it is worthwhile putting unused capacity to work.

Thus, Clark noted an important characteristic of incremental cost: when comparing alternatives, some costs are the same, and since they cancel each other out, they need not be calculated. Only the difference between variable costs needs to be considered.

As the volume of essays collected by Buchanan and Thirlby (1973) illustrates, a group of economists at the London School of Economics and Political Science came independently to a similar conclusion in the 1930s. Their interest was to analyze the opportunity cost of choosing one economic project over another. They argued that costs, to be relevant for decisionmaking, had to be measured against those of a forgone alternative, a counterfactual baseline. The cost of not choosing the alternative was defined as the opportunity cost. They, too, pointed out that some costs could be the same in alternative courses of action. Therefore, opportunity-cost analysis could exclude those identical costs and focus on the costs that differ across alternatives to establish whether the opportunity cost was higher than the expected net benefit from the chosen alternative.

Thus, the early formulations of the concept of incremental cost were intended to help decisionmakers choose among alternative courses of action the one that promised the most efficient resource utilization. And while efficient resource allocation is also an important consideration in prioritizing international cooperation initiatives, that is not the main use of the concept of incremental cost today in the international cooperation context. Its main purpose is to help identify the additional costs of contributing to a global public good—the costs that are additional to those a country would have incurred had it acted solely on the basis of national self-interest and national responsibility. This use of the concept of incremental cost began to emerge in international policy debates in the late 1980s and early 1990s, frequently in debates on the financing of corrective environmental action such as protection of the ozone layer, preservation of biodiversity, and maintenance of climate stability.

But not all countries valued these concerns equally. And since the richer, industrial countries had contributed most to the emergence of these environmental challenges, many believed that they had a greater obligation to support needed corrective action. Yet, the developing countries often held the key to resolving some of the problems (biodiversity preservation, for example) or could implement corrective action at a higher level of efficiency than the industrial countries. So industrial countries were interested in requesting that more effective and efficient developing countries undertake corrective actions on their behalf, either individually (in a sort of bilateral "trade") or collectively, on behalf of a wider group of countries. And since many global environmental issues have a public goods character, these actions would ultimately be taken in the interests of the international community as a whole.[1] This brought to the fore the issue of compensation and, linked to it, the new use of the concept of incremental cost as the cost of the extra effort that a country undertakes (beyond what it would do if guided solely by national interest) to contribute to a global public good.[2]

The concept of incremental cost provided a breakthrough in this debate in two ways. First, it offered an analytical framework for identifying national actions undertaken with additional external beneficiaries in mind. As King (1993) points out, determining the incremental cost of a national project designed to generate positive global spillovers does not unequivocally indicate how costs should be shared between the provider and other beneficiaries or among the many other beneficiaries that such projects often have. Consider how many actors would potentially benefit from the preservation of a plant species. The group of beneficiaries might not only be large, involving current and future generations, but also difficult to pinpoint. Still, by identifying the additional costs incurred, the concept provides a basis for negotiating cost-sharing arrangements that are perceived as economically efficient and fair by all concerned.

Second, the concept of incremental cost facilitates cost comparisons. The parsimony of its requirements is especially important in calculating the costs of enhanced provision of global public goods. These goods tend to call for a large number of highly complex and sometimes difficult-to-measure inputs. So if some of the component elements can be assumed to be fixed, whether a project has a national or a more global focus, cost estimation becomes much easier.

Box 1 summarizes the main features of the concept of incremental cost as applied to international cooperation. By highlighting some areas of application, it shows that incremental costs can arise in a diverse set of policy contexts, ranging from global environmental concerns to international peacekeeping, global communicable disease control, and the design and operation of national building blocks of international communication and transport networks.

THE TECHNICAL AND POLITICAL-ECONOMY CHALLENGES OF ESTIMATING INCREMENTAL COST

There are both technical and political-economy challenges—often closely intertwined—in determining incremental costs in the context of international

Box 1

THE CONCEPT OF INCREMENTAL COST

Incremental cost is the additional cost of pursuing one course of action rather than another, or the difference in cost between the alternative chosen and the alternative forgone in the case of mutually exclusive alternatives (for further detail, see King 1993).

Conventionally, one of the alternatives is regarded as the actual or proposed course of action. Let it be called alternative A. The other, alternative B, is called the baseline or reference course of action. A comparison of the costs of A and of B indicates the incremental cost of pursuing A rather than B. An important contribution of the literature on incremental cost has been to point out that a pair of alternatives usually includes items that are the same in both so that it often suffices to calculate the cost of the elements that differ.

The concept of incremental cost is now being employed in the context of international cooperation, when a country undertakes an action that contributes to the provision of a global public good to an extent that exceeds what the country would have done had it considered solely national interests and responsibilities.

The concept has found application in a variety of issue areas, from international peacekeeping to environmental challenges, ecotourism, and the provision of national building blocks of international transport and communications systems. Examples include:

- *Protecting the ozone layer.* The Multilateral Fund for Implementation of the Montreal Protocol to the Vienna Convention on Substances That Deplete the Ozone Layer makes financial payments to developing countries on the grounds that they could not otherwise afford to reduce emissions of ozone-depleting substances. These payments are compensation for the incremental cost of emission reductions incurred by these countries, paid on behalf of the international community.
- *Reducing emissions of greenhouse gases.* Countries that use more expensive substitutes for fossil fuels, that practice energy conservation to a greater extent than economically justified, or that sequester carbon in unwanted reforestation incur incremental costs for actions that mitigate climate change. The Global Environment Facility (GEF) finances this type of incremental costs in developing countries.
- *Conserving biodiversity.* The national benefits from conserving biodiversity may not be sufficient to justify conservation. The GEF can finance the incremental costs of biodiversity conservation in developing countries.
- *Minimizing the risk of radioactive fallout.* Replacing outdated nuclear reactors and upgrading others may be necessary to reduce the risk of

---

Box 1 (CONTINUED)

THE CONCEPT OF INCREMENTAL COST

nuclear accidents, affecting not only the country with the reactor but also neighboring countries. When it is not economically efficient for the country with the reactor to incur the incremental cost of the benefit to neighboring countries, this could be a basis for payments by industrial countries to economies in transition. For example, in 1997 the Group of Seven countries and the European Union created the Chernobyl Shelter Fund at the European Bank for Reconstruction and Development to help to stabilize the former nuclear reactor.

- *Protecting the world's cultural heritage.* While there are national benefits to protecting national cultural heritage, in some cases the benefits are global. The United Nations Educational, Scientific and Cultural Organization, through the World Heritage Fund, coordinates multilateral funding that is implicitly based on paying the net incremental costs of restoration or protection initiatives.

- *Controlling the spread of pests and communicable disease.* Actions to control the spread of pests or of communicable diseases provide benefits not only to the country taking these actions but also to neighboring countries and potentially the entire world. If the country where a new communicable disease emerges were to adopt a control strategy that was regionally or globally optimal, it might well incur net incremental costs (costs in excess of what it would be willing to spend based on the national damage alone). These incremental costs could be the basis for compensating the affected country. The outbreak of severe acute respiratory syndrome (SARS) in 2002 illustrates how quickly a new disease can spread internationally when the control strategy is not globally optimal.

Source: King 1993; www.thegef.org; www.ebrd.com/enviro/nuclear; http://whc.unesco.org/.

---

cooperation. The political-economy issues tend to arise when incremental costs are established as a reference point for international transfer payments.

Technical challenges

Some of the technical challenges in estimating incremental cost include identifying clear increments, especially for the incremental benefits that would justify the incremental expenditure; selecting appropriate planning horizons and system boundaries; dealing with the uncertainties in projecting future cost and benefit streams; and determining the counterfactual costs and benefits of the baseline alternative. Box 2 elaborates on each of these aspects.

Box 2

TECHNICAL ISSUES IN ESTIMATING INCREMENTAL COSTS AND BENEFITS

Several technical issues may arise when estimating the incremental cost of an activity or project compared with an alternative course of action. Among them:

Increments. Quantifying the costs and benefits not only of the course of action proposed but also of the course of action that would otherwise have taken place can increase technical complexity. But thinking in increments simplifies the estimation to the extent that certain hard-to-quantify costs and benefits occur in both the alternative and baseline cases. To the extent that they can be assumed to be fixed, they can be ignored because they cancel each other out.

Planning horizons and system boundaries. It is useful to choose the planning horizon (the period over which the incremental benefit will be sustained or the incremental costs incurred) and the system boundary (spatial scope of the action and its impact) in a way that captures all significant incremental costs and incremental benefits within the same analysis.

Expanding the system boundary can sometimes suggest radically new alternatives. For example, investing in agricultural intensification by indigenous groups may protect biodiversity by preventing encroachment on pristine areas within a watershed, while simultaneously reducing soil erosion. For historical and institutional reasons planning for these activities is separate, but treating both sets of activities within the same system may allow analysts to see and devise more cost-effective solutions.

Uncertainty. Typically, the investment costs of a project can be quantified as well as expenditures that occur over a brief period. However, a project designed to guarantee financial sustainability may require projections of recurrent costs and revenues over a longer period, which may be difficult to do with much certainty.

Counterfactuals. While projecting future benefits and costs is uncertain, for the selected alternative the actual costs and benefits will at least be revealed over time. More difficult is estimating the benefits and costs for the counterfactual alternative, especially when the chosen project is a substitute for this alternative. For example, the costs of a solar-thermal power station that emits no greenhouse gases can be measured, but the costs of the natural gas turbine plant for which it is a substitute have to be reasoned, perhaps using available information on the typical costs in the industry, the plant's operating characteristics, the location and costs of fuel supply, and the nature of the power grid into which the natural gas turbine plant would have been inserted.

Two examples demonstrate some of the technical challenges, based on projects whose intended objectives are to contribute to a global public good. The first example demonstrates how to estimate incremental cost of an additional project activity (see appendix). The example concerns a proposal to modify a cattle-raising project to protect wildlife in the Okavango Delta in southern Africa.[3] The second example describes a substitute activity, based on a project in Morocco aimed at contributing to a reduction in greenhouse gases (and thus to the global public good "climate stability") by substituting solar-thermal power for gas-fired power-generating capacity in Morocco (see appendix).[4] It demonstrates problems of costing a counterfactual baseline alternative.

These two examples show that estimating the net incremental costs of such projects may seem tremendously complex, yet it may be relatively simple and feasible when the analysis concentrates on estimating only the additional costs and benefits.

Political-economy challenges

Two situations are particularly prone to political-economy challenges. First, since there often is no unequivocal way of estimating incremental cost, reaching a methodological consensus can be difficult, especially if the stakeholder group is large and diverse. Second, when incremental cost becomes a basis for transfer payments from one group to another, the technical challenges may become an occasion for political gaming.

Methodological consensus. Consider, for example, the case of communicable disease control. Many rural clinics are involved in fighting a disease like HIV/AIDS, and their contribution to this goal is typically only one of many outputs they produce. The incremental cost of an additional effort to help prevent the disease from spreading across borders is extremely difficult to define and measure. Or consider the case of local farming communities protecting genetically diverse but lower yield varieties of crop species such as wheat and rice. In such cases it is important to reach a common understanding of incremental cost through participatory stakeholder dialogue, lest concerns about fairness arise.

One way to foster consensus is to help actors model incremental cost arguments on previous projects of a similar type. Another way is to develop a negotiation framework that shifts the emphasis from a general debate on methodology to specific issues of cost sharing.[5] But sometimes the only way to settle a matter is to have external experts assess the incremental cost of the project.

Political gaming. Suppose that the concern relates to using incremental cost as the basis for a transfer payment as distinct from using it in optimizing an investment decision for a single entity. The project proponent might have strong incentives to interpret any ambiguities in the incremental cost estimation in one of two strategic ways. One would be to maximize the likelihood of project selection, by arguing that the project requires extra cost and thus warrants being considered for a transfer payment. The second would be to maximize the amount of the extra cost—with a view to maximizing the compensation to be negotiated. The party that would make the payment has opposing incentives: to query the justification for a transfer payment and to lower the level of the compensation to be paid. It is important to bear these incentive structures in mind because data access is rarely symmetric and increments can be highly sensitive to small changes in assumptions about counterfactual and future situations.

To counter possible political gaming, it is useful to construct baselines from public information and data collected for other reasons, such as sector studies or investment plans. The substitute project case described in the appendix also addresses this issue. Another approach is to agree on a financing arrangement that tracks the time or risk profile of the activity so that payments can be based on incremental costs that are revealed over time rather than estimated up front, when uncertainties are greater.

DESIGNING AN APPROPRIATE COST-SHARING ARRANGEMENT

The incremental-cost concept provides a way to value the additional costs of generating positive externalities from a given project. However, it does not necessarily indicate how these costs are to be allocated. The question of "Who pays?" is to be determined outside the framework of incremental cost. Put differently, who is willing to pay—and how much—does not determine what the incremental costs are. The answers to these questions determine only to what extent and by whom the provider of the incremental effort will be reimbursed for the costs incurred, if at all.

The best arrangement for compensation depends on the nature of the benefits. Two basic models can be differentiated: the port model, applied in the context of airports and seaports, and the global-fund model of pooled compensation. Where a good has mixed public and private benefits, as in the port model, the recovery of incremental costs can often be left to the provider, because user fees and charges can be levied. In contrast, national contributions to global public goods with diffuse benefits, as in the global-fund model, are likely to call for the creation by the international community of a common, global fund.

The port model: mixed public-private benefits

Consider the case of an airport that provides a variety of services to airlines, freight-forwarders, passengers, ground-handling agents, and others. Now consider the need to choose between an airport investment and management plan to serve domestic demand only and one to make the airport a hub in the international civil aviation system, generating global public benefits (standardized levels of communication and improved connectivity and air safety). The incremental cost would include not only the additional resource costs of the supply but also such external costs as congestion, pollution, and noise, and the opportunity costs that arise when use of the service by one party prevents use by another—such as excess demand for runway capacity.

The beneficiaries of the international hub alternative would be national residents plus a large number of potential external agents, some of whom may arrive and depart from the airport and others who may enjoy the airport services only indirectly, say as consumers of a good shipped by air. For consumers who come to the airport, the operator can recover at least some of the incremental costs through user fees and charges. The incremental cost of upgrading, standardizing, and expanding airport services is an important reference value for the economic regulation of airport prices. Incremental cost is used to determine user fees and charges in various ways. For example, charges for aircraft takeoff, landing, and parking are determined according to the aircraft's length, weight, and other factors that influence the cost of providing terminal services and facilities (see, for example, UK Civil Aviation Authority 2001).

Thus, airports illustrate the case of projects that generate global public benefits while also introducing access barriers (for example, the need for tickets, which permits the airport operator to charge passengers according to the frequency of their airport use). The port model of user fees and charges for the recovery of incremental costs thus applies in cases where the good or service is an impure public good, with both public and private benefits (figure 1). Airport services are largely nonrival (at least up to the congestion point), which makes them public in nature, available for all to consume. But it is also feasible to make them exclusive, accessible only against payment of an airport tax or other levy.

A similar type of good can be found in ecotourism. The cost of maintaining wilderness that is of global significance or of preserving areas that are ecologically sensitive but attractive to tourists can, for example, be wholly or partially recovered from hotel operators and travelers. Hotel developers could be required to internalize the costs of incorporating environmental constraints in the design of barrages that control water levels near beachfront hotels. Such environmentally motivated tourism charges have been introduced in a number of countries.[6]

The global-fund model: diffuse benefits

Consider a national contribution toward the provision of the global public good international peace and security. Many countries support UN peacekeeping operations by providing a contingent of their national military forces. Canada's Department of National Defence estimates an incremental cost—costs additional to those needed to sustain the military forces in peacetime standby on Canadian soil—of C$395 million between 2001 and 2003 for Canada's participation in international security efforts such as Operation Appollo in Afghanistan (Canada

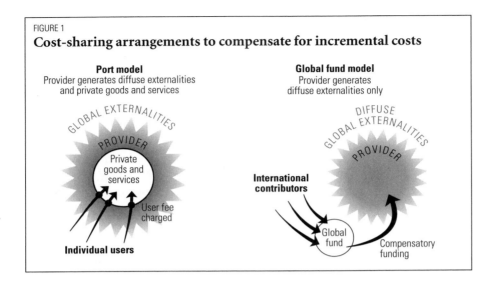

FIGURE 1
Cost-sharing arrangements to compensate for incremental costs

Port model
Provider generates diffuse externalities
and private goods and services

Global fund model
Provider generates
diffuse externalities only

Department of Finance 2003, p. 163). For the United States the incremental cost of engaging in military operations abroad to fight terrorism is estimated at $165 billion from September 11, 2001, through fiscal 2004 (U.S. GAO 2004, p. 5). Presumably other contributing countries make similar calculations, at least implicitly, as a reference point for comparing the costs incurred with any intangible national benefits they may derive from serving the global common good or for establishing the reimbursement due to them from the United Nations.

Promoting international peace and security tends to generate important diffuse public effects that benefit many parts of the world. That usually makes it difficult to follow the type of beneficiary-pays approach applied in the port model of cost-sharing incremental cost. When projects generate diffuse externalities, it is usually more appropriate to adopt a capacity-to-pay approach (see figure 1). UN peacekeeping missions are typically funded based on a common pool arrangement: UN member states contribute to the cost of these missions according to assessed contributions, which reflect mainly their level of income (UN 2001). Mission expenses are met from these common pool resources, including reimbursement of poorer countries that contribute military forces.

Many national projects addressing global environmental challenges are similar in nature. The cross-border externalities they help generate are also highly diffuse, benefiting the international community. To offer appropriate incentives and compensation to national providers, the international community has established several pooled financing arrangements.

The Global Environment Facility (GEF) is a prominent example.[7] It serves several international environmental conventions as a financing mechanism and mobilizes resources from donor countries in negotiated replenishment rounds every three to four years. The GEF estimates the overall level of resources required, which donor countries are then invited to meet. A basic framework has been agreed to, based on the shares of the 10th replenishment round of the World Bank Group's International Development Association. Contributions are closely related to a country's gross domestic product. However, donors can make additional contributions. And while some countries do so, others fail to contribute even their informally agreed-on share. GEF funding is meant to compensate providing countries for the extra efforts they undertake in the global interest. As a general rule recipients are developing countries and transition economies.[8]

CONCLUSION

A major message of this analysis is that the concept of incremental cost has different uses. Sometimes it is a tool for choosing between alternative courses of action. Sometimes it is a tool for determining the cost incurred by individual providers of a good when they are thinking beyond their self-interest or about their responsibility for internalizing various external costs. In the international cooperation context incremental cost tends to refer to the extra costs incurred by a national provider of a global public good or externality—beyond what the providing country would have contributed had it acted solely on national considerations.

Another message is that incremental cost constitutes but a reference point for negotiating cost-sharing arrangements. It can form the basis for various financing arrangements. A number of factors determine actual payments to the provider, which may be lower or higher depending on such factors as the provider's political bargaining skills and power. And different arrangements can be made to compensate the provider for the incremental cost incurred based on the nature of the good's benefits (whether mixed public-private benefits or diffuse). The port model illustrates one approach, relying on user fees and charges, among other financing sources. The global, or pooled compensation, fund illustrates another approach, relying especially on resource mobilization by an international financing facility.

The concept of incremental cost allows the international community to recognize that some national projects make significant contributions to solving a global problem. Compensating providers for these contributions creates an incentive for them to undertake the effort. The concept also enables those who help defray the incremental cost to realize that the resources they contribute are not conventional aid but a payment undertaken in their self-interest or at least in the mutual interests of the parties involved. In the port model this fact is often quite clear. In the global-fund model incremental cost payments are often confused with conventional aid. Distinguishing these two lines of financing more systematically could increase people's willingness to pay and generate additional resources for meeting global challenges.

APPENDIX. ESTIMATING THE INCREMENTAL COST OF AN ADDITIONAL
PROJECT AND A SUBSTITUTE PROJECT

The methodology for estimating incremental cost varies according to whether the
project is additional or a substitute. This appendix offers an example of each.

An example of an additional project: cattle raising and wildlife protection in the Okavango Delta

An additional project goes beyond what an actor would have undertaken based
only on private or national interest. Taking national, regional, or global public
concerns into account may generate additional activities that incur additional,
incremental cost.

Context. In response to an outbreak of contagious bovine pleuropneumonia
(CBP) in the Okavango Delta in Southern Africa, government authorities decided
to erect veterinary fences to prevent the cattle from mingling and spreading the
disease.[9] Such fences were known to be an effective device for containing the disease. However, the fences would intersect important wildlife corridors and prevent the migration of wildlife from core wetlands to dispersal areas outside the
delta. Because this would have a major impact on the ecosystem of the delta, a
replacement for the fences was considered.

Baseline. CBP is a serious livestock disease, which so far has not been transmitted
naturally or experimentally to wildlife. Wildlife has a natural resistance to CBP
and is neither a reservoir of infection nor a vector of transmission. When the new
outbreak occurred, the primary concern thus was to prevent the disease from
spreading through cattle herds.

Proposed alternatives. Two alternative courses of action were proposed. One was to
make the fences more wildlife friendly, taking into account the differences between
wildlife and cattle in size, physiology, and leaping ability. The other option was to
do without fences and to vaccinate cattle instead. To be effective, however, the vaccine must be kept frozen up to the point of inoculation. Each alternative implied
an extra, added effort in the global interest—and an incremental cost.

Both alternatives meet two conditions. First, the domestic benefits of the
baseline are maintained: CBP will be contained, exports of the animals can continue, and foreign exchange earnings will not be disrupted. Second, the threat to
the wildlife and the delta's ecosystem is minimized either by modifying the veterinary fences or by doing without them and vaccinating the cattle.

Determination of the net incremental cost. Only estimates of net incremental
costs—costs minus benefits—can provide a sound basis for comparing the alter-

natives. And consideration of both domestic and global benefits is important because international compensation for incremental cost should be provided net of the domestic benefits.

The incremental benefits of the two alternatives are the same (table A.1). Thus, comparison of the net incremental cost of the two alternatives does not require computation of the benefits: it is enough to establish that they are the same.

Both alternatives provide domestic incremental benefits relative to the baseline. A major potential advantage of shifting to either of the alternatives is that they would ensure higher populations of wild animals, which could provide a steady supply of bushmeat for local subsistence consumption. This would imply a cost savings over meat purchased from cattle ranches, which tends to be more expensive.

The incremental global benefit is the conservation of the biodiversity associated with the delta biome. The main stakeholder for this benefit is the global community. Since there are both incremental domestic and global benefits, determination of the net global benefits that are external to the country would

TABLE A.1

Benefit analysis for an additional project

Benefit	Baseline (B) Veterinary fences	Alternative 1 (A1) Annual vaccination, no fences	Alternative 2 (A2) Wildlife-friendly fences	Increment 1 (A1–B)	Increment 2 (A2–B)
Domestic	Cattle isolated, and threat of disease (CBP) contained	Cattle isolated, and threat of disease (CBP) contained	Cattle isolated, and threat of disease (CBP) contained	Nil	Nil
	Less free-ranging wildlife	More free-ranging wildlife	More free-ranging wildlife	More bush-meat for local consumption	More bush-meat for local consumption
Global biodiversity	Strangulation of wildlife and disruption of migration paths (negative benefits)	Movement and migration of wildlife not curtailed or threatened	Movement and migration of wildlife not curtailed or threatened	Improved probability of wildlife survival and migration to dispersal areas	Improved probability of wildlife survival and migration to dispersal areas

Source: GEF 1997.

require having estimates of both domestic and global benefits. Because of the lack of empirical information on this issue, this estimation is difficult to do.

Since the baseline and the alternatives have little in common, calculating the incremental cost requires estimating the full costs of the baseline and the alternatives (that is usually the situation when estimating costs of an additional project). For the baseline and for either alternative, there are capital (fixed) costs and recurrent (variable) costs to consider.

The incremental cost of the vaccination alternative is less than half the cost of the wildlife-friendly fences alternative (table A.2). Since the benefits are the same in both alternatives, the alternatives can be compared even though there are no estimates of the benefits. It is not, however, possible to say that these incremental costs are associated purely with global benefits, because both alternatives generate additional domestic benefits.

An example of a substitute project: substituting power sources to reduce greenhouse gas emissions

In the case of a substitute project an actor contemplates replacing the current practice with an alternative that considers not only the private or national interest but also the national, regional, or global public concerns. This substitute may generate additional activities and incur additional incremental cost.

Context. Morocco's energy demand had grown at an average annual rate of about 6 percent during the 1990s and was expected to continue growing at this pace for the foreseeable future.[10] To meet the growing demand, some 1,200 megawatts of additional generation capacity were needed over the following five years.

TABLE A.2

Cost estimates for an additional project
(U.S. dollars)

Cost	Baseline (B) Veterinary fences	Alternative 1 (A1) Annual vaccination, no fences	Alternative 2 (A2) Wildlife- friendly fences	Increment 1 (A1–B)	Increment 2 (A2–B)
Capital	900,000	1,000,000	3,050,000	100,000	2,150,000
Recurrent[a]	1,151,805	2,303,610	1,727,707	1,151,805	575,902
	[200,000]	[400,000]	[300,000]	[200,000]	[100,000]
Total	2,051,805	3,303,610	4,777,707	1,251,805	2,725,902

a. Present value of recurrent costs for years 2–10, at a 10 percent discount rate. Annual recurrent costs in brackets.
Source: GEF 1997.

TABLE A.3

Cost estimates for a substitute project
(millions of U.S. dollars)

Cost	Baseline (B) Integrated gas combined cycle	Alternative (A) Solar thermal–natural gas hybrid	Increment (A–B)
Capital costs	58.4	112.6	54.2
Site works and infrastructure	1.6	3.4	1.8
Solar field	0.0	34.9	34.9
Heat transfer system / boiler	0.0	2.8	2.8
Power block	41.4	36.3	−5.1
Balance of plant	7.9	19.0	11.1
Services	7.5	16.2	8.7
Fuel costs	120.7	105.3	−15.4
Operations and maintenance costs	35.1	39.5	4.4
Total	214.2	257.4	43.2

Note: Costs are based on an assumed lifetime of 25 years for both the baseline and substitute plants, each delivering 774 gigawatt hours of energy a year.
Source: GEF 1999b (pp. 4–5).

Coal and natural gas were expected to be used as the fuel sources for this expansion. But the government was also committed to developing renewable energy resources. A proposed GEF-financed project would build a hybrid solar-thermal and fossil fuel power plant as a substitute for a combined-cycle gas turbine plant that would otherwise have been economically preferred. The proposed plant would have the same energy output and, as far as possible, the same operating characteristics as the plant it would substitute for, but it would be more expensive, meaning that incremental costs would be incurred.

Baseline. Using a computer program to analyze the power system expansion plan, fuel supply and availability, and potential candidate plants, the government's planning authority identified combined-cycle gas turbine plants fueled with natural gas as the least-cost baseline course of action.

Proposed alternative. The proposed alternative was a solar thermal–fossil fuel hybrid power plant delivering the same amount of energy annually as the baseline. The plant would be located in an area with good solar resources and close to the natural gas pipeline. Calculations of cost, output, operating characteristics, and solar share were based on the findings of a prefeasibility study.

Determination of net incremental cost. Determination of incremental cost is based on a direct comparison of the proposed alternate plant and the least-cost conventional solution in the same capacity range (the baseline).

Since the annual power delivery is the same for both, there is no difference in domestic benefits for this aspect. Substituting solar-thermal for some of the fossil fuel will improve domestic air quality slightly, but the additional domestic benefits are small and can be ignored. The substitute project would generate two types of global environmental benefits, however. It would accelerate the commercial breakthrough of solar-thermal technology, and it would reduce the emission of carbon dioxide, a greenhouse gas, and thus mitigate climate change. Since all the incremental benefits of the substitute project are global, the international community should provide compensation equal to the incremental cost.

Capital costs are substantially higher for solar-thermal power (about $1,650 per kilowatt) than for conventional combined-cycle gas turbine with the same energy output ($450 per kilowatt). Variable costs—mainly operations and maintenance and fuel purchases—are lower, however. The typical operations and maintenance costs for a solar field are about 1¢ per kilowatt hour—compared with about 0.5¢ per kilowatt hour for a typical combined-cycle gas turbine plant. These higher operations and maintenance costs are more than offset by savings in fuel costs. The economic cost of natural gas from the pipeline is $2.5 per million British thermal units, or about 1.67¢ per kilowatt hour of output (assuming a reasonable plant efficiency of 51 percent).

On these assumptions, the incremental cost is estimated at $43.2 million (table A.3). This incremental cost generates incremental benefits that can be considered fully global in scope. As such, it provides a direct estimate of the compensation to be provided by the international community.

NOTES

1. For a discussion on the concept of global public goods and its application to various global environmental challenges, see Kaul, Grunberg, and Stern (1999); Kaul and others (2003); and Sandler (2004).

2. Paragraph 33.14 of Agenda 21 (UN 1992) explicitly endorses the use of the incremental cost concept to determine the compensation to be provided to developing countries for activities that yield global environmental benefits.

3. This proposal was discussed during the preparation of a GEF-financed project (GEF 1997). The project is the Regional (Angola, Botswana, Namibia) Environmental Protection and Sustainable Management of the Okavango Basin Project, approved as part of the July 24, 2000, GEF Intersessional Work Program and endorsed on the basis of a final project document posted on November 5, 2002 (GEF 2000). The proposal discussed was not part of the final approved project.

4. This GEF-financed project is the Morocco Solar-Based Thermal Plant Project, approved as project 18 in the May 5, 1999, GEF Work Program (GEF 1999a).

5. All of these have actually been used by the GEF. For paradigm cases see King and Giesen (1997) and International Institute for Environment and Development (1999). The GEF Small Grants Program balances incremental cost at the program level and does not impose this analytical burden on small grantees. Costs are also negotiated and agreed.

6. For example, Belize requires all foreign tourists to pay a $3.75 conservation fee at the airport to directly finance a trust for the conservation of protected areas. In the Turks and Caicos Islands hotel room taxes were increased from 8 percent to 9 percent, and the additional 1 percent goes directly into a conservation trust fund modeled on the one in Belize. The Tubbataha Reefs National Marine Park in the Philippines charges scuba divers a $50 per person reef conservation fee to protect Tubbataha's coral reefs. For more detailed descriptions and other examples see Conservation Finance Alliance (2003).

7. See www.thegef.org.

8. Eligibility varies somewhat in accordance with rules negotiated in the context of the environmental conventions.

9. This example is based on GEF (1997).

10. This example is based on GEF (1999a).

REFERENCES

Buchanan, James M., and George F. Thirlby, eds. 1973. *L.S.E. Essays on Cost.* London: London School of Economics and Political Science.

Canada, Department of Finance. 2003. *The Budget Plan 2003.* Ottawa.

Clark, John Maurice. 1923a. *The Economics of Overhead Costs.* Chicago, Ill.: University of Chicago Press.

———. 1923b. "Some Aspects of Overhead Costs: An Application of Overhead Cost to Social Accounting, with Special Reference to the Business Cycle." *American Economic Review* 13 (suppl. 1): 50–59.

Conservation Finance Alliance. 2003. *Conservation Finance Guide.* [http://guide.conservationfinance.org/index].

GEF (Global Environment Facility). 1997. "Paradigm Cases to Illustrate the Application of the Incremental Cost Assessment to Biodiversity." Washington, D.C. [www.thegef.org/Operational_Policies/Eligibiligy_Criteria/Incremental_Costs/paradigm.htm].

———. 1999a. "Morocco: Solar Based Thermal Power Plant." Washington, D.C. [www.gefonline.org/projectDetails.cfm?projID=647].

———. 1999b. "Project Document for WP Part 1." Washington, D.C. [www.gefweb.org/wprogram/May99/Climate/morocco_sol1.oc].

————. 2000. "Project Brief: Regional (Angola, Botswana, Namibia) Environmental Protection and Sustainable Management of the Okavango Basin." [www.gefweb.org/Documents/Work_Programs/wp_july2000/wp-c9-01.PDF].

International Institute for Environment and Development. 1999. "Clarifying and Simplifying Incremental Costs." Report of the GEF/IIED Workshop, March 25–26, London.

Jackson, Hugh. 1925. Book review of *The Economics of Overhead Costs* by John Maurice Clark. *The American Economic Review* 15 (1): 82–84.

Johnson, H. Thomas, and Robert S. Kaplan. 1987. *Relevance Lost: The Rise and Fall of Management Accounting.* Boston, Mass.: Harvard Business School Press.

Kaul, Inge, Isabelle Grunberg, and Marc A. Stern, eds. 1999. *Global Public Goods: International Cooperation in the 21st Century.* New York: Oxford University Press.

Kaul, Inge, Pedro Conceição, Katell Le Goulven, and Ronald U. Mendoza, eds. 2003. *Providing Global Public Goods: Managing Globalization.* New York: Oxford University Press.

King, Kenneth. 1993. "The Incremental Costs of Global Environmental Benefits." Working Paper 5. Global Environmental Facility, Washington, D.C.

King, Kenneth, and Wim Giesen. 1997. *Incremental Costs of Wetland Conservation: Case Studies in Asia and the Pacific.* Kuala Lumpur: Wetlands International.

Sandler, Todd. 2004. *Global Collective Action.* New York: Cambridge University Press.

UK Civil Aviation Authority. 2001. "Economic Regulation and Incremental Costs." Consultation Paper. London.

UN (United Nations). 1992. *Earth Summit Agenda 21: The United Nations Programme of Action from Rio.* New York.

————. 2001. *Scale of Assessments for the Apportionment of the Expenses of United Nations Peacekeeping Operations.* General Assembly Resolution A/RES/55/235. New York.

U.S. GAO (General Accounting Office). 2004. "Military Operations: Fiscal Year 2004 Costs for the Global War on Terrorism Will Exceed Supplemental, Requiring DOD to Shift Funds from Other Uses." GAO-04-915. Washington, D.C.

CREATING NEW MARKETS
THE CHICAGO CLIMATE EXCHANGE

RICHARD L. SANDOR

New markets have emerged throughout history not as accidental events but as responses to new economic realities. For example, in the sixteenth and seventeenth centuries in Europe the rapid growth in demand for capital to finance maritime explorations and overseas commerce led to the emergence of the world's first stock markets. Today, efforts are under way to develop markets for products based on carbon dioxide emissions and mitigation. This time, the challenge prompting market creation is the growing risk of global climate change or, more concretely, the growing interest in financing corrective action in a way that minimizes the aggregate costs. No doubt, different problems call for different solutions. Still, in exploring market-based solutions to the challenge of reducing greenhouse gas emissions and averting the risk of global warming, we can rely today on a rich stock of both theoretical insight into market creation and practical experience in creating markets.

Four lessons seem particularly relevant:

- To be desirable, markets must be reasonably cost-effective, and the gains from trade must clearly outweigh the costs.
- Successful market development typically follows a multistage process, from recognition of a new challenge to the launch of pilot trading schemes, formalization of the trading process, and organization of futures and over-the-counter markets.
- Voluntary efforts and pilot schemes are important in market creation. By experimenting with various institutional mechanisms, they generate data that contribute to informed policy debate and decisionmaking. They allow potential market participants to learn by doing, and they build human capital that will be essential to the market when it takes off.
- Market creation often requires—or comes associated with—financial innovation, the introduction or diffusion of new technologies for financial

This chapter is based on the "Minnesota Lecture" given by the author at the University of Minnesota in October 2003. The author would like to thank Dr. Lynne Kiesling, Michael Walsh, and Rafael Marques for their comments and assistance in the preparation of this chapter.

intermediation. To enhance acceptance and facilitate implementation, it is important that these financial innovations be intellectually ratified by thought leaders.

This chapter elaborates on these messages. It first discusses how to determine when markets might be a desirable response to a particular policy challenge. It then considers some examples of market creation and distills an "ideal-type," seven-stage framework of market development. Next it examines the special case of the Chicago Climate Exchange, applying the heuristic tool of the seven-stage framework. Finally, it looks ahead, considering some of the challenges in moving from pilot initiatives to a full-fledged market for greenhouse gas emissions trading.

Determining when markets are economically desirable: the intellectual tradition

The emission of pollutants such as greenhouse gases is a classical case of a negative externality—a harmful spillover from an economic activity (consumption or production) of one agent to the welfare of another agent or group of agents. What characterizes externalities is that the agents whose activities generate them do not include the costs of these spillovers in their calculations when determining how much of a particular activity to undertake or how much of the good or service to produce or consume.[1] Greenhouse gas emissions, notably those of carbon dioxide, change the gas composition of the atmosphere. Unchecked, they will intensify the risk of climate change—with potentially high cost implications for all. Greenhouse gas emissions reduce the availability of the global public good "climate stability."[2] Thus, by emitting greenhouse gases an agent, let us say a country, generates a serious risk for the international community as a whole, including most likely itself.

Economists identify three principal means to control and correct external effects. One is to apply a command-and-control approach, such as standard setting. A second is to supplement this approach with economic incentives, such as taxes and subsidies, in the tradition established by Pigou (1920). And the third is to assign property rights, as suggested by Coase (1960).

It is widely believed that the second and third approaches are often preferable to command-and-control regulations. Command-and-control regulations tend to be of a "one size fits all" type, unable to exploit differences among actors, and thus lead to misallocation of resources and inefficiency. But how to choose between "economic incentives" and "property rights?"

Chichilnisky and Heal (2000) argue that for Pigou externalities arise because of a difference between the private costs and the social costs of an activity. Accordingly, Pigou proposed taxes as a tool for increasing the cost of activities that generate negative externalities so as to discourage their supply, and he proposed subsidies for lowering the costs of activities that generate positive externalities so as to encourage their supply.

Coase saw externalities as stemming instead from an absence of property rights. For example, when the atmosphere is viewed as a free good, there for all to use, individual actors lack the incentive to limit air pollution. But matters change if there are property rights that define agent's right to pollute or, more cautiously, their allowances to emit, say, greenhouse gases. When a firm's emissions exceed its allowance, it would have two main options: to install new technology that reduces emissions or to find another actor with unused quotas and buy additional allowances. Introducing property rights or caps, such as allowances and quotas, is an important step toward possible trading and market creation.

Although approaching externalities from different directions, Pigou's and Coase's suggestions lead to a similar outcome: a price change. The Coasean property rights-based approach has been viewed as perhaps the more effective and efficient instrument for dealing with such problems as reducing greenhouse gas emissions (see Cordes 2002; Philibert and Reinaud 2004). The goal of a market-based approach is to introduce flexibility and encourage agents to exchange their products until they feel that the marginal benefits of doing so equal the marginal costs.

While the Pigouvian approach starts by determining the cost (the tax rate or the level of subsidy to be paid), the Coasean approach starts by defining a property right. How individual agents will respond to the Pigouvian incentives is an empirical matter and sometimes difficult to predict. Moreover, given the large number of actors and activities that generate greenhouse gas emissions, monitoring compliance with a Pigouvian tax would be extremely difficult. Thus, in the Pigouvian approach the final outcome, in this case the actual reduction in greenhouse gas emissions, can be highly uncertain.

By contrast, Coasean-type measures such as pollution permits or other tradable greenhouse gas-related products such as credits for certified reductions or offsets effectively allow policymakers to cap pollution levels. Within these limits— and assuming well designed, efficient markets—individual actors can trade to discover the real price of these products and how it compares with that of alternative courses of action, such as developing and installing cleaner technologies.[3]

The market-based approach treats the environment as a truly scarce resource. Certainty of ownership and legal title is fundamental to both the success of markets and proper valuation of the resource. This not only avoids Hardin's (1968) "tragedy of the commons" but also liberates new capital that can be dedicated to environmental improvement (De Soto 2000).

The market-based approach also aims at providing a cost-effective solution. Emissions trading exploits differences in pollution mitigation costs for different emission sources or actors (Newell and Stavins 2003; Stavins 1998). Trading uses a price signal and profit motive to encourage those who can cut pollution costs most efficiently to "cash in" on their comparative advantage. The goal is to help society find and move along the least-cost pollution reduction supply curve. Also, by lowering the unit price of cutting pollution, trading might increase the quantity of pollution reduction that agents are willing to purchase. As Tietenberg (2001, p. xii) notes: "a pivotal point…occurred when empirical cost-effectiveness studies were able to show that it was possible to reach the predetermined standards at a much lower cost than was the case with the traditional command-and-control regime." Sandor, Bettelheim, and Swingland (2002) and Sandor, Walsh, and Marques (2002) suggest that the prospect of improved affordability of environmental protection is a central reason why environmental trading schemes are gaining greater acceptance.

Coase (1960) did not only draw attention to the importance of property rights as an indispensable step toward market creation. He also underlined that market creation may be the most attractive policy option if the transaction costs of trading are low enough to make the market mechanism superior to other policy options. Similarly, Arrow (1969) noted that economic actors are likely to take the market route only if the costs are lower than the benefits to be derived from trading. Minimizing transaction costs and ensuring operational and informational efficiency thus ought to be important considerations of market design.[4]

How to proceed in organizing an efficient new market? The next section analyzes some examples of market formation and evolution—equity, commodity, and fixed-income markets. These markets did not start spontaneously. They responded to latent or overt demand and emerged from deliberate action aimed at testing their feasibility and desirability and then, if they proved successful, at seeing them through until they were fully fledged.

THE HISTORICAL EXPERIENCE WITH MARKET EVOLUTION

Analysis of four cases of market creation—share trading initiated by the Dutch East India Company at the Amsterdam Stock Exchange, early trading in agricultural commodity futures at the Chicago Board of Trade, the emergence of the market for mortgage-backed securities, and the launch of sulfur dioxide emission allowance trading in the United States—reveals that despite considerable diversity, the four followed a similar pattern of market evolution, progressing through a seven-stage process:[5]

1. Structural economic change that creates a new demand for capital.
2. Creation of uniform standards for a new commodity or security.
3. Development of a legal instrument providing evidence of ownership to the commodity or security.
4. Development of informal spot markets (for immediate delivery) and forward markets (nonstandardized agreements for future delivery) for trading receipts of ownership.
5. Emergence of commodities or securities exchanges as centralized trading mechanisms.
6. Creation of organized futures markets (standardized contracts for future delivery on organized exchanges) and options markets.
7. Proliferation of over-the-counter markets.

Not a rigid course that markets must pass through sequentially, this seven-stage process is an analytical construct that seems to describe well the steps from initial experimental and informal trading activities to the emergence of standardized spot markets and futures contracts markets at organized exchanges (table 1).

Case 1: trading of shares of the Dutch East India Company at the Amsterdam Stock Exchange

The maritime explorations from Europe in the late fifteenth century created a tremendous structural change in the financing needs for exploration and expansion of overseas trade. Outfitting ships was costly and beyond what most individual economic actors or smaller partnerships were willing or able to invest, leading to a rapidly growing yet unmet need for capital (stage 1 of the seven-stage framework).

As documented in the account of a seventeenth century Amsterdam broker, Josef Penso de la Vega, the Dutch East India Company devised an innovative approach, mobilizing funds by issuing shares (Stringham 2003; see also de la Vega [1688] 1996; Kellenbenz [1957] 1996; and Fridson 1996). With the creation of these discrete, uniform shares a new financial product was launched (stage 2).[6] What made the shares tradable was that they were standardized and transferable. They served as evidence of ownership that company clerks recognized and were willing to accept (stage 3).

Funds were raised between 1602 and 1606, making shareholders co-owners in the company and creating an early example of a limited liability corporation. In the following years an informal spot market for shares emerged in and around Amsterdam (stage 4). The nascent equity exchange, though it had its own employees, became an informal side activity of the Amsterdam Bourse, a commodity exchange created in 1611 (Stringham 2003; Stringham and Boettke 2004).

Nevertheless, the share trading quickly became more sophisticated, including spot trading, forward contracts, futures, and options, so that in this case stage 6 preceded stage 5, the creation of the Amsterdam Stock Exchange in 1876. "Ducaton" shares, worth a tenth of the underlying share, appeared in the early 1680s (Stringham 2003). Issued by intermediaries, these assets were more affordable than the original shares and allowed a wider group of less affluent investors to enter the market. This differentiation or deconstruction of the initial instrument, and the resultant expansion of over the counter trading, brought the evolution of share trading to the final stage 7 of market development after nearly eight decades.

Case 2: agricultural commodity futures trading at the Chicago Board of Trade

The market for agricultural commodity futures was spurred by England's repeal of its Corn Laws, which had restricted grain imports, and the disruptions of grain imports from Russia caused by the Crimean War (1854–56). These events, along

TABLE 1

Four examples of the seven stages of market development

Stage	Trading of shares of the Dutch East India Company (1602)	Agricultural commodities futures trading at the Chicago Board of Trade (1848)
1. Structural change	• Expansion in European maritime trade • Rising demand for capital to outfit ships	• Removal of restrictions on grain imports into the United Kingdom (1846) and Crimean War (1854–56), leading to rising U.S. demand for imports • U.S. population increase adds further demand—encouraging new investments and expanding trade
2. Emergence of uniform standards	• Issuance of standardized shares by the Dutch East India Company (1602–06)	• Standards for measuring and grading grains set by the Chicago Board of Trade
3. Development of legal instrument	• Shares recognized by the Dutch East India Company as evidence of ownership	• Warehouse receipts issued as proof of ownership and made legally enforceable as of 1859
4. Development of informal spot markets	• Emergence of a spot market, linked informally as of 1611 to the Amsterdam commodity exchange, the Amsterdam Bourse	• Trading based on warehouse receipts begins
5. Emergence of formalized exchanges	• Amsterdam Stock Exchange formally established (1876)	• Charter of the Chicago Board of Trade (1859)
6. Creation of organized futures or options markets	• Futures and options on single "stocks" were common although not legal according to the Dutch law	• Futures contracts formalized (1865)
7. Proliferation of over the counter markets	• "Ducaton" shares representing one-tenth of the value of the earlier shares issued in the early 1680s, encouraging over-the-counter trading	• Options ("privileges") and over-the-counter ("bucket shop") trading begins to take off (1879)

Source: Authors' compilation based on references cited in the text.

Trading of mortgage-backed securities (1970)	Sulfur dioxide trading under the U.S. Clean Air Act Amendments (1990)
• Widening gap between demand for and supply of housing finance in the late 1960s and early 1970s	• Rising concerns about the effects of sulfur dioxide emissions on human health and the environment • Tripling of U.S. pollution-control costs between 1972 and 1990 • Keen interest in least-cost solution to sulfur dioxide problem
• Mortgage-backed pass-through security issued by Ginnie Mae (1970)	• Sulfur dioxide allowance as defined by the Clean Air Act Amendments of 1990
• Mortgage-backed securities (pass-throughs and bonds) find growing acceptance as financial products	• Sulfer dioxide allowance • Registry of U.S. Environmental Protection Agency
• Informal trading between government-sponsored agencies and Wall Street dealers, mortgage originators, and investors	• Various trading pilots during 1970s and 1980s and private sales of allowances in early 1990s • Test auctions in 1993 and 1994
• Secondary Mortgage Market Enhancement Act of 1984 and Tax Reform Act of 1986	• Annual auctions conducted by Chicago Board of Trade on behalf of the U.S. Environmental Protection Agency
• Ginnie Mae futures introduced at Chicago Board of Trade (1975)	• Futures being used but not yet within an official framework
• Increasing number of private retailers in mortgage-backed securities markets	• Informal over-the-counter trades

with rising domestic demand for wheat, stimulated grain production in the United States. The United States expanded the cultivated area and increased productivity, developing into a large producer and exporter of agricultural commodities. Capital was needed to finance the storage and shipment of grain from the main wheat-growing area of the Midwest to the major population and export centers along the East Coast (stage 1).

Initially, physical sacks of grain were traded and inspected for quantity and quality. A tradable instrument called the warehouse receipt had emerged in the 1840s. It provided evidence of ownership and facilitated both capital raising and ownership transfer (stage 3).Created in 1848, the Chicago Board of Trade soon defined standard grain measures and grading procedures (stage 2).[7] The charter conceded by the legislature of the state of Illinois in 1859 made these standards legally enforceable (Lurie 1979).

While the trading of futures contracts had existed since 1849 and the earliest forward contracts were recorded in 1851 (stage 4), not until 1859 were the rules governing the settlement and clearing of contracts incorporated into the charter (stage 5). In 1865 the Board of Trade created standardized agreements called futures contracts (stage 6). Stage 7 was reached with the emergence of options trading (also called "trades in privileges") in 1879. These had existed since the 1860s but had been repeatedly discouraged by the Board of Trade. They reemerged, this time traded mostly in off-market "bucket shops" (Lurie 1979, p. 76). It is this proliferation of over the counter transactions using market standards that can be recognized as the last stage in the process of market evolution.

Case 3: mortgage-backed securities trading

Trading in mortgage-backed securities is a more recent example of market evolution.[8] The impetus came in the 1970s, when the demand for housing—and housing finance—in the United States began to outpace the supply of housing mortgages by the thrift institutions that had been the conventional providers of this type of financing (Brendsel 1996). The U.S. government deregulated—more precisely, began to re-regulate—the financial services industry in 1970, opening the door to a search for innovative instruments that could attract additional investments to the housing sector (stage 1).

Facing a growing demand for mortgages, the thrifts had already begun to issue bonds backed by future payments of the principal and interest they would receive from their borrowers. Also, the U.S. Federal Housing Authority and the U.S. Department of Veterans Affairs had begun to insure or guarantee certain housing loans to attract additional investments. But all these measures fell short of what was required. Mortgages were sold individually or in small bundles, so the high transaction costs prevented large-scale investors from entering the market.

In 1970 the Government National Mortgage Association (Ginnie Mae) pioneered the issuance of mortgage-backed securities, a security based on a pool of mortgages guaranteed by Ginnie Mae and issued by financial institutions approved by Ginnie Mae (stage 2). Issuers purchase the mortgages from the originators, giving the holder (investor) a proportional interest in the mortgage pool. Originators pass all payments (of principal and interest) through directly to the investor. One of the first homogeneous, tradable, pass-through instruments, these securities became the foundation for a secondary market for mortgages (stage 3) that ultimately evolved into spot and forward markets, primarily among Wall Street dealers and mortgage bankers (stage 4). These securities were mostly a one-size instrument, usually a 30-year security matching the typical 30-year length of a housing loan. Then in 1983 collateralized mortgage obligations emerged, offering a differentiated set of products with various rates and maturities and appealing to a wider group of investors, both short and longer term. Further innovations, such as adjustable-rate mortgages, have been introduced to meet new challenges.

Trading of mortgage-backed securities remained scattered until the world's first interest rate futures contract—based on the Ginnie Mae pass-through instrument—was launched at the Chicago Board of Trade in 1975. Through that action financial futures and eventually collateralized mortgage obligations secured acceptance on trading floors of exchanges. Federal legislation (the Secondary Mortgage Market Enhancement Act of 1984 and the Tax Reform Act of 1986) confirmed these trade instruments and practices (Ranieri 1996). They concurrently created the platform for formalized exchanges (stage 5) and the framework for organized futures and options trading (stage 6).

The three main agencies in the field of mortgage-backed securities, Ginnie Mae, Federal National Mortgage Association (Fannie Mae), and Federal Home Loan Mortgage Corporation (Freddie Mac), buy (or facilitate the buying of, in the case of Ginnie Mae), mortgages from originators, bundle them, guarantee the principal and interest payments, and then sell them to investment firms that, in turn, sell them to individual investors.[9] Over-the-counter trading in these instruments is proliferating. Some analysts predict that as computerization allows relevant databases to become linked and investors find it easier to access and process more information on their own, the market for mortgage-backed securities may deconcentrate even more (stage 7).[10]

Case 4: sulfur dioxide emission allowance trading under the U.S. Clean Air Act Amendment of 1990

To ameliorate the adverse effects on human health and the environment of sulfur dioxide emissions from the burning of high-sulfur coal by electric utilities, Title IV of the U.S. Clean Air Act Amendments of 1990 introduced an overall limit on the emissions.[11] Title IV sets out how, within this limit, emission allowances should be distributed across individual actors (mainly utilities) and requires the creation of a trading scheme for these allowances. With Title IV, latent demand turned into overt demand (stage 1).

The goal set forth in the legislation was to reduce emissions to 50 percent of their 1980s level by 2000. To start off the trading scheme, utilities received a certain number of emission allowances free of charge based on their past levels of electricity generation. Each allowance represented an authorization to emit 1 ton of sulfur dioxide. Thus, the legislation itself defined the tradable product (stage 2). In addition, the U.S. Environmental Protection Agency (EPA) set up an electronic tracking system to record information on each party's allowances and actual emission levels. Companies could find out precisely what their quota was, whether they had surplus allowances, or whether they needed to buy additional ones (stage 3).

Private sales and purchases of allowances began even before the Clean Air Act Amendments entered into force in 1995 (stage 4). Organized exchanges began when the EPA chose the Chicago Board of Trade to conduct annual auctions of allowances on its behalf in 1993. The auctions were intended to send price signals to the market (stage 5).[12] On December 2004 the Chicago Climate Futures Exchange began to offer futures contracts on sulfur dioxide emission allowances, marking the establishment of stage 6. Similarly, over-the-counter trades are taking place, mainly on the sidelines of the official exchanges (so that stage 7, too, is still nascent).[13]

The sulfur dioxide trading system has been highly successful.[14] It has achieved larger reductions than the law requires, at costs 75 percent lower than some initial forecasts,[15] and with nearly 100 percent compliance. Studies by the U.S. General Accounting Office (1994, p. 37) put the annual costs of the program at $1.4–$2.6 billion, while EPA estimates health benefits of $10.6–$40 billion a year (U.S. EPA 1995, pp. S-3 and S-4). Reducing sulfur dioxide emissions makes economic sense, and trading seems to be a cost-effective way to do it. There has been steady growth in the trading of sulfur dioxide allowances, from 700,000 tons in 1995 to some 8 million tons in 2004. The market has a value of more than $5 billion a year for registered trades and trades in derivatives (options, forwards, and swaps).

THE CHICAGO CLIMATE EXCHANGE: A PILOT SCHEME IN THE EMERGING GREENHOUSE GAS MARKET

Initiatives aimed at exploring market-based approaches to the challenge of reducing greenhouse gas emissions fall into two main groups. One type aims at facilitating the exchange of credits that result from project-based emission reductions. The buyer participates in the financing of a project that reduces greenhouse gas emissions and in return receives certified credits for some or all of the emission reductions generated. The Prototype Carbon Fund operates in this way.[16] The other type of trading scheme deals with the exchange of pollution allowances, such as in the EU Greenhouse Gas Emission Trading System (EU ETS).[17] Both types of products are traded at the Chicago Climate Exchange.[18]

From recognizing the challenge to establishing evidence of allowances: stages 1–3

The emergence of the market in greenhouse gas emissions is a response to an urgent structural economic change: the growing risk of global climate change and the rising interest in identifying effective, least-cost policy responses. The United Nations Framework Convention on Climate Change of 1992 and the subsequent Kyoto Protocol of 1997 are expressions of this demand for change.[19] These agreements suggest that the demand for reducing greenhouse gases will grow over time. Thus, toward the end of the 1990s it seemed to make increasingly good business sense to explore ways to limit emissions of these gases and to create value for the reductions that actors would make.

First, several obstacles had to be overcome:

- Regulatory uncertainty.
- Lack of a clear and widely accepted definition of the new commodity to be traded.
- Lack of standards for monitoring, verification, and trade documentation.
- Lack of organized markets and clear market prices.

A 2000 study concluded that a pilot market in North America for greenhouse gas emissions would be feasible, and the Chicago Climate Exchange initiative was launched.[20] Its mission was to develop a voluntary program of emission reductions and trading for emission sources and offset projects in the United States, Canada, Mexico, and, for offset projects only, Brazil (box 1).

While the market architecture had been shown to be feasible in principle, further steps were needed. First, the initiative had to be "intellectually ratified." In part to achieve this goal, a high-level advisory committee was formed of members of the academic community, scientists, the environmental community, self-regulatory organizations, and business leaders (appendix box A.1).

Then, the architecture had to be translated into a more detailed design. A group of some 50 companies in the power generation, forest products, manufacturing, oil and gas, and agricultural sectors and hundreds of experts in engineering, forestry, and agriculture was assembled to contribute to the design phase. The first companies to join, designated founding and charter members, were given financial incentives. Another 45 members have joined subsequently, including Roanoke Steel, IBM, Rolls Royce, and several liquidity providers representing proprietary trading firms, environmental brokerage firms, and hedge funds (appendix box A.2).

Two main products are traded at the Chicago Climate Exchange:

- *Exchange allowances.* Allowances are issued to exchange members in accordance with their emission baseline and emission reduction schedule. Members' average emission levels for 1998–2001 are the baseline, which can be adjusted to reflect the acquisition or disposition of facilities. The

---

Box 1

THE CHICAGO CLIMATE EXCHANGE: MISSION AND GOALS

The Chicago Climate Exchange is a self-regulatory, rules-based exchange designed and governed by its members. Members have made a voluntary, legally binding commitment to reduce their emissions of greenhouse gases to 4 percent below their 1998–2001 average baseline by 2006, the last year of the pilot program.

The goals of the exchange are to:
- Demonstrate the viability of a market-based emissions reduction program.
- Establish a mechanism for price discovery.
- Allow flexibility in the methods, location, and timing of emission reductions so that greenhouse gases can be reduced cost-effectively.
- Facilitate trading with low transaction costs.
- Build market institutions and infrastructure and develop human capital for greenhouse gas emission trading.
- Harmonize and integrate the exchange with other trading schemes.
- Disseminate the experience and information gained to support policymakers, corporations, and the public on the real costs of addressing climate change.

Source: www.chicagoclimatex.com.

---

reduction schedule involves a yearly reduction of emissions by 1 percent from the baseline, starting in 2003.
- *Emission offsets.* Offsets are generated when members undertake mitigation projects such as landfill methane destruction; agricultural methane destruction; or carbon sequestration through forestry or agricultural soil projects, agricultural methane destruction, and fuel switching.[21]

A major concern in the initial stages was to achieve uniform product standards to facilitate trading and lower transaction costs. Chicago Climate Exchange activities cover emissions of all six greenhouse gases,[22] several types of offsetting projects, and exchange allowances and offsets. For standardization, emissions of all gases are converted to metric tons of carbon dioxide equivalent using the 100-year global warming potential established by the Intergovernmental Panel on Climate Change.[23] This is the unit of emissions measurement, reporting, price quotation, and trading. The currency traded is the carbon financial instrument (CFI), with 1 CFI equal to 100 metric tons of carbon dioxide equivalent. Every participant, plant, and location is separately registered, as are all allowances and offset projects, offering members clarity about the products as well as their holdings.

To facilitate price discovery prior to commencing continuous trading, the Chicago Climate Exchange held an auction of carbon financial instruments in

September 2003. In the early stages of a market, when there is great uncertainty about price and participants may not have fully established trading and compliance strategies, auctions provide invaluable information on price and volume. In addition, they encourage market participants to get ready for trading. For example, companies may have to get their data on emissions or offsets audited by an independent agency, such as the National Association of Securities Dealers. The September auction was an important step toward a disciplined, rules-based trading operation (Sandor 2003).

From informal spot market to formalized exchange: stages 4 and 5

To operate efficiently even an informal spot market requires some basic elements of an institutional architecture. The main building blocks of the Chicago Climate Exchange architecture include the trading platform, the registry, the clearing and settlement platform, and governance components, including the rulebook and such bodies as standing committees, the external advisory board, and the membership meeting (see table 2 for the main features of the Chicago Climate Exchange).[24]

The trading platform is an Internet-based marketplace for executing trade among Chicago Climate Exchange registry account holders. The registry is an electronic database of the CFIs owned by its account holders. All activities on the trading platform are conveyed to the clearing and settlement platform each day for follow-up, such as netting out positions or producing payment instructions for settling trades. The three market pillars—the trading platform, the registry, and the clearance and settlement platform—are interlinked to support trading operations with real-time data.

Because an efficient, well functioning market requires rules to foster predictability and minimize transaction costs, it is important for those who are interested in the newly emerging market to participate in voluntary pilot schemes to help shape the rules that will govern future market operations. The Chicago Climate Exchange provides opportunities for its members to contribute to self-regulatory efforts. For example, through standing committees, members provide oversight of specific market functions, from certification of emission offsets to compliance. The emerging rules will enter the Chicago Climate Exchange rulebook. Members also contribute to the evolution of the market through annual membership meetings. However, because reliability and standardization are also important, the Chicago Climate Exchange also emphasizes independent audit and scrutiny by external advisors. As noted, the National Association of Security Dealers audits members' baselines and annual emissions and monitors Chicago Climate Exchange trading activity to prevent improper trading.

LOOKING AHEAD

In November 2004 the Chicago Climate Exchange reached the milestone of 2 million tons of carbon dioxide traded (Chicago Climate Exchange 2005). Daily volume

TABLE 2

Main features of the Chicago Climate Exchange

Feature	Description
Geographic coverage	Canada, Mexico, and the United States for emission sources and offset projects, and Brazil for offset projects
Emission targets and timetable	Emission reduction commitments for 2003 through 2006. Emission targets are 1 percent below baseline during 2003, 2 percent during 2004, 3 percent during 2005, 4 percent during 2006
Emission baseline	Average annual emissions during 1998–2001
Gases included	Carbon dioxide, methane, nitrous oxide, perfluorochemicals, hydrofluorocarbons, sulfur hexafluoride
Instruments	Carbon financial instruments (CFIs), with 1 CFI representing 100 metric tons carbon dioxide
Banking of surplus instruments	Banking limited during 2003; full banking during 2004, 2005, 2006
Exposure limits (economic growth provisions)	No firm required to buy (or allowed to sell), on a net basis, more than 3 percent of its baseline during 2003, 4 percent during 2004, 6 percent during 2005, and 7 percent during 2006
Emission offsets	Emission offsets generated when members undertake mitigation projects, such as landfill methane destruction; agricultural methane destruction; or carbon sequestration through forestry or agricultural soil projects, agricultural methane destruction, or, if in Brazil, fuel switching
Early action credits	Credits from specified early projects to be included starting in 2004
Facilities included, emissions monitoring, reporting	Entitywide coverage. Power plants above 25 megawatts to use continuous emission monitors. World Resources Institute protocols to be used to quantify process emissions and emissions from fuel-combustion devices and vehicles. Vehicles and other smaller emission sources can be opted in. Special protocols for methane and carbon sequestration. Annual emissions reporting
Electricity purchase opt-in	Allowances issued if electricity purchase reduction targets are exceeded

TABLE 2 CONTINUED

Main features of the Chicago Climate Exchange

Feature	Description
Market efficiency	Limits on sales by individual firms (5 percent of programwide mitigation) and use of offsets and early action credits (up to 50 percent of programwide mitigation) to avoid market congestion; limits will be escalated if programwide emissions rise above baseline
Registry, electronic trading platform	Registry serves as official holder and transfer mechanism and is linked with the electronic trading platform on which all trades occur
Exchange governance	Self-regulatory organization overseen by committees comprising exchange members, supported by directors and staff

has averaged 7,800 metric tons since trading began in December 2003 (Chicago Climate Exchange 2004). In addition, efforts are under way to link the Chicago marketplace with trading venues in other locations. The European Climate Exchange, a wholly owned subsidiary of the Chicago Climate Exchange, manages sales and marketing for European environmental instruments. ECX Carbon Financial Instruments (ECX CFIs) listed on the International Petroleum Exchange (IPE) are advanced, low-cost, and financially guaranteed tools for trading in the EU Emission Trading Scheme. ECX CFI contracts include both spot contracts (for prompt delivery) and a series of futures contracts that allow users to lock in prices for instruments delivered at set dates in the future. Each ECX Carbon Financial Instrument will be based on emission allowances issued under the EU Emission Trading Scheme. Trading began on April 22, 2005. A growing number of national, subnational, and intracompany trading schemes are also emerging (see IETA 2003 and appendix boxes A.3 and A.4 in this chapter). As the number of schemes increases, it becomes more important—and easier—to connect individual trading places into a more coherent, integrated market. For the Chicago Climate Exchange market conditions are progressing toward stages 6 and 7.

While the feasibility of emissions trading has been established, there are several hurdles, mainly political, in the way of further progress. The Chicago Climate Exchange is based on the voluntary commitment of members to reduce greenhouse gas emissions. Members were willing to make such a commitment and test how best to achieve the self-imposed target because they expected emissions to be capped by law in the future. Although follow-up to the Kyoto Protocol is somewhat uncertain, it still seems that the demand for reductions in greenhouse gas emissions will continue to rise. The risk of global warming is real. Greenhouse gas emissions are clearly a contributing factor. Corrective action is likely to be expensive. Therefore a dual policy challenge has to be met: to value emission reductions (price them correctly) and to create efficient markets to allow competitive trading and minimize aggregate costs.

Future progress will not occur automatically. It requires systematic design and deliberate exploration of alternatives. And it requires considerable diffusion of the idea of emission trading. From its inception the Chicago Climate Exchange has emphasized public outreach through links to universities, journalists, and policymakers. Outreach and dissemination remain important concerns. The risk of global climate change is universal, so everyone wants a say in how to address this challenge. At the same time broad-based technical and policy dialogues will continue, to ensure that the latest knowledge is brought to bear on the evolution of the Chicago Climate Exchange. Innovative pilots like the Chicago Climate Exchange can draw extensively from existing expertise and experience—and they can provide valuable information to support future policy debate and decisionmaking.

CONCLUSION

It is too early to reliably assess the Chicago Climate Exchange or any of the other pilot schemes for greenhouse gas emission trading. Yet many encouraging signs are emerging, echoing the experience of more solidly established markets that have passed through similar stages. When the business case is clear, private entrepreneurs step forward. They make available the services that a new market requires, and they bring their comparative advantage for innovation to bear on the development of derivative products and on the linking and expansion of markets.

APPENDIX BOX A.1
CHICAGO CLIMATE EXCHANGE ORIGINAL EXTERNAL ADVISORY BOARD MEMBERS

- The Honorable *Richard M. Daley,** Mayor, City of Chicago (Honorary Chairman)
- *Warren Batts,* Adjunct Professor, University of Chicago Graduate School of Business; former CEO of Tupperware Corporation, Premark International, and Mead
- *David Boren,* President, University of Oklahoma; former governor of Oklahoma; former U.S. Senator
- *Ernst Brugger,** President, Brugger, Hanser & Partner; Director, International Red Cross
- *Paula DiPerna,* Author and public policy analyst and consultant; former President, the Joyce Foundation

APPENDIX BOX A.1 CONTINUED
CHICAGO CLIMATE EXCHANGE ORIGINAL EXTERNAL ADVISORY BOARD MEMBERS

- *Elizabeth Dowdeswell,** Visiting Professor, University of Toronto; former Executive Director, United Nations Environment Program
- *Jeffrey Garten,** former Dean, Yale School of Management
- *Lucien Bronicki,** Chairman, ORMAT International
- *Donald Jacobs,** Dean Emeritus, Kellogg Graduate School of Management, Northwestern University
- *Jonathan Lash,* President, World Resources Institute
- *Joseph Kennedy II,** Chairman, Citizens Energy Group; former U.S. Representative (Massachusetts)
- *Israel Klabin,** President, Brazilian Foundation for Sustainable Development
- *Bill Kurtis,** Journalist and television producer
- *Thomas Lovejoy,** President, Heinz Center; former Chief Biodiversity Advisor, World Bank
- *David Moran,** former President, Dow Jones Indexes
- *R. K. Pachauri,** Chairman, Intergovernmental Panel on Climate Change; Director Tata Energy Institute
- *Michael Polsky,** President and CEO, Invenergy
- *Les Rosenthal,* Principal, Rosenthal Collins; former Chairman, Chicago Board of Trade
- *Donna Redel,** former Executive Director, World Economic Forum
- *Mary Schapiro,* Vice Chairman, National Association of Securities Dealers (NASD); President, Regulatory Policy and Oversight, NASD
- *Maurice Strong,* Chairman, the Earth Council; former United Nations Under-Secretary-General
- *James Thompson,* Chairman, Winston & Strawn; former Governor of Illinois
- *Sir Brian Williamson,** former Chairman, London International Financial Futures Exchange
- *Robert Wilmouth,** President and CEO, National Futures Association
- *Klaus Woltron,** Austrian entrepreneur; Vice President, Vienna Club
- *Michael Zammit Cutajar,** former Executive Secretary, UN Framework Convention on Climate Change

*Current Advisory Board member. For other current members, see www.chicagoclimateexchange.com/about/people_advisory.html. Members without an asterisk have left their Advisory Board positions due to other responsibilities with the Exchange.

MEMBERS OF THE CHICAGO CLIMATE EXCHANGE AS OF DECEMBER 20, 2004

Aerospace and equipment
Rolls Royce*

Automotive
Ford Motor Co.**

Chemicals
Dow Corning
DuPont**

Consulting
Domani LLC
Global Change Associates
Natural Capitalism, Inc.
Rocky Mountain Institute

Diversified manufacturing
Bayer Corporation

Electric power generation
American Electric Power**
Green Mountain Power
Manitoba Hydro**
TECO Energy, Inc.

Electronics
Motorola, Inc.**

Energy management services
Sieben Energy Associates

Environmental services
Waste Management, Inc.**

Food processing
Premium Standard Farms

Forest products
International Paper**
MeadWestvaco Corp.**

Stora Enso North America**
Temple-Inland Inc.**

Information technology
IBM
Open Finance LLC

Legal services
Foley & Lardner

Liquidity provider
AGS Specialists LLC
Amerex Power Ltd.
Michael R. Anderson
Raymond S. Cahnman
Calyon Financial Inc.
Thomas H. Dittmer
Eagle Market Makers, Inc.
Evolution Markets LLC
FCT Europe Limited
First New York Securities LLC
Goldenberg, Hehmeyer & Co.
ICAP Energy LLC
Chris J. Johnson
Kingstree Trading LLC
Kottke Associates LLC
The League Corporation
Marquette Partners LP
Glenn M. Miller
Douglas M. Monieson
Natsource LLC
Rand Financial Services, Inc.
Refco LLC
Serrino Trading Co., Inc.
Shatkin Arbor, Inc
C. Richard Stark, Jr
Jeffrey B. Stern
Lee B. Stern
Tradelink LLC
Tradition Financial Services

APPENDIX BOX A.2 CONTINUED
MEMBERS OF THE CHICAGO CLIMATE EXCHANGE AS OF DECEMBER 20, 2004

Transmarket Group LLC

Municipality
City of Chicago**

Nongovernmental organization
American Coal Ash
    Association
American Council on
    Renewable Energy
Houston Advanced Research
    Center
World Resources Institute

Offset aggregator
Iowa Farm Bureau

Offset provider
Klabin S.A.
Restoration Soil & Research, Ltd.

Pharmaceuticals
Baxter Healthcare Corporation**

Private university
Tufts University*

Public university
University of Oklahoma
University of Iowa

Religious organizations
Jesuit Community of Santa
    Clara University

Semiconductors
STMicroelectronics*

Steel
Roanoke Electric Steel Corp.*

Student organizations
Oberlin Student Cooperative
    Association

Technology
Ecoenergetics srl
Millennium Cell

Transportation
Amtrak*

* Charter Member. ** Founding Member.
Note: For current members, see also www.chicagoclimateexchange.com/about/members.html.

APPENDIX BOX A.3
SELECTED INTERNATIONAL AGENCIES AND COUNTRIES ENGAGED IN THE
DEVELOPMENT OF GREENHOUSE GASES EMISSION TRADING

International agencies
European Commission
International Energy Agency
Nordic Council
Organisation for Economic Co-operation and Development
United Nations Conference on Trade and Development
United Nations Development Programme
United Nations Environment Programme
United Nations Industrial Development Organization
World Bank Group

Plurilateral trading groups, proposed or ongoing
Baltic countries
Estonia
Latvia
Lithuania
European Union
North America
Canada
Mexico
United States
Umbrella Group
Australia
Canada
Iceland
Japan
New Zealand
Norway
Russia
Ukraine
United States

**National emissions trading and the Clean Development Mechanism and
Joint Implementation, proposed or ongoing**
Canada
China
Denmark
European Union
Germany
Ireland

**SELECTED INTERNATIONAL AGENCIES AND COUNTRIES ENGAGED IN THE
DEVELOPMENT OF GREENHOUSE GASES EMISSION TRADING**

Japan
Korea, Rep. of
Netherlands
New Zealand
Norway
Russian Federation
Slovak Republic
Switzerland
United Kingdom
United States
32 host countries with Clean Development Mechanism and
    Joint Implementation offices or projects

Source: IETA 2003; Philibert and Reinaud 2004; Sandor, Bettelheim, and Swingland 2002.

SELECTED SUBNATIONAL AND PRIVATE TRADING INITIATIVES, PROPOSED OR
ONGOING

Regional and local government schemes
Australia
New South Wales
Western Australia
Brazil
Amapá
Amazonas
Paraná
Canada
Alberta
British Columbia (Greenhouse Gas Emission Reduction Trading)
Ontario (Pilot Emission Reduction Trading)
United States
California
Illinois
Massachusetts
Michigan
New Hampshire
New Jersey
New York State
North Carolina
Oregon
Wisconsin
Wyoming
Midwest
West Coast (California, Oregon, and Washington)
Northeast (Connecticut, Delaware, Maine, Massachusetts, New
  Hampshire, New Jersey, New York, Pennsylvania, Rhode Island, and
  Vermont)

Private schemes and exchanges
Internal trading
BP
Pemex
Royal Dutch Shell
Corporations with emission targets
Alcan
Alcoa
DuPont
Ontario Power Generation

SELECTED SUBNATIONAL AND PRIVATE TRADING INITIATIVES, PROPOSED OR ONGOING

Pechiney
Suncor Energy
TransAlta
Exchanges
Chicago Climate Exchange
Dutch Electricity Board/FACE Foundation
Edison Electric Institute/Utilitree
Hancock Natural Resources Group

Parties to private transactions
American Electric Power–The Nature Conservancy
Arizona Public Service Company–Niagara Mohawk Power Corporation
BP–The Nature Conservancy
Consorcio Noruego–Costa Rica
Environmental Financial Products LLC–Costa Rica
ENERGI E2 A/S–Joensuun Energia Oy
Fortum–EPCOR
Illinova–Environmental Synergy
Nuon–GSF Energy
Ontario Power Generation–PetroSource
Ontario Power Generation–Zahren Alternative Power Corporation
Pacific Power Australia–New South Wales
Sumitomo Corporation–United Energy Systems
Suncor Energy–Niagara Mohawk Power Corporation
Tesco–Uganda forest
London office of Sustainable Forestry Management–Salish and
  Kootenai Tribes
Toyota–New South Wales
Waste Management Inc.–Enron

Source: IETA 2003; Philibert and Reinaud 2004; Sandor, Bettelheim, and Swingland 2002.

Notes

1. Similarly, agents do not take into account the external (social) benefits of the positive externalities that they generate. As a result, negative externalities tend to be overprovided and positive ones underprovided.

2. For a discussion of global climate change, see, among others, IPCC (1995, 1996).

3. As Stavins (1998) points out, the market-based approach to pollution control is sometimes criticized as giving some actors a right to pollute and compelling others to suffer the ill-effects of pollution. This risk could arise where pollution affects particular locales—where externalities are targeted. However, for sulfur dioxide, the case Stavins had primarily in mind, and for greenhouse gases, externalities are of a diffuse type: these gases rise and mix in the air, affecting whole regions in the case of sulfur dioxide or acid rain or the world as a whole in the case of greenhouse gases.

4. Informational efficiency exists if at any time (when the market is open for trading) all information available at that time is fully reflected in current prices. A precondition of informational efficiency is operational efficiency, defined as trades being executed at the lowest possible cost. For a detailed discussion of these two concepts, see Houthakker and Williamson (1996).

5. For a more detailed discussion of the four cases, see Sandor (1999) and Sandor, Bettelheim, and Swingland (2002).

6. There is evidence of earlier trade of shares in Italy and Germany but none of the magnitude, stability, and fluidity of the trade that developed in Amsterdam in the seventeenth century.

7. Kroszner (1999, p. 5) provides details on the evolution of standards: "The Board's earliest foray into standard-setting occurred in the early 1850s when it tried to promulgate a standard definition of a bushel based on weight rather than the traditional but more difficult to verify volume-based definition...The turning point in the Board's role as standard-setter came when, in 1856, it created three quality categories of wheat in the city and provided the criteria for the grading. Warehouse receipts quickly became 'denominated' in the particular grade and did not refer to a particular lot...In 1857, the Board members voted to appoint a grain inspector to police the grading standards used in the elevators and warehouses and gradually the number of inspectors grew."

8. According to Kendall (1996, pp. 1–2), securitization can be defined as "a process of packaging individual loans and other debt instruments, converting the package into a security or securities, and enhancing their credit status or rating to further their sale to third-party investors. The process converts illiquid individual loans or debt instruments which cannot be sold readily to third-party investors into liquid, marketable securities. These new debt instruments are often termed 'asset-backed securities'...." In the case of mortgage-backed securities the assets are the future payments to be made by the borrower as well as the housing unit for which the borrower took out a mortgage.

9. Ginnie Mae provides guarantees only, while Fannie Mae and Freddie Mac originate and package and sell mortgages to investors. Fannie Mae was created in 1938 and became a private corporation in 1968. Freddie Mac was chartered by the U.S. Congress in 1970 as a secondary-market conduit for residential services (see www.fanniemae.com, www.ginniemae.gov, and www.freddiemac.com).

10. The ideas underpinning mortgage-backed securities have been transferred to a number of other assets, including credit card receipts and automobile loans (see the chapter by Conceição and Rajan in this volume).

11. For further information, see U.S. Congress (1990).

12. In fact, the auctions are designed to be revenue neutral. The proceeds are returned to the participating utilities.

13. For accounts of how the market has evolved, see, among others, Joskow, Shmalensee, and Bailey (1998), Sandor, Bettelheim and Swingland (2002), and Stavins (2003).

14. Reductions have exceeded regulatory requirements by 30 percent. Median health benefits are estimated at $10.6 billion a year in 1997 up to $40 billion in 2010, while the estimated costs of the program range from $1.4 to $2.6 billion a year (U.S. EPA 1995, pp. S-3 and S-4; U.S. GAO 1994, pp. 25 and 37; McLean 1997).

15. A flexibility arrangement that has proved particularly effective is the rule allowing companies to achieve more reductions now and to "bank" them for possible future use. This rule, in particular, motivated companies to reduce emissions beyond what the law required them to do.

16. For further information see www.carbonfinance.org/pcf.

17. For more information see http://europa.eu.int/comm/environment/climat/emission.htm.

18. For further details on the issues discussed in this section see Sandor, Walsh, and LeBlanc (1999), Sandor, Bettelheim, and Swingland (2002), and Sandor, Walsh, and Marques (2002). The architecture of the Chicago Climate Exchange was first proposed by Sandor (1994).

19. See http://unfccc.int and http://unfccc.int/essential_background/convention/items/2627.php .

20. This study was undertaken by Environmental Financial Products and financed by the Chicago-based Joyce Foundation. The grant was administered by Northwestern University's Kellogg Graduate School of Management. See also www.chicagoclimatex.com/about.

21. To qualify, projects had to be undertaken on or after January 1, 1999, although some prior activities could also qualify.

22. Carbon dioxide, methane, nitrous oxide, hydrofluorocarbons, perfluorocarbons, and sulfur hexafluoride.

23. See www.ipcc.ch.

24. The board of directors is at the top of the governance structure. For a list of directors, see www.chicagoclimateexchange.com/about/people_board.html.

REFERENCES

Arrow, Kenneth J. 1969. "The Organization of Economic Activity: Issues Pertinent to the Choice of Market vs. Non-market Allocation." In Joint Economic Committee, *The Analysis of Public Expenditure: The PPB System.* Washington, D.C.: Government Printing Office.

Brendsel, Leland C. 1996. "Securitization's Role in Housing Finance: The Special Contributions of the Government-Sponsored Enterprises." In Leon T. Kendall and Michael J. Fishman, eds., *A Primer on Securitization.* Cambridge, Mass.: MIT Press.

Chicago Climate Exchange. 2004. "Chicago Climate Exchange Reaches Volume Milestone of 1 Million Tons of Carbon Dioxide Traded. Exchange Announces Results of First Conditional Compliance Period." Press release. July 1. [www.chicagoclimatex.com/news/CCXPressRelease_040701.html].

————. 2005. "Chicago Climate Exchange Market Data." Chicago, Ill. [www.chicagoclimateexchange.com/trading/marketData.html].

Chichilnisky, Graciela, and Geoffrey Heal. 2000. "Markets for Tradable Carbon Dioxide Emission Quotas: Principles and Practice." In Graciela Chichilnisky and Geoffrey Heal, eds., *Environmental Markets: Equity and Efficiency.* New York: Columbia University Press.

Coase, Ronald H. 1960. "The Problem of Social Cost." *Journal of Law and Economics* 3 (1): 1–44.

Cordes, Joseph J. 2002. "Corrective Taxes, Charges, and Tradable Permits." In Lester M. Salamon, ed., *The Tools of Government: A Guide to the New Governance.* New York: Oxford University Press.

De la Vega, Josef Penso. [1688] 1996. "Confusion de Confusiones." Reprinted in Martin S. Fridson, ed., *Extraordinary Popular Delusions and the Madness of Crowds and Confusion de Confusiones.* New York: John Wiley & Sons.

De Soto, Hernando. 2000. *The Mystery of Capital: Why Capitalism Triumphs in the West and Fails Everywhere Else.* New York: Basic Books.

Fridson, Martin. S., ed. 1996. *Extraordinary Popular Delusions and the Madness of Crowds and Confusion de Confusiones.* New York: John Wiley & Sons.

Hardin, Garrett. 1968. "The Tragedy of the Commons." *Science* 162 (3859): 1243–48.

Houthakker, Hendrik S., and Peter J. Williamson. 1996. *The Economics of Financial Markets.* New York: Oxford University Press.

IETA (International Emissions Trading Association). 2003. *Greenhouse Gas Market 2003: Emerging but Fragmented.* Geneva.

IPCC (Intergovernmental Panel on Climate Change). 1995. *IPCC Second Assessment: Climate Change 1995.* Geneva: World Meteorological Organization and United Nations Environment Programme.

————. 1996. *Climate Change 1995: Economic and Social Dimensions of Climate Change.* Cambridge: Cambridge University Press.

Joskow, Paul L., Richard Schmalensee, and Elizabeth M. Bailey. 1998. "The Market for Sulfur Dioxide Emissions." *American Economic Review* 88 (4): 669–85.

Kellenbenz, Hermann. [1957] 1996. "Introduction to Confusion de Confusiones." In Martin S. Fridson, ed., *Extraordinary Popular Delusions and the Madness of Crowds and Confusion de Confusiones.* New York: John Wiley & Sons.

Kendall, Leon T. 1996. "Securitization: A New Era in American Finance." In Leon T. Kendall, and Michael J. Fishman, eds., *A Primer on Securitization.* Cambridge, Mass.: MIT Press.

Kroszner, Randall. S. 1999. "Can the Financial Markets Privately Regulate Risk? The Development of Derivatives Clearing Houses and Recent Over-the-Counter Innovations." *Journal of Money, Credit, and Banking* 31 (3): 596–618.

Lurie, Jonathan. 1979. *The Chicago Board of Trade 1859–1905: the Dynamics of Self-Regulation.* Urbana: University of Illinois Press.

McLean, Brian J. 1997. "Evolution of Marketable Permits: The U.S. Experience with Sulfur Dioxide Allowance Trading." *International Journal of Environmental and Pollution* 8 (1–2): 19–36.

Newell, Richard G., and Robert N. Stavins. 2003. "Cost Heterogeneity and the Potential Savings from Market-Based Policies." *Journal of Regulatory Economics* 23 (1): 43–59.

Philibert, Cédric, and Julia Reinaud. 2004. "Emissions Trading: Taking Stock and Looking Forward." COM/ENV/EPOC/IEA/SLT(2004)3. Paris: Organisation for Economic Co-operation and Development and International Energy Agency.

Pigou, Arthur C. 1920. *The Economics of Welfare.* 1st edition. London: Macmillan.

Ranieri, Lewis S. 1996. "The Origins of Securitization, Sources of Its Growth, and Its Future Potential." In Leon T. Kendall and Michael J. Fishman, eds., *A Primer on Securitization.* Cambridge, Mass.: MIT Press.

Sandor, Richard L. 1994. "In Search of Market Trees: Market Architecture and Tradable Entitlements for CO2 Abatement." In United Nations Conference on Trade and Development, *Combating Global Warming: Possible Rules, Regulations, and Administrative Arrangements for a Global Market in CO2 Emission Entitlements.* New York.

————. 1999. "A Limited-scale Voluntary International Greenhouse Gas Emissions Trading Program." In David L. Boren and Edward J. Perkins, eds., *Preparing America's Foreign Policy for the Twenty-first Century.* Norman, Okla.: University of Oklahoma Press.

————. 2003. "The First Chicago Climate Exchange Auction: The Birth of the North American Carbon Market." In International Emissions Trading Association, *Greenhouse Gas Market 2003: Emerging but Fragmented.* Geneva.

Sandor, Richard L., Eric C. Bettelheim, and Ian R. Swingland. 2002. "An Overview of a Free-market Approach to Climate Change and Conservation." *Philosophical Transactions of the Royal Society A* 360 (1797):1607–20.

Sandor, Richard L., Michael J. Walsh and Alice M. LeBlanc. 1999. "Creating a Market for Carbon Emissions: Gas Industry Opportunities." *Natural Gas.* June 6.

Sandor, Richard L., Michael J. Walsh, and Rafael L. Marques. 2002. "Greenhouse Gas Trading Markets." *Philosophical Transactions of the Royal Society A* 360 (1797): 1889–1900.

Stavins, Robert. 1998. "What Can We Learn from the Grand Policy Experiment? Positive and Normative Lessons from SO2 Allowance Trading." *Journal of Economic Perspectives* 12 (3): 69–88.

————. 2003. "Experience with Market-Based Environmental Policy Instruments." In Karl-Göran Mäler and Jeffrey Vincent, eds., *Handbook of Environmental Economics,* Vol. I. Amsterdam: Elsevier Science.

Stringham, Edward. 2003. "The Extralegal Development of Securities Trading in Seventeenth Century Amsterdam." *Quarterly Review of Economics and Finance* 43 (2): 321–44.

Stringham, Edward, and Peter Boettke. 2004. "Brokers, Bureaucrats and the Emergence of Financial Markets." *Managerial Finance.* 30 (2): 57–71.

Tietenberg, Tom. 2001. *Emissions Trading Programs.* Vol. I, *Implementation and Evolution.* Aldershot, UK: Ashgate.

U.S. Congress. 1990. *Clean Air Act Amendments of 1990.* Public Law 101-549. Nobember 15.

U.S. EPA (Environmental Protection Agency). 1995. *Human Health Benefits from Sulfate Reductions under Title IV of the 1990 Clean Air Act Amendments.* Washington, D.C.

————. 2004. "Trading Activity Breakdown: Number of Allowances Transferred by Quarter (1994–2003, Millions of Allowances Transferred)." Washington, D.C. [www.epa.gov/airmarkets/trading/so2market/transtable.html].

U.S. GAO (General Accounting Office). 1994. *Air Pollution: Allowance Trading Offers an Opportunity to Reduce Emissions at Less Cost.* GAO/RCED-95–30. Washington, D.C.

USING MARKETS MORE EFFECTIVELY

DEVELOPING COUNTRY ACCESS TO COMMODITY FUTURES MARKETS

C. WYN MORGAN

Moderating the adverse effects of price instability for primary commodity producers has long been a concern in both industrial and developing countries. Market and nonmarket strategies have been pursued toward this end. The Chicago Board of Trade, one of the world's earliest "modern" agricultural commodity exchanges, was founded in 1848. Its two main purposes are fostering price discovery and price stabilization through futures trading.

During the 1950s and 1960s, when the political climate shifted in favor of greater state intervention, commodity price stabilization was attempted through state trading boards, guaranteed minimum prices, and subsidies at the national level and various international commodity agreements at the international level, including the International Sugar Agreement (1954), Tin Agreement (1954), Coffee Agreement (1962), and somewhat later the Cocoa Agreement (1972) and Natural Rubber Agreement (1980).

Since the 1970s and 1980s yet another major shift in policy stance has swept across the world, placing renewed emphasis on economic liberalization and the use of markets and market-based instruments. Some international commodity agreements collapsed, others were allowed to lapse (Gilbert 1996), and futures trading entered an era of impressive, continuous growth (Carlton 1984). Although much of this growth is due to trading in financial futures, trading in commodity futures has expanded as well as a risk management tool for commodity producers and consumers.

The participation of developing country actors in these markets is still limited, although they appear to face some of the greatest risks. Many developing countries and their farming populations are highly dependent on a few—often only one or two—crops, and they have extremely limited means for self-protection. This raises

---

The data in this chapter on the trading volumes of futures exchanges were provided by the Futures Industry Association.

the question of whether it is desirable to explore strategies for assisting developing country actors in making greater use of the risk management opportunities offered by futures markets, especially markets for commodity futures, and if so, how this could be done.

This chapter briefly outlines the role of futures markets in managing commodity price risk and examines the use of futures markets by industrial and developing country actors. It identifies factors that impede greater access by developing country producers and traders and explores strategies for enhancing their access. It highlights the importance of international intermediary services, which could play a dual facilitation role. One role would be to build know-how about hedging in developing countries and strengthen national intermediaries (such as banks or producers cooperatives). A second role would be to help create a relation of trust and confidence between international traders (such as brokers operating on international exchanges) and emerging national intermediaries.

Such international intermediation services already exist in a nascent way, in the International Task Force on Commodity Risk Management in Developing Countries.[1] However, the analysis makes clear that commodities futures trading is no panacea. It can reduce some price risk and thus some income risk for developing countries and their commodity-producing communities. Yet it is no substitute for development. Both have to advance in tandem. Also, enhanced use of market-based strategies such as futures trading depends on prior public interventions in developing legal frameworks, financial institutions, and norms and standards.

AN OVERVIEW OF THE ROLE OF FUTURES MARKETS

If futures markets are to have a major part in solving the problem of volatility in commodity prices, it is important to understand their role—and what they require of market participants.

Futures markets complement spot markets, the most common trading arrangement. Spot markets exist in more or less institutionalized form wherever goods or services are exchanged against payment of a price and the transaction between seller and buyer is expected to be completed immediately—on the spot. Futures markets are markets for derivative products, contract products derived from an underlying good or service, such as a commodity or currency. More specifically, futures are an agreement to buy or sell a certain amount of a particular item on a defined future date at a price specified at the time the agreement is concluded.

Futures belong to the category of forward-looking contracts, which also includes options and other instruments. While futures involve the commitment to deliver or buy, options give holders the right to purchase (for call options) or sell (for put options) but do not oblige them to do so. Options are thus attractive to hedgers because they protect against loss in value but do not force the hedger to give up potential gains.[2] There are only a relatively small number of futures exchanges. They typically have the following characteristics (Carlton 1984; Radetzki 1990; Telser 1981; and Tosini 2002):

* Trade is limited to exchange members, who can deal on their own or on others' behalf.
* Trade is strictly rule based, with the rules usually constituting self-regulation by exchange members and covering such aspects as standards of business conduct and contract terms and conditions.
* The products traded are highly standardized so as to enhance certainty, reduce search costs, and allow for speedy execution of trading operations.
* The exchange's clearinghouse acts as a contract partner, standing between buyers and sellers and freeing both from having to deal with the opposite side of the trade.
* Information is updated continuously and fed into the trading operations, contributing to price discovery and allowing market participants to be aware of the latest market trends.

Exchange members represent different actor groups, including commodity producers (farmers or farmers organizations such as cooperatives), buyers (such as export traders or grain millers), financial institutions (such as banks) that are involved in lending to commodity producers, and investors (often referred to as speculators). Each actor group may pursue a different purpose in trading futures and options (Thompson 1985).

Two of the main functions of futures markets are price stabilization and price discovery. Price stabilization is perhaps the most important for commodity producers and buyers. The need for managing or hedging price risk arises especially when there is a considerable time gap between the decision to produce or store a certain commodity and its actual sale in the spot market and when the product is subject to significant short-term price instability, as many commodities are. To offset some or all of this spot price risk, producers, traders (importers and exporters), processing agents, and consumers may want to hedge—to take a position in the futures or options markets that is opposite to that held in the spot market and thus to lock in a price for a commodity (figure 1).

Such risk sharing is possible only if there are other traders willing to accept risk. Speculators come to futures exchanges because they are prepared to assume risk—against a price.[3] However, the contract provides the holder of the option with the right—but not the obligation—to follow through on the contract. So if the futures price at the due date falls below the spot price, the holder lets the contract lapse, losing merely the premium. And if the futures price rises above the spot price, the premium might have been a small price to pay for guaranteeing—or even exceeding—a certain price level.

The two functions of price discovery and stabilization are important for decisionmaking on inventory management as well as on production issues. As futures

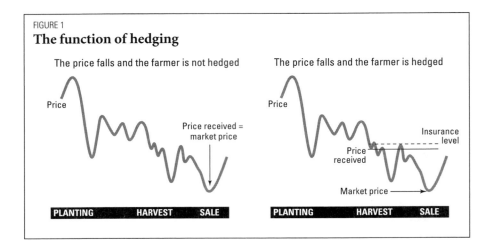

FIGURE 1

The function of hedging

The price falls and the farmer is not hedged

Price

Price received = market price

PLANTING   HARVEST   SALE

The price falls and the farmer is hedged

Price

Insurance level

Price received

Market price

PLANTING   HARVEST   SALE

markets collect and disseminate information and as price signals adjust to reflect such information, agents can make better informed decisions about holding stocks. As futures prices exceed spot prices, the incentive to store increases and vice versa. Futures thus foster more efficient storage. This, in turn, facilitates a smoother pattern of prices in the spot market, further reducing price volatility (Morgan 1999; Netz 1995).

The first futures markets were commodity based. Since the 1970s, however, when financial derivative markets started appearing and trading on futures exchanges began to grow exponentially into the multibillion dollar markets of today, financial futures began to outpace commodity futures (Carlton 1984; Futures Industry Association 2004; Santana-Boado 2001; see also table 1).

Only about 18 percent of futures contracts traded in 2004 were related to commodities (agricultural, energy, or metal products), reflecting the massive and continued growth in the use of financial derivatives in recent years (table 2). However, while commodity contracts make up a much smaller share of total trading volume than do financial contracts, use of commodities futures has grown substantially—the volume of agricultural commodities futures contracts alone more than doubled between 1998 and 2004. This suggests a buoyant market for these products (Santana-Boado 2001).

As do other markets, futures markets have strong properties of a public good. And since they cut across borders and serve economic actors around the world, they have some properties of a global public good. They are nonrival in consumption. Not only does one actor's use of the market not decrease its availability for others, but the larger the number of participants, the more competitive and efficient the market is likely to be. Therefore, futures markets seek a sufficiently large membership and trading volume. However, membership is exclusive, dependent on meeting certain criteria, notably those of excellent creditworthiness and

TABLE 1

Top 20 futures exchanges ranked by 2004 volume of contracts
(millions of contracts)

Exchange	1998	2003	2004
Korea Exchange[a]	50.2	2,899.9	2,586.8
Eurex	248.2	1,014.9	1,065.6
Chicago Mercantile Exchange	226.6	640.2	805.3
Euronext.liffe	nr	695.0	790.4
Chicago Board of Trade	nr	454.2	600.0
Chicago Board Options Exchange	206.9	283.9	361.1
International Securities Exchange (U.S.)	nr	245.0	360.9
Bovespa (Brazil)	nr	177.2	235.3
Mexican Derivatives Exchange	nr	173.8	210.4
American Stock Exchange	97.6	180.1	202.7
Bolsa de Mercadorias & Futuros (Brazil)	87.0	120.8	183.4
New York Mercantile Exchange	95.0	137.2	161.1
Philadelphia Stock Exchange	39.0	112.7	133.4
Pacific Stock Exchange (U.S.)	59.0	86.2	103.3
OMX Exchanges[b]	44.7	72.1	94.4
Dalian Commodity Exchange (China)	nr	75.0	88.0
National Stock Exchange of India	nr	nr	75.1
Tokyo Commodity Exchange	43.6	87.3	74.5
London Metal Exchange	53.1	72.3	71.9
Taiwan Futures Exchange	nr	nr	65.0

nr indicates that the exchange was not ranked in the top 20.
Note: Data include futures and options contracts.
a. Korea Stock Exchange and Korea Futures Exchange merged in 2004. Data for 1998 and 2003 are for Korea Stock Exchange.
b. OM Stockholm and HEX (Helsinki) merged in 2004. Data for 1998 and 2003 are for OM Stockholm.
Source: Futures Industry Association 2005.

proven ability to deliver cash. Futures exchanges thus have a strong "club good" character. And like other club goods they present an access problem for many actors—all who do not meet the key membership criteria of creditworthiness and availability of cash. Exchanges usually generate over-the-counter trade of the products they handle. So the market widens. But even then only qualifying (financially well positioned) traders find access.

So the question arises: who is trading on and benefiting from commodities futures markets?

TABLE 2

Trading volume on futures exchanges by type of contract ranked by 2004 volume of contracts

Contract type	1998 Number of contracts (millions)	1998 Share of total (percent)	1999 Number of contracts (millions)	1999 Share of total (percent)	2000 Number of contracts (millions)	2000 Share of total (percent)
Interest rate	759.9	58.4	674.0	53.5	736.6	51.0
Equity indices	178.1	13.7	207.5	16.5	250.7	17.4
Agricultural commodities	119.3	9.2	117.9	9.4	167.1	11.6
Energy products	82.8	6.4	103.0	8.2	139.0	9.6
Nonprecious metals	57.7	4.4	66.5	5.3	70.6	4.9
Foreign currency index	54.5	4.2	36.6	2.9	43.1	3.0
Individual equities	0.6	0.0	1.4	0.1	2.6	0.2
Precious metals	47.3	3.6	50.7	4.0	33.3	2.3
Other	1.2	0.1	1.3	0.1	1.3	0.1
Total	1,301.3	100.0	1,259.0	100.0	1,444.4	100.0

Note: Data include futures contracts only.
Source: Futures Industry Association 2005.

THE USE OF FUTURES MARKETS

Data on developing country use of futures markets are scarce. Studies of the proportion of open interest on U.S. exchanges accounted for by developing countries find it to be very low in all markets, ranging from 3.44 percent in currencies to 1.52 percent in grain and soybeans and 0.39 percent in livestock products (Debatisse and others 1993, pp. 49–52; Morgan, Rayner, and Vaillant 1999, p. 905).[4] While participation is thought to have grown since that study, no direct evidence is available to support this impression. Even among Organisation for Economic Co-operation and Development (OECD) countries, use of futures markets is not as high as it might be assumed or ought to be (Gardner 2000). Yet the theory of risk diversification and sharing is clear and predicts significant efficiency gains from risk management for the individual actor who hedges and for the economy as a whole.[5]

There are several possible explanations for this lower than expected participation rate. A major issue is often information about risk management products and how futures markets function. In addition, some actors are uncertain about the benefits of such markets. Several studies have found that some farmers are uneasy about getting involved in technical trading operations and with specula-

2001		2002		2003		2004	
Number of contracts (millions)	Share of total (percent)	Number of contracts (millions)	Share of total (percent)	Number of contracts (millions)	Share of total (percent)	Number of contracts (millions)	Share of total (percent)
1,034.1	57.4	1,154.0	52.6	1,579.4	53.2	1,910.9	55.2
331.8	18.4	527.3	24.1	688.0	23.2	747.3	21.6
121.5	6.7	127.3	5.8	240.1	8.1	250.7	7.2
151.1	8.4	185.3	8.5	197.0	6.6	219.4	6.3
66.9	3.7	73.2	3.3	86.6	2.9	100.3	2.9
44.8	2.5	43.4	2.0	62.7	2.1	91.5	2.6
14.7	0.8	32.5	1.5	56.8	1.9	88.0	2.5
36.5	2.0	48.5	2.2	59.3	2.0	54.5	1.6
0.7	0.0	0.8	0.0	0.6	0.0	0.8	0.0
1,802.2	100.0	2,192.2	100.0	2,970.5	100.0	3,463.3	100.0

tors (Ennew, Morgan, and Rayner 1992; Shiller 1993). In the past, government price supports have meant that farmers did not need to seek out risk management tools, and so many may be unfamiliar with them. In addition, the scale of farm enterprise has often been a limiting factor. Futures products tend to be tailored to the risk management requirements of larger farm operators (ITF 1999).

In addition to the reasons industrial country actors are hesitant to use futures markets, important additional obstacles face developing country actors. For many, accessing futures markets requires conducting business abroad, adding foreign exchange risk to the already considerable complexities of futures trading. For many, too, creditworthiness is a problem. And, especially important, national intermediaries are lacking (ITF 1999; Thompson 1985). In industrial countries many commodity producers or traders do not go directly to futures markets but deal through intermediaries, such as their financial institutions or specialized brokers. Thus, there are substantial barriers between commodity producers in developing countries, notably poor farmers, who urgently need protection against price volatility, and the sophisticated commodities futures markets in places like Chicago, London, and Singapore.

Still, there are some well established commodity exchanges in developing countries, including Argentina's Bolsa de Cereales (dating to 1854) and India's Bombay

Oilseeds and Oils Exchange (created in 1950). And many new commodity exchanges have been created in recent years in developing and transition economies, including the Budapest Commodity Exchange in 1989, the Romanian Commodities Exchange in 1992, the Zimbabwe Agricultural Commodity Exchange in 1994, and the Kenya Commodity Exchange in 1997 (Santana-Boado 2001). China's Zhengzhou Commodity Exchange, established in 1990, inaugurated a mungbean futures contract in 1993 (Williams and others 1998). In addition, exchanges were created in the 1970s and 1980s in Bolivia, Colombia, Costa Rica, Ecuador, El Salvador, Honduras, Nicaragua, Panama, and Peru to organize domestic agricultural trade flows as domestic trade was liberalized. Several of these exchanges are still in an early evolutionary phase and have not yet started futures trading.

One solution to the problem of the missing market would be for more developing countries to establish their own futures exchanges. But as Morgan, Rayner, and Vaillant (1999) show, establishing a domestic exchange is a very expensive and difficult policy route. Start-up costs are extremely high, and the opportunity cost of using scarce government funds for such projects would be high as well. Even if the political will were strong and the money could be found to support such a measure, there are a number of important prerequisites before futures markets can operate effectively. A country needs a well developed legal and financial system to underpin an exchange and provide credit and credibility for the brokers who would trade on it. Also, information flows and telecommunications systems must be good and uncorrupted to ensure clear market signals between spot and futures markets. Thus, it is not surprising that only a few middle-income developing countries such as Brazil and China have established their own futures exchanges.

For market participants in many developing countries, therefore, access to futures trading is still rare (Varangis, Larson, and Anderson 2002). What strategies could facilitate enhanced access? Leuthold (1994) argues that the barriers to establishing domestic markets are so substantial that many developing countries would be better advised to trade on existing exchanges. The next section explores ways to facilitate this policy path.

PROMOTING ACCESS TO INSTRUMENTS OF COMMODITY RISK MANAGEMENT FOR DEVELOPING COUNTRY ACTORS

In exploring a forward strategy for developing countries it is useful to draw on the experience of industrial countries and that of developing countries that have used exchanges to reduce commodity price risks. A range of such examples can be found in Claessens and Duncan (1993), Varangis and Larson (1996), ITF (1999), and Faruqee, Coleman, and Scott (1997). The key message that emerges is the need for a dual intermediation strategy to create national intermediaries, such as producers organizations or other broker services, and to provide international intermediation services to help strengthen national intermediaries.

Promoting national intermediaries

The experience of Mexico's Agricultural Trade Support and Services Office (ASERCA) helps to illustrate the role of a national intermediary. Established in 1994 to advance liberalization of the agricultural sector, the hedging program administered by ASERCA assists local commodity producers in using futures and options markets to reduce price risk.[6]

ASERCA acts as an intermediary between local producers and futures markets. Its regional representatives offer local producers a guaranteed price for their commodities at the time production or planting decisions have to be made. Without futures trading such forward contracting could be very costly for ASERCA's limited budget of about $22 million in 2002 to 2003 (Snowden and Benavides 2005, p. 5). ASERCA's national headquarters hedges its risks on exchanges in New York and Chicago, purchasing options to cover possible adverse price movements. ASERCA recovers about half the premium costs of these options from farmers who join the risk management scheme. A government subsidy covers the other half of the costs.

ASERCA demonstrates that it is not necessary for individual producers to trade directly on an established market. Intermediaries can bundle the risk management needs of smaller producers to reduce transaction costs. When intermediaries deal with several commodities, as ASERCA does, they can even pool risks and hedge across several commodities.

Various institutions could take on the job of intermediary, including producers associations and cooperatives, banks, and government facilities set up for that purpose, as in the case of ASERCA. However, intermediaries will take root and succeed only where there is a demand for their services. Local producers, traders, or processing agents must understand risk management and consider it an activity for which they are willing to pay a certain price. This requires education and training of all concerned actor groups—often among the first steps taken in national efforts to enhance the use of risk management instruments.[7]

Providing international intermediation services

In some cases developing countries will establish national intermediaries on their own initiative. In other cases international assistance can help to build the requisite national institutions and capacity.

The International Task Force on Commodity Risk Management in Developing Countries, a public-private partnership established under a World Bank initiative in 1999, seeks to aid developing countries in using market-based risk management tools to manage their exposure to commodity-related risks. It does so through three major types of activities:

* Providing technical assistance to developing countries to identify areas in which risk management would be useful and providing training and education in the design and implementation of risk management programs.

- Helping developing countries establish contacts with market actors through whom they can trade in offshore futures markets.
- Undertaking research and development on risk management products and strategies.

Box 1 provides an example of the task force's work in helping Tanzania access commodity futures markets to manage commodity risk in the coffee market.

For the first role of providing technical assistance, the challenge for an international intermediary is to help build national technical know-how and institutions and to share experience on how to ensure that small producers, the most vulnerable parties, also benefit from hedging operations. The local knowledge of government agencies, nongovernmental organizations (NGOs), aid agencies, and others can help to identify key nodes in the local transmission process, such as cooperatives and other collaborative groups, that might be willing to engage in price insurance schemes to benefit many smaller producers. What is important is finding a means of disseminating the benefits to all producers indirectly through such key nodes rather than trying to directly involve every producer in managing commodity price instability or other commodity-related risks.

Even with a policy commitment to broad-based benefit sharing, however, risk management will benefit primarily the more commercially oriented producers rather than the poorest subsistence farmers (Varangis, Larson, and Anderson 2002). If hedging takes off, however, some resources that today go to ad hoc compensation of farmers who suffer from severe price volatility could become available to assist the poorest farmers.

As to the second role of facilitating market relations, the original proposal for the creation of the task force highlighted the existence of a "trust gap" between suppliers and users of risk management tools (ITF 1999, p. 5). Thus even where developing country actors are willing to engage in trading, they might not have the opportunity because of an inability to prove their creditworthiness. As a public-private partnership involving both national and international actors, the task force can break down some of the information barriers between established players on commodity exchanges and those in developing countries seeking access.[8]

On the third role of research and development (R&D), the starting point should be the recognition that there are as yet no easy responses to the problem of commodity risk management. The initial focus of the task force has been on commodity price risk management. From a producer's viewpoint, however, managing price risks is only one of several risk management needs. Also important are products for hedging against weather-related and other output risks. The task force has identified weather risk management instruments as one of its substantive focus areas.[9] Producers also face income risks, another area that the international intermediary might explore for the feasibility and desirability of using various instruments that have been proposed as possible tools of income insurance.[10]

Box 1
HELPING TANZANIA ACCESS COMMODITY FUTURES MARKETS

Coffee accounts for about a fifth of Tanzania's export earnings. When world coffee prices hit a record low in 2001/02, some 400,000 of the country's low-income coffee producing households were severely affected.

The coffee market had already experienced considerable price volatility during much of the previous decade. So when the 2001/02 price drop occurred, it threatened the continued existence of one of the largest cooperative unions of smallholder coffee producers in Tanzania. At the beginning of the coffee season the union pays producers an advance on a guaranteed minimum price for their output. An additional payment is made later, should spot prices prove to be higher. The union gets the money for the first payments by taking a loan from a local bank. The prior volatility in coffee prices had already made it difficult for the union to meet its repayment obligations, and the renewed price drop in 2001/02 weakened its financial standing even further.

It was then that union management decided to explore price risk management and began collaboration with the World Bank's Commodity Risk Management Group, the implementing arm of the International Task Force on Commodity Risk Management in Developing Countries. A first phase aimed at familiarizing union and World Bank staff and other key players with the ins and outs of hedging, followed by explanations to union members of the general purpose and benefits of risk management. Union members would have to make the decision to allow union management to allocate funds to purchase risk management products.

Since the primary goal was to put in a price floor, the union decided to purchase put options. Then came the challenge of opening an account with a seller of risk instruments, in this case an international bank. The bank's concern was to meet all its due diligence requirements and to prove that it had full knowledge of the new client and that the client was fully aware of all the risks involved in futures trading. It would have been extremely difficult for the union to gain the bank's acceptance had the union not had a known international intermediary on its side.

All concerns were finally allayed, however, and the put options were purchased. The union is now better able to meet its difficult goal of offering price stabilization services to its members.

Source: Bryla and others 2003.

CONCLUSION

It can be argued that stabilizing the prices of globally important commodities has public goods properties, benefiting not only producers but many others in direct or diffuse ways. Devlin and Titman (2004), for example, show that global exter-nalities arise from using futures markets for oil. With locked-in prices, producers do not have to respond to lower spot market prices by raising output (as they would in the absence of futures trading), possibly causing a further drop in world market prices. All producers can gain from this smoothing of production.

However, the foregoing discussion makes clear that the first steps in achiev-ing enhanced risk management may not always be straightforward. As Kydd and Poulton (2000) also argue, the problems of missing markets often cannot be resolved by the private sector alone. Public intervention may be needed to remove information obstacles and to change incentive structures to encourage new insti-tutions to form or new actors to enter markets with new products.

This chapter has argued that futures markets have a lot to offer for managing commodity-related risks. However, many commodity producers, especially in developing countries, still lack access to these markets. They face enormous risks, because they tend to be highly dependent on one or two commodities. And being poor and resource-constrained, they lack the means for adequate self-insurance. Facilitating their access to futures markets and greater price stability could make a significant contribution to their economic security, improving their financial posi-tion and perhaps lifting them out of poverty. Facilitating such access would be desir-able both for individual producers and for developing country governments. Where commodity producers lack risk protection, governments have to shoulder high financial burdens should commodity prices fall or a weather-related calamity occur.

Moreover, futures markets have strong public goods properties, belonging to the category of public goods with access problems (see the chapter by Conceição and Mendoza in this volume). If the benefits of removing the access problems exceed the costs of doing so (as seems to be the case), it would be inefficient—and inequitable—to leave developing country actors out of markets for risk manage-ment products.

This chapter has suggested enhancing developing country access to futures markets through offshore markets, a low cost strategy relative to the costs to devel-opment that might result without improved risk protection for developing coun-try commodity producers. The proposed strategy calls for promoting the creation of national intermediaries to bundle and then hedge the risk management needs of smaller producers and for providing international intermediation services to support the creation of the national intermediaries.

Such international intermediation services are in some measure already being provided by the International Task Force on Commodity Risk Management in Developing Countries. However, there is plenty of scope to expand such services. A good way to use aid funds efficiently to reduce poverty is to use development assis-tance to help poor farmers deal with price and other risks, either directly, through subsidized premia, or indirectly, through education and information campaigns on the potential benefits of risk management (see, for example, Guillaumont 2005).

For some time to come, however, efforts to move toward greater use of market-based risk management will have to move in parallel with other measures to protect against external shocks, such as the Compensatory Financing Facility or emergency assistance of the International Monetary Fund,[11] the FLEX initiative of the European Union,[12] and the Common Fund for Commodities.[13] The challenge is to find the right balance between these measures for different groups of commodity producers and countries.

NOTES

1. See www.itf-commrisk.org.

2. For a concise discussion of futures and options instruments and markets, see Millman (2002).

3. For example, using data on individual futures contracts between 1959 and 2004 from the Commodities Research Bureau and the London Metals Exchange, Gorton and Rouwenhorst (2005, p. 12) estimate the average risk premium of commodity futures at about 5 percent a year—roughly equal to that of stocks and double that of bonds.

4. Open interest is an indication of the number of contracts in a market in a specified period that have yet to be delivered or cancelled by the trading party.

5. See, for example, theoretical studies by McKinnon (1967) and later by Shiller (1993).

6. The hedging scheme, Subprograma de apoyos directos a cobertura de precios agricolas, is part of the Agricultural Trade Support and Services Office (Apoyos y servicios a la comercializacion agropecuaria, or ASERCA), a Mexican federal government department within the Secretariat of Agriculture and Rural Development. Further information is available at www.infoaserca.gob.mx/notas01.htm and www.sagarpa.gob.mx.

7. See, for example, the country case studies available on the web site of the International Task Force on Commodity Risk Management in Developing Countries at www.itf-commrisk.org/DisplayContent.asp?ID=211.

8. To see how the International Task Force on Commodity Risk Management in Developing Countries has implemented the first two roles described here, go to www.itf-commrisk.org/itf.asp?page=15 for country assistance initiatives on "Price risk" and www.itf-commrisk.org/itf.asp?page=22 for initiatives on "Weather risk."

9. These could include weather-based index insurance that relies on objective observations of specific weather events. To illustrate, based on an established correlation between rainfall and crop yield, an agricultural producer can hedge production risk by purchasing a contract that pays in case rainfall falls below a minimum threshold. For an extended discussion of these instruments, see Bryla and others (2003); Skees, Hazell, and Miranda (1999); Skees and others (2001); and Miranda and Vedenov (2001).

10. The various risk management tools mentioned here are intended for managing short-term risks. They do not address the longer term problems of a deterioration in the terms of trade of certain commodities.

11. The Compensatory Financing Facility was created in 1963 to help International Monetary Fund (IMF) members withstand temporary export instability. IMF emergency assistance is provided to countries facing natural disasters (such as droughts) or emerging from conflict. See www.imf.org/external/np/exr/facts/howlend.htm.

12. The FLEX initiative was created in 2000 under EU African, Caribbean, and Pacific cooperation to assist governments that are facing sudden revenue declines due to losses in export earnings. It provides additional budgetary support to countries that have registered a 10 percent loss in export earnings (2 percent for the least developed countries) and a 10 percent worsening of the programmed public deficit. However, experience shows that these eligibility criteria have been too stringent. Proposals to make the criteria more flexible are being considered. See http://europa.eu.int/comm/trade/issues/global/development/pr120204_en.htm.

13. The mandate of the Common Fund for Commodities is to enhance the socioeconomic development of commodity producers and to advance overall development through commodity development measures (research and development, productivity and quality improvements, technology transfer, improvements in marketing and market access) and commodity market development activities (physical market development, enhancement of market infrastructure, facilitation of private sector initiatives, commodity price risk management). For further information see www.common-fund.org/.

References

Bryla, Erin, Julie Dana, Ulrich Hess, and Panos Varangis. 2003. "The Use of Price and Weather Risk Management Instruments." Paper presented at the Resource Center on Urban Agriculture and Forestry conference, "Paving the Way Forward for Rural Finance: An International Conference on Best Practices," June 3–5, Washington, D.C.

Carlton, Dennis W. 1984. "Futures Markets: Their Purpose, Their History, Their Growth, Their Successes and Failures." *Journal of Futures Markets* 4 (3): 237–72.

Claessens, Stijn, and Ronald Duncan, eds. 1993. *Managing Commodity Price Risk in Developing Countries.* Washington, D.C.: World Bank.

Debatisse, Michel L., Isabelle Tsakok, Dina Umali, Stijn Claessens, and Kutlu Somel. 1993. "Risk Management in Liberalising Economies: Issues of Access to Food and Agricultural Futures and Options Markets." Europe and Central Asia/Middle East and North Africa (ECA/MENA) Technical Department Report 12220. World Bank, Washington, D.C.

Devlin, Julia, and Sheridan Titman. 2004. "Managing Oil Price Risk in Developing Countries." *World Bank Research Observer* 19 (1): 119–39.

Ennew, Christine T., C. Wyn Morgan, and Anthony John Rayner. 1992. "Objective and Subjective Influences on the Decision to Trade Futures: The Case of the London Potato Futures Market." *Journal of Agricultural Economics* 43 (2): 160–74.

Faruqee, Rashid, Jonathan R. Coleman, and Tom Scott. 1997. "Managing Price Risk in the Pakistan Wheat Market." *World Bank Economic Review* 11 (2): 263–92.

Futures Industry Association. 2004. News release. March 17. Chicago, Ill. [www.futuresindustry.org/fiahome-1927.asp].

———. 2005. Email interviews with Will Acworth, editor of *Futures Industry Magazine,* and Megan De Grandis, web site manager. May 9.

Gardner, Bruce L. 2000. "Recent Risk Management Policy Development in North America and the Prospects for Commodity Price Insurance in Developing Countries." Paper prepared for the World Bank conference, "Development Thinking for the Millennium," June 26–28, Paris.

Gilbert, Christopher J. 1996. "International Commodity Agreements: An Obituary Notice." *World Development* 24 (1): 1–19.

Gorton, Gary, and K. Geert Rouwenhorst. 2005. "Facts and Fantasies about Commodity Futures." Yale International Center for Finance Working Paper 04-20. Yale University, School of Management, New Haven, Conn. [http://papers.ssrn.com/sol3/papers.cfm?abstract_id=560042]

Guillaumont, Patrick. 2005. "On the Economic Vulnerability of Low-Income Countries." In Lino Briguglio and Eliawony J. Kisanga, eds., *Vulnerability and Resilience of Small States.* Malta: Formatek Malta.

ITF (International Task Force on Commodity Risk Management in Developing Countries). 1999. "Dealing with Commodity Price Volatility in Developing Countries: A Proposal for a Market-based Approach." Discussion paper for the Roundtable on Commodity Risk Management in Developing Countries, September 24, Washington, D.C.

Kydd, Jonathan, and Colin Poulton. 2000. "Agricultural Liberalisation, Commercialisation and the Market Access Problem." In Tony Killick, Jonathan Kydd, and Colin Poulton, "The Rural Poor and the Wider Economy: The Problem of Market Access." Background report for the International Fund for Agricultural Development Rural Poverty Report. University of London, Wye College, Kent, UK.

Leuthold, Raymond M. 1994. "Evaluating Futures Exchanges in Liberalising Economies." *Development Policy Review* 12 (2): 149–63.

McKinnon, Ronald. 1967. "Futures Markets, Buffer Stocks, and Income Stability for Primary Producers." *Journal of Political Economy* 75 (6): 844–61.

Millman, Gregory J. 2002. "Futures and Options Markets." In David Henderson, ed., *The Concise Encyclopedia of Economics.* [www.econlib.org/library/CEE.html].

Miranda, Mario, and Dmitry V. Vedenov. 2001. "Innovations in Agriculture and Natural Disaster Insurance." *American Journal of Agricultural Economics* 83 (3): 650–55.

Morgan, C. Wyn. 1999. "Futures Markets and Spot Price Volatility: A Case Study." *Journal of Agricultural Economics* 50 (2): 247–57.

Morgan, C. Wyn, Anthony John Rayner, and Charlotte Vaillant. 1999. "Agricultural Futures Markets in LDCs: A Policy Response to Price Volatility?" *Journal of International Development* 11 (6): 893–910.

Netz, Janet S. 1995. "The Effect of Futures Markets and Corners on Storage and Spot Price Volatility." *American Journal of Agricultural Economics* 77 (1): 182–93.

Radetzki, Marian. 1990. *A Guide to Primary Commodities in the World Economy.* Oxford: Blackwell.

Santana-Boado, Leonela. 2001. "Overview of the World's Commodity Exchanges, 2001." Geneva: United Nations Conference on Trade and Development. [http://r0.unctad.org/infocomm/comm_docs/docs/meetings/burg/bu02UNCTAD.PDF].

Shiller. Robert J. 1993. *Macro Markets: Creating Institutions for Managing Society's Largest Economic Risks.* Oxford: Oxford University Press.

Skees, Jerry, Peter Hazell, and Mario Miranda. 1999. "New Approaches to Crop Yield Insurance in Developing Countries." IFPRI Environment, Technology, and Production Division Discussion Paper 55. International Food Policy Research Institute, Washington, D.C. [www.microinsurancecentre.org/resources/Documents/eptdp55.pdf]

Skees, Jerry, Panos Varangis, Rodney Lester, Stephanie Gover, and Vijay Kalavakonda. 2001. "Developing Rainfall-Based Index Insurance in Morocco." Policy Research Working Paper 2577. World Bank, Washington, D.C.

Snowden, Nicholas, and Guillermo Benavides 2005. "Futures for Farmers: Hedging Participation and the Mexican Corn Scheme." Lancaster University Management School Working Paper 2005/007. Lancaster University, UK. [www.lums.lancs.ac.uk/publications/viewpdf/002167/].

Telser, Lester G. 1981. "Why There Are Organised Futures Markets." *Journal of Law and Economics* 24 (1): 1–22.

Thompson, Sarahelen. 1985. "Use of Futures Markets for Exports by Less Developed Countries." *American Journal of Agricultural Economics* 67 (5): 986–91.

Tosini, Paula. 2002. "Considerations in the Regulation of Financial Futures." Background paper prepared for the China Securities Regulatory Commission and Organisation for Economic Co-operation and Development's Second International Roundtable on Securities Markets in China, June 6–7, Shanghai. [www.oecd.org/dataoecd/23/15/2756228.pdf].

Varangis, Panos, and Donald Larson. 1996. "Dealing with Commodity Price Uncertainty." Policy Research Working Paper 1167. World Bank, Washington, D.C.

Varangis, Panos, Donald Larson, and Jock R. Anderson. 2002. "Agricultural Markets and Risks: Management of the Latter, Not the Former." Policy Research Working Paper 2793. World Bank, Washington, D.C.

Williams, Jeffrey, Anne Peck, Albert Park, and Scott Rozelle. 1998. "The Emergence of a Futures Market: Mungbeans on the China Zhengzhou Commodity Exchange." *The Journal of Futures Markets* 18 (4): 427–48.

ASSESSING CONTRACTUAL AND STATUTORY APPROACHES

POLICY PROPOSALS FOR RESTRUCTURING UNSUSTAINABLE SOVEREIGN DEBT

BARRY EICHENGREEN

In a speech to the National Economists Club in 2001 Anne Krueger, the first deputy managing director of the International Monetary Fund (IMF), pointed to a flaw in the international financial architecture requiring urgent attention: "We lack incentives to help countries with unsustainable debts resolve them promptly and in an orderly way. At present the only available mechanism requires the international community to bail out the private creditors. It is high time this hole was filled" (Krueger 2001, p. 1).

This observation, coming as it did from the number two official at the time of the institution at the center of crisis management efforts, quickly became a flash point in the so-called architecture debate. It provoked a flurry of proposals for reform. It is easy enough to understand why. Krueger's "manifesto" spoke to the widespread belief that the market for emerging market debt is dangerously unstable. Even as private capital flows to emerging markets posted impressive gains in 2003 (expected to continue through 2005), these flows are still recovering from their low point of $125 billion in 2002 (table 1). Medium- to long-term net non-bank lending to emerging markets declined even more precipitously from its peak of $88 billion in 1997 and has been even slower to recover (IIF 2003, p. 14). A variety of factors may have contributed to these fluctuations. Still, there is a broadly shared sense that the frequency of sovereign debt crises—starting with Mexico in 1994, extending through the Russian Federation in 1998, and culminating in

An earlier draft of this chapter was published in the *Journal of Economic Perspectives* (Eichengreen 2003). Portions of that article are reproduced here with the permission of the American Economic Association. For helpful comments the author wishes to thank Lee Buchheit, Mitu Gulati, Andrei Shleifer, Timothy Taylor, and Michael Waldman.

TABLE 1

External financing of emerging market economies, 1999–2005
(billions of U.S. dollars)

Item	1999	2000	2001	2002	2003	2004[a]	2005[b]
Current account balance	30.1	47.9	32.8	79.0	120.8	159.9	127.5
External financing, net							
Private flows, net	148.2	185.6	125.7	124.9	210.6	279.0	275.8
Equity investment, net	164.1	149.9	144.5	117.6	122.5	165.3	176.6
Direct investment, net	149.1	135.6	134.3	116.5	90.6	129.5	142.8
Portfolio investment, net	15.0	14.3	10.2	1.1	31.8	35.8	33.8
Private creditors, net	−15.9	35.7	−18.8	7.3	88.1	113.8	99.3
Commercial banks, net	−51.6	−4.4	−26.3	−6.8	26.4	49.2	42.2
Nonbanks, net	35.8	40.1	7.5	14.1	61.8	64.6	57.1
Official flows, net	12.4	−3.0	14.7	−5.4	−21.0	−18.5	−35.7
International financial institutions	2.4	3.3	24.3	8.1	−7.0	−10.9	−16.6
Bilateral creditors	10.0	−6.2	−9.6	−13.6	−14.1	−7.6	−19.0
Resident lending and other, net[c]	−135.4	−159.5	−85.7	−46.9	6.8	−43.7	−56.2
Reserves[d]	−55.3	−71.1	−87.5	−151.6	−317.1	−376.6	−311.5

Note: Emerging markets include the principal recipients of capital flows in Eastern Europe (Bulgaria, Czech Republic, Hungary, Poland, Romania, Russian Federation, Slovak Republic, and Turkey); Latin America (Argentina, Brazil, Chile, Colombia, Ecuador, Mexico, Peru, Uruguay, and Venezuela); Africa and the Middle East (Algeria, Egypt, Morocco, South Africa and Tunisia); and Asia (China, India, Indonesia, Republic of Korea, Malaysia, Philippines, and Thailand).
a. Estimated.
b. Forecast.
c. Including net lending, monetary gold, and errors and omissions.
d. Minus values indicate an increase in reserves.
Source: IIF 2003 (p. 1), 2005 (p. 1).

Argentina in 2001—and the way they were dealt with by the private and public sectors have had much to do with the volatility of the market.

But while there is broad agreement on the kind of steps needed to limit the frequency of financial crises—strengthen macroeconomic policies, improve supervision and regulation of financial systems, and develop techniques for more promptly identifying looming risks (IMF 2002)—there is no similar consensus on how to manage and resolve crises. Some suggest that institutional reforms making it easier to restructure unsustainable sovereign debts are a more attractive alternative to IMF financial assistance and that getting the IMF out of the bailout business would reduce excessive risk taking and help to stabilize the international financial system (G-22 1998). Others object that such reforms would be superfluous (Roubini 2002) or even counterproductive (Porzecanski 2003). Some join Krueger in arguing that significant change would require creating a new statutory process—not exactly an international bankruptcy court, but a set of mechanisms and procedures inspired by it—and amending the IMF's Articles of Agreement, hardly a negligible task. Others prefer a more decentralized process that would specify the procedures for restructuring a sovereign debt instrument at the time it is issued (Hubbard 2002).

Not surprisingly, these conflicting positions are informed by very different views of the nature and pervasiveness of the distortion giving rise to financial crises in the first place.

This chapter discusses the rationale behind efforts to make sovereign debt restructuring more efficient, orderly, and predictable, looking in particular at the contractual and statutory approaches to debt restructuring. It compares the two approaches, emphasizing the implications for asset substitution, aggregation, transition, and borrowing costs and presents empirical evidence on how the two approaches work in practice.

MOTIVATIONS FOR RESTRUCTURING SOVEREIGN DEBT

Rogoff and Zettelmeyer (2002) distinguish two justifications for making sovereign debt restructuring more efficient, orderly, and predictable: deadweight losses for lenders and borrowers and moral hazard for lenders.

Deadweight losses for lenders and borrowers
Inefficiencies associated with current arrangements impose deadweight losses on lenders and borrowers. Information problems, such as uncertainty about the debtor's willingness and ability to pay, encourage lenders and borrowers to engage in costly wars of attrition, unnecessarily delaying agreement on restructuring terms. Even when disagreements between borrowers and lenders are put to rest, coordination problems among creditors may delay acceptance of a restructuring offer. For example, a dissenting creditor may block agreement until being bought out on favorable terms.

During this period lenders receive no interest, and the borrowing country has no access to international capital markets. An extended loss of access may cause the exchange rate to collapse and banks with foreign currency-denominated liabilities to fall into crisis. This extended loss of market access and the recession that it provokes have high costs for a country (higher than the costs of financial distress for a corporation, according to Bolton 2003, p. 58). Officials in the borrowing country may thus feel compelled to pursue costly policies to avoid this plight, running down reserves, raising interest rates, and putting the economy through a deflationary wringer.

These costs could be reduced if countries with unsustainable debts reorganized sooner and if debtors and creditors could agree more rapidly on restructuring terms. A more efficient mechanism for debt workouts that deals better with information and coordination problems is needed to make this possible.

But not everyone agrees that debt restructuring is so difficult or that the costs are prohibitive. Ecuador, Pakistan, the Russian Federation, and Ukraine were all able to restructure their bonded debts in recent years, securing substantial debt service relief and even significant write-downs of principal. Making imaginative use of such techniques as exchange (take it or leave it) offers, they achieved high acceptance rates among creditors: 97 percent for Ecuador, 99 percent for Pakistan, 99 percent for Ukraine, and 96–99 percent for the Russian Federation, where the exchange came in two stages (Emerging Markets Creditors Association and others 2002, p. 1). Several of these countries were able to reenter the international capital market with surprising speed.

Nor does everyone agree that the costs of debt restructuring are a deadweight loss. Dooley (2000) argues that output losses from default are a necessary incentive for governments to repay, given sovereign debtors' immunity from legal action. A more predictable restructuring process that involves less forgone output might tempt governments to declare themselves incapable of repaying, leaving investors reluctant to lend. In this view the distinctive weaknesses of the sovereign debt market—low liquidity, high volatility, substantial spreads—imply that the restructuring of unsustainable debts is too easy, not too difficult. Sovereign debt does not suddenly become "unsustainable." Rather, unsustainable debt can be a consequence of endogenous policy choices by the borrowing government, which might only be encouraged by a mechanism for more smoothly resolving defaults. The problem becomes less one of how to deal with unsustainable debt and more one of how to organize the market so that defaults are less frequent and interest rates are lower (Shleifer 2003).

This argument has limits. Bolton (2003) observes that a restructuring procedure that is too creditor friendly may discourage lending as much as a procedure that is too debtor friendly. Sometimes debts are rendered unsustainable for reasons beyond the borrower's control. If dire consequences flow from the debtor's inability to service its debts, the debtor may be reluctant to borrow in the first place, and attractive investment projects may go unfunded. The problem is to strike the appropriate balance.

Moral hazard for investors

The international policy community, for its part, apparently views the costs of default as unacceptably high, as evidenced by the frequency with which it intervenes, evidently to limit the costs. This brings up the second rationale for reform, limiting moral hazard. The same costs of restructuring that pressure the IMF to provide emergency assistance to sovereign borrowers encourage investors to lend to them. An IMF loan that allows a country to pay off its maturing credits makes it possible for holders of those obligations to exit without losses. And since the

IMF typically gets paid back (arrears on IMF loans are uncommon), the residents of the crisis country end up footing the bill. It is their taxes that ultimately guarantee private investors 100 cents on the dollar.

But reducing the frequency and magnitude of IMF rescue operations, as Miller and Zhang (2000) point out, requires creating an environment where a commitment by the official community to stand aside is credible. The IMF and its industrial country government shareholders, like a central bank that sees a distressed financial institution as too big to fail, are motivated by the concern that failure to intervene would have unacceptable costs. As Fischer (2003, p. 28) puts it, "when a country's debt burden is unsustainable, the international community—operating through the IMF—faces the choice of lending to it, or forcing it into a potentially extremely costly restructuring, whose outcome is unknown." One motivation for new approaches to sovereign debt restructuring is thus to open up less costly avenues for debt reorganization, thereby reducing the pressure on the IMF to lend and removing the incentive for investors to engage in additional lending in anticipation of official intervention.

In fact, however, there is considerable disagreement over whether the prospect of IMF rescues encourages risk taking by investors. Mussa (2002b) argues on a priori grounds that this danger has been overblown. He observes that investors still demand significant spreads over U.S. Treasury bonds for emerging market debt, as if they do not expect that official assistance will guarantee that they are paid off in full. The quantitative literature analyzing the determinants of emerging spreads as a way of identifying moral hazard effects among investors is inconclusive. While Sarno and Taylor (1999), Chang (2000), and Spadafora (2001) find evidence of investor moral hazard, Zhang (1999) and Kamin (2004) do not.

A study by Dell'Ariccia, Schnabel, and Zettelmeyer (2002) summarizes this literature and argues that the decision to let the Russian Federation default constituted a "natural experiment," useful for testing for investor moral hazard. A departure from previous policy toward countries like Mexico and the Republic of Korea, the decision to let the Russian Federation default implied a decline in the perceived probability of future bailouts. If the prospect of bailouts had previously affected pricing behavior in the market, investors should have responded by demanding a larger premium for holding risky credits. The study found that spread compression declined significantly after August 1998, suggesting the existence of moral hazard effects due to IMF programs in the preceding period. But the finding also implies that the severity of the moral hazard problem may have diminished in recent years.

WHY NOW?

Despite the open-ended nature of these disputes and the fact that sovereign defaults are hardly new, there has been a strong push in recent years by the international policy community to alter the mechanisms for restructuring sovereign debt. Why this sudden attention?

The current debate can be traced to a lesson drawn from the Mexican crisis of 1994–95 and subsequently reinforced by the Asian, Brazilian, and Argentine crises: recent developments in international financial markets heighten information and collective action problems. In the 1970s most sovereign debt was held as medium- to long-term syndicated bank loans. Syndicates had limited numbers of participants, facilitating communication, collective action, and the application of moral suasion by governments. Covenants attached to the loans, such as sharing clauses that required an investor initiating legal action to share the proceeds with other creditors, discouraged disruptive litigation (Buchheit 1990).

Then came the debt crisis of the 1980s, which was resolved at the end of the decade by the Brady Plan, with many bank claims converted into securitized instruments (Brady bonds). This created a liquid market in the international debt securities of developing countries. More than half of the outstanding public external debt owed to private creditors is now in bonds. Market participants see this as progress. Because securitized instruments are more liquid and widely held, they have better risk-sharing properties. But because bondholders are more numerous and heterogeneous than the members of the typical bank syndicate, securitization also creates holdout problems. Unlike syndicated bank loans, sovereign bonds issued in the United States do not include sharing clauses to discourage opportunistic litigation.[1] And official arm-twisting has been rendered less effective by the growth of the bond market. Whereas banks are subject to regulatory incentives and moral suasion, most bondholders are not.

These facts were highlighted in a postmortem on the Mexican crisis commissioned by the Bank of England (Eichengreen and Portes 1995) and in subsequent reports by the Group of 10 (G-10 1996) and by the Group of 22 (G-22 1998).[2] But it took the Argentine crisis of 2001–02 to drive the point home.

That crisis is now the subject of a large literature (Mussa 2002a). In August 2001 the IMF agreed to provide Argentina with an additional $8 billion in assistance. The IMF earmarked $3 billion, to be brought forward from later disbursements, to support a voluntary, market-based operation to improve Argentina's debt profile—in effect, a restructuring operation to reduce immediate debt-servicing obligations. Frustratingly, however, no one could figure out how to use that $3 billion. Collective action problems made it difficult to get creditors to participate in a voluntary restructuring—precisely because it was voluntary. They preferred to see whether the multilateral institutions would provide additional assistance (Eichengreen 2002). In the end the official community felt that it had no alternative but to lend: doing nothing and forcing the country into a messy restructuring risked endangering Argentina's neighbors and undermining a fragile international financial system. At the same time officials feared that this action only aggravated the problem of moral hazard, convincing them of the need for institutional reform.

Options include retaining the status quo, promoting more complete and efficient debt contracts, developing a statutory approach with some of the functions of an international bankruptcy mechanism, and creating a full-fledged international bankruptcy court. National and international officials evidently regard the status quo as untenable (Taylor 2002a; Krueger 2001). And while some nongovernmental organizations continue to plump for a full-fledged sovereign bankruptcy court (see, for example, Jubilee Plus 2002), academics and officials tend to be skeptical, fearing that a judicial entity with extensive powers to override national law and private debt contracts would significantly weaken creditor rights and make it more difficult for emerging markets to fund their development needs. The policy debate therefore centers on the merits of the contractual approach and the statutory approach.

THE CONTRACTUAL APPROACH

One reason that sovereign debt restructuring is costly and unpredictable is that intercreditor relations are governed by incomplete contracts. Until 2003 sovereign bond contracts in the United States provided only sketchy guidance on what to do in a default. They made no provision for communication among bondholders, restraints on disruptive litigation, or a majority vote by bondholders on changes in payment terms. The key to more orderly restructuring, then, was to encourage lenders and borrowers to lay out the procedures for restructuring at the time the debt obligation is incurred.

Virtually all sovereign bonds issued in London and subject to UK law include the relevant provisions:

- *Collective representation clauses.* These provide for the establishment of a bondholders meeting at which creditors may exchange views. Procedures are also typically specified for selecting a bondholders' representative, generally the trustee, who is empowered to communicate the bondholders' negotiating terms to the debtor.
- *Majority enforcement clauses.* These prohibit individual bondholders from initiating litigation. The power to do so is vested with the trustee, acting on the instruction of creditors holding a specified fraction of the principal and charged with distributing all recovered funds in proportion to the principal amount. De facto, these provisions have the effect of sharing clauses.
- *Majority restructuring clauses.* These specify the majority share of bondholders required to amend payment terms (timing, amount of principal and interest). Typical shares are two-thirds of the notes represented at a first meeting of the bondholders and smaller shares at subsequent bondholder meetings. Voted changes are then binding on all bondholders. As White (2002, pp. 303–04) observes, bonds containing such clauses "lend themselves to restructuring, because a minority of holdouts can be forced to accept changes in bond terms."

Collective action clauses is the omnibus term used to refer to these collective representation, majority enforcement, and majority restructuring provisions. At the end of 2001 nearly 70 percent of the $354 billion in international sovereign bonds outstanding was issued under U.S. or German law, virtually none of which include such clauses (table 2). Virtually all of the rest did.[3] In 2004, however, 90 percent of the total value of new sovereign bond issues under New York law included collective action clauses, and more than 40 percent of the value of the outstanding stock of bonds of emerging market countries issued under New York law also included such clauses (table 3).

Collective action clauses had not been widely used in the United States, in part because the convoluted capital structure of U.S. corporations rendered market-based restructuring all but infeasible (Skeel 2003).[4] Before the 1920s most U.S. corporate bonds were reorganized under the court-led procedure known as an equity receivership, and in the 1930s Congress amended the Bankruptcy Act to facilitate supervision of corporate reorganizations by a bankruptcy judge (Swaine 1927; Buchheit and Gulati 2002).

In the 1930s, before adoption of the Trust Indenture Act,[5] when use of collective action clauses was at an all-time high in the United States, they appear to

TABLE 2

Stock of outstanding bonds by jurisdiction, selected industrial countries, 2001

Jurisdiction	Share of total (percent)	Amount (millions of U.S. dollars)	Number of bonds
United States	59.07	209,199	233[a]
Brady bonds		73,837	
United Kingdom	24.05	85,182	156
Germany	10.13	35,864	89
Japan	5.85	20,716	59
France	0.30	1,060	4
Switzerland	0.29	1,034	10
Luxembourg	0.22	763	4
Spain	0.04	138	1
Italy	0.03	105	1
Austria	0.02	67	1
Total[b]	100.0	354,129	558

a. Includes the aggregate amount of Brady bonds, but not the number of separate bonds.
b. Data on jurisdiction were not available for two bonds, accounting for the difference in totals.
Source: Dealogic 2004; IMF 2002 (p. 5).

TABLE 3

Emerging markets sovereign bond issuance by jurisdiction, 2002–04

	2002				2003				2004[a]			
	Q1	Q2	Q3	Q4	Q1	Q2[b]	Q3	Q4	Q1	Q2	Q3	Q4
With collective action clause[c]												
Number of issuances	6	5	2	4	9	31	10	5	25	19	21	14
Under New York law	0	0	0	0	1	22	5	4	14	12	14	12
Volume of issuances												
(US$ billions)	2.6	1.9	0.9	1.4	5.6	18.0	6.4	4.3	18.5	15.9	12.2	9.1
Under New York law	0	0	0	0	1.0	12.8	3.6	4.0	10.6	9.5	7.7	7.7
Without collective action clause[d]												
Number of issuances	17	12	5	10	14	4	7	7	2	2	1	4
Volume of issuances												
(US$ billions)	11.6	6.4	3.3	4.4	8.1	2.5	3.5	4.2	1.5	0.4	0.3	2.7

a. Data as of January 3, 2005.
b. Includes issues of restructured bonds by Uruguay.
c. UK and Japanese laws, and New York law where relevant.
d. German and New York laws.
Source: IMF 2005 (p. 43).

have been included in about 10 percent of new issues. But even when used, they were regarded with suspicion. Rather than protecting the majority of creditors against free-riders, they were often seen as allowing a few corporate and Wall Street insiders, who might hold the majority of the bond issue and also equity claims on the firm, to redistribute surplus from bond to equity holders and from small creditors to themselves. William O. Douglas, member and then chairman of the Securities and Exchange Commission, held hearings and published articles that developed this view (see, for example, Douglas 1940). The result was section 316(b) of the Trust Indenture Act of 1939, which prohibited any reduction in the amount due under a publicly issued corporate bond without the consent of each bondholder. This restriction was feasible—it did not lead to a spate of inefficient liquidations—because provisions of U.S. bankruptcy law allowed the courts to substitute for the missing provisions.

This history helps to explain why collective action clauses have not been included in corporate bonds issued in the United States, but it cannot explain why such provisions were for so long excluded from sovereign bonds. The Trust Indenture Act of 1939 does not apply to sovereign issues. The rationale for applying it would be weak, since there is no court-led alternative for sovereign debt reorganization akin to that available to corporations under U.S. bankruptcy law. This of course is precisely the problem that recent initiatives seek to address.

That collective action clauses did not come into more widespread use in the United States until recently could suggest that the markets regarded them as undesirable. Allowing a majority vote to force restructuring terms on dissenting investors might tempt the debtor to buy back a sufficient share of the issue to engineer the necessary majority, or the government might exert moral suasion over domestic institutional investors that had purchased the bonds on the secondary market. Similarly, making it easier for creditors to agree to a restructuring might make it more tempting for debtors to restructure, since the length of time when relations with creditors were in disarray would be correspondingly reduced. If the result was a weakening of creditor rights, investors might have good reason to shun such contracts.

Of course, it is not obvious that making it easier for creditors to coordinate in forming a common front would weaken their position. Nor is it obvious that debtors would take advantage of collective action clauses by acting more opportunistically. Indeed, in cases where restructuring was unavoidable, for reasons beyond the control of the debtor, collective action mechanisms that allowed the situation to be normalized more smoothly by facilitating coordination among creditors would presumably help to avoid an extended period when no interest was paid and no principal was recovered. In other words, creditors would find their position strengthened, not undercut.

But if collective action clauses would make debt restructuring more efficient, why have markets been slow in adopting this practice? Allen and Gale (1994) suggest five reasons why socially desirable financial innovations may fail to emerge. First, product uncertainty may make investors uncertain about the performance characteristics of the new financial instrument—for example, the commentary of market participants suggests considerable uncertainty about whether easier restructuring will make restructuring more frequent. Second, there may be a first-mover disadvantage if the costs of designing the new clauses and educating investors are incurred by the originator and then other entrants can free ride on these investments and quickly compete away any higher returns. Third, there may be coordination problems if a number of borrowers must issue these instruments simultaneously to create deep and liquid secondary markets. Fourth, new financial instruments may have positive externalities for the stability of the international system, but individual borrowers have only weak incentives to internalize this externality by adopting such new provisions. Finally, political distortions can arise when politicians facing reelection have shorter time horizons than society as a whole and thus prefer inflexible provisions that reduce the cost of borrowing now, even if they create restructuring costs that are inefficiently high from a social point of view.

It is unclear to what extent these limitations actually slowed the addition of collective action clauses to sovereign debt instruments in the United States. Product uncertainty was often cited as an obstacle to their more widespread use, but a sizable minority of sovereign debt had already been issued with such clauses, notably in the London market, suggesting that the level of product uncertainty and first mover disadvantages were lower than for a completely untried financial innovation and therefore were overcome in recent years. Coordination problems and the need to create a more liquid secondary market can be addressed by encouraging a few advanced industrial countries and higher income emerging markets to move simultaneously. Thus, the governments of Canada and the United Kingdom agreed to include collective action clauses in their loan contracts, and Switzerland and the European Union committed to doing the same. Moreover, in 2003 Mexico issued $1 billion in global Eurobonds in New York that included collective action clauses, considered a response to pressure for an investment-grade country to set a precedent in the interests of the greater good. The first-mover disadvantage, too, proved to be surmountable. The inadequacy of incentives for individual financial firms to develop innovative clauses was addressed through the cooperation of institutional investors and others, such as the G-10, in the design of model clauses. The bonds issued by Mexico included collective action clauses that followed closely the G-10 model, including the use of a 75 percent voting threshold for bondholders.[6]

There is now considerable momentum for greater use of collective action clauses. And as market participants gain experience with the price and performance characteristics of these provisions, any remaining problems of product uncertainty or lack of deep and liquid secondary markets should also lessen and further reduce the traditional resistance to including collective action clauses in debt instruments issued in New York.

THE STATUTORY APPROACH

Elaborating the provisions of loan contracts is in some sense the obvious way of addressing information, coordination, and free-rider problems in a decentralized financial system. But some observers, such as Anne Krueger (2001) of the IMF, insist in addition on the need for a statutory framework—not a full-blown bankruptcy court but a legal framework that would bind all countries and supersede the conflicting provisions of private loan agreements, much in the way that Chapter 11 of the U.S. Bankruptcy Code supersedes the provisions of private loan contracts in the United States when a firm goes into bankruptcy.[7] The most prominent proposal along these lines is Krueger's (2002a) sovereign debt restructuring mechanism. One way of thinking about the competing proposals is that a statutory approach like the sovereign debt restructuring mechanism elaborates the traditional U.S.-style court-led approach to debt restructuring by relying on statutes to create a quasi-judicial process for debt reorganization, while collective action clauses attempt to extend the traditional UK-style approach that relies on contracting and on self-organizing creditors, with little if any court involvement.

Proposals for a statutory approach typically have four key features, which bear more than a passing resemblance to the central features of U.S. Chapter 11. First, restraints on litigation would be imposed, perhaps after approval by a super-majority of creditors. Second, creditors could agree to assign seniority and protection from restructuring to new private lending, including the provision of trade credit, to reduce the dangers of a cutoff of foreign credit. Third, a super-majority of creditors, regardless of the bond issues or loan obligations they hold, could vote to accept new terms of payment under a restructuring agreement. Minority creditors would be bound by the decision of the majority. Finally, a dispute resolution forum would be created to verify claims, guarantee the integrity of the voting process, and adjudicate disputes.

Full implementation of the statutory approach would require amending the IMF's Articles of Agreement. That requires support from three-fifths of the members holding 85 percent of total voting power—a formidable task. By design, the Articles of Agreement are difficult to change, for otherwise they would not provide an effective set of checks and balances on decisionmaking. In particular, amendment requires the support of the U.S. government, which holds 17.1 percent of the votes,[8] and ratification by the U.S. Congress. At the spring 2003 meetings of the IMF, it was acknowledged that support for amending the articles fell short of the requisite level[9]—in particular, the U.S. government failed to lend its support. To be sure, a similar statutory approach could also be created by enacting legislation in each national jurisdiction. But the advantages of universality and uniformity would be lost if all countries did not adopt the necessary legislation.

COMPARING THE CONTRACTUAL AND STATUTORY APPROACHES

On what basis might the statutory approach be preferred over the contractual approach? Comparisons of the two emphasize the implications for four problems: asset substitution, aggregation, transition, and borrowing costs.

Asset substitution

Borrowers and lenders might substitute away from bonds with collective action clauses in favor of bank loans and other credit instruments that do not include them. As noted, an advantage of a statutory mechanism put in place by an amendment to the IMF's Articles of Agreement would be its universality—in principle, it would cover all assets and countries. Proponents of collective action clauses argue that such clauses can address the asset substitution problem. Some, like Taylor (2002b), propose that collective action clauses be added to bank debt as well as to bonds, which could be done by modifying bank regulation and securities market rules. Some argue that if a few major markets alter their contractual provisions, borrowing is unlikely to shift to other significantly less liquid and more costly locales. Most issuers now prefer to issue global bonds that meet registration requirements in all major markets, as a way of maximizing the potential customer base (Roubini and Setser 2003). In particular, the size of the institutional investor market in the United States makes it unlikely that the market will migrate away from that country.

Aggregation

Existing contractual provisions, even in the UK market, do not address the need for cross-issue coordination, leading to the aggregation problem. Collective action clauses provide for a majority vote by the holders of an individual bond issue to modify the terms of payment due to holders of that issue, but the clauses have no effect on the amounts due to holders of other issues. A statutory approach, by providing for one grand supermajority vote of all the creditors, would solve the problems of cross-issue coordination and intercreditor equity at a stroke.

Those who prefer collective action clauses observe that, historically, holders of different issues have addressed problems of cross-issue coordination by forming representative committees. The international market in sovereign bonds was active in the nineteenth and early twentieth centuries, when there were frequent defaults and restructurings. Bonds were widely held, and countries had multiple issues in the market. Bondholders dealt with problems of cross-issue coordination by forming committees of representatives of various classes of creditors (Feis 1930; Eichengreen and Portes 1989; Mauro and Yafeh 2003). Proponents of collective action clauses observe that there is a renewed tendency to form creditor committees—as in the cases of Argentina, Côte d'Ivoire, Ecuador, and the Russian Federation—and argue that these can again be relied on to solve problems of cross-issue coordination. They also suggest that a code of conduct like that suggested by the Bank of France (2003) could encourage information sharing among holders of different bond issues and discourage strategic behavior.

Transition

Even if all countries immediately change their statutes to require all bond issues to include collective action clauses, a transition period will still be required for these new instruments to work their way into the market. The IMF (2002, p. 6) has estimated that if all sovereign bonds issued starting in 2002 included collective action clauses, but no existing bonds were amended or exchanged, 80 percent of international sovereign bonds would include collective action clauses by 2010 and 90 percent by 2019. Market-based debt exchanges could be used to replace the existing stock of bonds with instruments that included collective action clauses, but it is not clear how enthusiastically the exchange offers would be received. How much concern to attach to the speed of the transition is unclear. After all, proposals for getting collective action clauses into the market have been debated for at least eight years. Taking another eight years to get 80 percent of the way there might be regarded as a significant achievement.

Borrowing costs

If measures such as collective action clauses to make sovereign debt restructuring more orderly also make it more frequent, investors may be reluctant to lend to emerging markets, making it more difficult for them to fund their development needs. The rebuttal is that countries go to great lengths to avoid debt restructuring and that fears of borrower moral hazard are exaggerated. Consequently, creditors will appreciate having in place mechanisms that ease restructuring when sovereign debts are rendered unsustainable by circumstances not of the debtor's making.

It might be argued that the same factors that keep the cost of capital for corporations from rising because of the existence of a well functioning domestic bankruptcy and insolvency code should apply to sovereign borrowers. But this view may be too sanguine, because there is no equivalent in the sovereign context to provisions in national statutes that allow the courts to replace management and impose other sanctions on corporations that invoke bankruptcy opportunistically. If the effort to reach a mutually acceptable compromise under Chapter 11 is unsuccessful, the result is a wind-up of the firm under Chapter 7. The court as trustee takes over the proceeding. Under a statutory approach like the proposed sovereign debt restructuring mechanism, unsuccessful negotiations would result only in cessation of the temporary limits on private litigation. This difference could significantly tip the balance of bargaining power in the direction of the debtor (Cream 2002).

EVIDENCE ON THE CONTRACTUAL AND STATUTORY APPROACHES

The bond market is the obvious place to look for evidence about how realistic these fears are, since debt instruments with collective action clauses have historically been issued in London but not in New York. The impact of contractual provisions on borrowing costs has been studied by Eichengreen and Mody (2004), Petas and Rahman (1999), Becker, Richards, and Thaicharoen (2003), and Gugiatti and Richards (2003). Eichengreen and Mody studied more than 3,000 bonds, in principle the universe of all international bonds issued between 1991 and 2000 by emerging markets—corporate, municipal, state, and sovereign. While issued by emerging market borrowers, this debt is denominated in industrial country currencies. The bonds trade on a secondary market.

The key finding of Eichengreen and Mody (2004) is that low-risk countries pay a relatively lower interest rate if they borrow with collective action clauses, while high-risk countries pay a relatively higher one. An intuitive interpretation is that more creditworthy emerging market borrowers value their capital market access and are unlikely to renege on their debt obligations. The ability to resort to provisions facilitating the orderly restructuring of their obligations is viewed positively by the markets. For less creditworthy borrowers potential lenders fear that collective action clauses might encourage opportunistic default. Borrowers with low credit quality are consequently charged a premium when debt instruments include them.

Mexico's precedent-setting $1 billion in global Eurobonds issued in 2003, which featured collective action clauses despite being subject to U.S. law, can be used to gauge the plausibility of these results. The bonds, maturing in March 2015, were priced to yield 6.92 percent, a spread of 312 basis points over 10-year U.S. Treasuries. Mexico's 2016 bond, without collective action clauses, was yielding about 7.28 percent (Mexico Ministry of Finance 2003). The Eichengreen and Mody (2004) results suggest that a country that had just succeeded in obtaining an investment grade rating (Standard & Poor's rated Mexican debt BBB–, its lowest investment grade rating, and Moody's rated it Baa2, one step above the lowest investment grade) should have enjoyed a discount on bonds with collective action clauses of about 25 basis points.

It is not clear how these empirical results would apply to a statutory mechanism for addressing sovereign debt. Krueger (2002b) argues that the impact on borrowing costs of a procedure like the proposed sovereign debt restructuring mechanism should be similar to that of collective action clauses. That is, having a statutory procedure for more orderly debt restructuring should make claims on highly creditworthy countries more attractive, since the countries would not resort to the mechanism except in extraordinary circumstances not of their own making, while having a mechanism in place to resolve crises quickly would be attractive to all parties. In contrast, less creditworthy countries, tempted to act opportunistically, might have to pay more.

However, a hypothetical statutory approach is not quite parallel to the already existing collective action clauses. Any statutory process would be new and unproven, likely to lead to greater product uncertainty for a time. For example, investors who currently hold debt instruments requiring unanimous consent to any change in the terms of payment might worry that a new regime with limits on litigation and various supermajority requirements was less respectful of their contractual rights.

CONCLUSION

The frequency of financial crises in emerging markets has focused attention on the limitations of current approaches to crisis resolution. Some analysts have emphasized the economic burden placed on emerging markets by the cost and difficulty of restructuring unsustainable sovereign debts. Others have pointed to the pressure felt by the IMF to provide financial assistance and the moral hazard thereby created for investors and governments, which increases the likelihood of future crises. Both observations suggest the desirability of reforms to make debt restructuring more orderly, efficient, and predictable, the first for its own sake, the second to render time consistent a commitment by the IMF to limit its intervention.

Concrete proposals for reform, such as the more widespread use of collective action clauses, surfaced following the first crises in the modern era of bond finance some 10 years ago. Ultimately, Krueger's proposal for a sovereign debt restructuring mechanism became a focus of the debate because it came from the international financial institution most directly involved with sovereign debt restructuring. The proposal was useful for focusing thought and clarifying issues. At the same time, however, it was criticized as too ambitious, arbitrary, and corrosive of market forces.

Thus officials decided, for the time being, to push ahead with getting collective action clauses into the market while consigning the sovereign debt restructuring mechanism to further study. But the question is likely to be revisited—presumably in the wake of the next serious emerging market crisis. For scholars this suggests the need for further work. How serious is the moral hazard problem? Can collective action clauses be added to bank loans and other credit instruments as easily as to bonds? To speed the transition, can market-based debt exchanges be used to retire debt instruments lacking collective action clauses, and what would be the cost of such operations? How serious is the aggregation problem that some see as the basis for choosing the sovereign debt restructuring mechanism over the collective action clause? Efforts to address these questions are sure to occupy researchers for years to come.

NOTES

1. The immediacy of the threat of litigation is disputed. Observers such as Scott (2003, p. 27) continue to warn that "the chances of holdout creditors collecting on their debts is a real one." Others, such as Roubini (2002), have argued that successful litigation has been limited to a few ill-advised court judgments, which are unlikely to be repeated. Implicitly acknowledging the validity of the skeptics' arguments, proponents of institutional reform have begun to attach less weight to this justification for official initiatives.

2. The Group of 10 (G-10) refers to the group of countries that have agreed to participate in the International Monetary Fund's General Arrangements to Borrow (GAB). The GAB was established in 1962, when the governments of eight IMF member countries—Belgium, Canada, France, Italy, Japan, the Netherlands, the United Kingdom, and the United States—and the central banks of two others, Germany and Sweden, agreed to make resources available to the IMF for drawings by participants and, under certain circumstances, by nonparticipants. The establishment on a temporary basis of the Group of 22 (G-22), also referred to as the "Willard Group," was announced by the leaders of the Asia-Pacific Economic Cooperation (APEC) countries at their meeting in Vancouver in November 1997. APEC leaders agreed to organize a gathering of finance ministers and central bank governors to advance reform of the architecture of the global financial system. See www.imf.org/external/np/exr/facts/groups.htm#G10.

3. Of Argentina's $111.8 billion in foreign bonds outstanding in 2001, 89 percent contained unanimous action clauses, while the remaining 11 percent, issued in London, included collective action clauses (Bratton and Gulati 2003, p. 16).

4. And in part because a contract providing for post-issuance changes to payment terms might not qualify as "unconditional promise to pay" under the Negotiable Instruments Law, and consequently its marketability would be impaired.

5. For a discussion of the Trust Indenture Act of 1939 see http://uscode.house.gov/download/title_11.php.

6. In 2002 a G-10 Working Group was formed to consider how sovereign debt contracts could be modified so as to make resolution of debt crises more orderly. This group later issued recommendations on the design of collective action clauses that could help achieve this objective. For further discussion on the development of these model clauses, see, for example, IMF (2003).

7. Chapter 11 concerns the debts of private entities such as corporations. They can be reorganized by domestic bankruptcy courts, which have jurisdiction over domestic corporate affairs. In principle, the same is true of subnational government entities such as municipalities, which can obtain protection from their creditors and assistance in restructuring their debts by invoking Chapter 9 of the bankruptcy code. In practice, however, these provisions are not frequently invoked. The fear that default by a state or municipality might tarnish the creditworthiness of the sovereign often causes central or federal governments to assume responsibility for the distressed debts of lower levels of government, reintroducing the problems addressed in this chapter. For more detail on the U.S. Bankruptcy Code, see http://uscode.house.gov/download/title_11.php.

8. See www.imf.org/external/np/sec/memdir/eds.htm.

9. See www.imf.org/external/np/cm/2003/041203.htm.

REFERENCES

Allen, Franklin, and Douglas Gale. 1994. *Financial Innovation and Risk Sharing.* Cambridge, Mass.: MIT Press.

Bank of France. 2003. "Toward a Code of Good Conduct on Sovereign Debt Renegotiation." Paris.

Becker, Torbjörn, Anthony J. Richards, and Yungong Thaicharoen. 2003. "Bond Restructuring and Moral Hazard: Are Collective Action Clauses Costly?" *Journal of International Economics* 61 (1): 127–61.

Bolton, Patrick. 2003. "Towards a Statutory Approach to Sovereign Debt Restructuring: Lessons from Corporate Bankruptcy Practice Around the World." *IMF Staff Papers* 50 (Special Issue): 41–71.

Bratton, William W., and G. Mitu Gulati. 2003. *Sovereign Debt Restructuring and the Best Interest of the Creditors.* George Washington University Law School Public Law Research Paper 59 and Georgetown Law and Economics Research Paper 387880. George Washington University and Georgetown University, Washington, D.C. [http://ssrn.com/abstract=387880].

Buchheit, Lee C. 1990. "The Sharing Clause as a Litigation Shield." *International Financial Law Review* 9 (10): 15–16.

Buchheit, Lee C., and G. Mitu Gulati. 2002. "Sovereign Bonds and the Collective Will." *Emory Law Journal* 51 (4): 1317–63.

Chang, Ha-Joon. 2000. "The Hazard of Moral Hazard: Untangling the Asian Crisis." *World Development* 28 (4): 775–88.

Cream, John F. 2002. "Sovereign Debt Restructuring." Bank of Nova Scotia, Toronto.

Dealogic. 2004. Bondware Database. [www.dealogic.com].

Dell'Ariccia, Giovanni, Isabel Schnabel, and Jeromin Zettelmeyer. 2002. "Moral Hazard and International Crisis Lending: A Test." IMF Working Paper 02/181. International Monetary Fund, Washington, D.C. [www.imf.org/external/pubs/ft/wp/2002/wp02181.pdf].

Dooley, Michael. 2000. *Can Output Losses Following International Financial Crises Be Avoided?* NBER Working Paper 7531. Cambridge, Mass.: National Bureau of Economic Research.

Douglas, William O. 1940. *Democracy and Finance.* New Haven, Conn.: Yale University Press.

Eichengreen, Barry. 2002. *Financial Crises and What to Do About Them.* Oxford: Oxford University Press.

———. 2003. "Restructuring Sovereign Debt." *Journal of Economic Perspectives* 17 (4): 75–98.

Eichengreen, Barry, and Ashoka Mody. 2004. "Do Collective Action Clauses Raise Borrowing Costs?" *Economic Journal* 114 (495): 247–64.

Eichengreen, Barry, and Richard Portes. 1989. "After the Deluge: Default, Negotiation and Readjustment during the Interwar Years." In Barry Eichengreen and Peter Lindert, eds., *The International Debt Crisis in Historical Perspective.* Cambridge, Mass.: MIT Press.

———. 1995. *Crisis? What Crisis? Orderly Workouts for Sovereign Debtors.* London: Centre for Economic Policy Research.

Emerging Markets Creditors Association, EMTA, Institute of International Finance, International Primary Market Association, International Securities Market Association, Securities Industry Association, and the Bond Market Association. 2002. "Sovereign Debt Restructuring." Discussion Paper. Institute of International Finance, Washington, D.C. [www.iif.com/data/public/SDRM.pdf].

Feis, Herbert. 1930. *Europe, the World's Banker.* New Haven, Conn.: Yale University Press.

Fischer, Stanley. 2003. "Financial Crises and Reform of the International Financial System." *Review of World Economics* 139 (1): 1–37.

G-10 (Group of 10). 1996. *Resolving Sovereign Liquidity Crises.* Washington, D.C.

G-22 (Group of 22). 1998. *Report of the Working Group on International Financial Crises.* Washington, D.C.

Gugiatti, Mark, and Anthony Richards. 2003. "Do Collective Action Clauses Influence Bond Yields? New Evidence from Emerging Markets." Research Discussion Paper 2003-02. Reserve Bank of Australia, Sydney.

Hubbard, R. Glenn. 2002. "Enhancing Sovereign Debt Restructuring." Paper presented at the Conference on the IMF's Sovereign Debt Proposal, October 7, Washington, D.C.

IIF (Institute of International Finance). 2003. "Capital Flows to Emerging Market Economies." Washington, D.C. [www.iif.com/data/public/cf_0103.pdf].

———. 2005. "Capital Flows to Emerging Market Economies." Washington, D.C. [www.iif.com/verify/data/report_docs/cf_0105.pdf].

IMF (International Monetary Fund). 2002. "Collective Action Clauses in Sovereign Bond Contracts—Encouraging Greater Use." Washington, D.C. [www.imf.org/external/np/psi/2002/eng/060602a.pdf].

———. 2003. "Collective Action Clauses: Recent Developments and Issues." Washington, D.C. [www.imf.org/external/np/psi/2003/032503.pdf].

———. 2005. *Global Financial Stability Report: Market Developments and Issues.* Washington, D.C.

Jubilee Plus. 2002. "Chapter 9/11? Resolving International Debt Crises: The Jubilee Framework for International Insolvency." London. [www.jubilee2000uk.org/analysis/reports/jubilee_framework.pdf].

Kamin, Steven B. 2004. "Identifying the Role of Moral Hazard in International Financial Markets." *International Finance* 7 (1): 25–59.

Krueger, Anne. 2001. "International Financial Architecture for 2002: A New Approach to Sovereign Debt Restructuring." Paper presented at the National Economists' Club Annual Members' Dinner, November 26, Washington, D.C. [www.imf.org/external/np/speeches/2001/112601.htm].

———. 2002a. *A New Approach to Sovereign Debt Restructuring.* Washington, D.C.: International Monetary Fund.

———. 2002b. "New Approaches to Sovereign Debt Restructuring: An Update on Our Thinking." Paper presented at the Institute for International Economics Conference on Sovereign Debt Workouts, April 1, Washington, D.C. [www.imf.org/external/np/speeches/2002/040102.htm].

Mauro, Paolo, and Yishay Yafeh. 2003. "The Corporation of Foreign Bondholders." IMF Working Paper WP/03/107. International Monetary Fund, Washington, D.C.

Mexico, Ministry of Finance. 2003. "12-Year Global UMS Bond with Collective Action Clauses in the International Markets." Public Debt Documents of the Investor Relations Office. Mexico City. [www.shcp.gob.mx/english/docs/pr030226.pdf].

Miller, Marcus, and Lei Zhang. 2000. "Sovereign Liquidity Crises: The Strategic Case for a Payments Standstill." *Economic Journal* 110 (460): 335–62.

Mussa, Michael. 2002a. *Argentina and the Fund: From Triumph to Tragedy.* Washington, D.C.: Institute for International Economics.

————. 2002b. "Reflections on Moral Hazard and Private Sector Involvement in the Resolution of Emerging Market Financial Crises." Institute for International Economics, Washington, D.C.

Petas, Peter, and Rashique Rahman. 1999. "Sovereign Bonds—Legal Aspects That Affect Default and Recovery." In *Global Emerging Markets—Debt Strategy*. London: Deutsche Bank.

Porzecanski, Arturo C. 2003. "A Critique of Sovereign Bankruptcy Initiatives." *Business Economics* 38 (1): 39–45.

Rogoff, Kenneth, and Jeromin Zettelmeyer. 2002. "Bankruptcy Procedures for Sovereigns: A History of Ideas, 1976–2001." *IMF Staff Papers* 49 (3): 470–507.

Roubini, Nouriel. 2002. "Bail-Ins, Bailouts, Burden Sharing and Private Sector Involvement in Crisis Resolution: The G-7 Framework and Some Suggestions on the Open Unresolved Issues." In Miguel Sebastián, ed., *Ensayos sobre Colombia y America Latina. Libro en memoria de Nicolás Botero*. Madrid: BBVA.

Roubini, Nouriel, and Brad Setser. 2003. "Improving the Sovereign Debt Restructuring Process: Problems of Restructuring, Proposed Solutions, and a Roadmap for Reform." Paper prepared for the Conference on Improving the Sovereign Debt Restructuring Process, March 9, Paris.

Sarno, Lucio, and Mark P. Taylor. 1999. "Moral Hazard, Asset Price Bubbles, Capital Flows and the East Asian Crisis: The First Tests." *Journal of International Money and Finance* 18 (4): 637–57.

Scott, Hal S. 2003. "A Bankruptcy Procedure for Sovereign Debtors?" Public Law Working Paper 53. Harvard Law School, Cambridge, Mass.

Shleifer, Andrei. 2003. "Will the Sovereign Debt Market Survive?" *American Economic Review* 93 (2): 85–90.

Skeel, David A., Jr. 2003. "Can Majority Voting Provisions Do It All?" *Emory Law Journal* 52 (1): 417–25.

Spadafora, Francesco. 2001. "The Pricing of Syndicated Bank Loans to Emerging Markets: Some Further Results." Working Paper 438. Bank of Italy, Rome.

Swaine, Robert. 1927. "Reorganization of Corporations: Certain Developments of the Last Decade." *Columbia Law Review* 27: 901–31.

Taylor, John. 2002a. "Sovereign Debt Restructuring: A U.S. Perspective." *Treasury News*. U.S. Treasury. Washington, D.C. [www.treas.gov/press/releases/po2056.htm].

————. 2002b. "Using Clauses to Reform the Process for Sovereign Debt Workouts: Progress and Next Steps." PO-3672. U.S. Treasury, Office of Public Affairs, Washington, D.C.

White, Michelle J. 2002. "Sovereigns in Distress: Do They Need Bankruptcy?" *Brookings Papers on Economic Activity* 1: 287–320.

Zhang, Xioaming. 1999. "Testing for 'Moral Hazard' in Emerging Markets Lending." IIF Research Paper 99-1. Institute of International Finance, Washington, D.C.

PLACING THE EMPHASIS ON REGULATION

LESSONS FROM PUBLIC FINANCE IN THE EUROPEAN UNION

Brigid Laffan

The European Union's system of public finance is the result of a continuous search for agreement among member states on the resource base of the common budget, its size, and the distribution of revenue across sectors and member states. Underlying all the debates is the fundamental question of the role of common spending: what contribution can an EU budget make to fostering regional integration and supporting member states in their national endeavors?

This chapter analyzes the political considerations and dynamics that have influenced the EU budget and the decisionmaking processes surrounding it and derives policy lessons for the financing of international cooperation more generally.

The European Union is an interesting in-between institution. It is more than a conventional intergovernmental organization (such as the United Nations) and less than a nation state. Thus, the lessons that can be drawn from the EU experience may reveal the types of financing arrangements that may become possible as international cooperation deepens and moves toward integration. The lessons may also reveal the limits of international cooperation, despite deepened integration, and the issues that nation states prefer to retain under their policymaking sovereignty.

From more than 40 years of EU budgetary politics, several policy messages stand out.

First, despite some growth, EU budgetary resources remain limited. They are capped at 1.27 percent of the European Union's gross national product (GNP), or 1.24 percent of its gross national income (GNI) (EC 2002). The richer member states, net contributors to the EU budget, have been firm about capping the portion of their revenues that they are willing to channel through the EU budget. This means that most important areas of public spending remain national. National governments, accountable to domestic electorates, are sensitive to the financial costs of the EU budget. Even though it is relatively small, considerations of equity and ability to pay are an important part of the budgetary discourse. This also means that the main influence that the European Union has on national policy-making, including national public finance, occurs through regulatory measures rather than through direct spending.

Second, and closely related, financing of the EU budget has been controversial at times. There have been three traditional revenue sources: levies on agricultural imports, custom duties on other imports, and transfers from member states of a percentage of a harmonized base of value-added taxes (VATs) collected. A fourth source, added recently, requires member states to contribute a modest portion of their GNI. This has encouraged member states to think in terms of "their money" in the common budget. There have also been proposals to introduce a European tax, but these have failed to attract sufficient political support.

Third, there is broad-based acceptance of the importance of interstate transfers. Such financial assistance is meant to help lower income member states adjust to market integration and other common regulatory measures or to catch up with more economically advanced member states. There is no agreement, however, that the European Union should engage in permanent financial transfers of the kind common in federal systems.

Fourth, to avoid annual budget negotiations, member states agreed in the late 1980s to embed the annual budget in a multiyear framework. This step brought enhanced stability and predictability. It also linked expenditure to revenue, thus avoiding the resource problems of the early 1980s when having adequate resources to fund annual budgetary commitments was often in doubt. This framework also made it more difficult, however, for member states to respond to new, emerging challenges and demands for unforeseen expenditures.

Fifth, member states are expected to unanimously adopt the multiyear budget framework, to ensure that all member states accept the outcome of the budgetary bargain. However, agreement on the framework is often possible only if side payments are made, so that all member states feel that the bargain makes them better off.

Sixth, like all jurisdictions, the European Union finds it difficult to break away from past budgetary commitments once it has embarked on financing a particular activity or making a particular side payment. This explains in part, for example, why agriculture remains the largest item of EU spending, despite many attempts to reduce it.

Seventh, the design of EU public finance policies and modalities is not based primarily on economic analysis, notably the insights of fiscal federalism theory. Rather, EU public finance has evolved incrementally and has a strong bias toward the status quo.

In elaborating on these messages, this chapter traces the evolution of the EU's public finance and budgetary debates.

THE MAIN PHASES OF BUDGETARY DEVELOPMENT

The EU budget has evolved in four phases (Laffan and Shackleton 2000; box 1).[1] Phase I, from 1958 to 1970, marks the search for a constitutional framework for development of EU finances and for agreement on an independent budgetary resource. An agreement was achieved through the 1970 Budget Treaty, following a decision by the EC Council of Ministers (EC Council 1970). Phase II, from 1971 to 1984, was a period of continuing conflict over budgetary issues, resulting in stagnation of the European Union and deteriorating relations among member states.

In response to this experience, the European Commission, headed by President Jacques Delors, initiated two budgetary reform efforts, commonly referred to as Delors I (1988) and Delors II (1992). Delors I introduced the multiyear budget framework, and Delors II led to a stronger emphasis on fostering cohesion within the European Union. Phase III, from 1985 to 1998, was a period of stability and consolidation of EU public finance.

Phase IV, from 1999 to 2006, includes the enlargement of the European Union to East-central Europe. This increased the number of member states from 15 to 25 and shifted the north-south focus of some EU policies, notably its cohesion measures, to an east-west focus. So far, enlargement-related expenditures have been accommodated within the agreed-on budget ceiling of 1.24 percent of EU GNI (EC 2002).

The European Union will soon enter a fifth phase of budgetary politics from 2007 to 2013. The key question is whether current policy agreements can be sustained. Phase V will likely have to address two main challenges: continuing support to weaker member states, old and new, and a possible refocusing of policy priorities on new issues, such as strengthening research and development capacity to foster competitiveness and economic strength.

Phases II through V, which are most relevant to this chapter, are discussed in turn below.

THE EARLY YEARS OF CONFLICT-LADEN ANNUAL BUDGET NEGOTIATIONS

A number of conflicts emerged during the period following adoption of the 1970 and 1975 EU Budget Treaties and the first EU enlargement in 1973.[2] One axis of dispute concerned the distributional consequences of the common budget. The most intractable issue was the so-called UK problem, which had its roots in the structure of the EU budget. From the pattern of UK trade and the small size of its agricultural workforce it was apparent from the outset that the United Kingdom would be a major net contributor to the budget. The 1970 Budget Treaty reflects a desire by original member states to lock in this budgetary advantage before the United Kingdom became a member in 1973. As part of the

Box 1

Chronology of key dates in the evolution of the EU budget

Phase I

1958 Rome Treaty establishes the European Economic Community (EEC).

1961 Denmark, Ireland, and the United Kingdom apply for membership.

1965 President de Gaulle of France removes his country's ministers and officials from the EEC's Council of Ministers in part because of a dispute over the revenue base for the EEC budget.

Phase II

1970 The 1970 Budget Treaty establishes three main revenue sources (own resources) for the EEC budget.

1973 Denmark, Ireland, and the United Kingdom join the EEC. The prospect of a UK budgetary problem emerges.

1975 The 1975 Budget Treaty gives the European Parliament an important role in the annual budget cycle.

1984 At the Fontainebleau European Council meeting member states agree to a compensation mechanism for the United Kingdom.

Phase III

1985 European Council agrees to reform the EEC treaty.

1987 The 1986 Single European Act enters into force, and negotiations begin on a new budgetary package known as Delors I.

1988 Member states approve the Delors I reform measures, including the policy principle of a multiyear budget framework and a first financial package for 1988–92.

1992 Treaty on European Union is signed and agreement is reached on a second multiyear financial package known as Delors II, covering 1993–99.

1993 Member states establish the conditions for an eastern enlargement at the meeting of the European Council of Ministers in Copenhagen.

1997 Agenda 2000 is published, setting forth the European Commission's proposals for the European Union's financial perspective for 2000–06.

Phase IV

1999 Agreement is reached on the financial perspective contained in Agenda 2000.

2002 The euro is introduced.

2004 Ten new member states accede to the European Union.

Phase V

2003–04 Debate commences on the expenditure framework for 2007–13.

renegotiation of UK membership in 1975, a complex financial mechanism was agreed that would allow for rebates in the event of a heavy contribution. The agreed mechanism was not very effective, however, and by 1978 the United Kingdom was the second largest contributor although it was then one of the less prosperous member states. The European Union conceded ad hoc annual rebates from 1980 onward but not until 1984 did it agree on a more lasting formula that did not have to be renegotiated each year.

The 1984 rebate formula was inserted into the Delors I agreement of 1988 and has remained part of budgetary agreements since. The budget includes a compensation mechanism that reduces the UK annual contribution according to the agreed formula. However, the UK rebate has been increasingly questioned (see, for example, EC 2002, p. 79), and there are signs that the issue is ready to resurface.

A second axis of budgetary conflict concerned the division of powers over the budget among the European Parliament, the Council of Ministers, and the European Commission. Each year the tortuous annual budgetary process was conflict-ridden, with arcane debates on highly technical questions (Laffan 1997, pp. 79–88). Underlying these debates was a power struggle between the member states represented in the Council of Ministers and the directly elected Parliament, which sought to increase its influence.

This institutional conflict together with the distributional issues raised by the budgetary position of the United Kingdom dominated the politics of the European Union until 1988. It sapped political energies and led to a deterioration in relations among the member states at a time when they faced pressing economic problems. The lengthy and heated arguments were often about relatively small amounts of money, suggesting that it was less the money that was at issue than the underlying policy principles—questions of fairness, of which issues to delegate "upward," and of which body should have which powers in deciding these matters.

THE MULTIYEAR FRAMEWORK: A STEP TOWARD ENHANCED BUDGETARY STABILITY

The context of European budgetary politics changed with the entering into force of the 1987 Single European Act, with its core program of promoting the internal market (European Communities 1987). Without this renewed impetus toward integration, there might not have been sufficient political will to alter the framework of the EU budget. The European Commission under President Jacques Delors put forward an ambitious program of budgetary reform and expansion to:

- Establish a multiyear financial perspective for the annual budgets.
- Increase the budget and the amount of resources going to Europe's poorer regions.
- Establish a regulatory framework for budgetary discipline, particularly for containing agricultural expenditure.

These recommendations were adopted in the first financial perspective (a common decision taken by the European Commission, the Council, and the Parliament) in 1988. The first financial perspective (the Delors I package) was a critical juncture in EU budgetary history. In the negotiations the member states, assisted by the European Commission, hammered out a five-year budgetary framework that covered all aspects of expenditure and revenue. Although tough bargaining characterized these negotiations, the result was integrative rather than distributive, changing the way the European Union went about its budgetary business. After the years of conflict that had bogged down past budget debates, how did the member states manage to craft this agreement?

Several factors contributed to the emergence of a consensus. All member states were committed to the single-market program and did not want to see perpetual budgetary conflict undermine prospects for market integration. The key dimension of the 1988 agreement was the multiyear financial perspective, which embedded the annual budget in a predictable and agreed framework of commitments and payments. The revenue and expenditure sides of the budget were thus tackled together so that member states could see an integrated budget picture. A fourth source of budgetary revenue was added, requiring member states to contribute a percentage of their GNI. The percentage was to be set each year, so that this "fourth resource" would cover the expenditures that the other own resources were not sufficient to cover, up to the budget ceiling. The three own resources consisted of:

- The two traditional resources (collected since 1970) based on levies on agricultural imports and custom duties on other imports into member states.
- The VAT-based resource (collected since 1979), obtained from member states as national contributions to the budget, based on the transfer of a fixed percentage of a harmonised base of the VAT collected (box 2).

The Delors I agreement also codified the UK compensation mechanism, and Germany agreed to continue its role as "paymaster of the Union"—as the largest economy in the European Union, Germany would be the largest contributor to a budget increasingly relying on the GNI-based resource. Budgetary peace followed the 1988 Delors I agreement. The new arrangements seemed to benefit all member states, with each able to bring something home to its public. In addition, solidarity with Europe's less developed states and regions became an institutionalized value in the system.

Yet the key dimension of the 1988 agreement was the multiyear financial perspective, with agreement on the overall size of budget commitments and payments and on the broad headings of expenditure. This meant that the annual budget cycle was embedded in a predictable and agreed-on framework. Among other things, this helped bring agricultural expenditure under control, and it became an important tool for fostering greater cohesion within the European Union, a political and economic objective added to the European Union's mandates in the Single European Act.

Box 2
SIZE AND STRUCTURE OF THE BUDGET OF THE EUROPEAN UNION

Revenue. The 1970 EU Budget Treaty established three sources of revenue: customs duties on all EU imports, levies on agricultural imports, and up to 1 percent of a harmonized rate of the value-added tax (VAT) collected in member states. Member states are legally obliged to collect these resources and transfer them to the European Union minus a collection charge for the customs duties and agricultural levies.

The duties and levies are also known as the European Union's traditional "own resources." Revenue from these sources has steadily declined as trade liberalization has advanced. The 1988 Delors I budgetary reform package added a fourth income source to compensate for this loss. Member states are now required to help cover the gap between expenditure needs and revenue generated by the three traditional sources. Based on the actual budget gap, additional payments are determined annually as a uniform percentage of each country's GNI. As the figure shows, the revenue generated from this new source is fast becoming the main EU revenue source, contributing more than 60 percent of total revenue in 2004.

EU revenue by type, 1971–2004

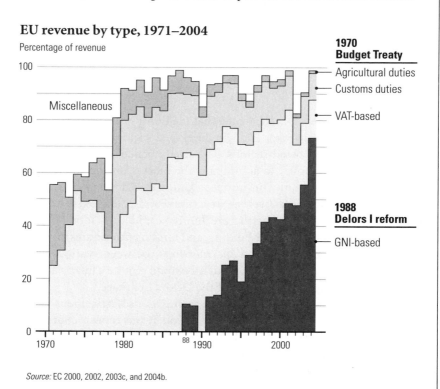

Source: EC 2000, 2002, 2003c, and 2004b.

SIZE AND STRUCTURE OF THE BUDGET OF THE EUROPEAN UNION

The EU budget remains relatively small, at about 1.27 percent of the combined GNP of its member states (1.24 percent of combined GNI). This is small compared with the 40–55 percent of GDP that EU member states channel through their national government budgets.

Expenditure. The multiyear financial perspective, which began with the 1988 Delors I reform package, determines the overall expenditure (and revenue) parameters of the EU budget. The first five-year framework agreed in 1988 was followed by a seven-year agreement in 1992. The current framework covers the years 2000–06. Annual budgets complement the multiyear framework. In the 1970s the Common Agricultural Policy emerged as the dominant expenditure item, reaching as high as 80 percent of the budget in 1985 (Laffan 1997, p. 100). The Delors I agreement established a framework for budgetary discipline in agriculture and greatly increased the money spent on structural or cohesion policy. Gradually, the share of agricultural expenditures declined. In the 2003 commitments budget, expenditures were distributed as follows: agriculture (46.3 percent), cohesion (33.2 percent), internal policies (6.6 percent), administration (5.1 percent), external policies (4.8 percent), pre-accession aid (3.3 percent), and reserves (0.7 percent) (EC 2003c, p. 7).

The Single European Act stipulated that the European Union has a responsibility to assist Europe's weaker and less developed regions to catch up with the more economically advanced regions. The strengthened emphasis on cohesion was in part a flanking policy to accompany the market integration contained in the internal market program. The European Union thus developed a range of policy instruments, known collectively as Structural Funds, designed to assist lagging regions and states to build infrastructure, human capital, and jobs. Specific eligibility criteria were established for funding, and funding procedures involved multiyear planning, evaluation, and partnerships between various levels of government and civil society actors. All of this would require a financial tool along the lines of the multiyear perspective of the Delors I package.[3]

A second financial perspective, known as the Delors II agreement, was agreed in December 1992. Spanning a seven-year period, it was more a continuation of the Delors I approach than a radical shift in budgetary policy or process. Again, the conclusion of a new treaty, the Treaty on European Union, informally known as the Maastricht Treaty, provided the political impetus for budgetary reform (European Communities 1992). The agreement urged a continuing commitment to Europe's less developed regions and the establishment of a new instrument, the Cohesion Fund.[4]

In addition, there was a significant increase in the resources allocated to external activities and a continuing emphasis on control of agricultural expenditures. Although the new reform measures were aimed largely at consolidating earlier change, negotiations proved more difficult than in the previous round. An important reason was that an emerging net-contributors club was beginning to make itself felt in the budgetary politics of the European Union.

CONSOLIDATION OF EXPENDITURE LEVELS

The enlargement of the European Union to East-Central Europe, which began casting its shadow over budgetary debates in the 1990s, and the clamor of the net-contributors club raised the specter of a return to the zero-sum, distributive bargaining that had marred the pre-1988 period. Member states faced a tradeoff between their collective interest in avoiding a return to budgetary conflict and their national interest in protecting their gains from the budget, the enlargement notwithstanding. It seemed that without restructuring several policy regimes, the enlargement could not be accommodated within existing resources.

The European Commission, aware of the competing concerns of the member states and the candidate states, crafted the broad outline of a budgetary framework for 1999–2006 called *Agenda 2000: For a Stronger and Wider Union* (EC 1997). A key purpose of Agenda 2000 was to ensure member states that the costs of enlargement could be absorbed without budgetary increases, despite concerns to the contrary. Member states could approve the new financial framework without seeking national parliamentary ratification and without going through bruising national debates on contributions to the EU budget. An important recommendation of Agenda 2000 called for capping Cohesion Fund spending (until then set as a proportion of the EU budget) at 0.46 percent of EU GNP (EC 1997, pp. 18–19). It also proposed reducing agricultural price supports and increasing compensation for farmers.

Despite these efforts, conflicts arose during the budget negotiations between coalitions of member states over the gains and losses arising from having to accommodate enlargement expenditures. Countries that were already net contributors did not want to bear the financial burden of the enlargement (table 1). German negotiators argued for austerity. Germany's net contribution to the EU budget had risen from 4 billion euros in 1988 to 11.5 billion euros in 1995 at a time when its per capita income was declining following reunification (Laffan 2001, p. 214). Austria, the Netherlands, Sweden, and the United Kingdom joined Germany in urging austerity. The United Kingdom was in an ambivalent position, since one of its primary goals was to retain the compensation mechanism agreed in the 1980s. A second group of countries, including France and Italy, were minor net contributors. They were expected to bear an increased burden in an enlarged European Union.

TABLE 1

The net budgetary position of EU member states, 2002

Member state	Share of GNI (percent)	Euros (millions)
Greece	2.39	3,387.9
Portugal	2.14	2,692.3
Ireland	1.50	1,576.7
Spain	1.29	8,870.8
Finland	0.00	−5.7
Denmark	−0.09	−165.0
Belgium	−0.10	−256.4
Austria	−0.11	−226.3
France	−0.14	−2,184.2
United Kingdom[a]	−0.17	−2,902.8
Italy	−0.23	−2,884.5
Germany	−0.24	−5,067.8
Luxembourg	−0.25	−48.9
Sweden	−0.29	−746.6
Netherlands	−0.51	−2,187.7

Note: To calculate the net budgetary position the European Commission deducts member states' contributions to the EU budget from the payments received from the EU budget. Administrative expenditures by EU institutions are not considered in the calculations; only operational expenditures.
a. Values take UK compensatory payment into account.
Source: EC 2003a (p.126).

Aligned against the net contributors club was a coalition of countries led by Spain that had benefited from the past spending patterns of the Cohesion and Structural Funds. Included in this group were Greece and Portugal. Ireland, following a period of high growth, was moving away from supporting this position but wanted to protect its allocations from the EU budget until at least 2006.

Finance ministries of member states and politicians in the net-contributing countries are ever vigilant about the size of their contributions. Yet as the European Commission is at pains to explain, the net budgetary position is an exercise in accounting and does not capture the full economic gains from EU membership.[5] Market share and volume of trade are other important variables that need to be considered. In addition, a significant share of the EU Structural Fund is spent on imports from other member states. For example, Greece spent 43 percent of EU investment on imports from other member states (EC 2003b, p. 6). A systematic calculation of net gains would also have to take into account the distributional impact of regulatory measures implemented on an EU-wide basis.

Despite all the concerns an agreement on the third financial perspective was finally hammered out in Berlin in March 1999 (table 2). Its key feature is the consolidation and stabilization of EU expenditure by capping agricultural expenditures at roughly the 1999 level and stabilizing rather than increasing expenditures on structural operations. All the member states, particularly the net contributors, pressed for an end to the UK rebate, but the rebate was retained.

The fact that agreement was achieved despite the level of conflict demonstrates that member states did not want to return to the annual budgetary negotiations of the late 1970s and early 1980s. They saw merit in retaining the multiyear approach and the principle of integrative bargaining.

New spending priorities to respond to new challenges?

The evolution of EU public finance and budgetary policies has been marked by changes in modality and process, such as the introduction of the multiyear framework, and in policy focus. As noted, there has long been concern about the level of agricultural spending, reflecting growing global concern about the European Union's agricultural subsidies. While expenditure levels on agriculture have not changed much, the focus of spending has changed, from price support to compensation of farmers. And expenditure on external activities has also increased.

With the new 2007–13 budget cycle fast approaching, deliberations have begun on the role of the new multiyear framework and the considerations that should shape it. The European Commission requested a high-level study group to analyze all economic instruments available to the European Union and their contributions to economic governance. The group, known as the Sapir Group, made a strong case for reallocating the internal EU budget, which absorbs 1 percent of the EU GDP, to three broad areas (Sapir 2003, pp. 198–205):

- *Growth,* including research and development, education and training, and infrastructure, which should receive about 45 percent of the internal budget.
- *Convergence,* including support for adjustment processes in the new member states (20 percent of available resources) and in other qualifying member states (10 percent of resources), with another 5 percent allocated to various other convergence measures.
- *Restructuring,* including support for displaced workers (5 percent), agriculture (5 percent), and the phasing out of agricultural expenditures (10 percent).

The overall recommendation is clearly to shift from agriculture, a declining industry and way of life, to new opportunities for growth and convergence. While it might be difficult for such a radical shift to win political support, there is no denying that the past pattern of agricultural expenditure is coming under pres-

TABLE 2

EU financial perspective for 2000–06 (millions of euros)

Budget category	Current prices				2004 prices		
	2000	2001	2002	2003	2004	2005	2006
Agriculture	41,738	44,530	46,587	47,378	49,305	50,431	50,575
Structural operations	32,678	32,720	33,638	33,968	41,035	41,685	42,932
Internal policies	6,031	6,272	6,558	6,796	8,722	8,967	9,093
External action	4,627	4,735	4,873	4,972	5,082	5,093	5,104
Administration	4,638	4,776	5,012	5,211	5,983	6,154	6,325
Reserves	906	916	676	434	442	442	442
Pre-accession strategy	3,174	3,240	3,328	3,386	3,455	3,455	3,455
Compensation	na	na	na	na	1,410	1,299	1,041
Total appropriations for commitments	93,792	97,189	100,672	102,145	115,434	117,526	118,967
Total appropriations for payments	91,322	94,730	100,078	102,767	111,380	112,260	114,740
Own-resources ceiling (percent of GNI)[a]	1.24	1.24	1.24	1.24	1.24	1.24	1.24
Margin for unforeseen expenditure (percent of GNI)	0.17	0.16	0.13	0.15	0.16	0.18	0.18
Ceiling appropriations for payments (percent of GNI)	1.07	1.08	1.11	1.09	1.08	1.06	1.06

na is not applicable.

Note: Data reflect the budgetary requirement of the enlarged 25-member European Union.

a. These are based on the 1995 European System of Accounts (ESA95) accounting standard that harmonizes measurement of GNI.

Source: EC 2004b (p. 8).

sure from the recent enlargement of the European Union and from international trade talks.

Another review group, the Solidarity Group, examined in 2003 the policies necessary to redress inequalities between member states, regions, and citizens and to reinforce economic and social cohesion within an enlarged European Union (EC 2003d). The Solidarity Group comprised commissioners and other officials under the chairmanship of then French Commission member Michel Barnier. Its main focus was on what kind of cohesion policy the European Union should have. Two concerns dominated deliberations: the increase in regional disparities following the recent enlargement and the need for economic and social restructuring arising from globalization and technological advances. The group's report suggests that the center of gravity of future policy will shift eastward, following enlargement, but that the needs of current weaker regions should not be ignored. The report supports development of a contingency reserve for responding to sectoral and local shocks. It emphasizes cooperation on justice and home affairs, particularly external border protection, as well as the traditional economic concerns of cohesion policy.

In February 2004 the European Commission published its own proposals for the fourth financial perspective covering 2007–13 (EC 2004a). The negotiations are bound to be difficult. New member states will bring new demands to the debates. The old member states are likely to defend the previous status quo. New global challenges call for new responses, including perhaps increased external expenditures. Yet the current net contributors will not want to shoulder a larger financial burden. Hence, the European Union faces the prospect of a difficult and perhaps lengthy budgetary debate.

LESSONS FOR INTERNATIONAL COOPERATION

What lessons for the financing of international cooperation can be drawn from this examination of the evolution of public finance and budgetary policy in the European Union? The analysis in this chapter has shown that despite the successes in political and economic integration, EU member states have maintained the nation state as the primary locus of public finance. At 1.24 of the EU members' GNI the EU budget is but a small fraction of the member states' combined income.[6] In contrast, the U.S. federal budget represents about 20 percent of U.S. GDP (Enderlein and others 2003, p. 6; U.S. OMB 2004, table 15.3), and EU member states' spending through national budgets is about 40 percent of GDP (IMF 2003, p. 14). Public spending on education, health, welfare, and defense has clearly remained a domestic matter in Europe. While seeking to promote fairness, member states also aim at deriving clear national benefits from international cooperation. Regulation through law is the primary instrument of public power in the European Union and that depends heavily on the ability to persuade member states to implement a common body of law.

Rather than look at international cooperation as purely a matter of distributional, win-lose bargaining, EU member states have tried to view enhanced integration as generating important net benefits for all. Thus financing integration programs is not wasting money but making a worthwhile investment. But while this useful policy principle of integrative bargaining has since the late 1980s underpinned many of the policy regimes and debates, past and current budgetary negotiations indicate that the principle may be more persuasive in theory than in practice, when it comes up against the many competing demands of home constituencies.

NOTES

1. For more extensive discussion of the political dynamics of the EU budget, see Shackleton (1990), Begg and Grimwade (1998), and Laffan (1997).

2. The 1970 Budget Treaty established EU financing through three types of own resources (that is, independent of national deliberation by each member state). The 1975 Budget Treaty provided for the creation of a Court of Auditors and strengthened the European Parliament's budgetary powers.

3. The 1988 reform of the Structural Funds established five objectives for funding, the most important being to provide assistance to regions whose GDP was 75 percent or less of the EU average. The number of objectives was reduced to three in 1998.

4. The Cohesion Fund was added to the existing Structural Funds to help finance large-scale infrastructure and environmental projects in member states whose GDP was less than 90 percent of the EU average. It was regarded as a side payment to Spain in return for Spain's agreement on the Treaty on European Union.

5. The European Union releases a report each year that calculates the funds given by member states and compares them with the funds received under the various community programs. These reports are available at http://europa.eu.int/comm/budget/agenda2000/reports_en.htm.

6. Determination of the level of the EU budget has not been grounded in economic analysis based on fiscal federalism. Fiscal federalism considerations have also had little impact on the assignment of public finance functions to the European Union, despite numerous attempts to apply them (see EC 1993 for the most extensive economic analysis of EU finances).

REFERENCES

Begg, Ian, and Nigel Grimwade. 1998. *Paying for Europe.* Sheffield, UK: Sheffield Academic Press.

Enderlein, Henrik, Johannes Lindner, Oscar Calvo-Gonzalez, and Raymond Ritter. 2003. "The EU Budget: How Much Scope for Institutional Reform?" Paper presented at the CESIFO-Delphi Konferenz, December 5–6, Munich.

EC Council (European Community Council). 1970. "Decision of 21 April 1970 on the Replacement of Financial Contributions from Member States by the Communities' Own Resources (70/243 ECSC, EEC, Euratom)." *Official Journal of the European Communities* April 28, L 94, p. 19. Luxembourg.

EC (European Commission). 1993. *The Economics of Community Public Finance.* European Economy Series 5. Brussels.

———. 1997. *Agenda 2000: For a Stronger and Wider Europe.* Com (97)/2000. Luxembourg: Official Publications.

———. 2000. *The Community Budget: The Facts in Figures.* Luxembourg: Official Publications.

———. 2002. *European Union: Public Finance.* Luxembourg: Official Publications.

———. 2003a. *Allocation of 2002 EU Operating Expenditure by Member State.* Luxembourg: Official Publications.

———. 2003b. *The Future of Cohesion Policy: Fact File.* Luxembourg: Official Publications.

———. 2003c. *General Budget of the European Union for the Financial Year 2003.* Luxembourg: Official Publications.

———. 2003d. "Sustainable Growth and Competitiveness for All: Financial Perspective Post 2006." Internal unpublished paper prepared by Commissioner Michel Barnier, Brussels.

———. 2004a. *Building Our Common Future: Policy Challenges and Budgetary Means of the Enlarged Union 2007–2013.* Com (2004) 101 final, 10.2.2004. Luxembourg: Official Publications.

———. 2004b. *General Budget of the European Union for the Financial Year 2004.* Luxembourg: Official Publications.

European Communities. 1987. "Single European Act." *Official Journal of the European Communities* June 29, L 169. Luxembourg.

———. 1992. "Treaty on European Union." *Official Journal of the European Communities* July 29, C 191. Luxembourg.

IMF (International Monetary Fund). 2003. *Government Finance Statistics Yearbook.* Washington, D.C.

Laffan, Brigid. 1997. *The Finances of the Union.* London: Macmillan.

———. 2001. "Finance and Budgetary Processes in the European Union." In Simon Bromley, ed., *Governing the European Union.* London: Sage.

Laffan, Brigid, and Michael Shackleton. 2000. "The Budget." In Helen Wallace and William Wallace, eds., *Policy Making in the European Union.* Oxford: Oxford University Press.

Sapir, André. 2003. *An Agenda for a Growing Europe: Making the European Economic System Deliver.* Oxford: Oxford University Press.

Shackleton, Michael. 1990. *Financing the European Community*. London: Pinter.

U.S. OMB (Office of Management and Budget). 2004. B*udget of the United States Government. Fiscal Year 2005. Historical Tables.* Washington, D.C. [www. whitehouse.gov/omb/budget/fy2005/hist.html].

4

THE NEW INTERNATIONAL PUBLIC FINANCE

ENHANCING AID EFFICIENCY

USING AID INSTRUMENTS MORE COHERENTLY
GRANTS AND LOANS
Paul Collier

•

RECTIFYING CAPITAL MARKET IMPERFECTIONS
THE CONTINUING RATIONALES FOR MULTILATERAL LENDING
Yilmaz Akyüz

•

PULLING NOT PUSHING REFORMS
DELIVERING AID THROUGH CHALLENGE GRANTS
Steve Radelet

OVERCOMING COORDINATION AND ATTRIBUTION PROBLEMS
MEETING THE CHALLENGE OF UNDERFUNDED REGIONALISM
Nancy Birdsall

•

REDUCING THE COSTS OF HOLDING RESERVES
A NEW PERSPECTIVE ON SPECIAL DRAWING RIGHTS
Jacques J. Polak and Peter B. Clark

•

CREATING INCENTIVES FOR PRIVATE SECTOR INVOLVEMENT IN POVERTY REDUCTION
PURCHASE COMMITMENTS FOR AGRICULTURAL INNOVATION
Michael Kremer and Alix Peterson Zwane

•

MITIGATING THE RISKS OF INVESTING IN DEVELOPING COUNTRIES
CURRENCY-RELATED GUARANTEE INSTRUMENTS FOR INFRASTRUCTURE PROJECTS
Stephany Griffith-Jones and Ana Teresa Fuzzo de Lima

USING AID INSTRUMENTS MORE COHERENTLY

GRANTS AND LOANS

PAUL COLLIER

Public resource transfers from richer industrial countries to poorer developing countries are a standard means of fostering development. These transfers, usually grants or loans, are administered by a variety of multilateral and bilateral agencies. For many years there has been concern that the efficiency of the resource transfers is being compromised by the multiplicity of agencies and insufficient coordination among them. Much less attention has been paid to the multiplicity of instruments, largely because until recently the instruments were precisely partitioned by agency, at least among the multilateral agencies. The European Union and the United Nations system provided primarily grants, and the World Bank and the International Monetary Fund (IMF) provided mainly loans. The issue of the appropriateness of each instrument was therefore subsumed under more general issues of agency rivalries and coordination.

In 2001, prompted by a U.S. initiative, the World Bank added a grant element alongside its concessional lending. The circumstances in which grants were introduced—disagreement at a senior political level between the United States and the United Kingdom—initially precluded sensible discussion of the criteria for using grants. Any suggestions about when grants would be particularly appropriate were treated in certain quarters as an argument for grants, while any suggestions about when loans would be particularly appropriate were treated in other quarters as an argument against grants.

With the key personalities on both sides of the argument now no longer in public office, it is both feasible and urgent to address the issue lest the passage of time appear to legitimize current practice among both donors and beneficiaries. Resources for development are so scarce that it is imperative that they be used as well as possible. The current pattern of using grants and loans has little economic rationale. Injecting economic analysis into the discussion of instrument choice should considerably increase development effectiveness.

The author would like to thank David Dollar and Anke Hoeffler for help with the data analysis, and Steve Radelet for comments on earlier drafts.

The key message here is that the characteristics for assessing whether a recipient is better suited to grants or to loans should determine the composition of resource transfers but not the overall volume of transfers. This proposition has powerful implications for the balance between grants and loans. A country with a high absorptive capacity for aid, but with low creditworthiness—such as many post-conflict countries—would receive large resource transfers in the form of grants. To avoid moral hazard, however, reforming governments with successful economies (and increasing creditworthiness) should not appear to be penalized by getting their aid as loans instead of grants. One way to avoid this is to make the grants and loans peak at the same time. Thus as a country progresses and the share of loans rises relative to that of grants, loans would not be substituted for grants, but both would rise and then fall together.

Before starting the analysis, this chapter provides a basic classification of the stages of development that a typical aid-recipient country goes through. It then considers the concept of poverty-efficient transfers for determining the overall size of the resource transfer and the appropriate allocation of grants and loans that a country can productively absorb at each stage of development. The emerging ideal-type pattern of combining grants and loans then serves as a frame of reference for evaluating the actual composition of grants and loans. The analysis reveals much scope for reforming the deployment of these aid instruments. Some policy options for enhancing coherence and for better combining grants and loans are also discussed.

BASIC PRINCIPLES OF AID ABSORPTION

A useful approach to aid allocation is to imagine a country's gradual transition from severe poverty and a dysfunctional state to middle-income status and a relatively well functioning state. Although still evolving, the Country Policy and Institutional Assessment (CPIA) of the World Bank is one way to make these stages more concrete.[1] The CPIA suggests country rankings according to some 20 indicators of policy and institutional performance, with rankings from 1, low, to 4, high. Combining these rankings with levels of per capita income creates a seven-stage classification of the development process (table 1).

At stage 1 a country has not only very low income but also extremely weak policies, governance, and institutions. It then begins a gradual process of reform, moving from stage 1 through stage 4 (shaded area of table 1). This is the first development phase, marked mainly by improvements in institutional and governance capacity and performance. To simplify the analysis, changes in per capita income during this initial reform phase are assumed to be sufficiently small to be ignored for purposes of aid allocation. This is roughly the sort of reform that Uganda went through from the end of the 1970s, when the country was in turmoil in the last stages of the Amin regime, and the end of

TABLE 1

Seven stylized stages of development

Stage	Country Policy and Institutional Assessment	Per capita income ($ PPP)
1	1	500
2	2	500
3	3	500
4	4	500
5	4	1,000
6	4	2,000
7	4	3,000

Note: PPP is purchasing power parity.

the 1990s, under the very different style of government of President Yoweri Museveni.

The second phase, stages 5 through 7, is one of growth following the reforms of phase one, which are assumed to continue. During this phase the country passes progressively from a per capita income of $500, right at the bottom of the range for developing countries, rising through $1,000, $2,000, and finally attaining $3,000, the threshold of middle-income status.

How much aid in the form of grants and loans can a country productively absorb at each of these stages? Answering this requires first understanding how to determine the overall size of the resource transfer that is appropriate at each development stage.

One criterion for determining how much of the available aid is to flow to a particular country is the poverty efficiency of such a transfer—the number of people who would be permanently lifted out of poverty as a result of the development financed by the transfer. A poverty-efficient allocation of aid would distribute aid between countries in a way that maximizes the reduction in poverty, with the marginal dollar of aid being equally effective in each aid-receiving country. Collier and Dollar (2001, 2002) have developed a simple empirical analysis of absorptive capacity that derives such a poverty-efficient allocation.[2] The analysis finds that aid is on average quite effective in reducing poverty, even at the margin. Additional aid would further reduce poverty. However, the effectiveness of aid could be considerably increased if it were better allocated across countries. The single biggest mistake in aid allocation from the perspective of poverty reduction is that too much is allocated to middle-income countries relative to low-income countries. Among low-income countries there is also a tendency for too little aid to go to countries with reasonable policies, governance, and institutions.

Building on the Collier and Dollar (2001, 2002) analysis, figure 1 shows roughly how aid would be allocated across the seven development stages if it were to be poverty efficient, as defined above. The resulting pattern is unsurprising in its general shape. In the first phase of development, such as in Somalia, where needs are great but the capacity to absorb aid effectively is extremely limited, the margin at which further aid is ineffective is reached quickly. With income held constant at this very low level but with policy, governance, and institutions improving, the need remains the same but the scope for aid to meet these needs increases and so aid should increase. In the second phase, as income rises, aid per capita should start to decline. Aid may still be highly effective in the growth process, but less poverty reduction accompanies that growth because there are fewer poor people in the country. Aid should be lower for a country at stage 7 than for a country at stage 2.

WHY BOTH GRANTS AND LOANS?

Before looking at how best to combine grants and loans, it is important to consider why any public resource transfers to developing countries are made in the form of loans. After all, in recent years there have been two rounds of debt forgiveness for low-income countries—the Heavily Indebted Poor Countries (HIPC) Debt Initiatives—and resource transfers in the form of loans are becoming increasingly problematic. Since each round of debt forgiveness undermines the credibility of sovereign credit, debt forgiveness inadvertently generates a global public bad. Would anything be lost if the current flow of resource transfers through loans were stopped and replaced by grants?

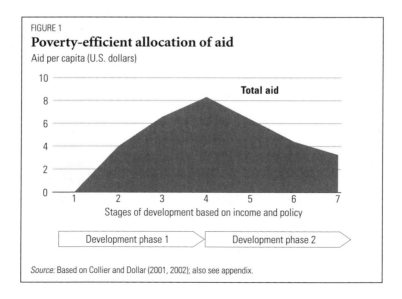

FIGURE 1
Poverty-efficient allocation of aid
Aid per capita (U.S. dollars)

Total aid

Stages of development based on income and policy

Development phase 1   Development phase 2

Source: Based on Collier and Dollar (2001, 2002); also see appendix.

Rationale for loans over grants
The arguments in favor of loans fall into three broad categories.

Economic convergence. Conditional on policies, lower income countries tend to grow more rapidly than do richer countries—they tend to converge on them. Looking to some distant future when once-poor countries have converged on rich countries, there is then nothing unreasonable in expecting these countries to repay resources that have assisted their catch-up growth. What converging countries need is not permanent charity but a temporary resource transfer. Donor country electorates may be willing to provide more funds on such a basis than they would be prepared to hand over as grants. However, convergence is far from certain. In 1960 Kenya and the Republic of Korea had the same level of income. Korea is now a member of the Organisation for Economic Co-operation and Development (OECD) whereas Kenya is still a low-income country. This could probably not have been anticipated in 1960, but clearly Korea is in a position to repay the public resource transfers it received when it was a low-income country, although Kenya is not.

Convergence provides some rationale for loans that are repayable conditional on performance in the growth of income. The main multilateral loan instrument, that of the International Development Association (IDA), indirectly has this feature. The rules governing repayments of IDA loans—IDA "reflows"—require that all repayments be returned to the IDA pot for further lending. IDA eligibility is defined by the level of per capita income—only low-income countries are eligible to borrow. In this sense, although not in the strict legal sense, IDA is a common pool resource of low-income countries and so is in effect collectively "owned" by them. Since IDA-eligible countries are the only ones to benefit from IDA repayments, IDA funds are like a rotating savings and credit association among poor households.

Such an arrangement has one obvious disadvantage compared with the same pool of resources being distributed as grants: the ambiguous "ownership" of an undetermined share of the IDA common pool does not constitute a creditworthy asset, and so a debt is generated—a legally clear structure of liabilities—with no offsetting structure of entitlements. There is an offset to this disadvantage, however. Since IDA membership is determined by the criterion of income, when a country grows out of poverty it ceases to be IDA-eligible. An important recent example of such an evolution is China. China is thus now in the position of repaying IDA loans but not being able to reborrow from IDA. This structure in effect provides a resource flow from middle-income countries to low-income countries, which would not be the case were IDA transfers all grants.

In the future this arrangement is liable to have desirable properties as many more substantial IDA borrowers, such as India, succeed in growing their way out of IDA eligibility, leaving the pool of IDA resources concentrated on a diminishing group of countries at the bottom of the economic ladder. On present growth patterns IDA will gradually become concentrated on Sub-Saharan Africa. The conversion of IDA loans to grants, unless accompanied by offsetting changes, would therefore amount to a transfer from a future low-income Africa to a future middle-income Asia: a poor Africa would be forgiving a richer Asia its debts. One obvious offsetting change would be an increase in overall aid flows from donor countries to compensate for the loss of IDA reflows. In effect, by undertaking to compensate in this way, donor countries would be avoiding the global public bad of further sovereign defaults.

Transition to capital markets. A much stronger rationale for loans over grants is that loans expand the size of resource transfers by enabling developing countries to tap into global credit markets. The loans provided by the World Bank Group's International Bank for Reconstruction and Development (IBRD) have such a rationale. IBRD loans are concessional only in the sense that, being ultimately guaranteed by all member governments, they have an AAA credit rating, enabling developing countries to borrow more cheaply than they would be able to do on their own. Other than this guarantee, which has never been exercised, there is no subsidy, so that IBRD loans are concessional but self-financing. They help introduce developing countries to the capital market, whereas grants, if provided for development purposes, tend to signal lack of creditworthiness.

Resources during a crisis. A third powerful rationale for loans is that developing countries periodically encounter economic crises brought on by the policy errors of their governments. At such times countries need external resources, but providing the resources as grants might create a moral hazard by rewarding policy errors. But even loans carry a risk of moral hazard. For example, if the repayment period were as generous as for an IDA loan, the government committing the error would not itself be burdened by the repayment, which takes place years in the future. Hence, the terms of such crisis lending need to be much more severe than for IDA loans.

The agency that specializes in such crisis lending is the IMF. Its concessional resources are much smaller and less readily supplemented than those of IDA. The advantage is that IMF resources can be provided very rapidly and in situations where a country is in economic difficulty—this style of operation is the core business of the IMF. By comparison, the core business of the World Bank has traditionally been project lending. Although the World Bank now also provides nonproject loans, the Bank lacks traditional expertise in lending in crisis situations, which are inherently ill-suited to lending operations.

Rationale for combining grants and loans
Loans should not be the only instrument for resource transfers. Grants are important precisely because the development process is so uncertain. After more than

50 years of development efforts some countries are as poor as they were at the outset—or even poorer. Some countries may be so badly endowed—in the broadest sense of physical and social resources—that for the foreseeable future they will not develop. In some high-risk, low-income environments, such as in countries after conflict, substantial lending is inappropriate for both creditor and borrower. The risk level is sufficiently high that default is likely, further damaging rather than restoring the reputation of the borrower. A resource transfer is needed, but not in the form of loans.

What, then, would be a desirable balance between grants and loans at each of the seven stages of development? Recall that poverty-efficient aid can be determined in total (grants plus loans) without reference to its composition. This has the powerful implication that if there is some appropriate ceiling to the amount of loans that a country should take on—notably because of creditworthiness—the residual between that and poverty-efficient aid should be in the form of grants. So what should determine the grant and loan composition of this amount?

One possible answer is that it depends on the purpose of the resource transfer. For example, objectives such as basic health care are better suited to grants than to loans if only because donor country electorates are better able to consider such expenditures as meeting basic human needs—for which they are willing to pay—than as investments. Since the case for aid cannot deviate too far from what electorates are willing to finance through taxation, this argument is compelling.

However, the high degree of the fungibility of aid, and the tendency of even basic social expenditures to be inefficient in some countries, suggest that much of the case for grants over loans will rest not with the ostensible use of the aid but rather with the characteristics of the user. The user should be identified at both the country and the agency level, which will usually be the government, but not always.

What, then, are the characteristics that make a user more or less suitable for a loan or a grant? The answer is clearest at each end of the spectrum depicted in figure 1. At the lowest of the seven stages—very low-income countries with very weak governments—aid should be entirely in the form of grants. At this end of the spectrum, where the government is very weak, it may be desirable that aid intended for the delivery of basic services should bypass the government, instead going directly to nongovernmental organizations (NGOs), local authorities, or churches. This is part of the World Bank's strategy for low-income countries under stress (World Bank 2002).[3] Since official lending can be only to governments, or guaranteed by governments, assistance must be in the form of grants if it is to go directly to such agencies instead. Loans are also not appropriate because these environments are highly risky. And because these are the areas of most manifest need, donor country electorates' support for grants is at its strongest.

At the other end of the spectrum aid should be entirely in the form of loans. At this end of the spectrum the country should be creditworthy and already transitioning into IBRD lending. Because per capita income is relatively high, such countries are the least likely to touch the hearts of donor country electorates on the basis of need, and so grants are difficult to justify.

Combining grants and loans coherently: the ideal-type allocation

At some level of income and competence higher than that which justifies grants, loans should commence, and at some point before loans cease, grants should cease. Within the range over which both instruments are used, the ratio should presumably change continuously, with the proportion of grants falling steadily.

A priori there is one further feature of a desirable system of deployment. In the early range in which loans start to come in, grants should still be increasing in absolute terms, to reduce the incentive problem that could arise if improvements in income were met by a substitution of loans for grants. If grants and loans peaked at the same level of income, there would never be a range over which better policies or income growth led to a substitution of loans for grants, which is the core fear of those concerned with the disincentive effects of allocating grants purposively.

Even with a common peak, loans would increase more rapidly than grants once the country entered the range in which it was creditworthy. Similarly, beyond the level of income at which grants and loans jointly peaked, grants would diminish more rapidly than loans until the all-loan point was reached. Such a coherent pattern of grants and loans is illustrated in figure 2. The outer envelope is simply replicated from the poverty-efficient allocation in figure 1, and the hypothetical disaggregation into grants and loans illustrates one possible pattern that is consistent with the criteria previously argued as desirable.

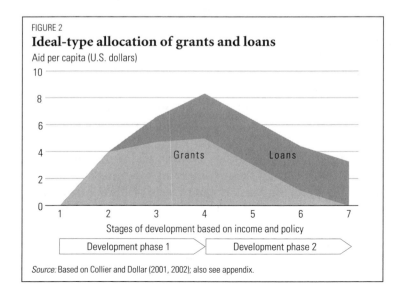

FIGURE 2
Ideal-type allocation of grants and loans
Aid per capita (U.S. dollars)

Stages of development based on income and policy

Development phase 1   Development phase 2

Source: Based on Collier and Dollar (2001, 2002); also see appendix.

There is no way for aid to avoid all incentive problems even were it entirely in the form of either grants or loans. At some stage aid has to taper off and then end in response to a rise in income, and this is a disincentive to such an improvement. In reality, though, it is a weak disincentive, since the implicit tax rate on increases in income can be set at very modest levels. However, by making the peak of aid coincident with the peaks for both grants and loans the disincentive effects of the composition of aid—the substitution of loans for grants as development proceeds—becomes subsidiary to the disincentive effect of reductions in the volume of aid.

Since aid should be tapered in during the first phase of development and tapered off during the second, its incentive effects will be favorable during the first phase and unfavorable during the second. This is true whatever the composition of aid between grants and loans. The overall incentive effect of aid is the difference between these two opposing effects. There is some evidence that each of these incentive effects of aid is modest, so that the net effect is likely to be small, with an ambiguous sign (see, for example, Collier and Dollar 2004). As suggested, the incentive effect of changes in the composition of aid can be designed so as not to alter the sign of the incentive effect of changes in the volume of aid. Thus although incentive effects often loom large in popular discussion, the proposed changes in the composition of aid are unlikely to have strong net incentive effects.

THE ACTUAL ALLOCATION OF GRANTS AND LOANS

How does the actual allocation of grants and loans compare with the allocation proposed in figure 2? At the beginning of this chapter total aid (grants plus loans) was shown to be misallocated when judged by the criterion of poverty efficiency. Here the focus is on the composition of aid, its allocation between grants and loans.

There is a large institutional problem that reduces the coherence of the deployment of grants and loans in aid allocation. The two largest multilateral aid institutions are the European Union and the World Bank. The European Union is a political multilateral organization, so its aid program is in part intended to strengthen relations between the European Union and recipients. Perhaps as a result, its allocation of aid has not been very poverty efficient, much of it being allocated to middle-income countries. This is particularly anomalous since EU aid is in the form of grants. By contrast, IDA is about the most poverty efficient of the large aid programs, with resources heavily targeted to low-income countries with reasonable institutional and policy ratings. Yet until very recently IDA has been entirely a lending institution.

Given their respective aid instruments, the European Union and the World Bank thus have remarkably ill-fitting strategies. In effect, the European Union is providing grants to middle-income countries while the World Bank is providing loans to low-income countries. This is precisely the opposite of what the analysis in this chapter suggests would be a coherent use of aid instruments.

And the problem of incoherence in the use of aid instruments is not limited to these two organizations. So it is not surprising to find that actual grant and loan allocations are both quite different from the proposed pattern (figure 3).

In the first phase of improving policy, the actual pattern has the same general shape as the ideal-type pattern, with grants and loans both rising and with loans rising more rapidly. However, except in stage 1 the ratio of grants to loans does not differ substantially across stages. In particular, it is surely questionable whether at stage 2, when governance, institutions, and policies are still very poor, it is appropriate for a country to receive as much as a third of its resource inflows as loans. However, the problems of the first phase are dwarfed by the problems of the second. While income increases from $500 per capita to $3,000 per capita, the ratio of grants to loans remains virtually constant. Worse, above $1,000 per capita the proportion of grants is even increasing.

So, while the pattern of grants and loans during the policy-improvement phase looks a little worrying, that during the income-growth phase looks wildly inappropriate—a gross misallocation. What would be the implications of a move to a more strategic deployment of grants and loans, with grants targeted to the lowest income countries?

MOVING TOWARD GREATER COHERENCE

The implications of the proposed, more coherent use of grants and loans that are likely to generate the most controversy are not those for poverty reduction but

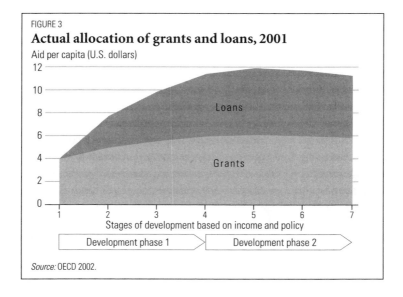

FIGURE 3

Actual allocation of grants and loans, 2001

Aid per capita (U.S. dollars)

Stages of development based on income and policy

Development phase 1

Development phase 2

Source: OECD 2002.

those for development agencies. Right now all the multilateral agencies are fairly heavily involved in all countries, the only limitation being geographic in the case of the regional development banks.

Suppose that grants were concentrated among the lowest income countries, while concessional loans were concentrated among the somewhat higher income countries. One implication is that the multilateral institutions that provide only grants (the European Union and the United Nations Development Programme) would concentrate on the lowest income countries, while those that make only loans (the regional development banks) would concentrate on the higher income countries. The IMF would have a specialized loan-making role, concentrating its resources on low-income countries that had just crossed the threshold from grant-only finance to borrowing. Since its concessional resources are quite limited, it would taper off its funding fairly rapidly once a country was judged suitable for credit from the development agencies. The World Bank, by virtue of its having both grant and loan instruments, would play a key role in getting coherence into the composition of aid. For this to happen, however, the Bank would need to unbundle its virtually fixed-coefficient packaging of grants and loans, so that some countries would get substantial grant-only financing.

Finally, there is the issue of whether some agency should be in charge of coordinating donors, so that overall aid and especially its composition between grants and loans broadly conformed to reasonable magnitudes. To an extent, donor coordination occurs without a coordinator. Each agency can see what the others are doing and infer the gaps that represent the highest returns to assistance. What is needed for such coordinatorless coordination to work is that all the agencies broadly share the same normative model of aid allocation and the same information. Historically, this has not worked very well.

The obvious coordinator for the grant and loan composition of aid is the IMF, since this is but a small extension of its existing role of assessing debt sustainability. Indeed, when a ceiling on debt sustainability was binding, the IMF might prefer to inform agencies that planned loans should be replaced by grants rather than telling them that the overall magnitude of development assistance needs to be reduced. The IMF would, in effect, attempt to guide donor agencies into collectively fulfilling the sort of aid allocation depicted in figure 2. The spectacular mismatch between the ideal-type pattern of figure 2 and the actual pattern of figure 3 suggests that it is time to give up on coordinatorless coordination.

The IMF would be assisted in this role by a change in its practice of accounting for fiscal deficits, which is biased against concessional loans relative to grants. When government expenditure is financed by grants, the amount of the grant is not treated as adding to the fiscal deficit, but when it is financed by a concessional loan, the face value of the loan is treated as adding to the deficit—its concessional nature is ignored. By contrast, in calculations of debt sustainability, concessional loans are correctly treated differently from nonconcessional loans. For example, an IDA loan adds to the net present value of debt by only about a third of the face value of the loan. Thus the impact on the fiscal deficit appears to be exaggerated by a factor of about three. Since EU aid is in the form of grants, whereas World Bank aid is in the form of loans, a country favored by the European Union will appear to have a much lower fiscal deficit than one favored by the World Bank, even if the impact of the total aid inflow on the net present value of their debt is identical.

Conclusion

Aid is transferred using the instruments of grants and loans in combinations that are difficult to justify. Loans have been made to countries with such low incomes and weak governance that the risk of default was extraordinarily high. If a resource transfer was justified in these situations—and sometimes it was—it would have more appropriately been in the form of grants. Conversely, grants have been distributed across the spectrum of per capita income, rather than being narrowly focused on high-risk countries in deepest poverty.

The main argument of the chapter is that the criterion of creditworthiness, which should clearly be one factor in the allocation of loans, should affect the composition rather than the amount of the total resource transfer. A country with a high absorptive capacity for aid, but with low creditworthiness—such as many post-conflict countries—should, on this analysis, receive large resource transfers in the form of grants.

There has been considerable reluctance to face the issue of the proper assignment of grants and loans, in part because historically some agencies have provided only grants and others only loans. While such institutional specialization may appear to assist proper focusing, in practice the bureaucratic temptation for each major agency to operate in virtually all countries leads to most countries receiving both grants and loans.

In part the reluctance to consider a more specialized use for each instrument is also a reaction to fears of moral hazard effects. Reforming governments with successful economies (and increasing creditworthiness) should not appear to be penalized by receiving aid as loans instead of grants. This problem could be overcome by letting the point at which grants peak coincide with the point at which loans peak. As a country progressed and the share of loans relative to that of grants rose, at no point would loans be substituted for grants—both would rise and then fall together.

APPENDIX. REGRESSIONS OF POVERTY-EFFICIENT AID, ACTUAL GRANTS,
AND ACTUAL LOANS ON INCOME AND POLICY, 2001

Table A.1 reports on regressions of poverty-efficient and actual aid on income and policy. The first two columns report regressions of poverty-efficient aid (per capita) on some basic country characteristics. Poverty-efficient aid is a hypothetical aid flow that would maximize global poverty reduction given the overall amount of global aid available. It is generated by the analysis reported in Collier and Dollar (2002). The second column adds the square of the log of per capita income and is reported for comparability with subsequent regressions. However, since the squared term is insignificant, the regression reported in column 1 is used in figure 1.

The third and fourth columns report regressions of actual aid per country on the same characteristics. Only the regressions with the addition of the quadratic effect of income are reported since the term is highly significant. The dependent variable is no longer poverty-efficient aid, but actual grants (column 3) or actual loans (column 4). The data relate to 2001 and are for aggregate aid, multilateral and bilateral, from all OECD countries (OECD 2002). Their implied allocation at each of the seven stages of development is depicted in figure 3. Thus, the regression in column 3 is used to infer the typical flow of grants that a country would receive at each of the seven stages, and the regression in column 4 is used to derive the typical flow of loans.

TABLE A.1

Regression results

Variable	Poverty-efficient aid 1	Poverty-efficient aid 2	Actual grants	Actual loans
Constant	15.666*	−5.997	−15.211*	−34.195*
	(5.26)	(0.32)	(2.99)	(3.57)
Log population	−0.006	0.008	0.484*	0.517*
	(0.05)	(0.06)	(13.83)	(7.98)
Log GNI per capita (PPP)	−2.817*	2.567	3.201*	7.310*
	(9.78)	(0.55)	(2.56)	(3.11)
Square of log GNI per capita (PPP)		−0.344	−0.230*	−0.515*
		(1.17)	(2.88)	(3.44)
Log CPIA	5.995*	6.510*	1.429**	3.926*
	(4.81)	(4.93)	(4.00)	(5.92)
R^2	0.462	0.468	0.694	0.539

*Significant at the 10 percent level. **Significant at the 5 percent level.
Note: Numbers in parentheses are t-statistics. All regressions are based on 120 observations. PPP is purchasing power parity.
Source: Author's calculation based on Collier and Dollar (2002) and data from OECD (2002) and World Bank, World Development Indicators, various years.

NOTES

1. The Country Policy and Institutional Assessment (CPIA) is undertaken annually by the World Bank (2003a,b) to determine its borrowers' policy and institutional performance in areas relevant to economic growth and poverty reduction. The assessment takes into account 20 criteria grouped into four clusters: economic management (management of inflation and macroeconomic imbalances; fiscal policy; management of public debt; management and sustainability of the development program); structural policies (trade policy and foreign exchange regime; financial stability; financial sector depth, efficiency, and resource mobilization; competitive environment for the private sector; goods and factor markets; policies and institutions for environmental sustainability); policies for social inclusion and gender equity (equity of public resource use, building human resources, social protection and labor, monitoring and analysis of poverty outcomes and impacts); and public sector management and institutions (property rights and rule-based governance; quality of budgetary and financial management; efficiency of revenue mobilization; quality of public administration; and transparency, accountability, and corruption in the public sector).

2. The Collier and Dollar analysis is based on four properties. One is that within a country and time period aid is subject to diminishing returns: the last $1 million of aid is less effective in raising growth than the average. Two, the contribution of aid-induced growth to poverty reduction in a country will tend to be greater the lower is the per capita income of the country and the more equally is income distributed. These two effects—diminishing returns and poverty—tend to offset each other. To avoid diminishing returns, aid per capita needs to be higher in higher income developing countries. To best reach the poor, aid per capita needs to be higher in lower income developing countries. Three, aid will tend to be more effective in inducing growth and in reducing poverty the better are policies, governance, and institutions. And four, although aid has various effects for good and for ill on policies, governance, and institutions, the net effect is on average sufficiently small to ignore.

3. The World Bank defines countries that rank lowest on the CPIA as low-income countries under stress. These countries tend to have weak policies, institutions, and governance and to lack the capacity or inclination to use finance effectively to reduce poverty. A special initiative, including a trust fund, was launched to move the development agenda in these countries forward despite the constraints to poverty reduction. The objective is to reduce the risk that these countries will become further marginalized by being excluded from aid that is becoming increasingly performance oriented. The initiative assists countries in strengthening institutions; initiating basic economic, social, and governance reforms; and building capacity for social service delivery—moving out of stage 1 and onto a path that might gradually lead the country through the seven stylized stages of the development process discussed in this chapter.

REFERENCES

Collier, Paul, and David Dollar. 2001. "Can the World Cut Poverty in Half?" *World Development* 28 (11): 1787–802.

―――. 2002. "Aid Allocation and Poverty Reduction." *European Economic Review* 46 (8): 1475–500.

―――. 2004. "Development Effectiveness: What Have We Learnt?" *Economic Journal* 114 (496): F244–71.

OECD (Organisation for Economic Co-operation and Development). 2002. *International Development Statistics.* Paris.

World Bank. 2002. "World Bank Group Work in Low Income Countries Under Stress: A Task Force Report." Washington, D.C. [www1.worldbank.org/operations/licus/documents/licus.pdf].

―――. 2003a. "Allocating IDA Funds Based on Performance: Fourth Annual Report on IDA's Country Assessment and Allocation Process." Washington, D.C. [http://siteresources.worldbank.org/IDA/Resources/PBAAR4.pdf].

―――. 2003b. "Country Policy and Institutional Assessment 2003: Assessment Questionnaire." Washington, D.C. [http://siteresources.worldbank.org/IDA/Resources/CPIA2003.pdf].

―――. Various years. *World Development Indicators.* Washington, D.C.

RECTIFYING CAPITAL MARKET IMPERFECTIONS

THE CONTINUING RATIONALES FOR MULTILATERAL LENDING

YILMAZ AKYÜZ

Multilateral lending has been a central instrument of international economic cooperation since the International Monetary Fund (IMF) and the International Bank for Reconstruction and Development (IBRD) were conceived at the United Nations Monetary and Financial Conference at Bretton Woods in 1944. These institutions had two distinct objectives: restoration and maintenance of international economic stability and national reconstruction and development.

The world economic and political landscape has changed significantly since then—communism rose and fell, colonialism ended, and global economic integration has increased. The Bretton Woods institutions have responded by realigning their activities. The changed realities have prompted an intense debate over the role of these institutions and the continuing need for multilateral lending with the rapid development of international capital markets (see, for instance, Walters 1994; U.S. IFIAC 2000).

This chapter reexamines the case for multilateral lending and distinguishes three types: countercyclical provision of liquidity to meet temporary current account imbalances, development finance (both concessional and nonconcessional loans), and lending to countries facing capital account crises in order to bail out private creditors.[1]

The rationale for countercyclical lending is stronger today in view of the increased instability of the international economic environment, greater vulnerability of developing countries to external shocks, and the procyclical behavior of international financial markets. The rationale for development finance is weaker today than in the immediate postwar era but continues to be valid for many low-income developing countries—the argument for development grants rather than loans is stronger than originally (see also the chapter by Collier in this volume).

The author is grateful to Richard Kozul-Wright and Jan Kregel for comments and suggestions.

And as in the immediate post–World War II era there continues to be little rationale today for lending to bail out private creditors.

THE RATIONALE BEHIND MULTILATERAL LENDING

Multilateral lending is a form of global collective action designed to provide external financing to developing countries pursuing certain agreed objectives. Collective action may be desirable on efficiency or humanitarian grounds. It may be needed when markets fail to generate Pareto-efficient outcomes because of such factors as externalities, public goods, imperfect and asymmetric information, monopolies or imperfect competition, and incomplete markets. It may also be desirable when there is broad agreement on certain social and humanitarian objectives that cannot be guaranteed even under efficient outcomes. Collective action may even be required for both efficiency and humanitarian reasons since "there are certain market failures which not only lead to inefficiencies (Pareto inefficient outcomes) but the incidence of those inefficiencies bears disproportionately on the poor" (Stiglitz 2003, p. 2).

Externalities, global public goods, and social and humanitarian objectives
One of the main reasons for international concern with the provision of external finance to developing countries is that lack of adequate financing has ramifications not only for the countries involved but also for the international community as a whole because of international externalities and global public goods.[2] When a country facing a tightened payments constraint as a result of trade shocks or higher international interest rates is forced to cut imports, its trading partners also suffer because of reductions in their exports and economic activity. Liquidity crises in emerging markets can lead to contagion or systemic risk. Environmental, health, and security problems associated with widespread poverty in poorer countries can generate negative externalities for the international community, requiring development finance to address the root causes of these problems. The increased significance of such international externalities associated with the growing interdependence of countries has resulted in a broadening of the concept of global public goods and greater public interest in their provision, which often requires global collective action.[3]

The pursuit of global humanitarian objectives and the provision of global public goods often require the provision of finance to poor countries in the form of grants or highly concessional loans and technical assistance rather than lending of the kind that capital markets provide. In this case the rationale for multilateral financing would be the global benefits attached to redistribution from richer to poorer countries rather than international capital market failures (Gilbert, Powell, and Vines 1999). By contrast, the rationale for nonconcessional multilateral lending should be sought primarily in international capital market failures, even though distributional considerations also come into play since such lending often contains a subsidy element.

International capital market failures

A main reason why rational behavior in unfettered private capital markets gives rise to inefficient outcomes is the presence of imperfect and asymmetric information (borrowers know more about their investment than lenders do, and information costs about borrowers' riskiness are high) and incomplete contracts (lenders cannot control all aspects of borrowers' behavior). These problems imply that lenders are generally unable to assess the quality of a loan and that defaults are costly. As loan rates are raised to cover risks, the average quality of loans falls because of adverse selection (lending to high-risk borrowers willing to pay high interest rates) and moral hazard (inducing "good" borrowers to invest in riskier projects). As a result, the expected rate of return net of default will decline once the loan rate reaches a certain level. Beyond that level the lender is inclined to ration borrowers rather than push up loan rates until the market clears. In other words, credit rationing would be an equilibrium outcome of rational behavior of lenders under conditions of imperfect and asymmetric information and incomplete contracts.[4]

Clearly, the problems of information and incomplete contracts are more acute for international lending to both public and private sectors in developing countries, which lack sophisticated financial institutions and markets and effective disclosure requirements, accounting standards, and prudential regulations. These problems lead to overestimation of risk, higher spreads and loan rates, shorter maturities, and severe credit rationing. Multilateral lending could rectify such capital market failures by extending long-term loans at below-market rates, including to countries with little or no access to international capital markets.

The second manifestation of capital market failure is instability in the volume and terms of international private capital flows, including boom-bust cycles and currency and debt crises, which have occurred with increasing frequency in emerging markets in recent years. These reflect abrupt and unexpected changes in market assessments of risks, which cannot always be attributed to policy shifts. A plausible explanation is provided by the theory of endogenous financial fragility developed by Minsky (1977), which sees financial cycles as an intrinsic feature of market economies.[5] Booms generated by improved opportunities for profitable investment lead to underestimation of risks, overexpansion of credit, and overindebtedness. Excessive risk taking eventually results in the deterioration of balance sheets and increases in nonperforming loans. Lenders respond by reassessing risks and sharply curtailing credit, leading to credit crunch, debt deflation, and defaults. However, while crises are almost always associated with some degree of financial fragility, they can take place in the absence of serious economic weaknesses because of the existence of multiple equilibria and the so-called self-fulfilling prophecies associated with herding behavior and collective action problems (Obstfeld 1996; Krugman 1996, 1998).

All this means that financial markets tend to behave procyclically and that countries may not have access to international liquidity when they need it most. Multilateral lending can help counter fluctuations and boom-bust cycles in international private capital flows. Such lending could serve two distinct purposes: allow countries to finance their imports of goods and services and factor income payments (current account financing) or help them maintain capital account convertibility and stay current on their external debt repayments (capital account financing).

It is also important to realize that capital market failures do not always necessitate multilateral lending. Other forms of collective action may be able to address such failures. For instance, an important part of the recent debate on reform of the international financial architecture has focused on whether private capital flows could be made more stable and thus more reliable sources of international liquidity and development finance (Akyüz 2002; CFRITF 1999; Goldstein 2000). Clearly, to the extent that this could be achieved, the rationale for multilateral lending would be weaker. Similarly, to the extent that multilateral finance institutions reduce information imperfections and asymmetries, improve risk assessment, and share in risks, resorting to multilateral lending for rectifying capital market failures would be lessened.

THE ORIGINAL DESIGN FOR MULTILATERAL LENDING

The main objective of the architects of the postwar international economic system was to avoid a recurrence of the problems that had led to the breakdown of international trade and payments in the interwar period.[6] Plans focused on establishing conditions for global economic stability and security and for sustained and broad-based growth in incomes and employment, drawing on three policy lessons from the interwar years:

*   *Market failure.* The Great Depression had shown that markets alone cannot resolve all economic problems. Markets may fail to bring about economically efficient outcomes, and they do not necessarily generate politically acceptable solutions.
*   *Interdependence.* Close linkages among trade, finance, investment, reconstruction, and development mean that solutions should not be sought in isolation.
*   *International cooperation.* Also because of cross-border dimensions and possible global spillover effects, these policy issues cannot be left to uncoordinated individual country actions. Furthermore, no country should be expected to put its house in order irrespective of global economic conditions and the possible negative spillovers they generate.

Thus the restoration of a stable global economic system was seen to require a shift from purely national policy formulation to a system of multilateral cooperation.

Negotiators finally reached agreement on only two institutions to deal with postwar financial problems, the IMF and the IBRD.[7] The main concern in 1944 was to address the challenges expected to emerge in the immediate postwar era: restoration and maintenance of international economic stability and reconstruction of war-ravaged countries (Mikesell 1994).

International economic stability: the rationale for IMF lending

For postwar planners the obvious lesson from the interwar years was that exchange rate stability and sustained expansion of output and employment were essential for avoiding tensions and disruptions in international trade. This, in turn, required global arrangements based on multilateral discipline over exchange rate policies, mechanisms for providing international liquidity, and restrictions on destabilizing capital flows. The IMF was created to ensure an orderly system of international payments at stable but multilaterally negotiated exchange rates under conditions of strictly limited international capital flows. Its most important function was to provide international liquidity to avoid deflationary adjustments and trade and exchange restrictions in deficit countries and to help maintain stable exchange rates in the face of temporary payments disturbances. These functions were designed primarily to secure the stability of external payments and exchange rates of the major industrial countries rather than to stabilize the balance of payments of developing countries.

The modalities for providing liquidity were one of the most controversial issues in the negotiations, particularly between the two architects of the postwar system, Harry Dexter White, head of the U.S. delegation, and John Maynard Keynes, head of the British delegation. White's scheme, outlining the basic design of the IMF, prevailed over Keynes' more ambitious plan for an International Clearing Union for both the multilateral clearing of national balances and the debiting and crediting of net balances (Oliver 1975, ch. 6; Dam 1982; Mikesell 1994). Agreement was reached on a fund to be financed through national contributions partly in gold and partly in domestic currencies, available for drawing on by those in need of international reserves. The IMF was also empowered to borrow from member countries to supplement its reserves in currencies in case of large demand.

While Keynes strongly argued that members should have unconditional access to reserves within the limits of their quotas[8] and that "it would be very unwise to try to make an untried institution too grandmotherly" (IMF 1969, vol.1, p.72), the United States resisted unconditional drawings on grounds that it would be the only source of net credit in the immediate postwar era since the dollar was then the only convertible currency.[9] The compromise agreed to in Article V entitled each member "to purchase the currencies of other members from the Fund in exchange for an equivalent amount of its own currency" when the member needed to "because of its balance of payments or its reserve position or developments in its reserves." Most countries interpreted this to mean that members had unconditional drawing rights within the limits of their quotas (Dell 1981), though there was considerable room for other interpretations.[10]

It was taken almost for granted that international financial markets could not be relied on for balance of payments financing, given the high degree of volatility in short-term capital flows during interwar years. Access to IMF liquidity was designed for current account transactions alone. Article IV permitted recourse to capital controls so long as they did not restrict payments for current transactions and even gave the IMF the authority to ask a member country to impose controls to avoid the use of IMF resources to finance large or sustained capital outflows. In effect, these arrangements discouraged reliance on private flows for balance of payment financing.

The IMF's assets and members' drawing rights and voting rights were all linked to the single concept of quotas (Dam 1982). Quotas were determined through a highly politicized exercise so as to give the United States veto power over key decisions (Mikesell 1994). Using the same criteria for countries' contributions and their drawing rights has ensured sufficient funding in reserve currencies from major industrial countries (Mikesell 1994), but it has also meant that the drawings of poorer countries with smaller quotas would be highly restricted.

Postwar reconstruction: the rationale for IBRD lending

The IBRD—now part of the World Bank Group—was established to facilitate capital investments to assist in postwar reconstruction.[11] Although "encouragement of the development of productive facilities and resources in less developed countries" is mentioned in Article I, financing development was almost an afterthought.[12] Most Europeans saw a tradeoff between reconstruction and development financing and emphasized the urgency of projects in war-torn areas. Attempts by Latin American countries to secure a balance between the two were met with resistance (Oliver 1975).

While postwar reconstruction required substantial imports, Europe had neither the financial resources nor the export capacity to pay for them. The war-torn countries had a structural trade imbalance that required long-term resource transfers far larger than the liquidity envisaged for the IMF. This presented the dilemma of how to reconcile the means with the objectives: the World Bank's capital base would have to be provided by the same countries it was designed to help. The solution was to have each member country pay only 20 percent of its subscription to the Bank's capital, with the rest being callable as the Bank ran out of resources to meet its obligations on funds borrowed from international markets.[13]

There was a consensus that the World Bank would not compete with private investors but would provide finance only "when private capital is not available on reasonable terms" (Article I). The rationale for World Bank lending was not simply the inadequacy of private capital for financing rapid reconstruction and meeting the needs of developing countries but also concern that the terms of private financing would not be appropriate for the conditions prevailing in the borrowing countries.

World Bank financing was to be provided as loans rather than grants. But these loans differed from private lending in two respects. First, they would carry lower interest rates. This would be possible because paid-in capital provided interest-free loanable funds, while the guarantee provided by shareholders allowed the World Bank to raise funds on international capital markets on highly favorable terms. Furthermore, the World Bank charged only a small commission over its borrowed funds in lending to its members, adding an element of subsidy to its loans. Second, unlike private lenders, which charged different rates for different borrowers based on differences in perceived risks, the World Bank would charge the same rate to all borrowers.

While Article III explicitly states that loans made or guaranteed by the World Bank shall be for specific reconstruction or development projects, exceptions were foreseen. This left discretion to the World Bank board for loans for currency stabilization and general balance of payments and even for countercyclical lending. Unlike the conditions governing access to IMF resources, there was little controversy over considerations governing the World Bank's lending decisions.

THE POSTWAR EVOLUTION OF MULTILATERAL LENDING

The world economic and political landscape has changed considerably since the Bretton Woods Conference, and the objectives pursued by the IMF and the World Bank and the modalities of their operation have changed as well, often in an ad hoc manner.

From countercyclical current account lending to crisis lending by the IMF

The past 60 years have seen a progressive distancing of the IMF from the initial objectives, particularly with respect to the automaticity of countercyclical current account financing. This is perhaps best seen in the evolution of the conditions governing members' drawings.[14] In 1947 the IMF board authorized challenging "representations" by members, thereby discarding the notion of automaticity. A key decision in 1952 formally adopted conditionality for drawings (borrowers commit to follow certain economic and financial policies)[15] and stipulated that drawings would be only for temporary problems and if proposed policies were deemed adequate to overcome them. Standby arrangements were introduced as the central operational modality (IMF 1969, vol. 3).[16] A 1956 decision introduced phased drawings, with loans disbursed in tranches contingent on satisfactory achievement of agreed targets. Performance criteria soon proliferated.[17]

As a result of these changes automatic drawing has been confined to the reserve tranche, with higher tranches entailing tighter conditionality. And since the IMF quotas have lagged considerably behind the growth of world trade, countries' access to balance of payments financing has come increasingly under IMF policy surveillance.

Perhaps the biggest divergence from the Bretton Woods objectives has been in the content of conditionality rather than the principle. Eligibility requirements for drawing from the IMF continue to be contentious. Through conditionality the IMF has effectively sought to impose exactly the kind of policies that the postwar planners tried to avoid in countries facing payments difficulties—austerity and destabilizing currency adjustments. Currency stability and maintenance of full employment have ceased to be the key components of international economic relations (Triffin 1976; UNCTAD 1987).

Austerity has been promoted even when payments difficulties resulted from external disturbances such as adverse terms of trade movements, hikes in international interest rates, or trade measures introduced by another country. Furthermore, the distinction between temporary and structural disequilibria has become blurred, often implying that a developing country should interpret every positive shock as temporary and thus refrain from using it as an opportunity for expansion and every negative shock as permanent and thus adjust to it by altering the domestic price structure and slowing growth.

Various soft-window facilities introduced to deal with temporary payment imbalances have also been hardened or discontinued.[18] The Compensatory Financing Facility, introduced in the early 1960s, enabled countries facing temporary shortfalls in primary export earnings to draw on the IMF beyond their normal drawing rights without the performance criteria required for upper credit tranches (Dam 1982). This semi-automaticity was subsequently removed (Dell 1985). Similarly, two oil facilities introduced in the 1970s as countercyclical devices to prevent oil price hikes from triggering a global recession have been discontinued (Dell 1986).[19]

In the mid-1970s the IMF's attention turned increasingly to development issues, leading to duplications with the World Bank. In 1974 the Extended Fund Facility was established as a nonconcessional lending facility to address persistent and structural balance of payments problems (Dam 1982; Ahluwalia 1999). This was followed by the Structural Adjustment Facility and the Enhanced Structural Adjustment Facility, which provided concessional lending to low-income countries for structural change. In 1999 the Enhanced Structural Adjustment Facility was replaced by a Poverty Reduction and Growth Facility, a concessional window for low-income countries.

In perhaps an even more important shift the IMF has become a crisis lender and manager for emerging markets. During the debt crisis in the 1980s many developing countries borrowed heavily from multilateral sources to finance debt servicing to private creditors (Sachs 1998). And since the financial crises in emerging markets in the 1990s, crisis lending has become the dominant financial activity of the IMF. The Supplemental Reserve Facility was established to provide financing above normal access limits to countries experiencing exceptional payments difficulties. The Contingent Credit Line was created as a precautionary line of defense for countries facing the threat of contagion but was discontinued in November 2003 because no country had applied for it, fearing that would give the wrong signal and impair their access to financial markets (Akyüz and Cornford 2002; Goldstein 2000; and IMF 2003). In March 2004 almost two-thirds of outstanding IMF credits were accounted for by crisis lending to Argentina, Brazil, and Turkey under standby agreements (IMF 2004b).

From reconstruction to development finance at the World Bank

As the task of addressing reconstruction financing for the war-torn European countries was effectively taken up by the Marshall Plan,[20] the World Bank's portfolio shifted throughout the 1950s from construction to development loans and from Europe to developing countries (Oliver 1975).[21] Most projects in the poorer developing countries did not prove to be viable at the moderately below-market rates applied to World Bank loans. An option would have been to extend the Marshall Plan to poorer countries, but this was not the course taken.

Instead, the International Development Association (IDA) was established in 1960 with contributions from industrial countries to provide very long-term credit to the poorest developing countries at exceptionally low costs. This was an important departure from the original design, which was that multilateral financing would take the form of loans rather than gifts or grants and that all borrowers would be charged the same interest rate. This was a clear recognition that a development agency could not simply operate as a bank, extending loans on market terms based on creditworthiness.

The shift to development finance was also associated with greater emphasis on working with the private sector. The International Finance Corporation (IFC) was created in 1956 to support private ventures without government guarantees. The Multilateral Investment Guarantee Agency (MIGA) was established in 1988 to facilitate foreign direct investment in developing countries by providing guarantees against noncommercial risks to investors.

An equally significant development was the creation of regional development banks, starting with the European Investment Bank in 1958.[22] These banks had their own soft windows for concessional lending and mandates to lend to the private sector without government guarantees. Their lending has expanded more rapidly than that of the World Bank and has focused on projects.

As the World Bank moved deeper into development financing, shortcomings in the original modalities of lending were laid bare. In its early years the World Bank had adopted a conservative stance, lending at close to market rates, insisting on the financial viability of projects, and directing loans to high-yielding infra-structure. This was due in part to the Bank's efforts to establish its own credit-worthiness in financial markets and in part to the emphasis placed on capital accumulation in development. It was also believed that infrastructure projects would attract private investment. As the complexities of development and the importance of development externalities became clearer, the World Bank's emphasis shifted to concessional lending and lending to social sectors and agriculture.

World Bank operations also started to focus on overall economic conditions and development priorities, moving from project lending to policy-based lending. This shift culminated in the introduction of ambitious market-friendly adjustment programs with the onset of the debt crisis in the 1980s. Under increased criticism from civil society for the neglect of key social and environmental concerns, the World Bank has continued to add new tasks to its mandate over the past two decades, and with them has come a proliferation of lending instruments (World Bank 2001; Einhorn 2001). This expansion has been accompanied by the ratcheting up of conditionality, in much the same way as in the IMF, and has encouraged collaboration between the two institutions.

The increased influence of the World Bank in key economic decisions in borrowing countries has not been matched by increased contributions to development finance. In real terms in the past two decades there has been barely any increase in net flows to developing countries from the World Bank, including both IBRD loans and IDA credits, because of declines in net flows from the IBRD (table 1). More important, net transfers from the IBRD have been negative in almost every year since 1990 for both low-income and middle-income countries. Thus, the IBRD has not made any contribution to the financial needs of developing countries as a whole in recent years, other than to provide finance to service its outstanding claims. The main contribution of the World Bank to development finance has taken the form of highly concessional IDA credits.

INTERNATIONAL FINANCIAL MARKETS: A CHANGING ENVIRONMENT FOR MULTILATERAL LENDING

The past 60 years have thus seen a gradual shift in the objectives and modalities of multilateral lending. The principal activity of the IMF is no longer lending to countries facing temporary difficulties in their current account payments but lending associated with capital account crises and concessional development finance to low-income countries. Similarly, the main contribution of the World Bank to development finance is concessional IDA credits rather than IBRD loans.

Are these changes desirable and indicative of a continuing rationale for multilateral lending? Answering these questions depends on the nature and effects of private capital flows to developing countries.

TABLE 1

World Bank lending to developing countries, 1970–2003
(billions of U.S. dollars)

Item	1970	1980	1990	1997	1998	1999	2000	2001	2002	2003
Disbursements	0.8	5.8	17.8	20.4	19.9	19.5	18.6	18.4	17.1	17.2
IBRD	0.7	4.2	13.4	14.5	14.4	14.1	13.4	12.3	10.3	11.1
IDA	0.2	1.6	4.3	5.9	5.6	5.4	5.2	6.1	6.8	6.1
Net flows	0.6	4.8	9.6	9.2	8.7	8.8	7.9	7.5	-0.2	-1.9
IBRD	0.4	3.2	5.5	3.9	3.9	4.2	3.6	2.5	-5.7	-6.4
IDA	0.2	1.6	4.1	5.3	4.8	4.5	4.3	5.0	5.5	4.6
Net transfers	0.3	3.0	2.4	1.9	1.5	0.9	-0.4	-0.5	-7.3	-7.7
IBRD	0.2	1.6	-1.4	-2.8	-2.7	-3.0	-4.1	-5.0	-12.1	-11.5
IDA	0.2	1.5	3.8	4.8	4.3	3.9	3.7	4.4	4.8	3.8

Note: Net flows equal disbursements minus principal repayments; net transfers equal net flows minus interest payments.
Source: World Bank 2004 (pp. 3–4).

The postwar era has seen two boom-bust cycles in private capital flows to developing countries: the first beginning in the early 1970s and ending with the debt crisis, and the second beginning in the early 1990s and ending with the East Asian and Russian financial crises (UNCTAD 2003; Kregel 2004).[23] The first boom was driven by the rapid expansion of international liquidity associated with oil surpluses and growing U.S. deficits and facilitated by financial deregulation in industrial countries and rapid growth of Eurodollar markets.[24] The second boom came after almost 10 years of suspension in private lending to developing countries and was encouraged by the success of the Brady Plan for sovereign debt restructuring, liberalization and stabilization in developing countries, and rapid expansion of liquidity in the United States and Japan in conditions of economic slowdown.

These cycles were thus driven by temporary and special factors rather than long-term fundamentals. Aggregate private flows to developing countries have manifested a degree of instability not justified by changes in the underlying fundamentals. This has also been true for spreads (UNCTAD 2003; Cunningham, Dixon, and Hayes 2001; Sy 2001). The increased instability of private flows explains why many developing countries keep excess reserves at the expense of imports and at high carry costs (UNCTAD 1999).

Although the terms and conditions of private loans vary widely, on average maturities are short and costs are high. Over the past 10 years or so the average maturity of private lending to middle-income countries was around half that of official lending (World Bank 2002, p. 249).

But not all emerging markets face similar conditions. After the debt crisis of the 1980s many East Asian developing countries continued to enjoy access to international capital markets despite the slowdown in aggregate lending to developing countries. During the recent bouts of instability contagion has been partial and markets have differentiated risks among sovereign borrowers (Cunningham, Dixon, and Hayes 2001; UNCTAD 2003). But even so, markets tend to overreact and behave procyclically, withdrawing capital from countries perceived to have high risks and generating fragility and vulnerability in the countries they favor.

In a world of inherently unstable capital flows the fundamental issue here is whether developing countries can, by their own policy action, avoid severe financial instability and crises while also securing adequate and sustained inflows of private capital. Clearly, maintaining a reasonable degree of financial stability calls for a policy of strategic integration into global capital markets as opposed to full and rapid integration. There is greater space to avoid boom-bust cycles and unsustainable financial bubbles through macroeconomic, exchange rate, and regulatory policies than developing countries have so far exploited (Akyüz 2004).

Under a policy of strategic integration the need for multilateral finance would vary by country group. The more successful developing countries with strong growth fundamentals would likely need only occasional IMF lending for current account financing on a countercyclical basis. Many of these countries, most located in Asia, already enjoy access to international capital markets at reasonable terms. But most other developing countries need large and continued injections of external finance for development. They cannot attract adequate private finance at reasonable terms because of deep-seated structural and institutional weaknesses and their high risk environments for lending. This is true not only of low-income countries with little or no access to international capital markets but of many middle-income countries as well.

Despite improving perceptions about emerging market risks and substantial compression of spreads, investment climates in more than half the 29 emerging market economies are rated as speculative, resulting in very high spreads (IIF various years). This group includes many Latin American countries with chronic savings and foreign exchange gaps, weak industrial export bases, and excessive debt. Attempts to rely on private flows have resulted in recurrent crises and stop-go development (UNCTAD 2003). Multilateral finance cannot be relied on indefinitely to fill savings and foreign exchange gaps in these countries. To escape this impasse, these countries must improve their savings, investment, and export performance.

THE WAY FORWARD FOR MULTILATERAL LENDING

The policy milieu today is quite different from that which gave rise to multilateral lending some 60 years ago, but some elements of the original rationale remain rel-

evant. There is a continuing, even strengthened, rationale for short-term, countercyclical lending for current account purposes by the IMF, and there is a continuing need for IDA-type concessional lending to low-income developing
countries.

Today's rationale for short-term, countercyclical current account lending

There is a consensus on the role of the IMF in providing short-term international
liquidity, but there is little agreement on the objectives of such lending. Some
major creditor governments continue to resist proposals for the enlargement of
IMF quotas and Special Drawing Rights (SDR) allocations to developing countries facing export shortfalls or rising import bills (see the chapter by Polak and
Clark in this volume). But these same creditor governments have been willing to
support lending in excess of official limits to many emerging markets facing capital account crises, for fear of the repercussions for international creditors and
investors should they fail to do so. Such assistance has often come as bailout operations designed to keep countries current on their debt repayments to private
creditors, to maintain capital account convertibility, and to prevent defaults.

Such lending fails to protect countries against the adverse consequences of
financial shocks and tends to aggravate market failures by creating creditor moral
hazard. It undermines market discipline and encourages imprudent lending since
private creditors are not required to bear the consequences of the risks they take
(Haldane and Scheibe 2004; Mina and Martinez-Vazquez 2002). Furthermore,
even when the external debt is owed by the private sector, the burden ultimately
falls on taxpayers because governments in debtor countries are often obliged to
serve as guarantors (Akyüz 2002).

There have been increased calls for the IMF to serve as lender of last resort
for emerging markets, to preempt crises as well as to resolve them (see, for example, Fischer 1999). The main idea is that if the IMF stands ready to provide liquidity to countries with sound policies, these countries would be protected from
contagion and financial panic. Such a step would involve a fundamental departure from the underlying premises of the Bretton Woods system. The report of
the U.S. International Financial Institutions Advisory Commission (U.S. IFIAC
2000) virtually proposes the elimination of all other forms of IMF lending.[25]

Such a shift in IMF lending would imply that only a small number of more
prosperous emerging economies would be eligible for IMF financing (Summers
2000). But in any case there are difficulties in transforming the IMF into a genuine international lender of last resort. The IMF would require discretion to create its own liquidity (or unconstrained access to international liquidity). While
various arrangements are possible in principle (such as a new role for the SDR or
allowing the IMF to go to markets), they are all problematic (Akyüz and Cornford
2002). The terms of access to such a facility pose additional problems. Genuine
lender of last resort financing would need to be accompanied by tightened global

supervision to ensure solvency, creating both technical and political difficulties. The creation of a lender of last resort may also aggravate rather than eliminate creditor moral hazard, and sound policies cannot always succeed in preventing imprudent lending.[26]

Given the persistent global economic instability and procyclical behavior of international financial markets, reform of IMF lending should focus on counter-cyclical financing in response to external trade and financial shocks. While it has to be recognized that money is fungible, it is important to ensure that resources be used to finance current account rather than capital account transactions.

Three areas deserve attention. First, IMF lending to counter sharp declines in private capital flows should aim at maintaining imports and the level of economic activity rather than repayment to private creditors and capital account convertibility. (These can be dealt with using other instruments; see Akyüz 2002 and the chapter by Eichengreen in this volume.) Such lending should be available to countries facing crises or threatened by contagion, with strict limits to avoid disincentives to private sector involvement (Peterson, Goldstein, and Hills 1999). It is also important to separate multilateral lending from bilateral arrangements, to reduce the scope for undue influence over IMF policies by some of its major shareholders. Crisis lending should be the sole responsibility of the IMF—the World Bank should stay out of provision of short-term liquidity (U.S. IFIAC 2000; Gilbert, Powell, and Vines 1999).

A second area of IMF lending is countercyclical support to countries facing temporary payments difficulties in their current accounts due to shortfalls in export earnings, surges in import prices, or hikes in interest rates on their external debt. Such lending should be available not only to poorer developing countries but also to emerging market economies, whose access to private finance is often impaired at times of current account difficulties because of the procyclical behavior of markets. Such lending is in line with the original tasks assigned to the IMF and should be semi-automatic.

Third, consideration should be given to the creation of a global counter-cyclical facility, to be available in times of sharp downturn in world economic growth and trade. The IMF performed this task during the 1970s through its two oil facilities. Access should be semi-automatic.

Determining the exact modalities of IMF lending in these areas is beyond the scope of this chapter. However, the fundamental point is that the IMF should limit itself to short-term, countercyclical lending for current account purposes. There is no sound rationale for IMF lending for capital account or development financing.

The continuing rationale for concessional lending and grants for low-income countries

There was considerable ambiguity during the Bretton Woods negotiations about the role that the IBRD was expected to play relative to private capital markets and investment. Thus it is no surprise that questions arise about the World Bank continuing its lending despite the rapid development of international capital markets. With the recovery of private capital flows to developing countries in the early 1990s, many claim that the original rationale for multilateral lending is no longer valid. While some argue that multilateral lending to countries with access to international capital markets should be discontinued, others find compelling reasons for such lending to continue.

An argument in favor of continued multilateral development lending is that multilateral development banks are better than private agents in generating and disseminating knowledge and promoting sound policies and that policy advice and technical assistance should be bundled together with multilateral lending to avoid incentive and agency problems. This view holds that since risk-return profiles of projects depend on the overall policy environment, conditionality that leads to improvements in policymaking provides a rationale for multilateral lending even in the absence of other types of market failure (Gavin and Rodrik 1995; Rodrik 1995). By financing projects that private lenders find too risky, multilateral development banks mobilize private capital by improving the risk-return profiles of private investment. Multilateral agencies could not achieve the same end by monitoring government policies on behalf of bilateral and private lenders since there may be severe incentive problems in the absence of direct lending.

These would be strong arguments if supported by the record. But evidence does not support the catalytic role of multilateral lending (Rodrik 1995; Ratha 2001). More important, there are serious questions about the effectiveness of conditionality and the success of projects financed by multilateral development banks (Stiglitz 2002a; Gilbert, Powell, and Vines 1999; Ocampo 2001; U.S. IFIAC 2000; and Meltzer 2001). Many policymakers argue that ex ante conditionality has not been successful in preventing policy failures and that such efforts to buy sound policies should be replaced by rewards for sound policies (see the chapter by Radelet in this volume). Some would like to see the World Bank become an effective "knowledge bank," focusing on the provision of knowledge, policy advice, and technical assistance while continuing to lend to middle-income countries. This lending is thought to be important to take advantage of complementarity between technical assistance and lending and to generate funding for IDA (Gilbert, Powell, and Vines 1999; Gilbert 2000).

However, many organizations in the United Nations system provide effective technical assistance to developing countries without combining it with lending. And IBRD loan-related income has not made significant contributions to IDA (Gilbert, Powell, and Vines 1999; Meltzer 2001). Promoting the already established practice of voluntary contributions by more advanced developing countries would be a better option.

The majority in the U.S. International Financial Institutions Advisory Commission took the proposition that middle-income countries now have access to international financial markets to its logical conclusion and recommended a phased graduation of these countries from multilateral lending and a conversion of IDA credits into grants (U.S. IFIAC 2000). Such reform would imply that the World Bank, and possibly other multilateral development banks, would be transformed from banks to development agencies.

While graduation is inevitable, there are difficulties in how the proposal is formulated. Experience clearly shows that investment-grade status is not an attribute inextricably linked to the long-term structural fundamentals of developing countries or strongly correlated with their levels of per capita income. If current ratings were taken as the basis for graduation, China and India would be excluded from IBRD lending while Argentina would continue to enjoy access. Credit ratings of emerging markets are capable of undergoing sharp and unexpected changes according to a country's success in managing volatile capital flows. A favorable rating at any point in time is no guarantee of uninterrupted future access to private finance.[27]

The proposal to provide grants rather than loans for the poorest countries has enjoyed considerable support, but many consider it impractical because funds are lacking or because it would jeopardize the World Bank's long-term financial viability (Summers 2000; Lerrick and Meltzer 2001, 2002; Sanford 2002, 2003; Salazar 2002). However, the IDA deputies eventually "recognized the advantages of increasing concessionality...and endorsed an expansion of IDA grants...in the range of 18 to 21 percent of overall IDA13 resources" (IDA 2002, p. 27).[28] More recently, 30 percent of IDA14 resources are expected to be provided on grant terms (IDA 2005).

One conclusion to be drawn from the recent debate on the rationale of multilateral lending is that the multilateral development banks, particularly the World Bank, should focus their activities on the poorest developing countries and adopt a graduation strategy for the more advanced developing countries. The World Bank could scale down its lending activities in the more successful middle-income countries that no longer need multilateral development finance. The main contribution of the Bretton Woods institutions to these countries could be to assist their strategic integration into international capital markets. This would call for a departure from the current approach to financial liberalization and openness.

Many middle-income countries continue to depend on multilateral finance because of misguided national development policies. These countries could be graduated from multilateral lending only if they were to achieve rapid economic growth leading to rising domestic savings and increased and stable flows of long-term private capital. Sustaining such a process calls not only for multilateral lending but also for a new approach to development policy, learning from the mistakes of the policies based on the Washington Consensus (Williamson 1990) and drawing on the lessons of the development experiences of some of the more successful developing countries.

For most poorer developing countries there is no alternative to multilateral finance—on strongly favorable terms. Many countries are already indebted and in need of a substantial debt writeoff. There is not much to be gained by adding to their stock of debt and interest payments, however concessional future development lending may be. Therefore, multilateral grant financing might even be preferable to concessional IDA credits.

NOTES

1. Multilateral financing is a part of official international financing, which also includes bilateral financing. There is wide agreement that multilateral lending is less driven by political considerations than is bilateral lending (see Gilbert, Powell, and Vines 1999; Kapur and Webb 1994; and Rodrik 1995). Without further discussion, this chapter maintains that to the extent that there is a need for official financing, it would, for that reason, be preferable to organize the lending on a multilateral basis.

2. For an earlier discussion of "externalities and international public goods...in the economic interactions of nations" see Bryant (1980, p. 473).

3. See Kaul, Grunberg, and Stern (1999); Phillips and Higgott (1999); Stiglitz (2002b); and Kaul and others (2003). What exactly constitutes global public goods seems to be highly contentious. However, the spectrum has been widening given the tendency of economics to invade and colonize other areas of social science (Kindleberger 1986, p. 1). Global security, global economic stability, global environment, knowledge, humanitarian assistance, and global health are now typically included among global public goods.

4. This analysis of credit rationing was first developed in a seminal article by Stiglitz and Weiss (1981). For a detailed discussion, see Davis (1992) and Mishkin (2004).

5. The approach goes back to Fisher's analysis of the Great Depression: see Davis (1992), which also surveys various explanations offered for financial instability and crises.

6. These problems were due primarily to the failure to provide for postwar reconstruction and potential balance of payments difficulties. For a brief account see Oliver (1975) and Dam (1982).

7. Two institutions that were to support the expansion of trade and prosperity under conditions of stability, the International Trade Organization and the International Commodity Stabilization Fund, were not created.

8. The quota-based system was supplemented in 1969 with the creation of the Special Drawing Right (SDR), a potential claim on the freely usable currencies of IMF members. Polak and Clark (in this volume) discuss the system in more detail.

9. See Dam (1982) and Dell (1981) for a discussion of the issues involved and the Anglo-American debate on conditionality.

10. For the full text of Article V today, see www.imf.org/external/pubs/ft/aa/aa05.htm.

11. The World Bank Group consists of five closely associated institutions: the IBRD, the International Development Association, the International Finance Corporation, the Multilateral Investment Guarantee Agency, and the International Centre for Settlement of Investment Disputes. The "World Bank" is the name that has come to be used for IBRD and IDA.

12. For the complete text of the IBRD Articles of Agreement, see http://siteresources.worldbank.org/EXTABOUTUS/Resources/ibrd-articlesofagreement.pdf.

13. See Article II, section 5 of the IBRD Articles of Agreement.

14. For an account of the rationale and evolution of IMF conditionality see Dell (1981). For more recent trends see Jungito (1994); Kapur and Webb (2000); and Buira (2003).

15. Conditionality is intended to provide assurance that the loan will be used to resolve the borrower's economic difficulties and that the country will be able to repay promptly; for details see IMF (2002).

16. Standby arrangements are designed to address short-term balance of payments problems. They are typically 12–18 months with repayment expected within 2–4 years (IMF 2004a).

17. Performance criteria are specific preconditions for disbursement of IMF credits. Quantitative performance criteria include macroeconomic policy variables such as international reserves, monetary and credit aggregates, and fiscal balances. Structural performance criteria vary widely, but could include specific measures to restructure key sectors such as energy, reform social security systems, or improve financial sector operations (see IMF 2002).

18. See also www.imf.org/external/np/exr/facts/howlend.htm.

19. In effect from 1974 to 1976, the oil facilities allowed the IMF to borrow from oil exporters and other countries in a strong external position and lend to oil importers to help finance their deficits (www.imf.org/external/pubs/ft/exrp/what.htm).

20. See www.marshallfoundation.org.

21. For an account of the evolution of the World Bank in its formative years see Oliver (1975). For a detailed history of the first 25 years of the World Bank see Mason and Asher (1973) and for its first half century see Kapur, Lewis, and Webb (1997).

22. For a detailed account see Kapur and Webb (1994) and Rwegasira and Kifle (1994).

23. Private capital flows now seem to be in the boom phase of a third cycle driven by historically low interest rates and high levels of liquidity, among other factors.

24. Established in 1957 the Eurodollar market involves limited-term dollar loans, generally with short repayment periods. Trading is in U.S. dollars and other convertible currencies and is conducted between banks outside the United States (see www.deutsche-bank.de/lexikon/2238_ENG_HTML.html).

25. The dissenting members of the commission pointed out that the most damaging proposals relate to the IMF's role in financial crises (Fidler 2000); see also Eichengreen and Portes (2000), Wolf (2000), and DeLong (2000, p. 2). See Meltzer (2001) for his comments on the critics.

26. Difficulties associated with IMF crisis lending have given rise to various proposals for the resolution of emerging market debt crises. Eichengreen (in this volume) discusses some of the key issues.

27. The fragility of the capital market access of developing countries is also noted by the U.S. Treasury (2000) in its response to the Meltzer Commission.

28. For a discussion of the rationale behind the use of grants and loans as development finance tools, see the chapter by Collier in this volume.

References

Ahluwalia, Montek S. 1999. "The IMF and the World Bank in the New Financial Architecture." In United Nations Conference on Trade and Development, *International Monetary and Financial Issues for the 1990s*. Vol. 9. Geneva.

Akyüz, Yilmaz. 2002. "Crisis Management and Burden Sharing." In Yilmaz Akyüz, ed., *Reforming the Global Financial Architecture. Issues and Proposals*. London: Zed Books.

———. 2004. "Managing Financial Instability and Shocks in a Globalizing World." Paper presented at a public lecture sponsored by Bank Negara and the University of Malaya, February 6, Kuala Lumpur.

Akyüz, Yilmaz, and Andrew Cornford. 2002. "Capital Flows to Developing Countries and the Reform of the International Financial System." In Deepak Nayyar, ed., *Governing Globalization*. New York: Oxford University Press.

Bryant, Ralph C. 1980. *Money and Monetary Policy in Interdependent Nations*. Washington, D.C.: The Brookings Institution.

Buira, Ariel. 2003. "An Analysis of IMF Conditionality." In Ariel Buira, ed., *Challenges to the World Bank and IMF: Developing Country Perspectives*. London: Anthem Press.

CFRITF (Council on Foreign Relations Independent Task Force). 1999. *Safeguarding Prosperity in a Global Financial System: The Future International Financial Architecture*. Washington, D.C.

Cunningham, Alastair, Liz Dixon, and Simon Hayes. 2001. "Analysing Yield Spreads on Emerging Market Sovereign Bonds." *Financial Stability Review* 11: 175–86.

Dam, Kenneth W. 1982. *The Rules of the Game: Reform and Evolution in the International Monetary System*. Chicago, Ill.: University of Chicago Press.

Davis, E. Philip. 1992. *Debt, Financial Fragility and Systemic Risk*. Oxford: Clarendon Press.

Dell, Sidney S. 1981. *On Being Grandmotherly: The Evolution of Fund Conditionality.* Essays in International Finance 144. Princeton, N.J.: Princeton University Press.

————. 1985. "The Fifth Credit Tranche." *World Development* 13 (2): 245–49.

————. 1986. "The History of the IMF." *World Development* 14 (9): 1203–12.

DeLong, John Bradford. 2000. Comment on "The Meltzer Report." [www.j-bradford-delong.net/TotW/meltzer.html].

Eichengreen, Barry, and Richard Portes. 2000. "A Shortsighted Vision for IMF Reform." *Financial Times.* March 9.

Einhorn, Jessica. 2001. "The World Bank's Mission Creep." *Foreign Affairs* 80 (September/October): 22–31.

Fidler, Stephen. 2000. "Report Urges Slimming Down of IMF and World Bank." *Financial Times.* March 8.

Fischer, Stanley. 1999. "On the Need for an International Lender of Last Resort." *Journal of Economic Perspectives* 13 (4): 85–104.

Gavin, Michael, and Dani Rodrik. 1995. "The World Bank in Historical Perspective." *American Economic Review Papers and Proceedings* 85 (2): 329–34.

Gilbert, Christopher, L. 2000. "Comments on the Meltzer Report." FEWEC, Vrije Universiteit, Amsterdam.

Gilbert, Christopher, Andrew Powell, and David Vines. 1999. "Positioning the World Bank." *Economic Journal* 109 (459): 598–633.

Goldstein, Morris. 2000. "Strengthening the International Financial Architecture. Where Do We Stand?" Institute of International Economics Working Paper 00-8. Washington, D.C.

Haldane, Andrew G., and Jorg Scheibe. 2004. "IMF Lending and Creditor Moral Hazard." Working Paper 216. Bank of England, London.

IDA (International Development Association). 2002. *Addition to IDA Resources: Thirteenth Replenishment.* Report from the Executive Directors of IDA to the Board of Governors. Washington, D.C.

————. 2005. "World Bank: Donors Agree to Substantial Increase in New Money for Poorest Countries." Accessed on March 21, 2005 from [www.worldbank.org/ida].

IIF (Institute of International Finance). Various years. "Capital Flows to Emerging Market Economies." Washington, D.C.

IMF (International Monetary Fund). 1969. *The International Monetary Fund 1945–1965.* Vol. 1–3. Washington, D.C.

————. 2002. *IMF Conditionality: A Factsheet.* Washington, D.C. [www.imf.org/external/np/exr/facts/conditio.htm].

————. 2003. "IMF Concludes Discussion on the Review of Contingent Credit Lines." *Public Information Notice* 03/146. Washington, D.C.

————. 2004a. *IMF Lending: A Factsheet.* Washington, D.C. [www.imf.org/external/np/exr/facts/howlend.htm].

————. 2004b. *IMF Financial Activities—Update March 26, 2004.* Washington, D.C. [www.imf.org/external/fin.htm].

Jungito, Roberto. 1994. "IMF–World Bank Policy Advice: The Coordination/Cross-Conditionality Question." In United Nations Conference on Trade and Development, *International Monetary and Financial Issues for the 1990s.* Vol. 4. Geneva.

Kapur, Davesh, and Richard Webb. 1994. "The Evolution of Multilateral Development Banks." In United Nations Conference on Trade and Development, *International Monetary and Financial Issues for the 1990s.* Vol. 4. Geneva.

————. 2000. "Governance-related Conditionalities of the International Financial Institutions." G-24 Discussion Paper 6. United Nations Conference on Trade and Development, Geneva.

Kapur, Devesh, John Lewis, and Richard Webb. 1997. *The World Bank: Its First Half Century.* Washington, D.C.: The Brookings Institution.

Kaul, Inge, Isabelle Grunberg, and Marc A. Stern, eds. 1999. *Global Public Goods: International Cooperation in the 21st Century.* New York: Oxford University Press.

Kaul, Inge, Pedro Conceição, Katell Le Goulven, and Ronald U. Mendoza, eds. 2003. *Providing Global Public Goods: Managing Globalization.* New York: Oxford University Press.

Kindleberger, Charles P. 1986. "International Public Goods without International Government." *American Economic Review* 76 (1): 1–13.

Kregel, Jan. 2004. "External Financing for Development and International Financial Stability—A Balance Sheet Approach." Paper presented at the G-24 Meeting, March 9, Geneva.

Krugman, Paul. 1996. "Are Currency Crises Self-Fulfilling?" In Ben S. Bernanke and Julio J. Rotemberg, eds., *NBER Macroeconomics Annual.* Cambridge, Mass.: MIT Press.

————. 1998. "Currency Crises." Massachusetts Institute of Technology, Department of Economics, Cambridge, Mass.

Lerrick, Adam, and Allan H. Meltzer. 2001. "The World Bank Is Wrong to Oppose Grants." *Wall Street Journal.* July 26.

————. 2002. *Grants: A Better Way to Deliver Aid.* Quarterly International Economics Report. Pittsburgh: Carnegie Mellon Gailliot Center for Public Policy.

Mason, Edward S., and Robert E. Asher. 1973. *The World Bank since Bretton Woods.* Washington, D.C.: The Brookings Institution.

Meltzer, Allan H. 2001. "The Report of the International Financial Institution Advisory Commission: Comments on the Critics." Carnegie Mellon Graduate

School of Industrial Administration, Pittsburgh. [www.gsia.cmu.edu/afs/andrew/gsia/meltzer/Spanishedition3.doc].

Mikesell, Raymond F. 1994. *The Bretton Woods Debates: A Memoir.* Essays in International Finance Series 192. Princeton, N.J.: Princeton University.

Mina, Wasseem, and Jorge Martinez-Vazquez. 2002. "IMF Lending, Maturity of International Debt and Moral Hazard." International Studies Program Working Paper Series 03-01. Georgia State University, Andrew Young School of Policy Studies, Atlanta.

Minsky, Hyman. 1977. "A Theory of Systemic Fragility." In Edward I. Altman and Arnold W. Sametz, eds., *Financial Crises.* New York: Wiley.

Mishkin, Frederic S. 2004. *The Economics of Money, Banking, and Financial Markets.* Boston, Mass.: Pearson, Addison Wesley.

Obstfeld, Maurice. 1996. "Models of Currency Crises with Self-Fulfilling Features." *European Economic Review* 40 (3–5): 1037–47.

Ocampo, José Antonio. 2001. "Recasting the International Financial Agenda." G-24 Discussion Paper 13. United Nations Conference on Trade and Development, Geneva.

Oliver, Robert W. 1975. *International Economic Co-Operation and the World Bank.* London: Macmillan.

Peterson, Peter G., Morris Goldstein, and Carla A. Hills. 1999. *Safeguarding Prosperity in a Global Financial System: The Future International Financial Architecture.* Washington, D.C.: Council on Foreign Relations.

Phillips, Nicola, and Richard Higgott. 1999. "Global Governance and the Public Domain: Collective Goods in a 'Post-Washington Consensus' Era." CSGR Working Paper 47/99. University of Warwick, Center for the Study of Globalisation and Regionalisation, Coventry, UK.

Ratha, Dilip. 2001. "Complementarity between Multilateral Lending and Private Flows to Developing Countries: Some Empirical Results." Policy Research Working Paper 2746. World Bank, Washington, D.C.

Rodrik, Dani. 1995. *Why Is There Multilateral Lending?* NBER Working Paper 5160. Cambridge, Mass.: National Bureau of Economic Research.

Rwegasira, Delphin G., and Henock Kifle. 1994. "Regional Development Banks and the Objectives of the Bretton Woods Institutions." In United Nations Conference on Trade and Development, *International Monetary and Financial Issues for the 1990s.* Vol. 4. Geneva.

Sachs, Jeffrey D. 1998. "External Debt, Structural Adjustment and Economic Growth." In United Nations Conference on Trade and Development, *International Monetary and Financial Issues for the 1990s.* Vol. 9. Geneva.

Salazar, Vander Caceres. 2002. *Taken for Granted? U.S. Proposals to Reform the World Bank's IDA Examined.* London: Bretton Woods Project.

Sanford, Jonathan, E. 2002. "World Bank: Funding IDA's Assistance Program." Report for Congress, Order Code RL31418. Congressional Research Service, Washington, D.C.

————. 2003. "Multilateral Development Banks: Issues for the 108th Congress." Issue Brief for Congress, Order Code IB96008. Congressional Research Service, Washington, D.C.

Stiglitz, Joseph E. 2002a. *Globalization and Its Discontents.* New York: W. W. Norton & Company.

————. 2002b. "Globalization and the Logic of Institutional Collective Action: Reexamining the Bretton Woods Institutions." In Deepak Nayyar, ed., *Governing Globalization.* New York: Oxford University Press.

————. 2003. "Ethics, Market and Government Failure, and Globalization." Paper presented at the Vatican Conference at the Ninth Plenary Session of the Pontifical Academy of Social Sciences, May 2–6, Casina Pio IV.

Stiglitz, Joseph E., and Andrew Weiss. 1981. "Credit Rationing in Markets with Imperfect Information." *American Economic Review* 71 (3): 393–410.

Summers, Lawrence H. 2000. "Testimony before the Banking Committee of the House of Representatives." *Treasury News.* March 23.

Sy, Amadou N. R. 2001. "Emerging Market Bond Spreads and Sovereign Credit Ratings: Reconciling Market View with Economic Fundamentals." IMF Working Paper WP/01/165. International Monetary Fund, Washington, D.C.

Triffin, Robert. 1976. "Jamaica: 'Major Revision' or Fiasco." In Edward M. Bernstein, Richard N. Cooper, Nurul Islam, Charles P. Kindleberger, Fritz Machlup, Robert V. Roosa, Robert Triffin, and John Williamson, eds., *Reflections on Jamaica.* Essays in International Finance Series 115. Princeton, N.J.: Princeton University Press.

UNCTAD (United Nations Conference on Trade and Development). 1987. "The Exchange Rate System." In *International Monetary and Financial Issues for the Developing Countries.* Geneva.

————. 1999. *Trade and Development Report.* Geneva.

————. 2003. *Trade and Development Report.* Geneva.

U.S. IFIAC (International Financial Institutions Advisory Commission). 2000. *Final Report of the International Financial Institutions Advisory Commission.* Washington, D.C.: U.S. Government Printing Office.

U.S. Treasury. 2000. "Response to the Report of the International Financial Institutions Advisory Commission." Washington, D.C.

Walters, Alan. 1994. *Do We Need the IMF and the World Bank?* London: Institute of Economic Affairs.

Williamson, John. 1990. "What Washington Means by Policy Reform." In J. Williamson, ed., *Latin American Adjustment: How Much Has Happened?* Washington, D.C.: Institute for International Economics.

Wolf, Martin. 2000. "Between Revolution and Reform—The Meltzer Commission's Vision." *Financial Times*. March 8.

World Bank. 2001. *World Bank Lending Instruments: Resources for Development Impact*. Washington, D.C.

———. 2002. *Global Development Finance*. Washington, D.C.

———. 2004. *Global Development Finance*. Washington, D.C.

PULLING NOT PUSHING REFORMS
DELIVERING AID THROUGH
CHALLENGE GRANTS

STEVE RADELET

Most donors deliver aid in very similar ways across recipient countries even though recipients vary widely in the quality of their governance, commitment to strong development policies, degree of political stability, and level of institutional capacity. This approach makes little sense. Aid effectiveness could be improved if donor systems were designed to take into account key differences in recipient countries.

Proponents of country selectivity argue that donors should provide more aid to countries with better policies and stronger institutions because they are likely to achieve better results.[1] But country selectivity could be used to influence more than the amount of aid. It could also influence the way aid is delivered, including the extent to which recipient countries set priorities and design activities, the mix of project and program aid, the breadth of aid-financed activities, the length of donor commitments, and the distribution of aid to governments, nongovernmental organizations (NGOs), and other groups. Donors could employ a differentiated strategy for aid delivery based on a country's quality of governance and commitment to development, as follows:

- *Strong-governance countries* would have significant say in establishing aid priorities and designing assistance programs, receive much of their aid as program funding, and benefit from larger and longer term financial commitments.
- *Weak-governance countries* would have limited say in setting priorities and designing aid activities, receive more aid as project finance rather than program funding, have a larger share of aid channeled through NGOs, and receive smaller and shorter term aid commitments.
- *Average-governance countries* would receive aid based on a mixed set of delivery strategies along the various dimensions noted for the other two categories.

The author thanks Sabeen Hassanali for her able research and other assistance.

Donors should make the distinctions between these strategies very clear and transparently assign recipient countries to receive aid through one of these channels. This approach would create incentives that would challenge recipients to strengthen institutions and policies. The pull or reward for demonstrating stronger governance would be greater national policy ownership, more flexible and attractive aid modalities, and larger, more predictable and longer term resource commitments. This approach differs significantly from traditional aid programs in which donors "push" countries to reform by negotiating aid disbursements in return for specific policy changes (sometimes known as "buying" reforms).

Some donors are beginning to differentiate their aid strategies along these lines. The UK Department for International Development provides financing to support sectorwide approaches in some countries, but not others.[2] The World Bank provides Poverty Reduction Support Credits to a small number of countries to finance their poverty reduction strategy and the associated social, institutional, and policy reforms.[3] Most recently, the United States has introduced the Millennium Challenge Account, a program to provide funding in innovative ways to a select group of low-income developing countries that (according to a defined set of criteria discussed later in this chapter) demonstrate good governance and introduce sound development policies.

This chapter considers what role such pull instruments or challenge programs could play within the overall framework of foreign aid, asking how they could be designed to function as effective and efficient incentive instruments and how they could best complement other aid modalities. It looks first at how challenge programs differ from more conventional aid approaches, taking the Millennium Challenge Account as an example, and shows how challenge programs fall conceptually within the pull rather than push incentives type. It then develops an argument for differentiated aid strategies across countries based on key characteristics of recipient countries.

AN OVERVIEW OF THE MILLENNIUM CHALLENGE ACCOUNT

The Millennium Challenge Account is designed to provide substantial financing to a select group of low-income countries that "rule justly, invest in their people, and encourage economic freedom."[4] The program has the potential to bring about the biggest change in U.S. foreign assistance policy since the Kennedy Administration, both because of its size (proposed to grow eventually to $5 billion a year) and because of the way aid could be delivered (Radelet 2003). Operations formally commenced in February 2004 with the creation of the new Millennium Challenge Corporation (MCC) to run the program. The first recipient country, Madagascar, signed a compact with the MCC in April 2005.[5] The idea is to select countries based on their demonstrated commitment to sound policies and good governance, give them more say in designing programs, provide them with larger sums of money, and hold them accountable for achieving results. Each of these four program dimensions is examined in turn and compared with conventional aid practices.

Country selectivity

The assessment and ranking of countries is based on 16 quantitative indicators drawn from publicly available databases (table 1). To qualify, a country must score above the median for low-income countries on half the indicators in each of the three categories—ruling justly, investing in people, encouraging economic

TABLE 1

Eligibility criteria for the Millennium Challenge Account

Indicator	Source
Ruling justly	
1. Control of corruption	World Bank Institute
2. Rule of law	World Bank Institute
3. Voice and accountability	World Bank Institute
4. Government effectiveness	World Bank Institute
5. Civil liberties	Freedom House
6. Political rights	Freedom House
Investing in people	
7. Immunization rate (DPT and measles)	World Health Organization/World Bank
8. Primary education completion rate	World Bank/United Nations Educational, Scientific, and Cultural Organization
9. Public primary education spending/GDP	National sources
10. Public expenditure on health/GDP	National sources
Encouraging economic freedom	
11. Country credit rating	Institutional Investor
12. Inflation	International Monetary Fund
13. Regulatory quality	World Bank Institute
14. Budget deficit/GDP	National sources
15. Trade policy	Heritage Foundation
16. Days to start a business	World Bank

Note: To qualify, countries must be above the median for countries in their income group on half the indicators in each of the three categories and above the median on corruption.
Source: MCC 2004d.

freedom—and it must score above the median on corruption.[6] Thus, a country that does poorly on, say, trade policy or budget balances can still qualify on other indicators.

The process is not entirely mechanical. The MCC Board has limited flexibility to adjust the list of qualifying countries to take account of gaps, lags, and weaknesses in the imperfect data. In May 2004 the MCC chose 16 qualifying countries for the first year: Armenia, Benin, Bolivia, Cape Verde, Georgia, Ghana, Honduras, Lesotho, Madagascar, Mali, Mongolia, Mozambique, Nicaragua, Senegal, Sri Lanka, and Vanuatu (MCC 2004b). In November it added one country—Morocco—for 2005. The number of qualifiers could reach 20–25 countries by 2006.

Many details of the selection process have been extensively debated, including the 16 indicators and their sources, the use of the median cutoff, the focus on the level of the indicators rather than changes, and the insistence on achieving a corruption score above the median (Radelet 2003; Brainard and others 2003). There are important concerns about the quality of the data, and whether the process is biased against the poorest countries, which would have difficulty scoring well on some of the indicators simply because of their poverty. Some observers see these indicators as an attempt by the U.S. government to push the "Washington Consensus."[7] However, since the Millennium Challenge Account includes indicators on immunization rates, school completion rates, and political rights and excludes indicators on tax reform, privatization, and foreign direct investment, that criticism is off base. Without repeating the details of these important debates, three key points about the selection process are worth emphasizing.

First, by using a public, transparent methodology, the Millennium Challenge Account is aimed at depoliticizing the process of selecting countries. Political considerations will undoubtedly creep into eligibility and allocation decisions, but the public selection process will limit the extent to which this happens. In turn, this process should strengthen the focus of the program on growth and poverty reduction and on issues that recipient governments see as their highest priorities.

Second, only a small number of countries will qualify each year. This is by design, to make the program more effective by concentrating resources where the United States believes they can achieve strong results. Nevertheless, most low-income countries will not qualify. Thus, while the Millennium Challenge Account has the potential to be a strong program for the countries that qualify, it does little for dozens of other countries that will not qualify and so leaves large gaps in what is necessary for a more complete foreign assistance strategy.

Third, qualification is based on policy and institutional changes that a country has already made, not on promises of future reforms. This makes the Millennium Challenge Account quite different from traditional conditionality-based aid in which donors disburse funds contingent on the recipient implementing specific policy changes and promising more in the future. In effect, the

Millennium Challenge Account is more a reward for sound policy choices than a downpayment on future reforms. Once a country qualifies and begins to receive funding, additional tranches are contingent on achieving specified results—such as distributing a targeted number of bednets or building a certain number of miles of roads. Basing continued funding on results is very different from using funds as an incentive to "buy" future policy reforms.

The Millennium Challenge Account is not the only aid program that uses a quantitative process for selecting countries. The World Bank, the Asian Development Bank, and the African Development Bank have all adopted performance-based allocation systems for distributing concessional loans among eligible borrowers. In the World Bank a country's allocation depends primarily on its Country Policy and Institutional Assessment (CPIA) score, through which Bank staff rank countries on 20 different policy and institutional criteria (World Bank 2003a,b; see also the chapter by Collier in this volume). The Asian and African Development Banks use similar systems (ADB 2001; AfDB 2004).

However, the Millennium Challenge Account differs from these systems in several ways. First, its indicators determine eligibility, whereas performance-based allocation systems are used to determine funding allocations across many countries, almost all of them eligible for some funding. Second, the Millennium Challenge Account uses publicly available data for its indicators, while the other systems use confidential data based on the opinions of agency staff. Third, Millennium Challenge Account countries will not only receive more money, they will receive it in very different ways.

Country ownership

Unlike most aid programs, in which donors take the lead role in shaping projects and proposals, the Millennium Challenge Account is intended to give recipient countries a much greater say in setting priorities and designing programs and to provide funds more flexibly. Guidelines issued by the MCC call for recipient countries to design their own programs and submit proposals for how they intend to use the funds (MCC 2004a). If proposals are approved, the MCC and the recipient country will enter into a multiyear agreement (typically three to five years) that specifies how the funds will be used and what targets the recipient will try to achieve.[8] Four such compacts had been signed by July 2005.[9] Countries can apply for new funding when the agreement expires so long as they maintain their eligibility and achieve the specified targets.

In giving recipient countries more say in defining priorities and designing programs, the Millennium Challenge Account resembles two other new and innovative aid delivery institutions: the Global Alliance for Vaccines and Immunizations and the Global Fund to Fight AIDS, Tuberculosis, and Malaria. Governments work closely with NGOs and the private sector to design programs that meet local needs and conditions and that give recipients a large stake in ensuring success.[10]

Millennium Challenge Account countries are likely to have substantial latitude in deciding which activities to fund (say, for rural roads, water systems, or worker training). Governments will be expected to work with NGOs, private companies, faith-based organizations, and other groups to specify how proposed activities fit in with their poverty reduction strategies, what targets they expect to achieve, and what role other donors have in related activities. In principle, some funding could be provided as budget support, but so far the MCC has resisted that option. The country ownership aspect of the Millennium Challenge Account is inseparable from the country selectivity approach: the United States is willing to grant extensive flexibility only to countries with good governance and not to countries with weak governance, high levels of corruption, or poor policies.

Scaling up

For the countries that qualify the Millennium Challenge Account could bring a significant scaling up of aid funds. According to its original design the program was supposed to reach $5 billion in funding by 2006, all of it to be disbursed as grants and fully additional to current assistance programs. This figure would have represented about a quarter of U.S. net official development assistance and about 6 percent of global net official development assistance in 2004. Only 20–25 countries are likely to qualify once the program reaches full speed, so with $5 billion the allocation to each country could be quite large. Radelet (2003, p. 126) calculates that for a set of 20 countries that are reasonably likely to qualify, the additional funds would constitute, on average, about a two-thirds increase in their capital inflow.

There is considerable doubt, however, that Millennium Challenge Account funding will ever reach $5 billion. With growing U.S. budget deficits, lawmakers are beginning to question the size of the Millennium Challenge Account. The administration requested $2.5 billion for the program in 2005 but Congress approved just $1.5 billion. At a more realistic $2.5 billion or so per year, the Millennium Challenge Account would still represent significant new resources, although not on its original scale.

The new funds may not be fully additional for the recipients, however, for two reasons. First, while recipient countries will still be eligible to receive other forms of U.S. assistance, they will likely receive less of it. The U.S. Agency for International Development will retain its presence in recipient countries but is likely to focus on a more limited set of activities. Second, other donors may reduce their funding to Millennium Challenge Account countries. The extent of this substitution will not be fully evident for several years.

Performance-based management

The United States claims that the Millennium Challenge Account will be performance based, with the MCC providing generous funding for initiatives that achieve their goals and reducing or eliminating funding for those that do not. Of course, many donors make the same pledge, while few actually implement it. Again, the Global Alliance for Vaccines and Immunizations and the Global Fund to Fight AIDS, Tuberculosis, and Malaria are two exceptions. For the Millennium Challenge Account this will require collecting good baseline data, establishing measurable benchmarks, and implementing a strong monitoring and evaluation program, none of which is easy.

CHALLENGE PROGRAMS: PUSH OR PULL?

A fundamental difference between challenge programs and most other aid programs is the incentive structure for introducing policy and institutional reforms. Traditional aid programs are push instruments, in two related ways. First, donor agencies typically allocate a certain amount of funding for each country and then design projects and programs to meet that funding level. The amounts allocated at senior levels drive the process, rather than need or the quality of the proposed project.

Second, since the early 1980s donors have used aid funds to push countries to implement reforms that donors see as desirable for the recipient country, its region, or the world. Typically, donors negotiate policy reforms that will be implemented as conditions for receiving the aid, matching a schedule of reforms with a schedule of aid disbursements. Countries are required to implement some of these reforms before they receive any aid (sometimes called "prior actions" or "condition precedents"), and they pledge to make the remaining reforms in line with aid flows. Sometimes specific reforms are matched precisely with new disbursements in individual funding agreements (as with International Monetary Fund and World Bank loans); at other times they are matched with entire aid programs (as through policy reform pledges to annual donor consultative group meetings).

The conditionality approach has not worked well (World Bank 1998; Collier 1997; Burnside and Dollar 2000; Easterly 2001). Collier (1997) points out that there is little relationship between aid flows and changes in policy. Donors have at times repeatedly "bought" the same reforms from recipient countries, paying for reforms that never materialize or that are soon reversed. In Kenya, for example, the World Bank provided four agricultural adjustment loans during the 1980s and 1990s based on government promises to implement the same basic set of reforms. Each time the government implemented the reforms, took the aid, and reversed the reforms (Collier 1997; Easterly 2001).

The failure of conditionality-based aid does not mean that recipient countries never introduce promised policy reforms. Many countries do. Rather, there is no relationship between aid disbursements and countries following through with promised policy changes: the evidence suggests that aid has played a very limited role as an incentive for countries to introduce reforms that they would otherwise not introduce. Countries reform when it is in their interest to do so, not otherwise. Aid disbursed as a quid pro quo for specific reforms plays only a minor role in shifting those interests and cannot significantly push countries into reform. This is especially the case if recipients see no real link between aid flows and the reforms, believing that they will receive the aid even if they do not implement the promised reforms.

The Millennium Challenge Account and other similar challenge programs work more as a pull instrument through the country selectivity process. Countries must have already implemented good policies to become eligible, and aid flows are not tied to specific reforms. Countries must score high enough on a minimum number of pre-established, publicly announced policy and institutional indicators to qualify. To be effective, these standards should not be negotiated and should not differ across country groups (although they might differ between low-income and middle-income countries). Subsequent disbursements are tied to achieving specified targets directly related to the aid flows (building a certain number of miles of roads, for example) rather than broad policy reforms. Thus, aid goes to countries that for their own reasons have introduced policy and institutional reforms, not to countries that only promise such reforms.

The performance-based allocation systems used by the multilateral development banks share some of these characteristics. They tie the level of financing to a country's rating on broad policy and institutional quality and not directly to promises of specific reforms. Thus, to some extent they are a pull instrument that rewards countries for previous policy choices. Most funding, however, continues to be tied to specific future policy changes and thus act like push instruments. In these mixed aid programs a pull system determines overall country allocations, while individual loans under that cap push countries toward further reforms. Challenge programs such as the Millennium Challenge Account go further in the direction of a pull instrument by using indicators to determine eligibility and by tying disbursements to results rather than to broad policy reforms.

While challenge programs may be a new idea within the foreign aid context, they are an established modality nationally, notably within the philanthropic context. For example, the Kresge Foundation offers challenge grant programs for building facilities and purchasing scientific equipment.[11] The U.S. Environmental Protection Agency offers challenge grants to nonprofit organizations to fund innovative solutions to specific environmental problems.[12] The U.S. Department of Education's Technology Innovation Challenge Grants provide funding to low-income areas for technology-based education initiatives.[13] In Australia the Landcare Greenhouse Challenge program provides grants to farmers, community groups, and businesses for programs to reduce agricultural greenhouse emissions.[14]

These facilities designate funds for a particular purpose and then invite potential recipients to apply for funds—large or small—for activities that the recipients design and that are aimed at achieving the intended goals. Within the international cooperation domain, the Global Fund to Fight AIDS, Tuberculosis, and Malaria and the Global Alliance for Vaccines and Immunization are similar to these challenge grant programs.

The Millennium Challenge Account goes beyond these programs and adds a further pull dimension by imposing strict eligibility requirements on potential recipients before they can apply for funding. Most other challenge grants do not restrict the applicant pool by measuring the "quality" of the recipient. Potential Millennium Challenge Account recipients must already have introduced demonstrable policy reforms of a certain standard before applying for funding for programs that they design in accordance with their highest priorities.

As a selectivity-based pull instrument the Millennium Challenge Account has many advantages, but its design also raises several important concerns. A critical issue is defining the eligibility criteria. There is considerable debate about just what policy and institutional conditions are necessary for aid to be effective and therefore what the eligibility requirements should be. Even with agreement on the indicators, weaknesses in the quality of the data lead to errors in measurement and inaccurate evaluations.

Performance-based allocation systems have been at the center of similar debates, such as those over the content and weighting of the components of the World Bank's CPIA scores. The same is true of private sector ratings systems, such as credit ratings by Standard & Poor's, Moody's, or Institutional Investor, which use slightly different systems to rate the creditworthiness of countries. Thus, although it might be desirable for donors to agree on a single rating system for all their aid programs, reaching agreement on such a system would be very difficult. Donors will differ on how selective programs should be as well as on issues of content and weighting.

Perhaps most important, selectivity-based programs by definition eliminate aid to countries that do not qualify. Taken to the extreme, selectivity-based aid would argue for halting aid to countries with weak policy and institutional environments. However, recent research has shown that certain types of aid can be effective even in these settings (Clemens, Radelet, and Bhavnani 2004). A more appropriate conclusion for selectivity-based aid is for donors to use different approaches in countries with weaker governance. In other words, donors could develop a more sophisticated toolkit with a range of approaches for delivering aid in different country circumstances.

EXPANDING THE TOOLKIT: DIFFERENTIATING AID STRATEGIES ACROSS COUNTRIES

The logic of the Millennium Challenge Account is that not only should better governed countries receive more aid but they also should receive it in ways that take advantage of their record of good governance. It takes the debate about country selectivity beyond simply reallocating funds to designing different aid-delivery instruments for different kinds of countries. This suggests that challenge programs could be at one end of a continuum of aid instruments that vary roughly in line with the quality of governance. Donors could deliver different quantities of aid and deliver it differently depending on quality of governance and commitment to strong development policies.

Varying aid delivery dimensions

At least five dimensions of aid delivery can be adjusted through gradation and phasing to better match aid delivery strategies to country conditions.

Recipient or donor control. Providing countries with more flexibility and ownership in determining national aid priorities makes sense in well governed countries, but not in poorly governed ones. Countries with stronger governance could be given responsibility for setting broad priorities and designing aid-financed programs. This should start with designing poverty reduction strategies and move on to specific donor-funded activities that grow out of that process. In weak, failing, and poorly governed countries, where governments have shown little commitment to good development policy, donors should retain a strong role in setting priorities and designing activities.

Program or project financing. Well governed countries should receive a greater share of aid as programmatic or budget support, while poorly governed countries should receive primarily (or exclusively) project financing. Programmatic or budget support gives countries greater flexibility to use funds for their highest priorities, adapt to changing needs, and finance recurrent as well as capital costs, as necessary. Budget support allows aid to be more consistent with the government's development strategy (since the budget provides a blueprint for allocating public sector resources) and more readily integrated with government financial resources for development. Aid in this form tends to strengthen government financial institutions, whereas project support can weaken them by pulling resources away from budget systems to individual satellite projects.

Well governed countries should be given the discretion that comes with programmatic financing and budget support, so long as they have adequate financial systems (including regularly published budgets, appropriate accounting and auditing standards, and regular public monitoring) and are able to continue to show results. Donors could still provide some funds to these countries as project aid, but most aid should be in the form of program assistance or budget support.[15]

In poorly governed countries with high levels of corruption, opaque budget procedures, and poor monitoring and auditing, programmatic funding and budget support make little sense. Instead, donors should continue to direct their funds to well defined projects that offer less discretion to recipient governments. Although project aid is partially fungible, it is less fungible than budget support, so donors can exert some control. In poorly governed countries more aid could go through NGOs than through the government, which should also reduce fungibility.

Delivery through central government or through local governments, NGOs, and civil society. In well governed countries most donor assistance should be channeled through the government, while in poorly governed countries a larger share could go through NGOs and civil society groups. Aid to the central government can be more easily aligned with the government's development strategy and better integrated into the budget. But not all aid should go through the central government, even in well governed countries, since the government is unlikely to have the capacity to implement all worthwhile projects. Doing so could create a larger than desirable public sector and would reduce the possibility of providing aid effectively through other channels. For some donor-financed programs provincial and local governments can provide services effectively.

In poorly governed countries more aid should go through NGOs or civil society groups, at least some of which may be more capable than the government to deliver basic social services to the poor. In countries with very weak governance, perhaps no aid should go through the government. While there is a possibility that a growing NGO sector will undermine government capacity building, governments in these countries have shown little commitment to strong development policies or little ability to use aid resources well. This approach permits more funds to be directed through institutions that can deliver stronger results.

NGOs are not a panacea. Some are more effective than others, and some may be even less effective and more corrupt than governments. Donors must carefully assess the NGOs they work with and how they work with them. The important point is that the most effective implementing partners for donors are likely to vary across countries, which should be recognized in donor strategies.

Broader or narrower range of activities. In well governed countries donors should support a broad range of activities consistent with programmatic and budget support. Donors could finance the poverty reduction strategy as a whole, including a wide array of activities in different sectors. This does not mean that everything can or should be funded. There is still a need to set priorities, perhaps with individual donors focusing on areas in which they have the strongest skills and experience. But donors as a group, working closely with the recipient government, should be thinking in terms of supporting a fully fledged development strategy rather than individual projects.

In poorly governed countries donors should narrowly focus on specific targets of opportunity. In the weakest states that could be basic consumption or social services for the poor, while in slightly stronger countries support could broaden to sectors in which the government has shown some commitment and potential for progress.

Longer or shorter term financial commitments. Donors should provide longer term financial commitments in well governed countries than in poorly governed countries. Achieving development goals can take many years, even in well governed countries. A country with an income of $300 per capita that records rapid economic growth per capita of 5 percent a year will take more than 30 years to reach a per capita income of $1,465, the historical cutoff for International Development Association eligibility.[16]

Aid funds are typically committed at most three years in advance—too short for planning purposes for many long-term investment projects in well governed countries. In well governed countries donors should consider making commitments over a five-year time frame, contingent on countries achieving their short- and medium-run targets and otherwise continuing with good governance. Funds could taper off over time as per capita incomes rise and recipients gain access to private capital markets (see the chapter by Collier in this volume). In poorly governed countries, shorter commitments are appropriate, especially for funds going through the government.

Linking assistance strategies with country characteristics

Some countries fall between well governed and poorly governed, and for them mixed strategies are appropriate. Thus donors might have three distinctive strategies to deliver aid to low-income countries based primarily on quality of governance (table 2).

Countries with good governance. Donors could provide large amounts of financing to countries with good governance, predominately as budget support or program aid. Recipients could be given much of the responsibility to set priorities and design activities consistent with their own development strategies. Most of the aid would be channeled through the central government, which should take the lead in coordinating donors. Depending on the country, local and provincial governments and NGOs could also receive significant funding. Donors could focus less on micromanaging activities and more on measuring and achieving broad results. Donors could commit funding for five years or more, subject to the strict requirement that recipients show continued good governance and achieve reasonable results. The amount of funding could gradually decline as these economies grow and gain access to private capital markets.

Countries with average governance. Governments in countries with average governance could receive less funding than those in well governed countries. Although recipients could play an active role in setting priorities and designing projects,

TABLE 2

Three strategies for aid modalities and country governance

Aid modality	Good governance	Average governance	Weak governance
Amount of funding	Large	Average	Small
Responsibility for setting priorities and designing projects and programs	Mostly with recipients (country ownership)	Combined donor and recipient	Mostly with donors
Program or project funding	Mainly program and budget support	Primarily projects, but some program and budget support	Almost entirely projects
Breadth of funded activities	Broad—support full poverty reduction and development strategy	Moderate—support areas with most promise for progress	Narrow—look for specific opportunities where some progress is possible; focus on humanitarian relief and providing basic services
Degree of donor flexibility	Most flexible	Limited flexibility	Very little flexibility
Recipients	Mostly government, with some to NGOs and private sector	Mix of government, NGOs, and private sector	Larger share to NGOs, with some to governments
Length of donor commitment	Long (5 years or more)	Moderate (3–5 years)	Short (1 year)
Monitoring and evaluation	Strong monitoring and evaluation with good baseline data; primarily focus on outputs and outcomes	Strong monitoring and evaluation with good baseline data; focus on inputs as well as outputs and outcomes	Strong monitoring and evaluation with good baseline data; very tight oversight and regular re-appraisal

donors could work to ensure broad-based participation and technical rigor. If used at all, budget and program support would be limited. Most funding could come in the form of well designed projects consistent with the country's overall development strategy, focusing on activities with demonstrable government commitment and with the potential for progress. Financial commitments could be for three to five years, contingent on progress. A larger share of funding could go through NGOs or civil society groups than in well governed countries. Project performance should be monitored carefully, with clear performance standards. Strong performance could lead to increased financial support and longer commitments, while weak results could lead to less aid. Donors must be prepared to reduce funding when agreed performance standards are not met.

Countries with weak governance. Countries with weak governance must be dealt with on a case-by-case basis since circumstances vary widely—some are failed states, others are failing, while still others are weak or fragile. Bilateral aid is likely to be heavily influenced by strategic and security considerations. For example, the United States has expressed strong concern about failed states as part of the war on terrorism and has allocated substantial sums to weak states that are its allies in that war. Assistance to poorly governed countries could be tightly focused on humanitarian relief and basic services for the poor. Donors could focus on a limited set of high priority activities with the potential for demonstrating quick results to policymakers and the public, to help consolidate the reform process (World Bank 2001).

Donors could play a greater role in setting priorities and designing activities than in countries with strong governance. Program aid and budget support should be used rarely, if ever. Where governance is particularly weak, aid should be provided through NGOs and civil society groups rather than the government. The World Bank (2001) and Collier (2002) have suggested establishing independent service authorities to oversee the delivery of basic services.[17] Working in these countries is much riskier than working elsewhere. Programs in poorly governed states require careful monitoring, regular reappraisal, flexible responses as initiatives begin to work or fail, and a higher tolerance for failure.

More pull than push
With three distinctive, graduated approaches that vary along several dimensions, donors will be relying more on pull instruments and less on push strategies. Since the first of the three approaches outlined above is more attractive to recipients than the second, and the second is more attractive than the third, this framework provides strong incentives for recipients to take the steps necessary to become eligible for the more favorable approach. Whether a recipient moves from one category to the next will depend on the demonstrated quality of governance and policy, not on promises of further reform. Within each strategy continued fund-

ing could be based more on achieving results directly related to the funding (building a certain number of roads, increasing the immunization rate by a prescribed amount) and less on promises for broad policy reforms. To the extent that push instruments continue, donors will have to be more firm about reducing funding when promises remain unfulfilled.

CONCLUSIONS

By and large donor programs have not differentiated their delivery instruments to countries based on good or bad policies or good or bad governance. Rather, donors have tied disbursements to promises for broad policy reforms in an attempt to push recipients to implement reforms that donors view as desirable.

The Millennium Challenge Account breaks with practice on both of these important dimensions. It takes country selectivity much further than previous programs by establishing high qualification standards based on good governance and strong policies, providing large amounts of funding to the countries that qualify, and delivering the assistance more flexibly and efficiently. By identifying policy standards for entry to the program rather than tying aid disbursements to promises for specific policy reforms, the Millennium Challenge Account serves as a pull instrument for development. Well governed countries that have already introduced policies that will benefit their country and region are thus rewarded with larger and more flexible assistance flows.

Challenge programs could be a first step toward designing distinct aid delivery approaches for different countries, depending on the quality of their governance and policy structure. Approaches could differ by size of flows, formulation as program (including budget support) or project support, role of recipient countries in setting priorities and designing programs and projects, reliance on governments or NGOs as implementing partners, and other aspects. If the Millennium Challenge Account succeeds, other donors may establish their own challenge programs. Ideally, donors would agree on the eligibility standards for such programs so that programs reinforced each other with a consistent message to recipients.

More differentiated strategies would allow donors to tailor aid delivery instruments more closely to the strengths and weaknesses of recipient countries, making aid more efficient and effective. Such strategies would also introduce more of a pull structure across the continuum of aid delivery instruments, rewarding countries that have better policies and stronger governance with more flexible and larger amounts of aid, without tying the aid to specific reform measures.

NOTES

1. The notion of country selectivity is based on research by Isham, Kaufmann, and Pritchett (1995); Burnside and Dollar (2000); and Collier and Dollar (2002) that

indicates that aid has a stronger relationship with growth in countries with stronger policies and institutions. The robustness of the results of the last two studies has recently been questioned, however (Easterly, Levine, and Roodman 2004). Clemens, Radelet, and Bhavnani (2004) find that subcategories of aid aimed primarily at growth have a positive impact on growth across all countries, but they find some evidence that the relationship is stronger in the presence of good institutions.

2. Under sectorwide approaches all significant government and donor funding for a sector supports a single sector policy and expenditure program, with the government leading the policymaking and implementation. Common approaches are adopted across the sector by all funding parties (government and donors), with increasing reliance on government procedures to disburse and account for donor funds. For further readings on sectorwide approaches in the health area see www.eldis.org/healthsystems/aid/#swaps.

3. Available to eligible borrowers from the International Development Association, the Poverty Reduction Support Credit is a quick-disbursing lending instrument. Uganda, Vietnam, and Burkina Faso are countries that have been approved for such lending (www.worldbank.org/ida).

4. See www.mca.gov/about_us/overview/index.shtml.

5. By July 2005 Honduras, Cape Verde, and Nicaragua joined Madagascar with signed compacts. For updates on the Millennium Challenge Account recipient countries, see the section on press releases on the MCC web site: www.mca.gov/public_affairs/press_releases/index.shtml. For independent updates and analysis see the Center for Global Development's MCA Monitor at www.cgdev.org.

6. For more detail on the qualification process, see Radelet (2003) and MCC (2004c,d).

7. The "Washington Consensus" is a term originally coined by John Williamson (1990) to summarize the set of 10 policy reforms that most of official Washington thought was the appropriate basis for reform in developing countries, including fiscal discipline, tax reform, trade and capital account liberalization, privatization and deregulation, and secure property rights. It has come to be used as a synonym for neoliberalism or market fundamentalism, although that was far from Williamson's intent.

8. However, in the case of Madagascar, the first Millennium Challenge Account recipient country, the $110 million compact was for four years. For further details see www.mca.gov/compacts/madagascar.shtml.

9. Madagascar (four years, $110 million), Cape Verde (5 years, $110 million), Honduras (5 years, $215 million), and Nicaragua (5 years, $175 million). See www.mca.gov/compacts.

10. The Global Alliance for Vaccines Immunization (GAVI) is a global public-private partnership that brings together governments in developing and industrial countries, established and emerging vaccine manufacturers, NGOs, research institutes, the United Nations Children's Fund (UNICEF), the World Health Organization (WHO), the Bill & Melinda Gates Foundation, and the World Bank. Through its

Vaccine Fund, GAVI provides financial resources to countries to purchase vaccines and other supplies and to support the operational costs of immunization. For further information, see www.vaccinealliance.org. The Global Fund is a global public-private partnership between governments, civil society, the private sector, and affected communities, and its purpose is to attract, manage, and disburse resources to fight AIDS, tuberculosis, and malaria. It does not implement programs directly, relying instead on the knowledge of local experts. For further information, see www.theglobal-fund.org.

11. See www.kresge.org/programs/index.htm.

12. See www.epa.gov/ecocommunity/sdcg.

13. See www.ed.gov/programs/techinnov/index.html.

14. See www.landcareaustralia.com.au.

15. Project aid has some practical advantages, even if it is inefficient. Overseers of donor budgets—parliamentarians and members of congress—like to be able to connect at least some of their money to specific activities. Moreover, project aid is less susceptible than program aid to politicized charges that the money was diverted to something else (such as a presidential airplane), even though the fungibility of money means that in reality there may be little difference between the two modes.

16. The figure is for 2005 and expressed in 2003 dollars. See www.worldbank.org/ida.

17. Collier (2002) likens these to an expenditure-side version of an Independent Revenue Authority. He describes six features of the independent service authority, suggesting that it would:
- Be autonomous from government with high standards of accountability to donors.
- Have an incentive system for its staff that motivates them to achieve the objectives of the donors (for example, in terms of health and education outcomes).
- Act as a "wholesaler" through which donors would channel their funds to "retail" providers of services.
- Contract with retail providers for a flow of services rather than pump-priming a project.
- Serve as a channel for funds, ideally equivalent to prior levels of spending on the services it would provide.
- Serve as a channel for all donor funding to the country for basic health care, primary education, or whatever it is providing.

REFERENCES

ADB (Asian Development Bank). 2001. "Policy on Performance-Based Allocation for Asian Development Fund Resources." Manila. [www.adb.org/Documents/Policies/ADF/Performance_Based_Allocation/Performance_Based_Allocation.pdf].

AfDB (African Development Bank). 2004. "Performance-Based Allocation of Resources." Presentation at Strategic Partnership with Africa (SPA) 6 Meeting, January 20–21, Tunis. [www.spa-psa.org/resources/pdf/jan04_plenary/present/quarcoo_afdb.pdf].

Brainard, Lael, Carol Graham, Nigel Purvis, Steven Radelet, and Gayle Smith. 2003. *The Other War: Global Poverty and The Millennium Challenge Account.* Washington, D.C.: Brookings Press and Center for Global Development.

Burnside, Craig, and David Dollar. 2000. "Aid, Policies, and Growth." *American Economic Review* 90 (4): 847–68.

Clemens, Michael, Steven Radelet, and Rikhil Bhavnani. 2004. "Counting Chickens When They Hatch: The Short-Term Effect of Aid on Growth." CGD Working Paper 44. Center for Global Development, Washington, D.C.

Collier, Paul. 1997. "The Failure of Conditionality." In Catherine Gwyn and Joan Nelson, eds., *Perspectives on Aid and Development.* Washington, D.C.: Overseas Development Council.

————. 2002. "Making Aid Smart: Institutional Incentives Facing Donor Organizations and Their Implications for Aid Effectiveness." Forum Series on the Roles of Institutions in Promoting Growth, Forum 2: The Institutional Economics Approach to Aid Effectiveness, Session on Incentives within Donor Organizations, February 25, Washington, D.C.

Collier, Paul, and David Dollar. 2002. "Aid Allocation and Poverty Reduction." *European Economic Review* 45 (1): 1–26.

Easterly, William. 2001. *The Elusive Quest for Growth: Economists' Adventures and Misadventures in the Tropics.* Cambridge, Mass.: MIT Press.

Easterly, William, Ross Levine, and David Roodman. 2004. "Aid, Policies, and Growth: Comment." *American Economic Review* 94 (3): 774–80.

Isham, Jonathan, Daniel Kaufmann, and Lant Pritchett. 1995. "Governance and Returns on Investment: An Empirical Investigation." Policy Research Working Paper 1550. World Bank, Washington, D.C. [http://econ.worldbank.org/files/619_wps1550.pdf].

MCC (Millennium Challenge Corporation). 2004a. "Guidance for Developing Proposals for MCA Assistance in FY 2004." Washington, D.C.

————. 2004b. "The Millennium Challenge Corporation Names MCA Eligible Countries." Washington, D.C.

————. 2004c. "Report on Countries that are Candidates for Millennium Challenge Account Eligibility in FY 2004 and Countries that Are Not Candidates Because of Legal Prohibitions." Washington, D.C.

————. 2004d. "Report on the Criteria and Methodology for Determining the Eligibility of Candidate Countries for Millennium Challenge Account Assistance in FY 2004." Washington, D.C.

OECD (Organisation for Economic Co-operation and Development). 2004. "Modest Increase in Development Aid in 2003." Paris.

Radelet, Steven. 2003. *Challenging Foreign Aid: A Policymakers Guide to the Millennium Challenge Account.* Washington, D.C.: Center for Global Development.

Williamson, John. 1990. "What Washington Means by Policy Reform." In *Latin American Adjustment: How Much Has Happened?* Washington, D.C.: Institute for International Economics.

World Bank. 1998. *Assessing Aid: What Works, What Doesn't, and Why.* Washington, D.C.

————. 2001. "World Bank Group Work in Low-Income Countries Under Stress: A Task Force Report." Washington, D.C.

————. 2003a. "Allocating IDA Funds Based on Performance: Fourth Annual Report on IDA's Country Assessment and Allocation Process." Report 27082. Washington, D.C.

————. 2003b. "IDA's Performance-Based Allocation System: Current and Emerging Issues." Washington, D.C. [http://siteresources.worldbank.org/IDA/Resources/MTRPBA.pdf].

Overcoming Coordination and Attribution Problems

Meeting the Challenge of Underfunded Regionalism

Nancy Birdsall

Global public goods—such as biodiversity preservation and improved management of international financial flows—have received considerable attention in recent years. Regional public goods—such as cross-border roads, dams, gas pipelines, power grids, and other physical infrastructure and multicountry measures to manage shared watersheds—have been relatively neglected, however.

Although many potential cross-border and other regional investments promise high returns, only very limited resources are currently spent on the provision of regional public goods. Thus regional public goods are probably undersupplied and underfunded in the developing world. This undersupply no doubt reflects the collective-action problems that beset public goods in general, including the problem of free-riding. However, regional public goods in the developing world face three additional challenges of coordination, attribution, and incentives.

First, producing regional infrastructure and goods and services and managing multicountry institutions require coordination among two or more governments. That is a tall order in the developing world, where the institutions of government are often poorly financed and staffed. The coordination problem is essentially a problem of underdevelopment and a challenge to national capacity building.

Second, the attribution of benefits to different countries is not straightforward, and thus how to share the costs of investing in regional goods is problematic. This attribution problem also discourages donors from supporting regional investments, especially given donors' strong country orientation and focus on country "ownership."

The author thanks William Cline, Alan Gelb, Todd Moss, and Steven Radelet for guidance and comments on an earlier version; Gunilla Pettersson and Sandip Sukhtankar for excellent help on the difficult task of finding, assessing, and organizing the limited data; and Barbara Lee and Rae Liu for help on finding rates of return information. This chapter is based on Center for Global Development Working Paper 49, available at www.cgdev.org/docs/WP%2049_1.pdf.

Third, because of these issues of coordination and attribution, both donors and recipient countries may view regional public goods as less desirable than national projects, which involve less complexity and hence less risk and uncertainty. Donors probably also perceive regional projects as less attractive than global public goods initiatives. Taxpayers in rich countries are more likely to be interested in helping Brazil and China minimize greenhouse gas emissions, which generates benefits for them as well, than in mounting a regional attack against Chagas disease, found only in Latin America, which would provide smaller and only indirect global benefits. These and other related factors contribute to the problem of incentives.

FUNDING OF REGIONAL INITIATIVES

Regional public goods are likely to call for financial inputs from a variety of actors: several national governments, intergovernmental organizations (notably when the public good affects developing countries), private actors (such as businesses), and perhaps even civil society organizations. However, the focus here is on foreign aid allocations to regional public goods.

For decades the principal recipients of official development assistance have been individual developing countries. This has shaped the system of statistics related to development assistance, including that of the Development Assistance Committee of the Organisation for Economic Co-operation and Development (OECD). There is thus no easy way of determining how much development assistance is allocated to regional initiatives.

Three different approaches were used here to estimate the share of development assistance going to purposes related to regional public goods. The first approach starts with the OECD's estimates based on donors' reports of the sectoral allocation of their annual commitments. Donors have agreed on the "sectors" for which their commitments would be classified as regional public goods or global public goods. The choice of sectors reflects a certain willingness to overstate rather than understate support for regional (and global) programs. This broad sectoral data set captures any support that might have spillover effects into neighboring countries. For example, support for waste management, road transport, and education/training are classified as regional public goods, even if all the support goes to a single country.[1] Based on these official donor-defined data, about 15 percent of all official development assistance during 1997–2001 went to support regional public goods (table 1).[2]

A second, narrower approach applies a stricter definition of a regional public good, limiting it to projects with clear transborder properties, such as regionwide air transport, river development, rail transport, protection and pest control, flood prevention and control, and support to institutions with regionwide activities. Even though this approach still requires considerable guessing about whether the support for these initiatives went to more than one country, it reduces

TABLE 1

Three estimates of regional public goods commitments by all donors as a share of total commitments to all developing countries, 1997 and 2002
(percent)

Data source	1997	2002
OECD Creditor Reporting System, broad sectoral set[a]	23.9	14.9
OECD Creditor Reporting System, strict sectoral set[b]	5.8	2.7
Bottom-up estimate[c]	—	3.4

— is not available.

a. Includes health policy and administrative management; medical education and training; medical services; health education; health personnel development; population and reproductive health; water resources policy and administrative management; education and training for water supply and sanitation; water resources protection; water supply and sanitation, large systems; river development; waste management and disposal; postconflict peace building (United Nations); demobilization; land mine clearance; reconstruction relief; road transport; rail transport; transport policy and administrative management; water transport and storage; education and training in transport and storage; communications policy and administrative management; telecommunications; radio, television, and print media; plant and postharvest protection and pest control; flood prevention and control; environmental education and training; rural development; aid to refugees (in recipient country); and support to local and regional nongovernmental organizations.

b. Includes water resources protection, river development, rail transport, air transport, plant protection and pest control, flood prevention and control, and support to local and regional nongovernmental organizations.

c. The sum of donor financing to the soft windows of the Inter-American Development Bank, the African Development Bank, and the Asian Development Bank plus donor commitments to regional programs and projects for selected donors (see table 2).

Source: Author's estimates based on OECD 2004 and Reisen, Soto, and Weithöner 2004.

the amount of development assistance for regional public goods to about 6 percent for 1997 and to less than 3 percent for 2002 (see table 1).

A third, bottom-up approach is to sum up disbursements to regional projects as shown in the annual reports and other publications of development agencies and institutions.[3] "Regional programs and projects" are often defined as those in which more than one country is legally engaged as a beneficiary, either for the specific program or project (such as the Greater Mekong Subregion program in Asia and the Puebla–Panama project in Latin America[4]), or as a member of a regional institution in which all other members are also aid recipients, such as the New Partnership for Africa's Development (NEPAD). To this it makes sense to add bilateral donor contributions to the soft windows of the regional development banks, although this inflates spending on regional programs and projects since the regional development banks spend only 0.4–2.7 percent of their resources on such activities.[5] When these contributions, which amounted to $1.3 billion in 2002, are added to the regional development bank commitments of $788 million, donor financing for regional programs in 2002 totals about $2 billion, or more than 3 percent of total donor commitments of $61.5 billion that year (table 2).

Table 1 shows the estimates of the share of development assistance spent on regional public goods using the three different approaches. Based on what are probably more realistic estimates (the strict sectoral set and the bottom-up

TABLE 2

Estimated commitments to regional programs and projects by selected multilateral and bilateral donors in 2002

Donor	Regional public goods commitments (millions of U.S. dollars)	Regional public goods commitments as share of total commitments (percent)
World Bank[a]	—	—
African Development Bank	30	1.2
Inter-American Development Bank[b]	20	0.4
Asian Development Bank[c]	45	0.7
European Bank for Reconstruction and Development[d]	99	2.7
United Nations Development Programme[e] (2001)	55	2.1
World Health Organization (1998/99)	138	7.1
United States[f]	303	2.4
United Kingdom[f]	98	2.6
Subtotal	788	—
Bilateral contributions to soft windows of regional development banks	1,300	—
Total	2,088	3.4

— is not available.

Note: Unless otherwise stated, data are for 2002. To the extent possible, commitments are for programs and projects managed by a regional organization such as the West African Monetary Union or the Central American Development Bank, regardless of the source. Commitments are expressed in nominal terms when reported by various sources.

a. The World Bank *Annual Report,* unlike those of the Inter-American Development Bank, the African Development Bank, the European Bank for Reconstruction and Development, and the Asian Development Bank, does not include a line item showing annual commitments to regional programs and projects.

b. In addition to regional commitments the Inter-American Development Bank also reports regional disbursements, which totaled $67 million in 2002. In the past it has also made concessional loans to the Central American Bank for Economic Integration and to other subregional development banks.

c. Regional commitments reflect one project only, the Trade Finance Facilitation Program.

d. This is the capital of six private equity or debt funds established to invest in or lend to private firms across two or more countries.

e. The United Nations Development Programme also granted $9.5 million for interregional and global projects in 2001 (and $16 million for intercountry programs in 2000).

f. These figures are probably inflated since they cover all "unspecified funds" going to a region and are likely to include funds that in fact went to individual countries.

Source: World Bank 2002; AfDB 2003; IDB 2003; ADB 2002; EBRD 2003; UN 2002; WHO 1999; USAID 2004;UK DFID 2004.

approach), between 3 percent and 4 percent of official development assistance goes to regional public goods.

Is this spending level adequate? Probably not. There are many areas in which regional cooperation and the provision of regional public goods could be improved, with potentially high social returns on investments.

Potential Gains from Enhanced Provision of Regional Public Goods: the Case of Sub-Saharan Africa

While examples of potentially good investments in enhancing the provision of regional public goods could be found in many regional groupings, Sub-Saharan Africa, as the poorest of all regional groupings, deserves special attention. Twenty-five of the 31 "top priority" countries (those that the United Nations has determined require urgent action to meet the Millennium Development Goals) are in Sub-Saharan Africa (UNDP 2003, p. 44). And this despite more than a decade of being the main recipient of development assistance. Clearly, more than the usual pattern of development assistance is required if the region is to achieve accelerated progress and meet the Millennium Development Goals on the targeted dates.

Thus, it is particularly noteworthy that Sub-Saharan Africa has characteristics that make the potential returns to further investments in regional public goods especially high. The region has a large number of small economies, with many at-the-border barriers and behind-the-border disparities (such as in policy approaches, norms, and standards) that impede economic activity. Strengthened regional cooperation could be an important force facilitating further development.

Addressing the small-economy challenge
Market size affects the potential for specialization and the ability of investors to achieve the economies of scale required to be competitive in global markets. Sub-Saharan Africa's economy as a whole is large enough (about the size of the economy of the Russian Federation) to support some specialization and scale investments. Were it fully integrated into a single market, Sub-Saharan Africa's economy would be close to the size of Chicago's (table 3). But the region's "internal" market is in fact highly divided among 48 countries, many of them very small indeed. Malawi's economy is approximately one one-hundredth the size of Sweden's. Even the largest economies—South Africa, Nigeria, and Sudan—are still relatively small. South Africa's economy is less than a third the size of Ohio's (or the Netherlands'). Imagine Chicago's economy with more than 40 different sets of tariffs and customs inspection systems, without any effective transport system linking its neighborhoods, and with legal barriers to citizens of one neighborhood working in another one.

The small size of the market in Sub-Saharan Africa inhibits investments in manufacturing and services that require minimum scale to be efficient and competitive. With most countries confined to producing primary goods and so without much value added or specialization, there is in turn little scope for intraregional trade. In 2003 trade within Africa was estimated at 10.2 percent of the entire region's trade, compared with 16 percent for Latin America and 50 percent for Asia (WTO 2004). South Africa was an exception, with 16 percent of its exports going to the region (IMF 2003). This dearth of intraregional trade both reflects and reinforces the lack of specialization and resulting lack of comple-

TABLE 3

Gross domestic product of selected countries, regions, states, and cities, 2001
(billions of U.S. dollars)

Region, country, or state	GDP
Netherlands	380
Ohio, United States[a]	374
Chicago[b]	349
Russian Federation	310
Sub-Saharan Africa	301
Sweden	210
Hong Kong	162
South Africa	113
Egypt	99
Peru	54
Nigeria	41
Sudan	13
Malawi	2

a. Refers to gross state product, which uses a similar methodology in calculation as the gross domestic product (GDP).
b. Refers to gross metropolitan product, which uses a similar methodology in calculation as the GDP.
Source: UNDP 2003 (pp. 278–81); for Ohio and Chicago, U.S. Bureau of Economic Analysis 2003 (table 3).

mentary demand across countries (Yeats 1998). In 2003 about 69 percent of Africa's exports were primary products, compared with 42 percent for Latin America and 14 percent for Asia (WTO 2004).

Small economies also imply that there are significant benefits to be derived from building regional (and more integrated) infrastructure networks, including for power and transport. Africa probably has the least-cost hydroelectric energy sources of any continent in the world.[6] But without shared electricity grids, energy use remains inefficient—producing $1 of output in Africa requires more energy than anywhere else in the world (UNECA 2004b, p. 137). High power costs keep local industries less competitive than they could be and hobble export diversification. In transport the opportunity cost of the lost network externalities in sea and air transport, because of the political difficulty of arranging efficient hubs (some countries would lose, requiring compensating transfers), is also high.[7]

Reducing the costs of many borders
Simply put, borders inhibit trade (McCallum 1995; Wei 1996). Sub-Saharan Africa copes with higher border costs than any other region, particularly when the off-

setting benefits of larger coast to land ratios and greater inland river access of other regions are taken into account. The region has an estimated 134,000 kilometers of national borders, more than half noncoastal.[8] By comparison, Europe has more borders overall (almost 200,000 kilometers), but fewer than 10 percent are non-coastal. It also has greater penetration of navigable rivers, as does the United States.[9] Estimated transit costs, including transport and insurance, are as high as 56 percent of the value of exports for Malawi, 36 percent for Uganda, and 25 percent or higher for eight other countries (in a sample of 14 countries) in a study by the United Nations Conference on Trade and Development (UNCTAD 2001, p. 4).[10]

Weak and nonintegrated transport infrastructure contributes heavily to these costs. An estimated 28 percent of multicountry highways in countries in the Economic Community of West African States are dysfunctional (called "missing links"), according to the United Nations Economic Commission for Africa (UNECA 2004a, p. 135). Estimated missing links in other regional groupings in Africa range from 14 percent in the East African Community to 47 percent in the Economic Community of Central African States.

Sub-Saharan Africa also suffers from extensive nongeographical barriers that add to border costs. Problems at the border include customs bribery and bureaucracy and legal and regulatory differences across markets. Fixing these problems requires institutionally demanding reforms within countries and complex policy harmonization between countries. The same is true for facilitating interconnectivity in telecommunications, energy, and transport systems.

In sum, Sub-Saharan Africa illustrates the high cost of political and geographic borders, especially for the small and landlocked economies in the region, and the related problem of small, poorly integrated economies.[11] Yet the economic disadvantage of many and costly borders can be overcome. Sub-Saharan Africa's situation suggests the potentially high returns to policy adjustments and new investments—in cross-border, multicountry infrastructure and in institutional integration—that would reduce the cost of borders. Those investments would also help to address the many other pressing development problems in Africa, including conflict, HIV/AIDS, and the high disease burden associated with tropical climates, that often require multicountry efforts to resolve.

Similar points could be made for economies in other parts of the world. Because almost all developing country economies are smaller than any industrial country economy (China and India are notable exceptions), regionalism ought to feature more prominently on the development agenda. One could even argue that lack of regional cooperation and integration adversely affects national-level aid and overall development effectiveness. Indeed, what is the right balance in different regions and subregions between national and regional projects is in itself an important question to explore.

Meanwhile, however, the evidence suggests that regional investments can generate high rates of return in Africa and elsewhere in the developing world where donor financing is important (box 1). (In Africa, where regional investments seem particularly attractive, donors are financing as much as half the government budgets in some countries and an even higher percentage of public investment.[12]) That raises the question of why donors have not been more engaged in financing regional programs and regional public goods.

DONOR FINANCING FOR REGIONAL PUBLIC GOODS

Regional public goods ought to be attractive to national governments and the international development community. So why is such limited development assistance being spent on such concerns?

Like other public goods, regional public goods tend to suffer from collective-action problems. But regional public goods that require both cooperation among developing countries and development assistance inputs encounter additional problems of coordination, attribution, and incentives.

The coordination challenge

Producing regional infrastructure and goods and services and managing multi-country institutions require coordination among two or more governments. Countries have to negotiate and agree on how much of the desired regional public good to provide, at what net cost or benefit and to whom, and who is expected to do what within a given time frame. Countries also need to decide on either close cooperation or more decentralized implementation.

That is a tall order, particularly in the developing world, where the institutions of government are often poorly financed and staffed. Also, it requires analytical capacities, for example, to undertake cost-benefit analyses that could help to estimate the net gain from a proposed regional project for all involved countries and for individual countries and how these gains compare with those of other potential projects. These analyses are complex yet indispensable for determining policy priorities and for enabling interventions to be seen not just as deserving highest attention but also as being just, generating a significant and fair net gain for all.

Ironically, recent donor reforms that focus on fostering and respecting developing country ownership of the programs supported by foreign aid do not help in this respect. Ownership is more difficult to achieve when more than one country is involved, and this difficulty probably multiplies rapidly as more than two countries are involved. In addition, aid recipients are increasingly subjected to various monitoring and assessment procedures, such as of their progress toward meeting the Millennium Development Goals (see, for example, the United Nations Development Programme's country reports on the Millennium Development Goals[13] and the World Bank's *Global Monitoring Reports*[14]). In fact, since the end of the cold war the donor community has become more focused on (and more transparent about) the need to ensure that aid goes to countries where it is most

Box 1
INVESTMENTS IN REGIONAL PUBLIC GOODS CAN YIELD HIGH RETURNS

Only about 3–4 percent of official development assistance goes to improving the provision of regional public goods. Yet the regional public goods that get financed tend to generate impressive returns. Consider the following examples:

The Southern Africa Power Pool. Created in 1995, the Southern Africa Power Pool (SAPP) is the first formal international power pool outside of North America and Western Europe. By integrating the power markets of its 12 member countries and taking advantage of economies of scale, SAPP is expected to generate net gains of $1.7 billion over the period 2000–16.

Baltic Sea clean-up. Because of an excessive supply of phosphorous, nitrogen, and other nutrients, eutrophication has been degrading the Baltic Sea and its coastline. The cost of reducing the nutrient load has been estimated at $4 billion a year. The nine affected Baltic countries have expressed a willingness to pay about $6 billion a year, thus suggesting a benefit-cost ratio of 1.5.

Controlling onchocerciasis. More commonly known as river blindness, onchocerciasis is the world's second leading infectious cause of blindness. In 1974 the World Health Organization launched the Onchocerciasis Control Program in 11 West African countries, in collaboration with the World Bank, the United Nations Development Programme, and the Food and Agriculture Organization. The program operated with an annual cost of less than $1 per person, and the annual rate of return was estimated at 20 percent, mainly due to increased agricultural output.

Controlling Chagas disease. Chagas disease is endemic in Latin America, affecting 14 countries. It affects 16–18 million people, and some 100 million people (about 25 percent of the population of Latin America) are at risk of acquiring it. Based on the benefits from reduced illness and savings in medical costs, the estimated rates of return are more than 64 percent for Argentina and 30 percent for Brazil alone. From 1975 to 1995 the government of Brazil invested more than $420 million in Chagas disease control, yielding benefits of well over $3 billion—or a return of about $7 for each $1 invested.

Note: The World Bank has economic rate of return data for only three regional infrastructure investment projects in Africa over the period 1979–92, although more data are available on single country projects (personal communication with World Bank staff, October 2004).
Source: Bowen and others 2003; Markowska and Zylicz 1999; Levine and the What Works Working Group 2004; Dias, Silveira, and Schofield 2002.

likely to be effective in fostering growth and reducing poverty (see, for example, the Development Assistance Committee's *Development Cooperation Reports*[15] and the chapter by Radelet in this volume). Donor reforms that encourage country ownership and country performance are consistent with country-focused approaches though not necessarily regional programming.

In short, recent donor reforms do not systematically encourage regional programs. They do not address the immense difficulties aid recipient countries face in cooperating among themselves or the resulting limits to their effective demand for financing of regional programs. Donor support aimed at strengthening developing countries' national capacity to cooperate regionally or globally receives surprisingly little attention, despite all the discussion about increased globalization and regionalization and the growing interdependence among countries.

The strong country focus of the current system of development assistance has its roots in the cold war era, when foreign aid often served as a foreign policy instrument to help bring or keep developing countries in either the Soviet or the Western bloc. Clearly, a change in focus would now be desirable. The aid system of the future should not only foster better linkages among interventions at the national, regional, and global levels but should also help countries strengthen their national capacity to cooperate.

The challenge of attribution

The challenge of attribution also follows from the country focus of the foreign aid system. For regional activities that are self-financed by the participating countries, the attribution of benefits and costs is part of the coordination challenge. For initiatives that involve donor funding, however, attribution creates an additional barrier to negotiating and managing an investment. This is particularly the case for the donor agencies involved.

For instance, the main instrument of the largest multilateral donor, the World Bank, is a loan to a single recipient government that must "guarantee" its repayment. As a result, the culture of the World Bank reflects its longstanding experience in supporting country-based programs. Only recently has this begun to change, with the use of its soft window (loans that in principle do not need such a guarantee) and its limited grant facility for global and regional programs.[16]

For much the same reason, the regional development banks have concentrated mostly on country-based loans and programs, despite their roots in a "regional" mission. This is the case even for the Inter-American Development Bank (IDB), which has long made fostering regional integration a high priority.[17] Only in late 2004 did the IDB board approve a new program of grant financing for regional programs, and this amounts to only $10 million a year of annual lending commitments of some $6 billion a year in 2003.[18]

For multilateral banks the attribution issue has in effect made lending to groups of developing countries for regional programs much more difficult than lending for single-country programs, since the borrowers must first agree among themselves on their respective debt obligations. This limited availability of grant financing has discouraged their greater involvement. And even though grant financing eliminates some of the problems of coordination and attribution, truly regional initiatives are rare. Many so-called regional programs are in essence a cluster of country programs.

Bilateral donors also face complications in developing and supporting multicountry programs, in both their loan and their grant activities. This hesitant use of the regional programming modality by all donor groups may also be related to donors' need for a single interlocutor who can be held accountable for managing a program. And multicountry programs pose the risk of a weak link in the chain of effectiveness. For example, a major program with the Southern African Development Community could be hurt if donors felt the need to cut off all aid to one participating country. The challenge of cooperation among recipients makes regional initiatives and their financing not only costlier for donors because of the higher transaction costs but also riskier in terms of their sustainability and ultimate results.

The incentive challenge

The current country focus of aid is also reflected in—and reinforced by—the lack of a clear sense of what organizational form regional projects could take. Implementation may take place at the country level or in a "regional" institution or both. It has been argued that regional development banks enjoy a comparative advantage as catalysts of collective action at the regional level through their ability to bring together potential participants, generate and transfer knowledge, provide assistance during negotiations, and transfer funding (Ferroni 2004). However, in fact, regional initiatives are being implemented through many different institutional arrangements. Regional projects receive external support from bilateral donors and from global as well as regional multilateral institutions. They are implemented by governments and often through public-private partnerships involving philanthropic foundations and other nonstate actors.[19] In short, many donors and government agencies are involved in providing some financing and supporting some management services for regional public goods, yet no one has a clear mandate. Regional public goods lack a "constituency."

Regional public goods share with many global public goods some of the uncertainty related to the "right" organizational form to provide them and in addition often lack the donor championship that global public goods enjoy. They are sometimes seen as remote and detached from the donor countries' self-interest, though some regional public goods (forestry preservation and development, for example) can generate important positive externalities beyond the regional level. Also, when regional public goods are severely undersupplied and impede development, poverty may become extreme and spill across borders into the global public domain.

The cause of the failure to see some of these spillover effects is often the same as the cause of the failure to see the links between national and regional public goods: the lack of credible cost-benefit analysis. Among donors and creditors, the early logic of estimating ex ante rates of return for infrastructure projects (taking into account shadow prices and so on) had by the 1980s yielded to a less technical and more practical calculus as financing for social programs (with less easily quantified benefits) became acceptable.[20] Moreover, for many donors, budget support has become the favored mode of development assistance. The implicit recognition is that differing priorities about public spending across sectors have to be resolved within countries through the political system and that only if the resulting priorities are "owned" locally will spending on them be sustained and effective. However, individual, national priority setting is unlikely to generate a strong demand for regional, cooperative initiatives—unless the general public is convinced that such initiatives would contribute significantly to their welfare and well-being. In the absence of detailed, issue-specific cost-benefit analyses, such a conviction is difficult to form. Hence regional initiatives may be sidelined both by developing countries' public and policymakers and by the donor community.

Thus lack of information, coupled with acute awareness of the coordination and attribution challenges facing such initiatives, leads to a lack of incentives to try them—despite the intuition that important development opportunities may remain untapped.

POLICY OPTIONS

If, as Kanbur (2003) also concluded, the international aid architecture, including its underlying incentive structures, is not conducive to funding multicountry initiatives, what can be done?

To better support regional (and perhaps also global) initiatives, aid policy reform would need to aim at three main objectives: strengthening regional institutions and national capacity for regional cooperation—to address the coordination challenge; creating new financial instruments to encourage regional programs without compromising accountability standards—to address attribution problems; and demonstrating that national economic growth and development often depend on the adequate provision of transnational, multicountry public goods—to address the incentive challenge.

Addressing the coordination challenge

Strengthening regional institutions and national-level capacity for international cooperation has to be a priority. The impetus is already there, as evidenced by the recent formation of the New Partnership for Africa's Development, the Macroeconomic and Financial Management Institute of Eastern and Southern

Africa, and the longstanding success of the Southern African Customs Union, all of which clearly have African ownership.[21]

The donor community also has an interest in strengthening genuine regional institutions, especially in Africa, because they are likely to form the backbone for high-return projects in reducing poverty and managing disease and other regional burdens and because they may also constitute the means for the region to participate in the production of global public goods. Regional bodies such as the United Nations Economic Commission for Africa and the African Development Bank could soon achieve the influence of their counterparts in Asia and Latin America, given the tremendous increase in the last few decades in the number of highly trained Africans.

There are several promising areas in which to begin a gradual shift of the current aid system from one with a strong country focus to one that offers greater possibilities for support of multicountry initiatives. In trade, African policymakers have clear incentives to move quickly, even unilaterally, to reduce the high costs they impose on themselves by maintaining barriers to free trade. The region would be immensely better off without the complications of a dozen trade agreements, all but three of them with no more than two or three members.[22] Resources to manage their customs institutions and harmonize their border arrangements ought to be a high priority for external financing in the context of discussions in the Doha Round of trade negotiations.

The principal priority, however, should probably be the financing of multicountry physical infrastructure. As already mentioned, the cost of borders is extremely high in Africa, an outcome of colonial investment patterns directed at European trade and post-independence underinvestment in physical infrastructure. Infrastructure development is an area where the need for regional cooperation is substantial and constrained more by lack of resources than of capacity.

Yet most donors (the International Development Association and the European Union are exceptions) have largely withdrawn from this domain in favor of the social sectors. Now, they could come back. Bringing in public resources to match and leverage possible private sector financing could make resulting joint endeavors more sustainable and successful, following the lessons of the first round of public-private partnerships in support of infrastructure development. Donors might also consider increasing their financing of the African Development Bank, enabling it to manage a much greater volume of regional infrastructure programs, using the kind of performance-based measures that the United States linked to incremental financing of the International Development Association in a recent replenishment.[23]

Addressing the attribution challenge

The multilateral development banks may have a much larger potential role in the financing of regionalism than can now be realized. They have all defined the issues well in regional strategy documents. Their critical constraint is the lack of an appropriate instrument that would allow them to use their existing capital to finance regional programs. Financing of regional initiatives to date has had to come mostly from concessional lending resources and from highly limited grant resources.

The bilateral donors could take the lead, especially in the regional banks, in creating new financial mechanisms to encourage regional lending. For example, they could promote greater use of net income to finance regional initiatives. Since that would affect the borrowing costs of middle-income countries, these countries would need more influence in setting the priorities for using such resources.[24] Bilateral donors could also develop facilities to finance guarantees for regional group borrowing from the multilateral development banks or on the private market or to subsidize the borrowing costs to individual countries participating in regional borrowing. The Development Assistance Committee of the OECD should require reporting on such support for regional programs and projects, a step that could advance progress on lending for regional public goods.

In addition, both bilateral and multilateral donors should examine the institutional innovations that have made some multicountry initiatives possible already, with an eye toward expanding their use. For example, a number of regional projects have been set up as public-private partnerships, with the private sector partners responsible for the financing and each government paying the special project vehicle (such as a concessionaire) a fee for services rendered. The Africa Trade Insurance Agency is an example of such an arrangement (see also the chapter by Kaul on global public-private partnerships in this volume).[25]

Addressing the incentives challenge

There is a need to demonstrate more clearly the potential net benefits of enhanced provision of regional public goods, such as those described in box 1, to persuade more national and international actors to consider regional initiatives and undertake the needed reforms to the current system of foreign aid. Even more helpful would be estimates of the distribution of the expected net benefits by country and even by population groups (along the lines suggested in the chapter by Conceição and Mendoza in this volume).

Such studies would make it possible to show what underprovision of these goods costs in terms of lost regional development opportunities and how severe underprovision could eventually create negative spillovers for the world, including donor countries. Witness, for instance, the international migration and refugee pressures that emerge as a result of conflict and insecurity. Between 1983 and 1991 the costs of administering asylum procedures and providing social welfare benefits to refugee claimants for a sample of 13 industrial countries increased from $500 million to $7 billion (UNHCR 1995, p. 199). Where feasible and appropriate, these types of externalities from severe underprovision could also be considered in cost-benefit analyses.

To improve statistics for longer term cost-benefit and comparative analysis, the donor community could establish common reporting requirements for all donors and creditors on their support for various regional programs and projects through the Development Assistance Committee of the OECD. Such reporting could also exert peer pressure on donors not to free ride on other donors by giving preference to bilateral and country-focused aid projects and sidelining regional or other multicountry initiatives.

Conclusion

All types of public goods suffer from a certain amount of free-riding and other collective-action problems, but three additional sets of problems afflict regional public goods, leading to their underfunding in developing country regions: lack of national and regional capacity to coordinate, the traditional country focus of the current foreign aid system, and the absence of both the strong recipient-country demand from which national public goods benefit and the donor self-interest from which global public goods often benefit. Tackling these challenges by enhancing the provision of regional public goods is important, both to accelerate development, especially in Sub-Saharan Africa, and to foster global progress and development more generally.

Notes

1. This refers to the OECD (2004) Creditor Reporting System, as explained and used by Reisen, Soto, and Weithöner (2004).

2. Global public goods received about 16 percent during the same period (Reisen, Soto, and Weithöner 2004).

3. Yet another approach would be to compile the annual disbursements of all creditors and donors to regional projects, but it would still be difficult to make a complete list of such projects and their financing. A partial listing of such projects can be found for the World Bank (World Bank 2004a).

4. For further information on these two programs, see www.adb.org/GMS/default.asp and www.iadb.org/ppp.

5. The donors also have capital paid in to back the hard windows of the regional development banks, but these amounts are a stock not an annual flow, and as discussed in this study, the hard windows provide loans that are not conducive to financing regional programs.

6. Hydropower from the Inga River in the Democratic Republic of the Congo could supply the growing electricity needs of all of southern Africa for the next seven years at 2 cents per kilowatt hour, according to World Bank staff (personal correspondence 2003).

7. Alan Gelb, World Bank chief economist for Africa, personal correspondence.

8. These figures (perhaps calculated for the first time) are from Sandip Sukhtankar. More detailed information can be obtained from him (ssukhtankar@brookings.edu) as well as from the author.

9. This is a point made by Adam Smith to explain England's domination of world trade into the twentieth century (Smith [1776] 2003, book 1, ch. 3, pp. 27–32).

10. These numbers are also reported in UNECA (2004a), which attributes these costs to "noncompliance and incomplete implementation of bilateral and multilateral agreements" (p. 141).

11. This group includes Burkina Faso, the Central African Republic, Chad, Ethiopia, Malawi, Mali, Niger, Uganda, Zambia, and Zimbabwe.

12. In 1999 donors financed more than half of central government expenditure in countries including Madagascar, Senegal, Sierra Leone, and Uganda (World Bank 2004b). They supply 40 percent or more of public resources in at least 30 developing countries, including Bolivia and Nepal (World Bank 2003, pp. 260–61). Since most donor financing is for investment, not operational costs or recurrent spending, it is clear that donors are financing the majority of public investment in countries relying heavily on aid.

13. See www.undp.org/mdg/countryreports.html.

14. For a list of these reports go to "Global Monitoring" at www.worldbank.org/html/extdr/thematic.htm

15. For a complete list of Development Cooperation Reports see www.oecd.org/findDocument/0,2350,en_2649_33721_1_119687_1_1_1,00.html.

16. See Birdsall and Rojas-Suarez (2004) and Ferroni (2004). The concessional window does not need the recipient government's guarantee, which has made financing of some regional projects possible—though such projects do require an agreement between at least two recipient governments on sharing the costs of borrowing.

17. The Inter-American Development Bank reports disbursements of ordinary capital of $1.98 billion to regional programs and projects over the period 1961–2002, while total commitments over the four decades were about $2.5 billion (IDB 2003, pp. 52–53).

18. Annual lending commitments are reported in IDB (2004a, p. 11). For further information on the Regional Public Goods Initiative see IDB (2004b).

19. See Birdsall (2004) for several examples of regional programs financed by separate country loans from multilateral banks. Reisen, Soto and Weithöner (2004) cite Sagasti and Bezanson (2001) on this point.

20. For investments in "public goods" such as education, rural roads, or strong property rights, credible cost-benefit analysis is impeded by the difficulty of measuring positive and negative externalities. The issue is well known in the case of education, for which private but not public returns to investments can be calculated. As a result there has long been debate about the right proportion of investment in primary and higher education, for example. The unmeasured benefits of each associated with

such externalities as the effects of primary education on mothers' and children's health and the effects of higher education on effective nation building, makes comparison of their relative social returns impossible (Birdsall 1996).

21. For a review of another half dozen African regional institutions, see USITC (2003).

22. Author's analysis based on Global Coalition for Africa, Economic Committee (2001, tables 1 and 2).

23. The United States agreed to increase its contribution to the International Development Association by $300 million during the 13th replenishment, subject to certain performance targets (see IDA 2002).

24. That marginal increase in influence would in itself be healthy, and consistent with the view that large emerging market economies are underrepresented in the multilateral banks (and the International Monetary Fund), given their increased share of the world economy.

25. See www.ati-aca.com.

REFERENCES

ADB (Asian Development Bank). 2002. *Annual Report 2001 Highlights.* Manila.

———. 2004. "Greater Mekong Subregion." Abidjan. [www.adb.org/GMS/default.asp].

AfDB (African Development Bank). 2003. "Statistical Appendix." *Annual Report.* Abidjan.

Birdsall, Nancy. 1996. "Public Spending on Higher Education in Developing Countries: Too Much or Too Little?" *Economics of Education Review* 15 (4): 407–19.

———. 2004. "Underfunded Regionalism in the Developing World." CGD Working Paper 49. Center for Global Development, Washington, D.C.

Birdsall, Nancy, and Liliana Rojas-Suarez, eds. 2004. *Financing Development: The Power of Regionalism.* Washington, D.C.: Center for Global Development.

Bowen, Brian H., Frederick T. Sparrow, Zuwei Yu, and Geoff Granum. 2003. "Benefits to South Asia from an Integrated Electricity Market Infrastructure." Paper presented at the South Asia Regional Initiative in Energy Training Program, July 19–23, Dhaka.

Dias, João Carlos Pinto, Antonio Carlos Silveira, and Christopher John Schofield. 2002. "The Impact of Chagas Disease Control in Latin America." *Memorias do Instituto Oswaldo Cruz* 97 (5): 603–12. [www.ovcnet.uoguelph.ca/popmed/ecosys/zoonoses/Chagas-Review.pdf].

EBRD (European Bank for Reconstruction and Development). 2003. "Financial Report." *Annual Report.* London.

Ferroni, Marco. 2004. "Regional Public Goods: The Comparative Edge of Regional Development Banks." In Nancy Birdsall and Liliana Rojas-Suarez, eds., *Financing Development: The Power of Regionalism*. Washington, D.C.: Center for Global Development.

Global Coalition for Africa, Economic Committee. 2001. "Regional Integration in Sub-Saharan Africa, Toward Rationalization and Greater Effectiveness." Report GCA/EC/02/4/2001. Pretoria. [www.gcacma.org/RegionalIntegation.htm].

IDA (International Development Association). 2002. "Additions to IDA Resources: Thirteenth Replenishment. Supporting Poverty Reduction Strategies." Washington, D.C. [http://siteresources.worldbank.org/IDA/Resources/ IDA13Report.pdf].

IDB (Inter-American Development Bank). 2003. *Annual Report 2002*. Washington, D.C.

———. 2004a. *Annual Report 2003*. Washington, D.C.

———. 2004b. "IDB Launches Call for Proposals to Promote Regional Public Goods September 15 to November 15." Press Release. Washington, D.C. [www.iadb.org/NEWS/Display/PRView.cfm?PR_Num=182_04&Language=English].

IMF (International Monetary Fund). 2003. *Direction of Trade Statistics*. Washington, D.C.

Kanbur, Ravi. 2003. "Cross-Border Externalities, International Public Goods, and Their Implications for Aid Agencies." In Lourdes Benería and Savitri Bisnath, eds., *Global Tensions: Challenges and Opportunities in the World Economy*. New York and London: Routledge.

Levine, Ruth, and the What Works Working Group with Molly Kinder. 2004. *Millions Saved: Proven Successes in Global Health*. Washington, D.C.: Center for Global Development.

Markowska, Agnieszka, and Tomasz Zylicz. 1999. "Costing an International Public Good: The Case of the Baltic Sea." *Ecological Economics* 30 (2): 301–16.

McCallum, John. 1995. "National Borders Matter: Canada-U.S. Regional Trade Patterns." *American Economic Review* 85 (3): 615–23.

OECD (Organisation for Economic Co-operation and Development). 2004. "Development Assistance Committee Creditor Reporting System." Paris. [www.oecd.org/dataoecd/50/17/5037721.htm].

Reisen, Helmut, Marcelo Soto, and Thomas Weithöner. 2004. "Financing Global and Regional Public Goods through ODA: Analysis and Evidence from the OECD Creditor Reporting System." OECD Working Paper 232. Organisation for Economic Co-operation and Development, Paris.

Sagasti, Francisco, and Keith Bezanson. 2001. *Financing and Providing Global Public Goods: Expectations and Prospects*. Stockholm: Institute of Development Studies and Ministry for Foreign Affairs of Sweden.

Smith, Adam. [1776] 2003. *The Wealth of Nations*. New York: Bantam Books.

UK DFID (Department for International Development). 2004. *Statistics on International Development 99/00–03/04*. London: Crown.

UN (United Nations). 2002. *Annual Report of the Administrator for 2001, Including the Results-Oriented Annual Report (ROAR)*. Statistical Annex. Executive Board of the United Nations Development Programme and of the United Nations Population Fund. DP/2002/15/Add.2. New York.

UNCTAD (United Nations Conference on Trade and Development). 2001. "Transit Systems of Landlocked and Transit Developing Countries: Recent Developments and Proposals for Future Action." TD/B/LDC/AC.1/17. New York. [www.unctad.org/en/docs//tbldcac1d16.en.pdf].

UNDP (United Nations Development Program). 2003. *Human Development Report 2003: Millennium Development Goals—A Compact among Nations to End Human Poverty*. New York: Oxford University Press.

UNECA (United Nations Economic Commission for Africa). 2004a. *Assessing Regional Integration in Africa*. ECA Policy Research Report. Addis Ababa. [www.uneca.org/aria/].

———. 2004b. *Economic Report on Africa 2004: Unlocking Africa's Trade Potential*. Addis Ababa. [www.uneca.org/era2004/].

UNHCR (United Nations High Commission on Refugees). 1995. *The State of the World's Refugees: In Search of Solutions*. New York: Oxford University Press. [www.unhcr.ch/cgi-bin/texis/vtx/publ?id=3ef99a814].

USAID (United States Agency for International Development). 2004. "US Overseas Loans and Grants." Washington, D.C. [http://qesdb.cdie.org/gbk].

U.S. Bureau of Economic Analysis. 2003. "Gross State Product by Industry for 2001: U.S. Economic Slowdown Widespread." News Release. U.S. Department of Commerce, Washington, D.C. [Accessed November 7, 2004, from www.bea.gov/bea/newsrelarchive/2003/gsp0503.pdf].

USITC (United States International Trade Commission). 2003. *U.S. Trade and Investment with Sub-Saharan Africa*. Fourth Annual Report. Washington, D.C.

Wei, Shang-Jin. 1996. *Intra-National versus International Trade: How Stubborn Are Nations in Global Integration*. NBER Working Paper 5531. Cambridge, Mass.: National Bureau of Economic Research.

WHO (World Health Organization). 1999. "Proposed Programme Budget for 2000–2001—Implementation of Resolution EB103.R6: Report by the Secretariat." Geneva.

World Bank. 2002. *Annual Report*. Vol. 2. *Financial Statements and Appendixes*. Washington, D.C.

———. 2003. *World Development Report 2004: Making Services Work for Poor People*. Washington, D.C. and New York: World Bank and Oxford University Press.

———. 2004a. "Projects Database." Washington, D.C. [www.worldbank.org/projects].

————. 2004b. World Development Indicators Database. [http://worldbank.org/data/].

WTO (World Trade Organization). 2004. *International Trade Statistics 2004*. Geneva. [www.wto.org/english/res_e/statis_e/its2004_e/its04_toc_e.htm].

Yeats, Alexander J. 1998. "What Can Be Expected From African Regional Trade Arrangements? Some Empirical Evidence." Policy Research Working Paper 2004. World Bank, Washington, D.C.

REDUCING THE COSTS OF HOLDING RESERVES
A NEW PERSPECTIVE ON SPECIAL DRAWING RIGHTS

JACQUES J. POLAK AND PETER B. CLARK

The First Amendment of the International Monetary Fund's (IMF) Articles of Agreement[1] (adopted in 1969) created a new facility, the Special Drawing Rights (SDRs) Account, that could issue a new type of international asset to compensate for shortfalls in the traditional reserve assets. The problem that the facility was intended to solve (the potential shortage of international reserves) vanished soon after the facility was created, with the shift to a floating exchange rate regime for the major currencies. International liquidity was further improved by the growth in international capital markets, which facilitated borrowing by creditworthy governments.

Allocations of SDRs ceased more than two decades ago, but the SDR facility could be resuscitated if there were a convincing rationale for doing so. This chapter argues that there are strong reasons to resume regular allocations of SDRs, an argument that follows on the recent advocacy of such allocations by the "Report of the High-Level Panel on Financing for Development" (UN 2001)[2] and George Soros (2002) in *On Globalization,* among others.

In recent years increasing attention has focused on the high cost to the majority of IMF members—those with no ensured access to the world's capital markets—of holding an adequate and secularly increasing amount of reserves. The IMF urges its members—and indeed, in the context of financial arrangements, requires them—to hold a stock of reserves that can protect them against balance of payments shocks without on every occasion having to negotiate a credit from the IMF. But for countries with no access to international capital markets or access only at interest rates far higher than the London interbank offered rate (LIBOR), acquiring and maintaining such reserves is costly and competes with the need for real capital.[3] Is there something that the IMF can do to reduce this cost?

The authors thank Graham Hacche for helpful comments on an earlier draft.

SDR allocations could reduce the costs for these members without imposing corresponding costs on other members. SDRs could do so because they are a monetary asset issued by the IMF and because the creation of money for which there is a demand to hold creates "seigniorage."[4] But the amount of seigniorage is limited by the demand (or absorptive capacity) for this type of money, thus constraining the extent to which the IMF can use the SDR facility to relieve the cost of holding reserves for its weaker members.

This chapter begins by recalling the original reasons for the introduction of the SDR mechanism at the end of the 1960s and the radical changes in the international monetary system since then that invalidated these reasons. It then looks at the evidence of the long-run increase in the demand for reserves by the great majority of IMF members and provides an indication of the high cost that many countries incur by holding a secularly increasing stock of such reserves. Next it considers the benefits and feasibility of a resumption of SDR allocations motivated by a new purpose: to take advantage of the fact that SDR allocations make the acquisition and holding of additional reserves costless for any country that receives an allocation. It further examines whether some of the original features of the SDR mechanism may need to be changed to serve this new objective and presents some tentative ideas on the magnitude of the allocations that could prudently be envisioned.[5]

THE CREATION OF THE SDR: TO MEET THE "SHORTAGE OF INTERNATIONAL LIQUIDITY"

The introduction of the SDR was the culmination of a massive intellectual and negotiating effort that occupied financial policymakers for most of the 1960s (box 1). It was designed as a definitive solution to a problem that had threatened the international monetary system since the end of World War I: the fear that the potential inadequacy of international liquidity might hamper the growth of the world economy. If countries collectively could not obtain sufficient reserves to meet the balance of payments deficits that they were likely to encounter from time to time, they would feel the need to throttle down the growth of their economies. And if many countries adopted such precautionary measures, the world economy might stagnate.

In recognition of this risk international negotiations that stretched over a six-year period, from 1963 to 1969, resulted in an agreed international solution: the creation of an international asset that (unlike gold or reserve currencies) would have no other function than to serve the need of the system for an adequate but not excessive quantity of international reserves. For this purpose a new facility was established in the IMF that was authorized, under strict safeguards against abuse, to create and annul ("allocate" and "cancel") a new form of reserve asset, with the awkward name of "Special Drawing Right." In accordance with its intended func-

Box 1

SPECIAL DRAWING RIGHTS

Special Drawing Rights (SDRs) are international reserve assets that the IMF is authorized to create when it considers that there is a long-term global need to supplement existing reserve assets. The IMF creates SDRs by "allocating" them to the SDR Accounts of its members. Allocations are made to members in proportion to their quota shares in the IMF. Decisions to allocate SDRs have been made only twice. The first allocation, distributed in 1970–72, was for SDR 9.3 billion. The second, distributed in 1979–81, was for SDR 12.1 billion, and brought the cumulative total to SDR 21.4 billion.

Under a proposed Fourth Amendment of the Articles of Agreement, a special one-time allocation of SDRs was approved by the Board of Governors of the IMF in September 1997. It would double cumulative SDR allocations to SDR 42.9 billion, with the new allocation distributed across the membership not in proportion to current quotas but to achieve cumulative allocations for each member that would be the same proportion of its 1997 quota. In this way the special allocation was designed to correct for the fact that countries that joined the IMF after 1981—more than one-fifth of the current membership—had never received an SDR allocation. This change in the distribution requires an amendment of the Articles of Agreement, and any amendment needs to be approved by three-fifths of IMF members with 85 percent of the total voting power. Because the United States, with 17 percent of the total voting power, has not yet approved the amendment, it has not yet been put into effect and the special allocation is still on hold.

Holders of SDRs can use them to make payments to other members and to the IMF. They can sell their SDRs for dollars or other freely usable currencies to other members, through voluntary exchanges or through IMF arrangements "designating" members with strong external positions to purchase their SDRs. In the last 20 years, designation by the IMF has not been necessary.

Members pay interest on their cumulative allocations and receive interest, at the same rate, on the SDRs. Thus, to the extent that a member continues to hold the SDRs allocated to it, it bears no net cost on this part of its reserves. If a member's SDR holdings rise above its allocation, it earns interest on the excess, and if its holdings fall below allocations, it pays net interest on the shortfall.

The IMF calculates the value of the SDR every day as the sum of the market values of specified amounts of four currencies: euro, pound sterling, U.S. dollar, and yen. It determines the SDR interest rate on a weekly basis as the weighted average of the market interest rates on short-term instruments in the same four currencies.

Source: IMF 2005b.

tion, the SDR would circulate in the official circuit only: it could be held only by governments, central banks, the IMF, and a narrowly defined group of other "official holders."

The creation of the SDR was not accompanied by the abolition of gold and reserve currencies as reserve assets (official discussions to this effect surfaced only later). But the future incremental role of these traditional reserve assets in official reserves was expected to be minor. Newly produced gold was expected to be absorbed almost entirely in industry and art, and the United States was expected to take any steps necessary to prevent foreign official holdings of dollars from increasing by more than modest amounts annually, lest diminishing confidence in the dollar lead to massive conversions into gold.

But in fact, a few months after the first allocation of SDRs was made on January 1, 1970, the assumption with respect to the supply of dollars proved to be wrong. In the course of 1970, U.S. Treasury securities held by nonresidents (essentially, foreign central banks) nearly doubled, from $10.3 billion to $19.8 billion, and in 1971 they more than doubled again, to $46.3 billion (Clark and Polak 2004, p. 55). Once the United States moved off gold in August 1971, protection of the gold stock ceased as a consideration for the prevention of an excessive flow of dollars into foreign reserves.

August 1971 also saw the beginning of the end of the par value system and the start of a movement toward floating exchange rates. In theory, truly floating exchange rates should dispense with the need for reserves and thus should do away with any problem of a shortage of international liquidity from the demand side. But empirical studies of the effect of floating on countries' actual reserve policies in the 1970s suggest that its impact was at most small.[6] The spread of floating since then has been accompanied by persistently large increases in world reserves. But the main impact of floating on the problem of international liquidity was not that it may have brought a modest reduction in the demand for reserves by many countries. Rather, it was that it liberated the United States from concern about the magnitude of the claims on its economy held by one category of foreign holders—central banks.

As a result of this fundamental change in the international monetary system, the concept of "international liquidity" has changed totally from that prevailing at the time the SDR was introduced. Two of the three components of international reserves have almost entirely ceased to function in that capacity. Gold is no longer a monetary asset. Even many of the most conservative central banks are in the process of selling their gold holdings in the market. The stock of SDRs has become very small relative to total reserves (about 1 percent), and SDRs have become almost exclusively a vehicle for transactions between the IMF and its members.

Consequently, the principle in the IMF Articles of Agreement that the allocation of SDRs should "meet the long-term global need, as and when it arises, to supplement existing reserve assets" can no longer serve as a guide for allocating

SDRs in the manner in which those words were interpreted in 1969. Any case for future allocations of SDRs will have to be based on grounds other than the need of the system as a whole for additional liquidity. Instead, "need" will have to be interpreted in terms of other benefits to the system, in particular the benefit of permitting low-income countries to acquire and hold reserves at a much lower interest rate than they would have to pay in the market and a reduced dependence of the system on borrowed reserves that are liable to be recalled when they are most needed.

THE DEMAND FOR RESERVES AND THE COST OF HOLDING THEM

Since international reserves are used primarily to finance external imbalances, the level of reserves that countries find necessary to hold would be expected to be fairly closely related to the factors that affect the magnitude of those imbalances. One relevant scale variable is the level of trade in goods and services. The ratio of reserves to imports of goods and services shows an upward trend for emerging markets and developing countries, but not for industrial countries (figure 1), which are closer to being pure floaters and can access the world capital markets when they need additional financial resources.

Moreover, as painfully brought home by recent crises in a number of emerging market economies, countries also need reserves to meet sudden changes in

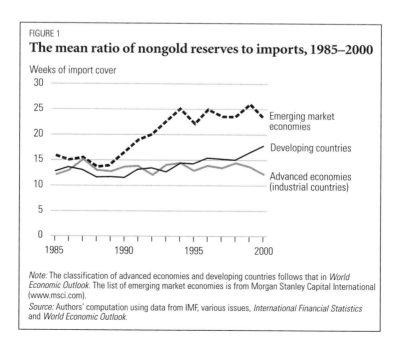

FIGURE 1

The mean ratio of nongold reserves to imports, 1985–2000

Weeks of import cover

Note: The classification of advanced economies and developing countries follows that in *World Economic Outlook*. The list of emerging market economies is from Morgan Stanley Capital International (www.msci.com).

Source: Authors' computation using data from IMF, various issues, *International Financial Statistics* and *World Economic Outlook*.

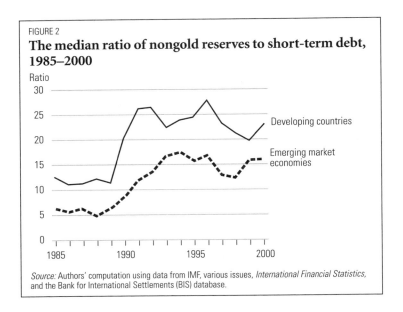

FIGURE 2

The median ratio of nongold reserves to short-term debt, 1985–2000

Source: Authors' computation using data from IMF, various issues, *International Financial Statistics,* and the Bank for International Settlements (BIS) database.

capital movements. Accordingly, the ratio of reserves to short-term debt may be another key indicator of reserve adequacy. This ratio also rose sharply in the early 1990s (figure 2).

The secular expansion of trade and the increased exposure to disturbances in the capital account that comes with greater financial openness are thus making it necessary for the nonindustrial countries, on average, to add substantial amounts to their reserves. The IMF has encouraged this tendency, urging members to pay greater attention to the need to hold sufficient reserves to reduce external vulnerability.

Holding reserves is costly for countries that have to pay high premiums above LIBOR to attract funds from the world's capital markets. It is even more costly for countries that have no access to these markets and for which the acquisition of $10 million in reserves implies sacrificing $10 million in consumption or investment. Only a general order of magnitude can be given of the costs of the reserves held by the nonindustrial countries collectively, but it is clear that the cost is very high. Considering that the cost of borrowing for emerging market economies has averaged 800 basis points above LIBOR over the past decade,[7] and absent any realistic estimates of the interest costs for countries without access to capital markets, an annual interest rate of 10 percent would almost certainly underestimate the cost of holding reserves for these two groups of countries.[8]

At the end of 2002 nonindustrial countries together held nongold reserves equal to about $1.5 trillion. Just over half of this amount was held by five economies in Asia (China, Taiwan Province of China, Republic of Korea, Hong

Kong SAR, and Singapore), whose reserves were probably at least in part a reflection of their "fear of floating," in particular their fear of currency appreciation.[9]

But even the poorest countries—those eligible for Poverty Reduction and Growth Facility loans from the IMF—collectively held about SDR 90 billion in reserves at the end of 2002, at an implied cost of more than $10 billion for that year.[10] Rough as they are, these figures suggest that these countries could benefit significantly from a mechanism that could alleviate the cost of holding reserves. Fortunately, such a mechanism already exists: the SDR facility introduced more than 30 years ago.

When an IMF member country receives an allocation of SDRs, it has to pay the SDR interest rate (about 2.46 percent[11]) on the amount received. If it keeps the SDRs in its reserves, it earns interest on them at the same rate. Thus, the cost of holding SDRs in an amount equal to the addition to a country's reserves from an SDR allocation is zero. And if the member uses the SDRs received to acquire reserve assets that have a somewhat higher yield than the SDR—for example, because of a somewhat longer maturity—the member may be able to hold this part of its reserve portfolio at a modest net profit.

Although the SDR mechanism is available, no allocations have been made for more than two decades, and there is no indication that there will be a sufficient majority of members in favor of an allocation (85 percent of the total voting power in the Board of Governors) in the foreseeable future. This is not surprising, considering that the problem that motivated the introduction of the SDR (a potential global shortage of international liquidity) no longer prevails and that the countries with high credit ratings can easily and cheaply obtain credit from the world's capital markets. (A "one-time special allocation" that was agreed unanimously by the Board of Governors in 1997, which differs in some respects from the "general allocations" envisioned in the Articles of Agreement and therefore requires an amendment to the Articles, has not yet taken place because the amendment still lacks ratification by the United States needed to achieve 85 percent of the total voting power.[12])

Thus, the development of the world monetary system since the introduction of the SDR in 1970 has put the grand design of that innovation—making the SDR the "principal reserve asset in the international monetary system" (Article VIII, Section 7)—out of reach, at least for the time being. Although the industrial countries no longer have a direct financial interest in SDR allocations, there nonetheless remains a strong case for them to use the SDR mechanism to help less wealthy members hold an adequate stock of reserves. In recent years, the industrial countries have spent about $70–$80 billion a year on aid to developing countries, a good part of it to increase these countries' real capital assets (OECD 2004, 2005). But an adequate stock of international reserves, which would help to insulate countries from the damaging effects of balance of payments disturbances, is just as important to development as are roads and factories. And while assisting countries to acquire physical assets is expensive and competes with pressing domestic needs in the donor countries, assisting countries to build up their reserves through the existing SDR mechanism can, if properly managed, be costless. Furthermore, to the extent that a developing country pays less for its reserves or increases them because they have become cheaper, the country reduces the credit risk of its commercial and official lenders.

This satisfactory outcome is predicated on the assumption that resumed allocations do not increase the total stock of SDRs beyond the point at which this stock is willingly held at the SDR interest rate. In that respect the proposal presented here differs from those sometimes made to use SDR allocations to achieve massive transfers of real resources for development assistance, the provision of global public goods, or debt relief.[13]

A FRESH LOOK AT THE SDR

Should the international community wish to use the SDR to facilitate the acquisition of sufficient reserves by low-income countries—an objective barely considered when the SDR was created—all aspects of the SDR mechanism should be reconsidered from the perspective of this new objective. The identification here of the features of the facility that may need to be changed does not at this stage address the question of whether any changes that appear desirable would require amendment of the Articles of Agreement, though that could become an important consideration.

One question relating to the Articles of Agreement needs to be mentioned, however. Article XVIII requires that allocations of SDRs "meet the long-term global need... to supplement existing reserve assets." If the members of the IMF accept the desirability of resuming the regular allocation of SDRs, they will have to decide whether "long-term global need" includes the need of a large part of the membership to increase their reserves as the scale of their international transactions increases or whether such action would require amendment of Article XVIII. IMF staff have generally favored the former approach, that is, that no amendment would be required. The case for the Fourth Amendment, on the other hand, was based in part on the opinion of some members that "long-term global need" in the sense of Article XVIII no longer existed.

Changes in the use of SDRs

Two of the original features of the SDR that were once considered extremely important are no longer operative. "Reconstitution"—each member's obligation to hold on average a certain proportion of the SDRs allocated to it—was abolished in 1980. And "designation"—the process by which the IMF directed the SDRs that some members wanted to sell to other members that had a sufficiently strong external position and relatively low holdings of SDRs—survives on a contingency basis only, since there are enough members willing to buy on a voluntary basis the moderate amounts of SDRs on offer.

With these two changes the SDR has shed a large part of its original *dirigiste* character. Contrary to the intentions of the drafters of the First Amendment, each member can now, in practice, decide on the amount of SDRs it wants to hold in its reserves. And while the 20 or so industrial countries were expected to hold more than 100 percent of their SDR allocations, only a handful of them do so (Germany, Japan, Norway, Portugal, and the United States among them). In recent years the largest holders of SDRs in proportion to their allocations are all to be found outside of the industrial world—as of April 2005 these included Singapore (which holds 1,160 percent of its allocation), Libya (816 percent), Botswana (796 percent), Paraguay (632 percent), Argentina (513 percent), Lebanon (487 percent), Kuwait (448 percent), Iraq (432 percent), and China (348 percent).[14]

Not contrary to the original expectations, many developing countries hold only a small part of their SDR allocations, but not (in the great majority of cases) because they have "spent" their allocations on additional imports. This is clear from the fact that their total reserves have increased well in excess of their allocations. The substitution of other reserve assets for SDRs must therefore be viewed as a portfolio choice, perhaps induced by the fact that reserve currencies, but not SDRs, can be used for direct interventions in exchange markets.[15]

The low interest rate that countries have to pay on SDR allocations reduces their cost of holding reserves, whether these reserves are held in SDRs or in other assets. To the (modest) extent that this makes these countries better off, they will be able to afford additional imports or to borrow on better terms in world capital markets.

Allocation to all members or to low-income members only?

If one concentrates on the benefits that SDR allocations can convey to nonindustrial countries, the most important issue to be decided is whether allocations should go to these countries only or to the entire membership, as envisaged under the present Articles of Agreement. Yaqub, Mohammed, and Zaidi (1996) argue that it is clearly suboptimal to create SDRs for countries that would not benefit from them and that have shown their lack of interest by consistently opposing the resumption of general allocations. The reduction in the size of allocations that would result from leaving out, roughly speaking, the industrial countries would, moreover, mitigate any potential long-term risk of creating more SDRs than the membership would collectively want to hold.

Allocation to the membership as a whole, on the other hand, would be in line with the original conception of the SDR mechanism. It would be more powerful in reducing the systemic risk to the international monetary system because SDRs are a permanent addition to the world's stock of reserves (except in the unlikely event of a decision to cancel outstanding SDRs), while reserves obtained by borrowing in capital markets may be recalled in the very circumstances when they are most needed.

Little weight should be given to the argument that parallel allocations to industrial countries are necessary to create additional "acceptance obligations" to ensure that members wanting to sell their newly acquired SDRs find buyers. With "designation" having become inoperative, members have become accustomed to determining themselves what proportion of reserves they want to hold as SDRs. Thus it seems unlikely that there would be broad support for the resumption of general allocations if that included a strong likelihood of the reactivation of the designation provisions.

A narrower allocation would, in any event, make the need for designation more remote. But one could envisage other ways to promote, and even ensure, balance between the supply and demand for SDRs. These could include creating an arrangement under which commercial banks might (in effect) hold SDRs and choosing a market rate of interest for the SDR that would balance supply and demand.[16]

The concept of a focused allocation also raises the question of how to select the countries that would be eligible to receive SDRs. Yaqub, Mohammed, and Zaidi (1996) suggest that, to qualify, a member would need to be eligible for assistance from the Enhanced Structural Adjustment Facility (now the Poverty Reduction and Growth Facility) and the International Development Association *or* have a credit rating below investment grade (or no rating at all), and have reserves below 50 percent of annual imports. They estimate that countries eligible by these criteria would account for only 16 percent of the total IMF quotas.[17] They also suggest that some of these countries might choose to opt out of allocations, perhaps in the belief that this would enhance their credit standing.

Any criteria this general would exclude, for no persuasive reason, some countries that believe that they would benefit from an SDR allocation. While there may be an advantage in narrowing SDR allocations to a set of countries accounting for, say, 25 percent of quotas, further narrowing them to a set of countries accounting for 20 percent or 15 percent of quotas would not likely be worth pursuing. Accordingly, if the benefits of an allocation concentrated on part of the membership were judged to outweigh the disadvantages, the simplest criterion would most likely carry the day: each member would choose whether to be included in allocations, with the choice made for a "basic period" of three or five years.

In form, therefore, the wording for participation in the special one-time allocation might well suffice (paragraphs 1 and 4 of Schedule M of the Fourth Amendment): "1. Subject to 4 below, each…participant…shall receive an allocation of SDRs…. 4. The Fund shall not allocate SDRs under this Schedule to those participants that have notified the Fund in writing prior to the date of the allocation of their desire not to receive the allocation."

In substance, however, an allocation intended to be restricted to the less affluent IMF members would require a prior understanding by the richer members that they would opt out of the allocation. Various definitions of richer members could be considered, such as per capita income, participation in the New Arrangements to Borrow,[18] or membership in the Organisation for Economic Co-operation and Development.[19]

One provision of the Fourth Amendment that differs from the existing Articles of Agreement, but indicates the prevailing view of the membership, is that an allocation for a member with overdue obligations in any of its accounts with the IMF will be kept in escrow until arrears in all IMF accounts are cleared. This provision should probably become part of any decision to resume allocations. It deviates from the principle in the current Articles of Agreement of separation between the General Resources Account and the SDR Account, which permits crediting an allocation to a member's SDR Account even though it has accumulated arrears in its General Resources Account.[20]

SOME OBSERVATIONS ON THE SIZE OF RESUMED ALLOCATIONS OF SDRs

The magnitude of the first round of SDR allocations (1970–72) was based on a forecast of the desired growth of global reserves, an estimate of the amount of gold becoming available for reserves, and what was believed to be an acceptable growth of reserves in the form of U.S. dollars. Given the fundamental changes in the international monetary system that have taken place in the intervening period, any such approach would no longer makes sense.

The primary focus should now be not on the total amount to be allocated but on the degree to which the rising demand for reserves of the nonindustrial world should be met by SDR allocations. The Articles of Agreement specify that allocations should be the same percentage of quotas for all members that participate in the allocation. This provision reflects the important principle that the size of a member's allocation should not be based on the strength or weakness of its payments position at the time of the allocation. That principle deserves to be preserved. The IMF's conditional credit mechanism is available to assist individual members when they require assistance tailored to their actual situation.

No simple formula could select that common percentage of quotas to be allocated to all nonindustrial members. (The same percentage would apply to industrial countries if they shared in the allocation, but because the benefit to them of an allocation would be marginal at most, the percentage chosen is of less importance to them.)

It would be useful to compare for each nonindustrial country alternative percentages of quota, for example 5 percent, 10 percent, and 15 percent, with the expected medium-term trend of their demand for reserves. These trends could be calculated on the basis of projections of trade and either historical or normative figures on reserves as a percentage of annual imports.

The common percentage of quota selected for allocations should not be so low as to make the exercise irrelevant nor so high as to provide much more than the amount that a significant part of the membership is prepared to hold as additions to their reserves. The percentage should also be low enough not to undermine the conditionality that the IMF applies in granting conditional credit. That credit is also measured as a percentage of quotas per year, with the current maximum for most forms of IMF credit set at 100 percent of quota per year.[21] The 5 percent, 10 percent, and 15 percent shares suggested as hypothetical choices for annual SDR allocations would appear to be far enough below that maximum to avoid any serious threat to the conditionality of IMF credits.

With so many considerations affecting the choice of an allocation percentage, not to mention the basic choice of whether to resume regular allocations at all, the selection of a percentage to be allocated will inevitably contain a large political element. Being aware of that in advance may temper any disappointment with the decision later.

Conclusion

The resumption of regular allocations of SDRs would make a substantial contribution to both the equity and the efficiency of the international monetary system, and it would thus have important qualities of a global public good. Equity would be served by enabling developing countries to acquire much needed reserves at a lower cost than they pay now. As noted above, the self-insurance cost for the poorest developing countries could amount to more than $10 billion a year—roughly 13–14 percent of total net official development assistance in recent years. Under current arrangements the proportionate cost of holding an adequate stock of reserves is much higher for the poorest developing countries than for the industrial countries with access to cheap credit from world capital markets.

Regular allocations also contribute to the efficiency of the system, by making it more robust against financial crises. Reserves in the form of SDRs, unlike reserves borrowed from world capital markets, are not at risk of recall whenever a wave of anxiety hits the system. The assurance of a crisis-proof supply of reserves would strengthen the system and promote both growth and development, for the benefit of industrial and developing countries alike.

Notes

1. See www.imf.org/external/pubs/ft/aa/index.htm.

2. Also known as the "Zedillo Report," after the Chairman of the Panel, Ernesto Zedillo.

3. LIBOR is the interest rate that the largest international banks charge each other for loans.

4. Seigniorage is the profit that results from the difference in the cost of printing money and the face value of that money.

5. For a more extensive discussion of international liquidity and development of the SDR since its inception in 1970, see Clark and Polak (2004).

6. See Clark and Polak (2004, pp. 57–60) for a discussion of these studies.

7. Based on authors' calculations of JP Morgan Chase emerging market bond index (Brady narrow) sovereign spread from 1992 to 2002.

8. Ten percent is the rate the Organisation for Economic Co-operation and Development uses as the demarcation between concessional and nonconcessional lending.

9. Reserves were $291 billion for China, $162 billion for Taiwan Province of China, $115 billion for Hong Kong SAR, $121 billion for the Republic of Korea, and $82 billion for Singapore (IMF, *International Financial Statistics*). For a recent analysis of the reserve-holding behavior of emerging market economies, in particular in Asia, see Edison (2003).

10. Based on an average exchange rate of 0.7 SDR = $1 for 2003, SDR 90 billion is about $129 billion.

11. The SDR interest rate is the weighted average of the interest rates on short-term liquid claims in the four reserve currencies: the euro, pound sterling, U.S. dollar, and yen. The figure cited is for the week of May 23–29, 2005. See www.imf.org/external/np/fin/rates/sdr_ir.cfm.

12. See www.imf.org/external/np/sec/memdir/eds.htm.

13. Soros (2002) has proposed using part of the SDRs created under the Fourth Amendment, as well as subsequent annual allocations, as a trust fund to finance the provision of global public goods and possibly other development assistance activities. There were also proposals to use allocations of SDRs to finance debt relief. For a discussion of these proposals, see Boughton (2001) and UN (1999).

14. The figures are as of April 30, 2005 (IMF 2005c).

15. There will always be some countries for which the opportunity cost of holding reserves is so high that even modest SDR allocations will exceed the secular increase in their demand for reserves (which may be close to zero), inducing them to spend most or all of any allocations they receive. For example, of all members that received allocations in 1969–71, 10 held smaller total reserves in 1989 than in 1969 (IMF, *International Financial Statistics*). Six of these were among the 11 countries that were in arrears to the IMF in 1989 (IMF 1989). Countries with overdue obligations to the IMF will not receive their allocations under the special one-time allocation agreed by the Board of Governors in 1997. (By 2003 the number of members in arrears had been reduced to six.)

16. Both of these modifications to the current SDR regime might be introduced without amendment because:

- Commercial banks cannot, under the current Articles, be accepted as "other holders." Neither can the Special Disbursement Account of the IMF. However, the IMF found a way around this prohibition. The Bank for International Settlements (BIS), a prescribed "other holder," holds SDRs "on behalf of" the IMF (IMF 1994, p. 145). Commercial banks should have no difficulty constructing a similar arrangement, if they were interested.

- The IMF currently sets the SDR interest rate as a weighted average of the market interest rates for short-term paper in the four currencies that make up the SDR (see note 10). It could presumably also set it at a market-determined rate for the SDR itself. If commercial banks held balances of SDR deposits with the BIS, an interbank market in these deposits could be developed, and hence an SDR LIBOR rate.

17. For a discussion of their calculations, see Yaqub, Mohammed, and Zaidi (1996, p. 212).

18. The New Arrangements to Borrow are a set of credit arrangements between the IMF and 26 member countries and institutions to provide supplementary resources to the IMF to help respond to financial instability. For further details, see IMF (2005a).

19. Under Article XVIII, Section (2) (e) (i), though not under paragraph 4 of Schedule M, a member cannot opt out unless it also voted against the allocation. Unless this condition is removed, a proposal to allocate could not be adopted if members holding more than 15 percent of total quotas intended to opt out.

20. Members' quota subscriptions make up the General Resources Account, which is the main source of most IMF lending.

21. For a discussion of access to IMF credit, see, for example, IMF (2004).

References

Boughton, James M. 2001. *Silent Revolution: The International Monetary Fund 1979–1989.* Washington, D.C.: International Monetary Fund.

Clark, Peter B., and Jacques J. Polak. 2004. "International Liquidity and the Role of the SDR in the International Monetary System." *IMF Staff Papers* 51 (1): 47–71.

Edison, Hali. 2003. "Are Foreign Exchange Reserves in Asia Too High?" In *World Economic Outlook: Public Debt in Emerging Markets.* Washington, D.C.: International Monetary Fund. [www.imf.org/external/pubs/ft/weo/2003/02/pdf/chapter2.pdf].

IMF (International Monetary Fund). 1989. *Annual Report of the Executive Board.* Washington, D.C.

———. 1994. *Annual Report of the Executive Board.* Washington, D.C.

———. 2004. "Report on Access to Fund Resources during 2003." Washington, D.C. [www.imf.org/external/np/fin/2004/access/eng/020504.pdf].

———. 2005a. "IMF Borrowing Arrangements: GAB and NAB." Washington, D.C.

———. 2005b. "Special Drawing Rights: A Factsheet." Washington, D.C. [www.imf.org/external/np/exr/facts/sdr.htm].

————. 2005c. "Special Drawing Rights (SDRs) Allocations and Holdings for All Members as of April 30, 2005." Washington, D.C. [www.imf.org/external/np/tre/tad/extsdr1.cfm].

————. Various issues. *International Financial Statistics.* Washington, D.C.

————. Various years. *World Economic Outlook.* Washington, D.C.

OECD (Organisation for Economic Co-operation and Development). 2004. "Modest Increase in Development Aid in 2003." Paris. [www.oecd.org/document/22/0,2340,en_2649_201185_31504022_1_1_1_1,00.html].

————. 2005. "Official Development Assistance Increases Further—But 2006 Targets Still a Challenge." Paris. [www.oecd.org/document/3/0,2340,en_2649_201185_34700611_1_1_1_1,00.html].

Soros, George. 2002. *On Globalization.* New York: Public Affairs.

United Nations. 1999. "Finding Solutions to the Debt Problems of Developing Countries." Report of the Executive Committee on Economic and Social Affairs of the United Nations. New York. [www.un.org/esa/coordination/ecesa/eces99-2.htm].

————. 2001. "Report of the High Level Panel on Financing for Development." ("Zedillo Report"). Document A/55/1000. New York. [www.un.org/esa/ffd/a55-1000].

Yaqub, Muhammad, Azizali Mohammed, and Iqbal Zaidi.1996. "A Focused SDR Allocation." In Michael Mussa, James M. Boughton, and Peter Isard, eds., *The Future of the SDR in Light of Changes in the International Monetary System.* Washington, D.C.: International Monetary Fund.

CREATING INCENTIVES FOR PRIVATE SECTOR INVOLVEMENT IN POVERTY REDUCTION

PURCHASE COMMITMENTS FOR AGRICULTURAL INNOVATION

MICHAEL KREMER AND ALIX PETERSON ZWANE

The economies of developing countries still depend heavily on agriculture, which employs more than half the population in low-income countries (World Bank 2002). Yet agricultural productivity remains strikingly low in these countries, and advances that are widely adopted have often proven elusive, particularly in the tropics. The International Institute for Tropical Agriculture has identified the limited adoption of new and improved technologies that have been developed by the research community as an important problem impeding the growth of food production in Sub-Saharan Africa (IITA 2002; see also Santaniello 2002), in addition to the lack of technologies themselves.

Funding for agricultural research and development (R&D) must respond to the challenge of technology diffusion in the tropics while simultaneously recognizing the increasing importance of the private sector and the tools and techniques of biotechnology as sources of productivity advances.[1] Private R&D in agriculture fails to focus on the tropical products produced by most developing countries, in part because of their lack of purchasing power.

This chapter considers a new approach to funding agricultural R&D for the tropics that could address this dual challenge of pro-poor R&D: creating incentives that ensure that the most socially valuable technologies attract private research effort and that the resulting technological innovations are actually diffused and used to enhance agricultural productivity. This approach, an advanced purchase commitment, rewards innovative agricultural advances based on their adoption in the tropics. Purchase commitments pay for research outputs and are appropriate for encouraging the development of specific, needed products. Purchase commitments can also potentially provide incentives throughout the product supply chain.[2] Several researchers have proposed that a promise to purchase a product once it has been developed is a potentially useful approach in trop- ical agriculture (Spillane 2002; Arends-Kuenning and Makundi 2000; Sachs 1999; World Bank 2001). Others have also considered this as a means of encouraging R&D in tropical diseases (see, for example, Kremer and Glennerster 2004 and Sachs and Kremer 1999).

THE MARKET FOR TROPICAL R&D

The R&D required to improve the productivity of tropical agriculture differs from that for temperate zone countries.[3] Not only do the technology needs differ, but agricultural research in tropical countries is also subject to significant distortions, leading to underinvestment by the private sector.

Different product and technology needs in the tropics
Some staple crops grown in tropical countries, such as cassava and millet, are not grown in industrial countries or imported in any significant amounts (Binenbaum and others 2003). Tropical countries have distinct agroecological sys- tems, including higher average temperatures, fragile soils, an absence of seasonal frost, and ecozone-specific weeds and pests (Masters and Wiebe 2000). For these reasons agricultural technologies spill over more easily within ecological zones than between them (Diamond 1997; Johnson and Evenson 2000). Thus temper- ate zone countries benefit more from research in other temperate countries than tropical countries do.[4] For example, advances in maize productivity in temperate regions cannot be immediately transferred to tropical regions.

Different farming technologies also create different R&D needs. Farming in developing countries is less likely to be irrigated, more likely to take place on hill- sides or degraded land, and likely to use few inputs (Pinstrup-Andersen and Cohen 2000). Livestock are often the main source of fertilizer. Most farming is on a small scale and unmechanized. Livestock are generally grazed on unmanaged pasture that is often a local common-property resource (Delgado and others 1999).

Thus, even if all technological advances were made freely available, agricul- tural research oriented toward industrial, temperate climate countries would not necessarily meet the needs of tropical countries.

Insufficient spending on agricultural R&D
Industrial countries invest nearly four times more in public sector agricultural research as a share of agricultural gross domestic product (GDP) than developing countries do (James 1996; Alston, Pardey, and Roseboom 1998; Pardey and Beintema 2001). Even accounting for the research on tropical agriculture per- formed under the umbrella of the Consultative Group on International Agricultural Research (CGIAR), public spending on tropical agriculture research

is dwarfed by public spending on temperate climate research.[5] In Latin America and Asia research intensity is catching up with that in industrial countries, while in Sub-Saharan Africa research intensity is declining (Pardey and Beintema 2001).

Private agricultural R&D is even more concentrated in industrial countries than is public sector research (Pray and Umali-Deininger 1998; Pardey and Beintema 2001). The private sector performs much of the biotechnology research, with proprietary claims to key tools and products (Byerlee and Fischer 2002). Virtually no private agricultural R&D investment is targeted toward smaller or economically stagnant developing countries. In the few tropical countries where private research intensity is relatively high, such as Colombia and Malaysia, the research is generally directed toward plantation crops intended primarily for export markets (Pray and Umali-Deininger 1998).[6]

Distortions in the research market for tropical agriculture

Appropriate policies and price signals can provide incentives to create products tailored to particular regions and their ecological and factor endowments (Hayami and Ruttan 1985; Ruttan and Hayami 1990). This has been difficult to achieve in many tropical countries, however. A key reason is that the market for agricultural R&D is highly distorted in developing countries, and there are particular disincentives to protect intellectual property in agriculture that industrial country governments do not confront.

Even if governments in developing countries wanted to protect intellectual property rights in agriculture, they would have great difficulty enforcing restrictions on the resale of seeds. This is technically difficult to do because plants and animals self-multiply. Under traditional technologies farmers may use and then multiply and sell their own seed or livestock after purchasing seed or animals once.[7] If farmers can sell seed, as well as reuse it, competition among sellers will drive seed prices close to marginal cost, eliminating the possibility for the seed developer to recoup R&D costs and thus quickly eliminating most of the incentives for investment in R&D. In both industrial and developing countries farmers reuse nonhybrid seeds, though there are efforts to prevent this in industrial countries, which also prohibit (if imperfectly) resale for some products.

If resale could be policed as effectively in developing countries, they would not suffer disproportionately from a lack of R&D. However, prohibiting the resale of agricultural products is difficult because farmers are dispersed across small, often remote plots and seeds are frequently sold in small amounts in rural markets (Byerlee 1996). Prohibiting resale would also disproportionately affect adoption rates in developing countries because farmers have little access to credit or insurance markets that make it feasible to pay for technologies with uncertain benefits up front.

Despite the evidence that intellectual property rights protection can lead to increased R&D (Pray 1992; Swanson and Göeschl 2000; Diwan and Rodrik 1991; Khan and Sokoloff 2001), most agricultural technology has traditionally been in

the public domain, with few patents sought or enforced (Herdt 1999). One reason countries do not protect intellectual property rights is that agricultural
research is subject to a "time-consistency" problem. In general, biotechnology and
agricultural research are risky and costly, but once a product has been developed,
it can be produced at a low unit cost. Without intellectual property rights protection, competition in production will drive price toward marginal cost, which is
optimal for governments ex post, though they may want to create incentives for
R&D ex ante. Governments therefore have little incentive to live up to commitments to protect intellectual property rights.[8]

Productivity improvements related to important food crops in tropical countries may be transnational public goods. For example, an improvement in cassava
productivity that is useful in Uganda may be useful in Nigeria and many other
countries as well, leaving inadequate incentives for protection of intellectual property rights by Uganda alone. This is true even though a particular advance will
need to be specialized to countries' own cassava varieties.

For products also grown in industrial countries, such as wheat, most small
developing countries can rely on the research done in industrial countries, and
their free-riding will have only a marginal effect on total research output. For
products not grown in industrial countries, such as cassava or millet, developing
countries cannot free ride on industrial country incentives. Because many small
countries would be the beneficiaries of such research, it is difficult to coordinate
the sharing of any gains made by offering incentives such as intellectual property
protection while excluding free-riders.[9]

When taken together, the empirical evidence that tropical countries have distinct R&D needs that are not being met and greater market distortions than industrial, temperate climate countries suggests that donor support for tropical
agricultural R&D may be appropriate.

WHAT FORMS CAN PUBLIC SUPPORT FOR AGRICULTURAL R&D TAKE?

Agricultural R&D has high social rates of return.[10] Because of the market failures
discussed above, private returns to R&D in agriculture are far smaller than these
social returns, and private developers cannot appropriate many of the benefits
associated with their research (Huffman and Evenson 1993; Pray and Umali-
Deininger 1998), especially in tropical countries. This suggests that public support to tropical agricultural R&D is justified.

But how should this public support be provided? Programs to encourage agricultural R&D can be broadly classified as "push" and "pull" interventions. Push
programs subsidize research inputs and pull programs pay for research outputs.
While the traditional response to encourage agricultural R&D has relied mostly
on push programs, pull programs are an important complement to push programs, particularly in situations in which the desired innovation can be clearly

defined. Push programs are especially important to encourage the private sector to invest in agricultural R&D.

Push programs

Examples of push programs are the grant-funded international agricultural research centers, under the umbrella of the CGIAR (Anderson 1997); national agricultural research systems and other government laboratories; and research tax credits and grants to researchers such as those provided by the U.S. National Science Foundation. All are cases of direct public funding of R&D. Another example is the system of grants provided by the U.S. Agency for International Development to U.S. land grant universities to perform research in tropical agriculture under the Collaborative Research Support Programs.

Direct public funding is typically the best way to stimulate basic research. Rewarding the development of applied products is unlikely to stimulate basic research, which generally seeks to provide information to other researchers rather than to develop specific products. In agriculture, basic research in genetics and plant physiology complements more applied research in plant breeding.

While critical for basic research, push programs are subject to information asymmetries, compounded by imperfectly aligned incentives between funders and scientists (Huffman and Just 2000) and by politicization. These difficulties mean that funds spent on push programs may be wasted and that unpromising avenues of research may continue to be funded.

Information asymmetries arise because scientists know their prospects for developing new products better than funders do. Scientists may overstate the usefulness of their work or the probability of success in appeals for funding. And scientists are likely to be more interested than funders are in pursuing lines of research that will achieve scientific rather than commercial goals.[11]

Some technologies developed under push programs have failed to be widely adopted in developing countries (IITA 2002) in part because scientists have failed to develop products that address the constraints faced by farmers (Christensen 1994; Santaniello 2002). Advances worthy of scientific acclaim and that have seemed promising in a controlled environment, such as improved cowpeas that defoliate, have not translated well to the mixed cropping environment in which farmers actually work (Carr 1989). And constraints that scientists have thought were important, such as infestations by the sweet potato weevil in Uganda, have been of secondary concern to farmers, who were more interested in improving root quality (Thiele, van de Fliert, and Campilan 2001). Adoption has also been slow because technological advances altered the taste or appearance of food crops. Farmers in Uganda did not adopt an improved variety of sweet potato because the plant was redder than the traditional variety (Thiele, van de Fliert, and Campilan 2001), and the inferior quality of hybrid bananas (high tannin, hard texture, poor taste) stalled their uptake by farmers in East Africa (Nowakunda and others 2002).[12]

The allocation of funds on the basis of political, rather than scientific, considerations is another difficulty.[13] Political considerations may also lead to inappropriate siting of facilities and may make firing staff or terminating particular research programs difficult (Greenland 1997). For example, many U.S. land grant universities are located in small towns in the interior of the country, where it can be difficult to attract researchers.

Public sector institutions and programs may be difficult to shut down. Bertram (1993) summarizes the experience of the International Maize and Wheat Improvement Center's (CIMMYT) work on triticale. In the 1960s CIMMYT began working on triticale, believing that it had good potential for adoption in developing countries. Much success was achieved in improving weight and grain quality, and the new variety has been widely adopted, but overwhelmingly in industrial countries. Determining when or whether CIMMYT, whose mandate is to meet the needs of developing countries, should cease working on triticale is a difficult decision to make.

There is an existing infrastructure for push research in tropical agriculture at the international CGIAR research centers, which usually perform research without seeking intellectual property rights protection for their innovations (Alston, Pardey, and Roseboom 1998). The CGIAR receives contributions of about $360 million a year (CGIAR 2003), about 12 percent of total spending on tropical agriculture (Pardey and Bientema 2001). The CGIAR has had important successes that have contributed to agricultural productivity gains in developing countries, including the suite of technologies responsible for the green revolution.

Those successes illustrate that there are potentially high returns to agricultural research for developing countries. Inefficiencies in push funding can make it difficult to realize these returns.

Pull programs

Pull programs increase rewards for the development of a particular technology. If policymakers can specify a desired technology, it may be cost effective to complement traditional push funding mechanisms with a pull program that rewards research outputs. Under pull programs, funders pay only for concrete research outputs that meet prespecified criteria. This creates strong incentives for researchers to carefully select research projects and to focus on developing viable products that respond to the needs of farmers. Policymakers and funders need not select the research approach but only the characteristics of the final product. Project selection is in the hands of those with the most information.

The history of pull efforts promising specific rewards for specific products suggests that these can be an effective tool for stimulating research. However, to work well, pull programs must be able to make credible commitments to reward appropriate products without committing the funder to pay for inappropriate products.

The importance of credibly guaranteeing that appropriate innovation will be rewarded is well illustrated by the British government's sponsoring of a competition in 1707 for developing a method of determining longitude at sea, setting a prize of £20,000. The Board of Longitude expected astronomers and mathematicians to develop a solution, but the winning solution used a chronometer that was sufficiently accurate to determine time even on rolling ships, so that longitude could be determined by comparing time at the port of departure with local time (Sobel 1995).

The development of the chronometer carries several lessons. First, contests intended to induce innovation should specify desired outputs, not methodologies. The chronometer solution did not fit the preconceptions of the Board of Longitude. Had the government created a push program run by the board, it likely would have funded only astronomers. Second, the conditions of the competition and the criteria and process for awarding the prize should be carefully specified in advance.

Private firms have been rewarded before by international organizations for research in tropical agriculture. Rausser, Ameden, and Simon (2000) describe a payment made by the Plant Sciences Research Programme of the UK Overseas Development Administration to a private company holding the relevant patents to produce transgenic germplasm expressing insect-resistant genes for potatoes and sweet potatoes. In return, a nonexclusive, royalty-free license to this technology is given to the Overseas Development Administration, allowing it to distribute the germplasm to breeders in developing countries. Brenner and Komen (1994) describe a similar arrangement in which the U.S. Agency for International Development funded research by a private company to develop virus-resistant sweet potatoes in return for a nonexclusive license to the product to be distributed in developing countries. These programs differ from the pull program considered here in that payment was not contingent on successful development and the funding agency determined the firm that would receive payment before the technology was developed.

For applied research in which desired outputs can be identified, the incentive mechanisms created by pull programs can relieve the pressure on funders to pick winners and can align the incentives of scientists and policymakers more effectively than can grant-funded research. Because the recipients of the reward are not prespecified, more productive firms may undertake the desired research even if it means licensing needed technologies. If rewards depend on use, developers have strong incentives to ensure that their technology will actually be adopted. However, the case for push funding mechanisms remains strong for research at the early stages and in cases in which it is impossible to specify the desired product.

A COMMITMENT TO REWARD INNOVATION UPTAKE: CREATING INCENTIVES FOR THE PRIVATE SECTOR TO REACH POOR FARMERS

This section considers the practical issues in whether pull programs can be used to create incentives for private tropical agriculture R&D. It focuses on the design features and challenges of such programs. Such programs directly address the twin challenges of tropical agricultural R&D: a shortfall of investment from the private sector and great uncertainty about whether innovations will be used to improve the productivity of tropical agriculture. The proposed tool is an explicit commitment to pay firms that disseminate advances in tropical agriculture.

Three major sets of issues emerge in designing such a program. First, for the pull program to work, policymakers must be able to identify the desired technologies, define the required health and safety characteristics, and determine the appropriate payment (based on an estimate of the social value of the prespecified innovations). Second, procedures for approving products and paying rewards need to be established. Third, potential funders need to be identified, along with the reasons why they would be inclined to support purchase commitments.

Identifying desired technologies and their social values

Serageldin and Persley (2000) have identified several constraints that limit the productivity of tropical agriculture (table 1). They contend that because of the nature of these constraints, advances are most likely to come from biotechnology, the portion of agricultural research that is dominated by the private sector. The Rockefeller Foundation (2002) has identified a similar set of problem areas. Prioritization exercises like these suggest the ability to identify specific desired advances that may be appropriate for funding with a purchase commitment. In general, the more narrowly and discretely donors and policymakers can define the desired product, the more appropriate a pull program will be.

To use a purchase commitment to overcome any of the constraints identified by Serageldin and Persley (2000), policymakers must know the productivity gains and profits per hectare that would result for a range of product lines. Kremer and Peterson Zwane (2005) provide illustrative calculations of the social value of the development of blast-resistant finger millet. Using 1994 production figures, they estimate the dollar value of the loss of the finger millet crop due to blast—one of the constraints identified by Serageldin and Persley—at $91 million annually and the social value of the desired trait at $28 for a hectare's worth of seed inputs.

Rewarding innovation and diffusion

In agriculture a pull program may be most effective if rewards are tied to adoption. This gives farmers a say in determining the characteristics of new products brought to the market and is attractive precisely because diffusion of new technologies has sometimes proven difficult in tropical agriculture in the past (Christensen 1994; Carr 1989; IITA 2002; Santaniello 2002).[14]

Of course, adoption rates would not be the only criterion for determining reward payments. To avoid providing a large reward for a new technology that is only slightly better than existing technologies, reward programs would need to establish a series of well defined technical criteria that a qualifying innovation

TABLE 1

Some key agricultural constraints in developing countries

Commodity	Problem	Affected regions
Banana and plantain	Black Sigatoka disease	Global
Cassava	Cassava mosaic virus	Sub-Saharan Africa
Maize	Low protein content	Global
	Drought	Global
Millet	Blast	South Asia and Africa
	Photoperiod response	Global
Sorghum	Drought, heat tolerance	South Asia and Africa
Rice	Blast, submergence	Global
	Low vitamin A content	Global
	Low yield potential	Global
Wheat	Heat tolerance	Africa and Asia
	Drought/salinity tolerance	Global
Cattle	Trypanosomosis	Global
	East coast fever	Africa
Sheep	Heat tolerance, helminths	Global
Goats	Helminths	Global
Chickens	Newcastle virus	Global
Pigs	Viral diseases	Global

Source: Serageldin and Persley 2000.

ought to meet. Thus in the case of a new food crop variety, an important dimension might be its drought tolerance, as determined by the mean and variance of the yield of the new technology relative to traditional varieties. A commitment could be structured so that it would be triggered only if a new variety satisfied a particular cost-effectiveness threshold. Thus, designing eligibility standards would be far from trivial. Kremer and Peterson Zwane (2005) discuss some of these design issues further.

Measuring uptake also presents challenges. Given the importance of paying for the new product on the basis of total demand, it is likely to be most feasible to pay the firm that has developed the desired trait on the basis of total hectares planted each year with material using the particular technology, rather than on the basis of total seeds or propagation material sold. This would allow the practice of saving seed to continue, potentially resolving some of the tension that has arisen in the struggle over genetic use-restriction technologies, while still providing a return to product developers that covers their research costs and compensates them for risk.[15] This would also mitigate the potential for firms to distort the seed market, for example, by offering gifts to those who purchase the product.

In practice, surveys could be conducted to estimate the prevalence of the new technology, and the firm could be compensated accordingly. For the developer to receive payments from the pull program, farmers would have to actually plant the seeds that they purchase.[16]

One possibility is to structure the payment to the firm as a percentage of the market price of the product grown using material that contains the new technology. In theory this could make many of the specification problems less onerous. The price of the product, relative to the price of products grown using traditional means, should summarize information about the appeal of the new product. The price should also reflect the fact that farmers will not be enthusiastic about adopting a technology that gives only a small gain.[17]

Under such a program researchers would have strong incentives to maximize commodity uptake and thus to develop technological advances that are useful and appropriate for smallholders, taking into account local ecologies and real world farming practices. Researchers would also have incentives to consider the strong influence of taste and appearance on adoption of new food crops. Tying rewards to adoption may be a more effective means of inducing the development of technologies that are responsive to small farmers' needs and tastes than requiring evidence from scientists that they have solicited farmers' opinions about needed technologies. As the track record for technology adoption suggests, scientists may fulfill this requirement with varying degrees of commitment and effectiveness.

Making rewards contingent on adoption could create incentives at many points in the supply chain. Tying awards to adoption rates means that private sector firms, with their access to venture capital, genetic material, and biotechnology tools and know-how, but with perhaps little capacity for seed multiplication in developing countries and little advantage in agricultural extension, must take the existing and potential seed supply chain into account when making research effort decisions.

One factor that firms will have to contend with is the weaknesses in national agricultural research systems in the poorest developing countries, which is a barrier to the diffusion of new technologies (Nottenberg, Pardey, and Wright 2002). Donor-supported capacity building efforts for national agricultural research systems would continue to be important if pull funding were introduced in tropical agriculture.

Likewise, the lack of local expertise in using and regulating modern biotechnology is a major constraint on its use and diffusion in developing countries (Nottenberg, Pardey, and Wright 2002). Many of the poorest countries have inadequate biosafety regulation and lack the infrastructure to ensure that new agricultural technologies developed using biotechnology meet health and environmental standards (Byerlee and Fischer 2002). This constraint on diffusion exists whether a pull funding mechanism is used or not. Uncertainty about local regulatory policies will be a disincentive to investment even if a pull program is introduced.

More generally, coordination and contracting difficulties would not disappear. But they would be no worse than under traditional public-private partnerships. If the contracting problem is too difficult to solve, or the risks imposed on developers are too great relative to the size of the expected reward, firms may decide that a difficult supply chain makes R&D on the specified product unprofitable. In that case, the program might not induce the development of desired technologies, and no donor resources will be spent. If inefficiencies in the supply chain are sufficiently great, it may be a socially inappropriate use of resources to fund this R&D by any means.

If the difficulties presented by the supply chain can be surmounted, the program provides strong incentives to figure out how to do so. Developers might decide to purchase or create seed firms in developing countries. Alternatively, they may find that a partnership with a tropical country firm is attractive for the adaptive stages of development or they may issue nonexclusive licenses. Public sector institutions will have an incentive to adapt products to local environments because of their research mandate, regardless of any formal partnerships (in which case payment could still be made to the first innovator), though gaining access to proprietary technology may still be difficult.

A pull program would provide strong incentives for combining public and private complementary assets to bring to farmers products that they actually want. By providing incentives to the entity eligible for the reward, the program provides incentives for this entity to provide rewards to other elements of the supply chain. In theory, payments could be made at any step in the formal supply chain, but missing intellectual property rights protection may require that rewards be provided earlier in the supply chain rather than later. Rules would be needed to ensure that breeders that illegally release varieties could not receive rewards.

The rules of the program could specify that payments be made to the entity that registers the first product meeting the desired specification in an eligible country, whether a foreign company, a domestic company, or a national research institute that performed adaptive research under contract or by agreement with a private developer. Division of the reward between the registrant and other entities that participated in the development process would then be a matter for the parties to resolve privately.

Funding the rewards

A pull program has two characteristics that may make it attractive both to those engaged in agricultural R&D and to potential funders of the program. First, an explicit commitment to help finance purchases of new agricultural products would not interfere with other initiatives to improve agricultural productivity—

it would represent a complementary approach for existing efforts. Second, it would not require that funds be set aside in an escrow account at the outset of the program, because the commitment need not be financed until a desired product is developed. The historical and legal records provide strong evidence that even without funds set aside at the outset the courts will interpret a suitably designed commitment as a legally binding contract (Morantz and Sloane 2001).

If research funding were balanced between push and pull mechanisms, donors might not only identify opportunities for budget reallocation but also could increase support for the CGIAR while committing to future rewards to firms under a pull program. The strong incentives created by pull programs may boost donors' enthusiasm for funding research for tropical agriculture since donors can be confident that resources will not be wasted. There is survey evidence from the United States that many people think a large portion of foreign aid is "wasted," and some suggestion that there would be more support for foreign aid if this waste could be reduced (PIPA 2001).

Commitments to pay the rewards could be undertaken by the governments of industrial countries, multilateral agencies like the World Bank (perhaps in cooperation with the CGIAR), and private foundations. Depending on the nature of the new technology to be developed and disseminated and the resource requirements, donor consortia could also be formed.

Some donors consider earmarking future funds for a particular purpose undesirable, fearing that this practice reduces their programming flexibility. Earmarking can help resolve the time-consistency problem inherent in convincing potential developers that governments will compensate them adequately once the developers have sunk funds into developing a desired product.

Private foundations could play a major role in creating markets for new agricultural products. They may find it easier than governments to credibly commit to future payments, given their greater continuity of leadership. For example, by law, private foundations in the United States are required to spend at least 5 percent of their assets annually on charitable purposes. This suggests a natural way for them to combine push and pull incentives for agricultural product development. The foundation could spend 5 percent of its assets annually on grants to help expand the use of existing products or to fund basic research in tropical agriculture. Meanwhile, the foundation could put its principal to use in encouraging private research, simply by pledging that if specified products were actually developed, the foundation would pay firms according to the product's deployment in tropical countries.

CONCLUSION

This chapter examined the potential for an innovative financing mechanism to encourage private R&D in tropical agriculture. International funding for this research is appropriate because the potential productivity advances could have beneficiaries in many countries in tropical regions. Public funding for the R&D is appropriate because rates of return to research in agriculture are high and because significant failures in the research market mean that too little research is done by the private sector. These problems are particularly acute in tropical developing countries.

Traditional government-funded push research programs in this sector have created outputs that have often been adopted slowly, if at all. One reason is that under traditional push programs researchers have incentives to pursue research activities that do not result in products farmers want. In contrast, pull funding programs seem to have tremendous potential to complement traditional publicly funded research in tropical agriculture—particularly in light of the importance of the private sector in biotechnology.

The purchase commitment proposed in this chapter is attractive because no resources are spent until the desired product is developed and approved by regulators, and it can be structured so that total expenditure depends on adoption rates. This creates strong incentives for researchers to select appropriate projects and to focus on developing products that farmers will want.

Notes

1. Alston, Pardey, and Roseboom (1998) estimate that the annual growth rate of private agriculture R&D expenditures in the United States, United Kingdom, and Japan was approximately 5 percent during 1981–93. Other researchers have suggested that increased private sector biotechnology research effort for the tropics is important and desirable (Pardey, Roseboom, and Beintema 1997; Byerlee and Fischer 2002; Arends-Kuenning and Makundi 2000; World Bank 2001; Spillane 2002; Anderson 1998; James and Krattiger 1999; Rausser, Ameden, and Simon 2000).

2. The chapter builds on Kremer and Peterson Zwane (2005). Masters (2003) considers a similar set of issues and proposes a funding tool for tropical agriculture that is related to the proposal made by Kremer (1998) for public buyout of socially valuable patents. More broadly, this chapter is related to the academic literature on research incentives, including Scotchmer (1999); Shavell and van Ypserle (2001); and Wright (1983). It is also related to the extensive literature on agricultural research, including Alston and Pardey (1996); Evenson and Kislev (1976); Evenson and Westphal (1995); Huffman and Just (1994, 2000); Huffman and Evenson (1993); and Sunding and Zilberman (2001).

3. Agricultural R&D in general faces two sets of factors that present difficulties to private investors in tropical agricultural R&D as well. The first is the fact that the potential for the reuse and resale of seed makes it difficult for developers to appropriate the costs of R&D in agriculture. Popular opposition is likely to block technological approaches to intellectual property protection such as gene use-restriction technologies, one version of which is popularly known as the "terminator technology" (Pollan 1998; National Academy of Sciences 2000; UNDP 1999; ISNAR 1998). These technologies could make the seeds sterile, requiring farmers to purchase new seeds each season or after a specified number of seasons in order to continue to use

seeds embodying a particular technology (Jefferson and others 1999). The second factor is the fragmentation of intellectual property rights, which can reduce access to the final product and incentives to invest in developing new technologies. Since several different firms hold complementary patents for a single desired final product, as may be the case if a series of sequential innovations or adaptations to local conditions is needed, the parties acting individually may set higher prices than would be beneficial to the group collectively. As a result, incentives for R&D are reduced (Green and Scotchmer 1995). Ex ante negotiations between developers can mitigate this problem, but such negotiations may be difficult to coordinate or costly in practice. While fragmentation of intellectual property rights can occur in many fields, it is particularly important in agriculture because agricultural technologies must be adapted to local conditions. This implies, for example, that a different developer from the firm that produced the initial innovation may perform the R&D needed to specialize a technology to local conditions (Evans 1993).

4. Of course, even within temperate regions R&D needs are distinct because of ecological conditions and factor endowments. Ruttan and Hayami (1990) show that the agricultural research needs of the United States and Japan have differed significantly, despite their common temperate climates, due to the far greater availability of land in the United States. Huffman and Just (1999) discuss how the mix of federal and state funding for agricultural research in the United States evolved to respond to distinct local needs.

5. The denominator of the calculation of CGIAR research intensity is the sum of agricultural value added in all nontransition economies classified by the World Bank as low income (World Bank 2002). The numerator is total annual member contributions to CGIAR (CGIAR 1999).

6. R&D in these sectors will arguably drive down world prices, making developing countries as a whole worse off. For R&D that is truly a global public good (such as cotton productivity advances), both industrial and developing countries would be negatively affected by lower world prices.

7. This is not true of other agricultural products, such as vaccines, medicines, and artificial reproduction technologies that can also improve productivity.

8. This is not a new issue. Eli Whitney, for example, made little money from the patent that he held for the cotton gin. Blacksmiths could easily reproduce the cotton gin, and Southern juries were creative in finding reasons not to decide in Whitney's favor in numerous patent infringement suits that he filed (Green 1956). Modern researchers anticipate analogous problems in protecting intellectual property rights in developing countries.

9. Theoretically, developing countries could provide property rights protection only to products that are uniquely suited to their region. This scenario is similar to the proposal made by Lanjouw (2002) for reforms to the patent system for pharmaceuticals. While writing such a property rights regime into law would be difficult, allowing parallel imports would effectively accomplish such a policy if industrial countries do not themselves allow the use of gene use-restriction technologies (GURTs).

To see this, suppose that African countries announced that they were allowing both the use of GURT seeds for cassava and the parallel import of seeds that did not have gene use-restriction capability. If industrial countries did not allow the use of GURTs, firms might develop some products for markets that did not have this technology, relying on legal and contractual protection of intellectual property rights in these countries. However, they might develop products for tropical climates that used GURTs, since enforcement of intellectual property rights would otherwise be difficult in these areas, and a market for GURTs products would be present. If seed imports were allowed, then African countries would have access to tropical products with GURTs and temperate products without them. Of course, each cassava-growing country would still have incentives to free ride off incentives provided by other cassava-growing countries, and this would make it difficult to secure agreement on such an approach.

10. Social rates of return to agricultural R&D in industrial and developing countries are above most private hurdle rates, in the range of 40–80 percent on average (Alston and others 2000; Evenson 2001; Fuglie and others 1996). Even in a potentially difficult environment, Masters, Bedingar, and Oehmke (1998) report that most rates of return to agricultural R&D in Africa exceed 20 percent.

11. Hiring scientists on a long-term basis at CGIAR institutions, for example, can mitigate this problem. Because these scientists are charged with performing applied research that will result in usable products, it is less tempting to engage in research that will not result in practical agricultural innovations. Merit increases can also function as an incentive component of scientists' contracts, which Huffman and Just (1999) argue is a strength of the compensation packages provided to U.S. state agricultural experiment station scientists.

12. In an effort to improve adoption rates, recent research programs such as the Cassava Biotechnology Network have attempted to identify attractive technological advances by interviewing farmers about their needs (Arends-Kuenning and Makundi 2000). While this may be an improvement over research programs that have no input from farmers, responses to survey questions may depend on how questions are asked, farmers may not know the scientific opportunities and challenges, and there may be opportunities for scientists to manipulate or ignore farmers' responses.

13. The World Bank and other donors have made recent efforts to increase the role of competitive bidding in funding decisions for research performed by African national agriculture research systems (SPAAR 1997), in part to alleviate this phenomenon. This constitutes a small portion of total funding. For a review, see Gill and Carney (1999). Industrial countries like the United States have also increased their use of competitive grant mechanisms to allocate federal agricultural research funds (Huffman and Just 1999).

14. Other pull program design issues are discussed in detail in Kremer and Glennerster (2004). Questions that must be addressed for a pull program to be made operational include the following: How will the awardee be selected? How will donors ensure that rewards remain with the first innovator of the desired trait if other developers can create marginally superior products after the initial innovation has been

made? Should tropical countries be expected to make a copayment to supplement donors' resources?

15. This is consistent with the result shown by Wright (1983); protection of intellectual property rights in the form of patents is not necessary when the government can identify a technology that is needed and its social value.

16. This proposal does expose firms to risk as a result of exogenous shocks. Suppose, for example, that exogenous shocks leave a country without fertilizer for a year. This might lead farmers not to plant the product that has received the pull program award that year, even if in all other years they chose to do so.

17. The price of the technology itself will not contain information about the desirability of the product if, as is likely, firms act strategically. Since total payment will be dependent on adoption, firms could set the price near zero or give away gifts to farmers to encourage purchase of the technology.

REFERENCES

Alston, Julian M., and Philip G. Pardey. 1996. *Making Science Pay: Economics of Agricultural R&D Policy.* Washington, D.C.: American Enterprise Institute for Public Policy Research.

Alston, Julian M., Philip G. Pardey, and Johannes Roseboom. 1998. "Financing Agricultural Research: International Investment Patterns and Policy Perspectives." *World Development* 26 (6): 1057–71.

Alston, Julian M., Connie Chan-Kang, Michelle C. Marra, Philip G. Pardey, and T. J. Wyatt. 2000. *A Meta-Analysis of Rates of Return to Agricultural R&D.* IFPRI Research Report 113. Washington, D.C.: International Food Policy Research Institute.

Anderson, Jock R. 1997. "Policy and Management Work within International Agricultural Research." *The Australian Journal of Agricultural and Resource Economics* 41 (4): 521–39.

———. 1998. "Selected Policy Issues in International Agricultural Research: On Striving for International Public Goods in an Era of Donor Fatigue." *World Development* 26 (6): 1149–62.

Arends-Kuenning, Mary, and Flora Makundi. 2000. "Agricultural Biotechnology for Developing Countries: Prospects and Policies." *American Behavioral Scientist* 44 (3): 318–49.

Bertram, Robert B. 1993. "New Crops and the International Agricultural Research Centers." In Jules Janick and James E. Simon, eds., *New Crops.* New York: Wiley.

Binenbaum, Eran, Philip Pardey, and Brian D. Wright. 2003. "The CIAT-Papalotla Agreement: Intellectual Property in a Partnership That May Help Transform Tropical Cattle Farming." Working paper. University of Adelaide.

Binenbaum, Eran, Carol Nottenburg, Philip Pardey, Brian D. Wright, and Patricia Zambrano. 2003. "South-North Trade, Intellectual Property Rights Jurisdictions, and Freedom to Operate in Agricultural Research on Staple Crops." *Economic Development and Cultural Change* 51 (2): 309–35.

Brenner, Carliene, and John Komen. 1994. *International Initiatives in Biotechnology for Developing Country Agriculture: Promises and Problems.* OECD Development Center Technical Paper 100. Paris: Organisation for Economic Co-operation and Development.

Byerlee, Derek. 1996. "Modern Varieties, Productivity, and Sustainability: Recent Experience and Emerging Challenges." *World Development* 24 (4): 697–718.

Byerlee, Derek, and Ken Fischer. 2002. "Accessing Modern Science: Policy and Institutional Options for Agricultural Biotechnology in Developing Countries." *World Development* 30 (6): 931–48.

Carr, Stephen J. 1989. *Technology for Small-Scale Farmers in Sub-Saharan Africa: Experiences with Food Crop Production in Five Major Ecologic Zones.* Washington, D.C.: World Bank.

CGIAR (Consultative Group on International Agricultural Research). 1999. *1999 Annual Report.* Washington, D.C.

———. 2003. *2003 Annual Report.* Washington, D.C.

Christensen, Cheryl. 1994. *Agricultural Research in Africa: A Review of USAID Strategies and Experience.* Sustainable Development Publication Series, Technical Bulletin 3. Washington, D.C.: U.S. Agency for International Development.

Delgado, Christopher, Mark Rosegrant, Henning Steinfeld, Simeon Ehui, and Claude Coubois. 1999. "Livestock to 2020: The Next Food Revolution." IFPRI Food, Agriculture, and the Environment Discussion Paper 28. International Food Policy Research Institute, Washington, D.C.

Diamond, Jared. 1997. *Guns, Germs, and Steel.* New York: W.W. Norton.

Diwan, Ishac, and Dani Rodrik. 1991. "Patents, Appropriate Technology, and North-South Trade." *Journal of International Economics* 30 (1–2): 27–47.

Evans, Lloyd T. 1993. *Crop Evolution, Adaptation, and Yield.* New York: Cambridge University Press.

Evenson, Robert E. 2001. "Economic Impacts of Agricultural Research and Extension." In Bruce Gardner and Gordon Rausser, eds., *Handbook of Agricultural Economics.* Vol. 1A. New York: Elsevier Science, North Holland.

Evenson, Robert E., and Yoav Kislev. 1976. "A Stochastic Model of Applied Research." *Journal of Political Economy* 84 (2): 265–81.

Evenson, Robert E., and Larry E. Westphal. 1995. "Technological Change and Technology Strategy." In Jere Behrman and T. N. Srinivasan, eds., *Handbook of Development Economics.* Vol. 3A. New York: Elsevier Science, North Holland.

Fuglie, Keith, Nicole Ballenger, Kelly Day, Cassandra Koltz, Michael Ollinger, John Reilly, Uptal Vasavada, and Jet Yee. 1996. *Agricultural Research and Development: Public and Private Investments under Alternative Markets and Institutions.*

Agricultural Economic Report 735. Washington, D.C.: U.S. Department of Agriculture, Economic Research Service.

Gill, Gerard J., and Diana Carney. 1999. "Competitive Agricultural Technology Funds in Developing Countries." Overseas Development Institute Natural Resource Perspectives 41. Overseas Development Institute, London.

Green, Constance. 1956. *Eli Whitney and the Birth of American Technology.* Boston, Mass.: Little Brown and Company.

Green, Jerry R., and Suzanne Scotchmer. 1995. "On the Division of Profit in Sequential Innovation." *Rand Journal of Economics* 26 (1): 20–33.

Greenland, D. J. 1997. "International Agricultural Research and the CGIAR System-Past, Present, and Future." *Journal of International Development* 9 (4): 459–82.

Hayami, Yujiro, and Vernon W. Ruttan. 1985. *Agricultural Development: An International Perspective.* Baltimore, Md.: Johns Hopkins University Press.

Herdt, Robert W. 1999. "Enclosing the Global Plant Genetic Commons." Paper prepared for delivery at the China Center for Economic Research, Peking University, May 24, Beijing. [www.rockfound.org/Documents/182/proprights.pdf].

Huffman, Wallace E., and Robert Evenson. 1993. *Science for Agriculture: A Long-Term Perspective.* Ames, Iowa: Iowa State University Press.

Huffman, Wallace E., and Richard E. Just. 1994. "Funding, Structure, and Management of Agricultural Research in the United States." *American Journal of Agricultural Economics* 76 (4): 744–59.

———. 1999. "The Organization of Agricultural Research in Western Developed Countries." *Agricultural Economics* 21 (1): 1–18.

———. 2000. "Setting Efficient Incentives for Agricultural Research: Lessons from Principal-Agent Theory." *American Journal of Agricultural Economics* 82 (4): 828–41.

IITA (International Institute of Tropical Agriculture). 2002. "The Eco-Regional Program for Humid and Sub-humid Tropics of Sub-Saharan Africa (EPHTA)." [www.iita.org/partner/ephta.htm].

ISNAR (International Service for National Agricultural Research). 1998. *Annual Report 1998: Managing Biotechnology in Developing Country Agricultural Research.* Washington, D.C.: Consultative Group on International Agricultural Research.

James, Clive. 1996. *Agricultural Research and Development: The Need for Public and Private Partnerships.* Issues in Agriculture 9. Washington, D.C.: Consultative Group on International Agricultural Research.

James, Clive, and Anatole Krattiger. 1999. "The Role of the Private Sector." *IFPRI 2020 Vision for Food, Agriculture, and the Environment* Focus 2, Brief 4. Washington, D.C.: International Food Policy Research Institute. [www.ifpri.org/2020/focus/focus02.htm].

Jefferson, Richard A., Don Blyth, Carlos Correa, Gerardo Otero, and Calvin Qualset. 1999. "Technical Assessment of the Set of New Technologies Which Sterilize or

Reduce the Agronomic Value of Second-Generation Seed, as Exemplified by U.S. Patent No. 5,723,765, and WO 94/03619." Expert paper prepared for the Secretariat of the Convention on Biological Diversity, Subsidiary Body on Scientific, Technical, and Technological Advice, Quebec. [www.biodiv.org/convention/sbstta.asp].

Johnson, Daniel K. N., and Robert E. Evenson. 2000. "How Far Away is Africa? Technology Spillovers to Agriculture and Productivity." *American Journal of Agricultural Economics* 82 (3): 743–49.

Khan, Zorina B., and Kenneth L. Sokoloff. 2001. "The Early Development of Intellectual Property Institutions in the United States." *Journal of Economic Perspectives* 15 (3): 233–46.

Kremer. Michael. 1998. "Patent Buy-Outs: A Mechanism for Encouraging Innovation." *Quarterly Journal of Economics* 113 (4): 1137–67.

Kremer, Michael, and Glennerster, Rachel. 2004. *Creating R&D Incentives for Vaccines for AIDS, Tuberculosis, and Malaria.* Princeton, N.J.: Princeton University Press.

Kremer, Michael, and Alix Peterson Zwane. 2005. "Encouraging Private Sector Research for Tropical Agriculture." *World Development* 33 (1): 87–105

Lanjouw, Jean O. 2002. "A Patent Policy Proposal for Global Diseases." In Boris Pleskovic and Nicholas Stern, eds., *Annual World Bank Conference on Development Economics, 2001/2002.* New York: Oxford University Press.

Masters, William A. 2003. "Research Prizes: A Mechanism for Innovation in African Agriculture." Paper presented at the International Consortium on Agricultural Biotechnology Research 7th International Conference on Public Goods and Public Policy for Agricultural Biotechnology, June 29–July 3, Ravello, Italy.

Masters, William A., and Keith D. Wiebe. 2000. "Climate and Agricultural Productivity." Harvard University Center for International Development, Cambridge, Mass., and U.S. Department of Agriculture, Economic Research Service, Washington, D.C.

Masters, William A., Touba Bedingar, and James F. Oehmke. 1998. "The Impact of Agricultural Research in Africa: Aggregate and Case Study Evidence." *Agricultural Economics* 19 (1–2): 81–86.

Morantz, Alison, and Robert Sloane. 2001. "Vaccine Purchase Commitment Contract: Legal Strategies for Ensuring Enforceability." Harvard University, Economics Department, Cambridge, Mass.

National Academy of Sciences. 2000. *Transgenic Plants and World Agriculture.* Washington, D.C.: National Academy Press.

Nottenburg, Carol, Philip G. Pardey, and Brian D. Wright. 2002. "Accessing Other People's Technology for Non-Profit Research." *Australian Journal of Agricultural and Resource Economics* 46 (3): 389–416.

Nowakunda, Kephas, Patrick R. Rubaihayo, Michael A. Ameny, and Wilberforce Tushemereirwe. 2002. "Consumer Acceptability of Introduced Bananas in Uganda." *INFOMUSA* 9 (2): 22–25.

Pardey, Phillip G., and Nienke M. Beintema. 2001. *Slow Magic: Agricultural R&D: A Century after Mendel.* IFPRI Food Policy Report. Washington, D.C.: International Food Policy Research Institute.

Pardey, Phillip G., Johannes Roseboom, and Nienke M. Beintema. 1997. "Investments in African Agricultural Research." *World Development* 25 (3): 409–23.

Pinstrup-Andersen, Pir, and Marc J. Cohen. 2000. "Modern Biotechnology for Food and Agriculture: Risks and Opportunities for the Poor." In Ismael Serageldin and Gabrielle J. Persley, eds., *Promethean Science: Agricultural Biotechnology, the Environment, and the Poor.* Washington, D.C.: Consultative Group on International Agricultural Research.

PIPA (Program on International Policy Attitudes). 2001. *Americans on Foreign Aid and World Hunger: A Study of U.S. Public Attitudes.* Washington, D.C.

Pollan, Michael. 1998. "Playing God in the Garden." *The New York Times Sunday Magazine.* October 25.

Pray, Carl E. 1992. "Plant Breeders' Rights Legislation, Enforcement and R&D: Lessons for Developing Countries." In G. H. Peters and B. F. Stanton, eds., *Sustainable Agricultural Development: The Role of International Cooperation. Proceedings of the Twenty First International Conference of Agricultural Economists,* Brookfield, Vt.: Dartmouth Publishing Company.

Pray, Carl E., and Dina Umali-Deininger. 1998. "The Private Sector in Agricultural Research Systems: Will It Fill the Gap?" *World Development* 26 (6): 1127–48.

Rausser, Gordon, Holly Ameden, and Leo Simon. 2000. "Public–Private Alliances in Biotechnology: Can They Narrow the Knowledge Gaps between Rich and Poor?" *Food Policy* 25 (4): 499–513.

Rockefeller Foundation. 2002. "Biotechnology, Breeding, and Seed Systems for African Crops: Program Strategy and Focus." [www.africancrops.net/Aboutprogram.htm].

Ruttan, Vernon W., and Yujiro Hayami. 1990. "Induced Innovation Model of Agricultural Development." In C. K. Eicher, and J. Staatz, eds., *Agricultural Development in the Third World.* Baltimore, Md.: Johns Hopkins University Press.

Sachs, Jeffrey 1999. "Helping the World's Poorest." *The Economist.* August 14.

Sachs, Jeffrey, and Michael Kremer. 1999. "A Cure for Indifference." *Financial Times.* May 5.

Santaniello, Vittorio. 2002. "Biotechnology and Traditional Breeding in Sub-Saharan Africa." In Timothy M. Swanson, ed., B*iotechnology, Agriculture and the Developing World: The Distributional Implications of Technological Change.* Northampton, Mass.: Edward Elgar.

Scotchmer, Suzanne. 1999. "On the Optimality of the Patent Renewal System." *Rand Journal of Economics* 30 (2): 181–96.

Serageldin, Ismail, and Gabrielle J. Persley. 2000. *Promethean Science: Agriculture, Biotechnology, the Environment, and the Poor.* Washington. D.C.: Consultative Group on International Agricultural Research Secretariat.

Shavell, Steven, and Tanguy van Ypserle. 2001. "Rewards versus Intellectual Property Rights." *Journal of Law and Economics* 44 (2): 525–47.

Sobel, Dava. 1995. *Longitude*. New York: Walker and Company.

SPAAR (Special Program for African Agricultural Research). 1997. *1997 Annual Report*. Washington, D.C.: World Bank.

Spillane, Charles. 2002. "Agricultural Biotechnology and Developing Countries: Proprietary Knowledge and Diffusion of Benefits." In Timothy M. Swanson, ed., *Biotechnology, Agriculture and the Developing World: The Distributional Implications of Technological Change*. Northampton, Mass.: Edward Elgar Publishing.

Sunding, David, and David Zilberman 2001. "The Agricultural Innovation Process: Research and Technology Adoption in a Changing Agricultural Sector." In Bruce Gardner and Gordon Rausser, eds., *Handbook of Agricultural Economics*. Vol. 1A. New York: Elsevier Science, North Holland.

Swanson, Timothy M., and Timo Göeschl. 2000. "Property Rights Issues Involving Plant Genetic Resources: Implications of Ownership for Economic Efficiency." *Ecological Economics* 32 (1): 75–92.

Thiele, Graham, Elske van de Fliert, and Dindo Campilan. 2001. "What Happened to Participatory Research at the International Potato Center?" *Agriculture and Human Values* 18 (4): 429–46.

UNDP (United Nations Development Program). 1999. *Human Development Report 1999*. New York: Oxford University Press.

World Bank. 2001. *Global Development Finance 2001: Building Coalitions for Effective Development Finance*. Washington, D.C.

———. 2002. *World Development Indicators* CD-ROM. Washington, D.C.

Wright, Brian D. 1983. "The Economics of Invention Incentives: Patents, Prizes, and Research Contracts." *American Economic Review* 73 (4): 691–707.

MITIGATING THE RISKS
OF INVESTING IN
DEVELOPING COUNTRIES
CURRENCY-RELATED GUARANTEE
INSTRUMENTS FOR
INFRASTRUCTURE PROJECTS

STEPHANY GRIFFITH-JONES AND ANA TERESA FUZZO DE LIMA

The provision of infrastructure services has undergone fundamental change. Until a few decades ago these services would have been mostly state provided. Since the 1980s, however, policy shifts toward economic liberalization and privatization have opened new opportunities for private sector involvement. Investments in infrastructure projects with private participation in developing countries—where demand for such investments is largest—jumped from about $18 billion in 1990 to around $131 billion in 1997. By 2003, however, investments had plummeted to about $50 billion, causing vital projects to be halted or canceled (Izaguirre 2004, pp. 2–3). Since then, developing countries have had difficulty re-attracting private investors and restoring infrastructure investments to their 1997 levels. Why?

Developing countries critically need more infrastructure development. In many instances, infrastructure development also promises potentially high private and social returns. Moreover, global capital markets are deep enough to mobilize the requisite resources. Yet investors remain hesitant. In the aftermath of the Asian financial crisis of 1997–98 many investors experienced first-hand the inability of some governments to fulfill their contractual obligations to investors

The authors thank the Ford Foundation for the grant that helped finance the research on which this chapter is based, including a series of interviews with investment bankers, senior executives of multilateral development banks, staff of finance ministries of developing countries and the United Kingdom, and academics concerned with innovative instruments for financing infrastructure in developing countries.

and sponsors of long-term infrastructure projects. Since then, private sector actors have been awaiting a firmer regulatory framework and enhanced credit-worthiness of local economic agents, public and private. These changes are essential, but they will require time.

Not all investors' concerns arise from first-hand experience. Sometimes problems of information lead to perceptions of risk where the issue may really be one of building a relationship and getting acquainted with a new business context. Again, overcoming such information problems may take time. It requires that at least some investors return to gather fresh first-hand experience that could help break through information barriers.

Thus an important issue is what is being done—and what more could be done—to re-attract private finance to infrastructure services in developing countries. This chapter seeks to clarify this question by examining how public investment guarantees can facilitate infrastructure investment in developing countries.[1] The focus is on guarantees by multilateral and bilateral agencies to debt investors in infrastructure projects—investors who provide loans or buy project-related bonds.

The chapter examines both the main risks that investors in infrastructure services in developing countries typically face and the main public guarantee instruments currently on offer. These instruments cover some of the existing risks, especially commercial risks. Currency-related and regulatory risks for foreign investments are inadequately covered. New instruments are also needed to help infrastructure projects better withstand such shocks as major devaluations or a change in investor sentiments and preferences. To help compensate for such shocks, the possibility of countercyclical guarantees is explored. The chapter also examines the scope for more risk pooling and issuance of joint guarantees by developing country governments, notably for regional or subregional projects. While guarantees have not yet been able to induce a noticeable return of private investors, they have been successful in enhancing credit conditions, lowering the cost of capital, and lengthening the maturity of debt.

Improved public investment guarantees are critically important if developing countries are to accelerate their development and meet such global objectives and targets as the Millennium Development Goals.[2] Achieving these goals requires significantly increased private sector involvement. In the longer run effective and efficient risk management calls for reducing the range and level of existing risks. Meanwhile, however, enhanced public investment guarantees are an important incentive for re-attracting private investment flows—at higher levels, more affordable prices, and maturities that better match the often long-term economic nature of infrastructure projects.

Initially, some governments may need the backing and support of international aid agencies to provide such guarantees. Multilateral development banks and bilateral export credit agencies already provide investment guarantees. The importance of this role is likely to grow as governments continue to shift from direct intervention in the economy to incentive provision and as modalities such as public-private partnerships and project finance become more established and widespread.

RISKS OF INVESTING IN INFRASTRUCTURE SERVICES IN DEVELOPING COUNTRIES

Economic activity involves risk taking. Some risks can be calculated and priced. A rapidly expanding insurance market offers economic actors a wide gamut of products for managing risks. However, some risks result from unforeseeable events, and so are difficult to price and to cover by standard insurance products. Furthermore, some risks are "real" and can be documented and measured, while others are "perceived," often stemming from lack of information. Infrastructure projects in developing countries are beset by all these risks.

Risk theory suggests that risks should be allocated to the actors that can manage them at least cost. When contracting out the construction or operation of public infrastructure projects to the private sector, governments try to spread the risks that they would otherwise have to bear alone—and reduce the costs.[3] National capacity building to promote enhanced contracting design and monitoring is no doubt critical to the success of infrastructure projects. And so is a strengthened role for civil society monitoring of both government and private sector agents, to reduce opportunities for collusion.[4] While these issues are extremely important, they are not the main focus of this chapter, which looks at how guarantee instruments could make infrastructure investments more attractive to private investors.

Before a discussion of these instruments, it is useful to identify the types of risks that private investors typically face when considering a financial involvement in infrastructure projects in developing countries. These include commercial, political, and currency-related risks.

Commercial and political risks

Commercial risks for infrastructure investments include such aspects as delivery delays, cost overruns, and shortfalls from agreed-on performance standards (see, for example, Fitch Ratings 2004). Political risks include expropriation, breach of contract, regulatory changes, war and civil disturbance, and restrictions on converting local currency into foreign exchange for transfer outside the host country (transfer restrictions).[5]

The commercial risks are largely within the control of the private sector parties to the project and therefore do not require much in terms of public guarantees. Only to the extent that the host country's government has to deliver certain inputs may the private business partners want some protection against commercial risks.

By contrast, political risks are mostly under the control or influence of the host government. They might be caused by government action (such as changes in laws that adversely affect project economics) or inaction (such as delays in approving or failure to approve an expected tariff increase). Each investment type and phase has a different risk profile and financing requirements. Because of these varying characteristics, equity and debt investors can be expected to seek different rewards and require different guarantees, depending on the phases in which they participate (Griffith-Jones 1993).

Many investors see infrastructure projects in developing countries as posing all of these risks in a magnified way because the overall business environment may still require further development (Gómez-Ibáñez, Lorrain, and Osius 2004). In addition, for some investors these projects constitute a first-mover or pioneer initiative, surrounded by a host of uncertainties (Moran 2003). For example, a government may announce plans to implement a new regulatory framework to complement the privatization of a public utility. But because the government does not have much of a track record in carrying through on its commitments to policy reform, investors willing to take on the commercial risks of the investment may need additional assurance of the government's commitment before doing so.

Large infrastructure projects have several features that present risks that are additional to those of many other productive investments in developing countries (Griffith-Jones 1993):

*   A combination of high capital costs and low operating costs implies that financing costs are a very large proportion of the total.
*   Long construction periods are often combined with a slow build-up of revenue.
*   The project's cash flow is the crucial element determining the returns to equity investors and the security of lenders (in the absence of public guarantees).

Most infrastructure projects share these risks, whether they are undertaken in industrial or developing countries. However, the risks are perceived as being particularly high in developing countries. Investors may be especially concerned that, given the long duration of infrastructure projects and their often politically sensitive nature, regulatory changes may upset their economic calculations (Dailami and Leipziger 1997; Irwin and others 1999; Wilson 1982).

Currency-related risks

Currency-related risks make international infrastructure investments particularly high risk, especially in developing countries. For projects with foreign investments, a devaluation of the host country's currency could lead to substantial mismatch between the revenue stream in local currency and debt repayments in foreign currency. Regulatory risks are also greater in this situation. In the event of a currency devaluation, developing country governments are often compelled to default on their contractual obligations, including offtake agreements (guaranteed purchases of project outputs).[6] Thus currency risks may cause perceived regulatory risks (contract breach) to rise. Also, the contagion effects of a financial crisis elsewhere may increase perceived currency-related risks and turn market sentiment against a country for no fault of its own.

It is not surprising then that a downturn in investment in infrastructure projects in developing countries occurred at the time of the 1997–98 Asian financial crisis, as well as afterwards (figure 1). The crisis led to major devaluations in some currencies and sent ripple effects throughout the world, dampening investor interest in emerging markets.[7] Many contracts had to be renegotiated, including those of independent private power producers in Indonesia, Pakistan, and the Philippines (Gómez-Ibáñez, Lorrain, and Osius 2004). There were also numerous contract renegotiations in other emerging market countries. For instance, between 1989 and 2000 at least 50 percent of the transport and water concessions in Argentina, Brazil, Chile, Colombia, and Mexico were renegotiated (Guasch, Laffont, and Straub 2003, pp. 22–23).[8] Some contracts were canceled, and in some cases services were renationalized, exposing governments to severe compensation claims.

Large risks and large needs

Infrastructure investments in developing countries have not yet fully recovered from these shocks. Yet the need for increased infrastructure investment is enormous. Asia alone is expected to need some $1.5 trillion in infrastructure investments over the next decade to maintain its rate of economic development (Malhotra 1997, p. 33). And Latin American countries are forecast to require more than $50 billion in infrastructure investment annually over the next decade (McCartney 2000, p. 1).

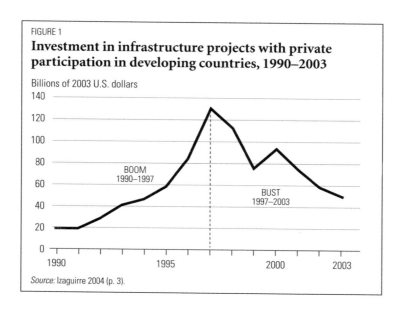

FIGURE 1

Investment in infrastructure projects with private participation in developing countries, 1990–2003

Billions of 2003 U.S. dollars

BOOM
1990–1997

BUST
1997–2003

Source: Izaguirre 2004 (p. 3).

Infrastructure projects in developing countries thus carry significant political, commercial, and currency risks. What is being done to protect investors against these risks, to help boost investment levels? More precisely, what investment guarantees are being offered, what risks do they cover, and with what effect?

PUBLIC INVESTMENT GUARANTEES FOR MANAGING THE RISKS OF FINANCING INFRASTRUCTURE SERVICES IN DEVELOPING COUNTRIES

An important rationale for public guarantees is that they can reduce the risks that the private sector cannot evaluate (because of uncertainty) or is unwilling to bear (because risk control, such as inflation control, has important externalities, for example). Guarantees should be catalytic, encouraging investors to explore new sectors and countries. They should also help to overcome information problems and signal commitment to public policy reforms or other types of government undertakings.

Effective guarantees would help attract more capital, at lower cost, and with extended maturities. Extended maturities are particularly important in infrastructure projects, because of their long duration. Public investment guarantees are not intended to provide windfall profits for private investors. As public policy instruments they should serve public purposes.

Whether public guarantees meet these conditions of economic desirability can reliably be determined only on a case-by-case basis.[9] The analysis here is limited to two main questions: Do current public guarantee schemes cover the relevant risks typical of infrastructure projects in developing countries? And do they achieve their stated purpose of attracting more and better (lower cost, longer maturity) private finance?

What public guarantee instruments are available?

Many developing country governments provide guarantees and other types of protection to foreign and domestic investors. In some instances, however, the government's capacity to deliver on these commitments is in doubt. In such cases the government has to seek a third party willing to provide the guarantee, with or without a sovereign counterguarantee. Multilateral development banks and bilateral export credit agencies often step in to provide this service. As described in box 1, their products consist mainly of political risk guarantees and partial credit guarantees.

Multilateral development banks. The multilateral development banks are in a unique position to help catalyze private finance for developing countries owing to their high creditworthiness and thus low-cost access to international capital. Their involvement has an additional attraction: investors feel that they can benefit from the extensive experience in dealing with developing countries that these banks have accumulated. Should a dispute arise and arbitrage become necessary,

Box 1

GUARANTEE INSTRUMENTS AVAILABLE TODAY: POLITICAL RISK AND PARTIAL CREDIT GUARANTEES

To attract private investors many governments in both industrial and developing countries offer guarantees to enhance the credit conditions of public infrastructure services projects. These projects are often organized as legally independent entities, following a project finance approach, with private sector investors responsible for mobilizing investment funds. In return, the government may commit to paying an annual fee to the project for the provision of agreed-on services for a certain period of time. Alternatively, the government may grant the project the right to levy user fees and charges to recoup its investment costs.

Because projects of this type pose many risks, governments can find it difficult to issue investment guarantees. They may lack the resources needed should the guarantee be called, and investors may lack confidence in these instruments. Multilateral development banks and bilateral credit agencies often step in as guarantors, with or without government counterguarantees, and offer two main types of guarantees:

- *Political risk guarantees,* covering specific events such as currency inconvertibility and transfer restrictions, confiscation, expropriation, and other forms of deprivation of project assets; political violence (sometimes including terrorist attacks); and breach of contract.
- *Partial credit guarantees,* providing comprehensive coverage against all risks for debt service default on a specified portion of the loan or debt.

Besides the risks of currency inconvertibility or transfer restrictions (which may result from regulatory changes), infrastructure projects can also suffer from other currency-related problems such as a major devaluation of the host country's currency. Such risks are only inadequately covered by today's guarantee instruments. It should be emphasized, however, that not all risks, certainly not all currency risk, should be covered by public guarantees.

Source: See notes 10–12.

they know that they can rely on the close relationships of confidence and trust that these banks have developed with their client governments or (as, for example, in the case of the International Finance Corporation) client corporations.

All regional development banks today offer investment guarantees.[10] Within the World Bank Group guarantees are available from the World Bank; the Multilateral Investment Guarantee Agency, which specializes in political risk guarantees for private investments in developing countries; and the International Finance Corporation, which offers partial credit guarantees for private sector companies.[11] In most instances, the guarantees can pertain to foreign currency investments or to investments made in local currency by national investors.

Bilateral export credit agencies. Bilateral export credit agencies are typically supported or owned by an industrial country government. Their mandate is to promote the sale of the home country's goods or services abroad. They provide government-backed loans, guarantees, and insurance to corporations from their own country seeking to do business abroad, notably in developing countries. Examples include Export Development Canada, Finnvera of Finland, Euler Hermes of Germany, Export Risk Guarantee Agency of Switzerland, Export Credits Guarantee Department of the United Kingdom, and Export-Import Bank of the United States. The Overseas Private Investment Corporation of the United Sates provides support for foreign investment that may not involve exports.[12] These bilateral agencies often work in partnership with their multilateral counterparts and employ many of the same risk-reducing instruments. Both sets of agencies have adjusted their risk management services as central governments in many countries have shifted more responsibility for infrastructure projects to subsovereign levels.

However, there is an important difference between bilateral and multilateral guarantees. Bilateral instruments need to meet the dual objectives of promoting the interests of the home country and fostering economic growth and development in the host country. Multilateral guarantees also tend to serve a dual purpose, in this case fostering the national objectives of developing countries and generating externalities that could promote global development, to the benefit of all.

Between 1994 and 1999 export credit agencies supported about half of all financing for energy projects in developing countries, with a heavy concentration in oil and gas development and fossil fuel-based power generation. The overwhelming share—roughly 90 percent—of support for energy-intensive exports and projects was provided by the world's seven leading industrial countries. During the mid- to late 1990s alone the Group of Seven governments, through their export credit agencies, cofinanced energy-intensive projects and exports valued at more than $103 billion (CIEL 2002, pp. 1–2; see also Maurer and Bhandari 2000).

What are the strengths and weaknesses of the current instruments?

Guarantee products appear to have succeeded in lowering the price of capital, as shown by the difference in interest spreads over U.S. treasury bonds of long-term loans for infrastructure projects in selected developing countries without and with guarantees (figure 2). In the case of Thailand, for example, the spread was 8.5 percent without guarantees and 2.9 percent with guarantees.[13] Guarantee schemes have also contributed to the lengthening of maturities of infrastructure finance (figure 3).

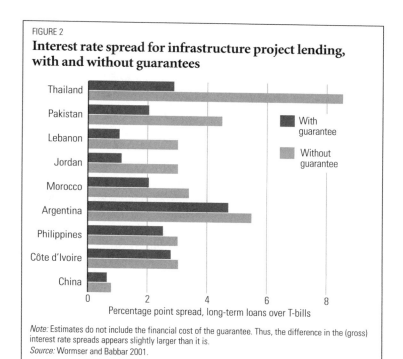

FIGURE 2

Interest rate spread for infrastructure project lending, with and without guarantees

Percentage point spread, long-term loans over T-bills

Note: Estimates do not include the financial cost of the guarantee. Thus, the difference in the (gross) interest rate spreads appears slightly larger than it is.
Source: Wormser and Babbar 2001.

FIGURE 3

Financing maturities of infrastructure projects in selected countries, with and without guarantees

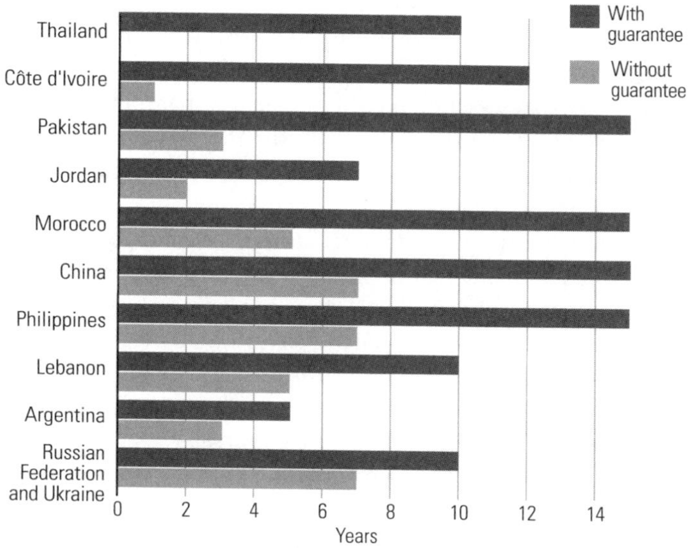

Years

Source: Wormser and Babbar 2001.

However, current guarantee instruments also have shortcomings. Processing for guarantee deals is often complex and time-consuming, so that transaction costs are higher than for straightforward loans. And use has remained limited by the lack of familiarity with these schemes on the part of developing country governments, international investors, and the staff of the multilateral development banks (see IDB 1999, for example).

Perhaps the most difficult issue is that guarantee schemes only very inadequately cover currency-related risks. Considering the severe impact that currency devaluations and crises have had on infrastructure projects, it is important to explore how exposure to these risks could be better covered, without generating too many potential liabilities to export credit agencies and multilateral development banks.

Also, most guarantee programs are designed for individual countries. Regional or subregional projects involving groups of countries with both high and with low sovereign risk ratings may be prevented from taking off because the high-risk countries cannot afford to go to capital markets. There is thus room for enhanced risk pooling that could make all the countries better off.

Expanding the set of guarantee instruments

Several policy options could enhance the protection of investors against currency risks and foster more risk sharing among developing countries on regional and subregional projects.

Responding to currency risks: contingent liquidity facilities and countercyclical guarantee instruments

As mentioned, infrastructure and utility projects (toll roads, power plants, telecommunications systems) often face serious difficulties because their revenues are in local currency and their debt payment obligations are largely in foreign currency. A major devaluation of the host country's currency or a swing in investor sentiment could generate serious financial difficulties for the project, including insolvency and default.

This risk could be mitigated through foreign exchange indexation of the tariff-setting formulas or through hedging in derivatives markets. But there are several limitations to these approaches. There are no derivatives markets for many currencies. Similarly, there are long-dated forward exchange rates for only a few developing country currencies. Also, it is unlikely that forward foreign exchange transactions with sufficient tenor could be arranged at an affordable cost to help finance infrastructure projects in developing countries.[14]

As noted, political risk and partial credit guarantees address some currency-related risks for infrastructure projects. For example, they can protect against convertibility problems and transfer restrictions that arise when such currency-related challenges emerge as a change in exchange rates or a swing in investor sentiment.

But these guarantee instruments protect mainly the interests of investors rather than those of the project. In the event of a crisis, projects all too often falter.

So what additional instruments could be put in place that would allow projects to continue to operate, despite temporary currency crises? Two possibilities are contingent liquidity facilities and countercyclical guarantees.

Contingent liquidity facilities. A contingent liquidity facility could assist infrastructure projects that have tapped international capital markets to continue to meet their foreign exchange payment obligations in the event of a major devaluation in the host country currency.[15] It is unlikely that the project would be able to significantly raise tariffs or prices for its services in the short term, yet the project must continue to meet its current debt service obligations. Contingent liquidity facilities could protect a project from insolvency by providing interim loan financing for, say, two years—sufficient time for the authorities to raise tariffs or prices and for the project to recover from an economic downturn. Contingent liquidity facility funds would allow the project to continue to operate—and to survive external shocks.

Two types of contingent liquidity facilities could be provided. A foreign exchange liquidity facility could be used to cover fluctuations in the foreign exchange value of the project's local currency revenue stream. A second type of facility could help projects meet shortfalls in their local currency revenue stream that may result because of political problems with raising tariffs or prices following a major devaluation.[16]

To illustrate, figure 4 shows how a foreign exchange liquidity facility would be drawn upon when the project's cash available for debt service (converted into U.S. dollars and shown by line 3), is below a pre-established "floor value" (shown by line 2) and is not enough to allow payment of the scheduled debt service. In turn, these withdrawals from the liquidity facility would be repaid within a specified period or as soon as the free cash flow permits (Sheppard 2003). Box 2 describes such a contingent liquidity facility provided by the U.S. Overseas Private Investment Corporation for the AES Tietê hydroelectric project in Brazil.

As Matsukawa, Sheppard, and Wright (2003) note, contingent liquidity facilities could be provided on a project-specific basis or for a series of projects. They suggest that responsibility for repayment could rest with either the project sponsor or the concerned government agency. Investors might prefer that the government assume this responsibility, because the required regulatory changes, such as a decision to increase tariffs, would have to be made by the government.

In the longer run, of course, the goal should be to reduce the risk of currency mismatch by developing domestic capital markets. If debt is financed in local—rather than foreign—currency, currency mismatches would not occur. Projects can contribute to the development of these markets by issuing bonds in local currency. But if these markets are not to be limited to local investors, the challenge becomes one of gaining the confidence of both national and international

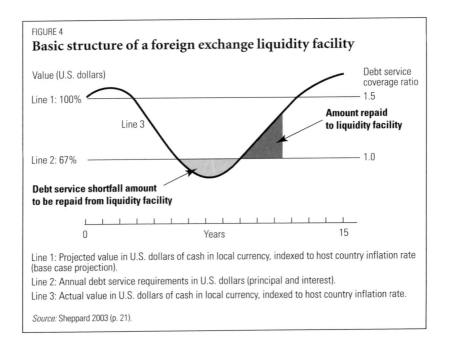

FIGURE 4

Basic structure of a foreign exchange liquidity facility

Line 1: Projected value in U.S. dollars of cash in local currency, indexed to host country inflation rate (base case projection).
Line 2: Annual debt service requirements in U.S. dollars (principal and interest).
Line 3: Actual value in U.S. dollars of cash in local currency, indexed to host country inflation rate.

Source: Sheppard 2003 (p. 21).

investors. Guarantees can play an important role. To encourage foreign investors to buy local currency instruments, partial credit guarantees and guarantees that protect investors against the usual political risk could include a feature that protects, to some extent, nonresident investors against foreign exchange risk.

Countercyclical guarantee instruments. One symptom of market failure is that private investors tend to overestimate risk in difficult times (during and immediately after currency crises) and underestimate it in good times. As a result, financial markets are prone to boom-bust patterns that are often determined more by changing preferences for risk aversion or by contagion effects than by country fundamentals (Eichengreen and Mody 1998; Henry and Lorentzen 2003). There is thus a strong case for public institutions to play an explicit countercyclical role.

Multilateral development banks could provide more explicit countercyclical lending, as Akyüz discusses in this volume. These banks and export credit agencies could also introduce an explicit countercyclical feature in their risk evaluations when issuing guarantees for lending to developing countries. Such guarantees could have a longer term perspective.

To elaborate, multilateral development banks and export credit agencies could increasingly use longer term models to assess risks. These models would allow them to "see through the cycle" by using measures of risk that are more focused on long-term fundamentals than on market-sensitive measures of short-term trends.

Box 2

AN EXAMPLE OF A CONTINGENT LIQUIDITY FACILITY: THE AES TIETÊ HYDROELECTRIC PROJECT IN BRAZIL

AES Tietê, a hydroelectric power generation company, operates 10 dams under a 30-year concession granted by the State of São Paulo, Brazil. The dams were built during 1958–97. Financing for their construction was obtained through corporate debt certificates, denominated in U.S. dollars and falling due in 2015. The issue benefited from coverage provided by the U.S. Overseas Private Investment Corporation (OPIC), which offered foreign investors protection against inconvertibility or devaluation of Brazil's currency—the currency of future power sales and so the source of revenue for servicing the debt.

The devaluation coverage is implemented through a contingent liquidity facility. OPIC guaranteed that the project would have a fixed amount of U.S. dollars available to support its debt service obligations during periods of depreciation. The guarantee stipulated that payments would cover only financial shortfalls due to changes in currency exchange rates, not those due to operational problems. The sponsor and OPIC agreed on a base financial forecast, defining the minimum cash generation by the project required to service its debt.

The OPIC liquidity facility, called the Real Exchange Rate Liquidity Facility, provides coverage of up to $30 million. It is organized as a revolving credit facility: for every devaluation claim to be paid by OPIC, a subordinated loan would be created to the sponsor in the same amount. Loan payments are to be made semi-annually from all excess cash available to the project.

Source: Matsukawa, Sheppard, and Wright 2003; Moran 2003; Sheppard 2002.

When market actors lower their exposure to a country, these public agencies would increase their level of guarantees if they considered the country's long-term fundamentals to be sound. Then, when private investors reenter the market, the public agencies could decrease their exposure, for example, by selling export credit guarantees in the secondary market. For such a system to function efficiently, however, secondary markets would need to be further developed.

Alternatively, stand-alone guarantee instruments with an explicit countercyclical element could be developed for long-term trade credit. This element could be activated in crisis periods or for countries facing a sharp decline or dramatic increase in the cost of capital. The aim would be to catalyze long-term trade credit, especially that linked to infrastructure.

Once the need for countercyclical guarantees is accepted, the decision has to be made about where best to place such guarantees institutionally. Bilateral export credit agencies have traditionally had an important role in providing such guarantees—and on a somewhat less procyclical basis than private lenders. Export credit agencies tend to guarantee more long-term projects, which implies a longer average time horizon than that of private banks and bondholders. They reschedule collectively through the Paris Club, which is assumed to give them more leverage to recover unpaid debts.[17] Furthermore, they have somewhat higher risk tolerance. Recent studies (Griffith-Jones and Spratt 2001) suggest, however, that the differences between the risk assessment of export credit agencies and that of private rating agencies is narrowing, thus diminishing the countercyclical role of the export credit agencies. And if bilateral export credit agencies are to play an explicit countercyclical role, they would need to modify their risk models.

Fostering enhanced risk sharing: sovereign guarantee pools

Another measure to attract infrastructure finance to developing countries is through regional or subregional guarantee agencies that act as sovereign guarantee pools to facilitate currency (and regulatory) risk sharing among countries with common interests and projects. These agencies could supply pooled guarantees to back the counterguarantees often required when multilateral development banks and export credit agencies provide guarantees. If carefully structured, such a risk-pooling arrangement could benefit both participating countries with lower credit ratings than their neighbors and those with better credit ratings. Why is this so?

If a regional project fails to take off because countries with low creditworthiness are unable to obtain investment funds on their own, all the involved countries are deprived of the benefits the project could have generated. So even the countries with better credit ratings may enjoy a net benefit by joining a risk-pooling arrangement that allows the project to be fully funded and so to move forward. Furthermore, the arrangement could be structured so that the more creditworthy country gets a higher proportion of the project's benefits. Because of factors such as proximity and political ties, the countries with higher creditworthiness might have better information on their lower rated neighbors than would international agencies, and so might be more willing to coguarantee.

Sovereign risk pooling is thus a public policy means of leveraging private capital. There are clear benefits from the use of this instrument. It can reduce perceived risks, make investment cheaper, and perhaps lengthen maturity. In the long run an extended good track record with the use of this guarantee product within a region should increase the credit rating of the region as a whole. This instrument is also likely to facilitate regional integration to the benefit of all countries within the region—and in some instances even the world as a whole. Sovereign risk pooling can serve as an important instrument for fostering the provision of regional public goods.[18]

CONCLUSION

This chapter has analyzed the role of public investment guarantees by multilateral banks and export credit agencies in attracting private debt finance to infrastructure projects in developing countries. Such guarantees are an important instrument for accelerating development—necessary if such objectives as the Millennium Development Goals are to be achieved on time.

Of course, multilateral or bilateral guarantees are no panacea. They will be available primarily where developing countries are committed to creating an attractive investment climate. These guarantees should perhaps be viewed as a transitional tool to facilitate foreign private investment in countries with which market actors are not yet fully familiar and while deep local currency markets are being developed.

Guarantee products currently available from multilateral development banks and bilateral export credit agencies include primarily political guarantees and partial credit guarantees that cover select commercial risks. While these products can lower the costs of capital and lengthen maturities, currency-related risks remain inadequately covered. In addition, because guarantee schemes are usually provided to individual countries, regional and subregional projects may be hard to finance when one of the involved countries suffers from low creditworthiness. Three complementary guarantee instruments were proposed in this chapter to respond to these shortcomings: contingent liquidity facilities, countercyclical guarantees, and sovereign risk pools.

Guarantees have to be offered with great care and after scrutiny of the proposed project and actors, to avoid problems of adverse selection. If the government bears the risk of project failure, private investors will select projects that are potentially more profitable but also more likely to fail. Knowing that a guarantee is available, the private investor may have limited interest in maximizing the project's chance of success. Moreover, guarantees can impose heavy costs on the host and source country taxpayers and consumers, particularly if contingent liabilities become very large and are realized.

Finally, because guarantees are rarely included in national accounts or budgets, public authorities may not know the full extent of their exposure. Therefore, contingent liabilities must be carefully monitored, and their use must be made more transparent (Brixi and Schick 2002). Progress in these areas is essential for allaying concerns and encouraging greater use of guarantee instruments.

Ideally, guarantees would be a confidence-building measure that would be used rarely and repaid on schedule.

NOTES

1. Guarantees are instruments that commit one party to answer for the obligations of another in case of a default on a payment to a third party.

2. See www.un.org/millenniumgoals.

3. Another important rationale for public-private partnering is public expenditure smoothing, by shifting responsibility for mobilizing investment funds to the private sector partners. On the rationales for public-private partnering, contracting out, and project financing, see Esty (2003); Irwin (2003); Spackman (2002); and the chapter on global public-private partnerships by Kaul in this volume.

4. For a discussion of the role of various actors in the provision of infrastructure services in developing countries, see, for instance, Fuzzo de Lima (2003) and Harris (2003).

5. See, for example, www.miga.org.

6. Offtake agreements are arrangements that guarantee purchases of the project output produced (such as, electricity) at an agreed price. Such agreements are typically required by project lenders as a precondition for lending.

7. For a further discussion of infrastructure-related financial flows, see Griffith-Jones (2003), Izaguirre (2004), and Vives (1999).

8. Renegotiation of concessions is not necessarily a bad sign, and it could lead to stronger deals insofar as it adjusts for the initial information asymmetry between governments and companies. During contractual negotiations, many investors had wanted to limit regulatory discretion and avoid exposing themselves to the politicized nature of pricing. In the early 1990s most contracts allowed for annual renegotiations without risking the contracts themselves. This proved appropriate, considering the number of renegotiations since then. For further discussion, see Guasch, Laffont, and Straub (2003).

9. For an analysis of financing infrastructure in the United States during the "railway age" and the lessons for infrastructure investments in developing countries today, see Eichengreen (1995); for an assessment of more recent experience with public guarantee programs, see Stanton (2002).

10. For overviews of the guarantee programs of the multilateral development banks, see the web sites of the following organizations: Asian Development Bank (www.adb.org/PrivateSector/Finance/guarantees.asp), African Development Bank (www.afdb.org/pls/portal/docs/page/adb_pagegroup/finance/financialproducts/productsinformation/guarantees/booklet%20guarantee.pdf), Inter-American Development Bank (www.iadb.org/pri/english/Products/cprg.htm), and the European Bank for Reconstruction and Development (www.ebrd.org/about/strategy/index.htm).

11. For more details, see www.worldbank.org/guarantees, http://ifcln1.ifc.org/ifcext/treasury.nsf/Content/PartialCreditGuarantee, and www.miga.org/screens/services/guarant/guarant.htm.

12. For details, visit the web sites of Export Development Canada (www.edc.ca), Finnvera (www.finnvera.fi), Euler Hermes (www.hermes-kredit.com), Export Risk Guarantee Agency of Switzerland (www.swiss-erg.com), Export Credits Guarantee Department of the United Kingdom (www.ecgd.gov.uk), Export-Import Bank of the United States (www.exim.gov), and the Overseas Private Investment Corporation of the United States (www.opic.gov). Harvard Business School's Project Finance Portal

contains additional examples of export credit agencies (www.hbs.edu/projfinportal/ecas.htm).

13. In addition, Gadanecz and Sorge (2004, p. 18) note that political risk guarantees and political risk insurance have a significant impact on credit spreads for project finance loans. They find evidence that these tools reduce ex ante credit spreads by almost one-third on average—or by about 50 basis points from an average spread in their sample of project finance loans of about 150 basis points.

14. For a more detailed discussion, see Matsukawa, Sheppard, and Wright (2003).

15. The International Finance Corporation already provides such a facility as part of its partial credit guarantee services. For more information, see http://www2.ifc.org/proserv/products/guarantees/guarantees.html.

16. See, in this connection, the proposal for a Devaluation Liquidity Backstopping Facility by the World Panel on Financing Water Infrastructure (Winpenny 2003) and the announcement of the Real Exchange Rate Liquidity (REX) product offered by Sovereign Risk Insurance Ltd. (2001).

17. The Paris Club is an informal group of official creditors whose role is to find coordinated and sustainable solutions to the payment difficulties of debtor countries (see www.clubdeparis.org).

18. For further discussion of regional public goods, see the chapter by Birdsall in this volume.

References

Brixi, Hana Polackova, and Allen Schick. 2002. *Government at Risk: Contingent Liabilities and Fiscal Risk.* Washington, D.C.: World Bank.

CIEL (Center for International Environmental Law). 2002. "Export Credit Agencies and Sustainable Development." Washington, D.C. [www.ciel.org/Publications/ECAs.pdf].

Dailami, Mansoor, and Danny Leipziger. 1997. *Infrastructure Finance and Capital Flows: A New Perspective.* Washington, D.C.: World Bank.

Eichengreen, Barry. 1995. "Financing Infrastructure in Developing Countries: Lessons from the Railway Age." *World Bank Research Observer* 10 (1): 75–91.

Eichengreen, Barry, and Ashoka Mody. 1998. *What Explains Changing Spreads on Emerging Market Debt: Fundamentals or Market Sentiment?* NBER Working Paper 6408. Cambridge, Mass.: National Bureau of Economic Research.

Esty, Benjamin C. 2003. "An Overview of Project Finance—2002 Update." Harvard Business School, Cambridge, Mass.

Fitch Ratings. 2004. "Rating Approach to Project Finance." Project Finance Criteria Report, August 12. [www.fitchratings.com/corporate/sectors/criteria_rpt.cfm?sector_flag=8&marketsector=1&detail=&body_content=crit_rpt].

Fuzzo de Lima, Ana Teresa. 2003. "The Relevance of Loan Guarantee Instruments in Project Finance for Developing Countries." Dissertation thesis. University of Sussex, Institute of Development Studies, Brighton, United Kingdom.

Gadanecz, Blaise, and Marco Sorge. 2004. "The Term Structure of Credit Spreads in Project Finance." BIS Working Paper 159. Basel: Bank for International Settlements. [www.bis.org/publ/work159.pdf].

Gómez-Ibáñez, José A., Dominique Lorrain, and Meg Osius. 2004. "The Future of Private Infrastructure." Working Paper. Harvard University, the John F. Kennedy School of Government, Cambridge, Mass. [http://ksghome.harvard.edu/~jgomezibanez/papers/Future_of_Private_Infrastructure.pdf].

Griffth-Jones, Stephany. 1993. *Loan Guarantees for Large Infrastructure Projects: The Issues and Possible Lessons for a European Facility.* Luxembourg: Office for Official Publications of the European Communities.

————. 2003. "Capital Flows to Emerging Economies: Does the Emperor Have Clothes?" In Ricardo Ffrench-Davis and Stephany Griffith-Jones, eds., *From Capital Surges to Drought: Seeking Stability for Emerging Economies.* Basingstoke, UK: Palgrave MacMillan.

Griffith-Jones, Stephany, and Stephen Spratt. 2001. "The Pro-Cyclical Effects of the New Basel Accord." In Jan Joost Teunissen, ed., *New Challenges of Crisis Prevention: Addressing Economic Imbalances in the North and Boom-Bust Cycles in the South.* The Hague: Forum on Debt and Development.

Guash, J. Luis, Jean-Jacques Laffont, and Stephane Straub. 2003. "Renegotiation of Concession Contracts in Latin America." Policy Research Working Paper 3011. World Bank, Washington, D.C. [http://econ.worldbank.org/files/25200_wps3011.pdf].

Harris, Clive. 2003. *Private Participation in Infrastructure in Developing Countries: Trends, Impacts, and Policy Lessons.* Washington, D.C.: World Bank.

Henry, Peter Blair, and Peter Lombard Lorentzen. 2003. "Domestic Capital Market Reform and Access to Global Finance: Making Markets Work." In Robert E. Litan, Michael Pomerleano, and V. Sundararajan, eds., *The Future of Domestic Capital Markets in Developing Countries.* Washington, D.C.: Brookings Institution Press.

IDB (Inter-American Development Bank). 1999. "Technical Discussion on Guarantees for Private Infrastructure." Washington, D.C. [www.iadb.org/sds/publication/publication_1172_e.htm].

Irwin, Timothy. 2003. *Public Money for Private Infrastructure: Deciding When to Offer Guarantees, Output-based Subsidies, and Other Fiscal Support.* Washington, D.C.: World Bank.

Irwin, Timothy, Michael Klein, Guillermo Perry, and Mateen Thobani. 1999. "Managing Government Exposure to Private Infrastructure Risks." *World Bank Research Observer* 14 (2): 229–45.

Izaguirre, Ada Karina. 2004. "Private Infrastructure: Activity Down by 13 Percent in 2003." Public Policy for the Private Sector Note 274. World Bank, Washington, D.C. [http://rru.worldbank.org/Documents/274izaguirre.pdf].

Malhotra, Anil K. 1997. "Private Participation in Infrastructure: Lessons from Asia's Power Sector." *Finance and Development* 34 (4): 33–35.

Matsukawa, Tomoko, Robert Sheppard, and Joseph Wright. 2003. "Foreign Exchange Risk Mitigation for Power and Water Projects in Developing Countries." Energy and Mining Sector Board Discussion Paper 9. World Bank, Washington, D.C. [www.worldbank.org/energy/pdfs/Energy_ExchangeCvr.pdf].

Maurer, Crescencia, and Ruchi Bhandari. 2000. "The Climate of Export Credit Agencies." *Climate Notes* May. World Resources Institute, Washington, D.C. [http://pdf.wri.org/eca.pdf].

McCartney, Eric. 2000. "Latin Report: Project Trends." *Project Finance Magazine.* [Accessed July 22, 2004, from www.projectfinancemagazine.com].

Moran, Theodore H. 2003. *Reforming OPIC for the 21st Century.* Washington, D.C.: Institute for International Economics.

Sheppard, Robert. 2002. "Case Study: AES Tietê Acquisition." *Infrastructure Journal* (February): 22–27.

———. 2003. "Using Capital Markets in the Financing of Infrastructure: The Use of Liquidity Facilities." Paper presented at the Inter-American Development Bank Business Seminar on Capital Markets for Development, June 3, Washington, D.C.

Sovereign Risk Insurance Ltd. 2002. "Sovereign Launches Innovative New Product to Protect Against Maxi-Devaluation Risk." Hamilton, Bermuda. [www.sovereignbermuda.com/Downloads/Sovereign-REX.pdf].

Spackman. Michael. 2002. "Public-Private Partnerships: Lessons from the British Approach." *Economic Systems* 26 (3): 283–301.

Stanton, Thomas H. 2002. "Loans and Loan Guarantees." In Lester M. Salamon, ed., *The Tools of Government: A Guide to the New Governance.* New York: Oxford University Press.

Vives, Antonio. 1999. *Pension Funds in Infrastructure Project Finance: Regulations and Instrument Design.* Washington D.C.: Inter-American Development Bank.

Wilson, Robert. 1982. "Risk Management of Public Projects." In Robert C. Lind, Gordon R. Cory, and Kenneth Arrow, ed., *Discounting for Time and Risk in Energy Policy.* Baltimore, Md.: Johns Hopkins University Press.

Winpenny, James. 2003. *Financing Water for All: Report of the World Panel on Financing Water Infrastructure.* Marseilles: World Water Council, 3rd World Water Forum, and Global Water Partnership. [www.gwpforum.org/gwp/library/FinPanRep.MainRep.pdf].

Wormser, Michel, and Suman Babbar. 2001. "Leveraging Private Finance in Frontier Markets." Presentation at the World Bank Guarantee Program Infrastructure Forum, May 2–4, Washington, D.C.

ANNEXES

FURTHER READING

·

GLOSSARY

·

ABOUT THE CONTRIBUTORS

·

INDEX

FURTHER READING

Addison, Anthony, and Alan Roe, eds. 2004. *Fiscal Policy for Development: Poverty, Reconstruction, and Growth.* Basingstoke, UK: Palgrave Macmillan.

Allen, Franklin, and Anthony M. Santomero. 1997. "The Theory of Financial Intermediation." *Journal of Banking and Finance* 21 (11–12): 1461–85.

Atkinson, Anthony B., ed. 2004. *New Sources of Development Finance.* Oxford: Oxford University Press.

Auerbach, Alan J., and Martin S. Feldstein, eds. 1987, 1991, 2002, and 2004. *Handbook of Public Economics.* Vol. 1–4. Amsterdam: Elsevier Science Publishers.

Bailey, Stephen J. 2003. *Strategic Public Finance.* New York: Palgrave MacMillan.

Basu, Kaushik, Pulin Nayak, and Ranjan Ray, eds. 2003. *Markets and Governments.* New Delhi: Oxford University Press.

Bell, Clive. 2003. *Development Policy as Public Finance.* New York: Oxford University Press.

Birdsall, Nancy, and Liliana Rojas-Suarez. 2004. *Financing Development: The Power of Regionalism.* Washington, D.C.: Center for Global Development.

Breton, Albert. 1998. *Competitive Governments: An Economic Theory of Politics and Public Finance.* Cambridge: Cambridge University Press.

Brinkerhoff, Jennifer M. 2002. *Partnership for International Development: Rhetoric or Results?* Boulder, Colo.: Lynne Rienner Publishers.

Buchanan, James M., and Richard A. Musgrave. 1999. *Public Finance and Public Choice: Two Contrasting Visions of the State.* Cambridge, Mass.: MIT Press.

Buljevich, Esteban C., and Yoon S. Park. 1999. *Project Finance and the International Financial Markets.* Dordrecht, Netherlands: Kluwer Academic Publishers.

Chang, Ha-Joon. 2003. *Globalization, Economic Development and the Role of the State.* London: Zed Books.

Cnossen, Sijbren, and Hans Werner Sinn, eds. 2003. *Public Finance and Public Policy in the New Century.* Cambridge, Mass.: MIT Press.

Commission for Africa. 2005. *Our Common Interest: Report of the Commission for Africa.* London. [www.commissionforafrica.org/english/report/thereport/english/11-03-05_cr_report.pdf].

Cornes, Richard, and Todd Sandler. 1996. *The Theory of Externalities, Public Goods, and Club Goods.* Cambridge: Cambridge University Press.

Cullis, John, and Philip Jones. 1998. *Public Finance and Public Choice: Alternative Perspectives.* New York: Oxford University Press.

De Ferranti, David, Guillermo E. Perry, Indermit S. Gill, and Luis Servén. 2000. *Securing Our Future in a Global Economy.* Washington, D.C.: World Bank.

Derviş, Kemal. 2005. *A Better Globalization: Legitimacy, Governance, and Reform.* Washington, D.C.: Center for Global Development.

Devarajan, Shantayanan, David Dollar, and Torgny Holmgren. 2001. *Aid and Reform in Africa.* Washington, D.C.: World Bank.

Easterly, William. 2002. *The Elusive Quest for Growth: Economists' Adventures and Misadventures in the Tropics.* Cambridge, Mass.: MIT Press.

Estevadeordal, Antoni, Brian Frantz, and Tam Robert Nguyen, eds. 2004. *Regional Public Goods: From Theory to Practice.* Washington, D.C.: Inter-American Development Bank.

Fabozzi, Frank J., Franco Modigliani, Frank J. Jones, and Michael G. Ferri. 2002. *Foundations of Financial Markets and Institutions.* 3rd edition. Upper Saddle River, N.J.: Prentice Hall.

Ferroni, Marco, and Ashoka Mody. 2002. *International Public Goods: Incentives, Measurement, and Financing.* Dordrecht, Netherlands: Kluwer Academic Publishers.

Froot, Kenneth A. ed. 1999. *The Financing of Catastrophe Risk.* Chicago, Ill.: University of Chicago Press.

Gupta, Sanjeev, Benedict Clements, Gabriela Inchauste, eds. 2004. *Helping Countries Develop: The Role of Fiscal Policy.* Washington, D.C.: International Monetary Fund.

Hillman, Arye L. 2003. *Public Finance and Public Policy.* Cambridge: Cambridge University Press.

Houthakker, Hendrik S., and Peter J. Williamson. 1996. *The Economics of Financial Markets.* New York: Oxford University Press.

Jha, Raghbendra. 1998. *Modern Public Economics.* London: Routledge.

Kahler, Miles, and David A. Lake, eds. 2003. *Governance in a Global Economy: Political Authority in Transition.* Princeton, N.J.: Princeton University Press.

Kaul, Inge, Isabelle Grunberg, and Marc A. Stern, eds. 1999. *Global Public Goods: International Cooperation in the 21st Century.* New York: Oxford University Press.

Kaul, Inge, Pedro Conceição, Katell Le Goulven, and Ronald U. Mendoza, eds. 2003. *Providing Global Public Goods: Managing Globalization.* New York: Oxford University Press.

Kendall, Leon T., and Michael J. Fishman, eds. 1996. *A Primer on Securitization.* Cambridge, Mass.: MIT Press.

Keohane, Robert O., and Marc A. Levy, eds. 1996. *Institutions for Environmental Aid.* Cambridge, Mass.: MIT Press.

Keohane, Robert O., and Helen V. Milner, eds. 1996. *Internationalization and Domestic Politics.* Cambridge: Cambridge University Press.

Kettl, Donald F. 2000. *The Global Public Management Revolution: A Report on the Transformation of Governance.* Washington, D.C.: Brookings Institution Press.

Labatt, Sonia, and Rodney R. White. 2002. *Environmental Finance: A Guide to Environmental Risk Assessment and Financial Products.* Hoboken, N.J.: Wiley and Sons.

Laffont, Jean-Jacques. 1988. *Fundamentals of Public Economics.* Cambridge, Mass.: MIT Press.

Lindblom, Charles E. 2001. *The Market System: What It Is, How It Works, and What To Make of It.* New Haven, Conn.: Yale University Press.

Lindert, Peter H. 2004. *Growing Public: Social Spending and Economic Growth since the 18th Century.* Vol. 1. Cambridge: Cambridge University Press.

————. 2004. *Growing Public: Further Evidence.* Vol. 2. Cambridge: Cambridge University Press.

Lomborg, Bjørn, ed. 2004. *Global Crises, Global Solutions.* Cambridge: Cambridge University Press.

Mäler, Karl-Göran, and Jeffrey R. Vincent, eds. 2003, 2005, and 2005. *Handbook of Environmental Economics.* Vol. 1–3. Amsterdam: Elsevier Science Publishers.

Miller, Merton H. 1986. "Financial Innovation: The Last Twenty Years and the Next." *Journal of Financial and Quantitative Analysis* 21 (4): 459–71.

Mosley, Layna. 2003. *Global Capital and National Governments.* Cambridge: Cambridge University Press.

Mueller, Dennis C. 2003. *Public Choice III.* Cambridge: Cambridge University Press.

Musgrave, Richard A. 1969. *Fiscal Systems.* New Haven, Conn.: Yale University Press.

Musgrave, Richard A., and Peggy B. Musgrave. 1989. *Public Finance in Theory and Practice.* 5th ed. New York: McGraw-Hill.

Nelson, Jane. 2002. *Building Partnerships: Cooperation between the United Nations System and the Private Sector.* New York: United Nations Department of Public Information.

Odedokun, Matthew, ed. 2004. *External Finance for Private Sector Development: Appraisals and Issues.* New York: Palgrave Macmillan.

Porter, Michael E., Klaus Schwab, Xavier Sala-I-Martin, and Augusto Lopez-Claros. 2004. *The Global Competitiveness Report 2004–2005.* Basingstoke, UK: Palgrave Macmillan.

Posner, Richard. 2004. *Catastrophe: Risk and Response.* New York: Oxford University Press.

Rajan, Raghuram, and Luigi Zingales. 2003. *Saving Capitalism from the Capitalists: Unleashing the Power of Financial Markets to Create Wealth and Spread Opportunity.* New York: Crown Business.

Razin, Assaf, and Efraim Sadka, eds. 1999. *The Economics of Globalization: Policy Perspectives from Public Economics.* Cambridge: Cambridge University Press.

Rosen, Harvey. 2004. *Public Finance.* 7th ed. New York: McGraw-Hill/Irwin.

Rosenau, Pauline Vaillancourt, ed. 2000. *Public-Private Policy Partnerships.* Cambridge, Mass.: MIT Press.

Sachs, Jeffrey D. 2005. *The End of Poverty: Economic Possibilities for Our Time.* New York: Penguin Press.

Sagasti, Francisco, Keith Bezanson and Fernando Prada. 2005. *The Future of Development Financing: Challenges and Strategic Choices.* Basingstoke, UK: Palgrave Macmillan.

Salamon, Lester M., ed. 2002. *The Tools of Government: A Guide to the New Governance.* Oxford: Oxford University Press.

Salanié, Bernard. 2000. *The Microeconomics of Market Failures.* Cambridge, Mass.: MIT Press.

Samuelson, Paul A. 1954. "The Pure Theory of Public Expenditure." *Review of Economics and Statistics* 36 (4): 387–89.

Sandler, Todd. 2004. *Global Collective Action.* Cambridge: Cambridge University Press.

Sandmo, Agnar. 2000. *The Public Economics of the Environment.* Oxford: Oxford University Press.

Shiller, Robert J. 2003. *The New Financial Order.* Princeton, N.J.: Princeton University Press.

Sinn, Hans Werner. 2003. *The New Systems Competition.* Malden, Mass.: Blackwell Publishers.

Södersten, Bo, ed. 2004. *Globalization and the Welfare State.* New York: Palgrave.

Spackman, Michael. 2002. "Public–Private Partnerships: Lessons from the British Approach." *Economic Systems* 26 (3): 283–301.

Stern, Nicholas, Jean-Jacques Dethier, and F. Halsey Rogers. 2005. *Growth and Empowerment: Making Development Happen.* Cambridge, Mass., and London: MIT Press.

Stiglitz, Joseph E. 2000. *Economics of the Public Sector.* 3rd ed. New York: W.W. Norton.

———. 2002. *Globalization and Its Discontents.* New York: W. W. Norton.

Tanzi, Vito. 1995. *Taxation in an Integrating World.* Washington, D.C.: Brookings Institution Press.

Tanzi, Vito, and Ludger Schuknecht. 2000. *Public Spending in the 20th Century: A Global Perspective.* Cambridge: Cambridge University Press.

Technical Group on Innovative Financing Mechanisms. 2004. *Action against Poverty: Final Report of the Technical Group on Innovative Financing Mechanisms.* New York: Technical Group on Innovative Financing Mechanisms.[www.mre.gov.br/ingles/politica_externa/temas_agenda/acfp/Reportfinal%20version.pdf].

Tietenberg, Thomas. 2003. *Environmental and Natural Resource Economics.* 6th ed. New York: Pearson Education.

United Nations. 2004. *A More Secure World: Our Shared Responsibility.* New York. [www.un.org/secureworld/report2.pdf].

United Nations Millennium Project. 2005. *Investing in Development: A Practical Plan to Achieve the Millennium Development Goals.* New York: United Nations Development Programme.

von Weizsäcker, Ernst Ulrich, Oran R. Young, and Matthias Finger with Marianne Beisheim, eds. 2005. *Limits to Privatization: How to Avoid Too Much of a Good Thing.* London: Earthscan Publications.

Widdus, Roy. 2001. "Public-Private Partnerships for Health: Their Main Targets, Their Diversity, and Their Future Directions." *Bulletin of the World Health Organisation* 79 (8): 713–20.

Wijen, Frank, Kees Zoeteman, and Jan Pieters, eds. 2005. *A Handbook of Globalization and Environmental Policy: Interventions of National Government in a Global Arena.* Cheltenham: Edward Elgar.

Wilensky, Harold L. 2002. *Rich Democracies: Political Economy, Public Policy, and Performance.* Berkeley, Calif.: University of California Press.

Wolf, Martin. 2004. *Why Globalization Works.* New Haven, Conn.: Yale University Press.

Working Group on New International Contributions to Finance Development. 2004. *Final Report of the Working Group on New International Contributions to Finance Development.* Paris. [www.france.diplomatie.fr/actual/pdf/landau_report.pdf].

World Bank. 1997. *World Development Report 1997: The State in a Changing World.* New York: Oxford University Press.

———. 1998. *Assessing Aid: What Works, What Doesn't and Why.* New York: Oxford University Press.

———. 2004. *World Development Report 2005: A Better Investment Climate for Everyone.* New York: Oxford University Press.

GLOSSARY

Allocative efficiency: The use of resources where they promise the highest relative returns, given existing technology and preferences.

Asymmetric information: A situation in which one or more parties to a transaction have better information than the other party or parties, as when the seller of a used car has more information about its quality than the buyer does.

Bond: An interest-bearing certificate issued by a government or corporation, promising to repay a sum of money (the principal) plus interest at a specified date or dates in the future.

Capital markets: Financial markets for *equity securities* and for *debt securities* with a maturity greater than one year.

Club good: An intermediate case between a *public good* and a *private good*. With a club good exclusion is feasible, but the optimal size of the club is generally larger than one individual.

Debt security: Security such as a *bond* representing borrowed money with a fixed repayment amount, specific maturity or maturities, and usually a specific interest rate or an original purchase discount.

Derivative: Financial instrument whose value is based on another security. For example, an option is a derivative instrument because its value derives from an underlying stock, stock index, or *futures contract.*

Definitions are drawn from John Downes and Jordan Elliot Goodman, 1991, *Dictionary of Finance and Investment Terms,* 3rd ed., New York: Barron's Educational Series; Frank J. Fabozzi, Franco Modigliani, Frank J. Jones, and Michael G. Ferri, 2002, *Foundations of Financial Markets and Institutions,* 3rd ed., New York: Prentice Hall; Inge Kaul, Pedro Conceição, Katell Le Goulven, and Ronald U. Mendoza, eds., 2003, *Providing Global Public Goods: Responding to Global Challenges,* New York: Oxford University Press; David W. Pearce, ed., 1992, *The MIT Dictionary of Modern Economics,* 4th ed., Cambridge, Mass: MIT Press. Paul A. Samuelson and William D. Nordhaus, 1989, *Economics,* 13th ed., New York: McGraw-Hill; Stephen W. Stein and Yves Miedzianogora, 1993, "International Project Finance—New Frontiers," *Project and Trade Finance* 128 (December): 36–41; Joseph E. Stiglitz and Carl E. Walsh, 2002, *Economics,* 3rd ed., New York: W.W.Norton.

Dynamic efficiency: The efficiency of an economy that appropriately balances short-run concerns (*static efficiency*) with long-run concerns (focusing on encouraging research and development).

Economies of scale: Reductions in the average cost of a product, resulting from an expanded level of output.

Economies of scope: The situation that exists when it is less expensive to produce two products together than to produce each one separately.

Equity security: Ownership interest possessed by shareholders in a corporation. Also known as a stock.

Exchange: Physical or electronic location where market participants who are members of the exchange trade stocks or other securities that are listed for trading on the exchange.

Externality: A phenomenon that arises when an individual or firm takes an action but does not bear all the costs (negative externality) or receive all the benefits (positive externality).

Final public good: *Public goods* (similar to *private goods*) can be differentiated by the stages of their production process. Final public goods are those desired for consumption, such as clean air, efficient markets, and peace and security. Producing final public goods often requires inputs of many different private goods, public goods, or both. Public goods that contribute to the production of a final public good are called intermediate public goods.

Financial intermediation: Placement of money with a financial intermediary like a broker or bank, which invests it in bonds, stocks, mortgages, or other loans, money market securities, or government obligations so as to achieve a targeted return.

Free rider: An actor such as an individual or a firm that enjoys the benefits of a public good without paying for it. Because of the difficulty of excluding anyone from using a *public* (nonexclusive) *good*, beneficiaries of the good have an incentive to avoid paying for it—that is, to be free-riders.

Futures contract: A standardized exchange-traded, legal agreement between a buyer and a seller in which the buyer agrees to take delivery of something at a specified price at the end of a designated period of time and the seller agrees to make delivery.

Global public good: A *public good* with benefits or costs that are strongly universal across countries, people, and generations.

Grant: Financing provided as a one-way transfer rather than an exchange by some agency or individual to other agencies or individuals.

Hedging: Strategy used to offset investment risk. A perfect hedge is one eliminating the possibility of future gain or loss.

Insurance: An instrument that enables the exchange of the risk of a large loss for the certainty of a small loss. The purchase of insurance, by payment of an insurance premium, spreads the risk associated with any specified contingency over a large number of individuals.

Intermediate public good: See *final public good.*

Market failure: Markets may fail to attain an efficient outcome under conditions such as lack of competition and existence of externalities, public goods, or information asymmetries.

Moral hazard: Arises under conditions of asymmetric information, when those with superior information alter their behavior in a way that benefits them while imposing costs on those with inferior information. Common examples of moral hazard involve insurance—those who purchase insurance could have a reduced incentive to avoid what they are insuring against.

Option: A contract in which the writer of the option grants the buyer the right, but not the obligation, to exercise some feature of the contract, usually to purchase from or to sell to the writer the contracted item, at a specified price within a specified period of time (or at a specified date).

Pareto efficient: A resource allocation is said to be Pareto efficient (or optimal) if there is no rearrangement that can make anyone better off without making someone else worse off.

Perfect information: The possession by market participants in a competitive economy of complete knowledge and foresight with regard to the array of present and future prices as well as the location of goods and services. Any divergence from such circumstances can be regarded as a state of imperfect information and is commonly cited as a source of market imperfection.

Principal-agent problem: Difficulties that can arise when the managers of an organization (for example, a firm or government), who are acting as agents for the organization's owners (for example, shareholders or constituencies) or principals, follow their own interests at the owners' expense.

Prisoner's dilemma: A situation in which the noncooperative pursuit of self-interest by two (or more) parties makes them both worse off.

Private good: Good with rival and exclusive benefits and/or costs.

Production efficiency: The condition in which more of some goods cannot be produced without producing less of other goods—or the production of goods at least cost.

Project finance: The financing of a stand-alone project in which the lenders of the debt finance for the project receive repayment solely or primarily from the revenue stream generated by the project.

Public good: Good with nonrival and/or nonexclusive benefits and/or costs. If a good possesses both these properties, it is a pure public good. If it exhibits only one of the properties, it is an impure public good. A good's benefits or costs are nonrival if one actor's use of the good does not reduce the benefits accruing to, or the costs to be borne by, others; and they are nonexclusive if no one can be or is being excluded from enjoying or having to bear them.

Regional public good: A *public good* whose benefits or costs span some or all countries within a geographic region.

Rent seeking: Behavior that seeks to obtain benefits by manipulating the economic environment, especially through government decisions or regulation.

Reinsurer: A financial intermediary that accepts insurance risks from a variety of primary insurers.

Securitization: The pooling of various types of debt (like mortgages or car loans) or other future flow receivables (like export earnings and workers' remittances in foreign currency or the future income to be generated by an infrastructure project such as a toll road) to back an issuance of securities.

Social benefit: The benefit to society resulting from an activity or good, as distinct from the private benefit to an individual actor or owner.

Social cost: The opportunity cost to society as a whole rather than just to one firm or individual. One of the major reasons that social costs differ from observed private costs is the existence of *externalities*.

Static efficiency: The efficiency of the economy with given technology.

Transnational public goods: An umbrella term covering both regional and global public goods.

Transaction costs: The extra costs (beyond the price of the purchase) of conducting a transaction, whether those costs are money, time, or inconvenience.

X-efficiency: See *production efficiency*.

ABOUT THE CONTRIBUTORS

YILMAZ AKYÜZ
Yilmaz Akyüz is an independent scholar. His current activities include advising the Third World Network on research in trade, finance, and development. He was director of the Division on Globalization and Development Strategies and Chief Economist at the United Nations Conference on Trade and Development (UNCTAD) until his retirement in July 2003. He was the principal author and head of the team preparing UNCTAD's *Trade and Development Report*. He was the Tun Ismail Ali Professor in Monetary and Financial Economics at the University of Malaya in 2003/04. He has taught at universities in Europe and published extensively in macroeconomics, finance, growth, and development.

SCOTT BARRETT
Scott Barrett is professor and director of International Policy at the School of Advanced International Studies, Johns Hopkins University, in Washington, D.C. He taught previously at the University of London and was educated in the United States, Canada, and the United Kingdom. He is the author of *Environment and Statecraft* (Oxford University Press, 2003) and numerous articles on international cooperation. His current research project is on the international control of infectious diseases.

NANCY BIRDSALL
Nancy Birdsall is the founding president of the Center for Global Development in Washington, D.C. Previously she served for three years as Senior Associate and Director of the Economic Reform Project at the Carnegie Endowment for International Peace. From 1993 to 1998 she was Executive Vice President of the Inter-American Development Bank. Before joining the Inter-American Development Bank, she spent 14 years in research, policy, and management positions at the World Bank. She is the author, coauthor, or editor of more than a dozen books, as well as numerous academic articles, and monographs including most recently, *Financing Development: The Power of Regionalism* (Center for Global Development, 2004) and *Delivering on Debt Relief: From IMF Gold to a New Aid Architecture* (Center for Global Development and Institute for International Economics, 2002).

PETER B. CLARK
Peter Clark is retired from the International Monetary Fund where he most recently served as a senior advisor in the Research Department. After teaching

economics at Duke University, he worked as an economist at the U.S. Treasury and at the Board of Governors of the Federal Reserve System in Washington. He then moved to the International Monetary Fund where he wrote extensively on macroeconomics and international monetary economics. He holds a PhD from the Massachusetts Institute of Technology.

PAUL COLLIER
Paul Collier is professor of Economics at the University of Oxford and director of the Centre for the Study of African Economies in the United Kingdom. During 1998–2003 he was director of the Development Research Group of the World Bank. He has worked on a wide range of problems in low-income Africa, most recently on violent conflict and the failure of the growth process. He has written extensively on aid issues.

PEDRO CONCEIÇÃO
Pedro Conceição is senior policy analyst and deputy director, Office of Development Studies, United Nations Development Programme. He was previously professor at the Technical University of Lisbon and researcher at the Center for Innovation, Technology, and Policy Research, in Lisbon. He holds a PhD from the Lyndon B. Johnson School of Public Affairs, University of Texas at Austin.

BARRY EICHENGREEN
Barry Eichengreen is the George C. Pardee and Helen N. Pardee Professor of Economics and of Political Science at the University of California, Berkeley. He is a research associate of the National Bureau of Economic Research and research fellow of the Centre for Economic Policy Research. In 1997–98 he was senior policy advisor at the International Monetary Fund. He is a fellow of the American Academy of Arts and Sciences and chairman of the Bellagio Group of academics and economic officials. He has published widely on the history and current operation of the international monetary and financial system. His books include *Capital Flows and Crises* (MIT Press, 2003), *Financial Crises and What to Do About Them* (Oxford University Press, 2002), and *Golden Fetters: The Gold Standard and the Great Depression, 1919–1939* (Oxford University Press, 1992).

ANA TERESA FUZZO DE LIMA
Ana Teresa Fuzzo de Lima holds an MPhil in development studies from the Institute of Development Studies at Sussex University. She has been a consultant for private sector development and infrastructure finance to various organizations including the Inter-American Development Bank, the European Commission, the Swedish Agency for International Development, and the UK Department for International Development. She worked previously as an invest-

ment banker for ABN Amro Bank with the project finance team and as a management consultant for Roland Berger Strategy Consultants.

STEPHANY GRIFFITH-JONES

Stephany Griffith-Jones is a professorial fellow at the Institute of Development Studies at Sussex University. She has been a senior consultant to numerous international organizations and national governments, including the World Bank, the European Commission, the Inter-American Development Bank, the Brazilian Presidency, and the Czech Central Bank. Currently, she is a principal officer with the United Nations, Department of Economic and Social Affairs, where she is working on financing for development for the high-level intergovernmental dialogue. She holds a PhD from Cambridge University and has published extensively on finance and macroeconomic policy in developing economies, including 18 books.

PETER S. HELLER

Peter Heller is deputy director of the Fiscal Affairs Department of the International Monetary Fund (IMF) and has served in various capacities with the IMF since 1977, including mission chief to Ethiopia, Kenya, and Somalia. Previously, he was assistant professor of economics at the University of Michigan. He has written extensively on issues of public finance, fiscal policy, health policy in developing countries, and economic development. He is the author of the recent book *Who Will Pay? Coping with Aging Societies, Climate Change, and Other Long-Run Fiscal Challenges* (International Monetary Fund, 2003).

PHILIP JONES

Philip Jones is professor of economics at the Department of Economics and International Development, University of Bath. He has published extensively on public finance and public choice in leading economics and political science journals including the *American Economic Review, Economic Journal, Journal of Public Economics, British Journal of Political Science,* and *Political Studies.* He has written a number of books and is coauthor (with John Cullis) of *Public Finance and Public Choice,* second edition (Oxford Economics Press, 1998). He holds a PhD from the University of Leicester.

INGE KAUL

Inge Kaul is director of the Office of Development Studies at the United Nations Development Programme. From 1990 to 1995 she was director of the Human Development Report Office at the United Nations Development Programme (UNDP), where she led a team of authors producing the annual *Human Development Report.* Before that she held other senior policy positions at UNDP. She has extensive research experience in developing countries and is the author of a number of publications on development finance and the lead editor of *Global Public Goods; International Cooperation in the 21st Century* (with Isabelle Grunberg and Marc A. Stern; Oxford University Press, 1999) and *Providing Global Public Goods; Managing Globalization* (with Pedro Conceição, Katell Le Goulven, and Ronald Mendoza; Oxford University Press, 2003).

KENNETH KING

Kenneth King is the manager for knowledge and learning partnerships at the World Bank Institute, where he mobilizes finance and international partnerships to support learning and capacity development in developing countries and economies in transition. Until 2004 he was deputy chief executive officer and chief operating officer of the Global Environment Facility, which finances global environmental benefits. He was educated in Australia, where he earned advanced degrees in environmental studies and nuclear physics.

MICHAEL KREMER

Michael Kremer is the Gates Professor of Developing Societies in the Department of Economics at Harvard University and senior fellow at the Brookings Institution in Washington, D.C. He is a fellow of the American Academy of Arts and Sciences and a recipient of a MacArthur Fellowship and a Presidential Faculty Fellowship. He and Rachel Glennerster recently published *Strong Medicine: Creating Incentives for Pharmaceutical Research on Neglected Diseases* (Princeton University Press, 2004). He has published in journals including the *American Economic Review, Econometrica,* and the *Quarterly Journal of Economics.* He previously taught in Kenya. He founded and was the first executive director of WorldTeach, a nonprofit organization that places more than 200 volunteer teachers annually in developing countries.

BRIGID LAFFAN

Brigid Laffan is Jean Monnet Professor of European Politics at University College Dublin. She has published widely on the dynamics of European integration. She was born in Cahirciveen, County Kerry, and educated at the Presentation Convent School, Cahirciveen. She has a degree in European studies from the University of Limerick and did graduate work at the College of Europe in Brugge and at Trinity College Dublin.

RONALD U. MENDOZA

Ronald U. Mendoza is a policy analyst for international trade and finance at the Office of Development Studies, United Nations Development Programme. He holds graduate degrees from Fordham University and Harvard University. His research and consultancy background includes work with the Federal Reserve Bank of Boston, the State of New Hampshire, the Economist Intelligence Unit in New York, and several nongovernmental organizations in Manila.

C. WYN MORGAN

Wyn Morgan is a senior lecturer in economics and research fellow in the Centre for Economic Development and International Trade (CREDIT) in the School of Economics at the University of Nottingham. He holds a PhD from Nottingham having taken a first degree at the University of Exeter. He has been a consultant for the Commonwealth Secretariat and was part of a UK discussion group for the World Bank's International Task Force on Commodity Risk Management. He has published work in a number of journals, including papers on primary commodity market analysis and the potential benefits of the use of futures markets by commodity producers.

PEGGY B. MUSGRAVE

Peggy Musgrave is an emerita professor of economics at the University of California, Santa Cruz. She previously taught at the University of Pennsylvania and Vassar College. She holds a doctorate from Johns Hopkins University and her doctoral dissertation (published in 1963) offered an early contribution to the field of international taxation. Her subsequent research was undertaken at the Harvard Tax Program and at the Fiscal Integration Project at Columbia University. She has served on the Board of Management of the International Institute of Public Finance and was coauthor (with Richard A. Musgrave) of one of the leading textbooks on public finance, *Public Finance in Theory and Practice* (McGraw-Hill, 1973).

ALIX PETERSON ZWANE

Alix Peterson Zwane is assistant cooperative extension specialist in the Department of Agricultural and Resource Economics at the University of California, Berkeley, and holds a PhD from Harvard University. Her recent research includes work on the impact of agricultural subsidies on poverty in developing countries and the causes of tropical deforestation. She is currently involved in evaluating the impact of investments in rural water quality on health and education in Kenya and a study of the impact of immigration reform on expenditure on public goods.

JACQUES J. POLAK

Jacques Polak is retired after a career spent almost entirely in international organizations: the League of Nations (1937–43), the United Nations Relief and Rehabilitation Administration (UNRRA; 1944–46), and the International Monetary Fund (IMF, 1947–86). At the IMF he was director of the Research Department and subsequently a member of the Executive Board. He holds a PhD in economics from Amsterdam University.

STEVEN RADELET

Steven Radelet is a senior fellow at the Center for Global Development, in Washington, D.C. He was deputy assistant secretary of the U.S. Treasury for Africa,

the Middle East, and Asia from January 2000 through June 2002. From 1990 to
2000 he was a fellow at the Harvard Institute for International Development and
a lecturer on economics and public policy at Harvard University. From 1991 to
1995 he was a resident advisor to the Indonesian Ministry of Finance. Earlier, he
served in a similar capacity with the Ministry of Finance in The Gambia. He is the
author of *Challenging Foreign Aid: A Policymaker's Guide to the Millennium
Challenge Account* (Center for Global Development, 2003) and coauthor of
Economics of Development, 5th edition (W.W. Norton, 2001).

HARI RAJAN

Hari Rajan is associate principal of J.P. Morgan Corsair Capital Partners, a private
equity investment firm in New York specializing in the global financial services
sector. He manages a diverse portfolio of investments in banking, insurance, and
consumer finance companies worldwide, with an emphasis on emerging markets
in Asia and Europe. He holds degrees from Yale University and the Wharton
School of the University of Pennsylvania.

TODD SANDLER

Todd Sandler is the Robert R. and Katheryn A. Dockson Chair of International
Relations and Economics at the University of Southern California, Los Angeles.
He has authored *Global Collective Action* (Cambridge University Press, 2004),
Economic Concepts for the Social Sciences (Cambridge University Press, 2001),
Global Challenges (Cambridge University Press, 1997) and *Collective Action:
Theory and Applications* (University of Michigan Press, 1992). He has coauthored
The Theory of Externalities, Public Goods, and Club Goods, 2nd edition
(Cambridge University Press, 1996). His articles have appeared in many journals
including the *Journal of Economic Literature, American Economic Review,
American Political Science Review, Quarterly Journal of Economics,* and *Journal of
Economic Theory.* He has done work for the Overseas Development Council,
Swedish Ministry for Foreign Affairs, U.S. Department of Defense, and World
Bank. In 2003 he was corecipient of the National Academy of Sciences Award for
Behavioral Research Relevant to the Prevention of Nuclear War, in recognition of
his work on terrorism.

RICHARD L. SANDOR

Richard L. Sandor is chairman and chief executive officer of the Chicago Climate
Exchange, a self-regulatory exchange that administers the world's first multinational and multisector marketplace for reducing and trading greenhouse gas
emissions. He is also a research professor at the Kellogg Graduate School of
Management at Northwestern University. He has been vice president and chief
economist of the Chicago Board of Trade. He was honored by the City of Chicago
and the Chicago Board of Trade for his contribution to the creation of financial

futures and his universal recognition as the "father of financial futures." In 2002 he was chosen by *Time* magazine as one of its "Heroes for the Planet." In 2004 he received the honorary degree of Doctor of Science, *honoris causa*, from the Swiss Federal Institute of Technology.

RAJIV SHAH

Rajiv Shah is deputy director for strategic opportunities at the Bill & Melinda Gates Foundation, in Seattle, Washington. He oversees the Vaccine Fund and shapes overall strategy for engaging with bilateral and multilateral financial institutions. He has also led efforts to develop the foundation's global health and global health advocacy strategies and created the Policy Research Network. He was health care policy advisor on the 2000 presidential campaign of Al Gore and on Philadelphia Mayor John Street's New Centuries Committee. He started, managed, and sold a health care consulting firm (Health Systems Analytics), whose clients included the U.S. government and some of the largest health systems in the country. In 1995 he cofounded Project IMPACT—an award-winning national nonprofit organization that conducts leadership, mentoring, media, and political activism activities and currently serves on its Board of Advisors.

ROBERT J. SHILLER

Robert J. Shiller is the Stanley B. Resor Professor of Economics at Yale University. He received his BA from the University of Michigan in 1967 and his PhD in economics from the Massachusetts Institute of Technology in 1972. He is cofounder and principal of Macro Securities Research, LLC, in the United States. He has written on financial markets, financial innovation, behavioral economics, and macroeconomics, among other topics. His books include *Macro Markets: Creating Institutions for Managing Society's Largest Economic Risks* (Oxford University Press, 1993), *Irrational Exuberance* (Princeton University Press, 2000, 2005), and *The New Financial Order: Risk in the 21st Century* (Princeton University Press, 2003).

VITO TANZI

Vito Tanzi is a consultant to the Inter-American Development Bank. Previously, he was director of the Fiscal Affairs Department (1981–2000) and Chief of the Tax Policy Division (1974–81) of the International Monetary Fund. He was undersecretary of the economy in the Italian government (2001–03) and professor of economics at the American University, Washington, D.C. (1967–76). He received his PhD in economics from Harvard University and honorary degrees from the University of Cordoba, University of Liege, University of Torino, and University of Bari. In 1990–94 he was president of the International Institute of Public Finance. He is the author of many books and articles in professional journals.

INDEX

Abbott, Kenneth W., 98n5

Abdelhamid, Doha, 87

Abed, George, 115

Ability-to-pay principle, 343

Absorptive capacity, 473

Accountability: of global public-private partnerships, 262n39; of the public sector, 78, 512, 540

Accretion principle, 168, 190n4

Accrual accounting, 142, 170

Acemoglu, Daron, 259n19

Action TB Programme, 260n26

Actor groups: comparative advantage of different, 259–60n19; in formulating global policy, 76; interventions in production of global public goods, 15

ADB. See Asian Development Bank

Addison, Anthony, 90

Adema, Willem, 120, 122

Adequate provision of global public goods, 45, 328–33; criteria for, 328

Adjustable-rate mortgages, 397

Adreoni, James, 280n5

Adserà, Alícia, 114

Advanced purchase commitments: 44, 51t, 59, 564; for agricultural innovation, 564–79

Adverse selection, 488

Aeras Global TB Vaccine Foundation, 236

AES Tietê hydroelectric project, 595, 597

AfDB. See African Development Bank

Africa Trade Insurance Agency, 542

African Agricultural Technology Foundation, 236

African Comprehensive HIV/AIDS Partnership, 237

African Development Bank (AfDB), 514, 532t, 541, 514, 600n10

African Growth and Opportunity Act, 23n14

African Programme for the Control of Onchocerciasis, 270

African Trade Insurance Agency (ATI), 234, 254

Agarwala, Ramgopal, 87

Agenda 2000: For a Stronger and Wider Union, 461

Aggregate net benefits from global public goods provision, 333, 335

Aggregative approaches: promoting fiscal sustainability, 138

Aggregation technologies in public good provision, 214n5, 358–64. See also Best shot aggregation technology; Summation aggregation technology; Weak-link aggregation technology

Agle, Bradley, 77

Agricultural commodity futures trading, 393, 394t, 396, 417–32

Agricultural R&D: difficulties to private investors, 576n3; forms of public support for, 567–70; funding for, 564; high social rates of return, 567, 578n10; insufficient spending on, 565–66

Agricultural Trade Support and Services Office. See ASERCA

Ahluwalia, Montek S., 493

Aid: allocating better across countries, 473; allocations to regional public goods, 530;building blocks of, 18; criteria for grants and loans allocation of, 476–79; differentiating across countries, 518–24; differentiated strategy for the delivery of, 510; dimensions of delivery of, 519–21; disbursements, 516; enhancing the efficiency of, 42–45; impact of, 18; incoherence in the use of, 480; involving national actions, 18, 19f; levels of expenditure on,

307; as the main operational system for international cooperation, 38; motivated by political interests, 153; motivation for, 23n13; overall incentive effect of, 479; phasing in tools for the delivery of, 44–45; policy reforms for regional initiatives, 540–43; poverty-efficient allocation of, 474f; recipient countries, 472–74; as a second-order priority, 284; shortcomings in, 23n17; trade and, 313

AIDS. See HIV/AIDS

AIG African Infrastructure Fund L.L.C., 234

Akyüz, Yilmaz, 43, 486–504, 489, 494, 497, 498, 499, 596

Albin, Cecilia, 335, 366

Aldrich, John, 306

Aldy, Joseph E., 368n3, 368n4

Alesina, Alberto, 23n13, 113, 153

Alexander, Yonah, 195, 210

Allen, Franklin, 442

Alliance USA, 183

Allocative efficiency, 10, 204, 612

Alston, Julian M., 565, 569, 576n1, 576n2, 578n10

Ameden, Holly, 258n6, 260n26, 570, 576n1

Amsterdam Stock Exchange, 393, 394t

Andanova, Liliana, 260n25

Andersen, Arthur, 260n20

Andersen, Søren Kaj, 258n5

Anderson, Jack R., 424, 426, 568, 576n1

Andrews, Richard N., 233

Anheier, Helmut, 76

Antimalarial drugs, 256. See also Malaria

Arce M., Daniel G., 199

Arellano, Cristina, 283

Arends-Kuenning, Mary, 565, 576n1, 578n12

Argentina: crisis lending to, 494; economic fortunes, 154; market-based operation to improve debt profile, 438; proposal to introduce GDP indexing, 159; SDR holdings of, 557

Arquilla, John, 210

Arrow, Kenneth J., 74, 392

Article IV consultations (IMF), 150n8

Articles of Agreement (IMF), 444, 556

ASERCA (Agricultural Trade Support and Services Office), 425, 429n6

Asher, Robert E., 503n21

Asian Development Bank (ADB), 514, 532t, 600n10

Asian financial crisis, 585

Asia-Pacific Economic Cooperation (APEC) 448n2, 214n7

Asset classes: creating new, 290, 292

Asset-backed securities, 287, 412n8

Asymmetric information, 488, 612

Aten, Bettina, 164n4

Athanasoulis, Stefano, 51t, 60, 155

ATI. See African Trade Insurance Agency

Atkinson, Anthony B., 23n22

Atradius, 254

Atta-Mensah, Joseph, 61n5

Attribution: for initiatives involving donor funding, 538–39; for regional public goods, 43, 529, 541–42

Audretsch, David, 237, 246f

Australia: Charter of Budget Honesty, 137; Landcare Greenhouse Challenge program, 517; New South Wales trading scheme, 62n15; Treasury, 137

Avi-Yonah, Reuven S., 173

Aylward, Bruce R., 348

Babbar, Suman, 51t, 59, 593f

Bahadur, Chandrika, 342

Bailey, Elizabeth M., 412n13

Bailey, Stephen J., 3, 308

Bailout operations: debt repayments to private creditors, 498; IMF getting out of, 434

Bakija, Jon, 184

Baldwin, Richard E., 111

Baldwin, Robert E., 313

Balls, Andrew, 300n17

Baltic Sea clean-up, 537

Banaian, King, 314

Banco do Brasil: securitization by, 300n13

Bandura, Romina, 73, 77, 80, 83, 85, 89, 98n10

Bangura, Yusuf, 88

Bank for International Settlements (BIS), 20f, 49f, 314; SDRs held by, 561–62n16

Bank of England, 438

Bank of France: code of conduct suggested by, 445

Bankruptcy court: in the United States, 449n7

Barlow, David, 88

Barnier, Michel, 465

Barr, Nicholas, 124

Barrett, Scott, 15, 23n9, 38, 39, 49f, 62n14, 261n35, 317n5, 317n9, 345, 347, 348, 357–68, 360, 364

Basel 2, 99n14

Basel Accord on the International Convergence of Capital Measures and Capital Standards (1987), 311, 312

Basu, Kaushik, 100n26

Batkibekov, Said, 87

Batts, Warren, 404

Baxter, Marianne, 164n6

Becker, Torbjörn, 446

Bedingar, Touba, 578n10

Begg, Ian, 466n1

Beghin, John C., 368n3

Behind-the-border economic openness, 78, 80

Beintema, Nienke M., 565, 566, 569, 576n1

Belize: conservation fee paid for, 387n6

Benavides, Guillermo, 425

Bendell, Jemm, 233

Beneficiary-pays principle, 343, 379

Benioff, Marc, 77

Benner, Thorsten, 258n5, 261n39

Bentley, Arthur, 310

Bergstrom, Theodore, 259n12

Berkley, Seth, 261n33

Bernstein, Steven, 261n39

Berrens, Robert P., 351n7

Bertram, Robert B., 569

Besley, Timothy, 259n19

Best shot aggregation technology, 15; 358

Best shot public goods, 358–60

Bettelheim, Eric C., 392, 409, 411, 412n5, 412n13, 412n18

Bezanson, Keith, 23n22, 544n19

Bhagwati, Jagdish, 92

Bhandari, Ruchi, 592

Bhattarai, Madhusudan, 352n17

Bhavnani, Rikhil, 518, 525n1

Bilateral donors, 532t, 539

Bilateral export credit agencies, 592, 597–98

Bilateral investment treaties (BITs), 76

Bill & Melinda Gates Foundation, 237, 270, 277

Binenbaum, Eran, 565

Biodiversity, 383–84; conserving, 374; Global Environment Facility facilitating preservation, 39; testing the market for products, 232–33

Biotechnology: lack of local expertise in using and regulating, 573; partnerships, 260n26

Bird, Richard M., 34, 172

Birdsall, Nancy, 23n19, 43, 529–45, 544n16, 544n19, 545n20, 601n18

BIS. See Bank for International Settlements

Blanchard, Olivier, 89, 99n23

Blending: domestic and external policy demands, 4, 28–30, 35, 58, 73–108; function of the state, 56. See also Intermediary state; International cooperation behind national borders

Blume, Lawrence, 259n12

Boadway, Robin, 178

Boerzel, Tania A., 221

Boettke, Peter, 393

Boix, Charles, 114

Bolho, Joelle, 87

Bolsa de Cereales, 423

Bolton, Patrick, 435, 436

Bombay Oilseeds and Oils Exchange, 423–24

Bond market, 438

Bonds, 612; corporate, 441; issued by governments, 286, 299n6; unindexed compared with GDP-indexed, 60

Bono, 153

Boogert, Kees den, 120

Boom-bust cycles: financial markets prone to, 596; in international private capital flows, 488; in private capital flows to developing countries, 496

Borcherding, Thomas E., 174

Borders. See National borders

Boren, David, 404

Borensztein, Eduardo, 51t, 60, 61n5, 159

Borrowing: by governments, 285; cost: 446; secured by donor commitments, 297

Boskin, Michael J., 21n1

Botswana, 237, 557

Bottazzi, Laura, 164n1

Boughton, James M., 63n18, 561n13

Bowen, Brian H., 537

Bowland, Bradley J., 368n3

Bowles, Roger, 313

Bradford, Colin I., 63n27

Bradford, David F., 182

Brady Plan, 438

Brain drain: from developing countries, 145

Brainard, Lael, 513

Bratton, William W., 448n3

Brazil: AES Tietê hydroelectric power generation company, 597; crisis lending to, 494

Brendsel, Leland C., 299n8, 396

Brennan, Geoffrey, 317n1

Brenner, Carliene, 570

Breton, Albert, 99n15

Bretton Woods institutions, 93, 270; role in multilateral lending, 486–509

Brinkerhoff, Derick, 259n19

Brinkerhoff, Jennifer M., 258n6, 259n19

Bristol-Myers Squibb Company and Foundation, 236, 260n26

British Social Attitudes Survey, 307, 308t

Brixi, Hana Polackova, 126n9, 142, 599

Broadwater, Ian, 219, 258n6, 258n8

Broecker, Wallace S., 149

Brokering special market deals, 223, 224–25t, 226, 235–36

Bruce, Neil, 178

Brugger, Ernst, 404

Bryant, Ralph C., 99n23, 283, 502n2

Bryla, Erin, 427, 429n9

Buchanan, James M., 22n3, 74, 304, 312, 317, 372

Buchheit, Lee, 433, 438, 440

Budapest Commodity Exchange, 424

Budget: long-term analytical perspective, 136–38; process, 141–43

Budget support, 519, 540

Budgetary development: in the European Union, 455

Budgetary rules: adjusting at the national level, 52–53

Buira, Ariel, 63n27, 93, 503n14

Bulgaria, 158

Bulíř, Aleš, 18, 283

Buljevich, Esteban C., 289

Burdekin, Richard C. K., 314

Burden- (or cost-) sharing: principle, 343; formula, 365

Bureaucracy: principal-agent theories of, 74; generating undue budget expansion, 175; in international agencies, 314–15

Burgess, Robin, 61n1

Burkina Faso, 525n3

Burnell, Peter, 313

Burnside, Craig, 318n12, 516, 524n1

Burt, Christopher D., 306

Buse, Kent, 259n15, 261n33

Bush, George W., 201, 202

Business actors. See Partnerships; Private sector

Business environment: national policy changes fostering, 88

Business ventures, 223, 224t, 229, 230–34

Byerlee, Derek, 566, 573, 576n1

Caballero, Ricardo J., 61n4, 61n5

Cadsby, C. Bram, 359, 366

Calder, Fanny, 234

Call options, 418

Cameron, David, 110

Campilan, Dindo, 568

Canada: incremental cost for international security efforts, 379; Department of Finance, 379–80

Canova, Fabio, 88

Capital: economic change creating a new demand for, 392, 394–95t; flows, 61n4; income, 174, 181; outflows, 170; raising for government spending, 285–86; tax competition to attract, 174

Capital markets: definition of, 612. See also Financial markets; International capital markets

Capital-export neutrality, 177; dividend-paid credit method and, 180; dividend-received credit method and, 179; dual income tax for and, 181

Capoor, Karan, 49f

Carbon dioxide: concentration in the atmosphere, 135, 20f

Carbon financial instrument (CFI), 400, 402t

Carbon reduction credits, 232

Carey, John, 88

Carlton, Dennis W., 417, 419, 420

Carney, Diana, 578n13

Carr, Stephen J., 568, 571

Carson, Richard T., 351n7

Casey, Bernard, 115

Cashore, Benjamin, 261n39

Cassava Biotechnology Network, 578n12

Catastrophe bonds, 90

Cauley, Jon, 206

CBP (contagious bovine pleuropneumonia), 382

Ceilings: on government spending, 283. See also Fiscal

CEPAL. See Comisión Económica para América Latina y el Caribe

CERN. See European Organization for Nuclear Research laboratory

Cernea, Michael, 343

CFI. See carbon financial instrument

CFRITF (Council on Foreign Relations Independent Task Force), 489

CGIAR (Consultative Group on International Agricultural Research), 565–66, 569, 577n5; grant-funded international agricultural research centers, 568; hiring scientists on a long-term basis, 578n11; international research centers, 569

Chagas disease, 537

Chalk, Nigel A., 287, 291

Challenge programs: incentive structure for introducing reforms, 516; working more as pull instruments, 517. See also Grants; Pull instruments

Chalmers, Malcolm, 315

Chang, Ha-Joon, 74, 437

Chapter 11: of the U.S. Bankruptcy Code, 443, 449n6

Charter of Budget Honesty: Australia, 137

Chernobyl Shelter Fund, 375

Chicago Board of Trade: agricultural commodity futures trading, 393, 394t, 396; clearing and settlement platform, 401; conducting annual auctions of allowances, 398; defining standard grain measures and grading, 396; evolution of standards, 412n7; founding of, 417

Chicago Climate Exchange, 39, 232, 398–401, 401; auction of carbon financial instruments in 2003, 400–401; detailed design of, 399; external advisory board members, 404–05; launching of, 399; main features of, 402–03t; members of (2004), 405–07; mission and goals, 400; products traded at, 399–400

Chichilnisky, Graciela, 390

China: potential to compete, 100n26; IDA loans, 475; SDR holdings of, 557

Choi, Joonook, 87

Christensen, Cheryl, 568, 571

Christian Aid, 240

Citibank N. A., 158

Civil society: 76, 77, 92, 236, 240

Claessens, Stijn, 424

Clark, John Maurice, 372

Clark, Peter B., 43, 498, 502n8, 549–62, 552, 561n5, 561n6

Clarke, Norman, 260n26

Clean Development Mechanism and Joint Implementation, 408–09

CleanTech Fund, 234

Clemens, Michael, 518, 525n1

Climate change. See Climate stability

Climate Investment Partnership, 232

Climate stability, 337, 339t, 340, 289, 390; benefits from international cooperation, 145; costs of corrective action, 134–36; fiscal implications of underproviding, 135; international negotiations, 351n11; fostering, 331–32; provision assessment for, 350; underprovision (overuse) provision problem, 331t

Cline, William R., 350

Clinton Foundation, 235, 255

Club good, 223, 224t, 421, 612

Cnossen, Sijbren, 23n20, 61n1, 88, 181

Coase, Ronald H., 7, 22n4, 390, 391

Coase theorem, 22n4

Coasean property rights-based approach, 390–21

Coatsworth, John H., 113

Code for Fiscal Sustainability (UK), 137

Code of Good Practices on Fiscal Transparency (IMF), 149n7

Cohen, Jonathan, 261n39

Cohen, Marc J., 565

Coherence of industrial country policies, 18, 42, 480–82

Coherent pattern of grants and loans, 478, 478f

Cohesion Fund, 156; added to the existing Structural Funds, 466n4; of the EU, 461

Cohesion policy: for the European Union, 465

Coleman, Jonathan R., 424

Collateralized mortgage obligations, 397

Collective action: 15, 33–34, 37–39, 41; at the international level, 18, 21; minus state coercion, 227; national compared with international, 14; problems, 351n4

Collective action clauses (CAC), 448n3; effects on low-risk versus high-risk countries, 446; making debt restructuring more efficient, 442; used in London markets and the United States, 440–41; in sovereign bond contracts, 440–43

Collier, Paul, 42, 471–84, 473, 474, 474f, 478f, 479, 483, 483t, 486, 504n28, 514, 516, 521, 523, 524n1, 526n17

COMESA. See Common Market for Eastern and Southern Africa

Comisión Económica para América Latina y el Caribe (CEPAL), 118

Command-and-control regulations, 390

Commercial risks: for infrastructure investments, 587–88

Commission for Africa, 18

Commission on Macroeconomics and Health, 62n12

Commission on the Private Sector and Development, 77, 241

Commitment to Development Index, 84, 99n20

Commodity exchanges, 392, 394–95t, 423–24

Commodity futures markets: developing country access to, 417–30; facilitating access to, 39–40

Commodity risk management, 424–27. See also International Task Force on Commodity

Risk Management in Developing Countries; Weather events

Commodity Risk Management Group, 427

Common Fund for Commodities, 429, 429n13

Common Market for Eastern and Southern Africa (COMESA), 254

Common pool approaches: financing international cooperation, 209; funding UN peacekeeping missions, 380

Communicable disease control: 375; incremental cost of controlling, 377; spending on, 90. See also Disease eradication

Comparative advantage: of different actor groups, 259–60n19; trading, 230

Compensation hypothesis, 109, 110; empirical evidence, 116; limited support for, 109; predictive value of, 111

Compensatory financing: of the Montreal Protocol, 363

Compensatory Financing Facility, 279n4, 429, 429n11, 493

Competition, 94; as fiscal discipline, 174–75; between intergovernmental organizations and global public-private partnerships, 241; reliance on, 4

Competitive government: national policy changes echoing, 88; theory of, 99n15

Competitiveness, 84, 92–93; indices of, 79–80; country rankings, 81

Conceição, Pedro, 3–23, 28–64, 36, 36f, 37, 38, 56, 59, 63n28, 63n29, 64n30, 138, 269–80, 278, 281–300, 284, 327–52, 328, 335, 343, 412n10, 428, 542

Concessional lending, 481; 499–502. See also Loans

Conditionality approach to aid disbursement, 516; content of, 493; evolution of, 76; for IMF drawings, 492, 503n15

Connolly, Stephen, 308

Conservation Finance Alliance, 387n6

Consumption taxation: cooperative coordination of, 185; entitlements, international equity, and efficiency for, 188t; entitlements with, 183–85; forms of, 183; international aspects of, 182–85, VAT, 183. See also VAT

Contagion effects: of a financial crisis, 589

Contagious bovine pleuropneumonia (CBP), 382

Contingent Credit Line, 494

Contingent liabilities, 142; from government guarantees, 137; monitoring for guarantees, 599

Contingent liquidity facilities, 595–97. See also Guarantee instruments

Contingent valuation, 351n7

Contracting out, 3, 7, 22n5, 81, 230–31, 251, 259n10, 260n21, 261n34, 587, 600n3

Contractual approach: comparing to the statutory approach, 444–46; evidence on, 446–47; to sovereign debt restructuring, 439–43. See also Collective action clauses, Debt restructuring

Cooperative rules: for economic efficiency and internation equity, 173–78

Coordination challenge: aid policy reform addressing for regional public goods, 540–41; of producing regional infrastructure and goods and services and managing multicountry institutions, 536; for regional public goods, 43, 529; of taxation of capital income, 174

Copenhagen Consensus: 335

Cordes, Joseph J., 259n17, 391

Cornes, Richard, 23n9, 23n11, 259n12, 333, 351n4, 351n6

Cornford, Andrew, 494, 498

Cornia, Giovanni Andrea, 100n28

Corporate income tax: falling average rate, 91–92; integrating with personal, 179–81; international administration of, 182; relation between countries' openness and tax rates, 92; source taxation of income implemented by, 172; treating as a separate tax, 178; as a withholding tax, 178

Corporate social responsibility: increasing importance attached to, 240; norms and standards, 233; protecting against potential risks, 231

Corporations: demonstrating social responsibility, 9; residency of, 190n7; taxation of, 170

Corruption score, 512t, 513

Cost comparisons: facilitated by incremental cost, 373

Costa Rica: rich biodiversity pool, 232–33

Cost-benefit analyses: considering externalities from severe underprovision, 542; difficulty of measuring positive and negative externalities, 544–45n20; as an indispensable step in rational decisionmaking, 52; lack of credible for regional public goods, 540

Cost-sharing arrangements: designing appropriate, 378–81; negotiating, 365–66

Council on Foreign Relations Independent Task Force (CFRITF), 489

Countercyclical tools: current account financing, 492; guarantee instruments, 596–98; lending, 486; role of public institutions in providing, 596

Countries, differentiating between 518–24. See Developing countries; Emerging market economies; Industrial countries; Low-income countries; OECD countries

Country performance and state behavior: measuring, 79–80, 82–83

Country Policy and Institutional Assessment (CPIA), 472, 484n1, 514; countries ranking lowest on, 484n3; score, 514

Country risks. See Risk(s)

Country selectivity: of the Millennium Challenge Account, 512–14; notion of, 524–25n1; using to influence more than the amount of aid, 510

CPIA. See Country Policy and Institutional Assessment

Credit rating agencies: criteria reflecting external policy expectations, 76; surveillance of long-term budget positions, 142

Credit ratings: of emerging markets, 501

Credit rationing: as an equilibrium outcome, 488

Creditor committees, 445

Crisis lending: by the IMF, 492–94, 499; terms of, 476

Cropper, Maureen L., 368n3

Cross-border externalities/spillovers. See Externalities

Cross-border flows: increase in, 19, 20f; sheer volume of, 194

Cullis, John G., 305, 308, 309, 314

Cultural heritage: protecting, 375

Cunningham, Alastair, 496, 497

Currency devaluation: impact on infrastructure projects, 588

Currency mismatch, 595–96

Currency-related guarantee instruments: for infrastructure projects, 585–601. See also Guarantee instruments

Cutajar, Michael Zammit, 405

Cutler, Claire A., 233

Dailami, Mansoor, 588

Daley, Richard M., 404

Dam, Kenneth W., 490, 491, 493, 502n6, 502n9

Daneshkhu, Scheherazade, 300n17

Daniels, Kenneth N., 299n7

Das, Tarun, 87

David Bowie bonds, 287

Davis, E. Phillip, 502n4, 502n5

Davis, Jeffrey, 89

Dawkins, Cedric, 77

De Ferranti, David, 88, 89, 121

De Jouvenel, Bertrand, 116

De la Vega, Josef Penso, 393

De Soto, Hernando, 391

De Tocqueville, Alexis, 309

Debatisse, Michel L., 422

Debt forgiveness: 153, 474. See also Heavily Indebted Poor Countries (HIPC) Debt Initiatives

Debt ratios: stabilizing in developing countries, 60

Debt restructuring, 435–37; of Argentina's debt, 438; deadweight losses, 435–36; Ecuador, Pakistan, the Russian Federation, and Ukraine restructuring, 436; statutory approach compared with the contractual approach, 444–46; evidence on, 446–47. See also Sovereign and sub-sovereign debt securities; Sovereign debt; Sovereign bonds

Debt securities, 285, 612

Debt sustainability, 42. See also Fiscal

Debt workout. See Debt restructuring

Debtor friendly restructuring procedure, 436

Decentralization, 46, 81, 85, 99n15, 114

Delgado, Christopher, 565

Dell, Sidney S., 491, 493, 502n9, 503n14

Dell'Ariccia, Giovanni, 437

DeLong, John Bradford, 504n25

Delors: President Jacques, 455, 457; I package (1988), 455, 458; II agreement (1992), 455, 460

Demographic challenges, 147. See also Long-term fiscal challenges; Population aging

Denmark: Ministry of Finance, 138

Derivative, 612; contracts, 299n4; products, 418

Derviş, Kemal, 18

Desai, Meghnad, 74

Detragiache, Enrica, 60

Deutsche Bank, 161

Devaluation coverage: for AES Tietê, 597. See also Currency devaluation

Devaluation Liquidity Backstopping Facility, 601n16

Developing countries: access to instruments of commodity risk management, 424–27; borrowing against future-flow receivables, 290; brain drain from, 145; capital market access, 504n27; commodity exchanges in, 423–24; declining tax revenues, 115; demographic challenges, 132–33; external financing to, 487; financial institutions and capital markets, 144–45; futures markets use, 422; guarantees to finance infrastructure in, 59; improving their business environment, 88; infrastructure development need, 585; instability of private flows to, 496; insufficient spending on agricultural R&D, 565–66; investing in infrastructure services, 587–90; lacking resources to enhance national security, 195; limited capacity to curb terrorism, 205; limited scope for direct social spending, 122; liquid market in the international debt securities of, 438; losses from tax havens, 61n6; median ratio of nongold reserves to short-term debt, 554f; public expenditure by regions (1980–1997), 113t; public investment guarantees, 590–94; public spending on pensions expected to rise, 115; ratio of nongold reserves to imports, 553f; reducing costly foreign reserve holdings, 43; social transfers in, 120; transference of terrorist attacks to, 206; as unfamiliar clients, 234; World Bank lending to (1970–2003), 496t. See also Low-income countries

Development, 15; achieving global security and stability, 17; advancing, 81; broadened global dimension of, 15, 17–18; external support for, 18; facilitating the involvement of private actors, 44; indices of, 82–83; opportunity costs, 17; production path of, 18–19

Development Assistance Committee: of the OECD, 89, 299n3, 530, 542, 543; *Development Cooperation Reports,* 538, 544n15

Development finance, 486, 494–95

Development venture capital funds, 234

Devereux, Michael P., 92, 169

Devlin, Julia, 428

DFID. See UK Department for International Development

DHS. See U.S. Department of Homeland Security

Diamond, Jared, 565

Diamond, Peter A., 351n7

Dias, João Carlos Pinto, 537

Differential contracting, 235

Differential cost, 372

Differential patenting, 235, 236; attracting private sector resources, 293; agreements negotiated by MMV, 256

Differentiating aid strategies: across countries, 518–24

Diffusion: of new technologies in tropical agriculture, 571

Dihel, Nora, 327

Dion, Michelle, 120

DiPerna, Paula, 404

Direct social spending. See Public social spending

Director, Aaron, 317n4

Director's Law, 309

Disaster Resource Network: of the World Economic Forum, 238

Disease eradication: as an example of a weakest link public good, 360; incentives for, 360; viewing in a binary way, 333. See also Communicable disease control; Polio eradication; Smallpox eradication

Distorted provision of public goods, 329

Distribution: activities of the state, 74; of net benefits of enhanced provision of global public goods across broad groups of countries, 336–37; of the net benefits from an international cooperation initiative, 335–36

Distribution branch of public finance, 10, 15

Distribution-sensitive global public goods assessment: designing, 336; full assessments of, 345–50; methodology for, 337–43; summary of results from, 338–39t

Diwan, Ishac, 566

Dixit, Arinash, 259n19

Dixon, Anna, 309

Dixon, Liz, 496, 497

Dodd, Randall, 283

Doha Round: of multilateral trade negotiations, 78

Dohrmann, Thomas, 99n15

Dollar, David, 23n13, 153, 318n12, 471, 473, 474, 474f, 478f, 479, 483, 483t, 516, 524n1

Donations: financing social ventures, 229

Donors, 343; borrowing against promises to pay, 294–98; coordinating, 481; financing for regional public goods, 538–40; financing public investment, 544n12; pushing countries to reform, 511; repeatedly buying the same reforms, 516; strengthening regional institutions, 541; support for tropical agriculture R&D, 567–70

Dooley, Michael, 436

Double bottom-line ventures, 223–24, 224t, 229, 234–35, 270

Double taxation: of dividend income, 178; of dividends, 179

Dougherty, Keith, 259n12

Douglas, William O., 441

Dowdeswell, Elizabeth, 405

Downs, Anthony, 306, 308, 317n2

Drehr, Axel, 307

Drèze, Jean, 342

Drezner, Daniel W., 99n23

Ducaton shares, 393, 394t

Duncan, Ronald, 424

Dynamic benefits: maximizing from new inventions, 332

Dynamic efficiency, 613

E7 Fund for Sustainable Energy Development, 234, 277

Easterly, William, 516, 525n1

Ebrill, Liam, 88

EC. See European Commission

Economic Community of Central African States, 535

Economic Community of West African States, 535

Economic derivatives market, 161

Economic openness: correlating with change in public spending, 116; expectations of, 30; indices of, 79–80; lower revenue for many developing countries, 116; multilayered notion of, 77; national policy reforms to promote, 31

Economic rationales: blending with foreign policy goals, 34–45, 35f

Economic risks: bearing long-term, 50; national policy changes regarding, 89. See also Risk(s); Risk management; National risk management

Economic unions: assigning responsibility for the corporate income tax to, 182; meeting the criterion of capital-export neutrality, 181

Economic volatility: protection and insurance against the consequences of, 83, 89

Economies of scale, 231, 613; benefiting from, 43–44

Economies of scope, 231, 613

Economy, Elizabeth C., 99n23

Ecuador, 436

ECX Carbon Financial Instruments (ECX CFIs), 403

Edison, Hali, 561n9

Edwards, Jeremy, 174

Edwards, Michael, 92

Effective tax rate, 190n8

Efficiency: enhancing for foreign aid, 42–45; gains possible with the new public finance tools, 58–60

Efficiency hypothesis, 109, 110; associated with declining public expenditures, 110; empirical evidence to support, 116; predictive value of, 111; some empirical support for, 109

Efficiency or allocation branch: of public finance, 10

Ehreth, Jennifer, 348, 349

Eichengreen, Barry, 40, 126n1, 433, 433–49, 438, 445, 446, 447, 499, 504n25, 504n26, 596, 600n9

Einhorn, Jessica, 495

Ekpo, Akpan H., 87

El Niño, 149

El Oraby, Nivine, 87

Elderly: cost of public benefits for in industrial countries, 133, 134f; increasing population share of, 147. See also Pensions; Population aging

Emerging Africa Infrastructure Fund, 234

Emerging market economies: contract renegotiations in, 589; cost of borrowing for, 554; credit ratings of, 501; external financing of, 434t; IMF as a crisis lender for, 493–94; investment climates rated as speculative, 497; median ratio of nongold reserves to short-term debt, 554f; ratio of nongold reserves to imports, 553f; reserve-holding behavior of, 561n9; risk management treaties, 155; sovereign bond issuance by jurisdiction, 441t; underrepresented in the multilateral banks, 545n24. See also Developing countries

Emerging Markets Creditors Association, 436

Emissions: allowances for sulfur dioxide, 397; offsets, 400; targets, 60; trading, 145, 391–92. see also Pollution permit trading

Emission reductions: credits purchased by the Prototype Carbon Fund, 252; exchange of credits that result from project-based, 398; valuing, 404

Enderlein, Henrik, 465

Enders, Walter, 195, 196, 206, 210, 214n3

Enhanced Structural Adjustment Facility: of the IMF, 493

Ennew, Christine T., 423

Enron Corporation, 299n12

Enterprise LSE, 260n20

EPA. See U.S. Environmental Protection Agency

Equity branch: of public finance, 10

Equity security, 613

Espinoza, Alvaro, 87

Esty, Benjamin C., 600n3

Esty, Daniel C., 38, 63n22

Ethical Trading Initiative, 233

EU. See European Union

EU Budget Treaty (1970), 459–60

EU Greenhouse Gas Emission Trading Scheme (EU ETS), 62n15, 90, 398, 403

Euler Hermes of Germany, 592

Eurobonds, 443

Eurodollar market, 503n24

European Bank for Reconstruction and Development (EBRD), 532t; Chernobyl Shelter Fund, 375; web site of, 600n10

European Climate Exchange, 403

European Commission (EC), 49f, 62n15, 231, 250, 258n1, 293, 453, 455, 457, 459, 460, 461, 462, 462t, 464t, 465, 466n6; budgetary reform and expansion, 457; budgetary reform efforts, 455; competing concerns of member states and candidate states, 461; Council, 455

European Investment Bank, 494

European Organization for Nuclear Research (CERN) laboratory, 360

European Space Agency, 231, 250, 293

European Union (EU), 144, 164n5; allocation of aid not poverty efficient, 479; annual budget negotiations, 455, 457; budgetary resources remaining limited, 453; concentrating on the lowest income countries, 481; consolidation of expenditure levels, 461–63; creating the Chernobyl Shelter Fund, 375; determination of the budget level of, 466n6; experience with regional public goods provision, 41; explicit provisions for effective risk sharing among member countries, 156; financial perspective for 2000–06, 464t; financing of the budget controversial at times, 454; as an in-between institution, 453; key dates in the evolution of the budget, 456; lessons for international cooperation, 465–66; main influence through regulatory measures, 454; multiyear framework for the annual budget, 454, 457–58, 460–61; net budgetary position of member states (2002), 462t; overall expenditure, 460; past budgetary commitments, 454; phases of budgetary development, 455; preoccupation with finance for programs that redistribute, 309; providing primarily grants, 471; public finance evolved incrementally, 454; public finance in, 453–66; purchasing excess supply to regulate output, 313; referring to a country, 214n17; revenue sources, 454; size and structure of the budget of, 459; spending priorities responding to new challenges, 463, 465; Stability and Growth Pact, 144; Structural Fund, 462; support for ATI, 254; system of public finance, 453

Eurostat, 300n18

Evans, Lloyd T., 577n3

Evenson, Robert E., 529, 565, 567, 576n2, 576n2, 578n10

Exchange allowances, 399–400

Export credit agencies, 596–97, 598

Export Credits Guarantee Department (UK), 592

Export Development Canada, 592

Export processing zones, 88

Export Risk Guarantee Agency (Switzerland), 592

Export-Import Bank (U.S.), 592

Extended fiscal accounting, 31, 37, 137

Extended Fund Facility (IMF), 279n4, 493

External policy expectations: clusters of, 77; contents of, 77–84; echoing in national public policy, 88–90; growth in, 87; origins and forms of, 75–77; purpose of, 84–85; sources of, 76

External shocks: protecting against, 83–84; resulting from negative cross-border spillovers, 84

Externalities, 31, 196, 224–25, 390–91, 613; internalizing cross-border, 10, 19, 29–31, 85, 90, 196, 304, 311. See also Negative cross-border externalities; Positive externalities

Fabozzi, Frank J., 286, 287

Factors of production: mobility of, 57. See also Tiebout effect

Fair Trade Labeling Organization, 233

Fairness: as a policy goal, 10; in international agreements, 176; in global public goods provision, 341–43; in international cooperation, 209, 363, 366, 377, 457, 465

Fankhauser, Samuel, 350

Fannie Mae, 286, 287, 397, 412n9

Faruqee, Rashid, 424

Fasano, Ugo, 89

Federal Home Loan Mortgage Corporation. See Freddie Mac

Federal National Mortgage Association. See Fannie Mae

Federal Reserve Bank of Kansas City, 99n17

Fehr, Ernst, 364

Feinstein, Osvaldo N., 258n5

Feis, Herbert, 445

Feldstein, Martin S., 149n5, 169, 185

Fenner, Frank, 347, 362

Ferris, James, 240

Ferroni, Marco, 23n9, 62n11, 309, 315, 539, 544n16

Fidler, Stephen, 504n25

Final public good, 613. See also Intermediate public good

Finance vehicles: role of, 291

Financial and insurance sectors: risk-taking behavior fostered by, 152

Financial crises, 12, 139, 147, 487–88

Financial innovations: market creation associated with, 389–90; efficiency gains from, 51; moving towards adoption, 47–58; socially desirable failing to emerge, 442

Financial intermediation, 240, 281–97, 389–90, 424–28, 613

Financial markets: behaving procyclically, 489; expanding global, 20f; failure of, 488; international, 495–97; introducing developing countries to, 476; overcoming resource constraints by turning to, 37. See also Capital markets; International capital markets

Financial stability: integration into global capital markets and, 497; international, 331t. See also International financial architecture

Financial Sustainability Forum, 49f

Financing: conventional notion for international cooperation, 283–85; of global public-private partnerships, 229; international cooperation, 281; required for the new public finance, 53–55; required to achieve internationally agreed goals, 62n12; as a strategic incentive, 357–68

Financing arrangements: issue-specific, 276, 290

Financing mechanisms: definition of, 269–70; created and cumulative number of, 275f;

established in the 1990s, 276; focusing on global public goods provision, 276; funding sources of new, 277f; growing diversification of, 269–80; issue-specific, 276; number and type of, 269; supporting international cooperation, 1930–present, 271–73t; to encourage regional lending, 542

Financing of global public goods: as different from foreign aid, 9–10, 38, 42; link with foreign aid, 4, 18, 35; hierarchy of policy interventions for, 40–42; mechanisms for, 276

Financing technologies: demand for and supply of, 53; demand for new, 52; new, 281–300; requiring institutional innovation, 290, 292; use of modern, 281. See also Financial intermediation; Indexation; Insurance

Financing tools: applications of new, 47, 51f; efficiency gains possible with the new, 58–60. See also Incentives; Public spending; Regulations

Finger, J. Michael, 312, 346

Finnvera of Finland, 592

Fiorina, Morris P., 317n1

First-responder grants, 202

Fiscal: accounting practices, 80, 137, 142–45, 148, 149n2; challenges, 131–50; deficit, 482; discipline, 3, 20, 29–32, 174–75; federalism, 466n6; illusion, 53, 305–08; projections, 137; rules, 143, 144; sustainability, 138–41, 143–45. See also Long-term fiscal challenges

Fiscal Responsibility Act (New Zealand), 137

Fiscal Strategy Report (New Zealand), 137

Fiscal termite hypothesis, 116, 117

Fischer, Ken, 566, 573, 576n1

Fischer, Stanley, 437, 498

Fitch Ratings, 98n9, 299n10, 587

Flat rate tax, 183

FLEX initiative, 429, 430n12

Flores, Nicholas E., 351n7

Florini, Ann, 261n31

Flypaper effect, 307–08

Ford Foundation, 270, 585

Foreign aid. See Aid

Foreign currency reserves, 32; holdings, 43. See also International reserves; Reserves

Foreign direct investment, 79, 88, 251, 494, 513; removal of regulations impeding, 88; confidence index, 89

Foreign exchange liquidity facility, 595, 596f. See also Guarantee instruments

Foreign investment, 88, 169, 171

Foreign tax: as a deduction from foreign-source income, 178; income taxes, 170, 171 net of, 169; treating the same as domestic tax, 177–78

Foreign trade taxes: as tax handles, 115. See also Tax(es); Tax handles

For-profit private investment fund, 270, 274f

Forward contracts: at the Chicago Board of Trade, 396

Forward markets, 392, 394–95t

Forward-looking contracts, 418

Foundation Center, 280n6

Foundations: differing from financing mechanisms, 270, 274f; as promoters of social venture partnerships, 240

Francois, Patrick, 259n19

Frankhauser, Samuel, 135

Freddie Mac, 286, 287, 397, 412n9

Free-riding, 351n4; incentive reduced by a weakest link aggregator, 209; international cooperation suffering from, 357; less risk of, 295–96; pure public good associated with, 199

Freedom House, 88, 89

Frey, Bruno S., 307, 314, 315

Fridson, Martin S., 393

Friedman, Thomas L., 93

Froot, Kenneth A., 22n6

Frost, Laura, 260n23

Fuglie, Keith, 578n10

Fujisaki, Tomoko, 260n23

Full provision of global public goods: determining, 330–33; not necessarily equivalent to optimal provision, 333; proposed definition of, 332; setting targets for, 334

Furubotn, Eirik G., 259n11

Future flow receivables, 287; role in project finance arrangements, 287; securitization of, 59, issuing securities backed by, 290

Futures: prices in relation to spot prices, 420

Futures contracts, 160,161, 403, 613; at the Chicago Board of Trade, 396; perpetual, 160, 161; settlement dates, 161

Futures exchanges: characteristics of, 419; club good character of, 421; listing of, 421t; trading volume on, 422–23t

Futures Industry Association, 417, 420, 421t, 422t

Futures markets: barriers to actors participating in, 422–23; creation of organized, 392, 394–95t; developing country access to, 417–30; functions of, 419; overview of the role of, 418–22; prerequisites, 424; use of, 422–24, facilitating access to, 39–40. See also Commodity futures markets

Fuzzo de Lima, Ana Teresa, 44, 286, 585–601, 600n4

G-7 (Group of Seven): creating the Chernobyl Shelter Fund, 375; energy-intensive projects and exports cofinanced by, 592; finance ministers, 300n19

G-8 (Group of Eight), 18, 99n17; list of activities, 214n7; summit meetings of, 83, 92, 93, 245

G-10 (Group of 10), 438, 443, 448n2, 449n6

G-20 (Group of 20) developing countries, 93

G-22 (Group of 22), 434, 438, 448n2

GAB (General Arrangements to Borrow), 448n2

Gabriel, Omon, 258n1

Gächter, Simon, 364

Gadanecz, Blaise, 289, 601n13

Galbraith, John Kenneth, 116, 306

Gale, Douglas, 442

Galileo satellite navigation system, 230–31, 250, 292; revenue stream arising from sales of private services, 293

Gallup International, 23n15

Game theory: asymmetric games, 213, 213f; burden sharing in formal, 365–66; equilibria in analytical, 359; representations countering terrorism, 199; symmetric games, 212f

Gardner, Bruce L., 422

Garrett, Geoffrey, 110, 114, 116, 126n5

Garten, Jeffrey, 405

GAVI (Global Alliance for Vaccines and Immunizations), 514, 525n10

Gavin, Michael, 500

GDP-indexed bonds, 51t, 60, 61n5, 159; as a precursor to macro markets, 160; as a precursor to more encompassing risk management options, 32

GEF. See Global Environment Facility

Gelb, Alan, 529, 543n7

Gemell, Norman, 306

Gene use-restriction technologies (GURTs), 572, 576–77n3, 577–78n9

General Agreement on Tariffs and Trade (GATT), 312

General obligation bonds, 286

Geradin, Damien, 63n22

Ghatak, Matreesh, 259n19

Gibson, Tom, 234

Giesen, Wim, 387n5

Gilardi, Fabrizio, 8f

Gilbert, Christopher J., 417, 487, 499, 500, 502n1

Gilbert, Christopher L., 62n16

Giles, Chris, 300n17

Gill, Gerard J., 578n13

Ginnie Mae, 286, 396–97, 412n9; as a part of the U.S. government, 287; pass-through instrument, 397

Glaeser, Edward, 113

Glasius, Marlies, 76

GlaxoSmithKline, 260n26

Glennerster, Rachel, 51t, 59, 294, 565, 578n14

Global Alliance for Tuberculosis Drug Development, 236

Global Alliance for Vaccines and Immunizations (GAVI), 514, 525n10

Global benefits of enhanced provision of global public goods: 333–35; assessment of 335–37; attached to redistribution, 487. See also Provision of global public goods

Global business and civil society: 94, 95; correcting government failure 96; promoting global efficiency and equity 94. See also: Civil society; Global markets; Nonstate actors

Global Business Coalition on HIV/AIDS, 239, 241, 257

Global challenges: 2,5,6f; addressing, 327–28; agenda of, 2; financing through international cooperation, 28–64; incorporating into national public finance, 29–34; increased public spending on, 85; international and national aspects of, 5, 6f

Global Climate and Energy Project, 237

Global climate change. See Climate stability

Global Coalition for Africa, Economic Committee, 545n22

Global Compact, 233–34, 261n29

Global costs: of corrective actions, 334; of current provision, 334

Global countercyclical facility, 499

Global Crop Diversity Trust, 245

Global development, 18, 24, production path 24. See also Development

Global Environment Facility (GEF), 39, 239, 276, 380–81, 383, 384, 385, 386n3, 387n9, 387n10; current structure and functioning, 261n36; financing incremental costs of biodiversity conservation, 374; financing incremental costs reducing emissions of greenhouse gases, 374; funding as additional, 315; payment of incremental costs by, 277; Small Grants Program, 387n5

Global equity: for development, 9–10, 15, 19f

Global fund model: as cost-sharing arrangements to compensate incremental costs 378–81; diffuse benefits, 379–81, 380f; of pooled compensation, 378

Global Fund to Fight AIDS, Tuberculosis, and Malaria, 209, 219, 235, 238–39, 239, 255, 257, 514, 526n10

Global HIV Vaccine Enterprise, 245

Global Institute for Partnership and Governance: of the World Economic Forum, 241

Global insurance industry. See Insurance

Global markets: 29, 136, 415n; collective action for the efficiency of 96; correcting public policy failure, 38–39; governments cooperation with 32, 46; failure of, 96; international organizations and, 10; in risk management 29, 30, trading in 54; competitiveness in 533. See also International capital markets; Markets

Global Monitoring Reports (World Bank), 536

Global natural commons, 329

Global Polio Eradication Initiative, 238

Global Programme on Maritime and Port Security, 209

Global public bads: 84, 91, 332

Global public finance, 5, 46. See also New public finance; Public finance theory

Global public goods, 10, 529, 614; considered to be remote, 284; efficient provision level of, 55–56; evolution of the provision of, 41–42; examples with provision problems, 330, 331t; fair and adequate provision of, 45; financing mechanisms for the provision of, 276; global net benefits of investing in, 333–35; identifying additional costs of contributing to, 372; improving the provision of, 334; link with globalization, 11; listing of, 502n3; preferences for, 57; production path of, 12, 14f; provision of, 487; subjecting provision to investment thinking, 38–42; underuse of, 328; hierarchy of policy interventions to provide, 40–42. See also Climate stability; Communicable disease control; Distribution-sensitive global public goods assessment; Financial stability; Financing of global public goods; Knowledge; Peace; Provision of global public goods; Security; Terrorism control; Transnational public goods

Global public policy networks, 58. See also Global business and civil society; Nonstate actors

Global public-private partnerships, 219–21; ad hoc origins, 244; advantages over intergovernmental organizations, 242; ambitious missions pursued by, 229; classes of, 223; contributing to global public goods provision and foreign aid, 35; defining, 221–22; enduring role for, 239; functional types of 224–39; modes of, 225–28, 225t, 243; growth in number of, 219, 239–41; intergovernmental organizations and, 241–42; judging the performance of different forms of, 243; listing with web addresses, 248–49; overview of the current landscape of, 221–29; profiles of, 229–39; types of, 226; typology for, 223, 224t. See also Public-private partnering; Public-private partnerships

Global R&D partnerships, 237

Global reporting initiatives, 233, 334

Global reports, 76

Global security, 33. See also Peace; Security

Global Water Partnership, 237

Globalization: from about 1870 to the beginning of World War I, 111; constraining public spending, 125; effects on tax systems, 167; examining earlier periods of, 111–13; fostering, 84; increasing a country's exposure to external risks, 110; intended, 11; link with global public goods, 11; link with public spending, 109; looking from the outside in, 21; new phase of, 4–5; pursuing policies of sustainable, 30; response to, 4; reversal in sentiments about, 92; risks intensified by, 140; systematic study of the links with public spending, 111; unintended, 11

GlobeScan Inc., 240

Göeschl, Timo, 566

Gold standard, 111, 126n1

Golden Rule of the United Kingdom, 144

Goldman Sachs, 161

Goldstein, Morris, 98n8, 489, 494, 499

Gómez-Ibáñez, José A., 588, 589

Gorton, Gary, 299n12, 429n3

Gottschalk, Ricardo, 60

Governance, 18, 43, 45, 75, 79–82, 318n12, 318n15; aid allocations and, 472–74, 480, 482, 484n1, 484n2, 484n3, 510–12, 515, 518–24; corporate, 22n5, 144, 150; of global public-private partnerships, 257, 261n31

Government(s): assigning new property rights, 40; changing programs to promote fiscal sustainability, 138–41; changing role of, 8f; cooperating with global markets, 32–33; contracting out arrangements, 230; from direct resource provider to incentive provider, 284; enabling project comparison to collect revenue, 289; entering into partnerships with each other, 222; expenditures providing social insurance against external risk, 110; as financial backstop for catastrophic situations, 140; hedging against commodity price volatility, 32; role in managing personal risk, 123; outsourcing of tasks by, 7; providing incentives to private actors, 284; potential fiscal implications of climate change, 135; pursuing policies of sustainable globalization, 30; regulation, 8; reluctant to sacrifice autonomy over security matters, 210; risk management treaties between, 154–55; role as the ultimate reinsurer, 134; scaling back direct ownership, 8; spending, 110; tapping into the pool of global resources, 46. See also Public spending; State(s)

Government debt securities, 286. See also Sovereign debt

Government failure: 37, 38, 74; correction by markets and NGOs, 37–38, 55–56; correction by nonstate actors 96; revisiting, 96; sources of, 7

Government National Mortgage Association. See Ginnie Mae

Government Petroleum Fund (Norway), 139

Grant assistance: as a development assistance tool, 45

Grants, 614; actual allocation of, 479–80, 480f; assessing a recipient's suitability, 472; challenge grants, 43, 510–26; characteristics, 477; clarifying rationales for, 42–43; combining with loans more coherently, 474, 478–79; EU aid in the form of, 479; for low-income countries, 499–502; proposed, more coherent use of, 480–82; as public resource transfers, 471; rationale for combining with loans, 476–78; regressions of actual, 483; to very low-income countries, 477. See also Loans

Great Depression, 116

Green, Constance, 577n8

Green, Jerry R., 577n3

Green Dot, 233

Green revolution, 569

Greenhouse gas emissions, 390; allowances trading in, 232; emergence of the market in, 399. See also Climate stability; Greenhouse gases

Greenhouse gases, 400, 402t, 413n22; costs of reducing, 135–36; emergence of the market in, 399; emission trading, 408–09; pilot scheme in the emerging market, 398–401; raising average global temperatures, 134; reducing emissions of, 374

Greenland, D. J., 569

Griffith, Rachel, 92

Griffith-Jones, Stephany, 44, 60, 286, 307, 585–601, 588, 598, 600n7

Grimwade, Nigel, 466n1

Grossman, Gene M., 352n17

Group of Seven (G-7): creating the Chernobyl Shelter Fund, 375; energy-intensive projects and exports cofinanced by, 592; finance ministers, 300n19

Group of Eight (G-8), 18, 99n17; list of activities, 214n7; summit meetings of, 83, 92, 93, 245

Group of 10 (G-10), 438, 443, 448n2, 449n6

Group of 20 (G-20) developing countries, 93

Group of 22 (G-22), 434, 438, 448n2

Growth-indexed bonds. See GDP-indexed bonds

Grubert, Harry, 169, 185, 190n11

Grunberg, Isabelle, 23n9, 352n22, 386n1, 502n3

Guarantee instruments: 45, 59, 142, 590, 599n1; advantages of 44; available today, 591; compared with advanced purchase commitments, 44; contingent liquidity facility 594–99; countercyclical 594, 599; for currency-related risks in developing countries 596–99; cushioning risks for private actors, 44; expanding the set of, 594–98; gains from issuing 51, 59; issued by aid agencies, 51t; leveraging private finance for public policy purposes, 286–87; by multilateral and bilateral agencies, 586; programs of the multilateral development banks, 600n10; reducing risks for the private sector, 590; shortcomings of current, 594; sovereign guarantees pool 598–99. See also Infrastructure development

Guasch, J. Luis, 589, 600n8

Gugiatti, Mark, 446

Guha-Khasnobis, Basudeb, 99n12

Guillaumont, Patrick, 428

Gulati, G. Mitu, 433, 440, 448n3

Gunningham, Niel, 258n1

GURTs (gene use-restriction technologies), 572, 576–77n3, 577–78n9

Haberham, Amir, 120

Habito, Cielito F., 87

Hacche, Graham, 549

Haldane, Andrew G., 498

Hall, Robert E., 183

Haller, Hana, 76, 98n7, 99n22, 351n12

Hamann, Javier, 18, 283

Handoussa, Heba, 87

Hansmann, Henry, 229

Hanson, James A., 99n23

Hardin, Garrett, 304, 391

Hari, Rajan, 281–300

Harmonization, 80, 84, 175. See also Policy harmonization

Harris, Clive, 22n5, 258n1, 600n4

Hart, Oliver, 259n11

Hartman, David G., 169

Hartz IV reforms, 100n27

Hassan, John, 316

Hassanali, Sabeen, 510

Hasseldine, John, 317n8

Hastie, Charlotte, 308t

Haufler, Virginia, 233

Hausman, Jerry A., 351n7

Hayami, Yujiro, 566, 577n4

Hayes, Simon, 496, 497

Hayibor, Sefa, 77

Hayter, Teresa, 317n6

Hazell, Peter, 429n9

Heady, Christopher, 88

Heal, Geoffrey, 199, 304, 390

Health insurance, 121, 140. See also Insurance; Social Protection

Heavily Indebted Poor Countries (HIPC) Debt Initiatives, 474. See also Debt forgiveness; Debt restructuring

Hedging, 158, 419, 614; functions of, 420f; options attractive to hedgers, 418–19; scheme, 429n6; against weather-related and other output risks, 426

Held, David, 99n23

Heller, Peter S., 31, 83, 124, 131–50, 149, 282

Henry, Peter Blair, 596

Herding behavior, 489

Herdt, Robert W., 567

Hertel, Thomas, 38, 345, 346

Heston, Alan, 164n4

Hewitt, Daniel, 308

Higgott, Richard, 502n3

High-Level Forum on Aid Effectiveness, 42

High-Level Forum on Harmonization, 42

High-Level Panel of the United Nations Secretary-General: on security challenges, 84

High-Level Panel on Threats, Challenges and Change, 17, 33

High-return investments: identifying, 328, 340–41

Hillman, Arye L., 3

Hills, Carla A., 499

Hills, John, 307

Hines, James R. Jr., 169, 170

Hinz, Richard, 121

HIPC. See Heavily Indebted Poor Countries Debt Initiatives

Hirschman, Albert, 228

Hirshleifer, Jack, 23n11, 214n5, 367n2

HIV/AIDS, 37, 82, 85, 245, 255, 277, 377, 535; partnerships, 237, 239, 245, 248, 257

Hoeffler, Anke, 471

Hoffman, Bruce, 195, 210

Holzmann, Robert, 121

Honohan, Patrick, 99n23, 126n6

Hookworm Vaccine Initiative, 236

Hopkins, Michael, 240

Horesh, Edward, 313

Houthakker, Hendrik S., 412n4

Howard, Christopher, 126n7

Howe, Neil, 133, 134f

Hubbard, R. Glenn, 435

Hudson, John, 317n2

Hueth, Darrell L., 351n13, 352n19

Huffman, Wallace E., 567, 568, 576n2, 577n4, 578n11, 578n13

Human development: reversals of, 81, 83; expenditures meeting basic, 477

Human rights, 9, 17, 76, 78, 81–82, 89, 96, 231, 234, 258n6

Hyman, David, 309

IBRD (International Bank for Reconstruction and Development): conception and realignment of, 486; declines in net flows from, 495; loans provided by, 476; postwar reconstruction as the rationale for, 491–92. See also World Bank

IDA (International Development Association), 254, 381, 501, 525n3, 545n23; converting credits into grants, 501; eligibility for assistance from, 558; establishment of, 494; expansion of grants, 501; historical cutoff for eligibility, 521; multilateral loan instruments, 475; as poverty efficient, 479. See also World Bank

IDB. See Inter-American Development Bank

IETA. See International Emissions Trading Association

IFC. See International Finance Corporation

Ihori, Toshihiro, 87

IFF. See International Finance Facility

IIF. See Institute for International Finance

IITA (International Institute of Tropical Agriculture), 564, 568, 571

IKEA Group, 251

Ikenberry, G. John, 94

ILO. See International Labour Organization

IMF (International Monetary Fund), 20f, 49f, 61n5, 98n8, 118t, 126n6, 139, 299n4, 300n17, 434, 445, 449n6, 465, 494, 503n15, 503n16, 503n17, 551, 553f, 554f, 561n14, 561n15, 562n16, 562n18, 562n21; accounting for fiscal deficits biased, 481; amending Articles of Agreement, 444; annual surveillance discussions, 143; Article IV consultations, 150n8; Code of Good Practices on Fiscal Transparency, 149n7; conception and realignment of, 486; conditions governing members' drawings, 492; coordinator for the grant and loan composition of aid, 481; countering sharp declines in private capital flows, 499; from coutercyclical current account lending to crisis lending, 492–94; credits, 560; emergency assistance, 429n11; emergency assistance of, 429; guaranteeing private investors, 437; high cost of reserves to members, 549; international economic stability as the rationale for, 490–91; as lender of last resort for emerging markets, 498–99; loan program conditions, 76; providing mainly loans, 471; providing short-term international liquidity, 498; reducing rescue operations,

437; resources transferring to developing countries, 311; specialized loan-making role, 481; specializing in crisis lending, 476; staff growth compared with the Bank for International Settlements, 314. See also Articles of Agreement; SDRs

INBio, 232–33

Incentives: challenge for regional projects, 539–40; changing structures, 63n18; for fostering international cooperation, 357; preferencers for the provision of, 41; problems and aid, 479; provision of 41; for regional public goods, 43, 542–43; supplementing command and control, 390; underlying public goods, 351n4

Income flows: securities representing, 157; not represented in securities markets, 152. See also Macro securities

Incomplete contracts, 226, 231, 488

Incremental cost: concept of, 56, 371, 374–75, 381, 386; baseline course of action in determining incremental cost, 374; evolution of the concept of, 371–73; facilitating costs comparisons, 373; helping decisionmakers choose, 372; methodologies for estimating, 382–86; offering an analytical framework, 373; for Okavango Delta alternatives, 382–84; payments between countries, 39; of preventing disease from spreading across borders, 377; reimbursement, 56; for a substitute project, 386; technical and political challenges of estimating, 373, 375–78; system boundaries during incremental cost estimation, 376

Index of future income, 49

Indexation, 52, 61n5

India: potential to compete, 100n26; study of a risk-sharing agreement for, 155

India-Brazil-South Africa Dialogue Forum, 93

Indices: of development and security, 82–83; of economic openness and competitiveness, 79–80; measuring country performance and state behavior, 76–77, 79–80, 82–83

Industrial countries: cost of public benefits for the elderly (2000 and 2004), 134f; government expenditures (1870–1980), 112f; impact of population aging, 133; under increasing competitive pressure, 93; leaving out of the SDR allocation, 557; ratio of nongold reserves to imports, 553f; requesting developing countries to undertake corrective actions on their behalf, 373

Informal spot market: institutional architecture of, 401

Information Analysis and Infrastructure Protection Directorate, 202

Information: asymmetries, 99n21, 568; costs lowered by harmonization 80; efficiency,392, 412n4; imperfect 97n4; incomplete, 306; perfect, 614; problems, 56; transparent and comprehensive for budget 471–72

Infrastructure development: currency-related guarantee instruments for, 585–601; financing of multicountry, 541; investment in with private participation in developing countries (1990–2003), 589f; investment needs, 589–90. See also Guarantee instruments

Infrastructure services, 585, 587–90

Ingram, Alan, 87

Ingram, Gregory, 258n5

Initiative on Public-Private Partnerships for Health, 258n6

Innovation, 570–75; in public finance, 47–58; states fostering, 88–89. See also Financial innovations

Innovators, 162

Institute for Financial Markets, 89

Institute for International Finance (IIF), 433, 434t

Institute for OneWorld Health, 237

Institutional Development Fund: of the World Bank, 254

Institutional innovation: enhancing resource mobilization, 292–98; financing technology requiring, 290, 292; overcoming public sector resource constraints, 292

Insurance, 117–24, 614; health, 121–22, 140; industry pressure from extreme weather events, 134, 135; livelihood, 49; markets, development of, 141; unemployment, 122–23. See also Risk management

Intellectual property: revenues, 287; rights, 240, 577n3

Intelsat Ltd., 260n22

Inter-American Development Bank (IDB), 532t, 538, 544n17, 544n18; disbursements to regional programs and projects, 544n17; web site of, 600n10

Interdependence, 91, 489

Interest rates: charged by the World Bank, 492; pressure on global, 133–34; spread for infrastructure project lending, 593f

Interest rate futures contract, 397

Intergovernmental cooperation: 201; failure, 37–38

Intergovernmental organizations: advantages of global public-private partnerships over, 242; deliberately encouraging partnerships, 242; global public-private partnerships and, 241–42; identifying qualifying tasks for partnerships, 244; potential for resource mobilization, 231; reengineering systematically, 53–54; supporting international cooperation, 1930–present, 271–73t

Intergovernmental Panel on Climate Change (IPCC), 134, 135f, 136, 149n1, 351n11, 400, 412n2

Intermediaries, 423, 425

Intermediary state, 52, 53, 93–97, 94–97, 95; rise of, 73–100. See also Blending; State(s)

Intermediate public goods, 613

Internalization: of cross-border externalities, 30, 31, 85, 90

Internation equity, 175; implications of the dividend-paid credit method, 180; implications of the dual income tax for, 181

International agreements: on intellectual property rights, 240; making risk sharing part of, 155–56; trade covered by WTO, 48f

International AIDS Vaccine Initiative, 236, 270

International Air Transport Association, 312

International Bank for Reconstruction and Development. See IBRD

International bankruptcy court, 439

International burden sharing: guideposts for, 343

International capital markets: access to 497, 498, 501, 549, 553, 555–57, 560, development of 486, 500, 549; dispersing risk trough 32; failures of, 488; tapping into 37, 144, 585, 595; transition to, 476. See also Capital markets; Financial markets

International Civil Aviation Organization (ICAO): assessed contribution, 366; conventions, 205

International Clearing Union, 490

International collective action, 304. See also Collective action

International commodity agreements, 417

International Commodity Stabilization Fund, 502n7

International Competition Network, 99n14

International Conference on Financing for Development, 282

International Convention for the Suppression of Terrorist Bombings, 206

International cooperation: behind and beyond borders, 58, 86–87; changes in perspective on, 284–85, 285t; to control transnational terrorism, 205–10; conventional notion of financing for, 283–85; dilemma of, 235; earmarking gains to domestic producers, 313–14; financing global challenges, 28–64; financing of, 315–17; fostering national fiscal responsibility, 143–45; implementing through regulation, 311–12; implications for the current system of, 239–42; inadequate availability of resources for, 282; incentives for fostering, 357; as an iterative, looping process, 33; means of supplying global public goods, 304; methodology for assessing, 327–52; motivations for, 91; needs exceeding available resources, 283; new actors, 277–78; new concerns requiring, 276–77; new perspective on financing, 285t; passing costs to citizens in other nations, 312–13; policy analysis of the costs of, 316; policy implementation side, 219; as a policy lesson from the interwar years, 489; potential to deliver rent, 310; public choice analysis of, 304–18; suffering from free-riding, 357; supply of transnational public goods, 358–64; transformation into a multiactor process, 4, 28–29, 36; types of efforts, 292; voters willingness to finance, 305–10; as a worthwhile investment, 284

International cooperation behind national borders; 4, 29–34, 52, 95; country studies on 86–87; by internalizing cross-border spillovers, 131–52; in international terrorism control, limits of, 205–06; through tax coordination, 167–94

International cooperation beyond national borders, 4, 34–46, 52; in international terrorism control, 206–10, through the use of

strategic incentives, 357–70; by compensating countries for incremental costs, 371–88; through market creation 389–416

International Development Association. See IDA

International economic stability, 490–91

International efficiency: in resource allocation, 182

International Emissions Trading Association (IETA), 90, 403

International equity: implications of the dividend-received credit method, 179

International externalities: global public goods and, 487. See also Externalitites

International Finance Corporation (IFC), 44, 234, 494; contingent liquidity facility provided by, 601n15; offering partial credit guarantees, 592; of the World Bank Group, 234

International Finance Facility (IFF), 278, 294–98, 300n17; accounting for borrowing under, 300n18; enabling the frontloading of foreign aid, 37; Immunization pilot project, 298; income and disbursement patterns for proposed, 295f; schematic representation of, 296f

International financial architecture, 433, 448n2

International Financial Facility for Aviation Safety, 209

International financial markets. See Financial markets

International financial stability. See Financial stability

International financing: as an incentive or compensation, 15, 199, 211, 371, 373–74, 378, 383, 386; necessary for weakest link global public goods, 361; provision of best shot public goods with, 359–60; public goods characteristics arrangements of, 365; of summation weakest link public goods, 362–63

International financing mechanisms. See Financing mechanisms.

International financing tools. See Financing tools

International Forum on Globalization, 99n15

International Institute for Environment and Development, 387n5

International Institute of Tropical Agriculture (IITA), 564, 568, 571

International intellectual property rights regime, 332

International intermediation services, 418, 425–26

International Labour Organization (ILO), 115t, 246

International Maize and Wheat Improvement Center (CIMMYT), 569

International Maritime Organization (IMO), 366

International Monetary Fund. See IMF

International Oil Pollution Compensation Fund, 276

International Organization for Standardization (ISO), 233, 253

International Petroleum Exchange (IPE), 403

International pollution permit trading, 51t, 60, 64n29

International private capital flows, 19, 21, 169, 174, 181, 433, 488–90, 495–99

International reserves, 553–54, 555. See also Foreign currency reserves; Reserves

International Service for National Agricultural Research (ISNAR), 576n3

International Space Station project, 260n21

International Task Force on Commodity Risk Management in Developing Countries (ITF), 418, 423, 424, 425–26, 427, 429n7

International Telecommunication Union (ITU), 246, 260n28, 366

International Telecommunications Satellite Organization, 260n22

International terrorism, 98n7, 207–08t. See also Terrorism control

International Trade Organization, 502n7

International Treaty on Plant Genetic Resources for Food and Agriculture, 233, 278

Internet: 331t

Internet Corporation for Assigned Names and Numbers, 233

Investment funds, 270, 279n3

Investment thinking: global public goods and, 38–42

Investments: identifying high-return, 328, 340–41

Investors: estimating risk, 596; moral hazard for, 436–37; risks in infrastructure projects in developing countries, 587

IPCC. See Intergovernmental Panel on Climate Change

Iraq: SDR holdings of, 557

Irwin, Timothy, 588, 600n3

Isard, Peter, 63n18

Isham, Jonathan, 524n1

ISNAR (International Service for National Agricultural Research), 576n3

ISO. See International Organization for Standardization

ITF. See International Task Force on Commodity Risk Management in Developing Countries

Izaguirre, Ada Karina, 59, 585, 600n7

Jackson, Hugh, 372

Jackson, Richard, 133, 134f

Jacobs, Donald, 405

James, Clive, 565, 576n1

Japan: support for ATI, 254

Jayaraman, Rajshri, 311, 352n22

Jefferson, Richard A., 577n3

Jepma, Catrinus J., 18, 317n6

Jermann, Urban, 164n6

Johnson, Daniel K. N., 565

Johnson, H. Thomas, 371

Joint ventures: between businesses, 222

Jolly, Richard, 100n28

Jones, Philip, 22n3, 37, 54, 141, 304–18, 305, 306, 308, 309, 313, 314, 316, 317n2, 318n11

Jordan, Scott, 236, 237

Joskow, Paul L., 412n13

Joyce Foundation, 412n20

Jubilee Debt Campaign, 153, 154; 2000: campaigns, 100n25; debt reduction secured by, 164n3; role of, 92

Jubilee Plus, 439

Jungito, Roberto, 503n14

Just, Richard E., 351n13, 352n19, 568, 576n2, 577n4, 578n11, 578n13

Kaempfer, William H., 313

Kahler, Miles, 94, 99n23

Kaldor, Mary, 76

Kaldor, Nicholas, 184

Kameri-Mbote, Patricia, 260n26

Kamin, Steven B., 437

Kamps, Christophe, 8f

Kanbur, Ravi, 23n9, 311, 352n19, 352n22, 352n22, 540

Kaplan, Robert S., 371

Kapstein, Ethan B., 81, 89, 100n23, 311

Kapur, Devesh, 76, 98n8, 502n1, 503n14, 503n21, 503n22

Kaufman, Nancy H., 168

Kaufman, Robert R., 120

Kaufmann, Daniel, 524n1

Kaul, Inge, 3–23, 23n9, 28–64, 30, 35, 57, 62n11, 63n26, 73–100, 219, 219–62, 238, 258n6, 258n8, 278, 284, 292, 300n15, 306, 309, 312, 315, 316, 328, 352n22, 365, 386n1, 502n3, 542, 600n3

Keen, Michael, 61n1, 88, 175

Kektar, Suhas, 51t

Kell, Georg, 258n6

Kellenbenz, Hermann, 393

Kelly, Gavin, 258n1

Kemp, Simon, 306

Kendall, Leon T., 412n8

Kennedy, Joseph II, 405

Kenya: Commodity Exchange, 424; compared with the Republic of Korea, 475; terrorist attacks in, 194–95, 213–14n2

Keohane, Robert O., 23n21, 99n23

Ketkar, Suhas, 59, 287, 291, 300n13

Kettler, Hannah, 236, 237

Keynes, John Maynard, 55, 126n2, 490

Khan, M Mahmud, 348, 349

Khan, Zorina B., 566

Khanna, Madhu, 233

Khattry, Barsha, 115

Kiesling, Lynne, 389

Kifle, Henock, 503n22

Kindleberger, Charles P., 502n3

King, Kenneth, 39, 96, 100n33, 371–87, 373, 374, 375, 387n5

King, Robert G., 299n5

Kisley, Yoav, 576n2

Klabin, Israel, 405

Klemm, Alexander, 92

Klenow, Peter J., 78

Klingebiel, Daniela, 126n6

Knight, Will, 351n2

Knowledge: with commercial potential, 236; identifying frontiers and milestones, 332; noncommercial or tacit, 261n32; related spillovers, 78; World Bank as a bank of, 500. See also Advanced purchase commitments

Kohn, Meir, 286

Komen, John, 570

Körber, Achim, 313

Korea. See Republic of Korea

Kozul-Wright, Richard, 486

KPMG Corporate Tax Rate Survey, 91

Krasner, Stephen D., 93

Krattiger, Anatole, 576n1

Krebs, Tom, 126n6

Kregel, Jan, 486, 496

Kremer, Michael, 23n20, 44, 51t, 59, 246, 259n19, 294, 564–79, 565, 571, 572, 576n2, 578n14

Kresge Foundation, 517

Krishna, Pravin, 126n6

Kroszner, Randall S., 412n7

Krueger, Alan B., 352n17

Krueger, Anne, 433, 439, 443, 447

Krugman, Paul, 185, 489

Kunreuther, Howard, 90, 199

Kurtis, Bill, 405

Kuwait, 557

Kydd, Jonathan, 428

Kyoto Protocol, 399; carbon dioxide emission targets suggested under, 84; compared with the Montreal Protocol, 318n9; costs of, 136, 149n1; follow-up to, 403–04; meeting emission targets, 60

La Ferrara, Eliana, 113

Labatt, Sonia, 22n6

Laffan, Brigid, 41, 156, 453–66, 455, 457, 460, 461, 466n1

Laffont, Jean-Jacques, 589, 600n8

Lake, David A., 94, 99n23

Lamb, Robert, 286

Lancaster, Carol, 87

Landau, Jean-Pierre, 23n22

Landau report, 23n22, 300n17

Landcare Greenhouse Challenge program, 517

Lane, Timothy, 283

Lanjouw, Jean O., 577n9

Larson, Donald, 424, 426

Lash, Jonathan, 405

Laudsburg, Steven E., 351n2

Le Goulven, Katell, 62n11, 238, 306, 309, 312, 315, 352n22, 365

Le Grand, Julian, 309

Lebanon, 557

Lecocq, Frank, 49f, 252

Lederberg, Joshua, 360

Ledyard, John O., 42

Lee, Barbara, 529

Lee, Dwight L., 318n11

Leipziger, Danny, 588

Lerner, Josh, 332

Lerrick, Adam, 501

Leuthold, Raymond M., 424

Leviathan: argument, 174; school 306

Levin, Jonathan D., 222

Levine, Ross, 63n24, 152, 299n5, 525n1

Levine, Ruth, 537

Levy, Marc A., 23n21, 260n25

Lewis, John, 503n21

LIBOR. See London interbank offered rate

Libya, 557

Liebenthal, Andres, 258n5

Liebman, Jeffrey, 149n5

Linder, Stephen, 258n5

Lindert, Peter H., 111, 114, 115, 118, 120

Link, Albert, 237, 246f

Linn, Johannes F., 63n27

Lipschitz, Leslie, 283

Lisbon Strategy of the European Union, 88–89

Lister, Graham, 87

Liu, Rae, 529

Loans: actual allocation of, 479–80, 480f; arguments in favor of, 475–76; assessing whether a recipient is suited for, 472; characteristics making users more or less suitable for, 477; clarifying rationales for, 42–43; combining with grants, 474, 478–79; IDA aid in the form of, 479; proposed, more coherent use of, 480–82; as public resource transfers, 471; rationale for combining with grants, 476–78; regressions of actual, 483; risk of moral hazard, 476; World Bank financing provided as, 492. See also Concessional lending; Grants

Lobbyist's perspective: politicians' response to political pressure, 310–14

Lomasky, Loren, 317n1

Lomborg, Bjørn, 62n13, 352n15

London interbank offered rate (LIBOR), 549, 560n3

London Metals Exchange, 429n3

London School of Economics and Political Science, 372

Long-term analytical perspective: for budget analysis, 136–38

Long-term fiscal challenges: consideration of in the budgetary process, 141; independent and competent assessments of, 142–43; mechanism for public debate on, 143; policy options for addressing, 131–50; range of, 147–49; safeguarding the interests of future generations, 143; solving, 136–45; transparent and comprehensive information about, 142; of the twenty-first century, 132–36.

Lord, Christopher, 307

Lorentzen, Peter Lombard, 596

Lorrain, Dominique, 588, 589

Lovejoy, Thomas, 405

Lowenbourg, Anton D., 313

Low-income countries:concentrating grants among, 481; continuing rationale for concessional lending and grants, 499–502; converging on richer countries, 475–76; IDA as a common pool resource of, 475; under stress, 484n3. See also Developing countries

Luce, Edward, 100n26

Lurie, Jonathan, 396

Ma, Yue, 315

Maastricht Treaty, 460

Macro markets, 32, 51t, 60, 157–60; for national risk management, 158

Macro securities, 160, 162, 164n7

Macroeconomic and Financial Management Institute of Eastern and Southern Africa, 540–41

Maddison, Angus, 111

Maddison, David, 352n17

Mailand, Mikkel, 258n5

Majnoni, Giovanni, 99n23

Majority enforcement clauses: in Sovereign bond contracts, 439

Majority restructuring clauses: in Sovereign bond contracts, 439

Majority voting bias, 305, 308–10

Makundi, Flora, 565, 576n1, 578n12

Malaria: control, 16–17t; funding R&D for antimalarial drugs, 256; vaccine for, 59

Malaria Vaccine Initiative, 276

Malawi: economy of, 533

Malena, Carmen, 258n6

Malhotra, Anil K., 589

Mallet, Victor, 100n26

Maloney, William, 126n6

Malprovision: of global public goods, 342–43; of public goods, 329. See also Provision of global public goods

Management Science, 237

Mansfield, Edward D., 313

Marine Stewardship Council, 233

Market(s): access, 435; actors, 37; approaches 39–40; creation and evolution 389–90, 392–98; determining when economically feasible, 390–92; emergence of new, 389; exercising de facto coercive power over states, 57; generating suboptimal outcomes, 97n3; interactive partnership with states 7; integrating as a global public good, 13; leaving the provision of goods and services to, 74; managing personal risk, 123; producing public goods and services, 9; as public goods, 12; rebalancing with states 7–9. See also Global markets

Market failure, 614; correcting, 54; correcting role of states, 85; factors causing the emer-
gence of, 21–22n2; as a justification for state intervention, 7; as a policy lesson from the interwar years, 489; public goods as a potential case of, 328; reasons for, 304; regulations correcting, 121; revisiting, 96

Market-based approaches, 391; aimed at providing a cost-effective solution, 391–92; to the challenge of reducing greenhouse gas emissions, 398; to national risk management, 156–60; to pollution control, 412n3; treating the environment as a truly scarce resource, 391

Market-based risk management tools, 425–26

Market-embedding national public goods, 84

Market-facilitating national public goods, 84

Markowska, Agnieszka, 537

Marques, Rafael L., 389, 392, 412n18

Martin, Juan, 81, 90

Martin, Lisa L., 305

Martin, Philippe, 111

Martinez-Vazquez, Jorge, 498

Maskus, Keith, 332

Mason, Edward S., 503n21

Masters, William A., 565, 576n2, 578n10

Mathiason, Nick, 164n3

Matsukawa, Tomoko, 595, 597, 601n14

Mattock, Nina, 256

Matusz, Steven, 346

Maurer, Crescencia, 592

Mauro, Paolo, 51t, 60, 61n5, 159, 445

Mavrotas, George, 300n17

May, Peter, 126n8

Maynes, Elizabeth, 359, 366

MCA Monitor, 525n5

MCC. See Millennium Challenge Corporation

McCallum, John, 534

McCartney, Eric, 589

McDonnell, Ida, 23n15

McGilvray, James, 315

McGregor, Richard, 100n26

McKibben, Warwick J., 51t, 60

McKinnon, Ronald, 429n5

McKinsey & Co., 234

McLean, Brian J., 412n14

McLure, Charles E. Jr., 172, 183, 190n16

McQuaid, Ronald W., 258n5

Meade, Norman F., 351n7

Médecins sans Frontières, 236

Medicines for Malaria Venture (MMV), 236–37, 242, 256, 276; drawing on non-monetary assets, 293; granting patent rights on intellectual property developed, 278

Mehta, Paras, 23n20

Meltzer, Allan H., 500, 501, 504n25

Mendonca, Lenny T., 99n15

Mendoza, Ronald U., 38, 56, 63n29, 64n30, 138, 284, 312, 327–52, 328, 342, 428, 542

Merchant, Khozem, 100n26

Merck & Co., Inc, 232–33, 237, 260n23

Merit wants: providing, 310

Merlen, Sylvain, 49f, 64n30, 90, 269

Messner, Dirk, 87

Mexican crisis (1994–95), 438

Mexico, 443, 447

Mi2g Intelligence Unit, 351n2

Mian, Atif, 259n19

Michel-Kerjan, Erwann, 90

Micklewright, John, 280n5

Middle-income countries. See Developing countries

MIGA. See Multilateral Investment Guarantee Agency

Migration, 133, 147–48; international frame-work for productive, 145; of jobs, 92

Mikesell, Raymond F., 490, 491

Milani, Andrea, 358

Milanovic, Branko, 81, 89, 100n23

Millennium Challenge Account, 511; concen-trating resources, 513; country ownership, 514–15; country selectivity of, 512–14; depoliticizing the process of selecting countries, 513; different from traditional conditionality-based aid, 513–14; eligibility criteria for, 512t, 518; further pull dimen-sion of strict eligibility requirements, 518; overview of, 511–16; performance-based management, 515–16; reward for sound policy choices, 514; scaling up of aid funds, 515; using publicly available data, 514

Millennium Challenge Corporation (MCC), 511, 512t, 513, 514, 525n6; Board, 513

Millennium Development Goals, 18; 2015 deadline for, 20, 62n12, 283, 293; achiev-ing, 37; as a decisive call by the interna-tional community, 81, 99n16; developing countries financing cooperation to achieve, 93; development assistance required, 299n2; financing required to meet, 62n12; Goal 1, 20, 332; International Finance Facility proposed to finance, 294; meeting, 17; progress toward, 98n7; public invest-ment guarantees important for meeting, 586; resources needed to meet, 283

Miller, Marcus, 437

Millman, Gregory J., 429n2

Mills, Anne, 51t, 59

Milner, Helen V., 99n23, 313, 317n7

Mina, Wasseem, 498

Minsky, Hyman, 488

Minstrom, Michael, 240

Mintz, Jack M., 34, 172, 178

MIPT (National Memorial Institute for the Prevention of Terrorism), 196

Miranda, Mario, 429n9

Mishkin, Frederic S., 502n4

Mkandawire, Thandika, 100n28

MMV. See Medicines for Malaria Venture

Mobile actors: encouraging certain behavior by the state, 96; taxing, 33

Mody, Ashoka, 23n9, 62n11, 142, 309, 315, 446, 447, 596

Mohammed, Azizali, 557, 558, 562n17

Mohieldin, Mahmoud, 87

Montreal Protocol: compared with the Kyoto Treaty, 318n9; compensation for the incre-mental cost of emission reductions, 374; participation nearly universal, 364; supply-ing ozone layer protection, 363; threat of restricting trade, 364

Montreal Protocol Fund. See Multilateral Fund for Implementation of the Montreal Protocol

Moody's ratings, 98n9

Moral hazard, 488, 614; aggravating creditor, 499; as a consideration in the insurance market, 141; creating creditor, 498; for investors, 436–37; loans and, 476

Moran, David, 405

Moran, Theodore H., 588, 597

Morantz, Alison, 575

Morgan, C. Wyn, 32, 89, 149n6, 245, 417–30, 420, 422, 423, 424

Morocco Solar-Based Thermal Plant Project, 387n4

Morrisey, Oliver, 313

Morrison, Kevin, 23n9

Morrissey, Oliver, 306

Mortgage-backed securities, 286; deconcentration of the market for, 397; trading, 396–97

Mortgages: secondary markets for selling, 286

Mosley, Layna, 99n23

Moss, Todd, 529

Mueller, Dennis, 309, 314

Multilateral development banks: guarantee programs of, 600n10; investment guarantees offered by, 590–92; longer term models to assess risks, 596–97; mobilizing private capital, 500; providing more explicit countercyclical lending, 596; role in the financing of regionalism, 541–42

Multilateral Fund for Implementation of the Montreal Protocol, 39, 374

Multilateral guarantees: dual purpose of, 592. See also Guarantee instruments

Multilateral Investment Guarantee Agency (MIGA), 44, 494; specializing in political risk guarantees, 591–92; of the World Bank Group, 234

Multilateral lending, 487; catalytic role of, 500; changing environment for, 495–97; continuing rationales for, 486–504; countering fluctuations and boom-bust cycles, 489; original design for, 489–92; postwar evolution of, 492–95; rationale behind, 487–89; rectifying capital market failures, 488; separating from bilateral arrangements, 499; types of, 486–87; way forward for, 497–502

Multilateral project facility approach, 295–96

Multilateral System of Access and Benefit-Sharing, 233

Multilateral trade regime: distribution-sensitive assessment methodology, 337, 338t; provision assessment for, 345–46; underprovision (malprovision) problem, 331t. See also Trade

Multiregional general equilibrium approach, 138

Multiyear financial perspective: for the EU, 457, 458

Mungbean futures contract, 424

Municipal bonds, 299n7

Murphy, David, 233

Museveni, Yoweri, 473

Musgrave, Peggy B., 3, 22n8, 33, 34, 74, 96, 167, 167–90, 169, 170, 172, 173, 175, 176, 182, 183, 184, 185, 189n1

Musgrave, Richard A., 3, 22n3, 22n7, 22n8, 58, 74, 126n3, 167, 172, 177, 309, 310

Mussa, Michael, 63n18, 437, 438

Mutti, John, 190n11

Mwega, Francis M., 87

Nabors, Robert, 311, 312

Nash, John, 335

Nash equilibriums, 199, 211; in asymmetric games, 213; for the weakest link scenario, 200; in a weakest link scenario, 212

NATO. See North Atlantic Treaty Organization

Nation states. See State(s)

National Academy of Sciences, 576n3

National agricultural research: in the poorest developing countries, 573; systems, 568

National Association of Securities Dealers, 401

National Biodiversity Institute (INBio), 232–33

National borders: increasing openness of, 3–5; international cooperation behind, 4, 11, 28, 30, 40, 46, 58, 86, 94–95; international cooperation beyond, 4, 6, 28, 34, 40, 46, 58, 95

National Council for Public-Private Partnerships (NCPPP), 258n1

National policy: agendas, 85; alignment, 85–93; changes, 88–90; making, 84–85; preferences, 74; public policy, 75–85

National public domains: interlocking of, 19

National public finance: incorporating global challenges, 29–34

National public goods: as building blocks of summation-type global public goods, 14; global public goods emerging from a summation of, 12; globalizing particular, 84; production path of, 12f

National risk management: macro markets for, 158; making effective happen, 160–64; private market responses to, 157–58; through decentralized market-based approaches, 156–60; through international risk-sharing agreements between governments, 153–56. See also Risk assessment; Risk management

National security, 89. See also Security

NCPPP (National Council for Public-Private Partnerships), 258n1

Negative cross-border externalities, 31, 84; generated by widespread poverty, 332, 487; greenhouse gases as a classical case of, 390; overprovided, 412n1; of security policies of industrial countries, 198. See also Externalities

Nelson, Jane, 258n5, 258n6

Net benefits: calculus, 336; determining burden-sharing principle, 343; enhancing the provision of global public goods, 333–35. See also Global benefits of enhanced provision of global public goods

NetMark Plus, 234

Netz, Janet S., 420

New actors: in international cooperation, 277–78. See also Financing mechanisms

New Arrangements to Borrow, 558–59, 562n18

New Deal, 126n4

New Partnership for Africa's Development (NEPAD), 222, 531, 540

New public finance, 5, 6f, 8, 46–47; comprehensive theory of, 58; costs of advancing, 47; implications for academics of, 55–58; implications for policymakers of, 47, 52–55; national measures required for the, 52–53; potential gains of, 2, 47

New South Wales, Australia, trading scheme, 62n15

New Zealand: Fiscal Responsibility Act, 137; Superannuation Fund, 139; Treasury, 137

Newell, Richard G., 391

Newlon, T. Scott, 185

Nickerson, David, 114

9/11: policy reforms after, 201–05; situation before, 201

Niskanen, William A., 74, 314

Nongovernmental organizations (NGOs), 253, 520

Non-OECD (Organisation for Economic Co-operation and Development) countries: cost of climate change, 135

Nonprofit international financing organizations, 279n2

Nonprofit organizations, 259n18, 270

Nonrivalry: benefiting from, 43–44

Nonstate actors: correcting failures of intergovernmental cooperation, 38; correcting global market failure and government failure 96; correcting public policy failure 38–39; as influential policymakers, 91; informal processes of norm and standard setting by, 30; involvement in international cooperation 277–79; joining forces in support of shared global concerns, 98n5; legitimacy of, 261n39

Normative analysis: countries as rational, utility-maximizing actors, 304–05; of efficient and inefficient outcomes, 305; for international cooperation, 304

Norms and standards: becoming self-enforcing, 233; at the international level, 205

North, Douglass, 221

North Atlantic Treaty Organization (NATO), 316

Norway, 139

Nottenberg, Carol, 573

Nowakunda, Kephas, 568

Nuclear Security Fund: of the International Atomic Energy Agency, 209, 276

OAS (Organization of American States), 160

Oates, Wallace E., 174, 306, 307

Oatley, Thomas, 311, 312

Obstfeld, Maurice, 164n6, 489

Ocampo, José Antonio, 81, 90, 500

ODA (official development assistance), 15, 18–19, 38, 45, 48, 62n11, 62 n12, 515, 530, 532, 537, 560

OECD (Organisation for Economic Co-operation and Development), 18, 42, 49f, 61n7, 112f, 114, 117t, 118t, 119t, 149n7, 169, 173, 174, 176, 280n6, 282, 351n3, 480f, 483, 483t, 531n1, 543n1, 555; code on budget transparency, 149n7; concessional and nonconcessional lending, 561n8; Development Assistance Committee (DAC), 89, 299n3, 530, 542, 543; membership in, 559; model for bilateral tax agreements, 34; model tax convention, 61–62n7; sectoral allocation of annual commitments, 530, 531t

OECD countries: correlation of change in openness and change in government outlay (1987–2002), 118t; cost of climate change, 135; general government expenditures (1987–2004), 112f; public social expenditure 1980–2001, 119t; use of futures markets, 422

Oehmke, James F., 578n10

Office of the United Nations High Commissioner for Refugees (UNHCR), 276

Official development assistance. See ODA

Offsets. See Emission offsets

Offtake agreements, 289, 294, 588, 600n6

Ohndorf, Markus, 87

Okavango Delta in Southern Africa: containing an outbreak of CBP in cattle, 382–84; modifying a cattle-raising project to protect wildlife, 377

Oliver, Robert W., 490, 491, 494, 502n6, 503n21

Olson, Mancur, 259n12, 304, 310, 316, 317n7

Onchocerciasis Control Programme, 260n23, 279n1

Open GIS Consortium, Inc., 233

Openness: combining with national security, 89; impact of, 20f; national policy changes echoing, 88; public challenges of greater, 3; requiring public investment in human capital, 110

Operation Appollo, 379

Operational efficiency, 412n4

OPIC (Overseas Private Investment Corporation), 592, 597

Optimal provision of global public goods: 55–56; compared with full provision, 332–33. See also Provision of global public goods

Options, 418, 614; created by the Economic Derivatives market, 161; markets, 392, 394–95t; trading, 396

Ordeshook, Peter C., 317n1

Organisation for Economic Co-operation and Development. See OECD

Osborne, Steven, 258n1

Osius, Meg, 588, 589

Ostrom, Elinor, 259n12

Outsourcing: by governments 7, 81, 231, 259n10; by private firms 28, 92, 145, 171

Over-the-counter markets, 393, 394–95t

Overseas Private Investment Corporation (OPIC), 592, 597

Overuse: of public goods, 329. See also Provision of global public goods

Oxfam Great Britain, 61n6

Ozone layer protection: 11, 357, 362–64, 368, 372, 374. See also Montreal Protocol

Pachauri, R.K., 405

Pakistan, 436

Palacios, Robert, 8f, 89

Pallage, Stéphane, 283

Panagarigy, Arvind, 92

Pappa, Evi, 88

Paraguay, 557

Pardey, Phillip G., 565, 566, 569, 573, 576n1, 576n2

Pareto optimality, 305, 330, 340–41, 352n20; efficiency, 487, 614

Paris Club, 598, 601n17

Parise, Gerald, 196

Park, Yoon S., 289

Parson, Edward A., 332

Partial credit guarantees, 44, 590–92, 594, 596, 599. See also Guarantee instruments

Partnerships: specific benefits, 230; typology of, 220. See also Global public private partnerships; Public private partnering; Public private partnerships

Patents, 329, 567, 570, 576, 576n2, 576n3, 579n15. See also Knowledge

Patient Capital Initiative, 234

PCF. See Prototype Carbon Fund

Peace: 95, 209–10, 225, 331–32, 345, 652n14, 373–74, 379–80, 61; underprovision (undersupply) problem, 331t. See also Security

Peltzman, Sam, 310

Pemex Finance Ltd., 291

Pensions: individual accounts, 8; pay as you go 149n5; public expenditure, 114, 114t. See also Elderly; Population aging; Social security

Performance-based allocation systems, 98n8, 472–84, 492–97, 503n17, 514, 517

Perman, Roger, 315

Permit trading. See Pollution permit trading

Persley, Gabrielle J., 571, 572t

Personal risk: managing, 123. See also Risk(s); Risk management

Pesenti, Paolo, 164n1

Petas, Peter, 446

Peterson, Peter G., 499

Peterson Zwane, Alix, 44, 246, 294, 564–79, 571, 572, 576n2

Petrei, Humberto, 87

Pettersson, Gunilla, 529

Philanthropic foundations, 270, 274

Philibert, Cedric, 391, 409, 411

Phillips, Nicola, 502n3

Physical infrastructure: financing of multicountry, 541; harmonizing, 80. See also Infrastructure development

Pieters, Jan, 100n23

Pigou, Arthur C., 390

Pigouvian approach, 390–91

Pinar, Abuzer, 306

Pinstrup-Andersen, Pir, 565

PIPA (Program on International Policy Attitudes), 307, 575

Plant Sciences Research Programme, 570

Pluchinsky, Dennis, 195, 210

Polak, Jacques J., 43, 498, 502n8, 549–62, 552, 561n5, 561n6

Policy demands/expectations: blending external and domestic, 29f, 30, 56; clusters of, 78f, 98n11; external sources of, 76

Policy harmonization: 11, 29, 42, 80, 148; behind borders, 34; tax systems, 175, 189n3

Policy reforms, 139–41; addressing, 31; after 9/11, 201–05

Policy-based lending, 495

Policymaking sovereignty: exclusive, 95; globalization and, 11, 19, 21, 81, 84–85, 91–92; as opposed to territorial, 73, 75, 91; responsive, 30, 53, 73, 85, 94, 95, 100n32

Polio eradication, 337, 339t, 340, 360; benefits of, 62n14; provision assessment for, 348–49; underprovision (undersupply) provision problem, 331t. See also Disease eradication; Global Polio Eradication Initiative

Political risk: guarantees, 591, 601n13; for infrastructure investments, 587–88; insurance, 601n13. See also Guarantee instruments; Risk(s)

Pollan, Michael, 576n3

Pollution permit trading, 31, 41, 51, 61, 64, 389–404

Polsky, Michael, 405

Pooled financing arrangements, 380–81

Population aging, 115, 132–34. See also Elderly; Pensions

Port model, 378–79, 380f

Porter, Michael E., 38, 80, 88

Porter, Tony, 233

Portes, Richard, 438, 445, 504n25

Porzecanski, Arturo C., 435

Positive analysis, 304

Positive externalities: resulting from changed behavior, 13; underprovided, 412n1. See also Externalities

Posner, Richard A., 52

Poulton, Colin, 428

Poverty: ill-effects of, 19, 20f; maximizing the reduction in, 473

Poverty efficient aid, 473–74, 474f, 483; regressions of, 483. See also Aid

Poverty reduction: 3, 7–9, 18–19, 42, 77–78, 84, 89; aid allocation for, 473–83; challenge grants and 511–24; loans, 555; private sector involvement, 564–76

Poverty Reduction Strategy Papers (PRSPs), 48, 89

Poverty Reduction Support Credits, 511, 525n3

Powell, Andrew, 487, 499, 500, 502n1

Prada, Fernando, 87

Pray, Carl E., 566, 567

Preemption strategy, 195, 198; asymmetric benefits from, 213; compared with enhanced security strategy, 198–200; as a pure public good, 198

Preferences: affecting the distribution of bene-
    fits, 335–36; for global public goods, 57,
    330; hierarchy for providing global public
    goods, 40

Prefunded defined contribution (investment
    based) systems, 149n5. See also Pensions

Prest, Alan R., 312

PricewaterhouseCoopers Corporate Finance,
    260n20

Principal-agent problem, 615; theories, 74

Prisoner's dilemma, 199, 211, 615; matrix of
    preemption, 211, 212f; properties of, 214n6

Pritchett, Lant, 524n1

Private actors: in development, 44

Private agents: insuring income, 158; purchas-
    ing the services of public agents, 251

Private cofinancing: of public programs, 8, 8f

Private finance: including in the pool of rev-
    enue sources, 284; initiative model, 230;
    leveraging with public guarantees, 286–87;
    re-attracting to infrastructure services, 586

Private Financing Initiative (UK), 287

Private goods, 223, 224t, 615; making essential
    affordable for all, 255; optimal consump-
    tion of, 351n6; turning into merit goods,
    235

Private provision of public goods. See Public
    goods

Private schemes and exchanges: in greenhouse
    gas emission trading, 410–11

Private sector: contracting, 231; development
    and 15–17, 44; global public goods and,
    11–15; managing adequate resource mobi-
    lization, 287–90; provision of infrastruc-
    ture projects, 585; rebalancing functions
    with the state 3–9, 31–38, 73, 80–85, 88;
    resource mobilization, 37; social welfare,
    31

Private spending: leveraging through tax
    expenditures, 31

Privatization, 8, 17, 31, 74–76, 88, 585–88. See
    also Public-private partnerships, State(s)

Product uncertainty: about new financial
    instruments, 442; greater for any statutory
    process, 447

Production efficiency, 615

Production of global public goods, 12–15. See
    also Financing of global public goods;

Global public goods; Provision of global
    public goods

Production path: of development, 18–19; of
    global public goods, 12; of national public
    goods, 12f

Program on International Policy Attitudes
    (PIPA), 307, 575

Program or project financing: as an aid delivery
    dimension, 519–20

Program (budget) aid, 519

Project aid, 519–20, 526n15

Project companies, 287, 289; enabling to collect
    cash flows, 288; role of, 289; structuring the
    roles of different actors, 288

Project facility approach, 295–96

Project finance, 281, 287–300, 615; financing
    arrangements, 288; guarantees and,
    587–99; originators, 289; revenue streams,
    293, 294–95; securitization and, 287–90;
    sponsors, 289

Property rights: assigning, 390; defining, 7;
    introducing, 391; regime, 99n21

Pro-poor R&D, 564; for agricultural innova-
    tion, 564–75. See also R&D

Prototype Carbon Fund (PCF), 54, 232, 242,
    252, 270, 279n3, 398

Provision of global public goods: access prob-
    lems, 328, 429; assessment of , 333–34,
    338–39; current, 333–34; determining full
    provision, 332; overprovision, 330; prob-
    lems, 328–30, 329f; scattered, 330; under-
    supply, 329; underuse, 328, 330. See also
    Adequate provision of global public goods;
    Distorted provision of global public goods;
    Full provision of global public goods;
    Malprovision; Optimal provision of global
    public goods; Underprovision

Prowle, Malcolm, 87

Proxy assets. See Macro securities

Public actors. See State(s)

Public agents: conferring a social license to
    operate, 231; insuring income, 158

Public choice analysis: focusing on decision-
    making processes, 305; of international
    agencies, 314; of international cooperation,
    37, 304–18; predicting that small producer
    groups will prove more effective, 310;
    revealing reasons for underfinancing inter-

national cooperation, 315; theorists, 74; yielding predictions, 304

Public debt: reducing, 138. See also Sovereign debt

Public expenditures. See Public spending

Public finance: branches of, 22n8; changing practice of, 20; current expectations for, 10; distinguishing characteristics of traditional, 9–10; evolution of, 3–4, 6f; gap between practice and standard theory, 10; international arm of the allocation branch of, 38; reengineering of, 3; response to the rebalancing of markets and states, 7–9; responses to the openness of national borders, 3

Public finance theory: conventional or traditional, 5–6, 9–10, 40; implications of the intermediary state for, 94–97; model of the state in, 74–75; future research agenda, 55–57; new linkages with practice, 96; response to growth of openness and globalization; 9–19 response to rebalancing markets and states, 5–9

Public goods, 328, 615; with access problems, 428; as available to all, 357; as a case of market failure, 99n21; determining the efficient provision level of, 55–56; final, 613; financing, 357; intermediate, 613; little room to trim outlays on, 139; physical or technical properties, 331; private provision of, 57, 74, 230; properties of norms and standards, 233; provision of, 10; restrictions limiting access to, 329; seeking to enhance the provision of, 235; as state-provided, 7; types of, 331, 358; voluntary provision of, 57, 243, 277. See also Global public goods

Public guarantee instruments. See Guarantee instruments

Public investment: declining, 8, 8f; guarantees, 586, 590–94; projects, 308

Public policy: failures, 38; goals, 7; instruments, 117–24; mechanisms, 244; outcomes, 8

Public revenue, 41

Public sector. See State(s)

Public social spending, 109, 118–20, 122, 124f

Public spending: benefits of underestimated, 306; capping, 283; limits to increased, 31;

links with globalization, 109, 111, 112–13; multiple drivers contributing to changes in, 113–15; overall levels of, 306; related to risks, 114; smoothing, 600n3; trends, 111–12

Public-private cooperation. See Public-private partnering

Public-private finance council: creating, 53, 54–55

Public-private partnering, 7–8; as a desirable and feasible policy options, 243; determining the desirability of, 246f; growing trend toward, 9; making risk management more affordable, 245; national, 219; ways of improving, 243–46. See also Global public private partnerships

Public-private partnerships, 3, 7–8, 12, 22n5, 34–35, 37, 40–41, 54, 219; definition, 221–22; role of state in, 227–28, 243; role of business in, 223–24, 227, 230–31; addressing global concerns, 219; advantages of, 22n5; multiple definitions in the current literature, 221; national 219, 237, 258n1; project companies set up as, 289; of a supply-driven nature, 260n25. See also Global public private partnerships; Partnerships

Puebla–Panama project, 531

Pull factors, 30

Pull instruments, 511, 523

Pull programs: to encourage agricultural R&D, 567–68, 569–70; making operational, 578–79n14

Purchase commitments. See Advanced purchase commitments

Pure public good, 615

Push factors, 30

Push instruments, 516

Push programs: to encourage agricultural R&D, 567, 568–69; subject to information asymmetries, 568

Push strategies, 523

Put options, 418, 427

Quantitative indicators: for the Millennium Challenge Account, 512

Quantitative performance criteria, 503n17

Quotas: selected for allocations, 559–60, IMF system originally linked to, 491

R&D (research and development): companies, 237; direct public funding of, 568; funding balancing between push and pull mechanisms, 575; insufficient spending on agricultural, 565–66; market for tropical agriculture, 565–67; private firms role in, 236; providers, 236

Rabushka, Alvin, 183

Radelet, Steve, 43, 471, 500, 510–26, 511, 513, 515, 518, 525n1, 525n6, 529, 538

Radetzki, Marian, 419

Radulescu, Roxana, 88

Raffer, Kunibert, 62n11, 76

Rahman, Rashique, 446

Rajan, Hari, 37, 59, 278, 412n10

Rajan, Raghuram G., 99n23

Ranieri, Lewis S., 299n8, 397

Rao, J. Mohan, 115, 335

Rappaport, Stephen P., 286

Ratha, Dilip, 51t, 59, 287, 291, 300n13, 500

Rausser, Gordon, 258n6, 260n26, 570, 576n1

Raynard, Peter, 261n39

Rayner, Anthony John, 422, 423, 424

Razin, Assaf, 23n20, 174

Real Exchange Rate Liquidity Facility, 597

Real Exchange Rate Liquidity (REX) product, 601n16

Recessions: amplified by underinsurance, 61n4; provoked by loss of market access, 435

Redel, Donna, 405

Regional development banks: bilateral donor contributions to, 531; country-based loans and programs, 538; creation of, 494

Regional projects: compiling annual disbursements, 543n3; guarantee agencies, 598; initiatives, 530, 530–32, 539; organizational form for, 539

Regional public goods, 18, 529, 615; challenges of coordination, attribution, and incentives, 529; donor financing for, 536, 538–40; fair and adequate provision of, 45; foreign aid allocations to, 530; high returns on investments in, 537; potential gains from enhanced provision of, 533–36; share

of development assistance going to, 530–32, 531t; sovereign risk pooling serving as an important instrument for fostering the provision of, 598; stricter definition of, 530–31, 531t; underfunded development opportunity, 43; undersupplied and underfunded in the developing world, 529; viewed as less desirable than national projects, 530. See also Transnational public goods

Regional trade agreements, 76, 312. See also Trade; Multilateral trade regime

Regulations, 8, 10, 29, 31, 40–41, 75, 80; command and control 390; complementing public spending, 109; in the European Union, 453–65; in global public private partnerships, 233–34; implementing international cooperation, 311–12, 316; information problems and, 488; international, 312; as an instrument of social protection, 121–22; reducing exposure to risk, 141; requiring preventive actions, 140; for social welfare, 109, 118, 121–25, 126n8, 141, 150n8

Regulatory costs, 312

Rehdanz, Katrin, 352n17

Reich, Michael R., 260n23

Reinaud, Julia, 391, 409, 411

Reinhold, Richard L., 34

Reinicke, Wolfgang H., 58, 261n39

Reinsurance, 140, 615. See also Insurance

Reisen, Helmut, 62n11, 531t, 543n1, 543n2, 544n19

Remittances, 19, 45, 145, 287, 290

Rent seeking, 74, 114, 318n11, 615

Reports on the Observance of Standards and Codes (IMF), 76

Republic of Korea: compared with Kenya, 475; economic fortunes, 154

Research and development. See R&D

Reserve adequacy: indicators of, 553–54

Reserves, 553–56. See also Foreign currency reserves; International reserves

Resource: constraints, 37, 285–92; flows, 283; mobilization, 292–98; scarcity, 241

Resource shortages: in international cooperation debates, 281; perceptions of, 282–85

Responsible sovereignty, 100n32

Responsive sovereignty, 53, 73; evolution toward, 94; exercising, 95; as the least-cost policy option, 85; notion of, 100n32; policy of, 30. See also Policymaking sovereignty

Revenue bonds, 286

Revised International Capital Adequacy Framework, 99n14

Richards, Anthony J., 446

Richards, John E., 305, 312

Richman, Peggy B., 169

Richter, Rudolf, 259n11

Ridley, Robert C., 256, 258n5

Riker, William H., 317n1

Risk(s): climate change, 9, 134, 147, 360–62, 389–404; country (aggregate), 79, 142, 446, 477; commercial 586–87; currency-related, 586–88; financial crises, 12, 139, 147, 487; fiscal, 140–42, 147–48; globalization, 4–5, 81, 110, 118, 147; investors in developing countries, 42–43, 437, 488, 523, 586–89; long-term risks, 131–32, 143; multilateral financial institutions, 489, 492, 492, 500, 590–92; mortgage market, 286; personal (idiosyncratic), 61n3, 74, 81–82, 109, 114, 123, 147; political 587; terrorism, 194–202

Risk assessment: country credit ratings, 30, 76, 80, 86, rankings, 86

Risk management: 152–63; as a task of states, 29–30, 52, 140, 118–20, 153–56, 244–45, 290–91; achieving enhanced, 428; allocating, 587; benefiting the more commercially oriented producers, 426; cooperating with the private sector, 32, 41, 89, 156–60; commodity risk, 39, 89, 418–26; cost of inadequate, 152; demand for, 118; instruments, 425; insurance industry and, 152; macro markets and, 51, 158–60; opportunities, 155; potential gains of, 47, 49–50; treaties, 154–55; vehicles, 163t. See also National risk management; Insurance; Social protection

Risk sharing: across countries, 153; allowing massive, 158; making part of international agreements, 155–56; politics of, 156; public advocacy of, 163–64

Risse-Kappen, Thomas, 87, 221

River blindness, 537

Robe, Michel A., 283

Rockefeller Foundation, 236, 270, 571

Rodríguez-Clare, Andrés, 78

Rodrik, Dani, 85, 99n23, 110, 116, 310, 500, 502n1, 566

Roe, Alan, 90

Rogoff, Kenneth, 435

Rojas-Suárez, Liliana, 23n19, 544n16

Roman, Ronald, 77

Romanian Commodities Exchange, 424

Romer, Thomas, 307

Ronfeldt, David, 210

Roodman, David, 525n1

Roosevelt, Franklin D., 126n4

Rose, Manfred, 182

Rose-Ackerman, Susan, 259n17

Roseboom, Johannes, 565, 569, 576n1

Rosen, Harvey S., 3, 22n7, 22n8, 309

Rosenau, Pauline Vaillan-Court, 258n5

Rosenthal, Howard, 307

Rosenthal, Les, 405

Rotary International, 238

Roubini, Nouriel, 435, 445, 448n1

Rouwenhorst, K. Geert, 429n3

Rowley, Charles R., 312

Rudra, Nita, 120

Ruggie, John Gerard, 75, 110, 261n29

Russian Federation, 436, 437

Russian Global Navigation Satellite System, 250

Ruttan, Vernon W., 566, 577n4

Rwegasira, Delphin G., 503n22

Sacerdote, Bruce, 113

Sachs, Jeffrey D., 18, 23n17, 42, 153, 164n6, 236, 283, 494, 565

Sadka, Efraim, 23n20, 174

Safe havens, 200

Sagasti, Francisco, 23n22, 87, 544n19

Sala-i-Martin, Xavier, 164n6

Salamon, Lester M., 3, 8

Salazar, Vander Caceres, 501

Samuelson, Paul A., 55, 330

Samuelson condition, 96, 55–56

Sander, Alison, 261n33

Sandler, Todd, 13, 23n9, 23n11, 23n21, 33, 62n10, 89, 194–214, 195, 196, 198, 199,

200, 206, 209, 210, 212, 213, 214n3, 214n5, 214n6, 259n12, 283, 308, 311, 329, 333, 351n4, 351n6, 367n2, 386n1

Sandmo, Agnar, 352n22

Sandor, Richard L., 39, 145, 286, 389–414, 392, 401, 409, 411, 412n5, 412n13, 412n18

Sanford, Jonathan E., 501

Santana-Boado, Leonela, 420, 424

Santaniello, Vittorio, 564, 568, 571

Sapir, André, 463

Sapir Group, 463

Sarno, Lucio, 437

SARS (severe acute respiratory syndrome), 327

Savings and stabilization funds, 19, 61n4

Schapiro, Mary, 405

Scheibe, Jorg, 498

Schervish, Paul G., 240

Schick, Allen, 599

Schmitz, Andrew, 351n13, 352n19

Schnabel, Albrecht, 92

Schnabel, Isabel, 437

Schneider, Friedrich, 315

Schofield, Christopher John, 537

Scholte, Jan Aart, 92

Scholz, Imme, 87

Schreurs, Miranda A., 99n23

Schubert, Renate, 87

Schuknecht, Ludger, 111, 112f, 114, 116, 120

Schuler, Philip, 346

Schulze, Günther G., 61n1, 114

Schweickart, Russell L., 358

Scorecards: measuring country performance and state behavior, 76–77, 79–80, 82–83

Scotchmer, Suzanne, 576n2, 577n3

Scott, Hal S., 448n1

Scott, John, 237, 246f

Scott, Tom, 424

SDRs (Special Drawing Rights), 502n8, 551; accounts of IMF members, 551; allocation to all or to low-income members only, 557–59; allocations of, 555; balance between the supply and demand for, 558; cessation of allocations of, 549; changes in the use of, 556–57; creation of, 549, 550–53; designation for, 556–57; fresh look

at, 556–59; interest rate, 555; issuance, 43; largest holders found outside of the industrial world, 557; LIBOR rate, 562n16; new perspective on, 549–62; reasons to resume regular allocations, 549; reconstitution of, 556; setting the interest rate, 562n16; size of resumed allocations of, 559–60; substitution of other reserve assets for, 557

Secondary Mortgage Market Enhancement Act (1984), 397

Securities exchanges: emergence of, 392, 394–95t

Securitization, 287, 412n8, 615; by Banco do Brasil, 300n13; creating holdout problems, 438; of future flow receivables, 51t, 59; making long-term funding available in the near term, 287; project finance and, 287–90; special-purpose facilities in, 291

Security: complementing with cross-border cooperation, 205; global, 33; improving, 81; indices of, 82–83; national, 89; passing on costs to customers, 204; toughening internal on a unilateral basis, 33; underprovision (undersupply) provision problem, 331t; as a weakest link public good, 199. See also Peace

Seed Initiative, 241

Seeds: difficulty enforcing restrictions on the resale of, 566; making sterile, 576–77n3; potential for the reuse and resale of, 576n3

Segura-Ubiergo, Alex, 120

Seigniorage, 550, 560n4

Sen, Amartya, 335, 352n19

Serageldin, Ismail, 571, 572t

Setser, Brad, 445

Setty, Gautam, 283

Shackleton, Michael, 455, 466n1

Shah, Rajiv, 37, 59, 278, 281–300

Shavell, Steven, 576n2

Shenkar, Oded, 100n26

Sheppard, Robert, 595, 596f, 597, 601n14

Shillcutt, Sam, 51t, 59

Shiller, Robert J., 32, 47, 50, 51t, 60, 92, 149n6, 152–65, 155, 158, 160, 161, 162, 164n1, 164n2, 165n8, 423, 429n5

Shleifer, Andrei, 55, 259n11, 259n19, 433, 436

Shmalensee, Richard, 412n13

Sidibe, Saidou, 87

Sidikou-Sow, Balkissa, 9

Silveira, Antonio Carlos, 537

Simon, Leo, 258n6, 260n26, 570, 576n1

Simon, Nathalie B., 368n3

Simone, Alejandro, 61n1, 88

Simonit, Silvia, 123

Sinclair, Darren, 258n1

Sinelnikov, Sergei, 87

Singapore, 557

Single European Act (1987), 457, 460

Sinn, Hans-Werner, 23n20, 61n1, 92, 96, 99n23, 169, 190n9

Siqueira, Kevin, 198

Sjölander, Stefan, 87

Skeel, David A., 440

Skees, Jerry, 429n9

Slemrod, Joel, 61n1, 92, 169, 170, 184

Sloane, Robert, 575

Small Enterprise Assistance Funds, 234

Smallpox eradication: application of a distribution-sensitive assessment methodology to, 337, 338t, 340; benefits of, 62n14; from developing countries, 361; huge returns to investment in, 362; provision assessment for, 347; underprovision (undersupply) problem, 331t. See also Disease eradication

Smith, Adam, 544n9

Smith, Brian, 313

Smith, David A., 99n23

Snidal, Duncan, 98n5, 305

Snowden, Nicholas, 425

Sobel, Dava, 570

Social benefit, 615

Social cost, 616

Social protection: 4, 82–85, 89; aging, 132–33, 137–38, 147; public policy instruments for, 109–25; and globalization, 114

Social rates of return, 246f; high for agricultural R&D, 567, 578n10

Social regulation, 122. See also Regulations

Social Security: debate in the United States, 100n27; national policy changes regarding, 89. See also Pensions

Social ventures, 223, 224, 224t, 229, 235–39

Social Watch, 258n1

Södersten, Bo, 89, 100n23

Sokoloff, Kenneth L., 566

Solidarity Group, 465

Solignac Lecomte, Henri-Bernard, 23n15

Solinger, Dorothy J., 99n23

Soludo, Charles C., 100n28

Sørensen, Georg, 94

Sørensen, Peter Birch, 23n20, 181

Sorge, Marco, 289, 601n13

Soros, George, 549, 561n13

Soto, Marcelo, 62n11, 531t, 543n1, 543n2, 544n19

Souleles, Nicholas S., 299n12

Southern Africa Power Pool (SAPP), 537

Southern African Customs Union, 541

Southwick, Karen, 77

Sovereign and subsovereign debt securities: raising capital, 285–86

Sovereign bonds: contracts, 439; international, 440t; issuing with collective action clauses, 440; relevant provisions on restructuring, 439–40. See also GDP-indexed bonds

Sovereign credit ratings: decoupling of loan transactions from, 291; as an incentive tool of market participants, 96

Sovereign debt: frequency of crises, 433–34; managing and resolving crises, 434; moving to a contractual and market-based solution, 40; market, 436; restructuring mechanism, 443; service, 159

Sovereign guarantee pools, 598. See also Guarantee instruments

Sovereignty. See Policymaking sovereignty

Spackman, Michael, 22n5, 258n1, 260n20, 288, 299n10, 600n3

Spadafora, Francesco, 437

Spain, 466n4

Special Drawing Rights. See SDRs

Special-purpose facilities: created to handle financing tools, 290; creating for the type 1 projects, 293; as an institutional go-between, 288, 290; in the international cooperation domain, 282; to mobilize private financing, 281; in securitization, 291

Special-purpose vehicles, 299n12

Spielman, David, 258n6, 260n26

Spilimbergo, Antonio, 60

Spillane, Charles, 565, 576n1

Spillovers, 11, 224–25. See also Externalities,

Spot markets: development of, 392, 394–95t; futures markets complementing, 418; informal, 401; prices, 420

Spratt, Stephen, 598

Srinivasan, T. N., 92

Stability and Growth Pact (EU), 144

Stabilization branch: of public finance, 22n8

Standard & Poor's rating, 98n9

Standards: international economic and financial, 48f

Standby arrangements: introduced to the IMF, 492

Stanton, Thomas H., 600n9

State(s): intermediary, 29–30, 39, 52–53, 93–97; coercive powers of, 75; competitiveness challenges accepted by, 88; core elements of, 74; competition among, 92–93; expanding market failure-correcting role, 85; increasing interdependence of, 91; model of, 74–75 as policymakers 90–91; as policytakers 90; rebalancing roles with markets, 3–9, 31–38, 73, 80–85, 88 ; role of 3–7, 9–14, 28–35, 46–58, 94; role in risk management, 29–30, 52, 118–20, 140, 153–56, 244–45, 290–91;Westphalian, 73, 75, 85, 93–97. See also Policymaking sovereignty

Static efficiency, 616

Statistical life, 359, 368n3

Statutory approach: comparing to the contractual approach, 444–46; evidence on, 446–47; with some of the functions of an international bankruptcy mechanism, 439; to sovereign debt restructuring, 443–44

Stavins, Robert N., 90, 391, 412n3, 412n13

Steinmo, Sven, 61n1

Stern, Marc A., 23n9, 352n22, 386n1, 502n3

Stern, Nicholas, 61n1

Steuerle, Eugene, 259n17

Stewart, Frances, 100n28

Stigler, George, 309, 317n4

Stiglitz, Joseph E., 7, 21n1, 22n2, 53, 97n3, 99n21, 222, 304, 342, 487, 500, 502n3, 502n4

Stock. See Equity security

Stock markets, 152, 157–58, 160, 162–63, 164n1

Stopford, John, 92

Strange, Susan, 92

Strategic Arms Limitations Talks (SALT), 351n5

Strategies for Enhancing Access to Medicines for Health, 237

Straub, Stephane, 589, 600n8

Streck, Charlotte, 258n5

Stringham, Edward, 393

Strong, Maurice, 405

Structural Adjustment Facility (IMF), 493

Structural Funds: developed by the European Union, 460, 466n3; to help poorer regions in Europe, 156

Sub-Saharan Africa: early structural adjustment programs, 100n28; provision of regional public goods to, 533; small and landlocked economies in the region, 535, 544n11

Subsidiarity, 189n3; applying, 40–42; in the European Union, 168

Subsovereign bonds, 286

Subsovereign debt securities, 285–86

Sukhtankar, Sandip, 529, 544n8

Sulfur dioxide emission allowance trading, 397–98, 413n14. See also Pollution permit trading

Summation aggregation technology, 15, 198

Summation public goods, 12–15, 358, 362–67

Summers, Lawrence H., 153, 498, 501

Summers, Robert, 164n4

Summit of the Americas (2004), 159–60

Sunding, David, 576n2

Superannuation Fund: New Zealand, 139

Supplemental Reserve Facility (IMF), 494

Swaine, Robert, 440

Swank, Duane, 61n1

Swanson, Timothy M., 566

Swift, Zhicheng Li, 126n9

Swingland, Ian R., 392, 409, 411, 412n5, 412n13, 412n18

Sy, Amadou N. R., 496

Tadelis, Steven, 222

Tanzania, 427

Tanzi, Vito, 7, 31, 61n1, 61n6, 109–26, 111, 112f, 114, 115, 116, 120, 121, 123, 126n3, 190n13

Tariffs: on agricultural imports in OECD countries, 63n21; unweighted average on the eve of World War I, 113

Tarr, David, 346

Task Force for Child Survival and Development, 260n23

Tax(es), 186–87; base, 172–73, 175–76, 184; consumption taxes, 182–85; dual income, 181; entitlements on income, 168–78; equity, 170; flat rate, 183; incentives, 173; on income 168–78, 179; neutrality, 171; personal expenditure tax, 184; progressive rates, 120, 181; sovereignty over source income, 168. See also Corporate income tax; VAT

Tax competition, 173, 174, 175

Tax cooperation: through bilateral negotiation, 33, 175, among national tax administrations, 178; necessary to achieve an international tax regime, 182; opportunities for among states, 91; source and residence countries, 168–71, 177, 182–83

Tax expenditures, 109, 120–21; 122–23, 126n9

Tax handles, 115, 115–16

Tax havens: losses from, 61n6

Tax revenue: financing public social expenditures, 120; loss or deferment of, 120; sacrifice of by the residence country, 177

Tax systems: recasting in areas sensitive to international differentials, 91; retaining or attracting transnational economic actors, 96; transforming into a common, globalized system, 33

Taylor, John, 439, 444

Taylor, Mark P., 437

Taylor, Timothy, 433

Taylor-Gooby, Peter, 308t

Technical Group on Innovative Financing Mechanisms, 300n17

Technology Innovation Challenge Grants, 517

Technology: licenses on a royalty-free basis, 236; energy technology: disseminating, 246

Telser, Lester G., 419

Terra Capital Fund, 234

Terrorism control, 33, 194–98; domestic, 196, 200–05; financing194–214; insurance, 90; international incentives for, 199; role of conventions, 205–07; as a weakest-link public good, 200

Tesar, Linda L., 164n6

Tessner, Sandrine, 258n6

Thaicharoen, Yungong, 446

Thiele, Graham, 568

Third-party government, 8. See also Government(s), State(s)

Thirlby, George F., 372

Thompson, James, 405

Thompson, Sarahelen, 419, 423

Thorbecke, Willem, 313

Tidjani Alou, Mahaman Sanoussi, 87

Tiebout, Charles M., 30

Tiebout effect, 30

Tied aid, 313, 317n6

Tietenberg, Tom, 392

Titman, Sheridan, 428

Tokarick, Stephen, 63n21

Topik, Steven C., 99n23

Tosini, Paula, 419

Tourism charges: 379

Trade: inhibited by borders in Sub-Saharan Africa, 534–36; insurance market, 254; liberalization, 115, 345; policy distortions, 345; policy reform, 341–42, 342f; sanctions, 313; threat of restricting, 364

Trade Policy Reviews: of the World Trade Organization, 98n7

Traditional public finance, 9–10. See also Public finance theory

Tragedy of the commons, 304, 391

Transaction costs, 296, 616

Transnational actors, 77; corporations, 240; growing political strength of, 91–92

Transnational public goods, 367n1, 616; requiring strategic manipulation, 364t; special challenges of, 357; success in the supply of, 358. See also Regional public goods; Transnational public goods

Transparency, 11, 78–80; in aid allocations 511–13, 536; in capital markets 144; in contingent liabilities, 599; contributing to the debate on long-term fiscal challenges

143; CPIA and 484m1; in IFF, 296; international codes of, 142–43, 149n7, 150n8; in special purpose vehicles, 282

Transparency codes: of the IMF and the OECD, 142

Transparency International, 77, 79, 234, 249

Triffin, Robert, 493

Triodos Renewable Energy for Development Fund, 234

Tropical agriculture: distortions in the research market for, 566–67; identifying desired technologies and their social values, 571; rewarding innovation tied to diffusion, 571–72; twin challenges of R&D, 571

Trust funds: established by intergovernmental entities, 279n4; using SDRs, 561n13

Trust Indenture Act, 440, 441

Tschirhart, John, 259n12

Tsunami catastrophe, 327

Tubbataha Reefs National Marine Park, 387n6

Tullock, Gordon, 74, 309, 310, 312

Turkey, 494

Turks and Caicos Islands, 387n6

Turner Foundation, 270

Twombly, Eric, 259n17

Uganda, 525n3

UK (United Kingdom): Code for Fiscal Sustainability, 137; Golden Rule, 144; private finance initiative model, 230

UK Department for International Development (DFID), 283, 296f, 300n16, 511, 532t

UK Emission Trading Scheme, 62n15

UK Her Majesty's Treasury, 137, 283, 287, 296f, 299n10, 300n16

Ukraine, 436

Umali-Deininger, Dina, 566, 567

UN. See United Nations

Unemployment insurance. See Insurance; Social protection

UN Foundation, 221, 258n5

UN General Assembly, 18, 283, 366

UN Millennium Project, 18, 23n17, 42, 62n12, 283, 284, 299n2

UNAIDS (Joint United Nations Programme on HIV/AIDS), 90

Unanimous action clauses, 448n3

Unemployment insurance. See Insurance; Social protection

UNCTAD. See United Nations Conference on Trade and Development

Underfunded regionalism: meeting the challenge of, 43, 529–45

Underhill, Geoffrey R. D., 100n23

Underprovision: assessing full costs of, 334; consequences of, 284; externalities from severe, 542; of a global public good, 330; of public goods, 328, 329. See also Provision of global public goods

UNDP. See United Nations Development Programme

UNECA. See United Nations Economic Commission for Africa

UNEP. See United Nations Environment Programme

UNESCO. See United Nations Educational, Scientific and Cultural Organization

UNFPA. See United Nations Population Fund

UNICEF. See United Nations Children's Fund

Unicode Consortium, 233

United Kingdom. See UK

United Nations (UN), 18, 20f, 49f, 61n5, 62n7, 84, 205, 208t, 234, 258n6, 260n25, 282, 380, 386n2, 532t, 549, 561n13; contributions of member states to, 366; dominating international financing, 270; maintaining a list of public-private partnerships, 258n6; multilateral treaties registered with, 76

United Nations Children's Fund (UNICEF), 237, 238, 255; developing countriese purchasing AIDS drugs and diagnostics, 235; relationship with IKEA, 251

United Nations Conference on Trade and Development (UNCTAD), 33, 49f, 76, 493, 496, 497, 535

United Nations Development Programme (UNDP), 89, 90, 279n1, 351n12, 533, 534t, 576n3; concentrating on the lowest income countries, 481

United Nations Economic Commission for Africa (UNECA), 534, 541, 544n10

United Nations Educational, Scientific and Cultural Organization (UNESCO), 375

United Nations Expanded Programme of Technical Assistance, 279n1

United Nations Environment Programme (UNEP), 90

United Nations Fund for International Partnerships, 241, 258n6

United Nations Model Double Taxation Convention, 62n7

United Nations Population Fund (UNFPA), 276

United Nations Security Council Resolution 1373, 98n7

United Nations Special Fund, 279n1

Universal Flour Fortification initiative, 261n35

Universal Postal Union (UPU), 276, 366

United Nations Research Institute for Social Development (UNRISD), 113t, 240

UNRISD. See United Nations Research Institute for Social Development

UPU (Universal Postal Union), 276, 366

Ursprung, Heinrich W., 61n1, 114

U.S. (United States): African Growth and Opportunity Act, 17; federal budget compared with the EU budget, 465; incremental cost of engaging in military operations abroad to fight terrorism, 380; intergovernmental cooperation challenges, 201; municipal bonds, 299n7; tax revenue loss to, 61n6

U.S. Agency for International Development (AID), 532t, 568, 570

U.S. Bankruptcy Code, 449n7

U.S. Centers for Disease Control and Prevention, 238

U.S. Department of Homeland Security (DHS), 201–05; 214n10; budgets by organization, 203t, 204

U.S. Department of Treasury, 169, 179, 182, 190n6, 504n27

U.S. Environmental Protection Agency (EPA), 398, 412n14; electronic tracking system, 398; offering challenge grants, 517

U.S. Global Positioning System, 250

USAID. See U.S. Agency for International Development

User fees, 289–90, 378–79, 381, 591

Utting, Peter, 241

Vaccine development. See Advance purchase commitments, R&D

Vaillancourt, François, 87

Vaillant, Charlotte, 422, 424

Valenduc, Christian, 126n9

Value: of a claim on GDP, 157

Value-added tax (VAT). See VAT

Van de Fliert, Elske, 568

Van de Linde, Erik, 214n7

Van den Berg, Hendrik, 313

Van den Ende, Leo, 120

Van Wincoop, Eric, 164n1

Van Ypserle, Tanguy, 576n2

Varangis, Panos, 424, 426

Variable costs, 372

Varian, Hal, 259n12

VAT (value-added tax), 31, 88, 122, 156, 172, 183–85, 188

Vaubel, Roland, 304, 307, 314

Vedenov, Dmitry V., 429n9

Verbon, Harrie A. A., 87

Vicary, Simon, 209, 213, 214n5

Vietnam, 525n3

Vijayakumar, Jayaraman, 299n7

Vijayaraghavan, Maya, 352n17

Vines, David, 100n23, 487, 499, 500, 502n1

Virmani, Arvind, 100n26

Viscusi, W. Kip, 368n3, 368n4

Vishny, Robert W., 55, 259n11

Vives, Antonio, 600n7

Voluntary cooperation: in market creation, 389; intergovernmental, 357; for public goods provision, 57, 227, 243

Voluntary provision of public goods. See Public goods

Von Grebmer, Klaus, 258n6, 260n26

Wacziarg, Romain, 113

Wafula, David, 260n26

Wagner's Law, 113

Waldman, Michael, 433

Walkenhorst, Peter, 327

Wallsten, Scott, 222

Walsh, Michael J., 389, 392, 412n18

Walters, Alan, 486

Washington Consensus, 501, 513, 525n7

Watson, Catherine, 317n6

Watson Wyatt Worldwide, 99n17

Waxman, Amalia, 261n33

Weak-link public goods, 33, 195, 360–62; matching behavior of, 212; scenario involving, 211–12; security as a, 199; supported by the common pool, 209; transnational terrorism, 195, 200

Weak-link aggregation technology, 311

Weather events: global costs of extreme (1950–1999), 135f; greater frequency and severity of extreme, 134, 135; risk management instruments, 426

Weather-based index insurance, 429n9

Webb, Richard, 502n1, 503n14, 503n21, 503n22

WEF (World Economic Forum) 83, 99n17, 221, 241, 258n5

Wegimont, Liam, 23n15

Wei, Shang-Jin, 534

Weisbrod, Burton, 259n17

Weiss, Allan N., 160, 162, 164n7, 502n4

Weiss, Linda, 94, 100n23

Weithöner, Thomas, 62n11, 531t, 543n1, 543n2, 544n19

Welfare state, 112

Werner, Ingrid, 164n6

Westphal, Larry E., 576n2

Westphalian state: exclusive political authority, 75; ideal-type, 73; replacing with the intermediary state, 93–97; transforming into an intermediary state, 73. See also State(s)

What Works Working Group, 537

Wheeler, Craig, 261n33

White, Harry Dexter, 490

White, Karen, 236, 237

White, Michelle J., 439

White, Rodney R., 22n6

WHO. See World Health Organization

Widdus, Roy, 261n33

Wiebe, Keith D., 565

Wieland, Hanneke, 87

Wijen, Frank, 100n23

Wilcoxen, Peter J., 51t, 60

Wilensky, Harold L., 63n23

Willard Group, 448n2

Willett, Thomas D., 314, 315

Williams, Jeffrey, 424

Williamson, Jeffrey G., 113

Williamson, John, 501, 525n7

Williamson, Oliver E., 226, 229, 259n11

Williamson, Peter J., 412n4

Williamson, Sir Brian, 405

Willingness to pay: for global public goods, 330

Wilmouth, Robert, 405

Wilson, John Douglas, 174

Wilson, Robert, 588

Winpenny, James, 241, 283, 601n16

Witholding taxes, 172, 176

Witte, Jan Martin, 258n5, 261n39

WMO (World Meteorological Organization), 352n17

Wolf, Martin, 81, 100n26, 299n5, 504n25

Woltron, Klaus, 405

Working Group on New International Contributions to Finance Development, 23n22, 300n17

World Bank, 38, 45, 49f, 62n11, 77, 88, 89, 90, 99n16, 117t, 235, 242, 254, 255, 283, 299n6, 300n17, 327, 368n4, 477, 483t, 484n1, 495, 496, 514, 516, 523, 532t, 543n3, 544n12, 564, 565, 576n1, 577n5; core business of, 476; defining low-income countries under stress, 484n3; disbursement of aid by, 315; grant element added by in 2001, 471; guarantees available from, 591; lending to developing countries (1970–2003), 496f; main instrument as a loan to a single recipient government, 538; performance-based allocation systems for distributing concessional loans, 514; playing a key role in getting coherence into the composition of aid, 481; providing finance only when private capital is not available, 491–92; providing mainly loans until recently, 471; from reconstruction to development finance at, 494–95; seed money for the Prototype Carbon Fund, 252; strategy for low-income countries under stress, 477

World Economic Forum (WEF), 83, 99n17, 221, 241, 258n5

World Federation of Exchanges (WFE), 20f

World Health Assembly: declaring smallpox eradicated in 1980, 347; resolution on polio eradication, 348

World Health Organization Framework Convention on Tobacco Control, 13

World Health Organization (WHO), 237, 238, 242, 327, 348, 532t; Onchocerciasis Control Programme, 537; pursuing partnership approaches, 246

World Heritage Fund, 276, 375

World Meteorological Organization (WMO), 352n17

World Panel on Financing Water Infrastructure, 241, 601n16

World Resources Institute (WRI), 90, 251

World Summit on Sustainable Development, 260n25

World Trade Organization (WTO), 20f, 49f, 92, 99n12, 190n13, 534

World Watch Institute, 90

World Water Council, 219

World Wide Fund for Nature (WWF), 251

Wormser, Michel, 51t, 59, 593f

Wright, Anna, 280n5

Wright, Brian D., 573, 576n2, 579n15

Wright, Joseph, 595, 597, 601n14

WTO. See World Trade Organization

Wyploz, Charles, 304

X-efficiency. See Production efficiency

Yafeh, Yishay, 445

Yale University, 236

Yandle, Bruce, 352n17

Yaqub, Mahammad, 557, 558, 562n17

Yeats, Alexander S., 534

Zadek, Simon, 92, 243, 258n5

Zaidi, Iqbal, 557, 558, 562n17

Zeckhauser, Richard, 304, 316, 317n7

Zedillo, Ernesto, 560n2

Zedillo Report, 560n2

Zee, Howell H., 61n1, 115

Zettelmeyer, Jeromin, 435, 437

Zhang, Lei, 437

Zhang, Xiaoke, 100n23

Zhang, Xioaming, 437

Zhengzhou Commodity Exchange, 424

Zilberman, David, 576n2

Zimbabwe Agricultural Commodity Exchange, 424

Zingales, Luigi, 99n23, 152

Zodrow, George, 174, 175, 183

Zoeteman, Kees, 100n23

Zylicz, Temasz, 537